ROUTLEDGE
STUDENT STATUTES

....

Contract, Tort and Restitution Statutes
2012–2013

'Focused content, layout and price – Routledge competes and wins in relation to all of these factors' – Craig Lind, University of Sussex, UK

'The best value and best format books on the market' – Ed Bates, Southampton University, UK

Routledge Student Statutes present all the legislation students need in one easy-to-use volume. Developed in response to feedback from lecturers and students, this book offers a fully up-to-date, comprehensive, and clearly presented collection of legislation – ideal for LLB and GDL course and exam use.

Routledge Student Statutes are:

- **Exam Friendly:** un-annotated and conforming to exam regulations
- **Tailored to fit your course:** 80% of lecturers we surveyed agree that Routledge Student Statutes match their course and cover the relevant legislation
- **Trustworthy:** Routledge Student Statutes are compiled by subject experts, updated annually and have been developed to meet student needs through extensive market research
- **Easy to use:** a clear text design, comprehensive table of contents, multiple indexes and highlighted amendments to the law make these books the more student-friendly Statutes on the market
- **Competitively Priced:** Routledge Student Statutes offer content and usability rated as good or better than our major competitor, but at a more competitive price
- **Supported by a Companion Website:** presenting scenario questions for interpreting Statutes, annotated web links, and multiple-choice questions, these resources are designed to help students to be confident and prepared.

James Devenney is Professor of Commercial Law at the University of Exeter.

Howard Johnson is a former Deputy Head of Bangor Law School and is currently a Professional Tutor at Cardiff Law School.

ROUTLEDGE STUDENT STATUTES

www.routledge.com/cw/statutes

Praise for Routledge Student Statutes

'The best value and best format books on the market' – Ed Bates, University of Southampton, UK

'Focused content, layout and price – Routledge competes and wins in relation to all of these factors' – Craig Lind, University of Sussex, UK

'comprehensive and reliable' – Andromachi Georgosouli, University of Leicester, UK

'user friendly and sensibly laid out' – John Stanton, Kingston University, UK

'An exciting and valuable selection of the key legislative material' – David Radlett, University of Kent, UK

'I prefer the layout of the Routledge statute book to other statute books that I have seen' – Nicola Haralambous, University of Hertfordshire, UK

'Well-presented and has thorough content [. . .] clearly a good competitor' – Brian Coggon, University of Lincoln, UK

'. . . given the addition of the useful web resource and the easy to read section headings, I would be more inclined to recommend this book than other statute texts' – Emma Warner-Reed, Leeds Metropolitan University, UK

'excellent and relevant' – Sarwan Singh, City University London, UK

'I personally prefer the Routledge series as it is better laid out and more accessible' – Jonathan Doak, University of Nottingham, UK

'*Routledge Student Statutes* are practical and carefully designed for the needs of the students' – Stelios Andreadakis, Oxford Brookes University, UK

'an excellent statute text' – Fang Ma, University of Hertfordshire, UK

'Other statute books are not as attractive in look or feel, not as easy to navigate, more expensive and amendments are less clear' – Jason Lowther, University of Plymouth, UK

'Gives good coverage and certainly includes all elements addressed on our current syllabus. I personally think this statute is more clearly set out than other statute books and is more user friendly for it' – Samantha Pegg, Nottingham Trent University, UK

'This statute book is a student friendly material. Index features as well as the overall content make this book a valuable contribution to student reading lists' – Orkun Akseli, Newcastle University, UK

'A very welcome publication' – Simon Barnett, University of Hertfordshire, UK

'I am sticking with *Routledge Student Statutes*' – Francis Tansinda, Manchester Metropolitan University, UK

ROUTLEDGE
STUDENT STATUTES

Contract, Tort and Restitution Statutes
2012–2013

JAMES DEVENNEY
Professor of Commercial Law at the University of Exeter

AND

HOWARD JOHNSON
Professional Tutor at Cardiff Law School

Routledge
Taylor & Francis Group

LONDON AND NEW YORK

First published 2013
by Routledge
2 Park Square, Milton Park, Abingdon, Oxon OX14 4RN

Simultaneously published in the USA and Canada
by Routledge
711 Third Avenue, New York, NY 10017

Routledge is an imprint of the Taylor & Francis Group, an informa business

British Library Cataloguing in Publication Data
A catalogue record for this book is available from the British Library

Library of Congress Catalog in Publication Data
A catalog record for this book has been requested

Parliamentary material is reproduced with the permission
of the Controller of HMSO on behalf of Parliament.

ISBN: 978–0–415–63381–9 (pbk)

Typeset in Sabon
by RefineCatch Limited, Bungay, Suffolk

MIX
Paper from
responsible sources
FSC® C004839
www.fsc.org

Printed and bound in Great Britain by
TJ International Ltd, Padstow, Cornwall

Contents

Preface

The aim of this book is to provide a selection of statutes and statutory instruments relevant to the study of Contract Law, Tort and Restitution in England, Wales and Scotland. Generally we have only sought to include provisions which were in force on 1st May 2012. However, we have also sought to include provisions – whether new or amending an existing provision – which we could ascertain would be in force before 31st December 2012. In most cases we have not included transitional provisions. The appendix contains provisions from a number of important statutes for which (at the time of writing) the commencement date was not known.

We are happy to acknowledge the copyright of the relevant holders and the publishers and editors thank the Scottish and UK Parliaments for their permission to reproduce material under copyright, reproduced under the terms of the Click-Use Licence. Please also note: Only European Union legislation printed in the paper edition of the *Official Journal of the European Union* is deemed authentic. We would also like to thank Damian Mitchell, Emma Nugent and Fiona Kinnear for making this book possible.

We welcome suggestions for the constitution of future editions of this book.

James Devenney and Howard Johnson
Exeter and Cardiff, May 2012

Guide to the Companion Website

....

www.routledge.com/cw/statutes

Visit the Companion Website for *Routledge Student Statutes* in order to:

- Understand how to use a statute book in tutorials and exams;

- Learn how to interpret statutes and other legislation to maximum effect;

- Gain essential practice in statute interpretation prior to your exams, through unique problem-based scenarios;

- Test your understanding of statutes through a set of Multiple Choice Questions for revision or to check your own progress;

- Understand how the law is developing with updates, additional information and links to useful websites.

Alphabetical Index

Chronological Index

Statutes

STATUTE OF FRAUDS 1677
(c.3)

IV NO ACTION AGAINST EXECUTORS, &C. UPON A SPECIAL PROMISE, OR UPON ANY AGREEMENT, OR CONTRACT FOR SALE OF LANDS, &C. UNLESS AGREEMENT, &C. BE IN WRITING AND SIGNED

No Action shall be brought . . . whereby to charge the Defendant upon any special promise to answer for the debt default or miscarriages of another person . . . unless the Agreement upon which such Action shall be brought or some Memorandum or Note thereof shall be in Writing and signed by the partie to be charged therewith or some other person thereunto by him lawfully authorized.

> *As amended by Law of Property Act 1925, sch. 7; Law Reform (Enforcement of Contracts) Act 1954, s. 1.*

FIRES PREVENTION (METROPOLIS) ACT 1774
(c.78)

86 NO ACTION SHALL LIE AGAINST A PERSON WHERE THE FIRE ACCIDENTALLY BEGINS

No action to lie against a person where the fire accidentally begins.

And no action, suit or process whatever shall be had, maintained or prosecuted against any person in whose house, chamber, stable, barn or other building, or on whose estate any fire shall, . . . accidentally begin, nor shall any recompence be made by such person for any damage suffered thereby, any law, usage or custom to the contrary notwithstanding; . . . provided that no contract or agreement made between landlord and tenant shall be hereby defeated or made void.

LIBEL ACT 1843
(c.96)

1 OFFER OF AN APOLOGY ADMISSIBLE IN EVIDENCE IN MITIGATION OF DAMAGES

In any action for defamation it shall be lawful for the defendant (after notice in writing of his intention so to do, duly given to the plaintiff at the time of filing or delivering the plea in such action), to give in evidence, in mitigation of damages, that he made or offered an apology to the plaintiff for such defamation before the commencement of the action, or as soon afterwards as he had an opportunity of doing so, in case the action shall have been commenced before there was an opportunity of making or offering such apology.

2 IN AN ACTION AGAINST A NEWSPAPER FOR LIBEL, THE DEFENDANT MAY PLEAD THAT IT WAS INSERTED WITHOUT MALICE AND WITHOUT NEGLECT, AND MAY PAY MONEY INTO COURT AS AMENDS

In an action for libel contained in any public newspaper or other periodical publication it shall be competent to the defendant to plead that such libel was inserted in such newspaper or other periodical publication without actual malice, and without gross negligence, and that before the commencement of the action, or at the earliest opportunity afterwards, he inserted in such newspaper or other periodical publication a full apology for the said libel, or, if the newspaper or periodical publication in which the said libel appeared should be ordinarily published at intervals exceeding one week, had offered to publish the said apology in any newspaper or periodical publication to be selected by the plaintiff in such action; . . . and to such plea to such action it shall be competent to the plaintiff to reply generally, denying the whole of such plea.

LIBEL ACT 1845
(c.75)

2 DEFENDANT NOT TO FILE SUCH PLEA WITHOUT PAYING MONEY INTO COURT BY WAY OF AMENDS

It shall not be competent to any defendant in such action, whether in England or in Ireland, to file any such plea, without at the same time making a payment of money into court by way of amends . . . but every such plea so filed without payment of money into court shall be deemed a nullity, and may be treated as such by the plaintiff in the action.

OFFENCES AGAINST THE PERSON ACT 1861
(c.100)

44 IF THE MAGISTRATES DISMISS THE COMPLAINT, THEY SHALL MAKE OUT A CERTIFICATE TO THAT EFFECT

If the justices, upon the hearing of any . . . . case of assault or battery upon the merits, where the complaint was preferred by or on behalf of the party aggrieved . . . shall deem the offence not to be proved, or shall find the assault or battery to have been justified, or so trifling as not to merit any punishment, and shall accordingly dismiss the complaint, they shall forthwith make out a certificate [. . .] stating the fact of such dismissal, and shall deliver such certificate to the party against whom the complaint was preferred.

45 CERTIFICATE OR CONVICTION SHALL BE A BAR TO ANY OTHER PROCEEDINGS

If any person against whom any such complaint as is mentioned in section 44 of this Act shall have been preferred by or on the behalf of the party aggrieved shall have obtained such certificate, or, having been convicted, shall have paid the whole amount adjudged to be paid, or shall have suffered the imprisonment . . . awarded, in every such case he shall be released from all further or other proceedings, civil or criminal, for the same cause.

LAW OF LIBEL AMENDMENT ACT 1888
(c.64)

5 CONSOLIDATION OF ACTIONS

It shall be competent for a judge or the court, upon an application by or on behalf of two or more defendants in actions in respect to the same, or substantially the same, libel brought by one and the same person, to make an order for the consolidation of such actions, so that they shall be tried together; and after such order has been made, and before the trial of the said actions, the defendants in any new actions instituted in respect of the same, or substantially the same, libel shall also be entitled to be joined in a common action upon a joint application being made by such new defendants and the defendants in the actions already consolidated.

In a consolidated action under this section the jury shall assess the whole amount of the damages (if any) in one sum, but a separate verdict shall be taken for or against each defendant in the same way as if the actions consolidated had been tried separately; and if the jury shall have found a verdict against the defendant or defendants in more than one of the actions so consolidated, they shall proceed to apportion the amount of damages which they shall have so found between and against the said last-mentioned defendants; and the judge at the trial, if he awards to the plaintiff the costs of the action, shall thereupon make such order as he shall deem just for the apportionment of such costs between and against such defendants.

FACTORS ACT 1889
(c.45)

Preliminary

1 DEFINITIONS

For the purposes of this Act—
(1) The expression "mercantile agent" shall mean a mercantile agent having in the customary course of his business as such agent authority either to sell goods, or to consign goods for the purpose of sale, or to buy goods, or to raise money on the security of goods:

(2) A person shall be deemed to be in possession of goods or of the documents of title to goods, where the goods or documents are in his actual custody or are held by any other person subject to his control or for him or on his behalf:

(3) The expression "goods" shall include wares and merchandise:

(4)   The expression "document of title" shall include any bill of lading, dock warrant, warehouse-keeper's certificate, and warrant or order for the delivery of goods, and any other document used in the ordinary course of business as proof of the possession or control of goods, or authorising or purporting to authorise, either by endorsement or by delivery, the possessor of the document to transfer or receive goods thereby represented:

(5)   The expression "pledge" shall include any contract pledging, or giving a lien or security on, goods, whether in consideration of an original advance or of any further or continuing advance or of any pecuniary liability:

(6)   The expression "person" shall include any body of persons corporate or unincorporate.

Dispositions by Mercantile Agents

2   POWERS OF MERCANTILE AGENT WITH RESPECT TO DISPOSITION OF GOODS

(1)   Where a mercantile agent is, with the consent of the owner, in possession of goods or of the documents of title to goods, any sale, pledge, or other disposition of the goods, made by him when acting in the ordinary course of business of a mercantile agent, shall, subject to the provisions of this Act, be as valid as if he were expressly authorised by the owner of the goods to make the same; provided that the person taking under the disposition acts in good faith, and has not at the time of the disposition notice that the person making the disposition has not authority to make the same.

(2)   Where a mercantile agent has, with the consent of the owner, been in possession of goods or of the documents of title to goods, any sale, pledge, or other disposition, which would have been valid if the consent had continued, shall be valid notwithstanding the determination of the consent: provided that the person taking under the disposition has not at the time thereof notice that the consent has been determined.

(3)   Where a mercantile agent has obtained possession of any documents of title to goods by reason of his being or having been, with the consent of the owner, in possession of the goods represented thereby, or of any other documents of title to the goods, his possession of the first-mentioned documents shall, for the purposes of this Act, be deemed to be with the consent of the owner.

(4)   For the purposes of this Act the consent of the owner shall be presumed in the absence of evidence to the contrary.

Dispositions by Sellers and Buyers of Goods

8   DISPOSITION BY SELLER REMAINING IN POSSESSION

Where a person, having sold goods, continues, or is, in possession of the goods or of the documents of title to the goods, the delivery or transfer by that person, or by a mercantile agent acting for him, of the goods or documents of title under any sale, pledge, or other disposition thereof, or under any agreement for sale, pledge, or other disposition thereof, to any person receiving the same in good faith and without notice of the previous sale, shall have the same effect as if the person making the delivery or transfer were expressly authorised by the owner of the goods to make the same.

9   DISPOSITION BY BUYER OBTAINING POSSESSION

Where a person, having bought or agreed to buy goods, obtains with the consent of the seller possession of the goods or the documents of title to the goods, the delivery or transfer, by that person or by a mercantile agent acting for him, of the goods or documents of title, under any sale, pledge, or other disposition thereof, or under any agreement for sale, pledge, or other disposition thereof, to any person receiving the same in good faith and without notice of any lien or other right of the original seller in respect of the goods, shall have the same effect as if the person making the delivery or transfer were a mercantile agent in possession of the goods or documents of title with the consent of the owner. For the purposes of this section—

(i)   the buyer under a conditional sale agreement shall be deemed not to be a person who has bought or agreed to buy goods, and

(ii)   "conditional sale agreement" means an agreement for the sale of goods which is a consumer credit agreement within the meaning of the Consumer Credit Act 1974 under which the purchase price or part of it is payable by instalments, and the property in the goods is to remain in the seller (notwithstanding that the buyer is to be in possession of the goods) until such conditions as to the payment of instalments or otherwise as may be specified in the agreement are fulfilled.

As amended by Consumer Credit Act 1974, s. 192 and Sch. 4, Pt. 1, para. 2.

SLANDER OF WOMEN ACT 1891
(c.51)

1 AMENDMENT OF LAW

Words spoken and published which impute unchastity or adultery to any woman or girl shall not require special damage to render them actionable.

Provided always, that in any action for words spoken and made actionable by this Act, a plaintiff shall not recover more costs than damages, unless the judge shall certify that there was reasonable ground for bringing the action.

2 SHORT TITLE AND EXTENT

This Act may be cited as the Slander of Women Act 1891, and shall not apply to Scotland.

LAW REFORM (MISCELLANEOUS PROVISIONS) ACT 1934
(c.41)

1 EFFECT OF DEATH ON CERTAIN CAUSES OF ACTION

(1)   Subject to the provisions of this section, on the death of any person after the commencement of this Act all causes of action subsisting against or vested in him shall survive against, or, as the case may be, for the benefit of, his estate. Provided that this subsection shall not apply to causes of action for defamation. . . . .

(1A)   The right of a person to claim under section 1A of the Fatal Accidents Act 1976 (bereavement) shall not survive for the benefit of his estate on his death.

(2)   Where a cause of action survives as aforesaid for the benefit of the estate of a deceased person, the damages recoverable for the benefit of the estate of that person—
    (a) shall not include—
        (i) any exemplary damages;
        (ii) any damages for loss of income in respect of any period after that person's death;]
    (b) ....
    (c) Where the death of that person has been caused by the act or omission which gives rise to the cause of action, shall be calculated without reference to any loss or gain to his estate consequent on his death, except that a sum in respect of funeral expenses may be included.

(3)   ....

(4)   Where damage has been suffered by reason of any act or omission in respect of which a cause of action would have subsisted against any person if that person had not died before or at the same time as the damage was suffered, there shall be deemed, for the purposes of this Act, to have been subsisting against him before his death such cause of action in respect of that act or omission as would have subsisted if he had died after the damage was suffered.

(5)   The rights conferred by this Act for the benefit of the estates of deceased persons shall be in addition to and not in derogation of any rights conferred on the dependants of deceased persons by the Fatal Accidents Acts 1976 . . . and so much of this Act as relates to causes of action against the estates of deceased persons shall apply in relation to causes of action under the said Acts as it applies in relation to other causes of action not expressly excepted from the operation of subsection (1) of this section.

(6)   In the event of the insolvency of an estate against which proceedings are maintainable by virtue of this section, any liability in respect of the cause of action in respect of which the proceedings are maintainable shall be deemed to be a debt provable in the administration of the estate, notwithstanding that it is a demand in the nature of unliquidated damages arising otherwise than by a contract, promise or breach of trust.

LAW REFORM (MARRIED WOMEN AND TORTFEASORS) ACT 1935
(c.30)

1 CAPACITY OF MARRIED WOMEN

Subject to the provisions of this Part of this Act, . . ., a married woman shall—

(a)   be capable of acquiring, holding, and disposing of, any property; and

(b)   be capable of rendering herself, and being rendered, liable in respect of any tort, contract, debt, or obligation; and

(c)   be capable of suing and being sued, either in tort or in contract or otherwise; and

(d)   be subject to the law relating to bankruptcy and to the enforcement of judgments and orders,

in all respects as if she were a feme sole.

3 ABOLITION OF HUSBAND'S LIABILITY FOR WIFE'S TORTS AND ANTE-NUPTIAL CONTRACTS DEBTS AND OBLIGATIONS

Subject to the provisions of this Part of this Act, the husband of a married woman shall not, by reason only of his being her husband, be liable—

(a) in respect of any tort committed by her whether before or after the marriage, or in respect of any contract entered into, or debt or obligation incurred, by her before the marriage; or

(b) to be sued, or made a party to any legal proceeding brought, in respect of any such tort, contract, debt, or obligation.

4 SAVINGS

(2) For the avoidance of doubt it is hereby declared that nothing in this Part of this Act—

    (a) renders the husband of a married woman liable in respect of any contract entered into, or debt or obligation incurred, by her after the marriage in respect of which he would not have been liable if this Act had not been passed;

    (b) exempts the husband of a married woman from liability in respect of any contract entered into, or debt or obligation (not being a debt or obligation arising out of the commission of a tort) incurred, by her after the marriage in respect of which he would have been liable if this Act had not been passed;

    (c) prevents a husband and wife from acquiring, holding, and disposing of, any property jointly or as tenants in common, or from rendering themselves, or being rendered, jointly liable in respect of any tort, contract, debt or obligation, and of suing and being sued either in tort or in contract or otherwise, in like manner as if they were not married;

    (d) prevents the exercise of any joint power given to a husband and wife.

LAW REFORM (FRUSTRATED CONTRACTS) ACT 1943
(c.40)

1 ADJUSTMENT OF RIGHTS AND LIABILITIES OF PARTIES TO FRUSTRATED CONTRACTS

(1) Where a contract governed by English law has become impossible of performance or been otherwise frustrated, and the parties thereto have for that reason been discharged from the further performance of the contract, the following provisions of this section shall, subject to the provisions of section two of this Act, have effect in relation thereto.

(2) All sums paid or payable to any party in pursuance of the contract before the time when the parties were so discharged (in this Act referred to as "the time of discharge") shall, in the case of sums so paid, be recoverable from him as money received by him for the use of the party by whom the sums were paid, and, in the case of sums so payable, cease to be so payable:

Provided that, if the party to whom the sums were so paid or payable incurred expenses before the time of discharge in, or for the purpose of, the performance of the contract, the court may, if it considers it just to do so having regard to all the circumstances of the case, allow him to retain or, as the case may be, recover the whole or any part of the sums so paid or payable, not being an amount in excess of the expenses so incurred.

(3) Where any party to the contract has, by reason of anything done by any other party thereto in, or for the purpose of, the performance of the contract, obtained a valuable

benefit (other than a payment of money to which the last foregoing subsection applies) before the time of discharge, there shall be recoverable from him by the said other party such sum (if any), not exceeding the value of the said benefit to the party obtaining it, as the court considers just, having regard to all the circumstances of the case and, in particular,—

(a) the amount of any expenses incurred before the time of discharge by the benefited party in, or for the purpose of, the performance of the contract, including any sums paid or payable by him to any other party in pursuance of the contract and retained or recoverable by that party under the last foregoing subsection, and

(b) the effect, in relation to the said benefit, of the circumstances giving rise to the frustration of the contract.

(4) In estimating, for the purposes of the foregoing provisions of this section, the amount of any expenses incurred by any party to the contract, the court may, without prejudice to the generality of the said provisions, include such sum as appears to be reasonable in respect of overhead expenses and in respect of any work or services performed personally by the said party.

(5) In considering whether any sum ought to be recovered or retained under the foregoing provisions of this section by any party to the contract, the court shall not take into account any sums which have, by reason of the circumstances giving rise to the frustration of the contract, become payable to that party under any contract of insurance unless there was an obligation to insure imposed by an express term of the frustrated contract or by or under any enactment.

(6) Where any person has assumed obligations under the contract in consideration of the conferring of a benefit by any other party to the contract upon any other person, whether a party to the contract or not, the court may, if in all the circumstances of the case it considers it just to do so, treat for the purposes of subsection (3) of this section any benefit so conferred as a benefit obtained by the person who has assumed the obligations as aforesaid.

2 PROVISION AS TO APPLICATION OF THIS ACT

(1) This Act shall apply to contracts, whether made before or after the commencement of this Act, as respects which the time of discharge is on or after the first day of July, nineteen hundred and forty-three, but not to contracts as respects which the time of discharge is before the said date.

(2) This Act shall apply to contracts to which the Crown is a party in like manner as to contracts between subjects.

(3) Where any contract to which this Act applies contains any provision which, upon the true construction of the contract, is intended to have effect in the event of circumstances arising which operate, or would but for the said provision operate, to frustrate the contract, or is intended to have effect whether such circumstances arise or not, the court shall give effect to the said provision and shall only give effect to the foregoing section of this Act to such extent, if any, as appears to the court to be consistent with the said provision.

(4) Where it appears to the court that a part of any contract to which this Act applies can properly be severed from the remainder of the contract, being a part wholly performed before the time of discharge, or so performed except for the payment in respect of that part of the contract of sums which are or can be ascertained under the contract, the court shall treat that part of the contract as if it were a separate contract and had not been frustrated and shall treat the foregoing section of this Act as only applicable to the remainder of that contract.

(5)   This Act shall not apply—
  (a) to any charterparty, except a time charterparty or a charterparty by way of demise, or to any contract (other than a charterparty) for the carriage of goods by sea; or
  (b) to any contract of insurance, save as is provided by subsection (5) of the foregoing section; or
  (c) to any contract to which section 7 of the Sale of Goods Act 1979 (which avoids contracts for the sale of specific goods which perish before the risk has passed to the buyer) applies, or to any other contract for the sale, or for the sale and delivery, of specific goods, where the contract is frustrated by reason of the fact that the goods have perished.

3 SHORT TITLE AND INTERPRETATION

(1)   This Act may be cited as the Law Reform (Frustrated Contracts) Act 1943.

(2)   In this Act the expression "court" means, in relation to any matter, the court or arbitrator by or before whom the matter falls to be determined.

As amended by Sale of Goods Act 1979, ss. 62–63 and Sch. 2, para. 2.

LAW REFORM (CONTRIBUTORY NEGLIGENCE) ACT 1945
(c.28)

1 APPORTIONMENT OF LIABILITY IN CASE OF CONTRIBUTORY NEGLIGENCE

(1)   Where any person suffers damage as the result partly of his own fault and partly of the fault of any other person or persons, a claim in respect of that damage shall not be defeated by reason of the fault of the person suffering the damage, but the damages recoverable in respect thereof shall be reduced to such extent as the court thinks just and equitable having regard to the claimant's share in the responsibility for the damage:

Provided that—
  (a) this subsection shall not operate to defeat any defence arising under a contract;
  (b) where any contract or enactment providing for the limitation of liability is applicable to the claim, the amount of damages recoverable by the claimant by virtue of this subsection shall not exceed the maximum limit so applicable.

(2)   Where damages are recoverable by any person by virtue of the foregoing subsection subject to such reduction as is therein mentioned, the court shall find and record the total damages which would have been recoverable if the claimant had not been at fault.

(3)   . . .

(4)   . . .

(5)   Where, in any case to which subsection (1) of this section applies, one of the persons at fault avoids liability to any other such person or his personal representative by pleading the Limitation Act 1939, or any other enactment limiting the time within which proceedings may be taken, he shall not be entitled to recover any damages from that other person or representative by virtue of the said subsection.

(6)   Where any case to which subsection (1) of this section applies is tried with a jury, the jury shall determine the total damages which would have been recoverable if the claimant had not been at fault and the extent to which those damages are to be reduced.

(7)   ...

4 INTERPRETATION

The following expressions have the meanings hereby respectively assigned to them, that is to say—

"court" means, in relation to any claim, the court or arbitrator by or before whom the claim falls to be determined;

"damage" includes loss of life and personal injury;

"fault" means negligence, breach of statutory duty or other act or omission which gives rise to a liability in tort or would, apart from this Act, give rise to the defence of contributory negligence.

5 APPLICATION TO SCOTLAND

In the application of this Act to Scotland—

(a)   the expression "dependant" means, in relation to any person, any person who would in the event of such first mentioned person's death through the fault of a third party be entitled to sue that third party for damages or solatium; and the expression "fault" means wrongful act, breach of statutory duty or negligent act or omission which gives rise to liability in damages, or would apart from this Act, give rise to the defence of contributory negligence;

(b)   section 3 of the Law Reform (Miscellaneous Provisions) (Scotland) Act 1940 (contribution among joint wrongdoers) shall apply in any case where two or more persons are liable, or would if they had all been sued be liable, by virtue of section 1(1) of this Act in respect of the damage suffered by any person.

(c)   for subsection (4) of section one the following subsection shall be substituted—

(4)   Where any person dies as the result partly of his own fault and partly of the fault of any other person or persons, a claim by any dependant of the first mentioned person for damages or solatium in respect of that person's death shall not be defeated by reason of his fault, but the damages or solatium recoverable shall be reduced to such extent as the court thinks just and equitable having regard to the share of the said person in the responsibility for his death.

CROWN PROCEEDINGS ACT 1947
(c.44)

2 LIABILITY OF THE CROWN IN TORT

(1)   Subject to the provisions of this Act, the Crown shall be subject to all those liabilities in tort to which, if it were a private person of full age and capacity, it would be subject:—
   (a) in respect of torts committed by its servants or agents;
   (b) in respect of any breach of those duties which a person owes to his servants or agents at common law by reason of being their employer; and

(c) in respect of any breach of the duties attaching at common law to the ownership, occupation, possession or control of property:

Provided that no proceedings shall lie against the Crown by virtue of paragraph (a) of this subsection in respect of any act or omission of a servant or agent of the Crown unless the act or omission would apart from the provisions of this Act have given rise to a cause of action in tort against that servant or agent or his estate.

(2) Where the Crown is bound by a statutory duty which is binding also upon persons other than the Crown and its officers, then, subject to the provisions of this Act, the Crown shall, in respect of a failure to comply with that duty, be subject to all those liabilities in tort (if any) to which it would be so subject if it were a private person of full age and capacity.

(3) Where any functions are conferred or imposed upon an officer of the Crown as such either by any rule of the common law or by statute, and that officer commits a tort while performing or purporting to perform those functions, the liabilities of the Crown in respect of the tort shall be such as they would have been if those functions had been conferred or imposed solely by virtue of instructions lawfully given by the Crown.

(4) Any enactment which negatives or limits the amount of the liability of any Government department, part of the Scottish Administration or officer of the Crown in respect of any tort committed by that department, part or officer shall, in the case of proceedings against the Crown under this section in respect of a tort committed by that department, part or officer, apply in relation to the Crown as it would have applied in relation to that department, part or officer if the proceedings against the Crown had been proceedings against that department, part or officer.

(5) No proceedings shall lie against the Crown by virtue of this section in respect of anything done or omitted to be done by any person while discharging or purporting to discharge any responsibilities of a judicial nature vested in him, or any responsibilities which he has in connection with the execution of judicial process.

(6) No proceedings shall lie against the Crown by virtue of this section in respect of any act, neglect or default of any officer of the Crown, unless that officer has been directly or indirectly appointed by the Crown and was at the material time paid in respect of his duties as an officer of the Crown wholly out of the Consolidated Fund of the United Kingdom, moneys provided by Parliament, the Scottish Consolidated Fund, . . . or any other Fund certified by the Treasury for the purposes of this subsection or was at the material time holding an office in respect of which the Treasury certify that the holder thereof would normally be so paid.

4 APPLICATION OF LAW AS TO INDEMNITY, CONTRIBUTION, JOINT AND SEVERAL TORTFEASORS, AND CONTRIBUTORY NEGLIGENCE

(1) Where the Crown is subject to any liability by virtue of this Part of this Act, the law relating to indemnity and contribution shall be enforceable by or against the Crown in respect of the liability to which it is so subject as if the Crown were a private person of full age and capacity.

. . .

(3) Without prejudice to the general effect of section one of this Act, the Law Reform (Contributory Negligence) Act 1945 (which amends the law relating to contributory negligence) shall bind the Crown.

LAW REFORM (PERSONAL INJURIES) ACT 1948
(c.41)

1 COMMON EMPLOYMENT

(1)   It shall not be a defence to an employer who is sued in respect of personal injuries caused by the negligence of a person employed by him, that that person was at the time the injuries were caused in common employment with the person injured.

...

(3)   Any provision contained in a contract of service or apprenticeship, or in an agreement collateral thereto, (including a contract or agreement entered into before the commencement of this Act) shall be void in so far as it would have the effect of excluding or limiting any liability of the employer in respect of personal injuries caused to the person employed or apprenticed by the negligence of persons in common employment with him.

2 MEASURE OF DAMAGES

...

(4)   In an action for damages for personal injuries (including any such action arising out of a contract), there shall be disregarded, in determining the reasonableness of any expenses, the possibility of avoiding those expenses or part of them by taking advantage of facilities available under the National Health Service Act 2006 or the National Health Service (Wales) Act 2006 or the National Health Service (Scotland) Act 1978, or of any corresponding facilities in Northern Ireland.

3 DEFINITION OF "PERSONAL INJURY"

In this Act the expression "personal injury" includes any disease and any impairment of a person's physical or mental condition, and the expression "injured" shall be construed accordingly.

4 APPLICATION TO CROWN

This Act shall bind the Crown.

DEFAMATION ACT 1952
(c.66)

2 SLANDER AFFECTING OFFICIAL, PROFESSIONAL OR BUSINESS REPUTATION

In an action for slander in respect of words calculated to disparage the plaintiff in any office, profession, calling, trade or business held or carried on by him at the time of the publication, it shall not be necessary to allege or prove special damage, whether or not the words are spoken of the plaintiff in the way of his office, profession, calling, trade or business.

3 SLANDER OF TITLE, ETC.

(1)   In an action for slander of title, slander of goods or other malicious falsehood, it shall not be necessary to allege or prove special damage—

(a) if the words upon which the action is founded are calculated to cause pecuniary damage to the plaintiff and are published in writing or other permanent form; or

(b) if the said words are calculated to cause pecuniary damage to the plaintiff in respect of any office, profession, calling, trade or business held or carried on by him at the time of the publication.

(2) Section one of this Act shall apply for the purposes of this section as it applies for the purposes of the law of libel and slander.

5 JUSTIFICATION

In an action for libel or slander in respect of words containing two or more distinct charges against the plaintiff, a defence of justification shall not fail by reason only that the truth of every charge is not proved if the words not proved to be true do not materially injure the plaintiff's reputation having regard to the truth of the remaining charges.

6 FAIR COMMENT

In an action for libel or slander in respect of words consisting partly of allegations of fact and partly of expression of opinion, a defence of fair comment shall not fail by reason only that the truth of every allegation of fact is not proved if the expression of opinion is fair comment having regard to such of the facts alleged or referred to in the words complained of as are proved.

9 EXTENSION OF CERTAIN DEFENCES TO BROADCASTING

(1) Section three of the Parliamentary Papers Act 1840 (which confers protection in respect of proceedings for printing extracts from or abstracts of parliamentary papers) shall have effect as if the reference to printing included a reference to broadcasting by means of wireless telegraphy.

10 LIMITATION ON PRIVILEGE AT ELECTION

A defamatory statement published by or on behalf of a candidate in any election to a local government authority, to the National Asssembly of Wales, to the Scottish Parliament or to Parliament shall not be deemed to be published on a privileged occasion on the ground that it is material to a question in issue in the election, whether or not the person by whom it is published is qualified to vote at the election.

11 AGREEMENTS FOR INDEMNITY

An agreement for indemnifying any person against civil liability for libel in respect of the publication of any matter shall not be unlawful unless at the time of the publication that person knows that the matter is defamatory, and does not reasonably believe there is a good defence to any action brought upon it.

12 EVIDENCE OF OTHER DAMAGES RECOVERED BY PLAINTIFF

In any action for libel or slander the defendant may give evidence in mitigation of damages that the plaintiff has recovered damages, or has brought actions for damages, for libel or slander in respect of the publication of words to the same effect as the words on which the action is founded, or has received or agreed to receive compensation in respect of any such publication.

13 CONSOLIDATION OF ACTIONS FOR SLANDER ETC.

Section five of the Law of Libel Amendment Act 1888 (which provides for the consolidation, on the application of the defendants, of two or more actions for libel by the same plaintiff) shall apply to actions for slander and to actions for slander of title, slander of goods or other malicious falsehood as it applies to actions for libel; and references in that section to the same, or substantially the same, libel shall be construed accordingly.

14 APPLICATION OF ACT TO SCOTLAND

This Act shall apply to Scotland subject to the following modifications, that is to say:—
   (a) sections one, two, eight and thirteen shall be omitted;
   (b) for section three there shall be substituted the following section—
        "Actions for verbal injury.
        3.   In any action for verbal injury it shall not be necessary for the pursuer to aver or prove special damage if the words on which the action is founded are calculated to cause pecuniary damage to the pursuer.";
   (c) subsection (2) of section four shall have effect as if at the end thereof there were added the words "Nothing in this subsection shall be held to entitle a defender to lead evidence of any fact specified in the declaration unless notice of his intention so to do has been given in the defences."; and
   (d) for any reference to libel, or to libel or slander, there shall be substituted a reference to defamation; the expression "plaintiff" means pursuer; the expression "defendant" means defender; for any reference to an affidavit made by any person there shall be substituted a reference to a written declaration signed by that person; for any reference to the High Court there shall be substituted a reference to the Court of Session or, if an action of defamation is depending in the sheriff court in respect of the publication in question, the sheriff; the expression "costs" means expenses; and for any reference to a defence of justification there shall be substituted a reference to a defence of veritas.

16 INTERPRETATION

(1)   Any reference in this Act to words shall be construed as including a reference to pictures, visual images, gestures and other methods of signifying meaning.

OCCUPIERS' LIABILITY ACT 1957
(c.31)

1 PRELIMINARY

(1)   The rules enacted by the two next following sections shall have effect, in place of the rules of the common law, to regulate the duty which an occupier of premises owes to his visitors in respect of dangers due to the state of the premises or to things done or omitted to be done on them.

(2)   The rules so enacted shall regulate the nature of the duty imposed by law in consequence of a person's occupation or control of premises and of any invitation or permission he gives (or is to be treated as giving) to another to enter or use the premises, but they shall not alter the rules of the common law as to the persons on whom a duty is so imposed or to whom it is owed; and accordingly for the purpose of the rules so enacted the persons

who are to be treated as an occupier and as his visitors are the same (subject to subsection (4) of this section) as the persons who would at common law be treated as an occupier and as his invitees or licensees.

(3) The rules so enacted in relation to an occupier of premises and his visitors shall also apply, in like manner and to the like extent as the principles applicable at common law to an occupier of premises and his invitees or licensees would apply, to regulate—
(a) the obligations of a person occupying or having control over any fixed or moveable structure, including any vessel, vehicle or aircraft; and
(b) the obligations of a person occupying or having control over any premises or structure in respect of damage to property, including the property of persons who are not themselves his visitors.

(4) A person entering any premises in exercise of rights conferred by virtue of—
(a) section 2(1) of the Countryside and Rights of Way Act 2000, or
(b) an access agreement or order under the National Parks and Access to the Countryside Act 1949,
is not, for the purposes of this Act, a visitor of the occupier of those premises.

2 EXTENT OF OCCUPIER'S ORDINARY DUTY

(1) An occupier of premises owes the same duty, the "common duty of care", to all his visitors, except in so far as he is free to and does extend, restrict, modify or exclude his duty to any visitor or visitors by agreement or otherwise.

(2) The common duty of care is a duty to take such care as in all the circumstances of the case is reasonable to see that the visitor will be reasonably safe in using the premises for the purposes for which he is invited or permitted by the occupier to be there.

(3) The circumstances relevant for the present purpose include the degree of care, and of want of care, which would ordinarily be looked for in such a visitor, so that (for example) in proper cases—
(a) an occupier must be prepared for children to be less careful than adults; and
(b) an occupier may expect that a person, in the exercise of his calling, will appreciate and guard against any special risks ordinarily incident to it, so far as the occupier leaves him free to do so.

(4) In determining whether the occupier of premises has discharged the common duty of care to a visitor, regard is to be had to all the circumstances, so that (for example)—
(a) where damage is caused to a visitor by a danger of which he had been warned by the occupier, the warning is not to be treated without more as absolving the occupier from liability, unless in all the circumstances it was enough to enable the visitor to be reasonably safe; and
(b) where damage is caused to a visitor by a danger due to the faulty execution of any work of construction, maintenance or repair by an independent contractor employed by the occupier, the occupier is not to be treated without more as answerable for the danger if in all the circumstances he had acted reasonably in entrusting the work to an independent contractor and had taken such steps (if any) as he reasonably ought in order to satisfy himself that the contractor was competent and that the work had been properly done.

(5) The common duty of care does not impose on an occupier any obligation to a visitor in respect of risks willingly accepted as his by the visitor (the question whether a risk was so accepted to be decided on the same principles as in other cases in which one person owes a duty of care to another).

(6)   For the purposes of this section, persons who enter premises for any purpose in the exercise of a right conferred by law are to be treated as permitted by the occupier to be there for that purpose, whether they in fact have his permission or not.

3 EFFECT OF CONTRACT ON OCCUPIER'S LIABILITY TO THIRD PARTY

(1)   Where an occupier of premises is bound by contract to permit persons who are strangers to the contract to enter or use the premises, the duty of care which he owes to them as his visitors cannot be restricted or excluded by that contract, but (subject to any provision of the contract to the contrary) shall include the duty to perform his obligations under the contract, whether undertaken for their protection or not, in so far as those obligations go beyond the obligations otherwise involved in that duty.

(2)   A contract shall not by virtue of this section have the effect, unless it expressly so provides, of making an occupier who has taken all reasonable care answerable to strangers to the contract for dangers due to the faulty execution of any work of construction, maintenance or repair or other like operation by persons other than himself, his servants and persons acting under his direction and control.

(3)   In this section "stranger to the contract" means a person not for the time being entitled to the benefit of the contract as a party to it or as the successor by assignment or otherwise of a party to it, and accordingly includes a party to the contract who has ceased to be so entitled.

(4)   Where by the terms or conditions governing any tenancy (including a statutory tenancy which does not in law amount to a tenancy) either the landlord or the tenant is bound, though not by contract, to permit persons to enter or use premises of which he is the occupier, this section shall apply as if the tenancy were a contract between the landlord and the tenant.

(5)   This section, in so far as it prevents the common duty of care from being restricted or excluded, applies to contracts entered into and tenancies created before the commencement of this Act, as well as to those entered into or created after its commencement; but, in so far as it enlarges the duty owed by an occupier beyond the common duty of care, it shall have effect only in relation to obligations which are undertaken after that commencement or which are renewed by agreement (whether express or implied) after that commencement.

5 IMPLIED TERM IN CONTRACTS

(1)   Where persons enter or use, or bring or send goods to, any premises in exercise of a right conferred by contract with a person occupying or having control of the premises, the duty he owes them in respect of dangers due to the state of the premises or to things done or omitted to be done on them, in so far as the duty depends on a term to be implied in the contract by reason of its conferring that right, shall be the common duty of care.

(2)   The foregoing subsection shall apply to fixed and moveable structures as it applies to premises.

(3)   This section does not affect the obligations imposed on a person by or by virtue of any contract for the hire of, or for the carriage for reward of persons or goods in, any vehicle, vessel, aircraft or other means of transport, or by or by virtue of any contract of bailment.

(4)   This section does not apply to contracts entered into before the commencement of this Act.

6 APPLICATION TO CROWN

This Act shall bind the Crown, but as regards the Crown's liability in tort shall not bind the Crown further than the Crown is made liable in tort by the Crown Proceedings Act 1947, and that Act and in particular section two of it shall apply in relation to duties under sections two to four of this Act as statutory duties.

OCCUPIERS' LIABILITY (SCOTLAND) ACT 1960
(c.30)

1 VARIATION OF RULES OF COMMON LAW AS TO DUTY OF CARE OWED BY OCCUPIERS

(1)   The provisions of the next following section of this Act shall have effect, in place of the rules of the common law, for the purpose of determining the care which a person occupying or having control of land or other premises (in this Act referred to as an "occupier of premises") is required, by reason of such occupation or control, to show towards persons entering on the premises in respect of dangers which are due to the state of the premises or to anything done or omitted to be done on them and for which he is in law responsible.

(2)   Nothing in those provisions shall be taken to alter the rules of the common law which determine the person on whom in relation to any premises a duty to show care as aforesaid towards persons entering thereon is incumbent.

(3)   Those provisions shall apply, in like manner and to the same extent as they do in relation to an occupier of premises and to persons entering thereon,—
   (a) in relation to a person occupying or having control of any fixed or moveable structure, including any vessel, vehicle or aircraft, and to persons entering thereon; and
   (b) in relation to an occupier of premises or a person occupying or having control of any such structure and to property thereon, including the property of persons who have not themselves entered on the premises or structure.

2 EXTENT OF OCCUPIER'S DUTY TO SHOW CARE

(1)   The care which an occupier of premises is required, by reason of his occupation or control of the premises, to show towards a person entering thereon in respect of dangers which are due to the state of the premises or to anything done or omitted to be done on them and for which the occupier is in law responsible shall, except in so far as he is entitled to and does extend, restrict, modify or exclude by agreement his obligations towards that person, be such care as in all the circumstances of the case is reasonable to see that that person will not suffer injury or damage by reason of any such danger.

(2)   Nothing in the foregoing subsection shall relieve an occupier of premises of any duty to show in any particular case any higher standard of care which in that case is incumbent on him by virtue of any enactment or rule of law imposing special standards of care on particular classes of persons.

(3)   Nothing in the foregoing provisions of this Act shall be held to impose on an occupier any obligation to a person entering on his premises in respect of risks which that person has willingly accepted as his; and any question whether a risk was so accepted shall be decided on the same principles as in other cases in which one person owes to another a duty to show care.

3 LANDLORD'S LIABILITY BY VIRTUE OF RESPONSIBILITY FOR REPAIRS

(1)   Where premises are occupied or used by virtue of a tenancy under which the landlord is responsible for the maintenance or repair of the premises, it shall be the duty of the landlord to show towards any persons who or whose property may from time to time be on the premises the same care in respect of dangers arising from any failure on his part in carrying out his responsibility aforesaid as is required by virtue of the foregoing provisions of this Act to be shown by an occupier of premises towards persons entering on them.

(2)   Where premises are occupied or used by virtue of a sub-tenancy, the foregoing subsection shall apply to any landlord who is responsible for the maintenance or repair of the premises comprised in the sub-tenancy.

(3)   Nothing in this section shall relieve a landlord of any duty which he is under apart from this section.

(4)   For the purposes of this section, any obligation imposed on a landlord by any enactment by reason of the premises being subject to a tenancy shall be treated as if it were an obligation imposed on him by the tenancy, "tenancy" includes a statutory tenancy which does not in law amount to a tenancy and includes also any contract conferring a right of occupation, and "landlord" shall be construed accordingly.

(5)   This section shall apply to tenancies created before the commencement of this Act as well as to tenancies created after its commencement.

4 APPLICATION TO CROWN

This Act shall bind the Crown, but as regards the liability of the Crown for any wrongful or negligent act or omission giving rise to liability in reparation shall not bind the Crown any further than the Crown is made liable in respect of such acts or omissions by the Crown Proceedings Act 1947, and that Act and in particular section two thereof shall apply in relation to duties under section two or section three of this Act as statutory duties.

LAW REFORM (HUSBAND AND WIFE) ACT 1962
(c.48)

1 ACTIONS IN TORT BETWEEN HUSBAND AND WIFE

(1)   Subject to the provisions of this section, each of the parties to a marriage shall have the like right of action in tort against the other as if they were not married.

(2)   Where an action in tort is brought by one of the parties to a marriage against the other during the subsistence of the marriage, the court may stay the action if it appears—
    (a) that no substantial benefit would accrue to either party from the continuation of the proceedings; or
    (b) that the question or questions in issue could more conveniently be disposed of on an application made under section seventeen of the Married Women's Property Act 1882 (determination of questions between husband and wife as to the title to or possession of property);

and without prejudice to paragraph (b) of this subsection the court may, in such an action, either exercise any power which could be exercised on an application under the said section seventeen, or give such directions as it thinks fit for the disposal under that section of any question arising in the proceedings.

(4)   This section does not extend to Scotland.

3 ... INTERPRETATION

(3)   The references in subsection (1) of section one and subsection (1) of section two of this Act to the parties to a marriage include references to the persons who were parties to a marriage which has been dissolved.

HIRE PURCHASE ACT 1964
(c.53)

Part III TITLE TO MOTOR VEHICLES ON HIRE-PURCHASE OR CONDITIONAL SALE

27 PROTECTION OF PURCHASERS OF MOTOR VEHICLES

(1)   This section applies where a motor vehicle has been bailed or (in Scotland) hired under a hire-purchase agreement, or has been agreed to be sold under a conditional sale agreement, and, before the property in the vehicle has become vested in the debtor, he disposes of the vehicle to another person.

(2)   Where the disposition referred to in subsection (1) above is to a private purchaser, and he is a purchaser of the motor vehicle in good faith without notice of the hire-purchase or conditional sale agreement (the "relevant agreement") that disposition shall have effect as if the creditor's title to the vehicle has been vested in the debtor immediately before that disposition.

(3)   Where the person to whom the disposition referred to in subsection (1) above is made (the "original purchaser") is a trade or finance purchaser, then if the person who is the first private purchaser of the motor vehicle after that disposition (the "first private purchaser") is a purchaser of the vehicle in good faith without notice of the relevant agreement, the disposition of the vehicle to the first private purchaser shall have effect as if the title of the creditor to the vehicle had been vested in the debtor immediately before he disposed of it to the original purchaser.

(4)   Where, in a case within subsection (3) above—
    (a)   the disposition by which the first private purchaser becomes a purchaser of the motor vehicle in good faith without notice of the relevant agreement is itself a bailment or hiring under a hire-purchase agreement, and
    (b)   the person who is the creditor in relation to that agreement disposes of the vehicle to the first private purchaser, or a person claiming under him, by transferring to him the property in the vehicle in pursuance of a provision in the agreement in that behalf,
the disposition referred to in paragraph (b) above (whether or not the person to whom it is made is a purchaser in good faith without notice of the relevant agreement) shall as well as the disposition referred to in paragraph (a) above, have effect as mentioned in sub-section (3) above.

(5)   The preceding provisions of this section apply—
    (a)   notwithstanding anything in section 21 of the Sale of Goods Act 1979 (sale of goods by a person not the owner), but

(b) without prejudice to the provisions of the Factors Acts (as defined by section 61(1) of the said Act of 1979) or of any other enactment enabling the apparent owner of goods to dispose of them as if he were the true owner.

(6) Nothing in this section shall exonerate the debtor from any liability (whether criminal or civil) to which he would be subject apart from this section; and, in a case where the debtor disposes of the motor vehicle to a trade or finance purchaser, nothing in this section shall exonerate—

(a) that trade or finance purchaser, or

(b) any other trade or finance purchaser who becomes a purchaser of the vehicle and is not a person claiming under the first private purchaser,

from any liability (whether criminal or civil) to which he would be subject apart from this section.

28 PRESUMPTIONS RELATING TO DEALINGS WITH MOTOR VEHICLES

(1) Where in any proceedings (whether criminal or civil) relating to a motor vehicle it is proved—

(a) that the vehicle was bailed or (in Scotland) hired under a hire-purchase agreement, or was agreed to be sold under a conditional sale agreement and

(b) that a person (whether a party to the proceedings or not) became a private purchaser of the vehicle in good faith without notice of the hire-purchase or conditional sale agreement (the "relevant agreement"),

this section shall have effect for the purposes of the operation of section 27 of this Act in relation to those proceedings.

(2) It shall be presumed for those purposes, unless the contrary is proved, that the disposition of the vehicle to the person referred to in subsection (1)(b) above (the "relevant purchaser") was made by the debtor.

(3) If it is proved that that disposition was not made by the debtor, then it shall be presumed for those purposes, unless the contrary is proved—

(a) that the debtor disposed of the vehicle to a private purchaser purchasing in good faith without notice of the relevant agreement, and

(b) that the relevant purchaser is or was a person claiming under the person to whom the debtor so disposed of the vehicle.

(4) If it is proved that the disposition of the vehicle to the relevant purchaser was not made by the debtor, and that the person to whom the debtor disposed of the vehicle (the "original purchaser") was a trade or finance purchaser, then it shall be presumed for those purposes, unless the contrary is proved—

(a) that the person who, after the disposition of the vehicle to the original purchaser, first became a private purchaser of the vehicle was a purchaser in good faith without notice of the relevant agreement, and

(b) that the relevant purchaser is or was a person claiming under the original purchaser.

(5) Without prejudice to any other method of proof, where in any proceedings a party thereto admits a fact, that fact shall, for the purposes of this section, be taken as against him to be proved in relation to those proceedings.

29 INTERPRETATION OF PART III

(1) In this Part of this Act—

"conditional sale agreement" means an agreement for the sale of goods under which the purchase price or part of it is payable by instalments, and the property in the goods is to remain in the seller (notwithstanding that the buyer is to be in possession of the goods) until such conditions as to the payment of instalments or otherwise as may be specified in the agreement are fulfilled;

"creditor" means the person by whom goods are bailed or (in Scotland) hired under a hire-purchase agreement or as the case may be, the seller under a conditional sale agreement, or the person to whom his rights and duties have passed by assignment or operation of law;

"disposition" means any sale or contract of sale (including a conditional sale agreement), any bailment or (in Scotland) hiring under a hire-purchase agreement and any transfer of the property in goods in pursuance of a provision in that behalf contained in a hire-purchase agreement, and includes any transaction purporting to be a disposition (as so defined) and "dispose of" shall be construed accordingly;

"hire-purchase agreement" means an agreement, other than a conditional sale agreement, under which—

(a) goods are bailed or (in Scotland) hired in return for periodical payments by the person to whom they are bailed or hired, and

(b) the property in the goods will pass to that person if the terms of the agreement are complied with and one or more of the following occurs—

    (i)   the exercise of an option to purchase by that person,

    (ii) the doing of any other specified act by any party to the agreement,

    (iii) the happening of any other specified events; and

"motor vehicle" means a mechanically propelled vehicle intended or adapted for use on roads to which the public has access.

(2)   In this Part of this Act "trade or finance purchaser" means a purchaser who, at the time of the disposition made to him, carries on a business which consists, wholly or partly,—

(a) of purchasing motor vehicles for the purpose of offering or exposing them for sale, or

(b) of providing finance by purchasing motor vehicles for the purpose of bailing or (in Scotland) hiring them under hire-purchase agreements or agreeing to sell them under conditional sale agreements,

and "private purchaser" means a purchaser who, at the time of the disposition made to him, does not carry on any such business.

(3)   For the purposes of this Part of this Act a person becomes a purchaser of a motor vehicle if, and at the time when, a disposition of the vehicle is made to him; and a person shall be taken to be a purchaser of a motor vehicle without notice of a hire-purchase agreement or conditional sale agreement if, at the time of the disposition made to him, he has no actual notice that the vehicle is or was the subject of any such agreement.

(4)   In this Part of this Act the "debtor" in relation to a motor vehicle which has been bailed or hired under a hire-purchase agreement, or, as the case may be, agreed to be sold under a conditional sale agreement, means the person who at the material time (whether the agreement has before that time been terminated or not) either—

(a) is the person to whom the vehicle is bailed or hired under that agreement, or

(b) is, in relation to the agreement, the buyer,

including a person who at that time is, by virtue of section 130(4) of the Consumer Credit Act 1974 treated as a bailee or (in Scotland) a custodier of the vehicle.

(5)   In this Part of this Act any reference to the title of the creditor to a motor vehicle which has been bailed or (in Scotland) hired under a hire-purchase agreement, or agreed to be sold under a conditional sale agreement, and is disposed of by the debtor, is a reference to such title (if any) to the vehicle as, immediately before that disposition, was vested in the person who then was the creditor in relation to the agreement.

As amended by Consumer Credit Act 1974, s. 192, Sch. 4 Pt 1 and Sch. 5 Pt 1; Sale of Goods Act 1979, s. 63 and Sch. 2, para. 4.

MISREPRESENTATION ACT 1967
(c.7)

1 REMOVAL OF CERTAIN BARS TO RESCISSION FOR INNOCENT MISREPRESENTATION

Where a person has entered into a contract after a misrepresentation has been made to him, and—

(a)   the misrepresentation has become a term of the contract; or

(b)   the contract has been performed;

or both, then, if otherwise he would be entitled to rescind the contract without alleging fraud, he shall be so entitled, subject to the provisions of this Act, notwithstanding the matters mentioned in paragraphs (a) and (b) of this section.

2 DAMAGES FOR MISREPRESENTATION

(1)   Where a person has entered into a contract after a misrepresentation has been made to him by another party thereto and as a result thereof he has suffered loss, then, if the person making the misrepresentation would be liable to damages in respect thereof had the misrepresentation been made fraudulently, that person shall be so liable notwithstanding that the misrepresentation was not made fraudulently, unless he proves that he had reasonable ground to believe and did believe up to the time the contract was made the facts represented were true.

(2)   Where a person has entered into a contract after a misrepresentation has been made to him otherwise than fraudulently, and he would be entitled, by reason of the misrepresentation, to rescind the contract, then, if it is claimed, in any proceedings arising out of the contract, that the contract ought to be or has been rescinded, the court or arbitrator may declare the contract subsisting and award damages in lieu of rescission, if of opinion that it would be equitable to do so, having regard to the nature of the misrepresentation and the loss that would be caused by it if the contract were upheld, as well as to the loss that rescission would cause to the other party.

(3)   Damages may be awarded against a person under subsection (2) of this section whether or not he is liable to damages under subsection (1) thereof, but where he is so liable any award under the said subsection (2) shall be taken into account in assessing his liability under the said subsection (1).

3 AVOIDANCE OF PROVISION EXCLUDING LIABILITY FOR MISREPRESENTATION

If a contract contains a term which would exclude or restrict—

(a)   any liability to which a party to a contract may be subject by reason of any misrepresentation made by him before the contract was made; or

(b)   any remedy available to another party to the contract by reason of such a misrepresentation, that term shall be of no effect except in so far as it satisfies the requirement of reasonableness as stated in section 11(1) of the Unfair Contract Terms Act 1977; and it is for those claiming that the term satisfies that requirement to show that it does.

5 SAVING FOR PAST TRANSACTIONS

Nothing in this Act shall apply in relation to any misrepresentation or contract of sale which is made before the commencement of this Act.

6 SHORT TITLE, COMMENCEMENT AND EXTENT

(1)   This Act may be cited as the Misrepresentation Act 1967.

(2)   This Act shall come into operation at the expiration of the period of one month beginning with the date on which it is passed.

(3)   This Act does not extend to Scotland.

. . .

As amended by Unfair Contract Terms Act 1977, s. 8(1) and Sale of Goods Act 1979, s. 62, s. 63 and Sch. 3.

CRIMINAL LAW ACT 1967
(c.58)

3 USE OF FORCE IN MAKING ARREST, ETC.

(1)   A person may use such force as is reasonable in the circumstances in the prevention of crime, or in effecting or assisting in the lawful arrest of offenders or suspected offenders or of persons unlawfully at large.

(2)   Subsection (1) above shall replace the rules of the common law on the question when force used for a purpose mentioned in the subsection is justified by that purpose.

14 CIVIL RIGHTS IN RESPECT OF MAINTENANCE AND CHAMPERTY

(1)   No person shall, under the law of England and Wales, be liable in tort for any conduct on account of its being maintenance or champerty as known to the common law, except in the case of a cause of action accruing before this section has effect.

(2)   The abolition of criminal and civil liability under the law of England and Wales for maintenance and champerty shall not affect any rule of that law as to the cases in which a contract is to be treated as contrary to public policy or otherwise illegal.

PARLIAMENTARY COMMISSIONER ACT 1967
(c.13)

10 REPORTS BY COMMISSIONER

(5)   For the purposes of the law of defamation, any such publication as is hereinafter mentioned shall be absolutely privileged, that is to say—
   (a) the publication of any matter by the Commissioner in making a report to either House of Parliament for the purposes of this Act;
   (b) the publication of any matter by a member of the House of Commons in communicating with the Commissioner or his officers for those purposes or by the Commissioner or his officers in communicating with such a member for those purposes;
   (c) the publication by such a member to the person by whom a complaint was made under this Act of a report or statement sent to the member in respect of the complaint in pursuance of subsection (1) of this section;
   (d) the publication by the Commissioner to such a person as is mentioned in subsection (2) or (2A) of this section of a report sent to that person in pursuance of that subsection.

THEATRES ACT 1968
(c.54)

4 AMENDMENT OF LAW OF DEFAMATION

(1)   For the purposes of the law of libel and slander . . . the publication of words in the course of a performance of a play shall, subject to section 7 of this Act, be treated as publication in permanent form.

(2)   The foregoing subsection shall apply for the purposes of section 3 (slander of title, etc.) of the Defamation Act 1952 as it applies for the purposes of the law of libel and slander.

(3)   In this section "words" includes pictures, visual images, gestures and other methods of signifying meaning.

(4)   This section shall not apply to Scotland.

7 EXCEPTIONS FOR PERFORMANCES GIVEN IN CERTAIN CIRCUMSTANCES

(1)   Nothing in sections 2 to 4 of this Act shall apply in relation to a performance of a play given on a domestic occasion in a private dwelling.

(2)   Nothing in sections 2 or 6 of this Act shall apply in relation to a performance of a play given solely or primarily for one or more of the following purposes, that is to say—
   (a) rehearsal; or
   (b) to enable—
      (i) a record or cinematograph film to be made from or by means of the performance; or
      (ii) the performance to be broadcast; or
      (iii) the performance to be included in a programme service (within the meaning of the Broadcasting Act 1990) other than a sound or television broadcasting service;

but in any proceedings for an offence under section 2, 5 or 6 of this Act alleged to have been committed in respect of a performance of a play. . . ., if it is proved that the performance was attended by persons other than persons directly connected with the giving of the performance or the doing in relation thereto of any of the things mentioned in paragraph (b) above, the performance shall be taken not to have been given solely or primarily for one or more of the said purposes unless the contrary is shown.

(3)   In this section—

"broadcast" means broadcast by wireless telegraphy (within the meaning of the Wireless Telegraphy Act 2006), whether by way of sound broadcasting or television;

"cinematograph film" means any print, negative, tape or other article on which a performance of a play or any part of such a performance is recorded for the purposes of visual reproduction;

"record" means any record or similar contrivance for reproducing sound, including the sound-track of a cinematograph film.

CIVIL EVIDENCE ACT 1968
(c.64)

11 CONVICTIONS AS EVIDENCE IN CIVIL PROCEEDINGS

(1)   In any civil proceedings the fact that a person has been convicted of an offence by or before any court in the United Kingdom or of a service offence (anywhere) shall (subject to subsection (3) below) be admissible in evidence for the purpose of proving, where to do so is relevant to any issue in those proceedings, that he committed that offence, whether he was so convicted upon a plea of guilty or otherwise and whether or not he is a party to the civil proceedings; but no conviction other than a subsisting one shall be admissible in evidence by virtue of this section.

(2)   In any civil proceedings in which by virtue of this section a person is proved to have been convicted of an offence by or before any court in the United Kingdom or of a service offence (anywhere)—
(a)   he shall be taken to have committed that offence unless the contrary is proved; and
(b)   without prejudice to the reception of any other admissible evidence for the purpose of identifying the facts on which the conviction was based, the contents of any document which is admissible as evidence of the conviction, and the contents of the information, complaint, indictment or charge-sheet on which the person in question was convicted, shall be admissible in evidence for that purpose.

(3)   Nothing in this section shall prejudice the operation of section 13 of this Act or any other enactment whereby a conviction or a finding of fact in any criminal proceedings is for the purposes of any other proceedings made conclusive evidence of any fact.

(4)   Where in any civil proceedings the contents of any document are admissible in evidence by virtue of subsection (2) above, a copy of that document, or of the material part thereof, purporting to be certified or otherwise authenticated by or on behalf of the court or authority having custody of that document shall be admissible in evidence and shall be taken to be a true copy of that document or part unless the contrary is shown.

. . .

(7)   In this section—

"service offence" has the same meaning as in the Armed Forces Ac 2006;

"conviction" includes anything that under s 376(1) and (2) of that Act is to be treated as a conviction, and "convicted" is to be read accordingly.

13 CONCLUSIVENESS OF CONVICTIONS FOR PURPOSES OF DEFAMATION ACTIONS

(1)   In an action for libel or slander in which the question whether the plaintiff did or did not commit a criminal offence is relevant to an issue arising in the action, proof that, at the time when that issue falls to be determined, he stands convicted of that offence shall be conclusive evidence that he committed that offence; and his conviction thereof shall be admissible in evidence accordingly.

(2)   In any such action as aforesaid in which by virtue of this section the plaintiff is proved to have been convicted of an offence, the contents of any document which is admissible as evidence of the conviction, and the contents of the information, complaint, indictment or charge-sheet on which he was convicted, shall, without prejudice to the reception of any other admissible evidence for the purpose of identifying the facts on which the conviction was based, be admissible in evidence for the purpose of identifying those facts.

(2A)   In the case of an action for libel or slander in which there is more than one plaintiff—
(a)   the references in subsections (1) and (2) above to the plaintiff shall be construed as references to any of the plaintiffs, and
(b)   proof that any of the plaintiffs stands convicted of an offence shall be conclusive evidence that he committed that offence so far as that fact is relevant to any issue arising in relation to his cause of action or that of any other plaintiff.

(3)   For the purposes of this section a person shall be taken to stand convicted of an offence if but only if there subsists against him a conviction of that offence by or before a court in the United Kingdom or (or in the case of a service offence) a conviction (anywhere) of that service offence;.

(4)   Subsections (4) to (7) of section 11 of this Act shall apply for the purposes of this section as they apply for the purposes of that section, but as if in the said subsection (4) the reference to subsection (2) were a reference to subsection (2) of this section.

EMPLOYERS' LIABILITY (DEFECTIVE EQUIPMENT) ACT 1969
(c.37)

1 EXTENSION OF EMPLOYER'S LIABILITY FOR DEFECTIVE EQUIPMENT

(1)   Where after the commencement of this Act—
(a)   an employee suffers personal injury in the course of his employment in consequence of a defect in equipment provided by his employer for the purposes of the employer's business; and
(b)   the defect is attributable wholly or partly to the fault of a third party (whether identified or not),

the injury shall be deemed to be also attributable to negligence on the part of the employer (whether or not he is liable in respect of the injury apart from this subsection), but without prejudice to the law relating to contributory negligence and to any remedy by way of contribution or in contract or otherwise which is available to the employer in respect of the injury.

(2)   In so far as any agreement purports to exclude or limit any liability of an employer arising under subsection (1) of this section, the agreement shall be void.

(3)   In this section—

"business" includes the activities carried on by any public body;

"employee" means a person who is employed by another person under a contract of service or apprenticeship and is so employed for the purposes of a business carried on by that other person, and "employer" shall be construed accordingly;

"equipment" includes any plant and machinery, vehicle, aircraft and clothing;

"fault" means negligence, breach of statutory duty or other act or omission which gives rise to liability in tort in England and Wales or which is wrongful and gives rise to liability in damages in Scotland; and

"personal injury" includes loss of life, any impairment of a person's physical or mental condition and any disease.

(4)   This section binds the Crown, and persons in the service of the Crown shall accordingly be treated for the purposes of this section as employees of the Crown if they would not be so treated apart from this subsection.

EMPLOYERS' LIABILITY (COMPULSORY INSURANCE) ACT 1969
(c.57)

1 INSURANCE AGAINST LIABILITY FOR EMPLOYEES

(1)   Except as otherwise provided by this Act, every employer carrying on any business in Great Britain shall insure, and maintain insurance, under one or more approved policies with an authorised insurer or insurers against liability for bodily injury or disease sustained by his employees, and arising out of and in the course of their employment in Great Britain in that business, but except in so far as regulations otherwise provide not including injury or disease suffered or contracted outside Great Britain.

(2)   Regulations may provide that the amount for which an employer is required by this Act to insure and maintain insurance shall, either generally or in such cases or classes of case as may be prescribed by the regulations, be limited in such manner as may be so prescribed.

(3)   For the purposes of this Act—
(a)   "approved policy" means a policy of insurance not subject to any conditions or exceptions prohibited for those purposes by regulations;
(b)   "authorised insurer" means—
(i)   a person who has permission under Part 4 of the Financial Services and Markets Act 2000 to effect and carry out contracts of insurance of a kind required by this Act and regulations made under this Act, or
(ii)   an EEA firm of the kind mentioned in paragraph 5(d) of Schedule 3 to the Financial Services and Markets Act 2000, which has permission under

paragraph 15 of that Schedule to effect and carry out contracts of insurance of a kind required by this Act and regulations made under this Act;

(c) "business" includes a trade or profession, and includes any activity carried on by a body of persons, whether corporate or unincorporate;

(d) except as otherwise provided by regulations, an employer not having a place of business in Great Britain shall be deemed not to carry on business there.

(3A) Subsection (3)(b) must be read with—

(a) section 22 of the Financial Services and Markets Act 2000;

(b) any relevant order under that section; and

(c) Schedule 2 to that Act.

2 EMPLOYEES TO BE COVERED

(1) For the purposes of this Act the term "employee" means an individual who has entered into or works under a contract of service or apprenticeship with an employer whether by way of manual labour, clerical work or otherwise, whether such contract is expressed or implied, oral or in writing.

(2) This Act shall not require an employer to insure—

(a) in respect of an employee of whom the employer is the husband, wife, civil partner, father, mother, grandfather, grandmother, step-father, step-mother, son, daughter, grandson, granddaughter, stepson, stepdaughter, brother, sister, half-brother or half-sister; or

(b) except as otherwise provided by regulations, in respect of employees not ordinarily resident in Great Britain.

AGE OF MAJORITY (SCOTLAND) ACT 1969
(c.39)

1 REDUCTION OF AGE OF MAJORITY TO 18

(1) As from the date on which this Act comes into force a person shall attain majority on attaining the age of eighteen instead of on attaining the age of twenty-one; and a person shall attain majority on that date if he has then already attained the age of eighteen but not the age of twenty-one.

FAMILY LAW REFORM ACT 1969
(c.46)

Part I REDUCTION OF AGE OF MAJORITY AND RELATED PROVISIONS

1 REDUCTION OF AGE OF MAJORITY FROM 21 TO 18

(1) As from the date on which this section comes into force a person shall attain full age on attaining the age of eighteen instead of on attaining the age of twenty-one; and a person shall attain full age on that date if he has then already attained the age of eighteen but not the age of twenty-one.

ANIMALS ACT 1971
(c.22)

Strict liability for damage done by animals

1 NEW PROVISIONS AS TO STRICT LIABILITY FOR DAMAGE DONE BY ANIMALS

(1) The provisions of sections 2 to 5 of this Act replace—
   (a) the rules of the common law imposing a strict liability in tort for damage done by an animal on the ground that the animal is regarded as ferae naturae or that its vicious or mischievous propensities are known or presumed to be known;
   (b) subsections (1) and (2) of section 1 of the Dogs Act 1906 as amended by the Dogs (Amendment) Act 1928 (injury to cattle or poultry); and
   (c) the rules of the common law imposing a liability for cattle trespass.

(2) Expressions used in those sections shall be interpreted in accordance with the provisions of section 6 (as well as those of section 11) of this Act.

2 LIABILITY FOR DAMAGE DONE BY DANGEROUS ANIMALS

(1) Where any damage is caused by an animal which belongs to a dangerous species, any person who is a keeper of the animal is liable for the damage, except as otherwise provided by this Act.

(2) Where damage is caused by an animal which does not belong to a dangerous species, a keeper of the animal is liable for the damage, except as otherwise provided by this Act, if—
   (a) the damage is of a kind which the animal, unless restrained, was likely to cause or which, if caused by the animal, was likely to be severe; and
   (b) the likelihood of the damage or of its being severe was due to characteristics of the animal which are not normally found in animals of the same species or are not normally so found except at particular times or in particular circumstances; and
   (c) those characteristics were known to that keeper or were at any time known to a person who at that time had charge of the animal as that keeper's servant or, where that keeper is the head of a household, were known to another keeper of the animal who is a member of that household and under the age of sixteen.

3 LIABILITY FOR INJURY DONE BY DOGS TO LIVESTOCK

Where a dog causes damage by killing or injuring livestock, any person who is a keeper of the dog is liable for the damage, except as otherwise provided by this Act.

4 LIABILITY FOR DAMAGE AND EXPENSES DUE TO TRESPASSING LIVESTOCK

(1) Where livestock belonging to any person strays on to land in the ownership or occupation of another and—
   (a) damage is done by the livestock to the land or to any property on it which is in the ownership or possession of the other person; or
   (b) any expenses are reasonably incurred by that other person in keeping the livestock while it cannot be restored to the person to whom it belongs or while it is detained in pursuance of section 7 of this Act, or in ascertaining to whom it belongs;

the person to whom the livestock belongs is liable for the damage or expenses, except as otherwise provided by this Act.

(2)   For the purposes of this section any livestock belongs to the person in whose possession it is.

5 EXCEPTIONS FROM LIABILITY UNDER SECTIONS 2 TO 4

(1)   A person is not liable under sections 2 to 4 of this Act for any damage which is due wholly to the fault of the person suffering it.

(2)   A person is not liable under section 2 of this Act for any damage suffered by a person who has voluntarily accepted the risk thereof.

(3)   A person is not liable under section 2 of this Act for any damage caused by an animal kept on any premises or structure to a person trespassing there, if it is proved either—
(a) that the animal was not kept there for the protection of persons or property; or
(b) (if the animal was kept there for the protection of persons or property) that keeping it there for that purpose was not unreasonable.

(4)   A person is not liable under section 3 of this Act if the livestock was killed or injured on land on to which it had strayed and either the dog belonged to the occupier or its presence on the land was authorised by the occupier.

(5)   A person is not liable under section 4 of this Act where the livestock strayed from a highway and its presence there was a lawful use of the highway.

(6)   In determining whether any liability for damage under section 4 of this Act is excluded by subsection (1) of this section the damage shall not be treated as due to the fault of the person suffering it by reason only that he could have prevented it by fencing; but a person is not liable under that section where it is proved that the straying of the livestock on to the land would not have occurred but for a breach by any other person, being a person having an interest in the land, of a duty to fence.

6 INTERPRETATION OF CERTAIN EXPRESSIONS USED IN SECTIONS 2 TO 5

(1)   The following provisions apply to the interpretation of sections 2 to 5 of this Act.

(2)   A dangerous species is a species—
(a) which is not commonly domesticated in the British Islands; and
(b) whose fully grown animals normally have such characteristics that they are likely, unless restrained, to cause severe damage or that any damage they may cause is likely to be severe.

(3)   Subject to subsection (4) of this section, a person is a keeper of an animal if—
(a) he owns the animal or has it in his possession; or
(b) he is the head of a household of which a member under the age of sixteen owns the animal or has it in his possession;
and if at any time an animal ceases to be owned by or to be in the possession of a person, any person who immediately before that time was a keeper thereof by virtue of the preceding provisions of this subsection continues to be a keeper of the animal until another person becomes a keeper thereof by virtue of those provisions.

(4)   Where an animal is taken into and kept in possession for the purpose of preventing it from causing damage or of restoring it to its owner, a person is not a keeper of it by virtue only of that possession.

(5)   Where a person employed as a servant by a keeper of an animal incurs a risk incidental to his employment he shall not be treated as accepting it voluntarily.

Detention and sale of trespassing livestock

7 DETENTION AND SALE OF TRESPASSING LIVESTOCK

(1)   The right to seize and detain any animal by way of distress damage feasant is hereby abolished.

(2)   Where any livestock strays on to any land and is not then under the control of any person the occupier of the land may detain it, subject to subsection (3) of this section, unless ordered to return it by a court.

(3)   Where any livestock is detained in pursuance of this section the right to detain it ceases—
    (a)   at the end of a period of forty-eight hours, unless within that period notice of the detention has been given to the officer in charge of a police station and also, if the person detaining the livestock knows to whom it belongs, to that person; or
    (b)   when such amount is tendered to the person detaining the livestock as is sufficient to satisfy any claim he may have under section 4 of this Act in respect of the livestock; or
    (c)   if he has no such claim, when the livestock is claimed by a person entitled to its possession.

(4)   Where livestock has been detained in pursuance of this section for a period of not less than fourteen days the person detaining it may sell it at a market or by public auction, unless proceedings are then pending for the return of the livestock or for any claim under section 4 of this Act in respect of it.

(5)   Where any livestock is sold in the exercise of the right conferred by this section and the proceeds of the sale, less the costs thereof and any costs incurred in connection with it, exceed the amount of any claim under section 4 of this Act which the vendor had in respect of the livestock, the excess shall be recoverable from him by the person who would be entitled to the possession of the livestock but for the sale.

(6)   A person detaining any livestock in pursuance of this section is liable for any damage caused to it by a failure to treat it with reasonable care and supply it with adequate food and water while it is so detained.

(7)   References in this section to a claim under section 4 of this Act in respect of any livestock do not include any claim under that section for damage done by or expenses incurred in respect of the livestock before the straying in connection with which it is detained under this section.

Animals straying on to highway

8 DUTY TO TAKE CARE TO PREVENT DAMAGE FROM ANIMALS STRAYING ON TO THE HIGHWAY

(1)   So much of the rules of the common law relating to liability for negligence as excludes or restricts the duty which a person might owe to others to take such care as is reasonable to see that damage is not caused by animals straying on to a highway is hereby abolished.

(2)   Where damage is caused by animals straying from unfenced land to a highway a person who placed them on the land shall not be regarded as having committed a breach of the duty to take care by reason only of placing them there if—

(a) the land is common land, or is land situated in an area where fencing is not customary, or is a town or village green; and

(b) he had a right to place the animals on that land.

Protection of livestock against dogs

9 KILLING OF OR INJURY TO DOGS WORRYING LIVESTOCK

(1) In any civil proceedings against a person (in this section referred to as the defendant) for killing or causing injury to a dog it shall be a defence to prove—

(a) that the defendant acted for the protection of any livestock and was a person entitled to act for the protection of that livestock; and

(b) that within forty-eight hours of the killing or injury notice thereof was given by the defendant to the officer in charge of a police station.

(2) For the purposes of this section a person is entitled to act for the protection of any livestock if, and only if—

(a) the livestock or the land on which it is belongs to him or to any person under whose express or implied authority he is acting; and

(b) the circumstances are not such that liability for killing or causing injury to the livestock would be excluded by section 5(4) of this Act.

(3) Subject to subsection (4) of this section, a person killing or causing injury to a dog shall be deemed for the purposes of this section to act for the protection of any livestock if, and only if, either—

(a) the dog is worrying or is about to worry the livestock and there are no other reasonable means of ending or preventing the worrying; or

(b) the dog has been worrying livestock, has not left the vicinity and is not under the control of any person and there are no practicable means of ascertaining to whom it belongs.

(4) For the purposes of this section the condition stated in either of the paragraphs of the preceding subsection shall be deemed to have been satisfied if the defendant believed that it was satisfied and had reasonable ground for that belief.

(5) For the purposes of this section—

(a) an animal belongs to any person if he owns it or has it in his possession; and

(b) land belongs to any person if he is the occupier thereof.

Supplemental

10 APPLICATION OF CERTAIN ENACTMENTS TO LIABILITY UNDER SECTIONS 2 TO 4

For the purposes of the Fatal Accidents Acts 1846 to 1959, the Law Reform (Contributory Negligence) Act 1945 and the Limitation Act 1980 any damage for which a person is liable under sections 2 to 4 of this Act shall be treated as due to his fault.

11 GENERAL INTERPRETATION

In this Act—

"common land" means—

(a) land registered as common land in a register of common land kept under Part 1 of the Commons Act 2006;

(b) land to which Part 1 of that Act does not apply and which is subject to rights of common within the meaning of that Act;

In Wales common land", and "town or village green" have the same meanings as in the Commons Registration Act 1965;

"damage" includes the death of, or injury to, any person (including any disease and any impairment of physical or mental condition);

"fault" has the same meaning as in the Law Reform (Contributory Negligence) Act 1945;

"fencing" includes the construction of any obstacle designed to prevent animals from straying;

"livestock" means cattle, horses, asses, mules, hinnies, sheep, pigs, goats and poultry, and also deer not in the wild state and, in sections 3 and 9, also, while in captivity, pheasants, partridges and grouse;

"poultry" means the domestic varieties of the following, that is to say, fowls, turkeys, geese, ducks, guinea-fowls, pigeons, peacocks and quails; and

"species" includes sub-species and variety.

"town or village green" means land registered as a town or village green in a register of town or village greens kept under Part 1 of the Commons Act 2006.

12 APPLICATION TO CROWN

(1) This Act binds the Crown, but nothing in this section shall authorise proceedings to be brought against Her Majesty in her private capacity.

(2) Section 38(3) of the Crown Proceedings Act 1947 (interpretation of references to Her Majesty in her private capacity) shall apply as if this section were contained in that Act.

13 SHORT TITLE, REPEAL, COMMENCEMENT AND EXTENT

(1) This Act may be cited as the Animals Act 1971.

(2) The following are hereby repealed, that is to say—
   (a) in the Dogs Act 1906, subsections (1) to (3) of section 1; and
   (b) in section 1(1) of the Dogs (Amendment) Act 1928 the words "in both places where that word occurs".

(3) This Act shall come into operation on 1st October 1971.

(4) This Act does not extend to Scotland or to Northern Ireland.

UNSOLICITED GOODS AND SERVICES ACT 1971
(c.30)

2 DEMANDS AND THREATS REGARDING PAYMENT

(1) A person who, not having reasonable cause to believe there is a right to payment, in the course of any trade or business makes a demand for payment, or asserts a present or prospective right to payment, for what he knows are unsolicited goods sent (after the commencement of this Act) to another person with a view to his acquiring them for the

purposes of his trade or business, shall be guilty of an offence and on summary conviction shall be liable to a fine . . .

(2) A person who, not having reasonable cause to believe there is a right to payment, in the course of any trade or business and with a view to obtaining any payment for what he knows are unsolicited goods sent as aforesaid—
  (a) threatens to bring any legal proceedings; or
  (b) places or causes to be placed the name of any person on a list of defaulters or debtors or threatens to do so; or
  (c) invokes or causes to be invoked any other collection procedure or threatens to do so, shall be guilty of an offence and shall be liable on summary conviction to a fine . . .

3 DIRECTORY ENTRIES

(1) A person ("the purchaser") shall not be liable to make any payment, and shall be entitled to recover any payment made by him, by way of charge for including or arranging for the inclusion in a directory of an entry relating to that person or his trade or business, unless—
  (a) there has been signed by the purchaser or on his behalf an order complying with this section,
  (b) there has been signed by the purchaser or on his behalf a note complying with this section of his agreement to the charge and before the note was signed, a copy of it was supplied, for retention by him, to him or a person acting on his behalf,
  (c) there has been transmitted by the purchaser or a person acting on his behalf an electronic communication which includes a statement that the purchaser agrees to the charge and the relevant condition is satisfied in relation to that communication, or
  (d) the charge arises under a contract in relation to which the conditions in section 3B(1) (renewed and extended contracts) are met.

(2) A person shall be guilty of an offence punishable on summary conviction with a fine . . . if, in a case where a payment in respect of a charge would be recoverable from him in accordance with the terms of subsection (1) above, he demands payment, or asserts a present or prospective right to payment, of the charge or any part of it, without knowing or having reasonable cause to believe that—
  (a) the entry to which the charge relates was ordered in accordance with this section,
  (b) a proper note of the agreement has been duly signed, or
  (c) the requirements set out in subsection (1)(c) or (d) above have been met.

(3) For the purposes of this section—
  (a) an order for an entry in a directory must be made by means of an order form or other stationery belonging to the purchaser, which may be sent electronically but which must bear his name and address (or one or more of his addresses); and
  (b) the note of a person's agreement to a charge must—
    (i) specify the particulars set out in Part 1 of the Schedule to the Regulatory Reform (Unsolicited Goods and Services Act 1971)(Directory Entries and Demands for Payment) Order 2005, and
    (ii) give reasonable particulars of the entry in respect of which the charge would be payable.

(3A) In relation to an electronic communication which includes a statement that the purchaser agrees to a charge for including or arranging the inclusion in a directory of any entry, the relevant condition is that—
  (a) before the electronic communication was transmitted the information referred to in subsection (3B) below was communicated to the purchaser, and

(b)   the electronic communication can readily be produced and retained in a visible and legible form.

(3B) that information is—
    (a)   the following particulars—
        (i)   the amount of the charge;
        (ii)   the name of the directory or proposed directory;
        (iii) the name of the person producing the directory;
        (iv)   the geographic address at which that person is established;
        (v)   if the directory is or is to be available in printed form, the proposed date of publication of the directory or of the issue in which the entry is to be included;
        (vi)   if the directory or the issue in which the entry is to be included is to be put on sale, the price at which it is to be offered for sale and the minimum number of copies which are to be available for sale;
        (vii) if the directory or the issue in which the entry is to be included is to be distributed free of charge (whether or not it is also to be put on sale), the minimum number of copies which are to be so distributed;
        (viii) if the directory is or is to be available in a form other than in printed form, adequate details of how it may be accessed; and
    (b)   reasonable particulars of the entry in respect of which the charge would be payable.

(3C) In this section "electronic communication" has the same meaning as in the Electronic Communications Act 2000.

   . . .

3B RENEWED AND EXTENDED CONTRACTS

(1)   The conditions referred to in section 3(1)(d) above are met in relation to a contract ("the new contract") if—
    (a)   a person ("the purchaser") has entered into an earlier contract ("the earlier contract") for including or arranging for the inclusion in a particular issue or version of a directory ("the earlier directory") of an entry ("the earlier entry") relating to him or his trade or business;
    (b)   the purchaser was liable to make a payment by way of a charge arising under the earlier contract for including or arranging for the inclusion of the earlier entry in the earlier directory;
    (c)   the new contract is a contract for including or arranging for the inclusion in a later issue or version of a directory ("the later directory") of an entry ("the later entry") relating to the purchaser or his trade or business;
    (d)   the form, content and distribution of the later directory is materially the same as the form, content and distribution of the earlier directory;
    (e)   the form and content of the later entry is materially the same as the form and content of the earlier entry;
    (f)   if the later directory is published other than in electronic form—
        (i)   the earlier directory was the last, or the last but one, issue or version of the directory to be published before the later directory, and
        (ii)   the date of publication of the later directory is not more than 13 months after the date of publication of the earlier directory;
    (g)   if the later directory is published in electronic form, the first date on which the new contract requires the later entry to be published is not more than the relevant period after the last date on which the earlier contract required the earlier entry to be published;

(h)   if it was a term of the earlier contract that the purchaser renew or extend the contract—

     (i)   before the start of the new contract the relevant publisher has given notice in writing to the purchaser containing the information set out in Part 3 of the Schedule to the Regulatory Reform (Unsolicited Goods and Services Act 1971) (Directory Entries and Demands for Payment) Order 2005; and

     (ii)   the purchaser has not written to the relevant publisher withdrawing his agreement to the renewal or extension of the earlier contract within the period of 21 days starting when he receives the notice referred to in sub-paragraph (i); and

(i)   if the parties to the earlier contract and the new contract are different—

     (i)   the parties to both contracts have entered into a novation agreement in respect of the earlier contract; or

     (ii)   the relevant publisher has given the purchaser the information set out in Part 4 of the Schedule to the Regulatory Reform (Unsolicited Goods and Services Act 1971) (Directory Entries and Demands for Payment) Order 2005.

(2)   For the purposes of subsection (1)(d) and (e), the form, content or distribution of the later directory, or the form or content of the later entry, shall be taken to be materially the same as that of the earlier directory or the earlier entry (as the case may be), if a reasonable person in the position of the purchaser would—

     (a)   view the two as being materially the same; or

     (b)   view that of the later directory or the later entry as being an improvement on that of the earlier directory or the earlier entry.

(3)   For the purposes of subsection (1)(g) "the relevant period" means the period of 13 months or (if shorter) the period of time between the first and last dates on which the earlier contract required the earlier entry to be published.

(4)   For the purposes of subsection (1)(h) and (i) "the relevant publisher" is the person with whom the purchaser has entered into the new contract.

(5)   The information referred to in subsection (1)(i)(ii) must be given to the purchaser prior to the conclusion of the new contract.

4   UNSOLICITED PUBLICATIONS

(1)   A person shall be guilty of an offence if he sends or causes to be sent to another person any book, magazine or leaflet (or advertising material for any such publication) which he knows or ought reasonably to know is unsolicited and which describes or illustrates human sexual techniques.

(2)   A person found guilty of an offence under this section shall be liable on summary conviction to a fine . . .

(3)   A prosecution for an offence under this section shall not in England and Wales be instituted except by, or with the consent of, the Director of Public Prosecutions.

5   OFFENCES BY CORPORATIONS

(1)   Where an offence under this Act which has been committed by a body corporate is proved to have been committed with the consent or connivance of, or to be attributable to any neglect on the part of, any director, manager, secretary, or other similar officer of the body corporate, or of any person who was purporting to act in any such capacity, he as well as the body corporate shall be guilty of that offence and shall be liable to be proceeded against and punished accordingly.

(2)   Where the affairs of a body corporate are managed by its members, this section shall apply in relation to the acts or defaults of a member in connection with his functions of management as if he were a director of the body corporate.

6 INTERPRETATION

(1)   In this Act, unless the context or subject matter otherwise requires,—

"acquire" includes hire;

"send" includes deliver, and "sender" shall be construed accordingly;

"unsolicited" means, in relation to goods sent to any person, that they are sent without any prior request made by him or on his behalf.

(2)   For the purposes of this Act, any invoice or similar document stating the amount of any payment shall be regarded as asserting a right to the payment unless it complies with the conditions set out in Part 2 of the Schedule to the Regulatory Reform (Unsolicited Goods and Services Act 1971)(Directory Entries and Demands for Payment) Order 2005.

(3)   Nothing in sections 3 or 3B shall affect the rights of any consumer under the Consumer Protection (Distance Selling) Regulations 2000.

As amended by Consumer Protection (Distance Selling Regulations) 2000, reg. 22(3); Unsolicited Goods and Services Act 1971 (Electronic Communications) Order 2001, art. 3, art. 4 and art. 6; Regulatory Reform (Unsolicited Goods and Services Act 1971) (Directory Entries and Demands for Payment) Order 2005, art. 2; Unsolicited Goods and Services Act 1971 (Electronic Commerce) (Amendment) Regulations 2005, reg. 2.

DEFECTIVE PREMISES ACT 1972
(c.35)

1 DUTY TO BUILD DWELLINGS PROPERLY

(1)   A person taking on work for or in connection with the provision of a dwelling (whether the dwelling is provided by the erection or by the conversion or enlargement of a building) owes a duty—
(a) if the dwelling is provided to the order of any person, to that person; and
(b) without prejudice to paragraph (a) above, to every person who acquires an interest (whether legal or equitable) in the dwelling;
to see that the work which he takes on is done in a workmanlike or, as the case may be, professional manner, with proper materials and so that as regards that work the dwelling will be fit for habitation when completed.

(2)   A person who takes on any such work for another on terms that he is to do it in accordance with instructions given by or on behalf of that other shall, to the extent to which he does it properly in accordance with those instructions, be treated for the purposes of this section as discharging the duty imposed on him by subsection (1) above except where he owes a duty to that other to warn him of any defects in the instructions and fails to discharge that duty.

(3)   A person shall not be treated for the purposes of subsection (2) above as having given instructions for the doing of work merely because he has agreed to the work being done in a specified manner, with specified materials or to a specified design.

(4)   A person who—
   (a)   in the course of a business which consists of or includes providing or arranging for the provision of dwellings or installations in dwellings; or
   (b)   in the exercise of a power of making such provision or arrangements conferred by or by virtue of any enactment;
   arranges for another to take on work for or in connection with the provision of a dwelling shall be treated for the purposes of this section as included among the persons who have taken on the work.

(5)   Any cause of action in respect of a breach of the duty imposed by this section shall be deemed, for the purposes of the Limitation Act 1939, the Law Reform (Limitation of Actions, &c.) Act 1954 and the Limitation Act 1963, to have accrued at the time when the dwelling was completed, but if after that time a person who has done work for or in connection with the provision of the dwelling does further work to rectify the work he has already done, any such cause of action in respect of that further work shall be deemed for those purposes to have accrued at the time when the further work was finished.

[NB The references in s 1(5) should now be read as to the Limitation Act 1980 – see Limitation Act 1980 and the Interpretation Act 1978 s 17(2)]

2 CASES EXCLUDED FROM THE REMEDY UNDER SECTION 1

(1)   Where—
   (a)   in connection with the provision of a dwelling or its first sale or letting for habitation any rights in respect of defects in the state of the dwelling are conferred by an approved scheme to which this section applies on a person having or acquiring an interest in the dwelling; and
   (b)   it is stated in a document of a type approved for the purposes of this section that the requirements as to design or construction imposed by or under the scheme have, or appear to have, been substantially complied with in relation to the dwelling;
   no action shall be brought by any person having or acquiring an interest in the dwelling for breach of the duty imposed by section 1 above in relation to the dwelling.

(2)   A scheme to which this section applies—
   (a)   may consist of any number of documents and any number of agreements or other transactions between any number of persons; but
   (b)   must confer, by virtue of agreements entered into with persons having or acquiring an interest in the dwellings to which the scheme applies, rights on such persons in respect of defects in the state of the dwellings.

(3)   In this section "approved" means approved by the Secretary of State, and the power of the Secretary of State to approve a scheme or document for the purposes of this section shall be exercisable by order, except that any requirements as to construction or design imposed under a scheme to which this section applies may be approved by him without making any order or, if he thinks fit, by order.

(4)   The Secretary of State—
   (a)   may approve a scheme or document for the purposes of this section with or without limiting the duration of his approval; and
   (b)   may by order revoke or vary a previous order under this section or, without such an order, revoke or vary a previous approval under this section given otherwise than by order.

(5)   The production of a document purporting to be a copy of an approval given by the Secretary of State otherwise than by order and certified by an officer of the Secretary of State to be a true copy of the approval shall be conclusive evidence of the approval, and without proof of the handwriting or official position of the person purporting to sign the certificate.

(6)   The power to make an order under this section shall be exercisable by statutory instrument which shall be subject to annulment in pursuance of a resolution by either House of Parliament.

(7)   Where an interest in a dwelling is compulsorily acquired—
   (a)   no action shall be brought by the acquiring authority for breach of the duty imposed by section 1 above in respect of the dwelling; and
   (b)   if any work for or in connection with the provision of the dwelling was done otherwise than in the course of a business by the person in occupation of the dwelling at the time of the compulsory acquisition, the acquiring authority and not that person shall be treated as the person who took on the work and accordingly as owing that duty.

3 DUTY OF CARE WITH RESPECT TO WORK DONE ON PREMISES NOT ABATED BY DISPOSAL OF PREMISES

(1)   Where work of construction, repair, maintenance or demolition or any other work is done on or in relation to premises, any duty of care owed, because of the doing of the work, to persons who might reasonably be expected to be affected by defects in the state of the premises created by the doing of the work shall not be abated by the subsequent disposal of the premises by the person who owed the duty.

(2)   This section does not apply—
   (a)   in the case of premises which are let, where the relevant tenancy of the premises commenced, or the relevant tenancy agreement of the premises was entered into, before the commencement of this Act;
   (b)   in the case of premises disposed of in any other way, when the disposal of the premises was completed, or a contract for their disposal was entered into, before the commencement of this Act; or
   (c)   in either case, where the relevant transaction disposing of the premises is entered into in pursuance of an enforceable option by which the consideration for the disposal was fixed before the commencement of this Act.

4 LANDLORD'S DUTY OF CARE IN VIRTUE OF OBLIGATION OR RIGHT TO REPAIR PREMISES DEMISED

(1)   Where premises are let under a tenancy which puts on the landlord an obligation to the tenant for the maintenance or repair of the premises, the landlord owes to all persons who might reasonably be expected to be affected by defects in the state of the premises a duty to take such care as is reasonable in all the circumstances to see that they are reasonably safe from personal injury or from damage to their property caused by a relevant defect.

(2)   The said duty is owed if the landlord knows (whether as the result of being notified by the tenant or otherwise) or if he ought in all the circumstances to have known of the relevant defect.

(3)   In this section "relevant defect" means a defect in the state of the premises existing at or after the material time and arising from, or continuing because of, an act or omission by the landlord which constitutes or would if he had had notice of the defect, have constituted a failure by him to carry out his obligation to the tenant for the maintenance

or repair of the premises; and for the purposes of the foregoing provision "the material time" means—

(a) where the tenancy commenced before this Act, the commencement of this Act; and

(b) in all other cases, the earliest of the following times, that is to say—

    (i) the time when the tenancy commences;

    (ii) the time when the tenancy agreement is entered into;

    (iii) the time when possession is taken of the premises in contemplation of the letting.

(4) Where premises are let under a tenancy which expressly or impliedly gives the landlord the right to enter the premises to carry out any description of maintenance or repair of the premises, then, as from the time when he first is, or by notice or otherwise can put himself, in a position to exercise the right and so long as he is or can put himself in that position, he shall be treated for the purposes of subsections (1) to (3) above (but for no other purpose) as if he were under an obligation to the tenant for that description of maintenance or repair of the premises; but the landlord shall not owe the tenant any duty by virtue of this subsection in respect of any defect in the state of the premises arising from, or continuing because of, a failure to carry out an obligation expressly imposed on the tenant by the tenancy.

(5) For the purposes of this section obligations imposed or rights given by any enactment in virtue of a tenancy shall be treated as imposed or given by the tenancy.

(6) This section applies to a right of occupation given by contract or any enactment and not amounting to a tenancy as if the right were a tenancy, and "tenancy" and cognate expressions shall be construed accordingly.

5 APPLICATION TO CROWN

This Act shall bind the Crown, but as regards the Crown's liability in tort shall not bind the Crown further than the Crown is made liable in tort by the Crown Proceedings Act 1947.

6 SUPPLEMENTAL

(1) In this Act—

"disposal", in relation to premises, includes a letting, and an assignment or surrender of a tenancy, of the premises and the creation by contract of any other right to occupy the premises, and "dispose" shall be construed accordingly;

"personal injury" includes any disease and any impairment of a person's physical or mental condition;

"tenancy" means—

(a) a tenancy created either immediately or derivatively out of the freehold, whether by a lease or underlease, by an agreement for a lease or underlease or by a tenancy agreement, but not including a mortgage term or any interest arising in favour of a mortgagor by his attorning tenant to his mortgagee; or

(b) a tenancy at will or a tenancy on sufferance; or

(c) a tenancy, whether or not constituting a tenancy at common law, created by or in pursuance of any enactment;

and cognate expressions shall be construed accordingly.

(2) Any duty imposed by or enforceable by virtue of any provision of this Act is in addition to any duty a person may owe apart from that provision.

(3)   Any term of an agreement which purports to exclude or restrict, or has the effect of excluding or restricting, the operation of any of the provisions of this Act, or any liability arising by virtue of any such provision, shall be void.

(4)   Section 4 of the Occupiers Liability Act 1957 (repairing landlords' duty to visitors to premises) is hereby repealed.

7 SHORT TITLE, COMMENCEMENT AND EXTENT

(1)   This Act may be cited as the Defective Premises Act 1972.

(2)   This Act shall come into force on 1st January 1974.

(3)   This Act does not extend to Scotland or Northern Ireland.

SUPPLY OF GOODS (IMPLIED TERMS) ACT 1973
(c.13)

Hire-purchase agreements

8 IMPLIED TERMS AS TO TITLE

(1)   In every hire-purchase agreement, other than one to which subsection (2) below applies, there is—
   (a) an implied term on the part of the creditor that he will have a right to sell the goods at the time when the property is to pass; and
   (b) an implied term that—
      (i)   the goods are free, and will remain free until the time when the property is to pass, from any charge or encumbrance not disclosed or known to the person to whom the goods are bailed or (in Scotland) hired before the agreement is made, and
      (ii) that person will enjoy quiet possession of the goods except so far as it may be disturbed by any person entitled to the benefit of any charge or encumbrance so disclosed or known.

(2)   In a hire-purchase agreement, in the case of which there appears from the agreement or is to be inferred from the circumstances of the agreement an intention that the creditor should transfer only such title as he or a third person may have, there is—
   (a) an implied term that all charges or encumbrances known to the creditor and not known to the person to whom the goods are bailed or hired have been disclosed to that person before the agreement is made; and
   (b) an implied term that neither—
      (i)   the creditor; nor
      (ii)   in a case where the parties to the agreement intend that any title which may be transferred shall be only such title as a third person may have, that person; nor
      (iii) anyone claiming through or under the creditor or that third person otherwise than under a charge or encumbrance disclosed or known to the person to whom the goods are bailed or hired, before the agreement is made;
   will disturb the quiet possession of the person to whom the goods are bailed or hired.

(3)   As regards England and Wales . . . the term implied by subsection (1)(a) above is a condition and the terms implied by subsections (1)(b), (2)(a) and (2)(b) above are warranties.

9 BAILING OR HIRING BY DESCRIPTION

(1)   Where under a hire-purchase agreement goods are bailed or (in Scotland) hired by description, there is an implied term that the goods will correspond with the description, and if under the agreement the goods are bailed or hired by reference to a sample as well as a description, it is not sufficient that the bulk of the goods corresponds with the sample if the goods do not also correspond with the description.

(1A)   As regards England and Wales . . . the term implied by subsection (1) above is a condition.

(2)   Goods shall not be prevented from being bailed or hired by description by reason only that, being exposed for sale, bailment or hire, they are selected by the person to whom they are bailed or hired.

10 IMPLIED UNDERTAKINGS AS TO QUALITY OR FITNESS

(1)   Except as provided by this section and section 11 below and subject to the provisions of any other enactment . . . there is no implied term as to the quality or fitness for any particular purpose of goods bailed or (in Scotland) hired under a hire-purchase agreement.

(2)   Where the creditor bails or hires goods under a hire purchase agreement in the course of a business, there is an implied term that the goods supplied under the agreement are of satisfactory quality.

(2A)   For the purposes of this Act, goods are of satisfactory quality if they meet the standard that a reasonable person would regard as satisfactory, taking account of any description of the goods, the price (if relevant) and all the other relevant circumstances.

(2B)   For the purposes of this Act, the quality of goods includes their state and condition and the following (among others) are in appropriate cases aspects of the quality of goods—
   (a)   fitness for all the purposes for which goods of the kind in question are commonly supplied,
   (b)   appearance and finish,
   (c)   freedom from minor defects,
   (d)   safety, and
   (e)   durability.

(2C)   The term implied by subsection (2) above does not extend to any matter making the quality of goods unsatisfactory—
   (a)   which is specifically drawn to the attention of the person to whom the goods are bailed or hired before the agreement is made,
   (b)   where that person examines the goods before the agreement is made, which that examination ought to reveal, or
   (c)   where the goods are bailed or hired by reference to a sample, which would have been apparent on a reasonable examination of the sample.

(2D)   If the person to whom the goods are bailed or hired deals as consumer or, in Scotland, if the goods are hired to a person under a consumer contract, the relevant circumstances mentioned in subsection (2A) above include any public statements on the specific characteristics of the goods made about them by the creditor, the producer or his representative, particularly in advertising or on labelling.

(2E)   A public statement is not by virtue of subsection (2D) above a relevant circumstance for the purposes of subsection (2A) above in the case of a contract of hire-purchase, if the creditor shows that—

(a) at the time the contract was made, he was not, and could not reasonably have been, aware of the statement,

(b) before the contract was made, the statement had been withdrawn in public or, to the extent that it contained anything which was incorrect or misleading, it had been corrected in public, or

(c) the decision to acquire the goods could not have been influenced by the statement.

(2F) Subsections (2D) and (2E) above do not prevent any public statement from being a relevant circumstance for the purposes of subsection (2A) above (whether or not the person to whom the goods are bailed or hired deals as consumer or, in Scotland, whether or not the goods are hired to a person under a consumer contract) if the statement would have been such a circumstance apart from those subsections.

(3) Where the creditor bails or hires goods under a hire-purchase agreement in the course of a business and the person to whom the goods are bailed or hired, expressly or by implication, makes known—

(a) to the creditor in the course of negotiations conducted by the creditor in relation to the making of the hire-purchase agreement, or

(b) to a credit-broker in the course of negotiations conducted by that broker in relation to goods sold by him to the creditor before forming the subject matter of the hire-purchase agreement,

any particular purpose for which the goods are being bailed or hired, there is an implied term that the goods supplied under the agreement are reasonably fit for that purpose, whether or not that is a purpose for which such goods are commonly supplied, except where the circumstances show that the person to whom the goods are bailed or hired does not rely, or that it is unreasonable for him to rely, on the skill or judgment of the creditor or credit-broker.

(4) An implied term as to quality or fitness for a particular purpose may be annexed to a hire-purchase agreement by usage.

(5) The preceding provisions of this section apply to a hire-purchase agreement made by a person who in the course of a business is acting as agent for the creditor as they apply to an agreement made by the creditor in the course of a business, except where the creditor is not bailing or hiring in the course of a business and either the person to whom the goods are bailed or hired knows that fact or reasonable steps are taken to bring it to the notice of that person before the agreement is made.

(6) In subsection (3) above and this subsection—

(a) "credit-broker" means a person acting in the course of a business of credit brokerage;

(b) "credit brokerage" means the effecting of introductions of individuals desiring to obtain credit—

(i) to persons carrying on any business so far as it relates to the provision of credit, or

(ii) to other persons engaged in credit brokerage.

(7) As regards England and Wales . . . the terms implied by subsections (2) and (3) above are conditions.

(8) In Scotland, "consumer contract" in this section has the same meaning as in section 12A(3) below.

11 SAMPLES

(1) Where under a hire-purchase agreement goods are bailed or (in Scotland) hired by reference to a sample, there is an implied term—

(a) that the bulk will correspond with the sample in quality; and

(b) that the person to whom the goods are bailed or hired will have a reasonable opportunity of comparing the bulk with the sample; and

(c) that the goods will be free from any defect, making their quality unsatisfactory, which would not be apparent on reasonable examination of the sample.

(2)   As regards England and Wales . . . the term implied by subsection (1) above is a condition.

11A MODIFICATION OF REMEDIES FOR BREACH OF STATUTORY CONDITION IN NON-CONSUMER CASES

(1)   Where in the case of a hire purchase agreement—

(a) the person to whom goods are bailed would, apart from this subsection, have the right to reject them by reason of a breach on the part of the creditor of a term implied by section 9, 10 or 11(1)(a) or (c) above, but

(b) the breach is so slight that it would be unreasonable for him to reject them,

then, if the person to whom the goods are bailed does not deal as consumer, the breach is not to be treated as a breach of condition but may be treated as a breach of warranty.

(2)   This section applies unless a contrary intention appears in, or is to be implied from, the agreement.

(3)   It is for the creditor to show—

(a) that a breach fell within subsection (1)(b) above, and

(b) that the person to whom the goods were bailed did not deal as consumer.

(4)   The references in this section to dealing as consumer are to be construed in accordance with Part I of the Unfair Contract Terms Act 1977.

(5)   This section does not apply to Scotland.

12 EXCLUSION OF IMPLIED TERMS

An express term does not negative a term implied by this Act unless inconsistent with it.

12A REMEDIES FOR BREACH OF HIRE-PURCHASE AGREEMENT AS RESPECTS SCOTLAND

(1)   Where in a hire-purchase agreement the creditor is in breach of any term of the agreement (express or implied), the person to whom the goods are hired shall be entitled—

(a) to claim damages, and

(b) if the breach is material, to reject any goods delivered under the agreement and treat it as repudiated.

(2)   Where a hire-purchase agreement is a consumer contract, then, for the purposes of subsection (1) above, breach by the creditor of any term (express or implied)—

(a) as to the quality of the goods or their fitness for a purpose,

(b) if the goods are, or are to be, hired by description, that the goods will correspond with the description,

(c) if the goods are, or are to be, hired by reference to a sample, that the bulk will correspond with the sample in quality,

shall be deemed to be a material breach.

(3)   In subsection (2) above "consumer contract" has the same meaning as in section 25(1) of the Unfair Contract Terms Act 1977; and for the purposes of that subsection the onus of

proving that a hire-purchase agreement is not to be regarded as a consumer contract shall lie on the creditor.

(4)   This section applies to Scotland only.

14 SPECIAL PROVISIONS AS TO CONDITIONAL SALE AGREEMENTS

(1)   Section 11(4) of the Sale of Goods Act 1979 (whereby in certain circumstances a breach of a condition in a contract of sale is treated only as a breach of warranty) shall not apply to a conditional sale agreement where the buyer deals as consumer within Part I of the Unfair Contract Terms Act 1977.

(2)   In England and Wales . . . a breach of a condition (whether express or implied) to be fulfilled by the seller under any such agreement shall be treated as a breach of warranty, and not as grounds for rejecting the goods and treating the agreement as repudiated, if (but only if) it would have fallen to be so treated had the condition been contained or implied in a corresponding hire-purchase agreement as a condition to be fulfilled by the creditor.

15 SUPPLEMENTARY

(1)   In sections 8 to 14 above and this section—

"business" includes a profession and the activities of any government department . . . or local or public authority;

"buyer" and "seller" includes a person to whom rights and duties under a conditional sale agreement have passed by assignment or operation of law;

"conditional sale agreement" means an agreement for the sale of goods under which the purchase price or part of it is payable by instalments, and the property in the goods is to remain in the seller (notwithstanding that the buyer is to be in possession of the goods) until such conditions as to the payment of instalments or otherwise as may be specified in the agreement are fulfilled;

"consumer sale" has the same meaning as in section 55 of the Sale of Goods Act 1979 (as set out in paragraph 11 of Schedule 1 to that Act)

"creditor" means the person by whom the goods are bailed or (in Scotland) hired under a hire-purchase agreement or the person to whom his rights and duties under the agreement have passed by assignment or operation of law; and

"hire-purchase agreement" means an agreement, other than conditional sale agreement, under which—
(a) goods are bailed or (in Scotland) hired in return for periodical payments by the person to whom they are bailed or hired, and
(b) the property in the goods will pass to that person if the terms of the agreement are complied with and one or more of the following occurs—
(i)   the exercise of an option to purchase by that person,
(ii) the doing of any other specified act by any party to the agreement,
(iii) the happening of any other specified event.
"producer" means the manufacturer of goods, the importer of goods into the European Economic Area or any person purporting to be a producer by placing his name, trade mark or other distinctive sign on the goods;

(3)   In section 14(2) above "corresponding hire-purchase agreement" means, in relation to a conditional sale agreement, a hire-purchase agreement relating to the same goods as the

conditional sale agreement and made between the same parties and at the same time and in the same circumstances and, as nearly as may be, in the same terms as the conditional sale agreement.

(4)   Nothing in sections 8 to 13 above shall prejudice the operation of any other enactment . . . or any rule of law whereby any term, other than one relating to quality or fitness, is to be implied in any hire-purchase agreement.

As amended by Consumer Credit Act 1974, s. 192 and Sch. 4 para. 35 and para. 36; Unfair Contract Terms Act 1977, Sch. 3; Sale of Goods Act 1979, s. 63 and Sch. 2, para. 16 and para. 17; Statute Law (Repeals) Act 1981, s. 1 and Sch. 1; Sale and Supply of Goods Act 1994, Sch.2, para. 4 and Sch. 3, para. 1; Sale and Supply of Goods to Consumers Regulations 2002. reg. 13.

HEALTH AND SAFETY AT WORK ACT 1974
(c.37)

2 GENERAL DUTIES OF EMPLOYERS TO THEIR EMPLOYEES

(1)   It shall be the duty of every employer to ensure, so far as is reasonably practicable, the health, safety and welfare at work of all his employees.

(2)   Without prejudice to the generality of an employer's duty under the preceding subsection, the matters to which that duty extends include in particular—
(a) the provision and maintenance of plant and systems of work that are, so far as is reasonably practicable, safe and without risks to health;
(b) arrangements for ensuring, so far as is reasonably practicable, safety and absence of risks to health in connection with the use, handling, storage and transport of articles and substances;
(c) the provision of such information, instruction, training and supervision as is necessary to ensure, so far as is reasonably practicable, the health and safety at work of his employees;
(d) so far as is reasonably practicable as regards any place of work under the employer's control, the maintenance of it in a condition that is safe and without risks to health and the provision and maintenance of means of access to and egress from it that are safe and without such risks;
(e) the provision and maintenance of a working environment for his employees that is, so far as is reasonably practicable, safe, without risks to health, and adequate as regards facilities and arrangements for their welfare at work.

(3)   Except in such cases as may be prescribed, it shall be the duty of every employer to prepare and as often as may be appropriate revise a written statement of his general policy with respect to the health and safety at work of his employees and the organisation and arrangements for the time being in force for carrying out that policy, and to bring the statement and any revision of it to the notice of all of his employees.

(4)   Regulations made by the Secretary of State may provide for the appointment in prescribed cases by recognised trade unions (within the meaning of the regulations) of safety representatives from amongst the employees, and those representatives shall represent the employees in consultations with the employers under subsection (6) below and shall have such other functions as may be prescribed.

3 GENERAL DUTIES OF EMPLOYERS AND SELF-EMPLOYED TO PERSONS OTHER THAN THEIR EMPLOYEES

(1)   It shall be the duty of every employer to conduct his undertaking in such a way as to ensure, so far as is reasonably practicable, that persons not in his employment who may be affected thereby are not thereby exposed to risks to their health or safety.

(2)   It shall be the duty of every self-employed person to conduct his undertaking in such a way as to ensure, so far as is reasonably practicable, that he and other persons (not being his employees) who may be affected thereby are not thereby exposed to risks to their health or safety.

(3)   In such cases as may be prescribed, it shall be the duty of every employer and every self-employed person, in the prescribed circumstances and in the prescribed manner, to give to persons (not being his employees) who may be affected by the way in which he conducts his undertaking the prescribed information about such aspects of the way in which he conducts his undertaking as might affect their health or safety.

4 GENERAL DUTIES OF PERSONS CONCERNED WITH PREMISES TO PERSONS OTHER THAN THEIR EMPLOYEES

(1)   This section has effect for imposing on persons duties in relation to those who—
(a) are not their employees; but
(b) use non-domestic premises made available to them as a place of work or as a place where they may use plant or substances provided for their use there,
and applies to premises so made available and other non-domestic premises used in connection with them.

(2)   It shall be the duty of each person who has, to any extent, control of premises to which this section applies or of the means of access thereto or egress therefrom or of any plant or substance in such premises to take such measures as it is reasonable for a person in his position to take to ensure, so far as is reasonably practicable, that the premises, all means of access thereto or egress therefrom available for use by persons using the premises, and any plant or substance in the premises or, as the case may be, provided for use there, is or are safe and without risks to health.

(3)   Where a person has, by virtue of any contract or tenancy, an obligation of any extent in relation to—
(a) the maintenance or repair of any premises to which this section applies or any means of access thereto or egress therefrom; or
(b) the safety of or the absence of risks to health arising from plant or substances in any such premises;
that person shall be treated, for the purposes of subsection (2) above, as being a person who has control of the matters to which his obligation extends.

(4)   Any reference in this section to a person having control of any premises or matter is a reference to a person having control of the premises or matter in connection with the carrying on by him of a trade, business or other undertaking (whether for profit or not).

6 GENERAL DUTIES OF MANUFACTURERS ETC., AS REGARDS ARTICLES AND SUBSTANCES FOR USE AT WORK

(1)   It shall be the duty of any person who designs, manufactures, imports or supplies any article for use at work or any article of fairground equipment—

(a) to ensure, so far as is reasonably practicable, that the article is so designed and constructed that it will be safe and without risks to health at all times when it is being set, used, cleaned or maintained by a person at work;

(b) to carry out or arrange for the carrying out of such testing and examination as may be necessary for the performance of the duty imposed on him by the preceding paragraph;

(c) to take such steps as are necessary to secure that persons supplied by that person with the article are provided with adequate information about the use for which the article is designed or has been tested and about any conditions necessary to ensure that it will be safe and without risks to health at all such times as are mentioned in paragraph (a) above and when it is being dismantled or disposed of; and

(d) to take such steps as are necessary to secure, so far as is reasonably practicable, that persons so supplied are provided with all such revisions of information provided to them by virtue of the preceding paragraph as are necessary by reason of its becoming known that anything gives rise to a serious risk to health or safety.

(1A) It shall be the duty of any person who designs, manufactures, imports or supplies any article of fairground equipment—

(a) to ensure, so far as is reasonably practicable, that the article is so designed and constructed that it will be safe and without risks to health at all times when it is being used for or in connection with the entertainment of members of the public;

(b) to carry out or arrange for the carrying out of such testing and examination as may be necessary for the performance of the duty imposed on him by the preceding paragraph;

(c) to take such steps as are necessary to secure that persons supplied by that person with the article are provided with adequate information about the use for which the article is designed or has been tested and about any conditions necessary to ensure that it will be safe and without risks to health at all times when it is being used for or in connection with the entertainment of members of the public; and

(d) to take such steps as are necessary to secure, so far as is reasonably practicable, that persons so supplied are provided with all such revisions of information provided to them by virtue of the preceding paragraph as are necessary by reason of its becoming known that anything gives rise to a serious risk to health or safety.

(2) It shall be the duty of any person who undertakes the design or manufacture of any article for use at work or of any article of fairground equipment to carry out or arrange for the carrying out of any necessary research with a view to the discovery and, so far as is reasonably practicable, the elimination or minimisation of any risks to health or safety to which the design or article may give rise.

(3) It shall be the duty of any person who erects or installs any article for use at work in any premises where that article is to be used by persons at work or who erects or installs any article of fairground equipment to ensure, so far as is reasonably practicable, that nothing about the way in which the article is erected or installed makes it unsafe or a risk to health at any such time as is mentioned in paragraph (a) of subsection (1) or, as the case may be, in paragraph (a) of subsection (1) or (1A) above.

(4) It shall be the duty of any person who manufactures, imports or supplies any substance—

(a) to ensure, so far as is reasonably practicable, that the substance will be safe and without risks to health at all times when it is being used, handled, processed, stored or transported by a person at work or in premises to which section 4 above applies;

(b) to carry out or arrange for the carrying out of such testing and examination as may be necessary for the performance of the duty imposed on him by the preceding paragraph,

(c) to take such steps as are necessary to secure that persons supplied by that person with the substance are provided with adequate information about any risks to health or safety to which the inherent properties of the substance may give rise, about the results of any relevant tests which have been carried out on or in connection with the substance and about any conditions necessary to ensure that the substance will be safe and without risks to health at all such times as are mentioned in paragraph (a) above and when the substance is being disposed of; and

(d) to take such steps as are necessary to secure, so far as is reasonably practicable, that persons so supplied are provided with all such revisions of information provided to them by virtue of the preceding paragraph as are necessary by reason of its becoming known that anything gives rise to a serious risk to health or safety.

(5) It shall be the duty of any person who undertakes the manufacture of any substance to carry out or arrange for the carrying out of any necessary research with a view to the discovery and, so far as is reasonable practicable, the elimination or minimisation of any risks to health or safety to which the substance may give rise at all such times as are mentioned in paragraph (a) of subsection (4) above.

(6) Nothing in the preceding provisions of this section shall be taken to require a person to repeat any testing, examination or research which has been carried out otherwise than by him or at his instance, in so far as it is reasonable for him to rely on the results thereof for the purposes of those provisions.

(7) Any duty imposed on any person by any of the preceding provisions of this section shall extend only to things done in the course of a trade, business or other undertaking carried on by him (whether for profit or not) and to matters within his control.

(8) Where a person designs, manufactures, imports or supplies an article for use at work or an article of fairground equipment and does so for or to another on the basis of a written undertaking by that other to take specified steps sufficient to ensure, so far as is reasonably practicable, that the article will be safe and without risks to health at all such times as are mentioned in paragraph (a) of subsection (1) or, as the case may be, in paragraph (a) of subsection (1) or (1A) above, the undertaking shall have the effect of relieving the first-mentioned person from the duty imposed by virtue of that paragraph to such extent as is reasonable having regard to the terms of the undertaking.

(8A) Nothing in subsection (7) or (8) above shall relieve any person who imports any article or substance from any duty in respect of anything which—

(a) in the case of an article designed outside the United Kingdom, was done by and in the course of any trade, profession or other undertaking carried on by, or was within the control of, the person who designed the article; or

(b) in the case of an article or substance manufactured outside the United Kingdom, was done by and in the course of any trade, profession or other undertaking carried on by, or was within the control of, the person who manufactured the article or substance.

(9) Where a person ("the ostensible supplier") supplies any article or substance to another ("the customer") under a hire-purchase agreement, conditional sale agreement or credit-sale agreement, and the ostensible supplier—

(a) carries on the business of financing the acquisition of goods by others by means of such agreements; and

(b) in the course of that business acquired his interest in the article or substance supplied to the customer as a means of financing its acquisition by the customer from a third person ("the effective supplier"),

the effective supplier and not the ostensible supplier shall be treated for the purposes of this section as supplying the article or substance to the customer, and any duty imposed by the preceding provisions of this section on suppliers shall accordingly fall on the effective supplier and not on the ostensible supplier.

(10) For the purposes of this section an absence of safety or a risk to health shall be disregarded in so far as the case in or in relation to which it would arise is shown to be one the occurrence of which could not reasonably be foreseen; and in determining whether any duty imposed by virtue of paragraph (a) of subsection (1), (1A) or (4) above has been performed regard shall be had to any relevant information or advice which has been provided to any person by the person by whom the article has been designed, manufactured, imported or supplied or, as the case may be, by the person by whom the substance has been manufactured.

47 CIVIL LIABILITY

(1) Nothing in this Part shall be construed—
   (a) as conferring a right of action in any civil proceedings in respect of any failure to comply with any duty imposed by sections 2 to 7 or any contravention of section 8; or
   (b) as affecting the extent (if any) to which breach of a duty imposed by any of the existing statutory provisions is actionable; or
   (c) as affecting the operation of section 12 of the Nuclear Installations Act 1965 (right to compensation by virtue of certain provisions of that Act).

(2) Breach of a duty imposed by health and safety regulations . . . shall, so far as it causes damage, be actionable except in so far as the regulations provide otherwise.

(3) No provision made by virtue of section 15(6)(b) shall afford a defence in any civil proceedings, whether brought by virtue of subsection (2) above or not; but as regards any duty imposed as mentioned in subsection (2) above health and safety regulations . . . may provide for any defence specified in the regulations to be available in any action for breach of that duty.

(4) Subsections (1)(a) and (2) above are without prejudice to any right of action which exists apart from the provisions of this Act, and subsection (3) above is without prejudice to any defence which may be available apart from the provisions of the regulations there mentioned.

(5) Any term of an agreement which purports to exclude or restrict the operation of subsection (2) above, or any liability arising by virtue of that subsection shall be void, except in so far as health and safety regulations . . . provide otherwise.

(6) In this section "damage" includes the death of, or injury to, any person (including any disease and any impairment of a person's physical or mental condition).

CONSUMER CREDIT ACT 1974
(c.39)

8 CONSUMER CREDIT AGREEMENTS

(1) A *consumer* credit agreement is an agreement between an individual ("the debtor") and any other person ("the creditor") by which the creditor provides the debtor with credit of any amount.

(3) A consumer credit agreement is a regulated agreement within the meaning of this Act if it is not an agreement (an "exempt agreement") specified in or under section 16, 16A, 16B or 16C.

. . .

Unfair relationships

140A UNFAIR RELATIONSHIPS BETWEEN CREDITORS AND DEBTORS

(1)   The court may make an order under section 140B in connection with a credit agreement if it determines that the relationship between the creditor and the debtor arising out of the agreement (or the agreement taken with any related agreement) is unfair to the debtor because of one or more of the following—
(a) any of the terms of the agreement or of any related agreement;
(b) the way in which the creditor has exercised or enforced any of his rights under the agreement or any related agreement;
(c) any other thing done (or not done) by, or on behalf of, the creditor (either before or after the making of the agreement or any related agreement).

(2)   In deciding whether to make a determination under this section the court shall have regard to all matters it thinks relevant (including matters relating to the creditor and matters relating to the debtor).

(3)   For the purposes of this section the court shall (except to the extent that it is not appropriate to do so) treat anything done (or not done) by, or on behalf of, or in relation to, an associate or a former associate of the creditor as if done (or not done) by, or on behalf of, or in relation to, the creditor.

(4)   A determination may be made under this section in relation to a relationship notwithstanding that the relationship may have ended.

(5)   An order under section 140B shall not be made in connection with a credit agreement which is an exempt agreement by virtue of section 16(6C).

140B POWERS OF COURT IN RELATION TO UNFAIR RELATIONSHIPS

(1)   An order under this section in connection with a credit agreement may do one or more of the following—
(a) require the creditor, or any associate or former associate of his, to repay (in whole or in part) any sum paid by the debtor or by a surety by virtue of the agreement or any related agreement (whether paid to the creditor, the associate or the former associate or to any other person);
(b) require the creditor, or any associate or former associate of his, to do or not to do (or to cease doing) anything specified in the order in connection with the agreement or any related agreement;
(c) reduce or discharge any sum payable by the debtor or by a surety by virtue of the agreement or any related agreement;
(d) direct the return to a surety of any property provided by him for the purposes of a security;
(e) otherwise set aside (in whole or in part) any duty imposed on the debtor or on a surety by virtue of the agreement or any related agreement;
(f) alter the terms of the agreement or of any related agreement;
(g) direct accounts to be taken, or (in Scotland) an accounting to be made, between any persons.

(2)   An order under this section may be made in connection with a credit agreement only—
(a) on an application made by the debtor or by a surety;
(b) at the instance of the debtor or a surety in any proceedings in any court to which the debtor and the creditor are parties, being proceedings to enforce the agreement or any related agreement; or

(c) at the instance of the debtor or a surety in any other proceedings in any court where the amount paid or payable under the agreement or any related agreement is relevant.

(3) An order under this section may be made notwithstanding that its effect is to place on the creditor, or any associate or former associate of his, a burden in respect of an advantage enjoyed by another person.

(4) An application under subsection (2)(a) may only be made—
(a) in England and Wales, to the county court;
(b) in Scotland, to the sheriff court;

. . .

140C INTERPRETATION OF SS. 140A AND 140B

(1) In this section and in sections 140A and 140B "credit agreement" means any agreement between an individual (the 'debtor') and any other person (the 'creditor') by which the creditor provides the debtor with credit of any amount.

(2) References in this section and in sections 140A and 140B to the creditor or to the debtor under a credit agreement include—
(a) references to the person to whom his rights and duties under the agreement have passed by assignment or operation of law;
(b) where two or more persons are the creditor or the debtor, references to any one or more of those persons.

. . .

(4) References in sections 140A and 140B to an agreement related to a credit agreement (the "main agreement") are references to—
(a) a credit agreement consolidated by the main agreement;
(b) a linked transaction in relation to the main agreement or to a credit agreement within paragraph (a);
(c) a security provided in relation to the main agreement, to a credit agreement within paragraph (a) or to a linked transaction within paragraph (b).

(5) In the case of a credit agreement which is not a regulated consumer credit agreement, for the purposes of subsection (4) a transaction shall be treated as being a linked transaction in relation to that agreement if it would have been such a transaction had that agreement been a regulated consumer credit agreement.

. . .

140D ADVICE AND INFORMATION

The advice and information published by the OFT under section 229 of the Enterprise Act 2002 shall indicate how the OFT expects sections 140A to 140C of this Act to interact with Part 8 of that Act.

As amended by Consumer Credit Act 2006, ss. 2(1), 5(1), 19, 20, 21 and 22(1), and Sch. 4, para. 1; Legislative Reform (Consumer Credit) Order 2008, art. 3(2).

GUARD DOGS ACT 1975
(c.50)

1 CONTROL OF GUARD DOGS

(1) A person shall not use or permit the use of a guard dog at any premises unless a person ("the handler") who is capable of controlling the dog is present on the premises and the dog is under the control of the handler at all times while it is being so used except while it is secured so that it is not at liberty to go freely about the premises.

(2) The handler of a guard dog shall keep the dog under his control at all times while it is being used as a guard dog at any premises except—
(a) while another handler has control over the dog; or
(b) while the dog is secured so that it is not at liberty to go freely about the premises.

(3) A person shall not use or permit the use of a guard dog at any premises unless a notice containing a warning that a guard dog is present is clearly exhibited at each entrance to the premises.

2 RESTRICTION ON KEEPING GUARD DOGS WITHOUT A LICENCE

(1) A person shall not keep a dog at guard dog kennels unless he holds a licence under section 3 of this Act in respect of the kennels.

(2) A person shall not use or permit the use at any premises of a guard dog if he knows or has reasonable cause to suspect that the dog (when not being used as a guard dog) is normally kept at guard dog kennels in breach of subsection (1) of this section.

5 OFFENCES, PENALTIES AND CIVIL LIABILITY

(1) A person who contravenes section 1 or 2 of this Act shall be guilty of an offence and liable on summary conviction to a fine not exceeding [F1 level 5 on the standard scale].

(2) The provisions of this Act shall not be construed as—
(a) conferring a right of action in any civil proceedings (other than proceedings for the recovery of a fine or any prescribed fee) in respect of any contravention of this Act or of any regulations made under this Act or of any of the terms or conditions of a licence granted under section 3 of this Act; or
(b) derogating from any right of action or other remedy (whether civil or criminal) in proceedings

7 INTERPRETATION

In this Act, unless the context otherwise requires—

. . .

"guard dog" means a dog which is being used to protect—
(a) premises; or
(b) property kept on the premises; or
(c) a person guarding the premises or such property.

CONGENITAL DISABILITIES (CIVIL LIABILITY) ACT 1976
(c.28)

1 CIVIL LIABILITY TO CHILD BORN DISABLED

(1) If a child is born disabled as the result of such an occurrence before its birth as is mentioned in subsection (2) below, and a person (other than the child's own mother) is under this section answerable to the child in respect of the occurrence, the child's disabilities are to be regarded as damage resulting from the wrongful act of that person and actionable accordingly at the suit of the child.

(2) An occurrence to which this section applies is one which—
    (a) affected either parent of the child in his or her ability to have a normal, healthy child; or
    (b) affected the mother during her pregnancy, or affected her or the child in the course of its birth, so that the child is born with disabilities which would not otherwise have been present.

(3) Subject to the following subsections, a person (here referred to as "the defendant") is answerable to the child if he was liable in tort to the parent or would, if sued in due time, have been so; and it is no answer that there could not have been such liability because the parent suffered no actionable injury, if there was a breach of legal duty which, accompanied by injury, would have given rise to the liability.

(4) In the case of an occurrence preceding the time of conception, the defendant is not answerable to the child if at that time either or both of the parents knew the risk of their child being born disabled (that is to say, the particular risk created by the occurrence); but should it be the child's father who is the defendant, this subsection does not apply if he knew of the risk and the mother did not.

(4A) In the case of a child who was a parent by virtue of section 42 or 43 of the Human Fertilisation and Embryology Act 2008, the reference in subsection (4) to the child's father includes a reference to the woman who is a parent by virtue of that section.

(5) The defendant is not answerable to the child, for anything he did or omitted to do when responsible in a professional capacity for treating or advising the parent, if he took reasonable care having due regard to then received professional opinion applicable to the particular class of case; but this does not mean that he is answerable only because he departed from received opinion.

(6) Liability to the child under this section may be treated as having been excluded or limited by contract made with the parent affected, to the same extent and subject to the same restrictions as liability in the parent's own case; and a contract term which could have been set up by the defendant in an action by the parent, so as to exclude or limit his liablility to him or her, operates in the defendant's favour to the same, but no greater, extent in an action under this section by the child.

(7) If in the child's action under this section it is shown that the parent affected shared the responsibility for the child being born disabled, the damages are to be reduced to such extent as the court thinks just and equitable having regard to the extent of the parent's responsibility.

[1A EXTENSION OF SECTION 1 TO COVER INFERTILITY TREATMENTS

(1)   In any case where—
(a)   a child carried by a woman as the result of the placing in her of an embryo or of sperm and eggs or her artificial insemination is born disabled,
(b)   the disability results from an act or omission in the course of the selection, or the keeping or use outside the body, of the embryo carried by her or of the gametes used to bring about the creation of the embryo, and
(c)   a person is under this section answerable to the child in respect of the act or omission,
the child's disabilities are to be regarded as damage resulting from the wrongful act of that person and actionable accordingly at the suit of the child.

(2)   Subject to subsection (3) below and the applied provisions of section 1 of this Act, a person (here referred to as "the defendant") is answerable to the child if he was liable in tort to one or both of the parents (here referred to as "the parent or parents concerned") or would, if sued in due time, have been so; and it is no answer that there could not have been such liability because the parent or parents concerned suffered no actionable injury, if there was a breach of legal duty which, accompanied by injury, would have given rise to the liability.

(3)   The defendant is not under this section answerable to the child if at the time the embryo, or the sperm and eggs, are placed in the woman or the time of her insemination (as the case may be) either or both of the parents knew the risk of their child being born disabled (that is to say, the particular risk created by the act or omission).

(4)   Subsections (5) to (7) of section 1 of ths Act apply for the purposes of this section as they apply for the purposes of that but as if references to the parent or the parent affected were references to the parent or parents concerned.]

2 LIABILITY OF WOMAN DRIVING WHEN PREGNANT

A woman driving a motor vehicle when she knows (or ought reasonably to know) herself to be pregnant is to be regarded as being under the same duty to take care for the safety of her unborn child as the law imposes on her with respect to the safety of other people; and if in consequence of her breach of that duty her child is born with disabilities which would not otherwise have been present, those disabilities are to be regarded as damage resulting from her wrongful act and actionable accordingly at the suit of the child.

3 DISABLED BIRTH DUE TO RADIATION

(1)   Section 1 of this Act does not affect the operation of the Nuclear Installations Act 1965 as to liability for, and compensation in respect of, injury or damage caused by occurrences involving nuclear matter or the emission of ionising radiations.

(2)   For the avoidance of doubt anything which—
(a)   affects a man in his ability to have a normal, healthy child; or
(b)   affects a woman in that ability, or so affects her when she is pregnant that her child is born with disabilities which would not otherwise have been present,
is an injury for the purposes of that Act.

(3)   If a child is born disabled as the result of an injury to either of its parents caused in breach of a duty imposed by any of sections 7 to 11 of that Act (nuclear site licensees and others to secure that nuclear incidents do not cause injury to persons, etc.), the child's disabilities are to be regarded under the subsequent provisions of that Act (compensation and other

matters) as injuries caused on the same occasion, and by the same breach of duty, as was the injury to the parent.

(4)   As respects compensation to the child, section 13(6) of that Act (contributory fault of person injured by radiation) is to be applied as if the reference there to fault were to the fault of the parent.

(5)   Compensation is not payable in the child's case if the injury to the parent preceded the time of the child's conception and at that time either or both of the parents knew the risk of their child being born disabled (that is to say, the particular risk created by the injury).

4 INTERPRETATION AND OTHER SUPPLEMENTARY PROVISIONS

(1)   References in this Act to a child being born disabled or with disabilities are to its being born with any deformity, disease or abnormality, including predisposition (whether or not susceptible of immediate prognosis) to physical or mental defect in the future.

(2)   In this Act—
(a) "born" means born alive (the moment of a child's birth being when it first has a life separate from its mother), and "birth" has a corresponding meaning; and
(b) "motor vehicle" means a mechanically propelled vehicle intended or adapted for use on roads,
and references to embryos shall be construed in accordance with section 1 of the Human Fertilisation and Embryology Act 1990.

(3)   Liability to a child under section 1 [1A] or 2 of this Act is to be regarded—
(a) as respects all its incidents and any matters arising or to arise out of it; and
(b) subject to any contrary context or intention, for the purpose of construing references in enactments and documents to personal or bodily injuries and cognate matters,
as liability for personal injuries sustained by the child immediately after its birth.

(4)   No damages shall be recoverable under any of those sections in respect of any loss of expectation of life, nor shall any such loss be taken into account in the compensation payable in respect of a child under the Nuclear Installations Act 1965 as extended by section 3, unless (in either case) the child lives for at least 48 hours.

(4A) In any case where a child carried by a woman as the result of the placing in her of an embryo or of sperm and eggs or her artificial insemination is born disabled, any reference in section 1 of this Act to a parent includes a reference to a person who would be a parent but for sections 27 to 29 of the Human Fertilisation and Embryology Act 1990, or sections 33 to 47 of the Human and Embryology Act 2008.

(5)   This Act applies in respect of births after (but not before) its passing, and in respect of any such birth it replaces any law in force before its passing, whereby a person could be liable to a child in respect of disabilities with which it might be born; but in section 1(3) of this Act the expression "liable in tort" does not include any reference to liability by virtue of this Act, or to liability by virtue of any such law.

(6)   References to the Nuclear Installations Act 1965 are to that Act as amended; and for the purposes of section 28 of that Act (power by Order in Council to extend the Act to territories outside the United Kingdom) section 3 of this Act is to be treated as if it were a provision of that Act.

5 CROWN APPLICATION

This Act binds the Crown.

FATAL ACCIDENTS ACT 1976
(c.30)

1 RIGHT OF ACTION FOR WRONGFUL ACT CAUSING DEATH

(1)   If death is caused by any wrongful act, neglect or default which is such as would (if death had not ensued) have entitled the person injured to maintain an action and recover damages in respect thereof, the person who would have been liable if death had not ensued shall be liable to an action for damages, notwithstanding the death of the person injured.

(2)   Subject to section 1A(2) below, every such action shall be for the benefit of the dependants of the person ("the deceased") whose death has been so caused.

(3)   In this Act "dependant" means—
(a) the wife or husband or former wife or husband of the deceased;
(aa) the civil partner or former civil partner of the deceased;
(b) any person who—
   (i)   was living with the deceased in the same household immediately before the date of the death; and
   (ii) had been living with the deceased in the same household for at least two years before that date; and
   (iii) was living during the whole of that period as the husband or wife of the deceased;
(c) any parent or other ascendant of the deceased;
(d) any person who was treated by the deceased as his parent;
(e) any child or other descendant of the deceased;
(f) any person (not being a child of the deceased) who, in the case of any marriage to which the deceased was at any time a party, was treated by the deceased as a child of the family in relation to that marriage;
(fa) any person (not being a child of the deceased) who, in the case of a civil partnership in which the deceased was at any time a civil partner, was treated by the deceased as a child of the family in relation to that civil partnership;
(g) any person who is, or is the issue of, a brother, sister, uncle or aunt of the deceased.

(4)   The reference to the former wife or husband of the deceased in subsection (3)(a) above includes a reference to a person whose marriage to the deceased has been annulled or declared void as well as a person whose marriage to the deceased has been dissolved.

(4A) The reference to the former civil partner of the deceased in subsection (3)(aa) above includes a reference to a person whose civil partnership with the deceased had been annulled as well as a person whose civil partnership with the deceased had been dissolved.

(5)   In deducing any relationship for the purposes of subsection (3) above—
(a) any relationship by affinity shall be treated as a relationship by consanguinity, any relationship of the half blood as a relationship of the whole blood, and the stepchild of any person as his child, and
(b) an illegitimate person shall be treated as the legitimate child of his mother and reputed father.

(6)   Any reference in this Act to injury includes any disease and any impairment of a person's physical or mental condition.

1A BEREAVEMENT

(1)   An action under this Act may consist of or include a claim for damages for bereavement.

(2)   A claim for damages for bereavement shall only be for the benefit—
(a) of the wife or husband or civil partner of the deceased; and
(b) where the deceased was a minor who was never married or a civil partner—
(i) of his parents, if he was legitimate; and
(ii) of his mother, if he was illegitimate.

(3)   Subject to subsection (5) below, the sum to be awarded as damages under this section shall be £11,800.

(4)   Where there is a claim for damages under this section for the benefit of both the parents of the deceased, the sum awarded shall be divided equally between them (subject to any deduction falling to be made in respect of costs not recovered from the defendant).

(5)   The Lord Chancellor may by order made by statutory instrument, subject to annulment in pursuance of a resolution of either House of Parliament, amend this section by varying the sum for the time being specified in subsection (3) above.

2 PERSONS ENTITLED TO BRING THE ACTION

(1)   The action shall be brought by and in the name of the executor or administrator of the deceased.

(2)   If—
(a) there is no executor or administrator of the deceased, or
(b) no action is brought within six months after the death by and in the name of an executor or administrator of the deceased,
the action may be brought by and in the name of all or any of the persons for whose benefit an executor or administrator could have brought it.

(3)   Not more than one action shall lie for and in respect of the same subject matter of complaint.

(4)   The plaintiff in the action shall be required to deliver to the defendant or his solicitor full particulars of the persons for whom and on whose behalf the action is brought and of the nature of the claim in respect of which damages are sought to be recovered.

3 ASSESSMENT OF DAMAGES

(1)   In the action such damages, other than damages for bereavement, may be awarded as are proportioned to the injury resulting from the death to the dependants respectively.

(2)   After deducting the costs not recovered from the defendant any amount recovered otherwise than as damages for bereavement shall be divided among the dependants in such shares as may be directed.

(3)   In an action under this Act where there fall to be assessed damages payable to a widow in respect of the death of her husband there shall not be taken account the re-marriage of the widow or her prospects of re-marriage.

(4)   In an action under this Act where there fall to be assessed damages payable to a person who is a dependant by virtue of section 1(3)(b) above in respect of the death of the person with whom the dependant was living as husband or wife there shall be taken into account

(together with any other matter that appears to the court to be relevant to the action) the fact that the dependant had no enforceable right to financial support by the deceased as a result of their living together.

(5) If the dependants have incurred funeral expenses in respect of the deceased, damages may be awarded in respect of those expenses.

(6) Money paid into court in satisfaction of a cause of action under this Act may be in one sum without specifying any person's share.

4 ASSESSMENT OF DAMAGES: DISREGARD OF BENEFITS

In assessing damages in respect of a person's death in an action under this Act, benefits which have accrued or may accrue to any person from his estate or otherwise as a result of his death shall be disregarded.

5 CONTRIBUTORY NEGLIGENCE

Where any person dies as the result partly of his own fault and partly of the fault of any other person or persons, and accordingly if an action were brought for the benefit of the estate under the Law Reform (Miscellaneous Provisions) Act 1934 the damages recoverable would be reduced under section 1(1) of the Law Reform (Contributory Negligence) Act 1945, any damages recoverable in an action . . . under this Act shall be reduced to a proportionate extent.

DANGEROUS WILD ANIMALS ACT 1976
(c.38)

1 LICENCES

(1) Subject to section 5 of this Act, no person shall keep any dangerous wild animal except under the authority of a licence granted in accordance with the provisions of this Act by a local authority.

(3) A local authority shall not grant a licence under this Act unless it is satisfied that—
  (a) it is not contrary to the public interest on the grounds of safety, nuisance or otherwise to grant the licence;
  (b) the applicant for the licence is a suitable person to hold a licence under this Act;
  (c) any animal concerned will at all times of its being kept only under the authority of the licence—
    (i) be held in accommodation which secures that the animal will not escape, which is suitable as regards construction, size, temperature, lighting, ventilation, drainage and cleanliness and which is suitable for the number of animals proposed to be held in the accommodation, and
    (ii) be supplied with adequate and suitable food, drink and bedding material and be visited at suitable intervals;
  (d) appropriate steps will at all such times be taken for the protection of any animal concerned in case of fire or other emergency;
  (e) all reasonable precautions will be taken at all such times to prevent and control the spread of infectious diseases;
  (f) while any animal concerned is at the premises where it will normally be held, its accommodation is such that it can take adequate exercise.

4 POWER TO SEIZE AND TO DISPOSE OF ANIMALS WITHOUT COMPENSATION

(1)   Where—

(a) an animal is being kept contrary to section 1(1) of this Act, or

(b) any condition of a licence under this Act is contravened or not complied with,

the local authority in whose area any animal concerned is for the time being may seize the animal, and either retain it in the authority's possession or destroy or otherwise dispose of it, and shall not be liable to pay compensation to any person in respect of the exercise of its powers under this subsection.

(2)   A local authority which incurs any expenditure in exercising its powers under subsection (1)(a) of this section shall be entitled to recover the amount of the expenditure summarily as a civil debt from any person who was at the time of the seizure a keeper of the animal concerned.

(3)   A local authority which incurs any expenditure in exercising its powers under subsection (1)(b) of this section shall be entitled to recover the amount of the expenditure summarily as a civil debt from the person to whom the licence concerned was granted.

TORTS (INTERFERENCE WITH GOODS) ACT 1977
(c.32)

Preliminary

1 DEFINITION OF "WRONGFUL INTERFERENCE WITH GOODS"

In this Act "wrongful interference", or "wrongful interference with goods", means—

(a)   conversion of goods (also called trover),

(b)   trespass to goods,

(c)   negligence so far at it results in damage to goods or to an interest in goods.

(d)   subject to section 2, any other tort so far as it results in damage to goods or to an interest in goods.

and references in this Act (however worded) to proceedings for wrongful interference or to a claim or right to a claim for wrongful interference shall include references to proceedings by virtue of Part I of the Consumer Protection Act 1987 or Part II of the Consumer Protection (Northern Ireland) Order 1987 (product liability) in respect of any damage to goods or to an interest in goods or, as the case may be, to a claim or right to claim by virtue of that Part in respect of any such damage.

Detention of goods

2 ABOLITION OF DETINUE

(1)   Detinue is abolished.

(2)   An action lies in conversion for loss or destruction of goods which a bailee has allowed to happen in breach of his duty to his bailor (that is to say it lies in a case which is not otherwise conversion, but would have been detinue before detinue was abolished).

3 FORM OF JUDGMENT WHERE GOODS ARE DETAINED

(1)   In proceedings for wrongful interference against a person who is in possession or in control of the goods relief may be given in accordance with this section, so far as appropriate.

(2)   The relief is—
      (a) an order for delivery of the goods, and for payment of any consequential damages, or
      (b) an order for delivery of the goods, but giving the defendant the alternative of paying damages by reference to the value of the goods, together in either alternative with payment of any consequential damages, or
      (c) damages.

(3)   Subject to rules of court—
      (a) relief shall be given under only one of paragraphs (a), (b) and (c) of subsection (2),
      (b) relief under paragraph (a) of subsection (2) is at the discretion of the court, and the claimant may choose between the others.

(4)   If it is shown to the satisfaction of the court that an order under subsection (2)(a) has not been complied with, the court may—
      (a) revoke the order, or the relevant part of it, and
      (b) make an order for payment of damages by reference to the value of the goods.

(5)   Where an order is made under subsection (2)(b) the defendant may satisfy the order by returning the goods at any time before execution of judgment, but without prejudice to liability to pay any consequential damages.

(6)   An order for delivery of the goods under subsection (2)(a) or (b) may impose such conditions as may be determined by the court, or pursuant to rules of court, and in particular, where damages by reference to the value of the goods would not be the whole of the value of the goods, may require an allowance to be made by the claimant to reflect the difference.

      For example, a bailor's action against the bailee may be one in which the measure of damages is not the full value of the goods, and then the court may order delivery of the goods, but require the bailor to pay the bailee a sum reflecting the difference.

(7)   Where under subsection (1) or subsection (2) of section 6 an allowance is to be made in respect of an improvement of the goods, and an order is made under subsection (2)(a) or (b), the court may assess the allowance to be made in respect of the improvement, and by the order require, as a condition for delivery of the goods, that allowance to be made by the claimant.

(8)   This section is without prejudice—
      (a) to the remedies afforded by section 133 of the Consumer Credit Act 1974, or
      (b) to the remedies afforded by sections 35, 42 and 44 of the Hire-Purchase Act 1965, or to those sections of the Hire-Purchase Act (Northern Ireland) 1966 (so long as those sections respectively remain in force), or
      (c) to any jurisdiction to afford ancillary or incidental relief.

4 INTERLOCUTORY RELIEF WHERE GOODS ARE DETAINED

(1)   In this section "proceedings" means proceedings for wrongful interference.

(2)   On the application of any person in accordance with rules of court, the High Court shall, in such circumstances as may be specified in the rules, have power to make an order providing for the delivery up of any goods which are or may become the subject matter of subsequent proceedings in the court, or as to which any question may arise in proceedings.

(3)   Delivery shall be, as the order may provide, to the claimant or to a person appointed by the court for the purpose, and shall be on such terms and conditions as may be specified in the order.

Damages

5 EXTINCTION OF TITLE ON SATISFACTION OF CLAIM FOR DAMAGES

(1)   Where damages for wrongful interference are, or would fall to be, assessed on the footing that the claimant is being compensated—
  (a) for the whole of his interest in the goods, or
  (b) for the whole of his interest in the goods subject to a reduction for contributory negligence,
payment of the assessed damages (under all heads), or as the case may be settlement of a claim for damages for the wrong (under all heads), extinguishes the claimant's title to that interest.

(2)   In subsection (1) the reference to the settlement of the claim includes—
  (a) where the claim is made in court proceedings, and the defendant has paid a sum into court to meet the whole claim, the taking of that sum by the claimant, and
  (b) where the claim is made in court proceedings, and the proceedings are settled or compromised, the payment of what is due in accordance with the settlement or compromise, and
  (c) where the claim is made out of court and is settled or compromised, the payment of what is due in accordance with the settlement or compromise.

(3)   It is hereby declared that subsection (1) does not apply where damages are assessed on the footing that the claimant is being compensated for the whole of his interest in the goods, but the damages paid are limited to some lesser amount by virtue of any enactment or rule of law.

(4)   Where under section 7(3) the claimant accounts over to another person (the "third party") so as to compensate (under all heads) the third party for the whole of his interest in the goods, the third party's title to that interest is extinguished.

(5)   This section has effect subject to any agreement varying the respective rights of the parties to the agreement, and where the claim is made in court proceedings has effect subject to any order of the court.

6 ALLOWANCE FOR IMPROVEMENT OF THE GOODS

(1)   If in proceedings for wrongful interference against a person (the "improver") who has improved the goods, it is shown that the improver acted in the mistaken but honest belief that he had a good title to them, an allowance shall be made for the extent to which, at the time as at which the goods fall to be valued in assessing damages, the value of the goods is attributable to the improvement.

(2)   If, in proceedings for wrongful interference against a person ("the purchaser") who has purported to purchase the goods—
  (a) from the improver, or
  (b) where after such a purported sale the goods passed by a further purported sale on one or more occasions, on any such occasion,
it is shown that the purchaser acted in good faith, an allowance shall be made on the principle set out in subsection (1).

For example, where a person in good faith buys a stolen car from the improver and is sued in conversion by the true owner the damages may be reduced to reflect the improvement, but if the person who bought the stolen car from the improver sues the improver for failure of consideration, and the improver acted in good faith, subsection (3) below will ordinarily make a comparable reduction in the damages he recovers from the improver.

(3) If in a case within subsection (2) the person purporting to sell the goods acted in good faith, then in proceedings by the purchaser for recovery of the purchase price because of failure of consideration, or in any other proceedings founded on that failure of consideration, an allowance shall, where appropriate, be made on the principle set out in subsection (1).

(4) This section applies, with the necessary modifications, to a purported bailment or other disposition of goods as it applies to a purported sale of goods.

Liability to two or more claimants

7 DOUBLE LIABILITY

(1) In this section "double liability" means the double liability of the wrongdoer which can arise—
  (a) where one of two or more rights of action for wrongful interference is founded on a possessory title, or
  (b) where the measure of damages in an action for wrongful interference founded on a proprietary title is or includes the entire value of the goods, although the interest is one of two or more interests in the goods.

(2) In proceedings to which any two or more claimants are parties, the relief shall be such as to avoid double liability of the wrongdoer as between those claimants.

(3) On satisfaction, in whole or in part, of any claim for an amount exceeding that recoverable if subsection (2) applied, the claimant is liable to account over to the other person having a right to claim to such extent as will avoid double liability.

(4) Where, as the result of enforcement of a double liability, any claimant is unjustly enriched to any extent, he shall be liable to reimburse the wrongdoer to that extent.

For example, if a converter of goods pays damages first to a finder of the goods, and then to the true owner, the finder is unjustly enriched unless he accounts over to the true owner under subsection (3); and then the true owner is unjustly enriched and becomes liable to reimburse the converter of the goods.

8 COMPETING RIGHTS TO THE GOODS

(1) The defendant in an action for wrongful interference shall be entitled to show, in accordance with rules of court, that a third party has a better right than the plaintiff as respects all or any part of the interest claimed by the plaintiff, or in right of which he sues, and any rule of law (sometimes called jus tertii) to the contrary is abolished.

(2) Rules of court relating to proceedings for wrongful interference may—
  (a) require the plaintiff to give particulars of his title,
  (b) require the plaintiff to identify any person who, to his knowledge, has or claims any interest in the goods,
  (c) authorise the defendant to apply for directions as to whether any person should be joined with a view to establishing whether he has a better right than the plaintiff, or has a claim as a result of which the defendant might be doubly liable,

(d) where a party fails to appear on an application within paragraph (c), or to comply with any direction given by the court on such an application, authorise the court to deprive him of any right of action against the defendant for the wrong either unconditionally, or subject to such terms or conditions as may be specified.

(3) Subsection (2) is without prejudice to any other power of making rules of court.

9 CONCURRENT ACTIONS

(1) This section applies where goods are the subject of two or more claims for wrongful interference (whether or not the claims are founded on the same wrongful act, and whether or not any of the claims relates also to other goods).

(2) Where goods are the subject of two or more claims under section 6 this section shall apply as if any claim under section 6(3) were a claim for wrongful interference.

(3) If proceedings have been brought in a county court on one of those claims, county court rules may waive, or allow a court to waive, any limit (financial or territorial) on the jurisdiction of county courts in the County Courts Act 1984 or the County Courts (Northern Ireland) Order 1980 so as to allow another of those claims to be brought in the same county court.

(4) If proceedings are brought on one of the claims in the High Court, and proceedings on any other are brought in a county court, whether prior to the High Court proceedings or not, the High Court may, on the application of the defendant, after notice has been given to the claimant in the county court proceedings—
(a) order that the county court proceedings be transferred to the High Court, and
(b) order security for costs or impose such other terms as the court thinks fit.

Conversion and trespass to goods

10 CO-OWNERS

(1) Co-ownership is no defence to an action founded on conversion or trespass to goods where the defendant without the authority of the other co-owner—
(a) destroys the goods, or disposes of the goods in a way giving a good title to the entire property in the goods, or otherwise does anything equivalent to the destruction of the other's interest in the goods, or
(b) purports to dispose of the goods in a way which would give a good title to the entire property in the goods if he was acting with the authority of all co-owners of the goods.

(2) Subsection (1) shall not affect the law concerning execution or enforcement of judgments, or concerning any form of distress.

(3) Subsection (1)(a) is by way of restatement of existing law so far as it relates to conversion.

11 MINOR AMENDMENTS

(1) Contributory negligence is no defence in proceedings founded on conversion, or on intentional trespass to goods.

(2) Receipt of goods by way of pledge is conversion if the delivery of the goods is conversion.

(3) Denial of title is not of itself conversion.

Uncollected goods

12 BAILEE'S POWER OF SALE

(1)   This section applies to goods in the possession or under the control of a bailee where—
(a)   the bailor is in breach of an obligation to take delivery of the goods or, if the terms of the bailment so provide, to give directions as to their delivery, or
(b)   the bailee could impose such an obligation by giving notice to the bailor, but is unable to trace or communicate with the bailor, or
(c)   the bailee can reasonably expect to be relieved of any duty to safeguard the goods on giving notice to the bailor, but is unable to trace or communicate with the bailor.

(2)   In the cases of Part I of Schedule 1 to this Act a bailee may, for the purposes of subsection (1), impose an obligation on the bailor to take delivery of the goods, or as the case may be to give directions as to their delivery, and in those cases the said Part I sets out the method of notification.

(3)   If the bailee—
(a)   has in accordance with Part II of Schedule 1 to this Act given notice to the bailor of his intention to sell the goods under this subsection, or
(b)   has failed to trace or communicate with the bailor with a view to giving him such a notice, after having taken reasonable steps for the purpose,
and is reasonably satisfied that the bailor owns the goods, he shall be entitled, as against the bailor, to sell the goods.

(4)   Where subsection (3) applies but the bailor did not in fact own the goods, a sale under this section, or under section 13, shall not give a good title as against the owner, or as against a person claiming under the owner.

(5)   A bailee exercising his powers under subsection (3) shall be liable to account to the bailor for the proceeds of sale, less any costs of sale, and—
(a)   the account shall be taken on the footing that the bailee should have adopted the best method of sale reasonably available in the circumstances, and
(b)   where subsection (3)(a) applies, any sum payable in respect of the goods by the bailor to the bailee which accrued due before the bailee gave notice of intention to sell the goods shall be deductible from the proceeds of sale.

(6)   A sale duly made under this section gives a good title to the purchaser as against the bailor.

(7)   In this section, section 13, and Schedule 1 to this Act,
(a)   "bailor" and "bailee" include their respective successors in title, and
(b)   references to what is payable, paid or due to the bailee in respect of the goods include references to what would be payable by the bailor to the bailee as a condition of delivery of the goods at the relevant time.

(8)   This section, and Schedule 1 to this Act, have effect subject to the terms of the bailment.

(9)   This section shall not apply where the goods were bailed before the commencement of this Act.

13 SALE AUTHORISED BY THE COURT

(1)   If a bailee of the goods to which section 12 applies satisfies the court that he is entitled to sell the goods under section 12, or that he would be so entitled if he had given any notice required in accordance with Schedule 1 to this Act, the court—

    (a) may authorise the sale of the goods subject to such terms and conditions, if any, as may be specified in the order, and

    (b) may authorise the bailee to deduct from the proceeds of sale any costs of sale and any amount due from the bailor to the bailee in respect of the goods, and

    (c) may direct the payment into court of the net proceeds of sale, less any amount deducted under paragraph (b), to be held to the credit of the bailor.

(2)   A decision of the court authorising a sale under this section shall, subject to any right of appeal, be conclusive, as against the bailor, of the bailee's entitlement to sell the goods, and gives a good title to the purchaser as against the bailor.

(3)   In this section "the court" means the High Court or a county court and a county court shall have jurisdiction in the proceedings save that, in Northern Ireland, a county court shall only have jurisdiction in proceedings if the value of the goods does not exceed the county court limit mentioned in Article 10(1) of the County Courts (Northern Ireland) Order 1980.

Supplemental

14 INTERPRETATION

(1)   In this Act, unless the context otherwise requires—

    ....

"goods" includes all chattels personal other than things in action and money.

16 EXTENT AND APPLICATION TO THE CROWN

(1)   Section 15 shall extend to Scotland, but otherwise this Act shall not extend to Scotland.

(2)   This Act, except section 15, extends to Northern Ireland.

(3)   This Act shall bind the Crown, but as regards the Crown's liability in tort shall not bind the Crown further than the Crown is made liable in tort by the Crown Proceedings Act 1947.

SCHEDULES
SCHEDULE 1

Section 12

Uncollected Goods

Part I POWER TO IMPOSE OBLIGATION TO COLLECT GOODS

1. (1) For the purposes of section 12(1) a bailee may, in the circumstances specified in this Part of this Schedule, by notice given to the bailor impose on him an obligation to take delivery of the goods.

    (2) The notice shall be in writing, and may be given either—
        (a) by delivering it to the bailor, or
        (b) by leaving it at his proper address, or
        (c) by post.

    (3) The notice shall—
        (a) specify the name and address of the bailee, and give sufficient particulars of the goods and the address or place where they are held, and

(b) state that the goods are ready for delivery to the bailor, or where combined with a notice terminating the contract of bailment, will be ready for delivery when the cont ract is terminated, and

(c) specify the amount, if any, which is payable by the bailor to the bailee in respect of the goods and which became due before the giving of the notice.

(4) Where the notice is sent by post it may be combined with a notice under Part II of this Schedule if the notice is sent by post in a way complying with paragraph 6(4).

(5) References in this Part of this Schedule to taking delivery of the goods include, where the terms of the bailment admit, references to giving directions as to their delivery.

(6) This Part of this Schedule is without prejudice to the provisions of any contract requiring the bailor to take delivery of the goods.

Goods accepted for repair or other treatment

2. If a bailee has accepted goods for repair or other treatment on the terms (expressed or implied) that they will be re-delivered to the bailor when the repair or other treatment has been carried out, the notice may be given at any time after the repair or other treatment has been carried out.

Goods accepted for valuation or appraisal

3. If a bailee has accepted goods in order to value or appraise them, the notice may be given at any time after the bailee has carried out the valuation or appraisal.

Storage, warehousing, etc.

4.—(1) If a bailee is in possession of goods which he has held as custodian, and his obligation as custodian has come to an end, the notice may be given at any time after the ending of the obligation, or may be combined with any notice terminating his obligation as custodian.

(2) This paragraph shall not apply to goods held by a person as mercantile agent, that is to say by a person having in the customary course of his business as a mercantile agent authority either to sell goods or to consign goods for the purpose of sale, or to buy goods, or to raise money on the security of goods.

Supplemental

5. Paragraphs 2, 3 and 4 apply whether or not the bailor has paid any amount due to the bailee in respect of the goods, and whether or not the bailment is for reward, or in the course of business, or gratuitous.

Part II NOTICE OF INTENTION TO SELL GOODS

6.—(1) A notice under section 12(3) shall—

(a) specify the name and address of the bailee, and give sufficient particulars of the goods and the address or place where they are held, and

(b) specify the date on or after which the bailee proposes to sell the goods, and

(c) specify the amount, if any, which is payable by the bailor to the bailee in respect of the goods, and which became due before the giving of the notice.

(2) The period between giving of the notice and the date specified in the notice as that on or after which the bailee proposes to exercise the power of sale shall be such as will afford the bailor a reasonable opportunity of taking delivery of the goods.

(3) If any amount is payable in respect of the goods by the bailor to the bailee, and become due before giving of the notice, the said period shall be not less than three months.

(4) The notice shall be in writing and shall be sent by post in a registered letter, or by the recorded delivery service.

7.—(1) The bailee shall not give a notice under section 12(3), or exercise his right to sell the goods pursuant to such a notice, at a time when he has notice that, because of a dispute concerning the goods, the bailor is questioning or refusing to pay all or any part of what the bailee claims to be due to him in respect of the goods.

(2) This paragraph shall be left out of account in determining under section 13(1) whether a bailee of goods is entitled to sell the goods under section 12, or would be so entitled if he had given any notice required in accordance with this Schedule.

Supplemental

8.   For the purposes of this Schedule, and of section 26 of the Interpretation Act 1889 in its application to this Schedule, the proper address of the person to whom a notice is to be given shall be—
   (a) in the case of a body corporate, a registered or principal office of the body corporate, and
   (b) in any other case, the last.

UNFAIR CONTRACT TERMS ACT 1977
(c.50)

Part I AMENDMENT OF LAW FOR ENGLAND AND WALES

Introductory

1 SCOPE OF PART I

(1) For the purposes of this Part of this Act, "negligence" means the breach—
   (a) of any obligation, arising from the express or implied terms of a contract, to take reasonable care or exercise reasonable skill in the performance of the contract;
   (b) of any common law duty to take reasonable care or exercise reasonable skill (but not any stricter duty);
   (c) of the common duty of care imposed by the Occupiers' Liability Act 1957 . . .

(2) This Part of this Act is subject to Part III; and in relation to contracts, the operation of sections 2 to 4 and 7 is subject to the exceptions made by Schedule 1.

(3) In the case of both contract and tort, sections 2 to 7 apply (except where the contrary is stated in section 6(4)) only to business liability, that is liability for breach of obligations or duties arising—
   (a) from things done or to be done by a person in the course of a business (whether his own business or another's); or
   (b) from the occupation of premises used for business purposes of the occupier;

and references to liability are to be read accordingly but liability of an occupier of premises for breach of an obligation or duty towards a person obtaining access to the premises for recreational or educational purposes, being liability for loss or damage suffered by reason of the dangerous state of the premises, is not a business liability of the occupier unless granting that person such access for the purposes concerned falls within the business purposes of the occupier.

(4)   In relation to any breach of duty or obligation, it is, immaterial for any purpose of this Part of this Act whether the breach was inadvertent or intentional, or whether liability for it arises directly or vicariously.

Avoidance of liability for negligence, breach of contract, etc.

2 NEGLIGENCE LIABILITY

(1)   A person cannot by reference to any contract term or to a notice given to persons generally or to particular persons exclude or restrict his liability for death or personal injury resulting from negligence.

(2)   In the case of other loss or damage, a person cannot so exclude or restrict his liability for negligence except in so far as the term or notice satisfies the requirement of reasonableness.

(3)   Where a contract term or notice purports to exclude or restrict liability for negligence a person's agreement to or awareness of it is not of itself to be taken as indicating his voluntary acceptance of any risk.

3 LIABILITY ARISING IN CONTRACT

(1)   This section applies as between contracting parties where one of them deals as consumer or on the other's written standard terms of business.

(2)   As against that party, the other cannot by reference to any contract term—
(a) when himself in breach of contract, exclude or restrict any liability of his in respect of the breach; or
(b) claim to be entitled—
(i)   to render a contractual performance substantially different from that which was reasonably expected of him, or
(ii) in respect of the whole or any part of his contractual obligation, to render no performance at all,
except in so far as (in any of the cases mentioned above in this subsection) the contract term satisfies the requirement of reasonableness.

4 UNREASONABLE INDEMNITY CLAUSES

(1)   A person dealing as consumer cannot by reference to any contract term be made to indemnify another person (whether a party to the contract or not) in respect of liability that may be incurred by the other for negligence or breach of contract, except in so far as the contract term satisfies the requirement of reasonableness.

(2)   This section applies whether the liability in question—
(a) is directly that of the person to be indemnified or is incurred by him vicariously;
(b) is to the person dealing as consumer or to someone else.

Liability arising from sale or supply of goods

5 "GUARANTEE" OF CONSUMER GOODS

(1)   In the case of goods of a type ordinarily supplied for private use or consumption, where loss or damage—
  (a)   arises from the goods proving defective while in consumer use; and
  (b)   results from the negligence of a person concerned in the manufacture or distribution of the goods,
  liability for the loss or damage cannot be excluded or restricted by reference to any contract term or notice contained in or operating by reference to a guarantee of the goods.

(2)   For these purposes—
  (a)   goods are to be regarded as "in consumer use" when a person is using them, or has them in his possession for use, otherwise than exclusively for the purposes of a business; and
  (b)   anything in writing is a guarantee if it contains or purports to contain some promise or assurance (however worded or presented) that defects will be made good by complete or partial replacement, or by repair, monetary compensation or otherwise.

(3)   This section does not apply as between the parties to a contract under or in pursuance of which possession or ownership of the goods passed.

6 SALE AND HIRE PURCHASE

(1)   Liability for breach of the obligations arising from—
  (a)   section 12 of the Sale of Goods Act 1979 (seller's implied undertakings as to title, etc.);
  (b)   section 8 of the Supply of Goods (Implied Terms) Act 1973 (the corresponding thing in relation to hire-purchase),
  cannot be excluded or restricted by reference to any contract term.

(2)   As against a person dealing as consumer, liability for breach of the obligations arising from—
  (a)   section 13, 14, or 15 of the 1979 Act (sellers's implied undertakings as to conformity of goods with description or sample, or as to their quality or fitness for a particular purpose);
  (b)   section 9, 10 or 11 of the 1973 Act (the corresponding things in relation to hire-purchase),
  cannot be excluded or restricted by reference to any contract term.

(3)   As against a person dealing otherwise than as consumer, the liability specified in subsection (2) above can be excluded or restricted by reference to a contract term, but only in so far as the term satisfies the requirement of reasonableness.

(4)   The liabilities referred to in this section are not only the business liabilities defined by section 1(3), but include those arising under any contract of sale of goods or hire-purchase agreement.

7 MISCELLANEOUS CONTRACTS UNDER WHICH GOODS PASS

(1)   Where the possession or ownership of goods passes under or in pursuance of a contract not governed by the law of sale of goods or hire-purchase, subsections (2) to (4) below apply as regards the effect (if any) to be given to contract terms excluding or restricting liability for breach of obligation arising by implication of law from the nature of the contract.

(2)   As against a person dealing as consumer, liability in respect of the goods' correspondence with description or sample, or their quality or fitness for any particular purpose, cannot be excluded or restricted by reference to any such term.

(3)   As against a person dealing otherwise than as consumer, that liability can be excluded or restricted by reference to such a term, but only in so far as the term satisfies the requirement of reasonableness.

(3A)   Liability for breach of the obligations arising under section 2 of the Supply of Goods and Services Act 1982 (implied terms about title etc. in certain contracts for the transfer of the property in goods) cannot be excluded or restricted by reference to any such term.

(4)   Liability in respect of—
(a) the right to transfer ownership of the goods, or give possession; or
(b) the assurance of quiet possession to a person taking goods in pursuance of the contract,
cannot (in a case to which subsection (3A) above does not apply) be excluded or restricted by reference to any such term except in so far as the term satisfies the requirement of reasonableness.

Other provisions about contracts

9 EFFECT OF BREACH

(1)   Where for reliance upon it a contract term has to satisfy the requirement of reasonableness, it may be found to do so and be given effect accordingly notwithstanding that the contract has been terminated either by breach or by a party electing to treat it as repudiated.

(2)   Where on a breach the contract is nevertheless affirmed by a party entitled to treat it as repudiated, this does not of itself exclude the requirement of reasonableness in relation to any contract term.

10 EVASION BY MEANS OF SECONDARY CONTRACT

A person is not bound by any contract term prejudicing or taking away rights of his which arise under, or in connection with the performance of, another contract, so far as those rights extend to the enforcement of another's liability which this Part of this Act prevents that other from excluding or restricting.

Explanatory provisions

11 THE "REASONABLENESS" TEST

(1)   In relation to a contract term, the requirement of reasonableness for the purposes of this Part of this Act, section 3 of the Misrepresentation Act 1967 . . . is that the term shall have been a fair and reasonable one to be included having regard to the circumstances which were, or ought reasonably to have been, known to or in the contemplation of the parties when the contract was made.

(2)   In determining for the purposes of section 6 or 7 above whether a contract term satisfies the requirement of reasonableness, regard shall be had in particular to the matters specified in Schedule 2 to this Act; but this subsection does not prevent the court or arbitrator from holding, in accordance with any rule of law, that a term which purports to exclude or restrict any relevant liability is not a term of the contract.

(3)   In relation to a notice (not being a notice having contractual effect), the requirement of reasonableness under this Act is that it should be fair and reasonable to allow reliance on it, having regard to all the circumstances obtaining when the liability arose or (but for the notice) would have arisen.

(4)   Where by reference to a contract term or notice a person seeks to restrict liability to a specified sum of money, and the question arises (under this or any other Act) whether the term or notice satisfies the requirement of reasonableness, regard shall be had in particular (but without prejudice to subsection (2) above in the case of contract terms) to—
    (a) the resources which he could expect to be available to him for the purpose of meeting the liability should it arise; and
    (b) how far it was open to him to cover himself by insurance.

(5)   It is for those claiming that a contract term or notice satisfies the requirement of reasonableness to show that it does.

12 "DEALING AS CONSUMER"

(1)   A party to a contract "deals as consumer" in relation to another party if—
    (a) he neither makes the contract in the course of a business nor holds himself out as doing so; and
    (b) the other party does make the contract in the course of a business; and
    (c) in the case of a contract governed by the law of sale of goods or hire-purchase, or by section 7 of this Act, the goods passing under or in pursuance of the contract are of a type ordinarily supplied for private use or consumption.

(1A) But if the first party mentioned in subsection (1) is an individual paragraph (c) of that subsection must be ignored.

(2)   But the buyer is not in any circumstances to be regarded as dealing as consumer—
    (a) if he is an individual and the goods are second hand goods sold at public auction at which individuals have the opportunity of attending the sale in person;
    (b) if he is not an individual and the goods are sold by auction or by competitive tender.

(3)   Subject to this, it is for those claiming that a party does not deal as consumer to show that he does not.

13 VARIETIES OF EXEMPTION CLAUSE

(1)   To the extent that this Part of this Act prevents the exclusion or restriction of any liability it also prevents—
    (a) making the liability or its enforcement subject to restrictive or onerous conditions;
    (b) excluding or restricting any right or remedy in respect of the liability, or subjecting a person to any prejudice in consequence of his pursuing any such right or remedy;
    (c) excluding or restricting rules of evidence or procedure;
    and (to that extent) sections 2 and 5 to 7 also prevent excluding or restricting liability by reference to terms and notices which exclude or restrict the relevant obligation or duty.

(2)   But an agreement in writing to submit present or future differences to arbitration is not to be treated under this Part of this Act as excluding or restricting any liability.

14 INTERPRETATION OF PART I

In this Part of this Act—

"business" includes a profession and the activities of any government department or local or public authority;

"goods" has the same meaning as in the Sale of Goods Act 1979;

"hire-purchase agreement" has the same meaning as in the Consumer Credit Act 1974;

"negligence" has the meaning given by section 1(1);

"notice" includes an announcement, whether or not in writing, and any other communication or pretended communication; and

"personal injury" includes any disease and any impairment of physical or mental condition.

Part II AMENDMENT OF LAW FOR SCOTLAND

15 SCOPE OF PART II

(1) This Part of this Act, is subject to Part III of this Act and does not affect the validity of any discharge or indemnity given by a person in consideration of the receipt by him of compensation in settlement of any claim which he has.

(2) Subject to subsection (3) below, sections 16 to 18 of this Act apply to any contract only to the extent that the contract—
  (a) relates to the transfer of the ownership or possession of goods from one person to another (with or without work having been done on them);
  (b) constitutes a contract of service or apprenticeship;
  (c) relates to services of whatever kind, including (without prejudice to the foregoing generality) carriage, deposit and pledge, care and custody, mandate, agency, loan and services relating to the use of land;
  (d) relates to the liability of an occupier of land to persons entering upon or using that land;
  (e) relates to a grant of any right or permission to enter upon or use land not amounting to an estate or interest in the land.

(3) Notwithstanding anything in subsection (2) above, sections 16 to 18—
  (a) do not apply to any contract to the extent that the contract—
    (i) is a contract of insurance (including a contract to pay an annuity on human life);
    (ii) relates to the formation, constitution or dissolution of any body corporate or unincorporated association or partnership;
  (b) apply to—
    a contract of marine salvage or towage;
    a charter party of a ship or hovercraft;
    a contract for the carriage of goods by ship or hovercraft; or,
    a contract to which subsection (4) below relates,
    only to the extent that—
    (i) both parties deal or hold themselves out as dealing in the course of a business (and then only in so far as the contract purports to exclude or restrict liability for breach of duty in respect of death or personal injury); or
    (ii) the contract is a consumer contract (and then only in favour of the consumer).

(4) This subsection relates to a contract in pursuance of which goods are carried by ship or hovercraft and which either—
  (a) specifies ship or hovercraft as the means of carriage over part of the journey to be covered; or

(b) makes no provision as to the means of carriage and does not exclude ship or hovercraft as that means,

in so far as the contract operates for and in relation to the carriage of the goods by that means.

16 LIABILITY FOR BREACH OF DUTY

(1) Subject to subsection (1A) below, Where a term of a contract, or a provision of a notice given to persons generally or to particular persons, purports to exclude or restrict liability for breach of duty arising in the course of any business or from the occupation of any premises used for business purposes of the occupier, that term or provision—
   (a) shall be void in any case where such exclusion or restriction is in respect of death or personal injury;
   (b) shall, in any other case, have no effect if it was not fair and reasonable to incorporate the term in the contract or, as the case may be, if it is not fair and reasonable to allow reliance on the provision.

(1A) Nothing in paragraph (b) of subsection (1) above shall be taken as implying that a provision of a notice has effect in circumstances where, apart from that paragraph, it would not have effect.

(2) Subsection (1)(*a*) above does not affect the validity of any discharge and indemnity given by a person, on or in connection with an award to him of compensation for pneumoconiosis attributable to employment in the coal industry, in respect of any further claim arising from his contracting that disease.

(3) Where under subsection (1) above a term of a contract or a provision of a notice is void or has no effect, the fact that a person agreed to, or was aware of, the term or provision shall not of itself be sufficient evidence that he knowingly and voluntarily assumed any risk.

17 CONTROL OF UNREASONABLE EXEMPTIONS IN CONSUMER OR STANDARD FORM CONTRACTS

(1) Any term of a contract which is a consumer contract or a standard form contract shall have no effect for the purpose of enabling a party to the contract—
   (a) who is in breach of a contractual obligation, to exclude or restrict any liability of his to the consumer or customer in respect of the breach;
   (b) in respect of a contractual obligation, to render no performance, or to render a performance substantially different from that which the consumer or customer reasonably expected from the contract;
   if it was not fair and reasonable to incorporate the term in the contract.

(2) In this section "customer" means a party to a standard form contract who deals on the basis of written standard terms of business of the other party to the contract who himself deals in the course of a business.

18 UNREASONABLE INDEMNITY CLAUSES IN CONSUMER CONTRACTS

(1) Any term of a contract which is a consumer contract shall have no effect for the purpose of making the consumer indemnify another person (whether a party to the contract or not) in respect of liability which that other person may incur as a result of breach of duty or breach of contract, if it was not fair and reasonable to incorporate the term in the contract.

(2)   In this section "liability" means liability arising in the course of any business or from the occupation of any premises used for business purposes of the occupier.

19 "GUARANTEE" OF CONSUMER GOODS

(1)   This section applies to a guarantee—
(a) in relation to goods which are of a type ordinarily supplied for private use or consumption; and
(b) which is not a guarantee given by one party to the other party to a contract under or in pursuance of which the ownership or possession of the goods to which the guarantee relates is transferred.

(2)   A term of a guarantee to which this section applies shall be void in so far as it purports to exclude or restrict liability for loss or damage (including death or personal injury)—
(a) arising from the goods proving defective while—
(i)   in use otherwise than exclusively for the purposes of a business; or
(ii) in the possession of a person for such use; and
(b) resulting from the breach of duty of a person concerned in the manufacture or distribution of the goods.

(3)   For the purposes of this section, any document is a guarantee if it contains or purports to contain some promise or assurance (however worded or presented) that defects will be made good by complete or partial replacement, or by repair, monetary compensation otherwise.

20 OBLIGATIONS IMPLIED BY LAW IN SALE AND HIRE-PURCHASE CONTRACTS

(1)   Any term of a contract which purports to exclude or restrict liability for breach of the obligations arising from—
(a) section 12 of the Sale of Goods Act 1979 (seller's implied undertakings as to title etc.);
(b) section 8 of the Supply of Goods (Implied Terms) Act 1973 (implied terms as to title in hire-purchase agreements),
shall be void.

(2)   Any term of a contract which purports to exclude or restrict liability for breach of the obligations arising from—
(a) section 13, 14 or 15 of the said Act of 1979 (seller's implied undertakings as to conformity of goods with description or sample, or as to their quality or fitness for a particular purpose);
(b) section 9, 10 or 11 of the said Act of 1973 (the corresponding provisions in relation to hire-purchase),
shall—
(i)   in the case of a consumer contract, be void against the consumer;
(ii) in any other case, have no effect if it was not fair and reasonable to incorporate the term in the contract.

21 OBLIGATIONS IMPLIED BY LAW IN OTHER CONTRACTS FOR THE SUPPLY OF GOODS

(1)   Any term of a contract to which this section applies purporting to exclude or restrict liability for breach of an obligation—

(a) such as is referred to in subsection (3)(a) below—
   (i) in the case of a consumer contract, shall be void against the consumer, and
   (ii) in any other case, shall have no effect if it was not fair and reasonable to incorporate the term in the contract;
(b) such as is referred to in subsection (3)(b) below, shall have no effect if it was not fair and reasonable to incorporate the term in the contract.

(2) This section applies to any contract to the extent that it relates to any such matter as is referred to in section 15(2)(*a*) of this Act, but does not apply to—
   (a) a contract of sale of goods or a hire-purchase agreement; or
   (b) a charterparty of a ship or hovercraft unless it is a consumer contract (and then only in favour of the consumer).

(3) An obligation referred to in this subsection is an obligation incurred under a contract in the course of a business and arising by implication of law from the nature of the contract which relates—
   (a) to the correspondence of goods with description or sample, or to the quality or fitness of goods for any particular purpose; or
   (b) to any right to transfer ownership or possession of goods, or to the enjoyment of quiet possession of goods.

(3A) Notwithstanding anything in the foregoing provisions of this section, any term of a contract which purports to exclude or restrict liability for breach of the obligations arising under section 11B of the Supply of Goods and Services Act 1982 (implied terms about title, freedom from encumbrances and quiet possession in certain contracts for the transfer of property in goods) shall be void.

22 CONSEQUENCE OF BREACH

For the avoidance of doubt, where any provision of this Part of this Act requires that the incorporation of a term in a contract must be fair and reasonable for that term to have effect—

(a) if that requirement is satisfied, the term may be given effect to notwithstanding that the contract has been terminated in consequence of breach of that contract;

(b) for the term to be given effect to, that requirement must be satisfied even where a party who is entitled to rescind the contract elects not to rescind it.

23 EVASION BY MEANS OF SECONDARY CONTRACT

Any term of any contract shall be void which purports to exclude or restrict, or has the effect of excluding or restricting—

(a) the exercise, by a party to any other contract, of any right or remedy which arises in respect of that other contract in consequence of breach of duty, or of obligation, liability for which could not by virtue of the provisions of this Part of this Act be excluded or restricted by a term of that other contract;

(b) the application of the provisions of this Part of this Act in respect of that or any other contract.

24 THE "REASONABLENESS" TEST

(1) In determining for the purposes of this Part of this Act whether it was fair and reasonable to incorporate a term in a contract, regard shall be had only to the circumstances which were, or ought reasonably to have been, known to or in the contemplation of the parties to the contract at the time the contract was made.

(2)   In determining for the purposes of section 20 or 21 of this Act whether it was fair and reasonable to incorporate a term in a contract, regard shall be had in particular to the matters specified in Schedule 2 to this Act; but this subsection shall not prevent a court or arbiter from holding, in accordance with any rule of law, that a term which purports to exclude or restrict any relevant liability is not a term of the contract.

(2A)   In determining for the purposes of this Part of this Act whether it is fair and reasonable to allow reliance on a provision of a notice (not being a notice having contractual effect), regard shall be had to all the circumstances obtaining when the liability arose or (but for the provision) would have arisen.

(3)   Where a term in a contract or a provision of a notice purports to restrict liability to a specified sum of money, and the question arises for the purposes of this Part of this Act whether it was fair and reasonable to incorporate the term in the contract or whether it is fair and reasonable to allow reliance on the provision, then, without prejudice to subsection (2) above in the case of a term in a contract, regard shall be had in particular to—
   (a)   the resources which the party seeking to rely on that term or provision could expect to be available to him for the purpose of meeting the liability should it arise;
   (b)   how far it was open to that party to cover himself by insurance.

(4)   The onus of proving that it was fair and reasonable to incorporate a term in a contract or that it is fair and reasonable to allow reliance on a provision of a notice shall lie on the party so contending.

25 INTERPRETATION OF PART II

(1)   In this Part of this Act—

"breach of duty" means the breach—

   (a)   of any obligation, arising from the express or implied terms of a contract, to take reasonable care or exercise reasonable skill in the performance of the contract;
   (b)   of any common law duty to take reasonable care or exercise reasonable skill;
   (c)   of the duty of reasonable care imposed by section 2(1) of the Occupiers' Liability (Scotland) Act 1960;

"business" includes a profession and the activities of any government department or local or public authority;

"consumer" has the meaning assigned to that expression in the definition in this section of "consumer contract";

"consumer contract" means subject to subsections (1A) and (1B) below a contract in which —
   (a)   one party to the contract deals, and the other party to the contract ("the consumer") does not deal or hold himself out as dealing, in the course of a business, and
   (b)   in the case of a contract such as is mentioned in section 15(2)(a) of this Act, the goods are of a type ordinarily supplied for private use or consumption;

and for the purposes of this Part of this Act the onus of proving that a contract is not to be regarded as a consumer contract shall lie on the party so contending;

"goods" has the same meaning as in the Sale of Goods Act 1979;

"hire-purchase agreement" has the same meaning as in section 189(1) of the Consumer Credit Act 1974;

"notice" includes an announcement, whether or not in writing, and any other communication or pretended communication;

"personal injury" includes any disease and any impairment of physical or mental condition.

(1A) Where the consumer is an individual, paragraph (b) in the definition of "consumer contract" in subsection (1) must be disregarded.

(1B) The expression of "consumer contract" does not include a contract in which—
  (a) the buyer is an individual and the goods are second hand goods sold by public auction at which individuals have the opportunity of attending in person; or
  (b) the buyer is not an individual and the goods are sold by auction or competitive tender.

(2) In relation to any breach of duty or obligation, it is immaterial for any purpose of this Part of this Act whether the act or omission giving rise to that breach was inadvertent or intentional, or whether liability for it arises directly or vicariously.

(3) In this Part of this Act, any reference to excluding or restricting any liability includes—
  (a) making the liability or its enforcement subject to any restrictive or onerous conditions;
  (b) excluding or restricting any right or remedy in respect of the liability, or subjecting a person to any prejudice in consequence of his pursuing any such right or remedy;
  (c) excluding or restricting any rule of evidence or procedure;
  but does not include an agreement to submit any question to arbitration.

(5) In sections 15 and 16 and 19 to 21 of this Act, any reference to excluding or restricting liability for breach of an obligation or duty shall include a reference to excluding or restricting the obligation or duty itself.

Part III PROVISIONS APPLYING TO WHOLE OF UNITED KINGDOM

Miscellaneous

26 INTERNATIONAL SUPPLY CONTRACTS

(1) The limits imposed by this Act on the extent to which a person may exclude or restrict liability by reference to a contract term do not apply to liability arising under such a contract as is described in subsection (3) below.

(2) The terms of such a contract are not subject to any requirement of reasonableness under section 3 or 4: and nothing in Part II of this Act shall require the incorporation of the terms of such a contract to be fair and reasonable for them to have effect.

(3) Subject to subsection (4), that description of contract is one whose characteristics are the following—
  (a) either it is a contract of sale of goods or it is one under or in pursuance of which the possession or ownership of goods passes; and
  (b) it is made by parties whose places of business (or, if they have none, habitual residences) are in the territories of different States (the Channel Islands and the Isle of Man being treated for this purpose as different States from the United Kingdom).

(4) A contract falls within subsection (3) above only if either—
  (a) the goods in question are, at the time of the conclusion of the contract, in the course of carriage, or will be carried, from the territory of one State to the territory of another; or
  (b) the acts constituting the offer and acceptance have been done in the territories of different States; or

(c) the contract provides for the goods to be delivered to the territory of a State other than that within whose territory those acts were done.

...

32 CITATION AND EXTENT

(1) This Act may be cited as the Unfair Contract Terms Act 1977.

(2) Part I of this Act extends to England and Wales . . . but it does not extend to Scotland.

(3) Part II of this Act extends to Scotland only.

(4) This Part of this Act extends to the whole of the United Kingdom.

SCHEDULES

SCHEDULE 1 SCOPE OF SECTIONS 2 TO 4 AND 7

1.   Sections 2 to 4 of this Act do not extend to—
(a) any contract of insurance (including a contract to pay an annuity on human life);
(b) any contract so far as it relates to the creation or transfer of an interest in land, or to the termination of such an interest, whether by extinction, merger, surrender, forfeiture or otherwise;
(c) any contract so far as it relates to the creation or transfer of a right or interest in any patent, trade mark, copyright or design right, registered design, technical or commercial information or other intellectual property, or relates to the termination of any such right or interest;
(d) any contract so far as it relates—
  (i) to the formation or dissolution of a company (which means any body corporate or unincorporated association and includes a partnership), or
  (ii) to its constitution or the rights or obligations of its corporators or members;
(e) any contract so far as it relates to the creation or transfer of securities or of any right or interest in securities.

2.   Section 2(1) extends to—
(a) any contract of marine salvage or towage;
(b) any charterparty of a ship or hovercraft; and
(c) any contract for the carriage of goods by ship or hovercraft;
but subject to this sections 2 to 4 and 7 do not extend to any such contract except in favour of a person dealing as consumer.

3.   Where goods are carried by ship or hovercraft in pursuance of a contract which either—
(a) specifies that as the means of carriage over part of the journey to be covered, or
(b) makes no provision as to the means of carriage and does not exclude that means, then sections 2(2), 3 and 4 do not, except in favour of a person dealing as consumer, extend to the contract as it operates for and in relation to the carriage of the goods by that means.

4.   Section 2(1) and (2) do not extend to a contract of employment, except in favour of the employee.

5.   Section 2(1) does not affect the validity of any discharge and indemnity given by a person, on or in connection with an award to him of compensation for pneumoconiosis attributable to employment in the coal industry, in respect of any further claim arising from his contracting that disease.

SCHEDULE 2 "GUIDELINES" FOR APPLICATION OF REASONABLENESS TEST

The matters to which regard is to be had in particular for the purposes of sections 6(3), 7(3) and (4), 20 and 21 are any of the following which appear to be relevant—

(a)   the strength of the bargaining positions of the parties relative to each other, taking into account (among other things) alternative means by which the customer's requirements could have been met;

(b)   whether the customer received an inducement to agree to the term, or in accepting it had an opportunity of entering into a similar contract with other persons, but without having to accept a similar term;

(c)   whether the customer knew or ought reasonably to have known of the existence and the extent of the term (having regard, among other things, to any custom of the trade and any previous course of dealing between the parties);

(d)   where the term excludes or restricts any relevant liability if some condition was not complied with, whether it was reasonable at the time of the contract to expect that compliance with that condition would be practicable;

(e)   whether the goods were manufactured, processed or adapted to the special order of the customer.

As amended by Sale of Goods Act 1979, ss. 62, 63 and Sch.2; Supply of Goods and Services Act 1982, ss. 11B, 17 and 20; Occupiers' Liability Act 1984, s. 2; Copyright, Designs and Patents Act 1988, s. 303 and Sch. 7, para.24; Law Reform (Miscellaneous Provisions) (Scotland) Act 1990, ss. 68, 74(2) and Sch. 9; Sale and Supply of Goods to Consumers Regulations 2002, reg. 14; Regulatory Reform (Trading Stamps) Order 2005, Sch. 1, para. 1.

STATE IMMUNITY ACT 1978

(c.33)

1 GENERAL IMMUNITY FROM JURISDICTION

(1)   A State is immune from the jurisdiction of the courts of the United Kingdom except as provided in the following provisions of this Part of this Act.

(2)   A court shall give effect to the immunity conferred by this section even though the State does not appear in the proceedings in question.

3 COMMERCIAL TRANSACTIONS AND CONTRACTS TO BE PERFORMED IN UNITED KINGDOM

(1)   A State is not immune as respects proceedings relating to—
      (a)   a commercial transaction entered into by the State; or
      (b)   an obligation of the State which by virtue of a contract (whether a commercial transaction or not) falls to be performed wholly or partly in the United Kingdom.

(2)   This section does not apply if the parties to the dispute are States or have otherwise agreed in writing; and subsection (1)(b) above does not apply if the contract (not being a commercial transaction) was made in the territory of the State concerned and the obligation in question is governed by its administrative law.

(3)   In this section "commercial transaction" means—
   (a)   any contract for the supply of goods or services;
   (b)   any loan or other transaction for the provision of finance and any guarantee or
         indemnity in respect of any such transaction or of any other financial obligation; and
   (c)   any other transaction or activity (whether of a commercial, industrial, financial,
         professional or other similar character) into which a State enters or in which it
         engages otherwise than in the exercise of sovereign authority;
   but neither paragraph of subsection (1) above applies to a contract of employment
   between a State and an individual.

5 PERSONAL INJURIES AND DAMAGE TO PROPERTY

A State is not immune as respects proceedings in respect of—
(a)   death or personal injury; or

(b)   damage to or loss of tangible property,

caused by an act or omission in the United Kingdom.

CIVIL LIABILITY (CONTRIBUTION) ACT 1978
(c.47)

Proceedings for contribution

1 ENTITLEMENT TO CONTRIBUTION

(1)   Subject to the following provisions of this section, any person liable in respect of any
       damage suffered by another person may recover contribution from any other person liable
       in respect of the same damage (whether jointly with him or otherwise).

(2)   A person shall be entitled to recover contribution by virtue of subsection (1) above
       notwithstanding that he has ceased to be liable in respect of the damage in question since
       the time when the damage occurred, provided that he was so liable immediately before he
       made or was ordered or agreed to make the payment in respect of which the contribution
       is sought.

(3)   A person shall be liable to make contribution by virtue of subsection (1) above
       notwithstanding that he has ceased to be liable in respect of the damage in question since
       the time when the damage occurred, unless he ceased to be liable by virtue of the expiry of
       a period of limitation or prescription which extinguished the right on which the claim
       against him in respect of the damage was based.

(4)   A person who has made or agreed to make any payment in bona fide settlement or
       compromise of any claim made against him in respect of any damage (including a
       payment into court which has been accepted) shall be entitled to recover contribution in
       accordance with this section without regard to whether or not he himself is or ever was
       liable in respect of the damage, provided, however, that he would have been liable
       assuming that the factual basis of the claim against him could be established.

(5)   A judgment given in any action brought in any part of the United Kingdom by or on
       behalf of the person who suffered the damage in question against any person from whom
       contribution is sought under this section shall be conclusive in the proceedings for
       contribution as to any issue determined by that judgment in favour of the person from
       whom the contribution is sought.

(6)   References in this section to a person's liability in respect of any damage are references to any such liability which has been or could be established in an action brought against him in England and Wales by or on behalf of the person who suffered the damage; but it is immaterial whether any issue arising in any such action was or would be determined (in accordance with the rules of private international law) by reference to the law of a country outside England and Wales.

2 ASSESSMENT OF CONTRIBUTION

(1)   Subject to subsection (3) below, in any proceedings for contribution under section 1 above the amount of the contribution recoverable from any person shall be such as may be found by the court to be just and equitable having regard to the extent of that person's responsibility for the damage in question.

(2)   Subject to subsection (3) below, the court shall have power in any such proceedings to exempt any person from liability to make contribution, or to direct that the contribution to be recovered from any person shall amount to a complete indemnity.

(3)   Where the amount of the damages which have or might have been awarded in respect of the damage in question in any action brought in England and Wales by or on behalf of the person who suffered it against the person from whom the contribution is sought was or would have been subject to—
   (a)   any limit imposed by or under any enactment or by any agreement made before the damage occurred;
   (b)   any reduction by virtue of section 1 of the Law Reform (Contributory Negligence) Act 1945 or section 5 of the Fatal Accidents Act 1976; or
   (c)   any corresponding limit or reduction under the law of a country outside England and Wales;
   the person from whom the contribution is sought shall not by virtue of any contribution awarded under section 1 above be required to pay in respect of the damage a greater amount than the amount of those damages as so limited or reduced.

Proceedings for the same debt or damage

3 PROCEEDINGS AGAINST PERSONS JOINTLY LIABLE FOR THE SAME DEBT OR DAMAGE

Judgment recovered against any person liable in respect of any debt or damage shall not be a bar to an action, or to the continuance of an action, against any other person who is (apart from any such bar) jointly liable with him in respect of the same debt or damage.

4 SUCCESSIVE ACTIONS AGAINST PERSONS LIABLE (JOINTLY OR OTHERWISE) FOR THE SAME DAMAGE

If more than one action is brought in respect of any damage by or on behalf of the person by whom it was suffered against persons liable in respect of the damage (whether jointly or otherwise) the plaintiff shall not be entitled to costs in any of those actions, other than that in which judgment is first given, unless the court is of the opinion that there was reasonable ground for bringing the action.

5 APPLICATION TO THE CROWN

Without prejudice to section 4(1) of the Crown Proceedings Act 1947 (indemnity and contribution), this Act shall bind the Crown, but nothing in this Act shall be construed as in any way affecting Her Majesty in Her private capacity (including in right of Her Duchy of Lancaster) or the Duchy of Cornwall.

6 INTERPRETATION

(1)   A person is liable in respect of any damage for the purposes of this Act if the person who suffered it (or anyone representing his estate or dependants) is entitled to recover compensation from him in respect of that damage (whatever the legal basis of his liability, whether tort, breach of contract, breach of trust or otherwise).

(2)   References in this Act to an action brought by or on behalf of the person who suffered any damage include references to an action brought for the benefit of his estate or dependants.

(3)   In this Act "dependants" has the same meaning as in the Fatal Accidents Act 1976.

(4)   In this Act, except in section 1(5) above, "action" means an action brought in England and Wales.

7 SAVINGS

(1)   Nothing in this Act shall affect any case where the debt in question became due or (as the case may be) the damage in question occurred before the date on which it comes into force.

(2)   A person shall not be entitled to recover contribution or liable to make contribution in accordance with section 1 above by reference to any liability based on breach of any obligation assumed by him before the date on which this Act comes into force.

(3)   The right to recover contribution in accordance with section 1 above supersedes any right, other than an express contractual right, to recover contribution (as distinct from indemnity) otherwise than under this Act in corresponding circumstances; but nothing in this Act shall affect—
(a) any express or implied contractual or other right to indemnity; or
(b) any express contractual provision regulating or excluding contribution;
which would be enforceable apart from this Act (or render enforceable any agreement for indemnity or contribution which would not be enforceable apart from this Act).

PNEUMOCONIOSIS ETC. (WORKERS' COMPENSATION) ACT 1979
(c.41)

1 LUMP SUM PAYMENTS

(1)   If, on a claim by a person who is disabled by a disease to which this Act applies, the Secretary of State is satisfied that the conditions of entitlement mentioned in section 2(1) below are fulfilled, he shall in accordance with this Act make to that person a payment of such amount as may be prescribed by regulations.

(2)   If, on a claim by the dependant of a person who, immediately before he died, was disabled by a disease to which this Act applies, the Secretary of State is satisfied that the conditions of entitlement mentioned in section 2(2) below are fulfilled, he shall in

accordance with this Act make to that dependant a payment of such amount as may be so prescribed.

(3)   The diseases to which this Act applies are pneumoconiosis, byssinosis and diffuse mesothelioma and any other disease which is specified by the Secretary of State for the purposes of this Act by order made by statutory instrument.

(4)   Regulations under this section may prescribe different amounts for different cases or classes of cases or for different circumstances.

2 CONDITIONS OF ENTITLEMENT

(1)   In the case of a person who is disabled by a disease to which this Act applies, the conditions of entitlement are—
   (a)   that disablement benefit is payable to him in respect of the disease or, subject to subsection (3A) below, would be payable to him in respect of it but for his disablement amounting to less than the appropriate percentage;
   (b)   that every relevant employer of his has ceased to carry on business; and
   (c)   that he has not brought any action, or compromised any claim, for damages in respect of the disablement.

(2)   In the case of the dependant of a person who, immediately before he died, was disabled by a disease to which this Act applies, the conditions of entitlement are—
   (a)   that no payment under this Act has been made to the deceased in respect of the disease;
   (b)   that disablement benefit was payable to the deceased in respect of the disease immediately before he died or, subject to subsection (3A) below, would have been so payable to him—
      (i)   but for his disablement amounting to less than the appropriate percentage; or
      (ii)   but for his not having claimed the benefit; or
      (iii)   but for his having died before he had suffered from the disease for the appropriate period; and
   (c)   that every relevant employer of the deceased has ceased to carry on business; and
   (d)   that neither the deceased nor his personal representatives nor any relative of his has brought any action, or compromised any claim, for damages in respect of the disablement or death.

(3A)   No amount is payable under this Act in respect of disablement amounting to less than 1 per cent.

(4)   For the purposes of this section any action which has been dismissed otherwise than on the merits (as for example for want of prosecution or under any enactment relating to the limitation of actions) shall be disregarded.

5 RECONSIDERATION OF DETERMINATIONS

(1)   Subject to subsection (2) below, the Secretary of State may reconsider a determination that a payment should not be made under this Act on the ground—
   (a)   that there has been a material change of circumstances since the determination was made; or
   (b)   that the determination was made in ignorance of, or was based on a mistake as to, some material fact;
   and the Secretary of State may, on the ground set out in paragraph (b) above, reconsider a determination that such a payment should be made.

(4)   If, whether fraudulently or otherwise, any person misrepresents or fails to disclose any material fact and in consequence of the misrepresentation or failure a payment is made under this Act, the person to whom the payment was made shall be liable to repay the amount of that payment to the Secretary of State unless he can show t hat the misrepresentation or failure occurred without his connivance or consent.

SALE OF GOODS ACT 1979
(c.54)

Part I CONTRACTS TO WHICH ACT APPLIES

1 CONTRACTS TO WHICH ACT APPLIES

(1)   This Act applies to contracts of sale of goods made on or after (but not to those made before) 1 January 1894.

. . .

Part II FORMATION OF THE CONTRACT

Contract of sale

2 CONTRACT OF SALE

(1)   A contract of sale of goods is a contract by which the seller transfers or agrees to transfer the property in goods to the buyer for a money consideration, called the price.

(2)   There may be a contract of sale between one part owner and another.

(3)   A contract of sale may be absolute or conditional.

(4)   Where under a contract of sale the property in the goods is transferred from the seller to the buyer the contract is called a sale.

(5)   Where under a contract of sale the transfer of the property in the goods is to take place at a future time or subject to some condition later to be fulfilled the contract is called an agreement to sell.

(6)   An agreement to sell becomes a sale when the time elapses or the conditions are fulfilled subject to which the property in the goods is to be transferred.

3 CAPACITY TO BUY AND SELL [ENGLAND AND WALES]

(1) Capacity to buy and sell is regulated by the general law concerning capacity to contract and to transfer and acquire property.

(2) Where necessaries are sold and delivered to a minor or to a person who by reason of drunkenness is incompetent to contract, he must pay a reasonable price for them.

(3) In subsection (2) above "necessaries" means goods suitable to the condition in life of the minor or other person concerned and to his actual requirements at the time of the sale and delivery.

3 CAPACITY TO BUY AND SELL [SCOTLAND]

(1) Capacity to buy and sell is regulated by the general law concerning capacity to contract and to transfer and acquire property.

(2) Where necessaries are sold and delivered to a person who by reason of mental incapacity or drunkenness is incompetent to contract, he must pay a reasonable price for them.

(3) In subsection (2) above "necessaries" means goods suitable to the condition in life of the person concerned and to his actual requirements at the time of the sale and delivery.

Formalities of contract

4 HOW CONTRACT OF SALE IS MADE

(1) Subject to this and any other Act, a contract of sale may be made in writing (either with or without seal), or by word of mouth, or partly in writing and partly by word of mouth, or may be implied from the conduct of the parties.

(2) Nothing in this section affects the law relating to corporations.

Subject matter of contract

5 EXISTING OR FUTURE GOODS

(1) The goods which form the subject of a contract of sale may be either existing goods, owned or possessed by the seller, or goods to be manufactured or acquired by him after the making of the contract of sale, in this Act called future goods.

(2) There may be a contract for the sale of goods the acquisition of which by the seller depends on a contingency which may or may not happen.

(3) Where by a contract of sale the seller purports to effect a present sale of future goods, the contract operates as an agreement to sell the goods.

6 GOODS WHICH HAVE PERISHED

Where there is a contract for the sale of specific goods, and the goods without the knowledge of the seller have perished at the time when the contract is made, the contract is void.

7 GOODS PERISHING BEFORE SALE BUT AFTER AGREEMENT TO SELL

Where there is an agreement to sell specific goods and subsequently the goods, without any fault on the part of the seller or buyer, perish before the risk passes to the buyer, the agreement is avoided.

The price

8 ASCERTAINMENT OF PRICE

(1) The price in a contract of sale may be fixed by the contract, or may be left to be fixed in a manner agreed by the contract, or may be determined by the course of dealing between the parties.

(2) Where the price is not determined as mentioned in sub-section (1) above the buyer must pay a reasonable price.

(3) What is a reasonable price is a question of fact dependent on the circumstances of each particular case.

9 AGREEMENT TO SELL AT VALUATION

(1) Where there is an agreement to sell goods on the terms that the price is to be fixed by the valuation of a third party, and he cannot or does not make the valuation, the agreement is avoided; but if the goods or any part of them have been delivered to and appropriated by the buyer he must pay a reasonable price for them.

(2) Where the third party is prevented from making the valuation by the fault of the seller or buyer, the party not at fault may maintain an action for damages against the party at fault.

Implied terms etc.

10 STIPULATIONS ABOUT TIME

(1) Unless a different intention appears from the terms of the contract, stipulations as to time of payment are not of the essence of a contract of sale.

(2) Whether any other stipulation as to time is or is not of the essence of the contract depends on the terms of the contract.

(3) In a contract of sale "month" prima facie means calendar month.

11 WHEN CONDITION TO BE TREATED AS WARRANTY

(1) This section does not apply to Scotland.

(2) Where a contract of sale is subject to a condition to be fulfilled by the seller, the buyer may waive the condition, or may elect to treat the breach of the condition as a breach of warranty and not as a ground for treating the contract as repudiated.

(3) Whether a stipulation in a contract of sale is a condition, the breach of which may give rise to a right to treat the contract as repudiated, or a warranty, the breach of which may give rise to a claim for damages but not to a right to reject the goods and treat the contract as repudiated, depends in each case on the construction of the contract; and a stipulation may be a condition, though called a warranty in the contract.

(4) Subject to section 35A below Where a contract of sale is not severable and the buyer has accepted the goods or part of them, the breach of a condition to be fulfilled by the seller can only be treated as a breach of warranty, and not as a ground for rejecting the goods and treating the contract as repudiated, unless there is an express or implied term of the contract to that effect.

(6)   Nothing in this section affects a condition or warranty whose fulfilment is excused by law by reason of impossibility or otherwise.

. . .

12 IMPLIED TERMS ABOUT TITLE, ETC.

(1)   In a contract of sale, other than one to which subsection (3) below applies, there is an implied term on the part of the seller that in the case of a sale he has a right to sell the goods, and in the case of an agreement to sell he will have such a right at the time when the property is to pass.

(2)   In a contract of sale, other than one to which subsection (3) below applies, there is also an implied term that—
(a)   the goods are free, and will remain free until the time when the property is to pass, from any charge or encumbrance not disclosed or known to the buyer before the contract is made, and
(b)   the buyer will enjoy quiet possession of the goods except so far as it may be disturbed by the owner or other person entitled to the benefit of any charge or encumbrance so disclosed or known.

(3)   This subsection applies to a contract of sale in the case of which there appears from the contract or is to be inferred from its circumstances an intention that the seller should transfer only such title as he or a third person may have.

(4)   In a contract to which subsection (3) above applies there is an implied term that all charges or encumbrances known to the seller and not known to the buyer have been disclosed to the buyer before the contract is made.

(5)   In a contract to which subsection (3) above applies there is also an implied term that none of the following will disturb the buyer's quiet possession of the goods, namely—
(a)   the seller;
(b)   in a case where the parties to the contract intend that the seller should transfer only such title as a third person may have, that person;
(c)   anyone claiming through or under the seller or that third person otherwise than under a charge or encumbrance disclosed or known to the buyer before the contract is made.

(5A)   As regards England and Wales . . . the term implied by subsection (1) above is a condition and the terms implied by subsections (2), (4) and (5) above are warranties.

. . .

13 SALE BY DESCRIPTION

(1)   Where there is a contract for the sale of goods by description, there is an implied term that the goods will correspond with the description.

(1A)   As regards England and Wales . . . the term implied by subsection (1) above is a condition.

(2)   If the sale is by sample as well as by description it is not sufficient that the bulk of the goods corresponds with the sample if the goods do not also correspond with the description.

(3)   A sale of goods is not prevented from being a sale by description by reason only that, being exposed for sale or hire, they are selected by the buyer.

. . .

14 IMPLIED TERMS ABOUT QUALITY OR FITNESS

(1) Except as provided by this section and section 15 below and subject to any other enactment, there is no implied term about the quality or fitness for any particular purpose of goods supplied under a contract of sale.

(2) Where the seller sells goods in the course of a business, there is an implied term that the goods supplied under the contract are of satisfactory quality.

(2A) For the purposes of this Act, goods are of satisfactory quality if they meet the standard that a reasonable person would regard as satisfactory, taking account of any description of the goods, the price (if relevant) and all the other relevant circumstances.

(2B) For the purposes of this Act, the quality of goods includes their state and condition and the following (among others) are in appropriate cases aspects of the quality of goods—
    (a) fitness for all the purposes for which goods of the kind in question are commonly supplied,
    (b) appearance and finish,
    (c) freedom from minor defects,
    (d) safety, and
    (e) durability.

(2C) The term implied by subsection (2) above does not extend to any matter making the quality of goods unsatisfactory—
    (a) which is specifically drawn to the buyer's attention before the contract is made,
    (b) where the buyer examines the goods before the contract is made, which that examination ought to reveal, or
    (c) in the case of a contract for sale by sample, which would have been apparent on a reasonable examination of the sample.

(2D) If the buyer deals as consumer or, in Scotland, if a contract of sale is a consumer contract, the relevant circumstances mentioned in subsection (2A) above include any public statements on the specific characteristics of the goods made about them by the seller, the producer or his representative, particularly in advertising or on labelling.

(2E) A public statement is not by virtue of subsection (2D) above a relevant circumstance for the purposes of subsection (2A) above in the case of a contract of sale, if the seller shows that—
    (a) at the time the contract was made, he was not, and could not reasonably have been, aware of the statement,
    (b) before the contract was made, the statement had been withdrawn in public or, to the extent that it contained anything which was incorrect or misleading, it had been corrected in public, or
    (c) the decision to buy the goods could not have been influenced by the statement.

(2F) Subsections (2D) and (2E) above do not prevent any public statement from being a relevant circumstance for the purposes of subsection (2A) above (whether or not the buyer deals as consumer or, in Scotland, whether or not the contract of sale is a consumer contract) if the statement would have been such a circumstance apart from those subsections.

(3) Where the seller sells goods in the course of a business and the buyer, expressly or by implication, makes known—
    (a) to the seller, or
    (b) where the purchase price or part of it is payable by instalments and the goods were previously sold by a credit-broker to the seller, to that credit-broker,

any particular purpose for which the goods are being bought, there is an implied term that the goods supplied under the contract are reasonably fit for that purpose, whether or not that is a purpose for which such goods are commonly supplied, except where the circumstances show that the buyer does not rely, or that it is unreasonable for him to rely, on the skill or judgment of the seller or credit-broker.

(4)   An implied term about quality or fitness for a particular purpose may be annexed to a contract of sale by usage.

(5)   The preceding provisions of this section apply to a sale by a person who in the course of a business is acting as agent for another as they apply to a sale by a principal in the course of a business, except where that other is not selling in the course of a business and either the buyer knows that fact or reasonable steps are taken to bring it to the notice of the buyer before the contract is made.

(6)   As regards England and Wales . . . the terms implied by subsections (2) and (3) above are conditions.

   . . .

Sale by sample

15 SALE BY SAMPLE

(1)   A contract of sale is a contract for sale by sample where there is an express or implied term to that effect in the contract.

(2)   In the case of a contract for sale by sample there is an implied term—
(a) that the bulk will correspond with the sample in quality;
(c) that the goods will be free from any defect, making their quality unsatisfactory, which would not be apparent on reasonable examination of the sample.

(3)   As regards England and Wales . . . the term implied by subsection (2) above is a condition.

   . . .

Miscellaneous

15A MODIFICATION OF REMEDIES FOR BREACH OF CONDITION IN NON-CONSUMER CASES

(1)   Where in the case of a contract of sale—
(a) the buyer would, apart from this subsection, have the right to reject goods by reason of a breach on the part of the seller of a term implied by section 13, 14 or 15 above, but
(b) the breach is so slight that it would be unreasonable for him to reject them,

then, if the buyer does not deal as consumer, the breach is not to be treated as a breach of condition but may be treated as a breach of warranty.

(2)   This section applies unless a contrary intention appears in, or is to be implied from, the contract.

(3)   It is for the seller to show that a breach fell within subsection (1)(b) above.

(4)   This section does not apply to Scotland.

15B REMEDIES FOR BREACH OF CONTRACT AS RESPECTS SCOTLAND

(1) Where in a contract of sale the seller is in breach of any term of the contract (express or implied), the buyer shall be entitled—
 (a) to claim damages, and
 (b) if the breach is material, to reject any goods delivered under the contract and treat it as repudiated.

(2) Where a contract of sale is a consumer contract, then, for the purposes of subsection (1) (b) above, breach by the seller of any term (express or implied)—
 (a) as to the quality of the goods or their fitness for a purpose,
 (b) if the goods are, or are to be, sold by description, that the goods will correspond with the description,
 (c) if the goods are, or are to be, sold by reference to a sample, that the bulk will correspond with the sample in quality,
 shall be deemed to be a material breach.

(3) This section applies to Scotland only.

Part III EFFECTS OF THE CONTRACT

Transfer of property as between seller and buyer

16 GOODS MUST BE ASCERTAINED

Subject to section 20A below Where there is a contract for the sale of unascertained goods no property in the goods is transferred to the buyer unless and until the goods are ascertained.

17 PROPERTY PASSES WHEN INTENDED TO PASS

(1) Where there is a contract for the sale of specific or ascertained goods the property in them is transferred to the buyer at such time as the parties to the contract intend it to be transferred.

(2) For the purpose of ascertaining the intention of the parties regard shall be had to the terms of the contract, the conduct of the parties and the circumstances of the case.

18 RULES FOR ASCERTAINING INTENTION

Unless a different intention appears, the following are rules for ascertaining the intention of the parties as to the time at which the property in the goods is to pass to the buyer.

Rule 1.— Where there is an unconditional contract for the sale of specific goods in a deliverable state the property in the goods passes to the buyer when the contract is made, and it is immaterial whether the time of payment or the time of delivery, or both, be postponed.

Rule 2.— Where there is a contract for the sale of specific goods and the seller is bound to do something to the goods for the purpose of putting them into a deliverable state, the property does not pass until the thing is done and the buyer has notice that it has been done.

Rule 3.— Where there is a contract for the sale of specific goods in a deliverable state but the seller is bound to weigh, measure, test, or do some other act or thing with reference to the goods for the purpose of ascertaining the price, the property does not pass until the act or thing is done and the buyer has notice that it has been done.

Rule 4.— When goods are delivered to the buyer on approval or on sale or return or other similar terms the property in the goods passes to the buyer—

  (a) when he signifies his approval or acceptance to the seller or does any other act adopting the transaction;

  (b) if he does not signify his approval or acceptance to the seller but retains the goods without giving notice of rejection, then, if a time has been fixed for the return of the goods, on the expiration of that time, and, if no time has been fixed, on the expiration of a reasonable time.

Rule 5.—(1) Where there is a contract for the sale of unascertained or future goods by description, and goods of that description and in a deliverable state are unconditionally appropriated to the contract, either by the seller with the assent of the buyer or by the buyer with the assent of the seller, the property in the goods then passes to the buyer; and the assent may be express or implied, and may be given either before or after the appropriation is made.

(2) Where, in pursuance of the contract, the seller delivers the goods to the buyer or to a carrier or other bailee or custodier (whether named by the buyer or not) for the purpose of transmission to the buyer, and does not reserve the right of disposal, he is to be taken to have unconditionally appropriated the goods to the contract.

(3) Where there is a contract for the sale of a specified quantity of unascertained goods in a deliverable state forming part of a bulk which is identified either in the contract or by subsequent agreement between the parties and the bulk is reduced to (or to less than) that quantity, then, if the buyer under that contract is the only buyer to whom goods are then due out of the bulk—

  (a) the remaining goods are to be taken as appropriated to that contract at the time when the bulk is so reduced; and

  (b) the property in those goods then passes to that buyer.

(4) Paragraph (3) above applies also (with the necessary modifications) where a bulk is reduced to (or to less than) the aggregate of the quantities due to a single buyer under separate contracts relating to that bulk and he is the only buyer to whom goods are then due out of that bulk.

19 RESERVATION OF RIGHT OF DISPOSAL

(1) Where there is a contract for the sale of specific goods or where goods are subsequently appropriated to the contract, the seller may, by the terms of the contract or appropriation, reserve the right of disposal of the goods until certain conditions are fulfilled; and in such a case, notwithstanding the delivery of the goods to the buyer, or to a carrier or other bailee or custodier for the purpose of transmission to the buyer, the property in the goods does not pass to the buyer until the conditions imposed by the seller are fulfilled.

(2) Where goods are shipped, and by the bill of lading the goods are deliverable to the order of the seller or his agent, the seller is prima facie to be taken to reserve the right of disposal.

(3) Where the seller of goods draws on the buyer for the price, and transmits the bill of exchange and bill of lading to the buyer together to secure acceptance or payment of the bill of exchange, the buyer is bound to return the bill of lading if he does not honour the bill of exchange, and if he wrongfully retains the bill of lading the property in the goods does not pass to him.

20 PASSING OF RISK

(1) Unless otherwise agreed, the goods remain at the seller's risk until the property in them is transferred to the buyer, but when the property in them is transferred to the buyer the goods are at the buyer's risk whether delivery has been made or not.

(2) But where delivery has been delayed through the fault of either buyer or seller the goods are at the risk of the party at fault as regards any loss which might not have occurred but for such fault.

(3) Nothing in this section affects the duties or liabilities of either seller or buyer as a bailee or custodier of the goods of the other party.

(4) In a case where the buyer deals as consumer or, in Scotland, where there is a consumer contract in which the buyer is a consumer, subsections (1) to (3) above must be ignored and the goods remain at the seller's risk until they are delivered to the consumer.

20A UNDIVIDED SHARES IN GOODS FORMING PART OF A BULK

(1) This section applies to a contract for the sale of a specified quantity of unascertained goods if the following conditions are met—
 (a) the goods or some of them form part of a bulk which is identified either in the contract or by subsequent agreement between the parties; and
 (b) the buyer has paid the price for some or all of the goods which are the subject of the contract and which form part of the bulk.

(2) Where this section applies, then (unless the parties agree otherwise), as soon as the conditions specified in paragraphs (a) and (b) of subsection (1) above are met or at such later time as the parties may agree—
 (a) property in an undivided share in the bulk is transferred to the buyer, and
 (b) the buyer becomes an owner in common of the bulk.

(3) Subject to subsection (4) below, for the purposes of this section, the undivided share of a buyer in a bulk at any time shall be such share as the quantity of goods paid for and due to the buyer out of the bulk bears to the quantity of goods in the bulk at that time.

(4) Where the aggregate of the undivided shares of buyers in a bulk determined under subsection (3) above would at any time exceed the whole of the bulk at that time, the undivided share in the bulk of each buyer shall be reduced proportionately so that the aggregate of the undivided shares is equal to the whole bulk.

(5) Where a buyer has paid the price for only some of the goods due to him out of a bulk, any delivery to the buyer out of the bulk shall, for the purposes of this section, be ascribed in the first place to the goods in respect of which payment has been made.

(6) For the purposes of this section payment of part of the price for any goods shall be treated as payment for a corresponding part of the goods.

20B DEEMED CONSENT BY CO-OWNER TO DEALINGS IN BULK GOODS

(1) A person who has become an owner in common of a bulk by virtue of section 20A above shall be deemed to have consented to—
 (a) any delivery of goods out of the bulk to any other owner in common of the bulk, being goods which are due to him under his contract;

(b) any dealing with or removal, delivery or disposal of goods in the bulk by any other person who is an owner in common of the bulk in so far as the goods fall within that co-owner's undivided share in the bulk at the time of the dealing, removal, delivery or disposal.

(2) No cause of action shall accrue to anyone against a person by reason of that person having acted in accordance with paragraph (a) or (b) of subsection (1) above in reliance on any consent deemed to have been given under that subsection.

(3) Nothing in this section or section 20A above shall—
(a) impose an obligation on a buyer of goods out of a bulk to compensate any other buyer of goods out of that bulk for any shortfall in the goods received by that other buyer;
(b) affect any contractual arrangement between buyers of goods out of a bulk for adjustments between themselves; or
(c) affect the rights of any buyer under his contract.

Transfer of title

21 SALE BY PERSON NOT THE OWNER

(1) Subject to this Act, where goods are sold by a person who is not their owner, and who does not sell them under the authority or with the consent of the owner, the buyer acquires no better title to the goods than the seller had, unless the owner of the goods is by his conduct precluded from denying the seller's authority to sell.

(2) Nothing in this Act affects—
(a) the provisions of the Factors Acts or any enactment enabling the apparent owner of goods to dispose of them as if he were their true owner;
(b) the validity of any contract of sale under any special common law or statutory power of sale or under the order of a court of competent jurisdiction.
. . .

23 SALE UNDER VOIDABLE TITLE

When the seller of goods has a voidable title to them, but his title has not been avoided at the time of the sale, the buyer acquires a good title to the goods, provided he buys them in good faith and without notice of the seller's defect of title.

24 SELLER IN POSSESSION AFTER SALE

Where a person having sold goods continues or is in possession of the goods, or of the documents of title to the goods, the delivery or transfer by that person, or by a mercantile agent acting for him, of the goods or documents of title under any sale, pledge, or other disposition thereof, to any person receiving the same in good faith and without notice of the previous sale, has the same effect as if the person making the delivery or transfer were expressly authorised by the owner of the goods to make the same.

25 BUYER IN POSSESSION AFTER SALE

(1) Where a person having bought or agreed to buy goods obtains, with the consent of the seller, possession of the goods or the documents of title to the goods, the delivery or transfer by that person, or by a mercantile agent acting for him, of the goods or documents of title, under any sale, pledge, or other disposition thereof, to any person

receiving the same in good faith and without notice of any lien or other right of the original seller in respect of the goods, has the same effect as if the person making the delivery or transfer were a mercantile agent in possession of the goods or documents of title with the consent of the owner.

(2)   For the purposes of subsection (1) above—
    (a)   the buyer under a conditional sale agreement is to be taken not to be a person who has bought or agreed to buy goods, and
    (b)   "conditional sale agreement" means an agreement for the sale of goods which is a consumer credit agreement within the meaning of the Consumer Credit Act 1974 under which the purchase price or part of it is payable by instalments, and the property in the goods is to remain in the seller (notwithstanding that the buyer is to be in possession of the goods) until such conditions as to the payment of instalments or otherwise as may be specified in the agreement are fulfilled.

    . . .

26 SUPPLEMENTARY TO SECTIONS 24 AND 25

In sections 24 and 25 above "mercantile agent" means a mercantile agent having in the customary course of his business as such agent authority either—

(a)   to sell goods, or

(b)   to consign goods for the purpose of sale, or

(c)   to buy goods, or

(d)   to raise money on the security of goods.

Part IV PERFORMANCE OF THE CONTRACT

27 DUTIES OF SELLER AND BUYER

It is the duty of the seller to deliver the goods, and of the buyer to accept and pay for them, in accordance with the terms of the contract of sale.

28 PAYMENT AND DELIVERY ARE CONCURRENT CONDITIONS

Unless otherwise agreed, delivery of the goods and payment of the price are concurrent conditions, that is to say, the seller must be ready and willing to give possession of the goods to the buyer in exchange for the price and the buyer must be ready and willing to pay the price in exchange for possession of the goods.

29 RULES ABOUT DELIVERY

(1)   Whether it is for the buyer to take possession of the goods or for the seller to send them to the buyer is a question depending in each case on the contract, express or implied, between the parties.

(2)   Apart from any such contract, express or implied, the place of delivery is the seller's place of business if he has one, and if not, his residence; except that, if the contract is for the sale of specific goods, which to the knowledge of the parties when the contract is made are in some other place, then that place is the place of delivery.

(3)   Where under the contract of sale the seller is bound to send the goods to the buyer, but no time for sending them is fixed, the seller is bound to send them within a reasonable time.

(4)   Where the goods at the time of sale are in the possession of a third person, there is no delivery by seller to buyer unless and until the third person acknowledges to the buyer that he holds the goods on his behalf; but nothing in this section affects the operation of the issue or transfer of any document of title to goods.

(5)   Demand or tender of delivery may be treated as ineffectual unless made at a reasonable hour; and what is a reasonable hour is a question of fact.

(6)   Unless otherwise agreed, the expenses of and incidental to putting the goods into a deliverable state must be borne by the seller.

30 DELIVERY OF WRONG QUANTITY

(1)   Where the seller delivers to the buyer a quantity of goods less than he contracted to sell, the buyer may reject them, but if the buyer accepts the goods so delivered he must pay for them at the contract rate.

(2)   Where the seller delivers to the buyer a quantity of goods larger than he contracted to sell, the buyer may accept the goods included in the contract and reject the rest, or he may reject the whole.

(2A) A buyer who does not deal as consumer may not—
    (a) where the seller delivers a quantity of goods less than he contracted to sell, reject the goods under subsection (1) above, or
    (b) where the seller delivers a quantity of goods larger than he contracted to sell, reject the whole under subsection (2) above,
if the shortfall or, as the case may be, excess is so slight that it would be unreasonable for him to do so.

(2B) It is for the seller to show that a shortfall or excess fell within subsection (2A) above.

(2C) Subsections (2A) and (2B) above do not apply to Scotland.

(2D) Where the seller delivers a quantity of goods—
    (a) less than he contracted to sell, the buyer shall not be entitled to reject the goods under subsection (1) above,
    (b) larger than he contracted to sell, the buyer shall not be entitled to reject the whole under subsection (2) above,
unless the shortfall or excess is material.

(2E) Subsection (2D) above applies to Scotland only.

(3)   Where the seller delivers to the buyer a quantity of goods larger than he contracted to sell and the buyer accepts the whole of the goods so delivered he must pay for them at the contract rate.

(5)   This section is subject to any usage of trade, special agreement, or course of dealing between the parties.

31 INSTALMENT DELIVERIES

(1)   Unless otherwise agreed, the buyer of goods is not bound to accept delivery of them by instalments.

(2)   Where there is a contract for the sale of goods to be delivered by stated instalments, which are to be separately paid for, and the seller makes defective deliveries in respect of one or more instalments, or the buyer neglects or refuses to take delivery of or pay for one or

more instalments, it is a question in each case depending on the terms of the contract and the circumstances of the case whether the breach of contract is a repudiation of the whole contract or whether it is a severable breach giving rise to a claim for compensation but not to a right to treat the whole contract as repudiated.

32 DELIVERY TO CARRIER

(1)   Where, in pursuance of a contract of sale, the seller is authorised or required to send the goods to the buyer, delivery of the goods to a carrier (whether named by the buyer or not) for the purpose of transmission to the buyer is prima facie deemed to be a delivery of the goods to the buyer.

(2)   Unless otherwise authorised by the buyer, the seller must make such contract with the carrier on behalf of the buyer as may be reasonable having regard to the nature of the goods and the other circumstances of the case; and if the seller omits to do so, and the goods are lost or damaged in course of transit, the buyer may decline to treat the delivery to the carrier as a delivery to himself or may hold the seller responsible in damages.

(3)   Unless otherwise agreed, where goods are sent by the seller to the buyer by a route involving sea transit, under circumstances in which it is usual to insure, the seller must give such notice to the buyer as may enable him to insure them during their sea transit; and if the seller fails to do so, the goods are at his risk during such sea transit.

(4)   In a case where the buyer deals as consumer or, in Scotland, where there is a consumer contract in which the buyer is a consumer, subsections (1) to (3) above must be ignored, but if in pursuance of a contract of sale the seller is authorised or required to send the goods to the buyer, delivery of the goods to the carrier is not delivery of the goods to the buyer.

33 RISK WHERE GOODS ARE DELIVERED AT DISTANT PLACE

Where the seller of goods agrees to deliver them at his own risk at a place other than that where they are when sold, the buyer must nevertheless (unless otherwise agreed) take any risk of deterioration in the goods necessarily incident to the course of transit.

34 BUYER'S RIGHT OF EXAMINING THE GOODS

Unless otherwise agreed, when the seller tenders delivery of goods to the buyer, he is bound on request to afford the buyer a reasonable opportunity of examining the goods for the purpose of ascertaining whether they are in conformity with the contract and, in the case of a contract for sale by sample, of comparing the bulk with the sample.

35 ACCEPTANCE

(1)   The buyer is deemed to have accepted the goods subject to subsection (2) below—
      (a)   when he intimates to the seller that he has accepted them, or
      (b)   when the goods have been delivered to him and he does any act in relation to them which is inconsistent with the ownership of the seller.

(2)   Where goods are delivered to the buyer, and he has not previously examined them, he is not deemed to have accepted them under subsection (1) above until he has had a reasonable opportunity of examining them for the purpose—
      (a)   of ascertaining whether they are in conformity with the contract, and
      (b)   in the case of a contract for sale by sample, of comparing the bulk with the sample.

(3)   Where the buyer deals as consumer or (in Scotland) the contract of sale is a consumer contract, the buyer cannot lose his right to rely on subsection (2) above by agreement, waiver or otherwise.

(4)   The buyer is also deemed to have accepted the goods when after the lapse of a reasonable time he retains the goods without intimating to the seller that he has rejected them.

(5)   The questions that are material in determining for the purposes of subsection (4) above whether a reasonable time has elapsed include whether the buyer has had a reasonable opportunity of examining the goods for the purpose mentioned in subsection (2) above.

(6)   The buyer is not by virtue of this section deemed to have accepted the goods merely because—
(a) he asks for, or agrees to, their repair by or under an arrangement with the seller, or
(b) the goods are delivered to another under a sub-sale or other disposition.

(7)   Where the contract is for the sale of goods making one or more commercial units, a buyer accepting any goods included in a unit is deemed to have accepted all the goods making the unit; and in this subsection "commercial unit" means a unit division of which would materially impair the value of the goods or the character of the unit.

. . .

35A RIGHT OF PARTIAL REJECTION

(1)   If the buyer—
(a) has the right to reject the goods by reason of a breach on the part of the seller that affects some or all of them, but
(b) accepts some of the goods, including, where there are any goods unaffected by the breach, all such goods,
he does not by accepting them lose his right to reject the rest.

(2)   In the case of a buyer having the right to reject an instalment of goods, subsection (1) above applies as if references to the goods were references to the goods comprised in the instalment.

(3)   For the purposes of subsection (1) above, goods are affected by a breach if by reason of the breach they are not in conformity with the contract.

(4)   This section applies unless a contrary intention appears in, or is to be implied from, the contract.

36 BUYER NOT BOUND TO RETURN REJECTED GOODS

Unless otherwise agreed, where goods are delivered to the buyer, and he refuses to accept them, having the right to do so, he is not bound to return them to the seller, but it is sufficient if he intimates to the seller that he refuses to accept them.

37 BUYER'S LIABILITY FOR NOT TAKING DELIVERY OF GOODS

(1)   When the seller is ready and willing to deliver the goods, and requests the buyer to take delivery, and the buyer does not within a reasonable time after such request take delivery of the goods, he is liable to the seller for any loss occasioned by his neglect or refusal to take delivery, and also for a reasonable charge for the care and custody of the goods.

(2)   Nothing in this section affects the rights of the seller where the neglect or refusal of the buyer to take delivery amounts to a repudiation of the contract.

Part V RIGHTS OF UNPAID SELLER AGAINST THE GOODS

Preliminary

38 UNPAID SELLER DEFINED

(1)   The seller of goods is an unpaid seller within the meaning of this Act—
(a)   when the whole of the price has not been paid or tendered;
(b)   when a bill of exchange or other negotiable instrument has been received as conditional payment, and the condition on which it was received has not been fulfilled by reason of the dishonour of the instrument or otherwise.

(2)   In this Part of this Act "seller" includes any person who is in the position of a seller, as, for instance, an agent of the seller to whom the bill of lading has been indorsed, or a consignor or agent who has himself paid (or is directly responsible for) the price.

39 UNPAID SELLER'S RIGHTS

(1)   Subject to this and any other Act, notwithstanding that the property in the goods may have passed to the buyer, the unpaid seller of goods, as such, has by implication of law—
(a)   a lien on the goods or right to retain them for the price while he is in possession of them;
(b)   in case of the insolvency of the buyer, a right of stopping the goods in transit after he has parted with the possession of them;
(c)   a right of re-sale as limited by this Act.

(2)   Where the property in goods has not passed to the buyer, the unpaid seller has (in addition to his other remedies) a right of withholding delivery similar to and co-extensive with his rights of lien or retention and stoppage in transit where the property has passed to the buyer.

Unpaid seller's lien

41 SELLER'S LIEN

(1)   Subject to this Act, the unpaid seller of goods who is in possession of them is entitled to retain possession of them until payment or tender of the price in the following cases:—
(a)   where the goods have been sold without any stipulation as to credit;
(b)   where the goods have been sold on credit but the term of credit has expired;
(c)   where the buyer becomes insolvent.

(2)   The seller may exercise his lien or right of retention notwithstanding that he is in possession of the goods as agent or bailee or custodier for the buyer.

42 PART DELIVERY

Where an unpaid seller has made part delivery of the goods, he may exercise his lien or right of retention on the remainder, unless such part delivery has been made under such circumstances as to show an agreement to waive the lien or right of retention.

43 TERMINATION OF LIEN

(1)   The unpaid seller of goods loses his lien or right of retention in respect of them—
(a)   when he delivers the goods to a carrier or other bailee or custodier for the purpose of transmission to the buyer without reserving the right of disposal of the goods;

(b)   when the buyer or his agent lawfully obtains possession of the goods;

(c)   by waiver of the lien or right of retention.

(2)   An unpaid seller of goods who has a lien or right of retention in respect of them does not lose his lien or right of retention by reason only that he has obtained judgment or decree for the price of the goods.

Stoppage in transit

44 RIGHT OF STOPPAGE IN TRANSIT

Subject to this Act, when the buyer of goods becomes insolvent the unpaid seller who has parted with the possession of the goods has the right of stopping them in transit, that is to say, he may resume possession of the goods as long as they are in course of transit, and may retain them until payment or tender of the price.

45 DURATION OF TRANSIT

(1)   Goods are deemed to be in course of transit from the time when they are delivered to a carrier or other bailee or custodier for the purpose of transmission to the buyer, until the buyer or his agent in that behalf takes delivery of them from the carrier or other bailee or custodier.

(2)   If the buyer or his agent in that behalf obtains delivery of the goods before their arrival at the appointed destination, the transit is at an end.

(3)   If, after the arrival of the goods at the appointed destination, the carrier or other bailee or custodier acknowledges to the buyer or his agent that he holds the goods on his behalf and continues in possession of them as bailee or custodier for the buyer or his agent, the transit is at an end, and it is immaterial that a further destination for the goods may have been indicated by the buyer.

(4)   If the goods are rejected by the buyer, and the carrier or other bailee or custodier continues in possession of them, the transit is not deemed to be at an end, even if the seller has refused to receive them back.

(5)   When goods are delivered to a ship chartered by the buyer it is a question depending on the circumstances of the particular case whether they are in the possession of the master as a carrier or as agent to the buyer.

(6)   Where the carrier or other bailee or custodier wrongfully refuses to deliver the goods to the buyer or his agent in that behalf, the transit is deemed to be at an end.

(7)   Where part delivery of the goods has been made to the buyer or his agent in that behalf, the remainder of the goods may be stopped in transit, unless such part delivery has been made under such circumstances as to show an agreement to give up possession of the whole of the goods.

46 HOW STOPPAGE IN TRANSIT IS EFFECTED

(1)   The unpaid seller may exercise his right of stoppage in transit either by taking actual possession of the goods or by giving notice of his claim to the carrier or other bailee or custodier in whose possession the goods are.

(2)   The notice may be given either to the person in actual possession of the goods or to his principal.

(3)   If given to the principal, the notice is ineffective unless given at such time and under such circumstances that the principal, by the exercise of reasonable diligence, may communicate it to his servant or agent in time to prevent a delivery to the buyer.

(4)   When notice of stoppage in transit is given by the seller to the carrier or other bailee or custodier in possession of the goods, he must re-deliver the goods to, or according to the directions of, the seller; and the expenses of the re-delivery must be borne by the seller.

Re-sale etc. by buyer

47 EFFECT OF SUB-SALE ETC. BY BUYER

(1)   Subject to this Act, the unpaid seller's right of lien or retention or stoppage in transit is not affected by any sale or other disposition of the goods which the buyer may have made, unless the seller has assented to it.

(2)   Where a document of title to goods has been lawfully transferred to any person as buyer or owner of the goods, and that person transfers the document to a person who take it in good faith and for valuable consideration, then—
    (a) if the last-mentioned transfer was by way of sale the unpaid seller's right of lien or retention or stoppage in transit is defeated; and
    (b) if the last-mentioned transfer was made by way of pledge or other disposition for value, the unpaid seller's right of lien or retention or stoppage in transit can only be exercised subject to the rights of the transferee.

Rescission: and re-sale by seller

48 RESCISSION: AND RE-SALE BY SELLER

(1)   Subject to this section, a contract of sale is not rescinded by the mere exercise by an unpaid seller of his right of lien or retention or stoppage in transit.

(2)   Where an unpaid seller who has exercised his right of lien or retention or stoppage in transit re-sells the goods, the buyer acquires a good title to them as against the original buyer.

(3)   Where the goods are of a perishable nature, or where the unpaid seller gives notice to the buyer of his intention to re-sell, and the buyer does not within a reasonable time pay or tender the price, the unpaid seller may re-sell the goods and recover from the original buyer damages for any loss occasioned by his breach of contract.

(4)   Where the seller expressly reserves the right of re-sale in case the buyer should make default, and on the buyer making default re-sells the goods, the original contract of sale is rescinded but without prejudice to any claim the seller may have for damages.

Part VA ADDITIONAL RIGHTS OF BUYER IN CONSUMER CASES

48A INTRODUCTORY

(1)   This section applies if—
    (a) the buyer deals as consumer or, in Scotland, there is a consumer contract in which the buyer is a consumer, and
    (b) the goods do not conform to the contract of sale at the time of delivery.

(2)   If this section applies, the buyer has the right—
    (a) under and in accordance with section 48B below, to require the seller to repair or replace the goods, or

(b) under and in accordance with section 48C below—
   (i) to require the seller to reduce the purchase price of the goods to the buyer by an appropriate amount, or
   (ii) to rescind the contract with regard to the goods in question.

(3) For the purposes of subsection (1)(b) above goods which do not conform to the contract of sale at any time within the period of six months starting with the date on which the goods were delivered to the buyer must be taken not to have so conformed at that date.

(4) Subsection (3) above does not apply if—
   (a) it is established that the goods did so conform at that date;
   (b) its application is incompatible with the nature of the goods or the nature of the lack of conformity.

48B REPAIR OR REPLACEMENT OF THE GOODS

(1) If section 48A above applies, the buyer may require the seller—
   (a) to repair the goods, or
   (b) to replace the goods.

(2) If the buyer requires the seller to repair or replace the goods, the seller must—
   (a) repair or, as the case may be, replace the goods within a reasonable time but without causing significant inconvenience to the buyer;
   (b) bear any necessary costs incurred in doing so (including in particular the cost of any labour, materials or postage).

(3) The buyer must not require the seller to repair or, as the case may be, replace the goods if that remedy is—
   (a) impossible, or
   (b) disproportionate in comparison to the other of those remedies, or
   (c) disproportionate in comparison to an appropriate reduction in the purchase price under paragraph (a), or rescission under paragraph (b), of section 48C(1) below.

(4) One remedy is disproportionate in comparison to the other if the one imposes costs on the seller which, in comparison to those imposed on him by the other, are unreasonable, taking into account—
   (a) the value which the goods would have if they conformed to the contract of sale,
   (b) the significance of the lack of conformity, and
   (c) whether the other remedy could be effected without significant inconvenience to the buyer.

(5) Any question as to what is a reasonable time or significant inconvenience is to be determined by reference to—
   (a) the nature of the goods, and
   (b) the purpose for which the goods were acquired.

48C REDUCTION OF PURCHASE PRICE OR RESCISSION OF CONTRACT

(1) If section 48A above applies, the buyer may—
   (a) require the seller to reduce the purchase price of the goods in question to the buyer by an appropriate amount, or
   (b) rescind the contract with regard to those goods,
   if the condition in subsection (2) below is satisfied.

(2) The condition is that—
   (a) by virtue of section 48B(3) above the buyer may require neither repair nor replacement of the goods; or
   (b) the buyer has required the seller to repair or replace the goods, but the seller is in breach of the requirement of section 48B(2)(a) above to do so within a reasonable time and without significant inconvenience to the buyer.

(3) For the purposes of this Part, if the buyer rescinds the contract, any reimbursement to the buyer may be reduced to take account of the use he has had of the goods since they were delivered to him.

48D RELATION TO OTHER REMEDIES ETC.

(1) If the buyer requires the seller to repair or replace the goods the buyer must not act under subsection (2) until he has given the seller a reasonable time in which to repair or replace (as the case may be) the goods.

(2) The buyer acts under this subsection if—
   (a) in England and Wales . . . he rejects the goods and terminates the contract for breach of condition;
   (b) in Scotland he rejects any goods delivered under the contract and treats it as repudiated;
   (c) he requires the goods to be replaced or repaired (as the case may be).

48E POWERS OF THE COURT

(1) In any proceedings in which a remedy is sought by virtue of this Part the court, in addition to any other power it has, may act under this section.

(2) On the application of the buyer the court may make an order requiring specific performance or, in Scotland, specific implement by the seller of any obligation imposed on him by virtue of section 48B above.

(3) Subsection (4) applies if—
   (a) the buyer requires the seller to give effect to a remedy under section 48B or 48C above or has claims to rescind under section 48C, but
   (b) the court decides that another remedy under section 48B or 48C is appropriate.

(4) The court may proceed—
   (a) as if the buyer had required the seller to give effect to the other remedy, or if the other remedy is rescission under section 48C
   (b) as if the buyer had claimed to rescind the contract under that section.

(5) If the buyer has claimed to rescind the contract the court may order that any reimbursement to the buyer is reduced to take account of the use he has had of the goods since they were delivered to him.

(6) The court may make an order under this section unconditionally or on such terms and conditions as to damages, payment of the price and otherwise as it thinks just.

48F CONFORMITY WITH THE CONTRACT

For the purposes of this Part, goods do not conform to a contract of sale if there is, in relation to the goods, a breach of an express term of the contract or a term implied by section 13, 14 or 15 above.

Part VI ACTIONS FOR BREACH OF THE CONTRACT

Seller's remedies

49 ACTION FOR PRICE

(1)   Where, under a contract of sale, the property in the goods has passed to the buyer and he wrongfully neglects or refuses to pay for the goods according to the terms of the contract, the seller may maintain an action against him for the price of the goods.

(2)   Where, under a contract of sale, the price is payable on a day certain irrespective of delivery and the buyer wrongfully neglects or refuses to pay such price, the seller may maintain an action for the price, although the property in the goods has not passed and the goods have not been appropriated to the contract.

(3)   Nothing in this section prejudices the right of the seller in Scotland to recover interest on the price from the date of tender of the goods, or from the date on which the price was payable, as the case may be.

50 DAMAGES FOR NON-ACCEPTANCE

(1)   Where the buyer wrongfully neglects or refuses to accept and pay for the goods, the seller may maintain an action against him for damages for non-acceptance.

(2)   The measure of damages is the estimated loss directly and naturally resulting, in the ordinary course of events, from the buyer's breach of contract.

(3)   Where there is an available market for the goods in question the measure of damages is prima facie to be ascertained by the difference between the contract price and the market or current price at the time or times when the goods ought to have been accepted or (if no time was fixed for acceptance) at the time of the refusal to accept.

Buyer's remedies

51 DAMAGES FOR NON-DELIVERY

(1)   Where the seller wrongfully neglects or refuses to deliver the goods to the buyer, the buyer may maintain an action against the seller for damages for non-delivery.

(2)   The measure of damages is the estimated loss directly and naturally resulting, in the ordinary course of events, from the seller's breach of contract.

(3)   Where there is an available market for the goods in question the measure of damages is prima facie to be ascertained by the difference between the contract price and the market or current price of the goods at the time or times when they ought to have been delivered or (if no time was fixed) at the time of the refusal to deliver.

52 SPECIFIC PERFORMANCE

(1)   In any action for breach of contract to deliver specific or ascertained goods the court may, if it thinks fit, on the plaintiff's application, by its judgment or decree direct that the contract shall be performed specifically, without giving the defendant the option of retaining the goods on payment of damages.

(2)   The plaintiff's application may be made at any time before judgment or decree.

(3)   The judgment or decree may be unconditional, or on such terms and conditions as to damages, payment of the price and otherwise as seem just to the court.

(4)   The provisions of this section shall be deemed to be supplementary to, and not in derogation of, the right of specific implement in Scotland.

53 REMEDY FOR BREACH OF WARRANTY

(1)   Where there is a breach of warranty by the seller, or where the buyer elects (or is compelled) to treat any breach of a condition on the part of the seller as a breach of warranty, the buyer is not by reason only of such breach of warranty entitled to reject the goods; but he may—
(a) set up against the seller the breach of warranty in diminution or extinction of the price, or
(b) maintain an action against the seller for damages for the breach of warranty.

(2)   The measure of damages for breach of warranty is the estimated loss directly and naturally resulting, in the ordinary course of events, from the breach of warranty.

(3)   In the case of breach of warranty of quality such loss is prima facie the difference between the value of the goods at the time of delivery to the buyer and the value they would have had if they had fulfilled the warranty.

(4)   The fact that the buyer has set up the breach of warranty in diminution or extinction of the price does not prevent him from maintaining an action for the same breach of warranty if he has suffered further damage.

(5)   This section does not apply to Scotland.

53A MEASURE OF DAMAGES AS RESPECTS SCOTLAND

(1)   The measure of damages for the seller's breach of contract is the estimated loss directly and naturally resulting, in the ordinary course of events, from the breach.

(2)   Where the seller's breach consists of the delivery of goods which are not of the quality required by the contract and the buyer retains the goods, such loss as aforesaid is prima facie the difference between the value of the goods at the time of delivery to the buyer and the value they would have had if they had fulfilled the contract.

(3)   This section applies to Scotland only.

Interest, etc.

54 INTEREST, ETC.

Nothing in this Act affects the right of the buyer or the seller to recover interest or special damages in any case where by law interest or special damages may be recoverable, or to recover money paid where the consideration for the payment of it has failed.

Part VII SUPPLEMENTARY

55 EXCLUSION OF IMPLIED TERMS

(1)   Where a right, duty or liability would arise under a contract of sale of goods by implication of law, it may (subject to the Unfair Contract Terms Act 1977) be negatived or

varied by express agreement, or by the course of dealing between the parties, or by such usage as binds both parties to the contract.

(2)   An express term does not negative a term implied by this Act unless inconsistent with it.

    . . .

57 AUCTION SALES

(1)   Where goods are put up for sale by auction in lots, each lot is prima facie deemed to be the subject of a separate contract of sale.

(2)   A sale by auction is complete when the auctioneer announces its completion by the fall of the hammer, or in other customary manner; and until the announcement is made any bidder may retract his bid.

(3)   A sale by auction may be notified to be subject to a reserve or upset price, and a right to bid may also be reserved expressly by or on behalf of the seller.

(4)   Where a sale by auction is not notified to be subject to a right to bid by or on behalf of the seller, it is not lawful for the seller to bid himself or to employ any person to bid at the sale, or for the auctioneer knowingly to take any bid from the seller or any such person.

(5)   A sale contravening subsection (4) above may be treated as fraudulent by the buyer.

(6)   Where, in respect of a sale by auction, a right to bid is expressly reserved (but not otherwise) the seller or any one person on his behalf may bid at the auction.

58 PAYMENT INTO COURT IN SCOTLAND

In Scotland where a buyer has elected to accept goods which he might have rejected, and to treat a breach of contract as only giving rise to a claim for damages, he may, in an action by the seller for the price, be required, in the discretion of the court before which the action depends, to consign or pay into court the price of the goods, or part of the price, or to give other reasonable security for its due payment.

59 REASONABLE TIME A QUESTION OF FACT

Where a reference is made in this Act to a reasonable time the question what is a reasonable time is a question of fact.

61 INTERPRETATION

(1)   In this Act, unless the context or subject matter otherwise requires,—

    "action" includes counterclaim and set-off, and in Scotland condescendence and claim and compensation;

    "bulk" means a mass or collection of goods of the same kind which—
    (a) is contained in a defined space or area; and
    (b) is such that any goods in the bulk are interchangeable with any other goods therein of the same number or quantity;

    "business" includes a profession and the activities of any government department . . . or local or public authority;

"buyer" means a person who buys or agrees to buy goods;

"consumer contract" has the same meaning as in section 25(1) of the Unfair Contract Terms Act 1977; and for the purposes of this Act the onus of proving that a contract is not to be regarded as a consumer contract shall lie on the seller;

"contract of sale" includes an agreement to sell as well as a sale;

"credit-broker" means a person acting in the course of a business of credit brokerage carried on by him, that is a business of effecting introductions of individuals desiring to obtain credit—

(a) to persons carrying on any business so far as it relates to the provision of credit, or

(b) to other persons engaged in credit brokerage;

"defendant" includes in Scotland defender, respondent, and claimant in a multiplepoinding;

"delivery" means voluntary transfer of possession from one person to another; except that in relation to sections 20A and 20B above it includes such appropriation of goods to the contract as results in property in the goods being transferred to the buyer;

"document of title to goods" has the same meaning as it has in the Factors Acts;

"Factors Acts" means the Factors Act 1889, the Factors (Scotland) Act 1890, and any enactment amending or substituted for the same;

"fault" means wrongful act or default;

"future goods" means goods to be manufactured or acquired by the seller after the making of the contract of sale;

"goods" includes all personal chattels other than things in action and money, and in Scotland all corporeal moveables except money; and in particular "goods" includes emblements, industrial growing crops, and things attached to or forming part of the land which are agreed to be severed before sale or under the contract of sale; and includes an undivided share in goods;

"plaintiff" includes pursuer, complainer, claimant in a multiplepoinding and defendant or defender counter-claiming;

"producer" means the manufacturer of goods, the importer of goods into the European Economic Area or any person purporting to be a producer by placing his name, trade mark or other distinctive sign on the goods;

"property" means the general property in goods, and not merely a special property;

"repair" means, in cases where there is a lack of conformity in goods for the purposes of section 48F of this Act, to bring the goods into conformity with the contract;

"sale" includes a bargain and sale as well as a sale and delivery;

"seller" means a person who sells or agrees to sell goods;

"specific goods" means goods identified and agreed on at the time a contract of sale is made and includes an undivided share, specified as a fraction or percentage, of goods identified and agreed on as aforesaid;

"warranty" (as regards England and Wales . . .) means an agreement with reference to goods which are the subject of a contract of sale, but collateral to the main purpose of such contract, the breach of which gives rise to a claim for damages, but not to a right to reject the goods and treat the contract as repudiated.

(3)   A thing is deemed to be done in good faith within the meaning of this Act when it is in fact done honestly, whether it is done negligently or not.

(4)   A person is deemed to be insolvent within the meaning of this Act if he has either ceased to pay his debts in the ordinary course of business or he cannot pay his debts as they become due.

(5)   Goods are in a deliverable state within the meaning of this Act when they are in such a state that the buyer would under the contract be bound to take delivery of them.

(5A)   References in this Act to dealing as consumer are to be construed in accordance with Part I of the Unfair Contract Terms Act 1977; and, for the purposes of this Act, it is for a seller claiming that the buyer does not deal as consumer to show that he does not.

    . . .

As amended by Insolvency Act 1985, s. 235, 236(2), Sch. 9, para 11, Sch. 10 Pt III; Bankruptcy (Scotland) Act 1985, s. 75(2) and Sch. 8; Age of Legal Capacity (Scotland) Act 1991, Sch. 2; Sale of Goods (Amendment) Act 1994, s. 1; Sale and Supply of Goods Act 1994, ss. 1–5, Sch. 2, para 5 and Sch. 3, para. 1; Sale of Goods (Amendment) Act 1995, ss. 1–2; Sale and Supply of Goods to Consumers Regulations 2002, regs. 3–6; Mental Capacity Act 2005, Sch. 6, para. 24.

LIMITATION ACT 1980
(c.58)

Part I ORDINARY TIME LIMITS FOR DIFFERENT CLASSES OF ACTION

1 TIME LIMITS UNDER PART I SUBJECT TO EXTENSION OR EXCLUSION UNDER PART II

(1)   This Part of this Act gives the ordinary time limits for bringing actions of the various classes mentioned in the following provisions of this Part.

(2)   The ordinary time limits given in this Part of this Act are subject to extension or exclusion in accordance with the provisions of Part II of this Act.

Actions founded on tort

2 TIME LIMIT FOR ACTIONS FOUNDED ON TORT

An action founded on tort shall not be brought after the expiration of six years from the date on which the cause of action accrued.

3 TIME LIMIT IN CASE OF SUCCESSIVE CONVERSIONS AND EXTINCTION OF TITLE OF OWNER OF CONVERTED GOODS

(1)   Where any cause of action in respect of the conversion of a chattel has accrued to any person and, before he recovers possession of the chattel, a further conversion take place, no action shall be brought in respect of the further conversion after the expiration of six years from the accrual of the cause of action in respect of the original conversion.

(2)   Where any such cause of action has accrued to any person and the period prescribed for bringing that action has expired and he has not during that period recovered possession of the chattel, the title of that person to the chattel shall be extinguished.

4 SPECIAL TIME LIMIT IN CASE OF THEFT

(1)   The right of any person from whom a chattel is stolen to bring an action in respect of the theft shall not be subject to the time limits under sections 2 and 3(1) of this Act, but if his title to the chattel is extinguished under section 3(2) of this Act he may not bring an action in respect of a theft preceding the loss of his title, unless the theft in question preceded the conversion from which time began to run for the purposes of section 3(2).

(2)   Subsection (1) above shall apply to any conversion related to the theft of a chattel as it applies to the theft of a chattel; and, except as provided below, every conversion following the theft of a chattel before the person from whom it is stolen recovers possession of it shall be regarded for the purposes of this section as related to the theft.

If anyone purchases the stolen chattel in good faith neither the purchase nor any conversion following it shall be regarded as related to the theft.

(3)   Any cause of action accruing in respect of the theft or any conversion related to the theft of a chattel to any person from whom the chattel is stolen shall be disregarded for the purpose of applying section 3(1) or (2) of this Act to his case.

(4)   Where in any action brought in respect of the conversion of a chattel it is proved that the chattel was stolen from the plaintiff or anyone through whom he claims it shall be presumed that any conversion following the theft is related to the theft unless the contrary is shown.

(5)   In this section "theft" includes—
(a)   any conduct outside England and Wales which would be theft if committed in England and Wales; and
(b)   obtaining any chattel (in England and Wales or elsewhere) by—
(i)   blackmail (within the meaning of section 21 of the Theft Act 1968), or
(ii)   fraud (within the meaning of the Fraud Act 2006);
and references in this section to a chattel being "stolen" shall be construed accordingly.

4A TIME LIMIT FOR ACTIONS FOR DEFAMATION OR MALICIOUS FALSEHOOD

The time limit under section 2 of this Act shall not apply to an action for—
(a)   libel or slander, or

(b)   slander of title, slander of goods or other malicious falsehood,

but no such action shall be brought after the expiration of one year from the date on which the cause of action accrued.

5 TIME LIMIT FOR ACTIONS FOUNDED ON SIMPLE CONTRACT

An action founded on simple contract shall not be brought after the expiration of six years from the date on which the cause of action accrued.

6 SPECIAL TIME LIMIT FOR ACTIONS IN RESPECT OF CERTAIN LOANS

(1)   Subject to subsection (3) below, section 5 of this Act shall not bar the right of action on a contract of loan to which this section applies.

(2)   This section applies to any contract of loan which—
    (a) does not provide for repayment of the debt on or before a fixed or determinable date; and
    (b) does not effectively (whether or not it purports to do so) make the obligation to repay the debt conditional on a demand for repayment made by or on behalf of the creditor or on any other matter;
except where in connection with taking the loan the debtor enters into any collateral obligation to pay the amount of the debt or any part of it (as, for example, by delivering a promissory note as security for the debt) on terms which would exclude the application of this section to the contract of loan if they applied directly to repayment of the debt.

(3)   Where a demand in writing for repayment of the debt under a contract of loan to which this section applies is made by or on behalf of the creditor (or, where there are joint creditors, by or on behalf of any one of them) section 5 of this Act shall thereupon apply as if the cause of action to recover the debt had accrued on the date on which the demand was made.

(4)   In this section "promissory note" has the same meaning as in the Bills of Exchange Act 1882.

    . . .

8 TIME LIMIT FOR ACTIONS ON A SPECIALTY

(1)   An action upon a specialty shall not be brought after the expiration of twelve years from the date on which the cause of action accrued.

(2)   Subsection (1) above shall not affect any action for which a shorter period of limitation is prescribed by any other provision of this Act.

Actions for sums recoverable by statute

9 TIME LIMIT FOR ACTIONS FOR SUMS RECOVERABLE BY STATUTE

(1)   An action to recover any sum recoverable by virtue of any enactment shall not be brought after the expiration of six years from the date on which the cause of action accrued.

(2)   Subsection (1) above shall not affect any action to which section 10 of this Act applies.

10 SPECIAL TIME LIMIT FOR CLAIMING CONTRIBUTION

(1)   Where under section 1 of the Civil Liability (Contribution) Act 1978 any person becomes entitled to a right to recover contribution in respect of any damage from any other person, no action to recover contribution by virtue of that right shall be brought after the expiration of two years from the date on which that right accrued.

(2)   For the purposes of this section the date on which a right to recover contribution in respect of any damage accrues to any person (referred to below in this section as "the relevant date") shall be ascertained as provided in subsections (3) and (4) below.

(3)   If the person in question is held liable in respect of that damage—
(a) by a judgment given in any civil proceedings; or
(b) by an award made on any arbitration;
the relevant date shall be the date on which the judgment is given, or the date of the award (as the case may be).

For the purposes of this subsection no account shall be taken of any judgment or award given or made on appeal in so far as it varies the amount of damages awarded against the person in question.

(4)   If, in any case not within subsection (3) above, the person in question makes or agrees to make any payment to one or more persons in compensation for that damage (whether he admits any liability in respect of the damage or not), the relevant date shall be the earliest date on which the amount to be paid by him is agreed between him (or his representative) and the person (or each of the persons, as the case may be) to whom the payment is to be made.

(5)   An action to recover contribution shall be one to which sections 28, 32 33A and 35 of this Act apply, but otherwise Parts II and III of this Act (except sections 34, 37 and 38) shall not apply for the purposes of this section.

Actions in respect of wrongs causing personal injuries or death

11 SPECIAL TIME LIMIT FOR ACTIONS IN RESPECT OF PERSONAL INJURIES

(1)   This section applies to any action for damages for negligence, nuisance or breach of duty (whether the duty exists by virtue of a contract or of provision made by or under a statute or independently of any contract or any such provision) where the damages claimed by the plaintiff for the negligence, nuisance or breach of duty consist of or include damages in respect of personal injuries to the plaintiff or any other person.

(1A) This section does not apply to any action brought for damages under section 3 of the Protection from Harassment Act 1997.

(2)   None of the time limits given in the preceding provisions of this Act shall apply to an action to which this section applies.

(3)   An action to which this section applies shall not be brought after the expiration of the period applicable in accordance with subsection (4) or (5) below.

(4)   Except where subsection (5) below applies, the period applicable is three years from
(a) the date on which the cause of action accrued; or
(b) the date of knowledge (if later) of the person injured.

(5)   If the person injured dies before the expiration of the period mentioned in subsection (4) above, the period applicable as respects the cause of action surviving for the benefit of his estate by virtue of section 1 of the Law Reform (Miscellaneous Provisions) Act 1934 shall be three years from—
(a) the date of death; or
(b) the date of the personal representative's knowledge;
whichever is the later.

(6)   For the purposes of this section "personal representative" includes any person who is or has been a personal representative of the deceased, including an executor who has not proved the will (whether or not he has renounced probate) but not anyone appointed only as a special personal representative in relation to settled land; and regard shall be had to any knowledge acquired by any such person while a personal representative or previously.

(7)   If there is more than one personal representative, and their dates of knowledge are different, subsection (5)(b) above shall be read as referring to the earliest of those dates.

11A ACTIONS IN RESPECT OF DEFECTIVE PRODUCTS

(1)   This section shall apply to an action for damages by virtue of any provision of Part I of the Consumer Protection Act 1987.

(2)   None of the time limits given in the preceding provisions of this Act shall apply to an action to which this section applies.

(3)   An action to which this section applies shall not be brought after the expiration of the period of ten years from the relevant time, within the meaning of section 4 of the said Act of 1987; and this subsection shall operate to extinguish a right of action and shall do so whether or not that right of action had accrued, or time under the following provisions of this Act had begun to run, at the end of the said period of ten years.

(4)   Subject to subsection (5) below, an action to which this section applies in which the damages claimed by the plaintiff consist of or include damages in respect of personal injuries to the plaintiff or any other person or loss of or damage to any property, shall not be brought after the expiration of the period of three years from whichever is the later of—
       (a) the date on which the cause of action accrued; and
       (b) the date of knowledge of the injured person or, in the case of loss of or damage to property, the date of knowledge of the plaintiff or (if earlier) of any person in whom his cause of action was previously vested.

(5)   If in a case where the damages claimed by the plaintiff consist of or include damages in respect of personal injuries to the plaintiff or any other person the injured person died before the expiration of the period mentioned in subsection (4) above, that subsection shall have effect as respects the cause of action surviving for the benefit of his estate by virtue of section 1 of the Law Reform (Miscellaneous Provisions) Act 1934 as if for the reference to that period there were substituted a reference to the period of three years from whichever is the later of—
       (a) the date of death; and
       (b) the date of the personal representative's knowledge.

(6)   For the purposes of this section "personal representative" includes any person who is or has been a personal representative of the deceased, including an executor who has not proved the will (whether or not he has renounced probate) but not anyone appointed only as a special personal representative in relation to settled land; and regard shall be had to any knowledge acquired by any such person while a personal representative or previously.

(7)   If there is more than one personal representative and their dates of knowledge are different, subsection (5)(b) above shall be read as referring to the earliest of those dates.

(8)   Expressions used in this section or section 14 of this Act and in Part I of the Consumer Protection Act 1987 have the same meanings in this section or that section as in that Part; and section 1(1) of that Act (Part I to be construed as enacted for the purpose of complying with the product liability Directive) shall apply for the purpose of construing

this section and the following provisions of this Act so far as they relate to an action by virtue of any provision of that Part as it applies for the purpose of construing that Part.

12 SPECIAL TIME LIMIT FOR ACTIONS UNDER FATAL ACCIDENTS LEGISLATION

(1)   An action under the Fatal Accidents Act 1976 shall not be brought if the death occurred when the person injured could no longer maintain an action and recover damages in respect of the injury (whether because of a time limit in this Act or in any other Act, or for any other reason).

Where any such action by the injured person would have been barred by the time limit in section 11 or 11A of this Act, no account shall be taken of the possibility of that time limit being overridden under section 33 of this Act.

(2)   None of the time limits given in the preceding provisions of this Act shall apply to an action under the Fatal Accidents Act 1976, but no such action shall be brought after the expiration of three years from—
(a) the date of death; or
(b) the date of knowledge of the person for whose benefit the action is brought; whichever is the later.

(3)   An action under the Fatal Accidents Act 1976 shall be one to which sections 28, 33, 33A and 35 of this Act apply, and the application to any such action of the time limit under subsection (2) above shall be subject to section 39; but otherwise Parts II and III of this Act shall not apply to any such action.

13 OPERATION OF TIME LIMIT UNDER SECTION 12 IN RELATION TO DIFFERENT DEPENDANTS

(1)   Where there is more than one person for whose benefit an action under the Fatal Accidents Act 1976 is brought, section 12(2)(b) of this Act shall be applied separately to each of them.

(2)   Subject to subsection (3) below, if by virtue of subsection (1) above the action would be outside the time limit given by section 12(2) as regards one or more, but not all, of the persons for whose benefit it is brought, the court shall direct that any person as regards whom the action would be outside that limit shall be excluded from those for whom the action is brought.

(3)   The court shall not give such a direction if it is shown that if the action were brought exclusively for the benefit of the person in question it would not be defeated by a defence of limitation (whether in consequence of section 28 of this Act or an agreement between the parties not to raise the defence, or otherwise).

14 DEFINITION OF DATE OF KNOWLEDGE FOR PURPOSES OF SECTIONS 11 AND 12

(1)   Subject to subsection (1A) below, in sections 11 and 12 of this Act references to a person's date of knowledge are references to the date on which he first had knowledge of the following facts—
(a) that the injury in question was significant; and
(b) that the injury was attributable in whole or in part to the act or omission which is alleged to constitute negligence, nuisance or breach of duty; and

(c) the identity of the defendant; and

(d) if it is alleged that the act or omission was that of a person other than the defendant, the identity of that person and the additional facts supporting the bringing of an action against the defendant;

and knowledge that any acts or omissions did or did not, as a matter of law, involve negligence, nuisance or breach of duty is irrelevant.

(1A) In section 11A of this Act and in section 12 of this Act so far as that section applies to an action by virtue of section 6(1)(a) of the Consumer Protection Act 1987 (death caused by defective product) references to a person's date of knowledge are references to the date on which he first had knowledge of the following facts—

(a) such facts about the damage caused by the defect as would lead a reasonable person who had suffered such damage to consider it sufficiently serious to justify his instituting proceedings for damages against a defendant who did not dispute liability and was able to satisfy a judgment; and

(b) that the damage was wholly or partly attributable to the facts and circumstances alleged to constitute the defect; and

(c) the identity of the defendant;

but, in determining the date on which a person first had such knowledge there shall be disregarded both the extent (if any) of that person's knowledge on any date of whether particular facts or circumstances would or would not, as a matter of law, constitute a defect and, in a case relating to loss of or damage to property, any knowledge which that person had on a date on which he had no right of action by virtue of Part I of that Act in respect of the loss or damage.

(2) For the purposes of this section an injury is significant if the person whose date of knowledge is in question would reasonably have considered it sufficiently serious to justify his instituting proceedings for damages against a defendant who did not dispute liability and was able to satisfy a judgment.

(3) For the purposes of this section a person's knowledge includes knowledge which he might reasonably have been expected to acquire—

(a) from facts observable or ascertainable by him; or

(b) from facts ascertainable by him with the help of medical or other appropriate expert advice which it is reasonable for him to seek;

but a person shall not be fixed under this subsection with knowledge of a fact ascertainable only with the help of expert advice so long as he has taken all reasonable steps to obtain (and, where appropriate, to act on) that advice.

Actions in respect of latent damage not involving personal injuries

14A SPECIAL TIME LIMIT FOR NEGLIGENCE ACTIONS WHERE FACTS RELEVANT TO CAUSE OF ACTION ARE NOT KNOWN AT DATE OF ACCRUAL

(1) This section applies to any action for damages for negligence, other than one to which section 11 of this Act applies, where the starting date for reckoning the period of limitation under subsection (4)(b) below falls after the date on which the cause of action accrued.

(2) Section 2 of this Act shall not apply to an action to which this section applies.

(3) An action to which this section applies shall not be brought after the expiration of the period applicable in accordance with subsection (4) below.

(4)   That period is either—
   (a) six years from the date on which the cause of action accrued; or
   (b) three years from the starting date as defined by subsection (5) below, if that period expires later than the period mentioned in paragraph (a) above.

(5)   For the purposes of this section, the starting date for reckoning the period of limitation under subsection (4)(b) above is the earliest date on which the plaintiff or any person in whom the cause of action was vested before him first had both the knowledge required for bringing an action for damages in respect of the relevant damage and a right to bring such an action.

(6)   In subsection (5) above "the knowledge required for bringing an action for damages in respect of the relevant damage" means knowledge both—
   (a) of the material facts about the damage in respect of which damages are claimed; and
   (b) of the other facts relevant to the current action mentioned in subsection (8) below.

(7)   For the purposes of subsection (6)(a) above, the material facts about the damage are such facts about the damage as would lead a reasonable person who had suffered such damage to consider it sufficiently serious to justify his instituting proceedings for damages against a defendant who did not dispute liability and was able to satisfy a judgment.

(8)   The other facts referred to in subsection (6)(b) above are—
   (a) that the damage was attributable in whole or in part to the act or omission which is alleged to constitute negligence; and
   (b) the identity of the defendant; and
   (c) if it is alleged that the act or omission was that of a person other than the defendant, the identity of that person and the additional facts supporting the bringing of an action against the defendant.

(9)   Knowledge that any acts or omissions did or did not, as a matter of law, involve negligence is irrelevant for the purposes of subsection (5) above.

(10) For the purposes of this section a person's knowledge includes knowledge which he might reasonably have been expected to acquire—
   (a) from facts observable or ascertainable by him; or
   (b) from facts ascertainable by him with the help of appropriate expert advice which it is reasonable for him to seek;
but a person shall not be taken by virtue of this subsection to have knowledge of a fact ascertainable only with the help of expert advice so long as he has taken all reasonable steps to obtain (and, where appropriate, to act on) that advice.

14B   OVERRIDING TIME LIMIT FOR NEGLIGENCE ACTIONS NOT INVOLVING PERSONAL INJURIES

(1)   An action for damages for negligence, other than one to which section 11 of this Act applies, shall not be brought after the expiration of fifteen years from the date (or, if more than one, from the last of the dates) on which there occurred any act or omission—
   (a) which is alleged to constitute negligence; and
   (b) to which the damage in respect of which damages are claimed is alleged to be attributable (in whole or in part).

(2)   This section bars the right of action in a case to which subsection (1) above applies notwithstanding that—
   (a) the cause of action has not yet accrued; or

(b) where section 14A of this Act applies to the action, the date which is for the purposes of that section the starting date for reckoning the period mentioned in subsection (4)
(b) of that section has not yet occurred;
before the end of the period of limitation prescribed by this section.

...

27A ACTIONS FOR RECOVERY OF PROPERTY OBTAINED THROUGH UNLAWFUL CONDUCT ETC.

(1)   None of the time limits given in the preceding provisions of this Act applies to any proceedings under Chapter 2 of Part 5 of the Proceeds of Crime Act 2002 (civil recovery of proceeds of unlawful conduct).

(2)   Proceedings under that Chapter for a recovery order in respect of any recoverable property shall not be brought after the expiration of the period of 20 years from the date on which the relevant person's cause of action accrued.

(3)   Proceedings under that Chapter are brought when—
(a) a claim form is issued, or
(aa) an application is made for a property freezing order, or
(b) an application is made for an interim receiving order,
whichever is the earliest.

(4)   The relevant person's cause of action accrues in respect of any recoverable property—
(a) in the case of proceedings for a recovery order in respect of property obtained through unlawful conduct, when the property is so obtained,
(b) in the case of proceedings for a recovery order in respect of any other recoverable property, when the property obtained through unlawful conduct which it represents is so obtained.

(5)   If—
(a) a person would (but for the preceding provisions of this Act) have a cause of action in respect of the conversion of a chattel, and
(b) proceedings are started under that Chapter for a recovery order in respect of the chattel, section 3(2) of this Act does not prevent his asserting on an application under section 281 of that Act that the property belongs to him, or the court making a declaration in his favour under that section.

(6)   If the court makes such a declaration, his title to the chattel is to be treated as not having been extinguished by section 3(2) of this Act.

(7)   Expressions used in this section and Part 5 of that Act have the same meaning in this section as in that Part.

(8)   In this section "relevant person" means –
(a) the Serious Organised Crime Agency,
(b) the Director of Public Prosecutios,
(c) the Director of Revenue and Customs Prosecutions, or
(d) the Director of the Serious Fraud Office.

27B ACTIONS FOR RECOVERY OF PROPERTY FOR PURPOSES OF AN EXTERNAL ORDER

(1)   None of the time limits given in the preceding provisions of this Act applies to any proceedings under Chapter 2 of Part 5 of the Proceeds of Crime Act 2002 (External

Requests and Orders) Order 2005 (civil proceedings for the realisation of property to give effect to an external order).

(2) Proceedings under that Chapter for a recovery order in respect of any recoverable property shall not be brought after the expiration of the period of 20 years from the date on which the relevant person's cause of action accrued.

(3) Proceedings under that Chapter are brought when—
   (a) a claim form is issued, or
   (b) an application is made for a property freezing order, or
   (c) an application is made for an interim receiving order,
       whichever is earliest.

(4) The relevant person's cause of action accrues in respect of any recoverable property—
   (a) in the case of proceedings for a recovery order in respect of property obtained, or believed to have been obtained, as a result of or in connection with criminal conduct, when the property is so obtained,
   (b) in the case of proceedings for a recovery order in respect of any other recoverable property, when the property obtained, or believed to have been obtained, as a result of or in connection with criminal conduct which it represents is so obtained.

(5) If—
   (a) a person would (but for the preceding provisions of this Act) have a cause of action in respect of the conversion of a chattel, and
   (b) proceedings are started under that Chapter for a recovery order in respect of the chattel,
   (c) section 3(2) of this Act does not prevent his asserting on an application under article 192 of that Order that the property belongs to him, or the court making a declaration in his favour under that article.

(6) If the court makes such a declaration, his title to the chattel is to be treated as not having been extinguished by section 3(2) of this Act.

(7) In this section—
   (a) "criminal conduct" is to be construed in accordance with section 447(8) of the Proceeds of Crime Act 2002, and
   (b) expressions used in this section which are also used in Part 5 of the Proceeds of Crime Act 2002 (External Requests and Orders) Order 2005 have the same meaning in this section as in that Part.

(8) In this section "relevant person" means—
   (a) the Serious Organised Crime Agency,
   (b) the Director of Public Prosecutions,
   (c) the Director of Revenue and Customs Prosecutions, or
   (d) the Director of the Serious Fraud Office.

27C ACTIONS FOR EXPLOITATION PROCEEDS ORDERS

(1) None of the time limits given in the preceding provisions of this Act applies to proceedings under Part 7 of the Coroners and Justice Act 2009 (criminal memoirs etc.) for an exploitation proceeds order.

(2) Proceedings under that Part for such an order are not to be brought after the expiration of 6 years from the date on which the enforcement authority's cause of action accrued.

(3)   Proceedings under that Part for such an order are brought when an application is made for the order.

(4)   Where exploitation proceeds have been obtained by a person from a relevant offence, an enforcement authority's cause of action under that Part in respect of those proceeds accrues when the enforcement authority has actual knowledge that the proceeds have been obtained.

(5)   Expressions used in this section and that Part have the same meaning in this section as in that Part.

Part II EXTENSION OR EXCLUSION OF ORDINARY TIME LIMITS

28 EXTENSION OF LIMITATION PERIOD IN CASE OF DISABILITY

(1)   Subject to the following provisions of this section, if on the date when any right of action accrued for which a period of limitation is prescribed by this Act, the person to whom it accrued was under a disability, the action may be brought at any time before the expiration of six years from the date when he ceased to be under a disability or died (whichever first occurred) notwithstanding that the period of limitation has expired.

(2)   This section shall not affect any case where the right of action first accrued to some person (not under a disability) through whom the person under a disability claims.

(3)   When a right of action which has accrued to a person under a disability accrues, on the death of that person while still under a disability, to another person under a disability, no further extension of time shall be allowed by reason of the disability of the second person.

(4)   No action to recover land or money charged on land shall be brought by virtue of this section by any person after the expiration of thirty years from the date on which the right of action accrued to that person or some person through whom he claims.

(4A)   If the action is one to which section 4A of this Act applies, subsection (1) above shall have effect—
   (a)   in the case of an action for libel or slander, as if for the words from "at any time" to "occurred" there were substituted the words "by him at any time before the expiration of one year from the date on which he ceased to be under a disability"; and
   (b)   in the case of an action for slander of title, slander of goods or other malicious falsehood, as if for the words "six years" there were substituted the words "one year".

(5)   If the action is one to which section 10 of this Act applies, subsection (1) above shall have effect as if for the words "six years" there were substituted the words "two years".

(6)   If the action is one to which section 11 or 12(2) of this Act applies, subsection (1) above shall have effect as if for the words "six years" there were substituted the words "three years".

(7)   If the action is one to which section 11A of this Act applies or one by virtue of section 6(1)(a) of the Consumer Protection Act 1987 (death caused by defective product), subsection (1) above—
   (a)   shall not apply to the time limit prescribed by subsection (3) of the said section 11A or to that time limit as applied by virtue of section 12(1) of this Act; and
   (b)   in relation to any other time limit prescribed by this Act shall have effect as if for the words "six years" there were substituted the words "three years".

28A EXTENSION FOR CASES WHERE THE LIMITATION PERIOD IS THE PERIOD UNDER SECTION 14A(4)(B)

(1)   Subject to subsection (2) below, if in the case of any action for which a period of limitation is prescribed by section 14A of this Act—

(a) the period applicable in accordance with subsection (4) of that section is the period mentioned in paragraph (b) of that subsection;

(b) on the date which is for the purposes of that section the starting date for reckoning that period the person by reference to whose knowledge that date fell to be determined under subsection (5) of that section was under a disability; and

(c) section 28 of this Act does not apply to the action;

the action may be brought at any time before the expiration of three years from the date when he ceased to be under a disability or died (whichever first occurred) notwithstanding that the period mentioned above has expired.

(2)   An action may not be brought by virtue of subsection (1) above after the end of the period of limitation prescribed by section 14B of this Act.

. . .

Acknowledgment and part payment

29 FRESH ACCRUAL OF ACTION ON ACKNOWLEDGMENT OR PART PAYMENT

. . .

(5)   Subject to subsection (6) below, where any right of action has accrued to recover—

(a) any debt or other liquidated pecuniary claim; or

(b) any claim to the personal estate of a deceased person or to any share or interest in any such estate;

and the person liable or accountable for the claim acknowledges the claim or makes any payment in respect of it the right shall be treated as having accrued on and not before the date of the acknowledgment or payment.

(6)   A payment of a part of the rent or interest due at any time shall not extend the period for claiming the remainder then due, but any payment of interest shall be treated as a payment in respect of the principal debt.

(7)   Subject to subsection (6) above, a current period of limitation may be repeatedly extended under this section by further acknowledgments or payments, but a right of action, once barred by this Act, shall not be revived by any subsequent acknowledgment or payment.

30 FORMAL PROVISIONS AS TO ACKNOWLEDGMENTS AND PART PAYMENTS

(1)   To be effective for the purposes of section 29 of this Act, an acknowledgment must be in writing and signed by the person making it.

(2)   For the purposes of section 29, any acknowledgment or payment—

(a) may be sent by the agent of the person by whom it is required to be made under that section; and

(b) shall be made to the person, or to an agent of the person, whose title or claim is being acknowledged or, as the case may be, in respect of whose claim the payment is being made.

31 EFFECT OF ACKNOWLEDGMENT OR PART PAYMENT ON PERSONS OTHER THAN THE MAKER OR RECIPIENT

. . .

(6)   An acknowledgment of any debt or other liquidated pecuniary claim shall bind the acknowledgor and his successors but not any other person.

(7)   A payment made in respect of any debt or other liquidated pecuniary claim shall bind all persons liable in respect of the debt or claim.

(8)   An acknowledgment by one of several personal representatives of any claim to the personal estate of a deceased person or to any share or interest in any such estate, or a payment by one of several personal representatives in respect of any such claim, shall bind the estate of the deceased person.

(9)   In this section "successor", in relation to any mortgagee or person liable in respect of any debt or claim, means his personal representatives and any other person on whom the rights under the mortgage or, as the case may be, the liability in respect of the debt or claim devolve (whether on death or bankruptcy or the disposition of property or the determination of a limited estate or interest in settled property or otherwise).

Fraud, concealment and mistake

32 POSTPONEMENT OF LIMITATION PERIOD IN CASE OF FRAUD, CONCEALMENT OR MISTAKE

(1)   Subject to subsections (3) and (4A) below, where in the case of any action for which a period of limitation is prescribed by this Act, either—
(a) the action is based upon the fraud of the defendant; or
(b) any fact relevant to the plaintiff's right of action has been deliberately concealed from him by the defendant; or
(c) the action is for relief from the consequences of a mistake;
the period of limitation shall not begin to run until the plaintiff has discovered the fraud, concealment or mistake (as the case may be) or could with reasonable diligence have discovered it.

References in this subsection to the defendant include references to the defendant's agent and to any person through whom the defendant claims and his agent.

(2)   For the purposes of subsection (1) above, deliberate commission of a breach of duty in circumstances in which it is unlikely to be discovered for some time amounts to deliberate concealment of the facts involved in that breach of duty.

(3)   Nothing in this section shall enable any action—
(a) to recover, or recover the value of, any property; or
(b) to enforce any charge against, or set aside any transaction affecting, any property;
to be brought against the purchaser of the property or any person claiming through him in any case where the property has been purchased for valuable consideration by an innocent third party since the fraud or concealment or (as the case may be) the transaction in which the mistake was made took place.

(4)   A purchaser is an innocent third party for the purposes of this section—
(a) in the case of fraud or concealment of any fact relevant to the plaintiff's right of action, if he was not a party to the fraud or (as the case may be) to the concealment

of that fact and did not at the time of the purchase know or have reason to believe that the fraud or concealment had taken place; and

(b) in the case of mistake, if he did not at that time of the purchase know or have reason to believe that the mistake had been made.

(4A) Subsection (1) above shall not apply in relation to the time limit prescribed by section 11A(3) of this Act or in relation to that time limit as applied by virtue of section 12(1) of this Act.

(5) Sections 14A and 14B of this Act shall not apply to any action to which subsection (1)(b) above applies (and accordingly the period of limitation referred to in that subsection, in any case to which either of those sections would otherwise apply, is the period applicable under section 2 of this Act).

Discretionary exclusion of time limit for actions for defamation or malicious falsehood

32A DISCRETIONARY EXCLUSION OF TIME LIMIT FOR ACTIONS FOR DEFAMATION OR MALICIOUS FALSEHOOD

(1) If it appears to the court that it would be equitable to allow an action to proceed having regard to the degree to which—
   (a) the operation of section 4A of this Act prejudices the plaintiff or any person whom he represents, and
   (b) any decision of the court under this subsection would prejudice the defendant or any person whom he represents,
the court may direct that that section shall not apply to the action or shall not apply to any specified cause of action to which the action relates.

(2) In acting under this section the court shall have regard to all the circumstances of the case and in particular to—
   (a) the length of, and the reasons for, the delay on the part of the plaintiff;
   (b) where the reason or one of the reasons for the delay was that all or any of the facts relevant to the cause of action did not become known to the plaintiff until after the end of the period mentioned in section 4A—
      (i) the date on which any such facts did become known to him, and
      (ii) the extent to which he acted promptly and reasonably once he knew whether or not the facts in question might be capable of giving rise to an action; and
   (c) the extent to which, having regard to the delay, relevant evidence is likely—
      (i) to be unavailable, or
      (ii) to be less cogent than if the action had been brought within the period mentioned in section 4A.

(3) In the case of an action for slander of title, slander of goods or other malicious falsehood brought by a personal representative
   (a) the references in subsection (2) above to the plaintiff shall be construed as including the deceased person to whom the cause of action accrued and any previous personal representative of that person; and
   (b) nothing in section 28(3) of this Act shall be construed as affecting the court's discretion under this section.

(4) In this section "the court" means the court in which the action has been brought.

Discretionary exclusion of time limit for actions in respect of personal injuries or death

33 DISCRETIONARY EXCLUSION OF TIME LIMIT FOR ACTIONS IN RESPECT OF PERSONAL INJURIES OR DEATH

(1)   If it appears to the court that it would be equitable to allow an action to proceed having regard to the degree to which—

   (a) the provisions of section 11 or 11A or 12 of this Act prejudice the plaintiff or any person whom he represents; and

   (b) any decision of the court under this subsection would prejudice the defendant or any person whom he represents;

   the court may direct that those provisions shall not apply to the action, or shall not apply to any specified cause of action to which the action relates.

(1A)   The court shall not under this section disapply—

   (a) subsection (3) of section 11A; or

   (b) where the damages claimed by the plaintiff are confined to damages for loss of or damage to any property, any other provision in its application to an action by virtue of Part I of the Consumer Protection Act 1987.

(2)   The court shall not under this section disapply section 12(1) except where the reason why the person injured could no longer maintain an action was because of the time limit in section 11 or subsection (4) of section 11A.

   If, for example, the person injured could at his death no longer maintain an action under the Fatal Accidents Act 1976 because of the time limit in Article 29 in Schedule 1 to the Carriage by Air Act 1961, the court has no power to direct that section 12(1) shall not apply.

(3)   In acting under this section the court shall have regard to all the circumstances of the case and in particular to—

   (a) the length of, and the reasons for, the delay on the part of the plaintiff;

   (b) the extent to which, having regard to the delay, the evidence adduced or likely to be adduced by the plaintiff or the defendant is or is likely to be less cogent than if the action had been brought within the time allowed by section 11, by section 11A or (as the case may be) by section 12;

   (c) the conduct of the defendant after the cause of action arose, including the extent (if any) to which he responded to requests reasonably made by the plaintiff for information or inspection for the purpose of ascertaining facts which were or might be relevant to the plaintiff's cause of action against the defendant;

   (d) the duration of any disability of the plaintiff arising after the date of the accrual of the cause of action;

   (e) the extent to which the plaintiff acted promptly and reasonably once he knew whether or not the act or omission of the defendant, to which the injury was attributable, might be capable at that time of giving rise to an action for damages;

   (f) the steps, if any, taken by the plaintiff to obtain medical, legal or other expert advice and the nature of any such advice he may have received.

(4)   In a case where the person injured died when, because of section 11or subsection (4) of section 11A, he could no longer maintain an action and recover damages in respect of the injury, the court shall have regard in particular to the length of, and the reasons for, the delay on the part of the deceased.

(5)   In a case under subsection (4) above, or any other case where the time limit, or one of the time limits, depends on the date of knowledge of a person other than the plaintiff, subsection (3) above shall have effect with appropriate modifications, and shall have effect

in particular as if references to the plaintiff included references to any person whose date of knowledge is or was relevant in determining a time limit.

(6)   A direction by the court disapplying the provisions of section 12(1) shall operate to disapply the provisions to the same effect in section 1(1) of the Fatal Accidents Act 1976.

(7)   In this section "the court" means the court in which the action has been brought.

(8)   References in this section to section 11or 11A include references to that section as extended by any of the preceding provisions of this Part of this Act or by any provision of Part III of this Act.

that death benefit is payable to or in respect of the dependant by reason of the deceased's death as a result of the disease,

33A.   EXTENSION OF TIME LIMITS BECAUSE OF MEDIATION IN CERTAIN CROSS-BORDER DISPUTES

(1)   In this section—
   (a)   "Mediation Directive" means Directive 2008/52/EC of the European Parliament and of the Council of 21 May 2008 on certain aspects of mediation in civil and commercial matters,
   (b)   "mediation"has the meaning given by article 3(a) of the Mediation Directive,
   (c)   "mediator"has the meaning given by article 3(b) of the Mediation Directive, and
   (d)   "relevant dispute" means a dispute to which article 8(1) of the Mediation Directive applies (certain cross-border disputes).

(2)   Subsection (3) applies where—
   (a)   a time limit under this Act relates to the subject of the whole or part of a relevant dispute,
   (b)   a mediation in relation to the relevant dispute starts before the time limit expires, and
   (c)   if not extended by this section, the time limit would expire before the mediation ends or less than eight weeks after it ends.

(3)   For the purposes of initiating judicial proceedings or arbitration, the time limit expires instead at the end of eight weeks after the mediation ends (subject to subsection (4)).

(4)   If a time limit has been extended by this section, subsections (2) and (3) apply to the extended time limit as they apply to a time limit mentioned in subsection (2)(a).

(5)   Where more than one time limit applies in relation to a relevant dispute, the extension by subsection (3) of one of those time limits does not affect the others.

(6)   For the purposes of this section, a mediation starts on the date of the agreement to mediate that is entered into by the parties and the mediator.

(7)   For the purposes of this section, a mediation ends on the date of the first of these to occur—
   (a)   the parties reach an agreement in resolution of the relevant dispute,
   (b)   a party completes the notification of the other parties that it has withdrawn from the mediation,
   (c)   a party to whom a qualifying request is made fails to give a response reaching the other parties within 14 days of the request,
   (d)   after the parties are notified that the mediator's appointment has ended (by death, resignation or otherwise), they fail to agree within 14 days to seek to appoint a replacement mediator,
   (e)   the mediation otherwise comes to an end pursuant to the terms of the agreement to mediate.

(8)   For the purpose of subsection (7), a qualifying request is a request by a party that another (A) confirm to all parties that A is continuing with the mediation.

(9)   In the case of any relevant dispute, references in this section to a mediation are references to the mediation so far as it relates to that dispute, and references to a party are to be read accordingly.

35 NEW CLAIMS IN PENDING ACTIONS: RULES OF COURT

(1)   For the purposes of this Act, any new claim made in the course of any action shall be deemed to be a separate action and to have been commenced—
   (a)   in the case of a new claim made in or by way of third party proceedings, on the date on which those proceedings were commenced; and
   (b)   in the case of any other new claim, on the same date as the original action.

(2)   In this section a new claim means any claim by way of set-off or counterclaim, and any claim involving either—
   (a)   the addition or substitution of a new cause of action; or
   (b)   the addition or substitution of a new party;
and "third party proceedings" means any proceedings brought in the course of any action by any party to the action against a person not previously a party to the action, other than proceedings brought by joining any such person as defendant to any claim already made in the original action by the party bringing the proceedings.

(3)   Except as provided by section 33 of this Act or by rules of court, neither the High Court nor any county court shall allow a new claim within subsection (1)(b) above, other than an original set-off or counterclaim, to be made in the course of any action after the expiry of any time limit under this Act which would affect a new action to enforce that claim.

For the purposes of this subsection, a claim is an original set-off or an original counterclaim if it is a claim made by way of set-off or (as the case may be) by way of counterclaim by a party who has not previously made any claim in the action.

(4)   Rules of court may provide for allowing a new claim to which subsection (3) above applies to be made as there mentioned, but only if the conditions specified in subsection (5) below are satisfied, and subject to any further restrictions the rules may impose.

(5)   The conditions referred to in subsection (4) above are the following—
   (a)   in the case of a claim involving a new cause of action, if the new cause of action arises out of the same facts or substantially the same facts as are already in issue on any claim previously made in the original action; and
   (b)   in the case of a claim involving a new party, if the addition or substitution of the new party is necessary for the determination of the original action.

(6)   The addition or substitution of a new party shall not be regarded for the purposes of subsection (5)(b) above as necessary for the determination of the original action unless either
   (a)   he new party is substituted for a party whose name was given in any claim made in the original action in mistake for the new party's name; or
   (b)   any claim already made in the original action cannot be maintained by or against an existing party unless the new party is joined or substituted as plaintiff or defendant in that action.

(7)   Subject to subsection (4) above, rules of court may provide for allowing a party to any action to claim relief in a new capacity in respect of a new cause of action notwithstanding that he had no title to make that claim at the date of the commencement of the action.

This subsection shall not be taken as prejudicing the power of rules of court to provide for allowing a party to claim relief in a new capacity without adding or substituting a new cause of action.

(8)   Subsections (3) to (7) above shall apply in relation to a new claim made in the course of third party proceedings as if those proceedings were the original action, and subject to such other modifications as may be prescribed by rules of court in any case or class of case.

Part III MISCELLANEOUS AND GENERAL

. . .

36 EQUITABLE JURISDICTION AND REMEDIES

(1)   The following time limits under this Act, that is to say—
(a) the time limit under section 2 for actions founded on tort;
(aa) the time limit under section 4A for actions for libel or slander, or for slander of title, slander of goods or other malicious falsehood;
(b) the time limit under section 5 for actions founded on simple contract;
(c) the time limit under section 7 for actions to enforce awards where the submission is not by an instrument under seal;
(d) the time limit under section 8 for actions on a specialty;
(e) the time limit under section 9 for actions to recover a sum recoverable by virtue of any enactment; and
(f) the time limit under section 24 for actions to enforce a judgment;
shall not apply to any claim for specific performance of a contract or for an injunction or for other equitable relief, except in so far as any such time limit may be applied by the court by analogy in like manner as the corresponding time limit under any enactment repealed by the Limitation Act 1939 was applied before 1st July 1940.

(2)   Nothing in this Act shall affect any equitable jurisdiction to refuse relief on the ground of acquiescence or otherwise.

37 APPLICATION TO THE CROWN AND THE DUKE OF CORNWALL

(1)   Except as otherwise expressly provided in this Act, and without prejudice to section 39, this Act shall apply to proceedings by or against the Crown in like manner as it applies to proceedings between subjects.

(2)   Notwithstanding subsection (1) above, this Act shall not apply to—
(a) any proceedings by the Crown for the recovery of any tax or duty or interest on any tax or duty;
(b) any forfeiture proceedings under the customs and excise Acts (within the meaning of the Customs and Excise Management Act 1979); or
(c) any proceedings in respect of the forfeiture of a ship.
In this subsection "duty" includes any debt due to Her Majesty under section 16 of the Tithe Act 1936, and "ship" includes every description of vessel used in navigation not propelled by oars.

(3)   For the purposes of this section, proceedings by or against the Crown include—
(a) proceedings by or against Her Majesty in right of the Duchy of Lancaster;
(b) proceedings by or against any Government department or any officer of the Crown as such or any person acting on behalf of the Crown; an
(c) proceedings by or against the Duke of Cornwall.

(4)   For the purpose of the provisions of this Act relating to actions for the recovery of land and advowsons, references to the Crown shall include references to Her Majesty in right of the Duchy of Lancaster; and those provisions shall apply to lands and advowsons forming part of the possessions of the Duchy of Cornwall as if for the references to the Crown there were substituted references to the Duke of Cornwall as defined in the Duchy of Cornwall Management Act 1863.

(5)   For the purposes of this Act a proceeding by petition of right (in any case where any such proceeding lies, by virtue of any saving in section 40 of the Crown Proceedings Act 1947, notwithstanding the general abolition by that Act of proceedings by way of petition of right) shall be treated as being commenced on the date on which the petition is presented.

(6)   Nothing in this Act shall affect the prerogative right of Her Majesty (whether in right of the Crown or of the Duchy of Lancaster) or of the Duke of Cornwall to any gold or silver mine.

38 INTERPRETATION

(1)   In this Act, unless the context otherwise requires—

"action" includes any proceeding in a court of law, including an ecclesiastical court (and see subsection 11 below);

"personal injuries" includes any disease and any impairment of a person's physical or mental condition, and "injury" and cognate expressions shall be construed accordingly;

(2)   For the purposes of this Act a person shall be treated as under a disability while he is an infant, or lacks capacity (within the meaning of the Mental Capacity Act 2005) to conduct legal proceedings.

. . .

39 SAVING FOR OTHER LIMITATION ENACTMENTS

This Act shall not apply to any action or arbitration for which a period of limitation is prescribed by or under any other enactment (whether passed before or after the passing of this Act) or to any action or arbitration to which the Crown is a party and for which, if it were between subjects, a period of limitation would be prescribed by or under any such other enactment.

41 SHORT TITLE, COMMENCEMENT AND EXTENT

(1)   This Act may be cited as the Limitation Act 1980.

. . .

(4)   . . . this Act does not extend to Scotland . . .

As amended by Latent Damage Act 1986, ss. 2(2) and 4; Consumer Protection Act 1987, ss. 6(6), 50(2) and Sch. 1; Defamation Act 1996, s. 5.

HIGHWAYS ACT 1980
(c.66)

41 DUTY TO MAINTAIN HIGHWAYS MAINTAINABLE AT PUBLIC EXPENSE

(1)   The authority who are for the time being the highway authority for a highway maintainable at the public expense are under a duty, subject to subsections (2) and (4) below, to maintain the highway.

(1A)   In particular, a highway authority are under a duty to ensure, so far as is reasonably practicable, that safe passage along a highway is not endangered by snow or ice.

58 SPECIAL DEFENCE IN ACTION AGAINST A HIGHWAY AUTHORITY FOR DAMAGES FOR NON-REPAIR OF HIGHWAY

(1)   In an action against a highway authority in respect of damage resulting from their failure to maintain a highway maintainable at the public expense it is a defence (without prejudice to any other defence or the application of the law relating to contributory negligence) to prove that the authority had taken such care as in all the circumstances was reasonably required to secure that the part of the highway to which the action relates was not dangerous for traffic.

(2)   For the purposes of a defence under subsection (1) above, the court shall in particular have regard to the following matters:—
    (a)   the character of the highway, and the traffic which was reasonably to be expected to use it;
    (b)   the standard of maintenance appropriate for a highway of that character and used by such traffic;
    (c)   the state of repair in which a reasonable person would have expected to find the highway;
    (d)   whether the highway authority knew, or could reasonably have been expected to know, that the condition of the part of the highway to which the action relates was likely to cause danger to users of the highway;
    (e)   where the highway authority could not reasonably have been expected to repair that part of the highway before the cause of action arose, what warning notices of its condition had been displayed;
but for the purposes of such a defence it is not relevant to prove that the highway authority had arranged for a competent person to carry out or supervise the maintenance of the part of the highway to which the action relates unless it is also proved that the authority had given him proper instructions with regard to the maintenance of the highway and that he had carried out the instructions.

(3)   This section binds the Crown.

102 PROVISION OF WORKS FOR PROTECTING HIGHWAYS AGAINST HAZARDS OF NATURE

(1)   The highway authority for a highway maintainable at the public expense may provide and maintain such barriers or other works as they consider necessary for the purpose of affording to the highway protection against snow, flood, landslide or other hazards of nature; and those works may be provided on the highway or on land which, or rights over

which, has or have been acquired by the highway authority in the exercise of highway land acquisition powers for that purpose.

(2)   The powers conferred by subsection (1) above to provide any works shall include power to alter or remove them.

(3)   A highway authority shall pay compensation to any person who suffers damage by reason of the execution by them under this section of any works on a highway.

SENIOR COURTS ACT 1981
[FORMERLY KNOWN AS SUPREME COURT ACT 1981]
(c.54)

32 ORDERS FOR INTERIM PAYMENT

(1)   As regards proceedings pending in the High Court, provision may be made by rules of court for enabling the court, in such circumstances as may be prescribed, to make an order requiring a party to the proceedings to make an interim payment of such amount as may be specified in the order, with provision for the payment to be made to such other party to the proceedings as may be so specified or, if the order so provides, by paying it into court.

(2)   Any rules of court which make provision in accordance with subsection (1) may include provision for enabling a party to any proceedings who, in pursuance of such an order, has made an interim payment to recover the whole or part of the amount of the payment in such circumstances, and from such other party to the proceedings, as may be determined in accordance with the rules.

(3)   Any rules made by virtue of this section may include such incidental, supplementary and consequential provisions as the rule-making authority may consider necessary or expedient.

(4)   Nothing in this section shall be construed as affecting the exercise of any power relating to costs, including any power to make rules of court relating to costs.

(5)   In this section "interim payment", in relation to a party to any proceedings, means a payment on account of any damages, debt or other sum (excluding any costs) which that party may be held liable to pay to or for the benefit of another party to the proceedings if a final judgment or order of the court in the proceedings is given or made in favour of that other party.

32A ORDERS FOR PROVISIONAL DAMAGES FOR PERSONAL INJURIES

(1)   This section applies to an action for damages for personal injuries in which there is proved or admitted to be a chance that at some definite or indefinite time in the future the injured person will, as a result of the act or omission which gave rise to the cause of action, develop some serious disease or suffer some serious deterioration in his physical or mental condition.

(2)   Subject to subsection (4) below, as regards any action for damages to which this section applies in which a judgment is given in the High Court, provision may be made by rules of

court for enabling the court, in such circumstances as may be prescribed, to award the injured person
- (a) damages assessed on the assumption that the injured person will not develop the disease or suffer the deterioration in his condition; and
- (b) further damages at a future date if he develops the disease or suffers the deterioration.

(3) Any rules made by virtue of this section may include such incidental, supplementary and consequential provisions as the rule-making authority may consider necessary or expedient.

(4) Nothing in this section shall be construed—
- (a) as affecting the exercise of any power relating to costs, including any power to make rules of court relating to costs; or
- (b) as prejudicing any duty of the court under any enactment or rule of law to reduce or limit the total damages which would have been recoverable apart from any such duty.

33 POWERS OF HIGH COURT EXERCISABLE BEFORE COMMENCEMENT OF ACTION

(1) On the application of any person in accordance with rules of court, the High Court shall, in such circumstances as may be specified in the rules, have power to make an order providing for any one or more of the following matters, that is to say—
- (a) the inspection, photographing, preservation, custody and detention of property which appears to the court to be property which may become the subject-matter of subsequent proceedings in the High Court, or as to which any question may arise in any such proceedings; and
- (b) the taking of samples of any such property as is mentioned in paragraph (a), and the carrying out of any experiment on or with any such property.

(2) On the application, in accordance with rules of court, of a person who appears to the High Court to be likely to be a party to subsequent proceedings in that court . . . the High Court shall, in such circumstances as may be specified in the rules, have power to order a person who appears to the court to be likely to be a party to the proceedings and to be likely to have or to have had in his possession, custody or power any documents which are relevant to an issue arising or likely to arise out of that claim—
- (a) to disclose whether those documents are in his possession, custody or power; and
- (b) to produce such of those documents as are in his possession, custody or power to the applicant or, on such conditions as may be specified in the order—
  - (i) to the applicant's legal advisers; or
  - (ii) to the applicant's legal advisers and any medical or other professional adviser of the applicant; or
  - (iii) if the applicant has no legal adviser, to any medical or other professional adviser of the applicant.

34 POWER OF HIGH COURT TO ORDER DISCLOSURE OF DOCUMENTS, INSPECTION OF PROPERTY ETC., IN PROCEEDINGS FOR PERSONAL INJURIES OR DEATH

. . .

(2) On the application, in accordance with rules of court, of a party to any proceedings to which this section applies], the High Court shall, in such circumstances as may be

specified in the rules, have power to order a person who is not a party to the proceedings and who appears to the court to be likely to have in his possession, custody or power any documents which are relevant to an issue arising out of the said claim—

(a) to disclose whether those documents are in his possession, custody or power; and

(b) to produce such of those documents as are in his possession, custody or power to the applicant or, on such conditions as may be specified in the order—

    (i) to the applicant's legal advisers; or

    (ii) to the applicant's legal advisers and any medical or other professional adviser of the applicant; or

    (iii) if the applicant has no legal adviser, to any medical or other professional adviser of the applicant.

(3) On the application, in accordance with rules of court, of a party to any proceedings . . . ., the High Court shall, in such circumstances as may be specified in the rules, have power to make an order providing for any one or more of the following matters, that is to say

(a) the inspection, photographing, preservation, custody and detention of property which is not the property of, or in the possession of, any party to the proceedings but which is the subject-matter of the proceedings or as to which any question arises in the proceedings;

(b) the taking of samples of any such property as is mentioned in paragraph (a) and the carrying out of any experiment on or with any such property.

69 TRIAL BY JURY

(1) Where, on the application of any party to an action to be tried in the Queen's Bench Division, the court is satisfied that there is in issue—

(a) a charge of fraud against that party; or

(b) a claim in respect of libel, slander, malicious prosecution or false imprisonment; or

(c) any question or issue of a kind prescribed for the purposes of this paragraph, the action shall be tried with a jury, unless the court is of opinion that the trial requires any prolonged examination of documents or accounts or any scientific or local investigation which cannot conveniently be made with a jury.

(2) An application under subsection (1) must be made not later than such time before the trial as may be prescribed.

(3) An action to be tried in the Queen's Bench Division which does not by virtue of subsection (1) fall to be tried with a jury shall be tried without a jury unless the court in its discretion orders it to be tried with a jury.

(4) Nothing in subsections (1) to (3) shall affect the power of the court to order, in accordance with rules of court, that different questions of fact arising in any action be tried by different modes of trial; and where any such order is made, subsection (1) shall have effect only as respects questions relating to any such charge, claim, question or issue as is mentioned in that subsection.

(5) Where for the purpose of disposing of any action or other matter which is being tried in the High Court by a judge with a jury it is necessary to ascertain the law of any other country which is applicable to the facts of the case, any question as to the effect of the evidence given with respect to that law shall, instead of being submitted to the jury, be decided by the judge alone.

CIVIL AVIATION ACT 1982
(C.16)

Trespass by aircraft and aircraft nuisance, noise, etc.

76 LIABILITY OF AIRCRAFT IN RESPECT OF TRESPASS, NUISANCE AND SURFACE DAMAGE

(1) No action shall lie in respect of trespass or in respect of nuisance, by reason only of the flight of an aircraft over any property at a height above the ground which, having regard to wind, weather and all the circumstances of the case is reasonable, or the ordinary incidents of such flight, so long as the provisions of any Air Navigation Order and of any orders under section 62 above have been duly complied with and there has been no breach of section 81 below.

(2) Subject to subsection (3) below, where material loss or damage is caused to any person or property on land or water by, or by a person in, or an article, animal or person falling from, an aircraft while in flight, taking off or landing, then unless the loss or damage was caused or contributed to by the negligence of the person by whom it was suffered, damages in respect of the loss or damage shall be recoverable without proof of negligence or intention or other cause of action, as if the loss or damage had been caused by the wilful act, neglect, or default of the owner of the aircraft.

(3) Where material loss or damage is caused as aforesaid in circumstances in which—
   (a) damages are recoverable in respect of the said loss or damage by virtue only of subsection (2) above, and
   (b) a legal liability is created in some person other than the owner to pay damages in respect of the said loss or damage,
   the owner shall be entitled to be indemnified by that other person against any claim in respect of the said loss or damage.

(4) Where the aircraft concerned has been bona fide demised, let or hired out for any period exceeding fourteen days to any other person by the owner thereof, and no pilot, commander, navigator or operative member of the crew of the aircraft is in the employment of the owner, ... this section shall have effect as if for references to the owner there were substituted references to the person to whom the aircraft has been so demised, let or hired out.

77 NUISANCE CAUSED BY AIRCRAFT ON AERODROMES

(1) An Air Navigation Order may provide for regulating the conditions under which noise and vibration may be caused by aircraft on aerodromes and may provide that subsection (2) below shall apply to any aerodrome as respects which provision as to noise and vibration caused by aircraft is so made.

(2) No action shall lie in respect of nuisance by reason only of the noise and vibration caused by aircraft on an aerodrome to which this subsection applies by virtue of an Air Navigation Order, as long as the provisions of any such Order are duly complied with.

SUPPLY OF GOODS AND SERVICES ACT 1982
(C.29)

Part I SUPPLY OF GOODS

Contracts for the transfer of property in goods

1 THE CONTRACTS CONCERNED

(1) In this Act in its application to England and Wales . . . a "contract for the transfer of goods" means a contract under which one person transfers or agrees to transfer to another the property in goods, other than an excepted contract.

(2) For the purposes of this section an excepted contract means any of the following—
    (a) a contract of sale of goods;
    (b) a hire-purchase agreement;
    (d) a transfer or agreement to transfer which is made by deed and for which there is no consideration other than the presumed consideration imported by the deed;
    (e) a contract intended to operate by way of mortgage, pledge, charge or other security.

(3) For the purposes of this Act in its application to England and Wales . . . a contract is a contract for the transfer of goods whether or not services are also provided or to be provided under the contract, and (subject to subsection (2) above) whatever is the nature of the consideration for the transfer or agreement to transfer.

2 IMPLIED TERMS ABOUT TITLE, ETC.

(1) In a contract for the transfer of goods, other than one to which subsection (3) below applies, there is an implied condition on the part of the transferor that in the case of a transfer of the property in the goods he has a right to transfer the property and in the case of an agreement to transfer the property in the goods he will have such a right at the time when the property is to be transferred.

(2) In a contract for the transfer of goods, other than one to which subsection (3) below applies, there is also an implied warranty that—
    (a) the goods are free, and will remain free until the time when the property is to be transferred, from any charge or encumbrance not disclosed or known to the transferee before the contract is made, and
    (b) the transferee will enjoy quiet possession of the goods except so far as it may be disturbed by the owner or other person entitled to the benefit of any charge or encumbrance so disclosed or known.

(3) This subsection applies to a contract for the transfer of goods in the case of which there appears from the contract or is to be inferred from its circumstances an intention that the transferor should transfer only such title as he or a third person may have.

(4) In a contract to which subsection (3) above applies there is an implied warranty that all charges or encumbrances known to the transferor and not known to the transferee have been disclosed to the transferee before the contract is made.

(5) In a contract to which subsection (3) above applies there is also an implied warranty that none of the following will disturb the transferee's quiet possession of the goods, namely—
 (a) the transferor;
 (b) in a case where the parties to the contract intend that the transferor should transfer only such title as a third person may have, that person;
 (c) anyone claiming through or under the transferor or that third person otherwise than under a charge or encumbrance disclosed or known to the transferee before the contract is made.

3 IMPLIED TERMS WHERE TRANSFER IS BY DESCRIPTION

(1) This section applies where, under a contract for the transfer of goods, the transferor transfers or agrees to transfer the property in the goods by description.

(2) In such a case there is an implied condition that the goods will correspond with the description.

(3) If the transferor transfers or agrees to transfer the property in the goods by sample as well as by description it is not sufficient that the bulk of the goods corresponds with the sample if the goods do not also correspond with the description.

(4) A contract is not prevented from falling within subsection (1) above by reason only that, being exposed for supply, the goods are selected by the transferee.

4 IMPLIED TERMS ABOUT QUALITY OR FITNESS

(1) Except as provided by this section and section 5 below and subject to the provisions of any other enactment, there is no implied condition or warranty about the quality or fitness for any particular purpose of goods supplied under a contract for the transfer of goods.

(2) Where, under such a contract, the transferor transfers the property in goods in the course of a business, there is an implied condition that the goods supplied under the contract are of satisfactory quality.

(2A) For the purposes of this section and section 5 below, goods are of satisfactory quality if they meet the standard that a reasonable person would regard as satisfactory, taking account of any description of the goods, the price (if relevant) and all the other relevant circumstances.

(2B) If the transferee deals as consumer, the relevant circumstances mentioned in subsection (2A) above include any public statements on the specific characteristics of the goods made about them by the transferor, the producer or his representative, particularly in advertising or on labelling.

(2C) A public statement is not by virtue of subsection (2B) above a relevant circumstance for the purposes of subsection (2A) above in the case of a contract for the transfer of goods, if the transferor shows that—
 (a) at the time the contract was made, he was not, and could not reasonably have been, aware of the statement,
 (b) before the contract was made, the statement had been withdrawn in public or, to the extent that it contained anything which was incorrect or misleading, it had been corrected in public, or
 (c) the decision to acquire the goods could not have been influenced by the statement.

(2D) Subsections (2B) and (2C) above do not prevent any public statement from being a relevant circumstance for the purposes of subsection (2A) above (whether or not the transferee deals as consumer) if the statement would have been such a circumstance apart from those subsections.

(3) The condition implied by subsection (2) above does not extend to any matter making the quality of goods unsatisfactory—
    (a) which is specifically drawn to the transferee's attention before the contract is made,
    (b) where the transferee examines the goods before the contract is made, which that examination ought to reveal, or
    (c) where the property in the goods is transferred by reference to a sample, which would have been apparent on a reasonable examination of the sample.

(4) Subsection (5) below applies where, under a contract for the transfer of goods, the transferor transfers the property in goods in the course of a business and the transferee, expressly or by implication, makes known—
    (a) to the transferor, or
    (b) where the consideration or part of the consideration for the transfer is a sum payable by instalments and the goods were previously sold by a credit-broker to the transferor, to that credit-broker,
    any particular purpose for which the goods are being acquired.

(5) In that case there is (subject to subsection (6) below) an implied condition that the goods supplied under the contract are reasonably fit for that purpose, whether or not that is a purpose for which such goods are commonly supplied.

(6) Subsection (5) above does not apply where the circumstances show that the transferee does not rely, or that it is unreasonable for him to rely, on the skill or judgment of the transferor or credit-broker.

(7) An implied condition or warranty about quality or fitness for a particular purpose may be annexed by usage to a contract for the transfer of goods.

(8) The preceding provisions of this section apply to a transfer by a person who in the course of a business is acting as agent for another as they apply to a transfer by a principal in the course of a business, except where that other is not transferring in the course of a business and either the transferee knows that fact or reasonable steps are taken to bring it to the transferee's notice before the contract concerned is made.

5 IMPLIED TERMS WHERE TRANSFER IS BY SAMPLE

(1) This section applies where, under a contract for the transfer of goods, the transferor transfers or agrees to transfer the property in the goods by reference to a sample.

(2) In such a case there is an implied condition—
    (a) that the bulk will correspond with the sample in quality; and
    (b) that the transferee will have a reasonable opportunity of comparing the bulk with the sample; and
    (c) that the goods will be free from any defect, making their quality unsatisfactory, which would not be apparent on reasonable examination of the sample.

(4) For the purposes of this section a transferor transfers or agrees to transfer the property in goods by reference to a sample where there is an express or implied term to that effect in the contract concerned.

5A MODIFICATION OF REMEDIES FOR BREACH OF STATUTORY CONDITION IN NON-CONSUMER CASES

(1)   Where in the case of a contract for the transfer of goods—
    (a)   the transferee would, apart from this subsection, have the right to treat the contract as repudiated by reason of a breach on the part of the transferor of a term implied by section 3, 4 or 5(2)(a) or (c) above, but
    (b)   the breach is so slight that it would be unreasonable for him to do so,
    then, if the transferee does not deal as consumer, the breach is not to be treated as a breach of condition but may be treated as a breach of warranty.

(2)   This section applies unless a contrary intention appears in, or is to be implied from, the contract.

(3)   It is for the transferor to show that a breach fell within subsection (1)(b) above.

Contracts for the hire of goods

6 THE CONTRACTS CONCERNED

(1)   In this Act in its application to England and Wales . . . a "contract for the hire of goods" means a contract under which one person bails or agrees to bail goods to another by way of hire, other than a hire-purchase agreement.

(3)   For the purposes of this Act in its application to England and Wales . . . a contract is a contract for the hire of goods whether or not services are also provided or to be provided under the contract, and whatever is the nature of the consideration for the bailment or agreement to bail by way of hire.

7 IMPLIED TERMS ABOUT RIGHT TO TRANSFER POSSESSION, ETC.

(1)   In a contract for the hire of goods there is an implied condition on the part of the bailor that in the case of a bailment he has a right to transfer possession of the goods by way of hire for the period of the bailment and in the case of an agreement to bail he will have such a right at the time of the bailment.

(2)   In a contract for the hire of goods there is also an implied warranty that the bailee will enjoy quiet possession of the goods for the period of the bailment except so far as the possession may be disturbed by the owner or other person entitled to the benefit of any charge or encumbrance disclosed or known to the bailee before the contract is made.

(3)   The preceding provisions of this section do not affect the right of the bailor to repossess the goods under an express or implied term of the contract.

8 IMPLIED TERMS WHERE HIRE IS BY DESCRIPTION

(1)   This section applies where, under a contract for the hire of goods, the bailor bails or agrees to bail the goods by description.

(2)   In such a case there is an implied condition that the goods will correspond with the description.

(3)   If under the contract the bailor bails or agrees to bail the goods by reference to a sample as well as a description it is not sufficient that the bulk of the goods corresponds with the sample if the goods do not also correspond with the description.

(4)   A contract is not prevented from falling within subsection (1) above by reason only that, being exposed for supply, the goods are selected by the bailee.

9 IMPLIED TERMS ABOUT QUALITY OR FITNESS

(1)   Except as provided by this section and section 10 below and subject to the provisions of any other enactment, there is no implied condition or warranty about the quality or fitness for any particular purpose of goods bailed under a contract for the hire of goods.

(2)   Where, under such a contract, the bailor bails goods in the course of a business, there is an implied condition that the goods supplied under the contract are of satisfactory quality.

(2A)   For the purposes of this section and section 10 below, goods are of satisfactory quality if they meet the standard that a reasonable person would regard as satisfactory, taking account of any description of the goods, the consideration for the bailment (if relevant) and all the other relevant circumstances.

(2B)   If the bailee deals as consumer, the relevant circumstances mentioned in subsection (2A) above include any public statements on the specific characteristics of the goods made about them by the bailor, the producer or his representative, particularly in advertising or on labelling.

(2C)   A public statement is not by virtue of subsection (2B) above a relevant circumstance for the purposes of subsection (2A) above in the case of a contract for the hire of goods, if the bailor shows that—
    (a)   at the time the contract was made, he was not, and could not reasonably have been, aware of the statement,
    (b)   before the contract was made, the statement had been withdrawn in public or, to the extent that it contained anything which was incorrect or misleading, it had been corrected in public, or
    (c)   the decision to acquire the goods could not have been influenced by the statement.

(2D)   Subsections (2B) and (2C) above do not prevent any public statement from being a relevant circumstance for the purposes of subsection (2A) above (whether or not the bailee deals as consumer) if the statement would have been such a circumstance apart from those subsections.

(3)   The condition implied by subsection (2) above does not extend to any matter making the quality of goods unsatisfactory—
    (a)   which is specifically drawn to the bailee's attention before the contract is made,
    (b)   where the bailee examines the goods before the contract is made, which that examination ought to reveal, or
    (c)   where the goods are bailed by reference to a sample, which would have been apparent on a reasonable examination of the sample.

(4)   Subsection (5) below applies where, under a contract for the hire of goods, the bailor bails goods in the course of a business and the bailee, expressly or by implication, makes known—
    (a)   to the bailor in the course of negotiations conducted by him in relation to the making of the contract, or
    (b)   to a credit-broker in the course of negotiations conducted by that broker in relation to goods sold by him to the bailor before forming the subject matter of the contract,
    any particular purpose for which the goods are being bailed.

(5)   In that case there is (subject to subsection (6) below) an implied condition that the goods supplied under the contract are reasonably fit for that purpose, whether or not that is a purpose for which such goods are commonly supplied.

(6)   Subsection (5) above does not apply where the circumstances show that the bailee does not rely, or that it is unreasonable for him to rely, on the skill or judgment of the bailor or credit-broker.

(7)   An implied condition or warranty about quality or fitness for a particular purpose may be annexed by usage to a contract for the hire of goods.

(8)   The preceding provisions of this section apply to a bailment by a person who in the course of a business is acting as agent for another as they apply to a bailment by a principal in the course of a business, except where that other is not bailing in the course of a business and either the bailee knows that fact or reasonable steps are taken to bring it to the bailee's notice before the contract concerned is made.

10 IMPLIED TERMS WHERE HIRE IS BY SAMPLE

(1)   This section applies where, under a contract for the hire of goods, the bailor bails or agrees to bail the goods by reference to a sample.

(2)   In such a case there is an implied condition—
   (a)   that the bulk will correspond with the sample in quality; and
   (b)   that the bailee will have a reasonable opportunity of comparing the bulk with the sample; and
   (c)   that the goods will be free from any defect, making their quality unsatisfactory, which would not be apparent on reasonable examination of the sample.

(4)   For the purposes of this section a bailor bails or agrees to bail goods by reference to a sample where there is an express or implied term to that effect in the contract concerned.

10A MODIFICATION OF REMEDIES FOR BREACH OF STATUTORY CONDITION IN NON-CONSUMER CASES

(1)   Where in the case of a contract for the hire of goods—
   (a)   the bailee would, apart from this subsection, have the right to treat the contract as repudiated by reason of a breach on the part of the bailor of a term implied by section 8, 9 or 10(2)(a) or (c) above, but
   (b)   the breach is so slight that it would be unreasonable for him to do so,
        then, if the bailee does not deal as consumer, the breach is not to be treated as a breach of condition but may be treated as a breach of warranty.

(2)   This section applies unless a contrary intention appears in, or is to be implied from, the contract.

(3)   It is for the bailor to show that a breach fell within subsection (1)(b) above.

Exclusion of implied terms, etc.

11 EXCLUSION OF IMPLIED TERMS, ETC.

(1)   Where a right, duty or liability would arise under a contract for the transfer of goods or a contract for the hire of goods by implication of law, it may (subject to subsection (2) below and the 1977 Act) be negatived or varied by express agreement, or by the course of dealing between the parties, or by such usage as binds both parties to the contract.

(2)   An express condition or warranty does not negative a condition or warranty implied by the preceding provisions of this Act unless inconsistent with it.

(3)   Nothing in the preceding provisions of this Act prejudices the operation of any other enactment or any rule of law whereby any condition or warranty (other than one relating to quality or fitness) is to be implied in a contract for the transfer of goods or a contract for the hire of goods.

Part IA SUPPLY OF GOODS AS RESPECTS SCOTLAND

Contracts for the transfer of property in goods

11A THE CONTRACTS CONCERNED

(1)   In this Act in its application to Scotland a "contract for the transfer of goods" means a contract under which one person transfers or agrees to transfer to another the property in goods, other than an excepted contract.

(2)   For the purposes of this section an excepted contract means any of the following—
(a)   a contract of sale of goods;
(b)   a hire-purchase agreement;
(d)   a transfer or agreement to transfer for which there is no consideration;
(e)   a contract intended to operate by way of mortgage, pledge, charge or other security.

(3)   For the purposes of this Act in its application to Scotland a contract is a contract for the transfer of goods whether or not services are also provided or to be provided under the contract, and (subject to subsection (2) above) whatever is the nature of the consideration for the transfer or agreement to transfer.

11B IMPLIED TERMS ABOUT TITLE, ETC.

(1)   In a contract for the transfer of goods, other than one to which subsection (3) below applies, there is an implied term on the part of the transferor that in the case of a transfer of the property in the goods he has a right to transfer the property and in the case of an agreement to transfer the property in the goods he will have such a right at the time when the property is to be transferred.

(2)   In a contract for the transfer of goods, other than one to which subsection (3) below applies, there is also an implied term that—
(a)   the goods are free, and will remain free until the time when the property is to be transferred, from any charge or encumbrance not disclosed or known to the transferee before the contract is made, and
(b)   the transferee will enjoy quiet possession of the goods except so far as it may be disturbed by the owner or other person entitled to the benefit of any charge or encumbrance so disclosed or known.

(3)   This subsection applies to a contract for the transfer of goods in the case of which there appears from the contract or is to be inferred from its circumstances an intention that the transferor should transfer only such title as he or a third person may have.

(4)   In a contract to which subsection (3) above applies there is an implied term that all charges or encumbrances known to the transferor and not known to the transferee have been disclosed to the transferee before the contract is made.

(5)   In a contract to which subsection (3) above applies there is also an implied term that none of the following will disturb the transferee's quiet possession of the goods, namely—
(a)   the transferor;
(b)   in a case where the parties to the contract intend that the transferor should transfer only such title as a third person may have, that person;

(c) anyone claiming through or under the transferor or that third person otherwise than under a charge or encumbrance disclosed or known to the transferee before the contract is made.

. . .

11C IMPLIED TERMS WHERE TRANSFER IS BY DESCRIPTION

(1) This section applies where, under a contract for the transfer of goods, the transferor transfers or agrees to transfer the property in the goods by description.

(2) In such a case there is an implied term that the goods will correspond with the description.

(3) If the transferor transfers or agrees to transfer the property in the goods by reference to a sample as well as by description it is not sufficient that the bulk of the goods corresponds with the sample if the goods do not also correspond with the description.

(4) A contract is not prevented from falling within subsection (1) above by reason only that, being exposed for supply, the goods are selected by the transferee.

11D IMPLIED TERMS ABOUT QUALITY OR FITNESS

(1) Except as provided by this section and section 11E below and subject to the provisions of any other enactment, there is no implied term about the quality or fitness for any particular purpose of goods supplied under a contract for the transfer of goods.

(2) Where, under such a contract, the transferor transfers the property in goods in the course of a business, there is an implied term that the goods supplied under the contract are of satisfactory quality.

(3) For the purposes of this section and section 11E below, goods are of satisfactory quality if they meet the standard that a reasonable person would regard as satisfactory, taking account of any description of the goods, the price (if relevant) and all the other relevant circumstances.

(3A) If the contract for the transfer of goods is a consumer contract, the relevant circumstances mentioned in subsection (3) above include any public statements on the specific characteristics of the goods made about them by the transferor, the producer or his representative, particularly in advertising or on labelling.

(3B) A public statement is not by virtue of subsection (3A) above a relevant circumstance for the purposes of subsection (3) above in the case of a contract for the transfer of goods, if the transferor shows that—
(a) at the time the contract was made, he was not, and could not reasonably have been, aware of the statement,
(b) before the contract was made, the statement had been withdrawn in public or, to the extent that it contained anything which was incorrect or misleading, it had been corrected in public, or
(c) the decision to acquire the goods could not have been influenced by the statement.

(3C) Subsections (3A) and (3B) above do not prevent any public statement from being a relevant circumstance for the purposes of subsection (3) above (whether or not the contract for the transfer of goods is a consumer contract) if the statement would have been such a circumstance apart from those subsections.

(4) The term implied by subsection (2) above does not extend to any matter making the quality of goods unsatisfactory—

    (a) which is specifically drawn to the transferee's attention before the contract is made,

    (b) where the transferee examines the goods before the contract is made, which that examination ought to reveal, or

    (c) where the property in the goods is, or is to be, transferred by reference to a sample, which would have been apparent on a reasonable examination of the sample.

(5)   Subsection (6) below applies where, under a contract for the transfer of goods, the transferor transfers the property in goods in the course of a business and the transferee, expressly or by implication, makes known—

    (a) to the transferor, or

    (b) where the consideration or part of the consideration for the transfer is a sum payable by instalments and the goods were previously sold by a credit-broker to the transferor, to that credit-broker,

    any particular purpose for which the goods are being acquired.

(6)   In that case there is (subject to subsection (7) below) an implied term that the goods supplied under the contract are reasonably fit for the purpose, whether or not that is a purpose for which such goods are commonly supplied.

(7)   Subsection (6) above does not apply where the circumstances show that the transferee does not rely, or that it is unreasonable for him to rely, on the skill or judgment of the transferor or credit-broker.

(8)   An implied term about quality or fitness for a particular purpose may be annexed by usage to a contract for the transfer of goods.

(9)   The preceding provisions of this section apply to a transfer by a person who in the course of a business is acting as agent for another as they apply to a transfer by a principal in the course of a business, except where that other is not transferring in the course of a business and either the transferee knows that fact or reasonable steps are taken to bring it to the transferee's notice before the contract concerned is made.

(10)   For the purposes of this section, "consumer contract" has the same meaning as in section 11F(3) below.

11E IMPLIED TERMS WHERE TRANSFER IS BY SAMPLE

(1)   This section applies where, under a contract for the transfer of goods, the transferor transfers or agrees to transfer the property in the goods by reference to a sample.

(2)   In such a case there is an implied term—

    (a) that the bulk will correspond with the sample in quality;

    (b) that the transferee will have a reasonable opportunity of comparing the bulk with the sample; and

    (c) that the goods will be free from any defect, making their quality unsatisfactory, which would not be apparent on reasonable examination of the sample.

(3)   For the purposes of this section a transferor transfers or agrees to transfer the property in goods by reference to a sample where there is an express or implied term to that effect in the contract concerned.

11F REMEDIES FOR BREACH OF CONTRACT

(1)   Where in a contract for the transfer of goods a transferor is in breach of any term of the contract (express or implied), the other party to the contract (in this section referred to as "the transferee") shall be entitled—

(a) to claim damages; and

(b) if the breach is material, to reject any goods delivered under the contract and treat it as repudiated.

(2) Where a contract for the transfer of goods is a consumer contract and the transferee is the consumer, then, for the purposes of subsection (1)(b) above, breach by the transferor of any term (express or implied)—

(a) as to the quality of the goods or their fitness for a purpose;

(b) if the goods are, or are to be, transferred by description, that the goods will correspond with the description;

(c) if the goods are, or are to be, transferred by reference to a sample, that the bulk will correspond with the sample in quality, shall be deemed to be a material breach.

(3) In subsection (2) above, "consumer contract" has the same meaning as in section 25(1) of the 1977 Act; and for the purposes of that subsection the onus of proving that a contract is not to be regarded as a consumer contract shall lie on the transferor.

Contracts for the hire of goods

11G THE CONTRACTS CONCERNED

(1) In this Act in its application to Scotland a "contract for the hire of goods" means a contract under which one person ("the supplier") hires or agrees to hire goods to another, other than a hire-purchase agreement.

(3) For the purposes of this Act in its application to Scotland a contract is a contract for the hire of goods whether or not services are also provided or to be provided under the contract, and whatever is the nature of the consideration for the hire or agreement to hire.

11H IMPLIED TERMS ABOUT RIGHT TO TRANSFER POSSESSION ETC.

(1) In a contract for the hire of goods there is an implied term on the part of the supplier that—

(a) in the case of a hire, he has a right to transfer possession of the goods by way of hire for the period of the hire; and

(b) in the case of an agreement to hire, he will have such a right at the time of commencement of the period of the hire.

(2) In a contract for the hire of goods there is also an implied term that the person to whom the goods are hired will enjoy quiet possession of the goods for the period of the hire except so far as the possession may be disturbed by the owner or other person entitled to the benefit of any charge or encumbrance disclosed or known to the person to whom the goods are hired before the contract is made.

(3) The preceding provisions of this section do not affect the right of the supplier to repossess the goods under an express or implied term of the contract.

11I IMPLIED TERMS WHERE HIRE IS BY DESCRIPTION

(1) This section applies where, under a contract for the hire of goods, the supplier hires or agrees to hire the goods by description.

(2) In such a case there is an implied term that the goods will correspond with the description.

(3)   If under the contract the supplier hires or agrees to hire the goods by reference to a sample as well as by description it is not sufficient that the bulk of the goods corresponds with the sample if the goods do not also correspond with the description.

(4)   A contract is not prevented from falling within subsection (1) above by reason only that, being exposed for supply, the goods are selected by the person to whom the goods are hired.

11J IMPLIED TERMS ABOUT QUALITY OR FITNESS

(1)   Except as provided by this section and section 11K below and subject to the provisions of any other enactment, there is no implied term about the quality or fitness for any particular purpose of goods hired under a contract for the hire of goods.

(2)   Where, under such a contract, the supplier hires goods in the course of a business, there is an implied term that the goods supplied under the contract are of satisfactory quality.

(3)   For the purposes of this section and section 11K below, goods are of satisfactory quality if they meet the standard that a reasonable person would regard as satisfactory, taking account of any description of the goods, the consideration for the hire (if relevant) and all the other relevant circumstances.

(3A)   If the contract for the hire of goods is a consumer contract, the relevant circumstances mentioned in subsection (3) above include any public statements on the specific characteristics of the goods made about them by the hirer, the producer or his representative, particularly in advertising or on labelling.

(3B)   A public statement is not by virtue of subsection (3A) above a relevant circumstance for the purposes of subsection (3) above in the case of a contract for the hire of goods, if the hirer shows that—
    (a)   at the time the contract was made, he was not, and could not reasonably have been, aware of the statement,
    (b)   by the time the contract was made, the statement had been withdrawn in public or, to the extent that it contained anything which was incorrect or misleading, it had been corrected in public, or
    (c)   the decision to acquire the goods could not have been influenced by the statement.

(3C)   Subsections (3A) and (3B) above do not prevent any public statement from being a relevant circumstance for the purposes of subsection (3) above (whether or not the contract for the hire of goods is a consumer contract) if the statement would have been such a circumstance apart from those subsections.

(4)   The term implied by subsection (2) above does not extend to any matter making the quality of goods unsatisfactory—
    (a)   which is specifically drawn to the attention of the person to whom the goods are hired before the contract is made, or
    (b)   where that person examines the goods before the contract is made, which that examination ought to reveal; or
    (c)   where the goods are hired by reference to a sample, which would have been apparent on reasonable examination of the sample.

(5)   Subsection (6) below applies where, under a contract for the hire of goods, the supplier hires goods in the course of a business and the person to whom the goods are hired, expressly or by implication, makes known—
    (a)   to the supplier in the course of negotiations conducted by him in relation to the making of the contract; or

(b) to a credit-broker in the course of negotiations conducted by that broker in relation to goods sold by him to the supplier before forming the subject matter of the contract,

any particular purpose for which the goods are being hired.

(6) In that case there is (subject to subsection (7) below) an implied term that the goods supplied under the contract are reasonably fit for that purpose, whether or not that is a purpose for which such goods are commonly supplied.

(7) Subsection (6) above does not apply where the circumstances show that the person to whom the goods are hired does not rely, or that it is unreasonable for him to rely, on the skill or judgment of the hirer or credit-broker.

(8) An implied term about quality or fitness for a particular purpose may be annexed by usage to a contract for the hire of goods.

(9) The preceding provisions of this section apply to a hire by a person who in the course of a business is acting as agent for another as they apply to a hire by a principal in the course of a business, except where that other is not hiring in the course of a business and either the person to whom the goods are hired knows that fact or reasonable steps are taken to bring it to that person's notice before the contract concerned is made.

(10) For the purposes of this section, "consumer contract" has the same meaning as in section 11F(3) above.

11K IMPLIED TERMS WHERE HIRE IS BY SAMPLE

(1) This section applies where, under a contract for the hire of goods, the supplier hires or agrees to hire the goods by reference to a sample.

(2) In such a case there is an implied term—
(a) that the bulk will correspond with the sample in quality; and
(b) that the person to whom the goods are hired will have a reasonable opportunity of comparing the bulk with the sample; and
(c) that the goods will be free from any defect, making their quality unsatisfactory, which would not be apparent on reasonable examination of the sample.

(3) For the purposes of this section a supplier hires or agrees to hire goods by reference to a sample where there is an express or implied term to that effect in the contract concerned.

Exclusion of implied terms, etc.

11L EXCLUSION OF IMPLIED TERMS ETC.

(1) Where a right, duty or liability would arise under a contract for the transfer of goods or a contract for the hire of goods by implication of law, it may (subject to subsection (2) below and the 1977 Act) be negatived or varied by express agreement, or by the course of dealing between the parties, or by such usage as binds both parties to the contract.

(2) An express term does not negative a term implied by the preceding provisions of this Part of this Act unless inconsistent with it.

(3) Nothing in the preceding provisions of this Part of this Act prejudices the operation of any other enactment or any rule of law whereby any term (other than one relating to quality or fitness) is to be implied in a contract for the transfer of goods or a contract for the hire of goods.

Part IB ADDITIONAL RIGHTS OF TRANSFEREE IN CONSUMER CASES

11M INTRODUCTORY

(1)   This section applies if—
    (a) the transferee deals as consumer or, in Scotland, there is a consumer contract in which the transferee is a consumer, and
    (b) the goods do not conform to the contract for the transfer of goods at the time of delivery.

(2)   If this section applies, the transferee has the right—
    (a) under and in accordance with section 11N below, to require the transferor to repair or replace the goods, or
    (b) under and in accordance with section 11P below—
        (i) to require the transferor to reduce the amount to be paid for the transfer by the transferee by an appropriate amount, or
        (ii) to rescind the contract with regard to the goods in question.

(3)   For the purposes of subsection (1)(b) above, goods which do not conform to the contract for the transfer of goods at any time within the period of six months starting with the date on which the goods were delivered to the transferee must be taken not to have so conformed at that date.

(4)   Subsection (3) above does not apply if—
    (a) it is established that the goods did so conform at that date;
    (b) its application is incompatible with the nature of the goods or the nature of the lack of conformity.

(5)   For the purposes of this section, "consumer contract" has the same meaning as in section 11F(3) above.

11N REPAIR OR REPLACEMENT OF THE GOODS

(1)   If section 11M above applies, the transferee may require the transferor—
    (a) to repair the goods, or
    (b) to replace the goods.

(2)   If the transferee requires the transferor to repair or replace the goods, the transferor must—
    (a) repair or, as the case may be, replace the goods within a reasonable time but without causing significant inconvenience to the transferee;
    (b) bear any necessary costs incurred in doing so (including in particular the cost of any labour, materials or postage).

(3)   The transferee must not require the transferor to repair or, as the case may be, replace the goods if that remedy is—
    (a) impossible,
    (b) disproportionate in comparison to the other of those remedies, or
    (c) disproportionate in comparison to an appropriate reduction in the purchase price under paragraph (a), or rescission under paragraph (b), of section 11P(1) below.

(4)   One remedy is disproportionate in comparison to the other if the one imposes costs on the transferor which, in comparison to those imposed on him by the other, are unreasonable, taking into account—
    (a) the value which the goods would have if they conformed to the contract for the transfer of goods,

(b) the significance of the lack of conformity to the contract for the transfer of goods, and

(c) whether the other remedy could be effected without significant inconvenience to the transferee.

(5) Any question as to what is a reasonable time or significant inconvenience is to be determined by reference to—

(a) the nature of the goods, and

(b) the purpose for which the goods were acquired.

11P REDUCTION OF PURCHASE PRICE OR RESCISSION OF CONTRACT

(1) If section 11M above applies, the transferee may—

(a) require the transferor to reduce the purchase price of the goods in question to the transferee by an appropriate amount, or

(b) rescind the contract with regard to those goods,
if the condition in subsection (2) below is satisfied.

(2) The condition is that—

(a) by virtue of section 11N(3) above the transferee may require neither repair nor replacement of the goods, or

(b) the transferee has required the transferor to repair or replace the goods, but the transferor is in breach of the requirement of section 11N(2)(a) above to do so within a reasonable time and without significant inconvenience to the transferee.

(3) If the transferee rescinds the contract, any reimbursement to the transferee may be reduced to take account of the use he has had of the goods since they were delivered to him.

11Q RELATION TO OTHER REMEDIES ETC.

(1) If the transferee requires the transferor to repair or replace the goods the transferee must not act under subsection (2) until he has given the transferor a reasonable time in which to repair or replace (as the case may be) the goods.

(2) The transferee acts under this subsection if—

(a) in England and Wales . . . he rejects the goods and terminates the contract for breach of condition;

(b) in Scotland he rejects any goods delivered under the contract and treats it as repudiated; or

(c) he requires the goods to be replaced or repaired (as the case may be).

11R POWERS OF THE COURT

(1) In any proceedings in which a remedy is sought by virtue of this Part the court, in addition to any other power it has, may act under this section.

(2) On the application of the transferee the court may make an order requiring specific performance or, in Scotland, specific implement by the transferor of any obligation imposed on him by virtue of section 11N above.

(3) Subsection (4) applies if—

(a) the transferee requires the transferor to give effect to a remedy under section 11N or 11P above or has claims to rescind under section 11P, but

(b) the court decides that another remedy under section 11N or 11P is appropriate.

(4)   The court may proceed—
   (a) as if the transferee had required the transferor to give effect to the other remedy, or if the other remedy is rescission under section 11P,
   (b) as if the transferee had claimed to rescind the contract under that section.

(5)   If the transferee has claimed to rescind the contract the court may order that any reimbursement to the transferee is reduced to take account of the use he has had of the goods since they were delivered to him.

(6)   The court may make an order under this section unconditionally or on such terms and conditions as to damages, payment of the price and otherwise as it thinks just.

11S CONFORMITY WITH THE CONTRACT

(1)   Goods do not conform to a contract for the supply or transfer of goods if—
   (a) there is, in relation to the goods, a breach of an express term of the contract or a term implied by section 3, 4 or 5 above or, in Scotland, by section 11C, 11D or 11E above, or
   (b) installation of the goods forms part of the contract for the transfer of goods, and the goods were installed by the transferor, or under his responsibility, in breach of the term implied by section 13 below or (in Scotland) in breach of any term implied by any rule of law as to the manner in which the installation is carried out.

Part II SUPPLY OF SERVICES

12 THE CONTRACTS CONCERNED

(1)   In this Act a "contract for the supply of a service" means, subject to subsection (2) below, a contract under which a person ("the supplier") agrees to carry out a service.

(2)   For the purposes of this Act, a contract of service or apprenticeship is not a contract for the supply of a service.

(3)   Subject to subsection (2) above, a contract is a contract for the supply of a service for the purposes of this Act whether or not goods are also—
   (a) transferred or to be transferred, or
   (b) bailed or to be bailed by way of hire,
   under the contract, and whatever is the nature of the consideration for which the service is to be carried out.

(4)   The Secretary of State may by order provide that one or more of sections 13 to 15 below shall not apply to services of a description specified in the order, and such an order may make different provision for different circumstances.

. . .

13 IMPLIED TERM ABOUT CARE AND SKILL

In a contract for the supply of a service where the supplier is acting in the course of a business, there is an implied term that the supplier will carry out the service with reasonable care and skill.

14 IMPLIED TERM ABOUT TIME FOR PERFORMANCE

(1)   Where, under a contract for the supply of a service by a supplier acting in the course of a business, the time for the service to be carried out is not fixed by the contract, left to be

fixed in a manner agreed by the contract or determined by the course of dealing between the parties, there is an implied term that the supplier will carry out the service within a reasonable time.

(2) What is a reasonable time is a question of fact.

15 IMPLIED TERM ABOUT CONSIDERATION

(1) Where, under a contract for the supply of a service, the consideration for the service is not determined by the contract, left to be determined in a manner agreed by the contract or determined by the course of dealing between the parties, there is an implied term that the party contracting with the supplier will pay a reasonable charge.

(2) What is a reasonable charge is a question of fact.

16 EXCLUSION OF IMPLIED TERMS, ETC.

(1) Where a right, duty or liability would arise under a contract for the supply of a service by virtue of this Part of this Act, it may (subject to subsection (2) below and the 1977 Act) be negatived or varied by express agreement, or by the course of dealing between the parties, or by such usage as binds both parties to the contract.

(2) An express term does not negative a term implied by this Part of this Act unless inconsistent with it.

(3) Nothing in this Part of this Act prejudices—
    (a) any rule of law which imposes on the supplier a duty stricter than that imposed by section 13 or 14 above; or
    (b) subject to paragraph (a) above, any rule of law whereby any term not inconsistent with this Part of this Act is to be implied in a contract for the supply of a service.

(4) This Part of this Act has effect subject to any other enactment which defines or restricts the rights, duties or liabilities arising in connection with a service of any description.

18 INTERPRETATION: GENERAL

(1) In the preceding provisions of this Act and this section—

"bailee", in relation to a contract for the hire of goods means (depending on the context) a person to whom the goods are bailed under the contract, or a person to whom they are to be so bailed, or a person to whom the rights under the contract of either of those persons have passed;

"bailor", in relation to a contract for the hire of goods, means (depending on the context) a person who bails the goods under the contract, or a person who agrees to do so, or a person to whom the duties under the contract of either of those persons have passed;

"business" includes profession and the activities of any government department or local or public authority;

"credit-broker" means a person acting in the course of a business of credit brokerage carried on by him;

"credit brokerage" means the effecting of introductions—
    (a) of individuals desiring to obtain credit to persons carrying on any business so far as it relates to the provision of credit; or

(b) of individuals desiring to obtain goods on hire to persons carrying on a business which comprises or relates to the bailment or as regards Scotland the hire of goods under a contract for the hire of goods; or

(c) of individuals desiring to obtain credit, or to obtain goods on hire, to other credit-brokers;

"enactment" means any legislation (including subordinate legislation) of the United Kingdom . . .;

"goods" includes all personal chattels, other than things in action and money, and as regards Scotland all corporeal moveables; and in particular "goods" includes emblements, industrial growing crops, and things attached to or forming part of the land which are agreed to be severed before the transfer bailment or hire concerned or under the contract concerned;

"hire-purchase agreement" has the same meaning as in the 1974 Act;

"producer" means the manufacturer of goods, the importer of goods into the European Economic Area or any person purporting to be a producer by placing his name, trade mark or other distinctive sign on the goods;

"property", in relation to goods, means the general property in them and not merely a special property;

"repair" means, in cases where there is a lack of conformity in goods for the purposes of this Act, to bring the goods into conformity with the contract.

"transferee", in relation to a contract for the transfer of goods, means (depending on the context) a person to whom the property in the goods is transferred under the contract, or a person to whom the property is to be so transferred, or a person to whom the rights under the contract of either of those persons have passed;

"transferor", in relation to a contract for the transfer of goods, means (depending on the context) a person who transfers the property in the goods under the contract, or a person who agrees to do so, or a person to whom the duties under the contract of either of those persons have passed.

(2) In subsection (1) above, in the definitions of bailee, bailor, transferee and transferor, a reference to rights or duties passing is to their passing by assignment assignation, operation of law or otherwise.

(3) For the purposes of this Act, the quality of goods includes their state and condition and the following (among others) are in appropriate cases aspects of the quality of goods—
(a) fitness for all the purposes for which goods of the kind in question are commonly supplied,
(b) appearance and finish,
(c) freedom from minor defects,
(d) safety, and
(e) durability.

(4) References in this Act to dealing as consumer are to be construed in accordance with Part I of the Unfair Contract Terms Act 1977; and, for the purposes of this Act, it is for the transferor or bailor claiming that the transferee or bailee does not deal as consumer to show that he does not.

. . .

20 CITATION, TRANSITIONAL PROVISIONS, COMMENCEMENT AND EXTENT

(1)   This Act may be cited as the Supply of Goods and Services Act 1982.

. . .

(6)   This Act except Part IA, which extends only to Scotland extends to Northern Ireland and Parts I and II do not extend to Scotland.

As amended by Sale and Supply of Goods Act 1994, Sch. 1, Sch. 2, para. 6, Sch. 3, para.1; Sale and Supply of Goods to Consumers Regulations 2002, regs. 7–12; Regulatory Reform (Trading Stamps) Order 2005, art. 5.

FORFEITURE ACT 1982
(c.34)

1 THE "FORFEITURE RULE"

(1)   In this Act, the "forfeiture rule" means the rule of public policy which in certain circumstances precludes a person who has unlawfully killed another from acquiring a benefit in consequence of the killing.

(2)   References in this Act to a person who has unlawfully killed another include a reference to a person who has unlawfully aided, abetted, counselled or procured the death of that other and references in this Act to unlawful killing shall be interpreted accordingly.

2 POWER TO MODIFY THE RULE

(1)   Where a court determines that the forfeiture rule has precluded a person (in this section referred to as "the offender") who has unlawfully killed another from acquiring any interest in property mentioned in subsection (4) below, the court may make an order under this section modifying the effect of that rule.

(2)   The court shall not make an order under this section modifying the effect of the forfeiture rule in any case unless it is satisfied that, having regard to the conduct of the offender and of the deceased and to such other circumstances as appear to the court to be material, the justice of the case requires the effect of the rule to be so modified in that case.

(3)   In any case where a person stands convicted of an offence of which unlawful killing is an element, the court shall not make an order under this section modifying the effect of the forfeiture rule in that case unless proceedings for the purpose are brought before the expiry of the period of three months beginning with his conviction.

(4)   The interests in property referred to in subsection (1) above are—
(a)   any beneficial interest in property which (apart from the forfeiture rule) the offender would have acquired—
(i)   under the deceased's will (including, as respects Scotland, any writing having testamentary effect) or the law relating to intestacy or by way of ius relicti, ius relictae or legitim;
(ii)   on the nomination of the deceased in accordance with the provisions of any enactment;

(iii) as a donatio mortis causa made by the deceased; or

(iv) under a special destination (whether relating to heritable or moveable property); or

(b) any beneficial interest in property which (apart from the forfeiture rule) the offender would have acquired in consequence of the death of the deceased, being property which, before the death, was held on trust for any person.

(5) An order under this section may modify the effect of the forfeiture rule in respect of any interest in property to which the determination referred to in subsection (1) above relates and may do so in either or both of the following ways, that is—

(a) where there is more than one such interest, by excluding the application of the rule in respect of any (but not all) of those interests; and

(b) in the case of any such interest in property, by excluding the application of the rule in respect of part of the property.

(6) On the making of an order under this section, the forfeiture rule shall have effect for all purposes (including purposes relating to anything done before the order is made) subject to the modifications made by the order.

(8) In this section—

"property" includes any chose in action or incorporeal moveable property; and

"will" includes codicil.

5 EXCLUSION OF MURDERERS

Nothing in this Act or in any order made under section 2 or referred to in section 3(1) of this Act or in any decision made under section 4(1A) of this Act shall affect the application of the forfeiture rule in the case of a person who stands convicted of murder.

ADMINISTRATION OF JUSTICE ACT 1982
(c.53)

Part I DAMAGES FOR PERSONAL INJURIES ETC.

Abolition of certain claims for damages etc.

1 ABOLITION OF RIGHT TO DAMAGES FOR LOSS OF EXPECTATION OF LIFE

(1) In an action under the law of England and Wales or the law of Northern Ireland for damages for personal injuries—

(a) no damages shall be recoverable in respect of any loss of expectation of life caused to the injured person by the injuries; but

(b) if the injured person's expectation of life has been reduced by the injuries, the court, in assessing damages in respect of pain and suffering caused by the injuries, shall take account of any suffering caused or likely to be caused to him by awareness that his expectation of life has been so reduced.

(2) The reference in subsection (1)(a) above to damages in respect of loss of expectation of life does not include damages in respect of loss of income.

2 ABOLITION OF ACTIONS FOR LOSS OF SERVICES ETC.

No person shall be liable in tort under the law of England and Wales or the law of Northern Ireland—

(a)   to a husband on the ground only of his having deprived him of the services or society of his wife;

(b)   to a parent (or person standing in the place of a parent) on the ground only of his having deprived him of the services of a child; or

(c)   on the ground only—
   (i)   of having deprived another of the services of his menial servant;
   (ii) of having deprived another of the services of his female servant by raping or seducing her; or
   (iii) of enticement of a servant or harbouring a servant.

Maintenance at public expense

5 MAINTENANCE AT PUBLIC EXPENSE TO BE TAKEN INTO ACCOUNT IN ASSESSMENT OF DAMAGES

In an action under the law of England and Wales or the law of Northern Ireland for damages for personal injuries (including any such action arising out of a contract) any saving to the injured person which is attributable to his maintenance wholly or partly at public expense in a hospital, nursing home or other institution shall be set off against any income lost by him as a result of his injuries.

OCCUPIERS' LIABILITY ACT 1984
(c.3)

1 DUTY OF OCCUPIER TO PERSONS OTHER THAN HIS VISITORS

(1)   The rules enacted by this section shall have effect, in place of the rules of the common law, to determine —
   (a)   whether any duty is owed by a person as occupier of premises to persons other than his visitors in respect of any risk of their suffering injury on the premises by reason of any danger due to the state of the premises or to things done or omitted to be done on them; and
   (b)   if so, what that duty is.

(2)   For the purposes of this section, the persons who are to be treated respectively as an occupier of any premises (which, for those purposes, include any fixed or movable structure) and as his visitors are —
   (a)   any person who owes in relation to the premises the duty referred to in section 2 of the Occupiers' Liability Act 1957 (the common duty of care), and
   (b)   those who are his visitors for the purposes of that duty.

(3)   An occupier of premises owes a duty to another (not being his visitor) in respect of any such risk as is referred to in subsection (1) above if —
   (a)   he is aware of the danger or has reasonable grounds to believe that it exists;
   (b)   he knows or has reasonable grounds to believe that the other is in the vicinity of the danger concerned or that he may come into the vicinity of the danger (in either case, whether the other has lawful authority for being in that vicinity or not); and

(c) the risk is one against which, in all the circumstances of the case, he may reasonably be expected to offer the other some protection.

(4) Where, by virtue of this section, an occupier of premises owes a duty to another in respect of such a risk, the duty is to take such care as is reasonable in all the circumstances of the case to see that he does not suffer injury on the premises by reason of the danger concerned.

(5) Any duty owed by virtue of this section in respect of a risk may, in an appropriate case, be discharged by taking such steps as are reasonable in all the circumstances of the case to give warning of the danger concerned or to discourage persons from incurring the risk.

(6) No duty is owed by virtue of this section to any person in respect of risks willingly accepted as his by that person (the question whether a risk was so accepted to be decided on the same principles as in other cases in which one person owes a duty of care to another).

(6A) At any time when the right conferred by section 2(1) of the Countryside and Rights of Way Act 2000 is exercisable in relation to land which is access land for the purposes of Part I of that Act, an occupier of the land owes (subject to subsection (6C) below) no duty by virtue of this section to any person in respect of—
(a) a risk resulting from the existence of any natural feature of the landscape, or any river, stream, ditch or pond whether or not a natural feature, or
(b) a risk of that person suffering injury when passing over, under or through any wall, fence or gate, except by proper use of the gate or of a stile.

(6AA) Where the land is coastal margin for the purposes of Part 1 of that Act (including any land treated as coastal margin by virtue of section 16 of that Act), subsection (6A) has effect as if for paragraphs (a) and (b) of that subsection there were substituted "a risk resulting from the existence of any physical feature (whether of the landscape or otherwise)."

(6B) For the purposes of subsection (6A) above, any plant, shrub or tree, of whatever origin, is to be regarded as a natural feature of the landscape.

(6C) Subsection (6A) does not prevent an occupier from owing a duty by virtue of this section in respect of any risk where the danger concerned is due to anything done by the occupier—
(a) with the intention of creating that risk, or
(b) being reckless as to whether that risk is created.

(7) No duty is owed by virtue of this section to persons using the highway, and this section does not affect any duty owed to such persons.

(8) Where a person owes a duty by virtue of this section, he does not, by reason of any breach of the duty, incur any liability in respect of any loss of or damage to property.

(9) In this section —

"highway" means any part of a highway other than a ferry or waterway;

"injury" means anything resulting in death or personal injury, including any disease and any impairment of physical or mental condition; and

"movable structure" includes any vessel, vehicle or aircraft.

1A SPECIAL CONSIDERATIONS RELATING TO ACCESS LAND

In determining whether any, and if so what, duty is owed by virtue of section 1 by an occupier of land at any time when the right conferred by section 2(1) of the Countryside and Rights of Way Act 2000 is exercisable in relation to the land, regard is to be had, in particular, to—

(a)   the fact that the existence of that right ought not to place an undue burden (whether financial or otherwise) on the occupier,

(b)   the importance of maintaining the character of the countryside, including features of historic, traditional or archaeological interest, and

(c)   any relevant guidance given under section 20 of that Act.

. . .

3 APPLICATION TO CROWN

Section 1 of this Act shall bind the Crown, but as regards the Crown's liability in tort shall not bind the Crown further than the Crown is made liable in tort by the Crown Proceedings Act 1947.

BUILDING ACT 1984
(c.55)

1 POWER TO MAKE BUILDING REGULATIONS

(1)   The Secretary of State may, for any of the purposes of—
  (a)   securing the health, safety, welfare and convenience of persons in or about buildings and of others who may be affected by buildings or matters connected with buildings,
  (b)   furthering the conservation of fuel and power, and
  (c)   preventing waste, undue consumption, misuse or contamination of water,
  (d)   furthering the protection and enhancement of the environment,
  (e)   facilitating sustainable development, or
  (f)   furthering the prevention or detection of crime,
  make regulations with respect to the matters mentioned in subsection 1A below.

1(A)   Those matters are—
  (a)   the design and construction of buildings;
  (b)   the demolition of buildings;
  (c)   services, fittings ad equipment provided in or in connection with buildings.

(2)   Regulations made under subsection (1) above are known as building regulations.

(3)   Schedule 1 to this Act has effect with respect to the matters as to which building regulations may provide.

(4)   The power to make building regulations is exercisable by statutory instrument, which is subject to annulment in pursuance of a resolution of either House of Parliament.

38 CIVIL LIABILITY

(1)   Subject to this section—
  (a)   breach of a duty imposed by building regulations, so far as it causes damage, is actionable, except in so far as the regulations provide otherwise, and
  (b)   as regards such a duty, building regulations may provide for a prescribed defence to be available in an action for breach of that duty brought by virtue of this subsection.

(2)   Subsection (1) above, and any defence provided for in regulations made by virtue of it, do not apply in the case of a breach of such a duty in connection with a building erected before the date on which that subsection comes into force unless the regulations imposing

the duty apply to or in connection with the building by virtue of section 2(2) or 2A above or paragraph 8 of Schedule 1 to this Act.

(3)　This section does not affect the extent (if any) to which breach of—
   (a) a duty imposed by or arising in connection with this Part of this Act or any other enactment relating to building regulations, or
   (b) a duty imposed by building regulations in a case to which subsection (1) above does not apply,
   is actionable, or prejudice a right of action that exists apart from the enactments relating to building regulations.

(4)　In this section, "damage" includes the death of, or injury to, any person (including any disease and any impairment of a person's physical or mental condition).

LAW REFORM (MISCELLANEOUS PROVISIONS) (SCOTLAND) ACT 1985
(c.73)

10 NEGLIGENT MISREPRESENTATION

(1)　A party to a contract who has been induced to enter into it by negligent misrepresentation made by or on behalf of another party to the contract shall not be disentitled, by reason only that the misrepresentation is not fraudulent, from recovering damages from the other party in respect of any loss or damage he has suffered as a result of the misrepresentation; and any rule of law that such damages cannot be recovered unless fraud is proved shall cease to have effect.

(2)　Subsection (1) applies to any proceedings commenced on or after the date on which it comes into force, whether or not the negligent misrepresentation was made before or after that date, but does not apply to any proceedings commenced before that date.

LATENT DAMAGE ACT 1986
(c.37)

Accrual of cause of action to successive owners in respect of latent damage to property

3 ACCRUAL OF CAUSE OF ACTION TO SUCCESSIVE OWNERS IN RESPECT OF LATENT DAMAGE TO PROPERTY

(1)　Subject to the following provisions of this section, where—
   (a) a cause of action ("the original cause of action") has accrued to any person in respect of any negligence to which damage to any property in which he has an interest is attributable (in whole or in part), and
   (b) another person acquires an interest in that property after the date on which the original cause of action accrued but before the material facts about the damage have become known to any person who, at the time when he first has knowledge of those facts, has any interest in the property;
   a fresh cause of action in respect of that negligence shall accrue to that other person on the date on which he acquires his interest in the property.

(2)   A cause of action accruing to any person by virtue of subsection (1) above—
    (a)   shall be treated as if based on breach of a duty of care at common law owed to the person to whom it accrues; and
    (b)   shall be treated for the purposes of section 14A of the 1980 Act (special time limit for negligence actions where facts relevant to cause of action are not known at date of accrual) as having accrued on the date on which the original cause of action accrued.

(3)   Section 28 of the 1980 Act (extension of limitation period in case of disability) shall not apply in relation to any such cause of action.

(4)   Subsection (1) above shall not apply in any case where the person acquiring an interest in the damaged property is either—
    (a)   a person in whom the original cause of action vests by operation of law; or
    (b)   a person in whom the interest in that property vests by virtue of any order made by a court under s 145 Insolvency Act 1986 (vesting of company property in liquidator).

(5)   For the purposes of subsection (1)(b) above, the material facts about the damage are such facts about the damage as would lead a reasonable person who has an interest in the damaged property at the time when those facts become known to him to consider it sufficiently serious to justify his instituting proceedings for damages against a defendant who did not dispute liability and was able to satisfy a judgment.

(6)   For the purposes of this section a person's knowledge includes knowledge which he might reasonably have been expected to acquire—
    (a)   from facts observable or ascertainable by him; or
    (b)   from facts ascertainable by him with the help of appropriate expert advice which it is reasonable for him to seek;
but a person shall not be taken by virtue of this subsection to have knowledge of a fact ascertainable by him only with the help of expert advice so long as he has taken all reasonable steps to obtain (and, where appropriate, to act on) that advice.

(7)   This section shall bind the Crown, but as regards the Crown's liability in tort shall not bind the Crown further than the Crown is made liable in tort by the Crown Proceedings Act 1947.

MINORS' CONTRACTS ACT 1987
(c.13)

2 GUARANTEES

Where—
(a)   a guarantee is given in respect of an obligation of a party to a contract made after the commencement of this Act, and

(b)   the obligation is unenforceable against him (or he repudiates the contract) because he was a minor when the contract was made, the guarantee shall not for that reason alone be unenforceable against the guarantor.

3 RESTITUTION

(1)   Where—
    (a)   a person ("the plaintiff") has after the commencement of this Act entered into a contract with another ("the defendant"), and

(b)   the contract is unenforceable against the defendant (or he repudiates it) because he was a minor when the contract was made, the court may, if it is just and equitable to do so, require the defendant to transfer to the plaintiff any property acquired by the defendant under the contract, or any property representing it.

(2)   Nothing in this section shall be taken to prejudice any other remedy available to the plaintiff.

. . .

5   SHORT TITLE, COMMENCEMENT AND EXTENT

(1)   This Act may be cited as the Minors' Contracts Act 1987.

(2)   This Act shall come into force at the end of the period of two months beginning with the date on which it is passed.

(3)   This Act extends to England and Wales only.

CONSUMER PROTECTION ACT 1987
(c.43)

Part I   PRODUCT LIABILITY

1   PURPOSE AND CONSTRUCTION OF PART I

(1)   This Part shall have effect for the purpose of making such provision as is necessary in order to comply with the product liability Directive and shall be construed accordingly.

(2)   In this Part, except in so far as the context otherwise requires—

"agricultural produce" means any produce of the soil, of stock-farming or of fisheries;

"dependant" and "relative" have the same meaning as they have in, respectively, the Fatal Accidents Act 1976 and the Damages (Scotland) Act 2011;

"producer", in relation to a product, means—
(a)   the person who manufactured it;
(b)   in the case of a substance which has not been manufactured but has been won or abstracted, the person who won or abstracted it;
(c)   in the case of a product which has not been manufactured, won or abstracted but essential characteristics of which are attributable to an industrial or other process having been carried out (for example, in relation to agricultural produce), the person who carried out that process;
"product" means any goods or electricity and (subject to subsection (3) below) includes a product which is comprised in another product, whether by virtue of being a component part or raw material or otherwise; and

"the product liability Directive" means the Directive of the Council of the European Communities, dated 25th July 1985, (No. 85/374/EEC) on the approximation of the laws, regulations and administrative provisions of the member States concerning liability for defective products.

(3)   For the purposes of this Part a person who supplies any product in which products are comprised, whether by virtue of being component parts or raw materials or otherwise,

shall not be treated by reason only of his supply of that product as supplying any of the products so comprised.

2 LIABILITY FOR DEFECTIVE PRODUCTS

(1) Subject to the following provisions of this Part, where any damage is caused wholly or partly by a defect in a product, every person to whom subsection (2) below applies shall be liable for the damage.

(2) This subsection applies to—
  (a) the producer of the product;
  (b) any person who, by putting his name on the product or using a trade mark or other distinguishing mark in relation to the product, has held himself out to be the producer of the product;
  (c) any person who has imported the product into a member State from a place outside the member States in order, in the course of any business of his, to supply it to another.

(3) Subject as aforesaid, where any damage is caused wholly or partly by a defect in a product, any person who supplied the product (whether to the person who suffered the damage, to the producer of any product in which the product in question is comprised or to any other person) shall be liable for the damage if—
  (a) the person who suffered the damage requests the supplier to identify one or more of the persons (whether still in existence or not) to whom subsection (2) above applies in relation to the product;
  (b) that request is made within a reasonable period after the damage occurs and at a time when it is not reasonably practicable for the person making the request to identify all those persons; and
  (c) the supplier fails, within a reasonable period after receiving the request, either to comply with the request or to identify the person who supplied the product to him.

(5) Where two or more persons are liable by virtue of this Part for the same damage, their liability shall be joint and several.

(6) This section shall be without prejudice to any liability arising otherwise than by virtue of this Part.

3 MEANING OF "DEFECT"

(1) Subject to the following provisions of this section, there is a defect in a product for the purposes of this Part if the safety of the product is not such as persons generally are entitled to expect; and for those purposes "safety", in relation to a product, shall include safety with respect to products comprised in that product and safety in the context of risks of damage to property, as well as in the context of risks of death or personal injury.

(2) In determining for the purposes of subsection (1) above what persons generally are entitled to expect in relation to a product all the circumstances shall be taken into account, including—
  (a) the manner in which, and purposes for which, the product has been marketed, its get-up, the use of any mark in relation to the product and any instructions for, or warnings with respect to, doing or refraining from doing anything with or in relation to the product;
  (b) what might reasonably be expected to be done with or in relation to the product; and
  (c) the time when the product was supplied by its producer to another;

and nothing in this section shall require a defect to be inferred from the fact alone that the safety of a product which is supplied after that time is greater than the safety of the product in question.

4 DEFENCES

(1)   In any civil proceedings by virtue of this Part against any person ("the person proceeded against") in respect of a defect in a product it shall be a defence for him to show—
  (a) that the defect is attributable to compliance with any requirement imposed by or under any enactment or with any EU obligation; or
  (b) that the person proceeded against did not at any time supply the product to another; or
  (c) that the following conditions are satisfied, that is to say—
    (i)   that the only supply of the product to another by the person proceeded against was otherwise than in the course of a business of that person's; and
    (ii) that section 2(2) above does not apply to that person or applies to him by virtue only of things done otherwise than with a view to profit; or
  (d) that the defect did not exist in the product at the relevant time; or
  (e) that the state of scientific and technical knowledge at the relevant time was not such that a producer of products of the same description as the product in question might be expected to have discovered the defect if it had existed in his products while they were under his control; or
  (f) that the defect—
    (i)   constituted a defect in a product ("the subsequent product") in which the product in question had been comprised; and
    (ii) was wholly attributable to the design of the subsequent product or to compliance by the producer of the product in question with instructions given by the producer of the subsequent product.

(2)   In this section "the relevant time", in relation to electricity, means the time at which it was generated, being a time before it was transmitted or distributed, and in relation to any other product, means—
  (a) if the person proceeded against is a person to whom subsection (2) of section 2 above applies in relation to the product, the time when he supplied the product to another;
  (b) if that subsection does not apply to that person in relation to the product, the time when the product was last supplied by a person to whom that subsection does apply in relation to the product.

5 DAMAGE GIVING RISE TO LIABILITY

(1)   Subject to the following provisions of this section, in this Part "damage" means death or personal injury or any loss of or damage to any property (including land).

(2)   A person shall not be liable under section 2 above in respect of any defect in a product for the loss of or any damage to the product itself or for the loss of or any damage to the whole or any part of any product which has been supplied with the product in question comprised in it.

(3)   A person shall not be liable under section 2 above for any loss of or damage to any property which, at the time it is lost or damaged, is not—
  (a) of a description of property ordinarily intended for private use, occupation or consumption; and
  (b) intended by the person suffering the loss or damage mainly for his own private use, occupation or consumption.

(4) No damages shall be awarded to any person by virtue of this Part in respect of any loss of or damage to any property if the amount which would fall to be so awarded to that person, apart from this subsection and any liability for interest, does not exceed £275.

(5) In determining for the purposes of this Part who has suffered any loss of or damage to property and when any such loss or damage occurred, the loss or damage shall be regarded as having occurred at the earliest time at which a person with an interest in the property had knowledge of the material facts about the loss or damage.

(6) For the purposes of subsection (5) above the material facts about any loss of or damage to any property are such facts about the loss or damage as would lead a reasonable person with an interest in the property to consider the loss or damage sufficiently serious to justify his instituting proceedings for damages against a defendant who did not dispute liability and was able to satisfy a judgment.

(7) For the purposes of subsection (5) above a person's knowledge includes knowledge which he might reasonably have been expected to acquire—
    (a) from facts observable or ascertainable by him; or
    (b) from facts ascertainable by him with the help of appropriate expert advice which it is reasonable for him to seek;
    but a person shall not be taken by virtue of this subsection to have knowledge of a fact ascertainable by him only with the help of expert advice unless he has failed to take all reasonable steps to obtain (and, where appropriate, to act on) that advice.

(8) Subsections (5) to (7) above shall not extend to Scotland.

6 APPLICATION OF CERTAIN ENACTMENTS ETC.

(1) Any damage for which a person is liable under section 2 above shall be deemed to have been caused—
    (a) for the purposes of the Fatal Accidents Act 1976, by that person's wrongful act, neglect or default;
    (b) for the purposes of section 3 of the Law Reform (Miscellaneous Provisions)(Scotland) Act 1940 (contribution among joint wrongdoers), by that person's wrongful act or negligent act or omission;
    (c) for the purposes of sections 3 to 6 of the Damages (Scotland) Act 2011 (rights of relatives of a deceased), by that person's act or omission; and
    (d) for the purposes of Part II of the Administration of Justice Act 1982 (damages for personal injuries, etc.—Scotland), by an act or omission giving rise to liability in that person to pay damages.

(2) Where—
    (a) a person's death is caused wholly or partly by a defect in a product, or a person dies after suffering damage which has been so caused;
    (b) a request such as mentioned in paragraph (a) of subsection (3) of section 2 above is made to a supplier of the product by that person's personal representatives or, in the case of a person whose death is caused wholly or partly by the defect, by any dependant or relative of that person; and
    (c) the conditions specified in paragraphs (b) and (c) of that subsection are satisfied in relation to that request,
    this Part shall have effect for the purposes of the Law Reform (Miscellaneous Provisions) Act 1934, the Fatal Accidents Act 1976 and the Damages (Scotland) Act 2011 as if liability of the supplier to that person under that subsection did not depend on that person having requested the supplier to identify certain persons or on the said conditions having been satisfied in relation to a request made by that person.

(3)   Section 1 of the Congenital Disabilities (Civil Liability) Act 1976 shall have effect for the purposes of this Part as if—

     (a)   a person were answerable to a child in respect of an occurrence caused wholly or partly by a defect in a product if he is or has been liable under section 2 above in respect of any effect of the occurrence on a parent of the child, or would be so liable if the occurrence caused a parent of the child to suffer damage;

     (b)   the provisions of this Part relating to liability under section 2 above applied in relation to liability by virtue of paragraph (a) above under the said section 1; and

     (c)   subsection (6) of the said section 1 (exclusion of liability) were omitted.

(4)   Where any damage is caused partly by a defect in a product and partly by the fault of the person suffering the damage, the Law Reform (Contributory Negligence) Act 1945 and section 5 of the Fatal Accidents Act 1976 (contributory negligence) shall have effect as if the defect were the fault of every person liable by virtue of this Part for the damage caused by the defect.

(5)   In subsection (4) above "fault" has the same meaning as in the said Act of 1945.

(6)   Schedule 1 to this Act shall have effect for the purpose of amending the Limitation Act 1980 and the Prescription and Limitation (Scotland) Act 1973 in their application in relation to the bringing of actions by virtue of this Part.

(7)   It is hereby declared that liability by virtue of this Part is to be treated as liability in tort for the purposes of any enactment conferring jurisdiction on any court with respect to any matter.

(8)   Nothing in this Part shall prejudice the operation of section 12 of the Nuclear Installations Act 1965 (rights to compensation for certain breaches of duties confined to rights under that Act).

7 PROHIBITION ON EXCLUSIONS FROM LIABILITY

The liability of a person by virtue of this Part to a person who has suffered damage caused wholly or partly by a defect in a product, or to a dependant or relative of such a person, shall not be limited or excluded by any contract term, by any notice or by any other provision.

8 POWER TO MODIFY PART I

(1)   Her Majesty may by Order in Council make such modifications of this Part and of any other enactment (including an enactment contained in the following Parts of this Act, or in an Act passed after this Act) as appear to Her Majesty in Council to be necessary or expedient in consequence of any modification of the product liability Directive which is made at any time after the passing of this Act.

9 APPLICATION OF PART I TO CROWN

(1)   Subject to subsection (2) below, this Part shall bind the Crown.

Part II CONSUMER SAFETY

11 SAFETY REGULATIONS

(1)   The Secretary of State may by regulations under this section ("safety regulations") make such provision as he considers appropriate . . . for the purpose of securing—

(a) that goods to which this section applies are safe;

(b) that goods to which this section applies which are unsafe, or would be unsafe in the hands of persons of a particular description, are not made available to persons generally or, as the case may be, to persons of that description; and

(c) that appropriate information is, and inappropriate information is not, provided in relation to goods to which this section applies.

(2) Without prejudice to the generality of subsection (1) above, safety regulations may contain provision—

(a) with respect to the composition or contents, design, construction, finish or packing of goods to which this section applies, with respect to standards for such goods and with respect to other matters relating to such goods;

(b) with respect to the giving, refusal, alteration or cancellation of approvals of such goods, of descriptions of such goods or of standards for such goods;

(c) with respect to the conditions that may be attached to any approval given under the regulations;

(d) or requiring such fees as may be determined by or under the regulations to be paid on the giving or alteration of any approval under the regulations and on the making of an application for such an approval or alteration;

(e) with respect to appeals against refusals, alterations and cancellations of approvals given under the regulations and against the conditions contained in such approvals;

(f) for requiring goods to which this section applies to be approved under the regulations or to conform to the requirements of the regulations or to descriptions or standards specified in or approved by or under the regulations;

(g) with respect to the testing or inspection of goods to which this section applies (including provision for determining the standards to be applied in carrying out any test or inspection);

(h) with respect to the ways of dealing with goods of which some or all do not satisfy a test required by or under the regulations or a standard connected with a procedure so required;

(i) for requiring a mark, warning or instruction or any other information relating to goods to be put on or to accompany the goods or to be used or provided in some other manner in relation to the goods, and for securing that inappropriate information is not given in relation to goods either by means of misleading marks or otherwise;

(j) for prohibiting persons from supplying, or from offering to supply, agreeing to supply, exposing for supply or possessing for supply, goods to which this section applies and component parts and raw materials for such goods;

(k) for requiring information to be given to any such person as may be determined by or under the regulations for the purpose of enabling that person to exercise any function conferred on him by the regulations.

12 OFFENCES AGAINST THE SAFETY REGULATIONS

(1) Where safety regulations prohibit a person from supplying or offering or agreeing to supply any goods or from exposing or possessing any goods for supply, that person shall be guilty of an offence if he contravenes the prohibition.

(2) Where safety regulations require a person who makes or processes any goods in the course of carrying on a business—

(a) to carry out a particular test or use a particular procedure in connection with the making or processing of the goods with a view to ascertaining whether the goods satisfy any requirements of such regulations; or

(b) to deal or not to deal in a particular way with a quantity of the goods of which the whole or part does not satisfy such a test or does not satisfy standards connected with such a procedure, that person shall be guilty of an offence if he does not comply with the requirement.

41 CIVIL PROCEEDINGS

(1) An obligation imposed by safety regulations shall be a duty owed to any person who may be affected by a contravention of the obligation and, subject to any provision to the contrary in the regulations and to the defences and other incidents applying to actions for breach of statutory duty, a contravention of any such obligation shall be actionable accordingly.

(2) This Act shall not be construed as conferring any other right of action in civil proceedings, apart from the right conferred by virtue of Part I of this Act, in respect of any loss or damage suffered in consequence of a contravention of a safety provision. . . .

(3) Subject to any provision to the contrary in the agreement itself, an agreement shall not be void or unenforceable by reason only of a contravention of a safety provision . . . .

(4) Liability by virtue of subsection (1) above shall not be limited or excluded by any contract term, by any notice or (subject to the power contained in subsection (1) above to limit or exclude it in safety regulations) by any other provision.

(5) Nothing in subsection (1) above shall prejudice the operation of section 12 of the Nuclear Installations Act 1965 (rights to compensation for certain breaches of duties confined to rights under that Act).

(6) In this section "damage" includes personal injury and death.

45 INTERPRETATION

(1) In this Act, except in so far as the context otherwise requires—

. . .

"business" includes a trade or profession and the activities of a professional or trade association or of a local authority or other public authority;

"conditional sale agreement", "credit—sale agreement" and "hire-purchase agreement" have the same meanings as in the Consumer Credit Act 1974 but as if in the definitions in that Act "goods" had the same meaning as in this Act;

. . .

"goods" includes substances, growing crops and things comprised in land by virtue of being attached to it and any ship, aircraft or vehicle;

. . .

"personal injury" includes any disease and any other impairment of a person's physical or mental condition;

"premises" includes any place and any ship, aircraft or vehicle;

"safety provision" means . . . any provision of safety regulations, a prohibition notice or a suspension notice;

"safety regulations" means regulations under section 11 above;

. . .

"substance" means any natural or artificial substance, whether in solid, liquid or gaseous form or in the form of a vapour, and includes substances that are comprised in or mixed with other goods;

"supply" and cognate expressions shall be construed in accordance with section 46 below;

46 MEANING OF "SUPPLY"

(1) Subject to the following provisions of this section, references in this Act to supplying goods shall be construed as references to doing any of the following, whether as principal or agent, that is to say
   (a) selling, hiring out or lending the goods;
   (b) entering into a hire-purchase agreement to furnish the goods;
   (c) the performance of any contract for work and materials to furnish the goods;
   (d) providing the goods in exchange for any consideration . . . other than money;
   (e) providing the goods in or in connection with the performance of any statutory function; or
   (f) giving the goods as a prize or otherwise making a gift of the goods;
   and, in relation to gas or water, those references shall be construed as including references to providing the service by which the gas or water is made available for use.

(2) For the purposes of any reference in this Act to supplying goods, where a person ("the ostensible supplier") supplies goods to another person ("the customer") under a hire-purchase agreement, conditional sale agreement or credit-sale agreement or under an agreement for the hiring of goods (other than a hire-purchase agreement) and the ostensible supplier—
   (a) carries on the business of financing the provision of goods for others by means of such agreements; and
   (b) in the course of that business acquired his interest in the goods supplied to the customer as a means of financing the provision of them for the customer by a further person ("the effective supplier"),
   the effective supplier and not the ostensible supplier shall be treated as supplying the goods to the customer.

(3) Subject to subsection (4) below, the performance of any contract by the erection of any building or structure on any land or by the carrying out of any other building works shall be treated for the purposes of this Act as a supply of goods in so far as, but only in so far as, it involves the provision of any goods to any person by means of their incorporation into the building, structure or works.

(4) Except for the purposes of, and in relation to, notices to warn . . ., references in this Act to supplying goods shall not include references to supplying goods comprised in land where the supply is effected by the creation or disposal of an interest in the land.

(5) Except in Part I of this Act references in this Act to a person's supplying goods shall be confined to references to that person's supplying goods in the course of a business of his, but for the purposes of this subsection it shall be immaterial whether the business is a business of dealing in the goods.

(6) For the purposes of subsection (5) above goods shall not be treated as supplied in the course of a business if they are supplied, in pursuance of an obligation arising under or in connection with the insurance of the goods, to the person with whom they were insured.

(7)   Except for the purposes of, and in relation to, prohibition notices or suspension notices, references in Parts 2 or 4 of this Act to supplying goods shall not include—

(a)   references to supplying goods where the person supplied carries on a business of buying goods of the same description as those goods and repairing or reconditioning them;

(b)   references to supplying goods by a sale of articles as scrap (that is to say, for the value of materials included in the articles rather than for the value of the articles themselves).

(8)   Where any goods have at any time been supplied by being hired out or lent to any person, neither a continuation or renewal of the hire or loan (whether on the same or different terms) nor any transaction for the transfer after that time of any interest in the goods to the person to whom they were hired or lent shall be treated for the purposes of this Act as a further supply of the goods to that person.

(9)   A ship, aircraft or motor vehicle shall not be treated for the purposes of this Act as supplied to any person by reason only that services consisting in the carriage of goods or passengers in that ship, aircraft or vehicle, or in its use for any other purpose, are provided to that person in pursuance of an agreement relating to the use of the ship, aircraft or vehicle for a particular period or for particular voyages, flights or journeys.

COPYRIGHT, DESIGNS AND PATENTS ACT 1988
(c.48)

85 RIGHT TO PRIVACY OF CERTAIN PHOTOGRAPHS AND FILMS

(1)   A person who for private and domestic purposes commissions the taking of a photograph or the making of a film has, where copyright subsists in the resulting work, the right not to have—

(a)   copies of the work issued to the public,

(b)   the work exhibited or shown in public, or

(c)   the work communicated to the public;

and, except as mentioned in subsection (2), a person who does or authorises the doing of any of those acts infringes that right.

(2)   The right is not infringed by an act which by virtue of any of the following provisions would not infringe copyright in the work—

(a)   section 31 (incidental inclusion of work in an artistic work, film, or broadcast);

(b)   section 45 (parliamentary and judicial proceedings);

(c)   section 46 (Royal Commissions and statutory inquiries);

(d)   section 50 (acts done under statutory authority);

(e)   section 57 or 66A (acts permitted on assumptions as to expiry of copyright, &c.).

ROAD TRAFFIC ACT 1988
(c.52)

38 THE HIGHWAY CODE

(7)   A failure on the part of a person to observe a provision of the Highway Code shall not of itself render that person liable to criminal proceedings of any kind but any such failure may in any proceedings (whether civil or criminal, and including proceedings for an

offence under the Traffic Acts, the Public Passenger Vehicles Act 1981 or sections 18 to 23 of the Transport Act 1985) be relied upon by any party to the proceedings as tending to establish or negative any liability which is in question in those proceedings.

143 USERS OF MOTOR VEHICLES TO BE INSURED OR SECURED AGAINST THIRD-PARTY RISKS

(1) Subject to the provisions of this Part of this Act—

  (a) a person must not use a motor vehicle on a road or other public place] unless there is in force in relation to the use of the vehicle by that person such a policy of insurance or such a security in respect of third party risks as complies with the requirements of this Part of this Act, and

  (b) a person must not cause or permit any other person to use a motor vehicle on a road or other public place unless there is in force in relation to the use of the vehicle by that other person such a policy of insurance or such a security in respect of third party risks as complies with the requirements of this Part of this Act.

(2) If a person acts in contravention of subsection (1) above he is guilty of an offence.

(3) A person charged with using a motor vehicle in contravention of this section shall not be convicted if he proves—

  (a) that the vehicle did not belong to him and was not in his possession under a contract of hiring or of loan,

  (b) that he was using the vehicle in the course of his employment, and

  (c) that he neither knew nor had reason to believe that there was not in force in relation to the vehicle such a policy of insurance or security as is mentioned in subsection (1) above.

(4) This Part of this Act does not apply to invalid carriages.

144 EXCEPTIONS FROM REQUIREMENT OF THIRD-PARTY INSURANCE OR SECURITY

(1) Section 143 of this Act does not apply to a vehicle owned by a person who has deposited and keeps deposited with the Accountant General of the Senior Courts the sum of £500,000, at a time when the vehicle is being driven under the owner's control.

(1A) The Secretary of State may by order made by statutory instrument substitute a greater sum for the sum for the time being specified in subsection (1) above.

(1B) No order shall be made under subsection (1A) above unless a draft of it has been laid before and approved by resolution of each House of Parliament.]

(2) Section 143 does not apply—

  (a) to a vehicle owned—

    (i) by the council of a county or county district in England and Wales, the Broads Authority, the Common Council of the City of London, the council of a London borough a National Park authority], the Inner London Education Authority the London Fire and Emergency Planning Authority, an authority established for an area in England by an order under s 207 of the Local Government and Public Involvement in Health Act 2007 (joint waste authorities), or a joint authority established by Part IV of the Local Government Act 1985, an economic prosperity board established under s 88 of the Local Democracy, Economic Development and Construction Act 2009 or a combined authority established under s 103 of that Act

(ii) by a council constituted under section 2 of the Local Government etc. (Scotland) Act 1994 in Scotland, or]

(iii) by a joint board or committee in England or Wales, or joint committee in Scotland, which is so constituted as to include among its members representatives of any such council,

at a time when the vehicle is being driven under the owner's control,

(b) to a vehicle owned by a local policing body or police authority . . . at a time when it is being driven under the owner's control, or to a vehicle at a time when it is being driven for police purposes by or under the direction of a constable, by a member of a police and crime commissioner's staff (within the meaning of Part 1 of the Police Reform and Social Responsibility Act 2011), by a member of the staff of the Mayor's Office for Policing and Crime (within the meaning of that Part of that Act), by a member of the civilian staff of a police force (within the meaning of that Part of that Act), by a member of the civilian staff of the metropolitan police force (within the meaning of that Part of that Act), by a person employed by the Common Council of the City of London in its capacity as a police authority, or by a person employed by a police authority, or

(c) a vehicle at a time when it is being driven on a journey to or from any place undertaken for salvage purposes pursuant to Part IX of the Merchant Shipping Act 1995,

(da) to a vehicle owned by a health service body, as defined in section 60(7) of the National Health Service and Community Care Act 1990 by a Primary Care Trust established under section 18 of the National Health Service Act 2006, by a Local Health Board established under section 11 of the National Health Service (Wales) Act 2006, at a time when the vehicle is being driven under the owner's control.

(db) to an ambulance owned by a National Health Service trust established under section 25 of the National Health Service Act 2006, section 18 of the National Health Service (Wales) Act 2006 or the National Health Service (Scotland) Act 1978, at a time when a vehicle is being driven under the owner's control]

(dc) to an ambulance owned by an NHS foundation trust, at a time when the vehicle is being driven under the owner's control,

(e) to a vehicle which is made available by the Secretary of State or the Welsh Ministers to any person, body or local authority in pursuance of section 12 or 80 of the National Health Service Act 2006, or section 10 or 38 of the National Health Service (Wales) Act 2006, at a time when it is being used in accordance with the terms on which it is so made available,

(f) to a vehicle which is made available by the Secretary of State to any local authority, education authority or voluntary organisation in Scotland in pursuance of section 15 or 16 of the National Health Service (Scotland) Act 1978 at a time when it is being used in accordance with the terms on which it is so made available.

(g) to a vehicle owned by the Care Quality Commission, at a time when the vehicle is being driven under the owner's control.

145 REQUIREMENTS IN RESPECT OF POLICIES OF INSURANCE

(1) In order to comply with the requirements of this Part of this Act, a policy of insurance must satisfy the following conditions.

(2) The policy must be issued by an authorised insurer.

(3) Subject to subsection (4) below, the policy—

(a) must insure such person, persons or classes of persons as may be specified in the policy in respect of any liability which may be incurred by him or them in respect of the death of or bodily injury to any person or damage to property caused by, or arising out of, the use of the vehicle on a road or other public place] in Great Britain, and (aa) must, in the case of a vehicle normally based in the territory of another member State, insure him or them in respect of any civil liability which may be incurred by him or them as a result of an event related to the use of the vehicle in Great Britain if,—

    (i)   according to the law of that territory, he or they would be required to be insured in respect of a civil liability which would arise under that law as a result of that event if the place where the vehicle was used when the event occurred were in that territory, and

    (ii) the cover required by that law would be higher than that required by paragraph (a) above, and

(b) must in the case of a vehicle normally based in Great Britain insure him or them in respect of any liability which may be incurred by him or them in respect of the use of the vehicle and of any trailer, whether or not coupled, in the territory other than Great Britain and Gibraltar of each of the member States of the Communities according to

    (i)   the law on compulsory insurance against civil liability in respect of the use of vehicles of the State in whose territory the event giving rise to the liability occurred; or

    (ii) if it would give higher cover, the law which would be applicable under this Part of this Act if the place where the vehicle was used when that event occurred were in Great Britain; and

(c) must also insure him or them in respect of any liability which may be incurred by him or them under the provisions of this Part of this Act relating to payment for emergency treatment.

(4)   The policy shall not, by virtue of subsection (3)(a) above, be required—

    (a) to cover liability in respect of the death, arising out of and in the course of his employment, of a person in the employment of a person insured by the policy or of bodily injury sustained by such a person arising out of and in the course of his employment, or

    (b) to provide insurance of more than £1,000,000 in respect of all such liabilities as may be incurred in respect of damage to property caused by, or arising out of, any one accident involving the vehicle, or

    (c) to cover liability in respect of damage to the vehicle, or

    (d) to cover liability in respect of damage to goods carried for hire or reward in or on the vehicle or in or on any trailer (whether or not coupled) drawn by the vehicle, or

    (e) to cover any liability of a person in respect of damage to property in his custody or under his control, or

    (f) to cover any contractual liability.

(4A) In the case of a person—

    (a) carried in or upon a vehicle, or

    (b) entering or getting on to, or alighting from, a vehicle,

the provisions of paragraph (a) of subsection (4) above do not apply unless cover in respect of the liability referred to in that paragraph is in fact provided pursuant to a requirement of the Employers' Liability (Compulsory Insurance) Act 1969.

148   AVOIDANCE OF CERTAIN EXCEPTIONS TO POLICIES OR SECURITIES

(1)   Where a certificate of insurance or certificate of security has been delivered under section 147 of this Act to the person by whom a policy has been effected or to whom a security has been given, so much of the policy or security as purports to restrict—

    (a) the insurance of the persons insured by the policy, or

(b) the operation of the security,

(as the case may be) by reference to any of the matters mentioned in subsection (2) below shall, as respects such liabilities as are required to be covered by a policy under section 145 of this Act, be of no effect.

(2)   Those matters are—

(a) the age or physical or mental condition of persons driving the vehicle,

(b) the condition of the vehicle,

(c) the number of persons that the vehicle carries,

(d) the weight or physical characteristics of the goods that the vehicle carries,

(e) the time at which or the areas within which the vehicle is used,

(f) the horsepower or cylinder capacity or value of the vehicle,

(g) the carrying on the vehicle of any particular apparatus, or

(h) the carrying on the vehicle of any particular means of identification other than any means of identification required to be carried by or under the Vehicle Excise and Registration Act 1994.

(3)   Nothing in subsection (1) above requires an insurer or the giver of a security to pay any sum in respect of the liability of any person otherwise than in or towards the discharge of that liability.

(4)   Any sum paid by an insurer or the giver of a security in or towards the discharge of any liability of any person which is covered by the policy or security by virtue only of subsection (1) above is recoverable by the insurer or giver of the security from that person.

(5)   A condition in a policy or security issued or given for the purposes of this Part of this Act providing—

(a) that no liability shall arise under the policy or security, or

(b) that any liability so arising shall cease,

in the event of some specified thing being done or omitted to be done after the happening of the event giving rise to a claim under the policy or security, shall be of no effect in connection with such liabilities as are required to be covered by a policy under section 145 of this Act.

(6)   Nothing in subsection (5) above shall be taken to render void any provision in a policy or security requiring the person insured or secured to pay to the insurer or the giver of the security any sums which the latter may have become liable to pay under the policy or security and which have been applied to the satisfaction of the claims of third parties.

(7)   Notwithstanding anything in any enactment, a person issuing a policy of insurance under section 145 of this Act shall be liable to indemnify the persons or classes of persons specified in the policy in respect of any liability which the policy purports to cover in the case of those persons or classes of persons

149 AVOIDANCE OF CERTAIN AGREEMENTS AS TO LIABILITY TOWARDS PASSENGERS

(1)   This section applies where a person uses a motor vehicle in circumstances such that under section 143 of this Act there is required to be in force in relation to his use of it such a policy of insurance or such a security in respect of third-party risks as complies with the requirements of this Part of this Act.

(2)   If any other person is carried in or upon the vehicle while the user is so using it, any antecedent agreement or understanding between them (whether intended to be legally binding or not) shall be of no effect so far as it purports or might be held—

(a) to negative or restrict any such liability of the user in respect of persons carried in or upon the vehicle as is required by section 145 of this Act to be covered by a policy of insurance, or

(b) to impose any conditions with respect to the enforcement of any such liability of the user.

(3) The fact that a person so carried has willingly accepted as his the risk of negligence on the part of the user shall not be treated as negativing any such liability of the user.

(4) For the purposes of this section—

(a) references to a person being carried in or upon a vehicle include references to a person entering or getting on to, or alighting from, the vehicle, and

(b) the reference to an antecedent agreement is to one made at any time before the liability arose.

151 DUTY OF INSURERS OR PERSONS GIVING SECURITY TO SATISFY JUDGMENT AGAINST PERSONS INSURED OR SECURED AGAINST THIRD-PARTY RISKS

(1) This section applies where, after a certificate of insurance or certificate of security has been delivered under section 147 of this Act to the person by whom a policy has been effected or to whom a security has been given, a judgment to which this subsection applies is obtained.

(2) Subsection (1) above applies to judgments relating to a liability with respect to any matter where liability with respect to that matter is required to be covered by a policy of insurance under section 145 of this Act and either—

(a) it is a liability covered by the terms of the policy or security to which the certificate relates, and the judgment is obtained against any person who is insured by the policy or whose liability is covered by the security, as the case may be, or

(b) it is a liability, other than an excluded liability, which would be so covered if the policy insured all persons or, as the case may be, the security covered the liability of all persons, and the judgment is obtained against any person other than one who is insured by the policy or, as the case may be, whose liability is covered by the security.

(3) In deciding for the purposes of subsection (2) above whether a liability is or would be covered by the terms of a policy or security, so much of the policy or security as purports to restrict, as the case may be, the insurance of the persons insured by the policy or the operation of the security by reference to the holding by the driver of the vehicle of a licence authorising him to drive it shall be treated as of no effect.

(4) In subsection (2)(b) above "excluded liability" means a liability in respect of the death of, or bodily injury to, or damage to the property of any person who, at the time of the use which gave rise to the liability, was allowing himself to be carried in or upon the vehicle and knew or had reason to believe that the vehicle had been stolen or unlawfully taken, not being a person who—

(a) did not know and had no reason to believe that the vehicle had been stolen or unlawfully taken until after the commencement of his journey, and

(b) could not reasonably have been expected to have alighted from the vehicle.

In this subsection the reference to a person being carried in or upon a vehicle includes a reference to a person entering or getting on to, or alighting from, the vehicle.

(5) Notwithstanding that the insurer may be entitled to avoid or cancel, or may have avoided or cancelled, the policy or security, he must, subject to the provisions of this section, pay to the persons entitled to the benefit of the judgment—

(a) as regards liability in respect of death or bodily injury, any sum payable under the judgment in respect of the liability, together with any sum which, by virtue of any enactment relating to interest on judgments, is payable in respect of interest on that sum,

(b) as regards liability in respect of damage to property, any sum required to be paid under subsection (6) below, and

(c) any amount payable in respect of costs.

(6) This subsection requires—

(a) where the total of any amounts paid, payable or likely to be payable under the policy or security in respect of damage to property caused by, or arising out of, the accident in question does not exceed £1,000,000, the payment of any sum payable under the judgment in respect of the liability, together with any sum which, by virtue of any enactment relating to interest on judgments, is payable in respect of interest on that sum,

(b) where that total exceeds £1,000,000, the payment of either—

(i) such proportion of any sum payable under the judgment in respect of the liability as £1,000,000 bears to that total, together with the same proportion of any sum which, by virtue of any enactment relating to interest on judgments, is payable in respect of interest on that sum, or

(ii) the difference between the total of any amounts already paid under the policy or security in respect of such damage and £1,000,000, together with such proportion of any sum which, by virtue of any enactment relating to interest on judgments, is payable in respect of interest on any sum payable under the judgment in respect of the liability as the difference bears to that sum,

whichever is the less, unless not less than £1,000,000 has already been paid under the policy or security in respect of such damage (in which case nothing is payable).

(7) Where an insurer becomes liable under this section to pay an amount in respect of a liability of a person who is insured by a policy or whose liability is covered by a security, he is entitled to recover from that person—

(a) that amount, in a case where he became liable to pay it by virtue only of subsection (3) above, or

(b) in a case where that amount exceeds the amount for which he would, apart from the provisions of this section, be liable under the policy or security in respect of that liability, the excess.

(8) Where an insurer becomes liable under this section to pay an amount in respect of a liability of a person who is not insured by a policy or whose liability is not covered by a security, he is entitled to recover the amount from that person or from any person who—

(a) is insured by the policy, or whose liability is covered by the security, by the terms of which the liability would be covered if the policy insured all persons or, as the case may be, the security covered the liability of all persons, and

(b) caused or permitted the use of the vehicle which gave rise to the liability.

(9) In this section—

(a) "insurer" includes a person giving a security,

(c) "liability covered by the terms of the policy or security" means a liability which is covered by the policy or security or which would be so covered but for the fact that the insurer is entitled to avoid or cancel, or has avoided or cancelled, the policy or security.

(10) In the application of this section to Scotland, the words "by virtue of any enactment relating to interest on judgments" in subsections (5) and (6)(in each place where they appear) shall be omitted.

153 BANKRUPTCY, ETC., OF INSURED OR SECURED PERSONS NOT TO AFFECT CLAIMS BY THIRD PARTIES

(1)   Where, after a certificate of insurance or certificate of security has been delivered under section 147 of this Act to the person by whom a policy has been effected or to whom a security has been given, an event which results in that person being a relevant person for the purposes of the Third Parties (Rights against Insurers) Act 2010 happens, the happening of that event shall, notwithstanding anything in thatAct not affect any such liability of that person as is required to be covered by a policy of insurance under section 145 of this Act . . .

(3)   Nothing in subsection (1) above affects any rights conferred by the Third Parties (Rights Against Insurers) Act 2010 on the person to whom the liability was incurred, being rights so conferred against the person by whom the policy was issued or the security was given.

Payments for treatment of traffic casualties

157 PAYMENT FOR HOSPITAL TREATMENT OF TRAFFIC CASUALTIES

(1)   Subject to subsection (2) below, where—
  (a) a payment, other than a payment under section 158 of this Act, is made (whether or not with an admission of liability) in respect of the death of, or bodily injury to, any person arising out of the use of a motor vehicle on a road or in some other public place, and
  (b) the payment is made—
    (i)   by an authorised insurer, the payment being made under or in consequence of a policy issued under section 145 of this Act, or
    (ii) by the owner of a vehicle in relation to the use of which a security under this Part of this Act is in force, or
    (iii) by the owner of a vehicle who has made a deposit under this Part of this Act, and
  (c) the person who has so died or been bodily injured has to the knowledge of the insurer or owner, as the case may be, received treatment at a hospital, whether as an in-patient or as an out-patient, in respect of the injury so arising,
the insurer or owner must pay the expenses reasonably incurred by the hospital in affording the treatment, after deducting from the expenses any moneys actually received in payment of a specific charge for the treatment, not being moneys received under any contributory scheme.

(2)   The amount to be paid shall not exceed £2,949.00 for each person treated as an in-patient or £295.00 for each person treated as an out-patient.

(3)   For the purposes of this section "expenses reasonably incurred" means—
  (a) in relation to a person who receives treatment at a hospital as an in-patient, an amount for each day he is maintained in the hospital representing the average daily cost, for each in-patient, of the maintenance of the hospital and the staff of the hospital and the maintenance and treatment of the in-patients in the hospital, and
  (b) in relation to a person who receives treatment at a hospital as an out-patient, reasonable expenses actually incurred.

158 PAYMENT FOR EMERGENCY TREATMENT OF TRAFFIC CASUALTIES

(1)   Subsection (2) below applies where—
  (a) medical or surgical treatment or examination is immediately required as a result of bodily injury (including fatal injury) to a person caused by, or arising out of, the use of a motor vehicle on a road or in some other public place], and

(b) the treatment or examination so required (in this Part of this Act referred to as "emergency treatment") is effected by a legally qualified medical practitioner.

(2) The person who was using the vehicle at the time of the event out of which the bodily injury arose must, on a claim being made in accordance with the provisions of section 159 of this Act, pay to the practitioner (or, where emergency treatment is effected by more than one practitioner, to the practitioner by whom it is first effected)—
   (a) a fee of £21.30 in respect of each person in whose case the emergency treatment is effected by him, and
   (b) a sum, in respect of any distance in excess of two miles which he must cover in order—
      (i) to proceed from the place from which he is summoned to the place where the emergency treatment is carried out by him, and
      (ii) to return to the first mentioned place,
   equal to 41 pence for every complete mile and additional part of a mile of that distance.

(3) Where emergency treatment is first effected in a hospital, the provisions of subsections (1) and (2) above with respect to payment of a fee shall, so far as applicable, but subject (as regards the recipient of a payment) to the provisions of section 159 of this Act, have effect with the substitution of references to the hospital for references to a legally qualified medical practitioner.

(4) Liability incurred under this section by the person using a vehicle shall, where the event out of which it arose was caused by the wrongful act of another person, be treated for the purposes of any claim to recover damage by reason of that wrongful act as damage sustained by the person using the vehicle.

159 SUPPLEMENTARY PROVISIONS AS TO PAYMENTS FOR TREATMENT

(1) A payment falling to be made under section 157 or 158 of this Act in respect of treatment in a hospital must be made to the hospital.

(2) A claim for a payment under section 158 of this Act may be made at the time when the emergency treatment is effected, by oral request to the person who was using the vehicle, and if not so made must be made by request in writing served on him within seven days from the day on which the emergency treatment was effected.

(3) Any such request in writing—
   (a) must be signed by the claimant or, in the case of a hospital, by an executive officer of the hospital claiming the payment.
   (b) must state the name and address of the claimant, the circumstances in which the emergency treatment was effected, and that it was first effected by the claimant or, in the case of a hospital, in the hospital, and
   (c) may be served by delivering it to the person who was using the vehicle or by sending it in a prepaid registered letter, or the recorded delivery service, addressed to him at his usual or last known address.

(4) A payment made under section 158 of this Act shall operate as a discharge, to the extent of the amount paid, of any liability of the person who was using the vehicle, or of any other person, to pay any sum in respect of the expenses or remuneration of the practitioner or hospital concerned of or for effecting the emergency treatment.

(5) A chief officer of police must, if so requested by a person who alleges that he is entitled to claim a payment under section 158 of this Act, provide that person with any information at the disposal of the chief officer—

(a) as to the identification marks of any motor vehicle which that person alleges to be a vehicle out of the use of which the bodily injury arose, and

(b) as to the identity and address of the person who was using the vehicle at the time of the event out of which it arose.

ROAD TRAFFIC (CONSEQUENTIAL PROVISIONS) ACT 1988
(c.54)

7 SAVING FOR LAW OF NUISANCE

Nothing in the Road Traffic Acts authorises a person to use on a road a vehicle so constructed or used as to cause a public or private nuisance, or in Scotland a nuisance, or affects the liability, whether under statute or common law, of the driver or owner so using such a vehicle.

LAW OF PROPERTY (MISCELLANEOUS PROVISIONS) ACT 1989
(c.34)

1 DEEDS AND THEIR EXECUTION

(1) Any rule of law which—
   (a) restricts the substances on which a deed may be written;
   (b) requires a seal for the valid execution of an instrument as a deed by an individual; or
   (c) requires authority by one person to another to deliver an instrument as a deed on his behalf to be given by deed,
   is abolished.

(2) An instrument shall not be a deed unless—
   (a) it makes it clear on its face that it is intended to be a deed by the person making it or, as the case may be, by the parties to it (whether by describing itself as a deed or expressing itself to be executed or signed as a deed or otherwise); and
   (b) it is validly executed as a deed
      (i) by that person or a person authorised to execute it in the name or on behalf of that person, or
      (ii) by one or more of those parties or a person authorised to execute it in the name or on behalf of one or more of those parties.

(2A) For the purposes of subsection (2)(a) above, an instrument shall not be taken to make it clear on its face that it is intended to be a deed merely because it is executed under seal.

(3) An instrument is validly executed as a deed by an individual if, and only if—
   (a) it is signed—
      (i) by him in the presence of a witness who attests the signature; or
      (ii) at his direction and in his presence and the presence of two witnesses who each attest the signature; and
   (b) it is delivered as a deed.

(4) In subsections (2) and (3) above "sign", in relation to an instrument, includes
   (a) an individual signing the name of the person or party on whose behalf he executes the instrument; and

(b) making one's mark on the instrument,
and "signature" is to be construed accordingly.

(4A) Subsection (3) above applies in the case of an instrument executed by an individual in the name or on behalf of another person whether or not that person is also an individual.

(5) Where a relevant lawyer, or an agent or employee of a relevant lawyer, in the course of or in connection with a transaction, purports to deliver an instrument as a deed on behalf of a party to the instrument, it shall be conclusively presumed in favour of a purchaser that he is authorised so to deliver the instrument.

(6) In subsection (5) above—

"purchaser" has the same meaning as in the Law of Property Act 1925;

"relevant lawyer" means a person who, for the purposes of the Legal Services Act 2007, is an authorised person in relation to an activity which constitutes a reserved instrument activity (within the meaning of that Act).

(7) Where an instrument under seal that constitutes a deed is required for the purposes of an Act passed before this section comes into force, this section shall have effect as to signing, sealing or delivery of an instrument by an individual in place of any provision of that Act as to signing, sealing or delivery.

. . .

(10) The references in this section to the execution of a deed by an individual do not include execution by a corporation sole and the reference in subsection (7) above to signing, sealing or delivery by an individual does not include signing, sealing or delivery by such a corporation.

(11) Nothing in this section applies in relation to instruments delivered as deeds before this section comes into force.

2 CONTRACTS FOR SALE ETC. OF LAND TO BE MADE BY SIGNED WRITING

(1) A contract for the sale or other disposition of an interest in land can only be made in writing and only by incorporating all the terms which the parties have expressly agreed in one document or, where contracts are exchanged, in each.

(2) The terms may be incorporated in a document either by being set out in it or by reference to some other document.

(3) The document incorporating the terms or, where contracts are exchanged, one of the documents incorporating them (but not necessarily the same one) must be signed by or on behalf of each party to the contract.

(4) Where a contract for the sale or other disposition of an interest in land satisfies the conditions of this section by reason only of the rectification of one or more documents in pursuance of an order of a court, the contract shall come into being, or be deemed to have come into being, at such time as may be specified in the order.

(5) This section does not apply in relation to—
(a) a contract to grant such a lease as is mentioned in section 54(2) of the Law of Property Act 1925 (short leases);
(b) a contract made in the course of a public auction; or

(c) a contract regulated under the Financial Services and Markets Act 2000, other than a regulated mortgage contract, a regulated home reversion plan, a regulated home purchase plan or a regulated sale and rent back agreement;

and nothing in this section affects the creation or operation of resulting, implied or constructive trusts.

(6) In this section—

"disposition" has the same meaning as in the Law of Property Act 1925;

"interest in land" means any estate, interest or charge in or over land;

"regulated mortgage contract", "regulated home reversion plan", "regulated home purchase plan" and "regulated sale and rent back agreement". must be read with—

(a) section 22 of the Financial Services and Markets Act 2000,
(b) any relevant order under that section, and
(c) Schedule 2 to that Act.

(7) Nothing in this section shall apply in relation to contracts made before this section comes into force.

(8) Section 40 of the Law of Property Act 1925 (which is superseded by this section) shall cease to have effect.

3 ABOLITION OF RULE IN BAIN V. FOTHERGILL

The rule of law known as the rule in Bain v. Fothergill is abolished in relation to contracts made after this section comes into force.
. . .

6 CITATION

(1) This Act may be cited as the Law of Property (Miscellaneous Provisions) Act 1989.

(2) This Act extends to England and Wales only.

As amended by Courts and Legal Services Act 1990, s. 125(2) and Sch. 17, para. 20; Trusts of Land and Appointment of Trustees Act 1996, Sch. 4, para. 1; Financial Services and Markets Act 2000 (Consequential Amendments and Repeals) Order 2001, Pt. 8, art. 317; Regulatory Reform (Execution of Deeds and Documents) Order 2005, arts. 7–8, Sch. 1 and Sch. 2; Financial Services and Markets Act 2000 (Regulated Activities) (Amendment) (No. 2) Order 2006, Pt. 3, art 27; Legal Services Act 2007, Sch. 21; Financial Services and Markets Act 2000 (Regulated Activities) (Amendment) Order 2009, Art. 24.

EMPLOYMENT ACT 1989
(c.38)

11 EXEMPTION OF SIKHS FROM REQUIREMENTS AS TO WEARING OF SAFETY HELMETS ON CONSTRUCTION SITES

(1) Any requirement to wear a safety helmet which (apart from this section) would, by virtue of any statutory provision or rule of law, be imposed on a Sikh who is on a construction site shall not apply to him at any time when he is wearing a turban.

(2)   Accordingly, where—
    (a) a Sikh who is on a construction site is for the time being wearing a turban, and
    (b) (apart from this section) any associated requirement would, by virtue of any statutory provision or rule of law, be imposed—
        (i) on the Sikh, or
        (ii) on any other person,
in connection with the wearing by the Sikh of a safety helmet, that requirement shall not apply to the Sikh or (as the case may be) to that other person.

(3)   In subsection (2) "associated requirement" means any requirement (other than one falling within subsection (1)) which is related to or connected with the wearing, provision or maintenance of safety helmets.

(4)   It is hereby declared that, where a person does not comply with any requirement, being a requirement which for the time being does not apply to him by virtue of subsection (1) or (2)—
    (a) he shall not be liable in tort to any person in respect of any injury, loss or damage caused by his failure to comply with that requirement; and
    (b) in Scotland no action for reparation shall be brought against him by any person in respect of any such injury, loss or damage.

(5)   If a Sikh who is on a construction site—
    (a) does not comply with any requirement to wear a safety helmet, being a requirement which for the time being does not apply to him by virtue of subsection (1), and
    (b) in consequence of any act or omission of some other person sustains any injury, loss or damage which is to any extent attributable to the fact that he is not wearing a safety helmet in compliance with the requirement,
that other person shall, if liable to the Sikh in tort (or, in Scotland, in an action for reparation), be so liable only to the extent that injury, loss or damage would have been sustained by the Sikh even if he had been wearing a safety helmet in compliance with the requirement.

(6)   Where—
    (a) the act or omission referred to in subsection (5) causes the death of the Sikh, and
    (b) the Sikh would have sustained some injury (other than loss of life) in consequence of the act or omission even if he had been wearing a safety helmet in compliance with the requirement in question,
the amount of any damages which, by virtue of that subsection, are recoverable in tort (or, in Scotland, in an action for reparation) in respect of that injury shall not exceed the amount of any damages which would (apart from that subsection) be so recoverable in respect of the Sikh's death.

(7)   In this section—

"building operations" and "works of engineering construction" have the same meaning as in the

"injury" includes loss of life, any impairment of a person's physical or mental condition and any disease;

"safety helmet" means any form of protective headgear; and

"statutory provision" means a provision of an Act or of subordinate legislation.

(8)   In this section—
    (a) any reference to a Sikh is a reference to a follower of the Sikh religion; and
    (b) any reference to a Sikh being on a construction site is a reference to his being there whether while at work or otherwise.

COURTS AND LEGAL SERVICES ACT 1990
(c.41)

8 POWERS OF COURT OF APPEAL TO AWARD DAMAGES

(1)   In this section "case" means any case where the Court of Appeal has power to order a new trial on the ground that damages awarded by a jury are excessive or inadequate.

(2)   Rules of court may provide for the Court of Appeal, in such classes of case as may be specified in the rules, to have power, in place of ordering a new trial, to substitute for the sum awarded by the jury such sum as appears to the court to be proper.

(3)   This section is not to be read as prejudicing in any way any other power to make rules of court.

BROADCASTING ACT 1990
(C.42)

166 DEFAMATORY MATERIAL

(1)   For the purposes of the law of libel and slander . . . the publication of words in the course of any programme included in a programme service shall be treated as publication in permanent form.

(2)   Subsection (1) above shall apply for the purposes of section 3 of each of the Defamation Acts (slander of title etc.) as it applies for the purposes of the law of libel and slander.

. . . .

(4)   In this section "the Defamation Acts" means the Defamation Act 1952 and the Defamation Act (Northern Ireland) 1955.

SCHEDULE 20

Section 203(1)

MINOR AND CONSEQUENTIAL AMENDMENTS

Section 3 (protection in respect of proceedings for printing extracts from or abstracts of parliamentary papers) shall have effect as if the reference to printing included a reference to including in a programme service.

AGE OF LEGAL CAPACITY (SCOTLAND) ACT 1991
(c.50)

1 AGE OF LEGAL CAPACITY

(1)   As from the commencement of this Act—
    (a)   a person under the age of 16 years shall, subject to section 2 below, have no legal capacity to enter into any transaction;

(b) a person of or over the age of 16 years shall have legal capacity to enter into any transaction.

. . .

2 EXCEPTIONS TO GENERAL RULE

(1) A person under the age of 16 years shall have legal capacity to enter into a transaction—
(a) of a kind commonly entered into by persons of his age and circumstances, and
(b) on terms which are not unreasonable.

. . .

(4A) A person under the age of sixteen years shall have legal capacity to instruct a solicitor, in connection with any civil matter, where that person has a general understanding of what it means to do so; and without prejudice to the generality of this subsection a person twelve years of age or more shall be presumed to be of sufficient age and maturity to have such understanding.

(4B) A person who by virtue of subsection (4A) above has legal capacity to instruct a solicitor shall also have legal capacity to sue, or to defend, in any civil proceedings.

(4C) Subsections (4A) and (4B) above are without prejudice to any question of legal capacity arising in connection with any criminal matter.

(5) Any transaction—
(a) which a person under the age of 16 years purports to enter into after the commencement of this Act, and
(b) in relation to which that person does not have legal capacity by virtue of this section, shall be void.

3 SETTING ASIDE OF TRANSACTIONS

(1) A person under the age of 21 years ("the applicant") may make application to the court to set aside a transaction which he entered into while he was of or over the age of 16 years but under the age of 18 years and which is a prejudicial transaction.

(2) In this section "prejudicial transaction" means a transaction which—
(a) an adult, exercising reasonable prudence, would not have entered into in the circumstances of the applicant at the time of entering into the transaction, and
(b) has caused or is likely to cause substantial prejudice to the applicant.

(3) Subsection (1) above shall not apply to—
(a) the exercise of testamentary capacity;
(b) the exercise by testamentary writing of any power of appointment;
(c) the giving of consent to the making of an adoption order;
(d) the bringing or defending of, or the taking of any step in, civil proceedings;
(e) the giving of consent to any surgical, medical or dental procedure or treatment;
(f) a transaction in the course of the applicant's trade, business or profession;
(g) a transaction into which any other party was induced to enter by virtue of any fraudulent misrepresentation by the applicant as to age or other material fact;
(h) a transaction ratified by the applicant after he attained the age of 18 years and in the knowledge that it could be the subject of an application to the court under this section to set it aside; or
(j) a transaction ratified by the court under section 4 below.

(4)   Where an application to set aside a transaction can be made or could have been made under this section by the person referred to in subsection (1) above, such application may instead be made by that person's executor, trustee in bankruptcy, trustee acting under a trust deed for creditors or curator bonis at any time prior to the date on which that person attains or would have attained the age of 21 years.

. . .

4   RATIFICATION BY COURT OF PROPOSED TRANSACTION

(1)   Where a person of or over the age of 16 years but under the age of 18 years proposes to enter into a transaction which, if completed, could be the subject of an application to the court under section 3 above to set aside, all parties to the proposed transaction may make a joint application to have it ratified by the court.

. . .

As amended by Children (Scotland) Act 1995, Sch. 4.

WATER INDUSTRY ACT 1991
(c.56)

209   CIVIL LIABILITY OF UNDERTAKERS FOR ESCAPES OF WATER ETC.

(1)   Where an escape of water, however caused, from a pipe vested in a water undertaker causes loss or damage, the undertaker shall be liable, except as otherwise provided in this section, for the loss or damage.

(2)   A water undertaker shall not incur any liability under subsection (1) above if the escape was due wholly to the fault of the person who sustained the loss or damage or of any servant, agent or contractor of his.

(3)   A water undertaker shall not incur any liability under subsection (1) above in respect of any loss or damage for which the undertaker would not be liable apart from that subsection and which is sustained—
    (a) by the Environment Agency], a relevant undertaker or any statutory undertakers, within the meaning of section 336(1) of the Town and Country Planning Act 1990;
    (b) by any public gas supplier within the meaning of Part I of the Gas Act 1986 or the holder of a licence under section 6(1) of the Electricity Act 1989;
    (c) by any highway authority; or
    (d) by any person on whom a right to compensation is conferred by section 82 of the New Roads and Street Works Act 1991.

(4)   The Law Reform (Contributory Negligence) Act 1945, the Fatal Accidents Act 1976 and the Limitation Act 1980 shall apply in relation to any loss or damage for which a water undertaker is liable under this section, but which is not due to the undertaker's fault, as if it were due to its fault.

(5)   Nothing in subsection (1) above affects any entitlement which a water undertaker may have to recover contribution under the Civil Liability (Contribution) Act 1978; and for

the purposes of that Act, any loss for which a water undertaker is liable under that subsection shall be treated as if it were damage.

(6)   Where a water undertaker is liable under any enactment or agreement passed or made before 1st April 1982 to make any payment in respect of any loss or damage the undertaker shall not incur liability under subsection (1) above in respect of the same loss or damage.

(7)   In this section "fault" has the same meaning as in the Law Reform (Contributory Negligence) Act 1945.

SOCIAL SECURITY CONTRIBUTIONS AND BENEFITS ACT 1992
(c.4)

94 RIGHT TO INDUSTRIAL INJURIES BENEFIT

(1)   Industrial injuries benefit shall be payable where an employed earner suffers personal injury caused after 4th July 1948 by accident arising out of and in the course of his employment, being employed earner's employment.

(2)   Industrial injuries benefit consists of the following benefits—
(a)   disablement benefit payable in accordance with sections 103 to 105 below, paragraphs 2 and 3 of Schedule 7 below and Parts II and III of that Schedule;
(b)   reduced earnings allowance payable in accordance with Part IV;
(c)   retirement allowance payable in accordance with Part V; and
(d)   industrial death benefit, payable in accordance with Part VI.

(3)   For the purposes of industrial injuries benefit an accident arising in the course of an employed earner's employment shall be taken, in the absence of evidence to the contrary, also to have arisen out of that employment.

(4)   Regulations may make provision as to the day which, in the case of night workers and other special cases, is to be treated for the purposes of industrial injuries benefit as the day of the accident.

(5)   Subject to sections 117, 119 and 120 below, industrial injuries benefit shall not be payable in respect of an accident happening while the earner is outside Great Britain.

(6)   In the following provisions of this Part of this Act "work" in the contexts "incapable of work" and "incapacity for work" means work which the person in question can be reasonably expected to do.

97 ACCIDENTS IN COURSE OF ILLEGAL EMPLOYMENTS

(1)   Subsection (2) below has effect in any case where—
(a)   a claim is made for industrial injuries benefit in respect of an accident, or of a prescribed disease or injury; or
(b)   an application is made under section 29 of the Social Security Act 1998 for a declaration that an accident was an industrial accident, or for a corresponding declaration as to a prescribed disease or injury.

(2)   The Secretary of State may direct that the relevant employment shall, in relation to that accident, disease or injury, be treated as having been employed earner's employment

notwithstanding that by reason of a contravention of, or non-compliance with, some provision contained in or having effect under an enactment passed for the protection of employed persons or any class of employed persons, either—

(a) the contract purporting to govern the employment was void; or

(b) the employed person was not lawfully employed in the relevant employment at the time when, or in the place where, the accident happened or the disease or injury was contracted or received.

(3) In subsection (2) above "relevant employment" means —

(a) in relation to an accident, the employment out of and in the course of which the accident arises; and

(b) in relation to a prescribed disease or injury, the employment to the nature of which the disease or injury is due.

99 EARNER TRAVELLING IN EMPLOYER'S TRANSPORT

(1) An accident happening while an employed earner is, with the express or implied permission of his employer, travelling as a passenger by any vehicle to or from his place of work shall, notwithstanding that he is under no obligation to his employer to travel by that vehicle, be taken to arise out of and in the course of his employment if—

(a) the accident would have been taken so to have arisen had he been under such an obligation; and

(b) at the time of the accident, the vehicle—

(i) is being operated by or on behalf of his employer or some other person by whom it is provided in pursuance of arrangements made with his employer; and

(ii) is not being operated in the ordinary course of a public transport service.

(2) In this section references to a vehicle include a ship, vessel, hovercraft or aircraft.

100 ACCIDENTS HAPPENING WHILE MEETING EMERGENCY

An accident happening to an employed earner in or about any premises at which he is for the time being employed for the purposes of his employer's trade or business shall be taken to arise out of and in the course of his employment if it happens while he is taking steps, on an actual or supposed emergency at those premises, to rescue, succour or protect persons who are, or are thought to be or possibly to be, injured or imperilled, or to avert or minimise serious damage to property.

101 ACCIDENT CAUSED BY ANOTHER'S MISCONDUCT ETC.

An accident happening after 19th December 1961 shall be treated for the purposes of industrial injuries benefit, where it would not apart from this section be so treated, as arising out of an employed earner's employment if—

(a) the accident arises in the course of the employment; and

(b) the accident either is caused—

(i) by another person's misconduct, skylarking or negligence, or

(ii) by steps taken in consequence of any such misconduct, skylarking or negligence, or

(iii) by the behaviour or presence of an animal (including a bird, fish or insect),

or is caused by or consists in the employed earner being struck by any object or by lightning; and

(c) the employed earner did not directly or indirectly induce or contribute to the happening of the accident by his conduct outside the employment or by any act not incidental to the employment.

107 ADJUSTMENTS FOR SUCCESSIVE ACCIDENTS

(1)   Where a person suffers two or more successive accidents arising out of and in the course of his employed earner's employment—

   (a) he shall not for the same period be entitled (apart from any increase of benefit mentioned in subsection (2) below) to receive industrial injuries benefit by way of two or more disablement pensions at an aggregate weekly rate exceeding the appropriate amount specified in Schedule 4, Part V, paragraph 4; and

   (b) regulations may provide for adjusting—

      (i)   disablement benefit, or the conditions for the receipt of that benefit, in any case where he has received or may be entitled to a disablement gratuity;

      (ii) any increase of benefit mentioned in subsection (2) below, or the conditions for its receipt.

SOCIAL SECURITY ADMINISTRATION ACT 1992
(c5)

Recovery of benefit payments

71ZB

Recovery of overpayments of certain benefits

(1)   The Secretary of State may recover any amount of the following paid in excess of entitlement—

   (a) universal credit,

   (b) jobseeker's allowance,

   (c) employment and support allowance, and

   (d) except in prescribed circumstances, housing credit (within the meaning of the State Pension Credit Act 2002).

(2)   An amount recoverable under this section is recoverable from—

   (a) the person to whom it was paid, or

   (b) such other person (in addition to or instead of the person to whom it was paid) as may be prescribed.

(3)   An amount paid in pursuance of a determination is not recoverable under this section unless the determination has been—

   (a) reversed or varied on an appeal, or

   (b) revised or superseded under section 9 or section 10 of the Social Security Act 1998, except where regulations otherwise provide.

(4)   Regulations may provide that amounts recoverable under this section are to be calculated or estimated in a prescribed manner.

(5)   Where an amount of universal credit is paid for the sole reason that a payment by way of prescribed income is made after the date which is the prescribed date for payment of that income, that amount is for the purposes of this section paid in excess of entitlement.

(6)   In the case of a benefit referred to in subsection (1) which is awarded to persons jointly, an amount paid to one of those persons may for the purposes of this section be regarded as paid to the other.

(7)   An amount recoverable under this section may (without prejudice to any other means of recovery) be recovered—

   (a) by deduction from benefit (section 71ZC);

   (b) by deduction from earnings (section 71ZD);

(c) through the courts etc (section 71ZE);

(d) by adjustment of benefit (section 71ZF).

Editor's Note: this subsection introduced by s 105 Welfare Reform Act 2012 to be brought into force on a day appointed by order.

TRADE UNION AND LABOUR RELATIONS (CONSOLIDATION) ACT 1992
(c.50)

Meaning of "trade union"

1 MEANING OF "TRADE UNION"

In this Act a "trade union" means an organisation (whether temporary or permanent)—

(a) which consists wholly or mainly of workers of one or more descriptions and whose principal purposes include the regulation of relations between workers of that description or those descriptions and employers or employers' associations; or

(b) which consists wholly or mainly of—
   (i) constituent or affiliated organisations which fulfil the conditions in paragraph (a) (or themselves consist wholly or mainly of constituent or affiliated organisations which fulfil those conditions), or
   (ii) representatives of such constituent or affiliated organisations,
   and whose principal purposes include the regulation of relations between workers and employers or between workers and employers' associations, or the regulation of relations between its constituent or affiliated organisations.

10 QUASI-CORPORATE STATUS OF TRADE UNIONS

(1) A trade union is not a body corporate but—
   (a) it is capable of making contracts;
   (b) it is capable of suing and being sued in its own name, whether in proceedings relating to property or founded on contract or tort or any other cause of action; and
   (c) proceedings for an offence alleged to have been committed by it or on its behalf may be brought against it in its own name.

(2) A trade union shall not be treated as if it were a body corporate except to the extent authorised by the provisions of this Part.

20 LIABILITY OF TRADE UNION IN CERTAIN PROCEEDINGS IN TORT

(1) Where proceedings in tort are brought against a trade union—
   (a) on the ground that an act—
      (i) induces another person to break a contract or interferes or induces another person to interfere with its performance, or
      (ii) consists in threatening that a contract (whether one to which the union is a party or not) will be broken or its performance interfered with, or that the union will induce another person to break a contract or interfere with its performance, or
   (b) in respect of an agreement or combination by two or more persons to do or to procure the doing of an act which, if it were done without any such agreement or combination, would be actionable in tort on such a ground,

then, for the purpose of determining in those proceedings whether the union is liable in respect of the act in question, that act shall be taken to have been done by the union if, but only if, it is to be taken to have been authorised or endorsed by the trade union in accordance with the following provisions.

(2) An act shall be taken to have been authorised or endorsed by a trade union if it was done, or was authorised or endorsed—
  (a) by any person empowered by the rules to do, authorise or endorse acts of the kind in question, or
  (b) by the principal executive committee or the president or general secretary, or
  (c) by any other committee of the union or any other official of the union (whether employed by it or not).

(3) For the purposes of paragraph (c) of subsection (2)—
  (a) any group of persons constituted in accordance with the rules of the union is a committee of the union; and
  (b) an act shall be taken to have been done, authorised or endorsed by an official if it was done, authorised or endorsed by, or by any member of, any group of persons of which he was at the material time a member, the purposes of which included organising or co-ordinating industrial action.

(4) The provisions of paragraphs (b) and (c) of subsection (2) apply notwithstanding anything in the rules of the union, or in any contract or rule of law, but subject to the provisions of section 21 (repudiation by union of certain acts).

(5) Where for the purposes of any proceedings an act is by virtue of this section taken to have been done by a trade union, nothing in this section shall affect the liability of any other person, in those or any other proceedings, in respect of that act.

(6) In proceedings arising out of an act which is by virtue of this section taken to have been done by a trade union, the power of the court to grant an injunction or interdict includes power to require the union to take such steps as the court considers appropriate for ensuring—
  (a) that there is no, or no further, inducement of persons to take part or to continue to take part in industrial action, and
  (b) that no person engages in any conduct after the granting of the injunction or interdict by virtue of having been induced before it was granted to take part or to continue to take part in industrial action.
  The provisions of subsections (2) to (4) above apply in relation to proceedings for failure to comply with any such injunction or interdict as they apply in relation to the original proceedings.

(7) In this section "rules", in relation to a trade union, means the written rules of the union and any other written provision forming part of the contract between a member and the other members.

22 LIMIT ON DAMAGES AWARDED AGAINST TRADE UNIONS IN ACTIONS IN TORT

(1) This section applies to any proceedings in tort brought against a trade union, except—
  (a) proceedings for personal injury as a result of negligence, nuisance or breach of duty;
  (b) proceedings for breach of duty in connection with the ownership, occupation, possession, control or use of property;
  (c) proceedings brought by virtue of Part I of the Consumer Protection Act 1987 (product liability).

(2)   In any proceedings in tort to which this section applies the amount which may awarded against the union by way of damages shall not exceed the following limit—

Number of members of union	Maximum award of damages
Less than 5,000	£10,000
5,000 or more but less than 25,000	£50,000
25,000 or more but less than 100,000	£125,000
100,000 or more	£250,000

(3)   The Secretary of State may by order amend subsection (2) so as to vary any of the sums specified; and the order may make such transitional provision as the Secretary of State considers appropriate.

(4)   Any such order shall be made by statutory instrument which shall be subject to annulment in pursuance of a resolution of either House of Parliament.

(5)   In this section—

"breach of duty" means breach of a duty imposed by any rule of law or by or under any enactment;

"personal injury" includes any disease and any impairment of a person's physical or mental condition; and

"property" means any property, whether real or personal (or in Scotland, heritable or moveable).

Part IV INDUSTRIAL RELATIONS

Chapter I COLLECTIVE BARGAINING

Introductory

178 COLLECTIVE AGREEMENTS AND COLLECTIVE BARGAINING

(1)   In this Act "collective agreement" means any agreement or arrangement made by or on behalf of one or more trade unions and one or more employers or employers' associations and relating to one or more of the matters specified below; and "collective bargaining" means negotiations relating to or connected with one or more of those matters.

(2)   The matters referred to above are—
   (a) terms and conditions of employment, or the physical conditions in which any workers are required to work;
   (b) engagement or non-engagement, or termination or suspension of employment or the duties of employment, of one or more workers;
   (c) allocation of work or the duties of employment between workers or groups of workers;
   (d) matters of discipline;
   (e) a worker's membership or non-membership of a trade union;
   (f) facilities for officials of trade unions; and
   (g) machinery for negotiation or consultation, and other procedures, relating to any of the above matters, including the recognition by employers or employers' associations of the right of a trade union to represent workers in such negotiation or consultation or in the carrying out of such procedures.

(3)   In this Act "recognition", in relation to a trade union, means the recognition of the union by an employer, or two or more associated employers, to any extent, for the purpose of

collective bargaining; and "recognised" and other related expressions shall be construed accordingly.

Enforceability of collective agreements

179 WHETHER AGREEMENT INTENDED TO BE A LEGALLY ENFORCEABLE CONTRACT

(1) A collective agreement shall be conclusively presumed not to have been intended by the parties to be a legally enforceable contract unless the agreement—
(a) is in writing, and
(b) contains a provision which (however expressed) states that the parties intend that the agreement shall be a legally enforceable contract.

(2) A collective agreement which does satisfy those conditions shall be conclusively presumed to have been intended by the parties to be a legally enforceable contract.

(3) If a collective agreement is in writing and contains a provision which (however expressed) states that the parties intend that one or more parts of the agreement specified in that provision, but not the whole of the agreement, shall be a legally enforceable contract, then—
(a) the specified part or parts shall be conclusively presumed to have been intended by the parties to be a legally enforceable contract, and
the remainder of the agreement shall be conclusively presumed not to have been intended by the parties to be such a contract.

(4) A part of a collective agreement which by virtue of subsection (3)(b) is not a legally enforceable contract may be referred to for the purpose of interpretating a party of the agreement which is such a contract.

Protection of acts in contemplation or furtherance of trade dispute

219 PROTECTION FROM CERTAIN TORT LIABILITIES

(1) An act done by a person in contemplation or furtherance of a trade dispute is not actionable in tort on the ground only—
(a) that it induces another person to break a contract or interferes or induces another person to interfere with its performance, or
(b) that it consists in his threatening that a contract (whether one to which he is a party or not) will be broken or its performance interfered with, or that he will induce another person to break a contract or interfere with its performance.

(2) An agreement or combination by two or more persons to do or procure the doing of an act in contemplation or furtherance of a trade dispute is not actionable in tort if the act is one which if done without any such agreement or combination would not be actionable in tort.

(3) Nothing in subsections (1) and (2) prevents an act done in the course of picketing from being actionable in tort unless it is done in the course of attendance declared lawful by section 220 (peaceful picketing)

(4) Subsections (1) and (2) have effect subject to sections 222 to 225 (action excluded from protection) and to sections 226 (requirement of ballot before action by trade union) and 234A (requirement of notice to employer of industrial action); and in those sections "not protected" means excluded from the protection afforded by this section or, where the expression is used with reference to a particular person, excluded from that protection as respects that person.]

220 PEACEFUL PICKETING

(1) It is lawful for a person in contemplation or furtherance of a trade dispute to attend—
    (a) at or near his own place of work, or
    (b) if he is an official of a trade union, at or near the place of work of a member of the union whom he is accompanying and whom he represents,
for the purpose only of peacefully obtaining or communicating information, or peacefully persuading any person to work or abstain from working.

(2) If a person works or normally works—
    (a) otherwise than at any one place, or
    (b) at a place the location of which is such that attendance there for a purpose mentioned in subsection (1) is impracticable,
his place of work for the purposes of that subsection shall be any premises of his employer from which he works or from which his work is administered.

(3) In the case of a worker not in employment where—
    (a) his last employment was terminated in connection with a trade dispute, or
    (b) the termination of his employment was one of the circumstances giving rise to a trade dispute,
in relation to that dispute his former place of work shall be treated for the purposes of subsection (1) as being his place of work.

(4) A person who is an official of a trade union by virtue only of having been elected or appointed to be a representative of some of the members of the union shall be regarded for the purposes of subsection (1) as representing only those members; but otherwise an official of a union shall be regarded for those purposes as representing all its members.

221 RESTRICTIONS ON GRANT OF INJUNCTIONS AND INTERDICTS

(1) Where—
    (a) an application for an injunction or interdict is made to a court in the absence of the party against whom it is sought or any representative of his, and
    (b) he claims, or in the opinion of the court would be likely to claim, that he acted in contemplation or furtherance of a trade dispute,
the court shall not grant the injunction or interdict unless satisfied that all steps which in the circumstances were reasonable have been taken with a view to securing that notice of the application and an opportunity of being heard with respect to the application have been given to him.

(2) Where—
    (a) an application for an interlocutory injunction is made to a court pending the trial of an action, and
    (b) the party against whom it is sought claims that he acted in contemplation or furtherance of a trade dispute,
the court shall, in exercising its discretion whether or not to grant the injunction, have regard to the likelihood of that party's succeeding at the trial of the action in establishing any matter which would afford a defence to the action under section 219 (protection from certain tort liabilities) or section 220 (peaceful picketing).

This subsection does not extend to Scotland.

244 MEANING OF "TRADE DISPUTE" IN PART V

(1) In this Part a "trade dispute" means a dispute between workers and their employer which relates wholly or mainly to one or more of the following—

(a) terms and conditions of employment, or the physical conditions in which any workers are required to work;

(b) engagement or non-engagement, or termination or suspension of employment or the duties of employment, of one or more workers;

(c) allocation of work or the duties of employment between workers or groups of workers;

(d) matters of discipline;

(e) a worker's membership or non-membership of a trade union;

(f) facilities for officials of trade unions; and

(g) machinery for negotiation or consultation, and other procedures, relating to any of the above matters, including the recognition by employers or employers' associations of the right of a trade union to represent workers in such negotiation or consultation or in the carrying out of such procedures.

(2) A dispute between a Minister of the Crown and any workers shall, notwithstanding that he is not the employer of those workers, be treated as a dispute between those workers and their employer if the dispute relates to matters which—

(a) have been referred for consideration by a joint body on which, by virtue of provision made by or under any enactment, he is represented, or

(b) cannot be settled without him exercising a power conferred on him by or under an enactment.

(3) There is a trade dispute even though it relates to matters occurring outside the United Kingdom, so long as the person or persons whose actions in the United Kingdom are said to be in contemplation or furtherance of a trade dispute relating to matters occurring outside the United Kingdom are likely to be affected in respect of one or more of the matters specified in subsection (1) by the outcome of the dispute.

(4) An act, threat or demand done or made by one person or organisation against another which, if resisted, would have led to a trade dispute with that other, shall be treated as being done or made in contemplation of a trade dispute with that other, notwithstanding that because that other submits to the act or threat or accedes to the demand no dispute arises.

(5) In this section—

"employment" includes any relationship whereby one person personally does work or performs services for another; and

"worker", in relation to a dispute with an employer, means—

(a) a worker employed by that employer; or

(b) a person who has ceased to be so employed if his employment was terminated in connection with the dispute or if the termination of his employment was one of the circumstances giving rise to the dispute.

301 EXTENT

(1) This Act extends to England and Wales and (apart from section 212A(6)) to Scotland.

As amended by Employment Rights (Dispute Resolution) Act 1998, Sch. 1.

RAILWAYS ACT 1993
(c.43)

122 STATUTORY AUTHORITY AS A DEFENCE TO ACTIONS IN NUISANCE ETC.

(1) Subject to the following provisions of this section—
    (a) any person shall have authority—
        (i) to use, or to cause or permit any agent or independent contractor of his to use, rolling stock on any track, or
        (ii) to use, or to cause or permit any agent or independent contractor of his to use, any land comprised in a network, station or light maintenance depot for or in connection with the provision of network services, station services or light maintenance services, and
    (b) any person who is the owner or occupier of any land shall have authority to authorise, consent to or acquiesce in—
        (i) the use by another of rolling stock on any track comprised in that land, or
        (ii) the use by another of that land for or in connection with the provision of network services, station services or light maintenance services,
    if and so long as the qualifying conditions are satisfied in the particular case.

(2) For the purposes of this section, the "qualifying conditions" are—
    (a) in relation to any use of rolling stock on track—
        (i) that the track is comprised in a network, station or light maintenance depot, and
        (ii) that the operator of that network, station or light maintenance depot is the holder of an appropriate licence or has the benefit of an appropriate licence exemption; and
    (b) in relation to any use of land for or in connection with the provision of network services, station services or light maintenance services, that the operator of the network, station or light maintenance depot in question is the holder of an appropriate licence or has the benefit of an appropriate licence exemption.

(3) The authority conferred by this section is conferred only for the purpose of providing a defence of statutory authority—
    (a) in England and Wales—
        (i) in any proceedings, whether civil or criminal, in nuisance; or
        (ii) in any civil proceedings, other than proceedings for breach of statutory duty, in respect of the escape of things from land;
    (b) in Scotland, in any civil proceedings on the ground of nuisance where the rule of strict liability applies, other than proceedings for breach of statutory duty.

(4) Nothing in this section shall be construed as excluding a defence of statutory authority otherwise available under or by virtue of any enactment.

(5) The owner or occupier of any land shall be regarded for the purposes of this section as "acquiescing" in—
    (a) any use by another of rolling stock on track comprised in that land, or
    (b) any use of that land by another for or in connection with the provision of network services, station services or light maintenance services,
    notwithstanding that it is not within his power to put an end to that use by that other.

(6)   For the purposes of this section—
   (a)   any reference to the use of rolling stock on track includes a reference to the carriage of any passengers or other persons, or any goods, of any class or description for any purpose on or by means of that rolling stock on that track; and
   (b)   rolling stock shall be regarded as "used" on any track at any time when it is present on that track, irrespective of whether the rolling stock is comprised in a train or not, whether the rolling stock is moving or stationary and, if moving, irrespective of the means by which the motion is caused.

(7)   In this section—

"appropriate licence", in relation to the operator of a network, station or light maintenance depot, means a licence which authorises him to be the operator of that network, station or light maintenance depot;

"appropriate licence exemption", in relation to the operator of a network, station or light maintenance depot, means any such licence exemption as exempts him from the requirement to hold the licence that would otherwise be the appropriate licence in his case;

and expressions used in this section and in Part I above have the same meaning in this section as they have in that Part.

REQUIREMENTS OF WRITING (SCOTLAND) ACT 1995
(c.7)

1 WRITING REQUIRED FOR CERTAIN CONTRACTS, OBLIGATIONS, TRUSTS, CONVEYANCES AND WILLS

(1)   Subject to subsection (2) below and any other enactment, writing shall not be required for the constitution of a contract, unilateral obligation or trust.

(2)   Subject to subsections (2A) and (3) below, a written document complying with section 2 of this Act shall be required for—
   (a)   the constitution of—
       (i)   a contract or unilateral obligation for the creation, transfer, variation or extinction of a real right in land;
       (ii)   a gratuitous unilateral obligation except an obligation undertaken in the course of business; and
       (iii) a trust whereby a person declares himself to be sole trustee of his own property or any property which he may acquire;
   (b)   the creation, transfer, variation or extinction of a real right in land otherwise than by the operation of a court decree, enactment or rule of law; and
   (c)   the making of any will, testamentary trust disposition and settlement or codicil.

(2A)   An electronic document complying with section 2A shall be valid for–
   (a)   the constitution of a contract or unilateral obligation for the creation, transfer, variation or extinction of a real right in land;
   (b)   the constitution of a gratuitous unilateral obligation; and
   (c)   the creation, transfer, variation or extinction of a real right in land.

(2B)   In this section, "electronic document" means a document created as an electronic communication within the ARTL system.

(3) Where a contract, obligation or trust mentioned in subsections (2)(a) or (2A) above is not constituted in a written document complying with section 2 or, as the case may be, an electronic document complying with section 2A, of this Act, but one of the parties to the contract, a creditor in the obligation or a beneficiary under the trust ("the first person") has acted or refrained from acting in reliance on the contract, obligation or trust with the knowledge and acquiescence of the other party to the contract, the debtor in the obligation or the truster ("the second person")—
   (a) the second person shall not be entitled to withdraw from the contract, obligation or trust; and
   (b) the contract, obligation or trust shall not be regarded as invalid,
on the ground that it is not so constituted, if the condition set out in subsection (4) below is satisfied.

(4) The condition referred to in subsection (3) above is that the position of the first person—
   (a) as a result of acting or refraining from acting as mentioned in that subsection has been affected to a material extent; and
   (b) as a result of such a withdrawal as is mentioned in that subsection would be adversely affected to a material extent.

(5) In relation to the constitution of any contract, obligation or trust mentioned in subsections (2)(a) or (2A) subsection (2)(a) above, subsections (3) and (4) above replace the rules of law known as *rei interventus* and homologation.

(6) This section shall apply to the variation of a contract, obligation or trust as it applies to the constitution thereof but as if in subsections (3) and (4) for the references to acting or refraining from acting in reliance on the contract, obligation or trust and withdrawing therefrom there were substituted respectively references to acting or refraining from acting in reliance on the variation of the contract, obligation or trust and withdrawing from the variation.

(7) In this section "real right in land" means any real right in or over land, including any right to occupy or to use land or to restrict the occupation or use of land, but does not include—
   (a) a tenancy;
   (b) a right to occupy or use land; or
   (c) a right to restrict the occupation or use of land,
if the tenancy or right is not granted for more than one year, unless the tenancy or right is for a recurring period or recurring periods and there is a gap of more than one year between the beginning of the first, and the end of the last, such period.

(8) For the purposes of subsection (7) above "land" does not include—
   (a) growing crops; or
   (b) a moveable building or other moveable structure.

2 TYPE OF WRITING REQUIRED FOR FORMAL VALIDITY OF CERTAIN DOCUMENTS

(1) No document required by section 1(2) of this Act shall be valid in respect of the formalities of execution unless it is subscribed by the granter of it or, if there is more than one granter, by each granter, but nothing apart from such subscription shall be required for the document to be valid as aforesaid.

(2) A contract mentioned in section 1(2)(a)(i) of this Act may be regarded as constituted or varied (as the case may be) if the offer is contained in one or more documents and the acceptance is contained in another document or other documents, and each document is subscribed by the granter or granters thereof.

(3)   Nothing in this section shall prevent a document which has not been subscribed by the granter or granters of it from being used as evidence in relation to any right or obligation to which the document relates.

(4)   This section is without prejudice to any other enactment which makes different provision in respect of the formalities of execution of a document to which this section applies.

2A FORMALITIES OF EXECUTION OF ELECTRONIC DOCUMENTS

(1)   An electronic document shall be valid in respect of the formalities of execution if that document has been authenticated by the granter, or if there is more than one granter by each granter, in accordance with subsection (2).

(2)   An electronic document is authenticated by a person if the digital signature of that person—
    (a) is incorporated into or logically associated with the electronic document;
    (b) was created by the person by whom it purports to have been created;
    (c) was created in accordance with such requirements as may be set out in directions made by the Keeper of the Registers of Scotland; and
    (d) is certified in accordance with—
        (i) subsection (3); and
        (ii) such requirements as may be set out in directions made by the Keeper of the Registers of Scotland.

(3)   For the purpose of this section a digital signature incorporated into or logically associated with an electronic document is certified by any person if that person (whether before or after the creation of the electronic document) has made a statement confirming that—
    (a) the signature;
    (b) a means of producing, communicating or verifying the signature; or
    (c) a procedure applied to the signature,
is (either alone or in combination with other factors) a valid means of establishing the authenticity of the document, the integrity of the document or both.

2B DIRECTIONS BY THE KEEPER OF THE REGISTERS OF SCOTLAND

A direction made by the Keeper of the Registers of Scotland under section 2A—
(a)   shall be published in such manner as the Keeper considers appropriate for the purpose of bringing it to the attention of the persons affected by it;

(b)   may make different provision for different purposes;

(c)   may include incidental, supplementary, saving and transitional provisions; and

(d)   may be varied or revoked by a subsequent direction.

2C AUTHENTICATION OF AN ELECTRONIC DOCUMENT BY A PERSON GRANTING IN MORE THAN ONE CAPACITY

Where a person grants an electronic document in more than one capacity authentication of that document by that person in accordance with this Act shall be sufficient to bind that person in all such capacities.

As amended by Abolition of Feudal Tenure etc (Scotland) Act 2000, Sch. 12; Automated Registration of Title to Land (Electronic Communications) (Scotland) Order 2006, art. 3.

POLICE ACT 1996
(c.16)

88 LIABILITY FOR WRONGFUL ACTS OF CONSTABLES

(1)   The chief officer of police for a police area shall be liable in respect of any unlawful conduct of constables under his direction and control in the performance or purported performance of their functions in like manner as a master is liable in respect of torts committed by his servants in the course of their employment, and accordingly shall, in the case of a tort, be treated for all purposes as a joint tortfeasor.

(2)   There shall be paid out of the police fund—
  (a) any damages or costs awarded against the chief officer of police in any proceedings brought against him by virtue of this section and any costs incurred by him in any such proceedings so far as not recovered by him in the proceedings; and
  (b) any sum required in connection with the settlement of any claim made against the chief officer of police by virtue of this section, if the settlement is approved by the police authority.

(3)   Any proceedings in respect of a claim made by virtue of this section shall be brought against the chief officer of police for the time being or, in the case of a vacancy in that office, against the person for the time being performing the functions of the chief officer of police; and references in subsections (1) and (2) to the chief officer of police shall be construed accordingly.

(4)   A local policing body may, in such cases and to such extent as appear to it to be appropriate, pay out of the police fund—
  (a) any damages or costs awarded against a person to whom this subsection applies in proceedings for any unlawful conduct of] that person,
  (b) any costs incurred and not recovered by such a person in such proceedings, and
  (c) any sum required in connection with the settlement of a claim that has or might have given rise to such proceedings.

(5)   Subsection (4) applies to a person who is—
  (a) a member of the police force maintained by the police authority,
  (b) a constable for the time being required to serve with that force by virtue of section 24 or 98 of this Act . . . ., or
  (c) a special constable appointed for the authority's police area.

(5A) This section shall have effect where, by virtue of section 23 or 24 of the Serious Organised Crime and Police Act 2005, a member of the staff of the Serious Organised Crime Agency who is neither a constable nor an employee of the local policing body is provided to a police force as if—
  (a) any unlawful conduct of his in the performance or purported performance of his functions were unlawful conduct of a constable under the direction and control of the chief officer of police of that force; and
  (b) subsection (4) applied to him in the case of the local policing body maintaining that force.

(6)   This section shall have effect where an international joint investigation team has been formed under the leadership of a constable who is a member of a police force as if—
  (a) any unlawful conduct, in the performance or purported performance of his functions as such, of any member of that team who is neither a constable nor an employee of the local policing body were unlawful conduct of a constable under the direction and control of the chief officer of police of that force; and

(b) subsection (4) applied, in the case of the local policing body maintaining that force, to every member of that team to whom it would not apply apart from this subsection.

(7) In this section "international joint investigation team" means any investigation team formed in accordance with—

(a) any framework decision on joint investigation teams adopted under Article 34 of the Treaty on European Union;

(b) the Convention on Mutual Assistance in Criminal Matters between the Member States of the European Union, and the Protocol to that Convention, established in accordance with that Article of that Treaty; or

(c) any international agreement to which the United Kingdom is a party and which is specified for the purposes of this section in an order made by the Secretary of State.

(8) A statutory instrument containing an order under subsection (7) shall be subject to annulment in pursuance of a resolution of either House of Parliament.

ARBITRATION ACT 1996
(c.23)

Consumer arbitration agreements

89 APPLICATION OF UNFAIR TERMS REGULATIONS TO CONSUMER ARBITRATION AGREEMENTS

(1) The following sections extend the application of the Unfair Terms in Consumer Contracts Regulations 1994 in relation to a term which constitutes an arbitration agreement.

For this purpose "arbitration agreement" means an agreement to submit to arbitration present or future disputes or differences (whether or not contractual).

(2) In those sections "the Regulations" means those regulations and includes any regulations amending or replacing those regulations.

(3) Those sections apply whatever the law applicable to the arbitration agreement.

90 REGULATIONS APPLY WHERE CONSUMER IS A LEGAL PERSON

The Regulations apply where the consumer is a legal person as they apply where the consumer is a natural person.

91 ARBITRATION AGREEMENT UNFAIR WHERE MODEST AMOUNT SOUGHT

(1) A term which constitutes an arbitration agreement is unfair for the purposes of the Regulations so far as it relates to a claim for a pecuniary remedy which does not exceed the amount specified by order for the purposes of this section.

. . .

108 EXTENT

(1) The provisions of this Act extend to England and Wales . . .

. . .

(3)   Sections 89, 90 and 91 (consumer arbitration agreements) extend to Scotland and the provisions of Schedules 3 and 4 (consequential amendments and repeals) extend to Scotland so far as they relate to enactments which so extend, subject as follows.

. . .

DEFAMATION ACT 1996
(C.31)

Responsibility for publication

1 RESPONSIBILITY FOR PUBLICATION

(1)   In defamation proceedings a person has a defence if he shows that—
   (a)   he was not the author, editor or publisher of the statement complained of,
   (b)   he took reasonable care in relation to its publication, and
   (c)   he did not know, and had no reason to believe, that what he did caused or contributed to the publication of a defamatory statement.

(2)   For this purpose "author", "editor" and "publisher" have the following meanings, which are further explained in subsection (3)—

"author" means the originator of the statement, but does not include a person who did not intend that his statement be published at all;

"editor" means a person having editorial or equivalent responsibility for the content of the statement or the decision to publish it; and

"publisher" means a commercial publisher, that is, a person whose business is issuing material to the public, or a section of the public, who issues material containing the statement in the course of that business.

(3)   A person shall not be considered the author, editor or publisher of a statement if he is only involved—
   (a)   in printing, producing, distributing or selling printed material containing the statement;
   (b)   in processing, making copies of, distributing, exhibiting or selling a film or sound recording (as defined in Part I of the Copyright, Designs and Patents Act 1988) containing the statement;
   (c)   in processing, making copies of, distributing or selling any electronic medium in or on which the statement is recorded, or in operating or providing any equipment, system or service by means of which the statement is retrieved, copied, distributed or made available in electronic form;
   (d)   as the broadcaster of a live programme containing the statement in circumstances in which he has no effective control over the maker of the statement;
   (e)   as the operator of or provider of access to a communications system by means of which the statement is transmitted, or made available, by a person over whom he has no effective control.
   In a case not within paragraphs (a) to (e) the court may have regard to those provisions by way of analogy in deciding whether a person is to be considered the author, editor or publisher of a statement.

(4)   Employees or agents of an author, editor or publisher are in the same position as their employer or principal to the extent that they are responsible for the content of the statement or the decision to publish it.

(5)   In determining for the purposes of this section whether a person took reasonable care, or had reason to believe that what he did caused or contributed to the publication of a defamatory statement, regard shall be had to—
   (a)   the extent of his responsibility for the content of the statement or the decision to publish it,
   (b)   the nature or circumstances of the publication, and
   (c)   the previous conduct or character of the author, editor or publisher.

(6)   This section does not apply to any cause of action which arose before the section came into force.

Offer to make amends

2 OFFER TO MAKE AMENDS

(1)   A person who has published a statement alleged to be defamatory of another may offer to make amends under this section.

(2)   The offer may be in relation to the statement generally or in relation to a specific defamatory meaning which the person making the offer accepts that the statement conveys ("a qualified offer").

(3)   An offer to make amends—
   (a)   must be in writing,
   (b)   must be expressed to be an offer to make amends under section 2 of the Defamation Act 1996, and
   (c)   must state whether it is a qualified offer and, if so, set out the defamatory meaning in relation to which it is made.

(4)   An offer to make amends under this section is an offer—
   (a)   to make a suitable correction of the statement complained of and a sufficient apology to the aggrieved party,
   (b)   to publish the correction and apology in a manner that is reasonable and practicable in the circumstances, and
   (c)   to pay to the aggrieved party such compensation (if any), and such costs, as may be agreed or determined to be payable.
   The fact that the offer is accompanied by an offer to take specific steps does not affect the fact that an offer to make amends under this section is an offer to do all the things mentioned in paragraphs (a) to (c).

(5)   An offer to make amends under this section may not be made by a person after serving a defence in defamation proceedings brought against him by the aggrieved party in respect of the publication in question.

(6)   An offer to make amends under this section may be withdrawn before it is accepted; and a renewal of an offer which has been withdrawn shall be treated as a new offer.

3 ACCEPTING AN OFFER TO MAKE AMENDS

(1)   If an offer to make amends under section 2 is accepted by the aggrieved party, the following provisions apply.

(2)   The party accepting the offer may not bring or continue defamation proceedings in respect of the publication concerned against the person making the offer, but he is entitled to enforce the offer to make amends, as follows.

(3)   If the parties agree on the steps to be taken in fulfilment of the offer, the aggrieved party may apply to the court for an order that the other party fulfil his offer by taking the steps agreed.

(4)   If the parties do not agree on the steps to be taken by way of correction, apology and publication, the party who made the offer may take such steps as he thinks appropriate, and may in particular—

(a)   make the correction and apology by a statement in open court in terms approved by the court, and

(b)   give an undertaking to the court as to the manner of their publication.

(5)   If the parties do not agree on the amount to be paid by way of compensation, it shall be determined by the court on the same principles as damages in defamation proceedings.

The court shall take account of any steps taken in fulfilment of the offer and (so far as not agreed between the parties) of the suitability of the correction, the sufficiency of the apology and whether the manner of their publication was reasonable in the circumstances, and may reduce or increase the amount of compensation accordingly.

(6)   If the parties do not agree on the amount to be paid by way of costs, it shall be determined by the court on the same principles as costs awarded in court proceedings.

(7)   The acceptance of an offer by one person to make amends does not affect any cause of action against another person in respect of the same publication, subject as follows.

(8)   In England and Wales or Northern Ireland, for the purposes of the Civil Liability (Contribution) Act 1978—

(a)   the amount of compensation paid under the offer shall be treated as paid in bona fide settlement or compromise of the claim; and

(b)   where another person is liable in respect of the same damage (whether jointly or otherwise), the person whose offer to make amends was accepted is not required to pay by virtue of any contribution under section 1 of that Act a greater amount than the amount of the compensation payable in pursuance of the offer.

(9)   In Scotland—

(a)   subsection (2) of section 3 of the Law Reform (Miscellaneous Provisions)(Scotland) Act 1940 (right of one joint wrongdoer as respects another to recover contribution towards damages) applies in relation to compensation paid under an offer to make amends as it applies in relation to damages in an action to which that section applies; and

(b)   where another person is liable in respect of the same damage (whether jointly or otherwise), the person whose offer to make amends was accepted is not required to pay by virtue of any contribution under section 3(2) of that Act a greater amount than the amount of compensation payable in pursuance of the offer.

(10)   Proceedings under this section shall be heard and determined without a jury.

4 FAILURE TO ACCEPT OFFER TO MAKE AMENDS

(1)   If an offer to make amends under section 2, duly made and not withdrawn, is not accepted by the aggrieved party, the following provisions apply.

(2)   The fact that the offer was made is a defence (subject to subsection (3)) to defamation proceedings in respect of the publication in question by that party against the person making the offer.' A qualified offer is only a defence in respect of the meaning to which the offer related.

(3)   There is no such defence if the person by whom the offer was made knew or had reason to believe that the statement complained of—
(a) referred to the aggrieved party or was likely to be understood as referring to him, and
(b) was both false and defamatory of that party;
but it shall be presumed until the contrary is shown that he did not know and had no reason to believe that was the case.

(4)   The person who made the offer need not rely on it by way of defence, but if he does he may not rely on any other defence.

If the offer was a qualified offer, this applies only in respect of the meaning to which the offer related.

(5)   The offer may be relied on in mitigation of damages whether or not it was relied on as a defence.

The meaning of a statement

7 RULING ON THE MEANING OF A STATEMENT

In defamation proceedings the court shall not be asked to rule whether a statement is arguably capable, as opposed to capable, of bearing a particular meaning or meanings attributed to it.

Summary disposal of claim

8 SUMMARY DISPOSAL OF CLAIM

(1)   In defamation proceedings the court may dispose summarily of the plaintiff's claim in accordance with the following provisions.

(2)   The court may dismiss the plaintiff's claim if it appears to the court that it has no realistic prospect of success and there is no reason why it should be tried.

(3)   The court may give judgment for the plaintiff and grant him summary relief (see section 9) if it appears to the court that there is no defence to the claim which has a realistic prospect of success, and that there is no other reason why the claim should be tried.

Unless the plaintiff asks for summary relief, the court shall not act under this subsection unless it is satisfied that summary relief will adequately compensate him for the wrong he has suffered.

(4)   In considering whether a claim should be tried the court shall have regard to—
(a) whether all the persons who are or might be defendants in respect of the publication complained of are before the court;
(b) whether summary disposal of the claim against another defendant would be inappropriate;
(c) the extent to which there is a conflict of evidence;
(d) the seriousness of the alleged wrong (as regards the content of the statement and the extent of publication); and
(e) whether it is justifiable in the circumstances to proceed to a full trial.

(5)   Proceedings under this section shall be heard and determined without a jury.

9 MEANING OF SUMMARY RELIEF

(1)   For the purposes of section 8 (summary disposal of claim) "summary relief" means such of the following as may be appropriate—

(a) a declaration that the statement was false and defamatory of the plaintiff;

(b) an order that the defendant publish or cause to be published a suitable correction and apology;

(c) damages not exceeding £10,000 or such other amount as may be prescribed by order of the Lord Chancellor;

(d) an order restraining the defendant from publishing or further publishing the matter complained of.

(2) The content of any correction and apology, and the time, manner, form and place of publication, shall be for the parties to agree.

If they cannot agree on the content, the court may direct the defendant to publish or cause to be published a summary of the court's judgment agreed by the parties or settled by the court in accordance with rules of court.

If they cannot agree on the time, manner, form or place of publication, the court may direct the defendant to take such reasonable and practicable steps as the court considers appropriate.

(2A) The Lord Chancellor must consult the Lord Chief Justice of England and Wales before making any order under subsection (1)(c) in relation to England and Wales.

(2B) The Lord Chancellor must consult the Lord Chief Justice of Northern Ireland before making any order under subsection (1)(c) in relation to Northern Ireland.

(2C) The Lord Chief Justice may nominate a judicial office holder (as defined in section 109(4) of the Constitutional Reform Act 2005) to exercise his functions under this section.

(2D) The Lord Chief Justice of Northern Ireland may nominate any of the following to exercise his functions under this section–

(a) the holder of one of the offices listed in Schedule 1 to the Justice (Northern Ireland) Act 2002;

(b) a Lord Justice of Appeal (as defined in section 88 of that Act).

(3) Any order under subsection (1)(c) shall be made by statutory instrument which shall be subject to annulment in pursuance of a resolution of either House of Parliament.

10 SUMMARY DISPOSAL: RULES OF COURT

(1) Provision may be made by rules of court as to the summary disposal of the plaintiff's claim in defamation proceedings.

(2) Without prejudice to the generality of that power, provision may be made—

(a) authorising a party to apply for summary disposal at any stage of the proceedings;

(b) authorising the court at any stage of the proceedings—

(i) to treat any application, pleading or other step in the proceedings as an application for summary disposal, or

(ii) to make an order for summary disposal without any such application;

(c) as to the time for serving pleadings or taking any other step in the proceedings in a case where there are proceedings for summary disposal;

(d) requiring the parties to identify any question of law or construction which the court is to be asked to determine in the proceedings;

(e) as to the nature of any hearing on the question of summary disposal, and in particular—

(i) authorising the court to order affidavits or witness statements to be prepared for use as evidence at the hearing, and

(ii) requiring the leave of the court for the calling of oral evidence, or the introduction of new evidence, at the hearing;

(f) authorising the court to require a defendant to elect, at or before the hearing, whether or not to make an offer to make amends under section 2.

13 EVIDENCE CONCERNING PROCEEDINGS IN PARLIAMENT

(1) Where the conduct of a person in or in relation to proceedings in Parliament is in issue in defamation proceedings, he may waive for the purposes of those proceedings, so far as concerns him, the protection of any enactment or rule of law which prevents proceedings in Parliament being impeached or questioned in any court or place out of Parliament.

(2) Where a person waives that protection—

(a) any such enactment or rule of law shall not apply to prevent evidence being given, questions being asked or statements, submissions, comments or findings being made about his conduct, and

(b) none of those things shall be regarded as infringing the privilege of either House of Parliament.

(3) The waiver by one person of that protection does not affect its operation in relation to another person who has not waived it.

(4) Nothing in this section affects any enactment or rule of law so far as it protects a person (including a person who has waived the protection referred to above) from legal liability for words spoken or things done in the course of, or for the purposes of or incidental to, any proceedings in Parliament.

(5) Without prejudice to the generality of subsection (4), that subsection applies to—

(a) the giving of evidence before either House or a committee;

(b) the presentation or submission of a document to either House or a committee;

(c) the preparation of a document for the purposes of or incidental to the transacting of any such business;

(d) the formulation, making or publication of a document, including a report, by or pursuant to an order of either House or a committee; and

(e) any communication with the Parliamentary Commissioner for Standards or any person having functions in connection with the registration of members' interests.

In this subsection "a committee" means a committee of either House or a joint committee of both Houses of Parliament.

Statutory privilege

14 REPORTS OF COURT PROCEEDINGS ABSOLUTELY PRIVILEGED

(1) A fair and accurate report of proceedings in public before a court to which this section applies, if published contemporaneously with the proceedings, is absolutely privileged.

(2) A report of proceedings which by an order of the court, or as a consequence of any statutory provision, is required to be postponed shall be treated as published contemporaneously if it is published as soon as practicable after publication is permitted.

(3) This section applies to—

(a) any court in the United Kingdom,

(b) the European Court of Justice or any court attached to that court,

(c) the European Court of Human Rights, and

(d) any international criminal tribunal established by the Security Council of the United Nations or by an international agreement to which the United Kingdom is a party.

In paragraph (a) "court" includes any tribunal or body exercising the judicial power of the State.

15 REPORTS, &C. PROTECTED BY QUALIFIED PRIVILEGE

(1)   The publication of any report or other statement mentioned in Schedule 1 to this Act is privileged unless the publication is shown to be made with malice, subject as follows.

(2)   In defamation proceedings in respect of the publication of a report or other statement mentioned in Part II of that Schedule, there is no defence under this section if the plaintiff shows that the defendant—

(a) was requested by him to publish in a suitable manner a reasonable letter or statement by way of explanation or contradiction, and

(b) refused or neglected to do so.

For this purpose "in a suitable manner" means in the same manner as the publication complained of or in a manner that is adequate and reasonable in the circumstances.

(3)   This section does not apply to the publication to the public, or a section of the public, of matter which is not of public concern and the publication of which is not for the public benefit.

(4)   Nothing in this section shall be construed—

(a) as protecting the publication of matter the publication of which is prohibited by law, or

(b) as limiting or abridging any privilege subsisting apart from this section.

Supplementary provisions

17 INTERPRETATION

(1)   In this Act—

"publication" and "publish", in relation to a statement, have the meaning they have for the purposes of the law of defamation generally, but "publisher" is specially defined for the purposes of section 1;

"statement" means words, pictures, visual images, gestures or any other method of signifying meaning; and

"statutory provision" means—

(a) a provision contained in an Act or in subordinate legislation within the meaning of the Interpretation Act 1978

(aa) a provision contained in an Act of the Scottish Parliament or in an instrument made under such an Act, or

(b) a statutory provision within the meaning given by section 1(f) of the Interpretation Act (Northern Ireland) 1954.

20 SHORT TITLE AND SAVING

(1)   This Act may be cited as the Defamation Act 1996.

SCHEDULES

SCHEDULE 1

Section 15

QUALIFIED PRIVILEGE

Part I STATEMENTS HAVING QUALIFIED PRIVILEGE WITHOUT EXPLANATION OR CONTRADICTION

1.   A fair and accurate report of proceedings in public of a legislature anywhere in the world.

2.   A fair and accurate report of proceedings in public before a court anywhere in the world.

3.   A fair and accurate report of proceedings in public of a person appointed to hold a public inquiry by a government or legislature anywhere in the world.

4.   A fair and accurate report of proceedings in public anywhere in the world of an international organisation or an international conference.

5.   A fair and accurate copy of or extract from any register or other document required by law to be open to public inspection.

6.   A notice or advertisement published by or on the authority of a court, or of a judge or officer of a court, anywhere in the world.

7.   A fair and accurate copy of or extract from matter published by or on the authority of a government or legislature anywhere in the world.

8.   A fair and accurate copy of or extract from matter published anywhere in the world by an international organisation or an international conference.

Part II STATEMENTS PRIVILEGED SUBJECT TO EXPLANATION OR CONTRADICTION

9.—(1)   A fair and accurate copy of or extract from a notice or other matter issued for the information of the public by or on behalf of—
(a)   a legislature in any member State or the European Parliament;
(b)   the government of any member State, or any authority performing governmental functions in any member State or part of a member State, or the European Commission;
(c)   an international organisation or international conference.

(2)   In this paragraph "governmental functions" includes police functions.

10.   A fair and accurate copy of or extract from a document made available by a court in any member State or the European Court of Justice (or any court attached to that court), or by a judge or officer of any such court.

11.—(1)   A fair and accurate report of proceedings at any public meeting or sitting in the United Kingdom of—
(a)   a local authority, local authority committee;
(aa) in the case of a local authority which are operating executive arrangements the executive of that authority or a committee of that executive;
(b)   a justice or justices of the peace acting otherwise than as a court exercising judicial authority;
(c)   a commission, tribunal, committee or person appointed for the purposes of any inquiry by any statutory provision, by Her Majesty or by a Minister of the

Crown, a member of the Scottish Executive, the Welsh Ministers or the Counsel General to the Welsh Assembly Government or a Northern Ireland Department;

(d) a person appointed by a local authority to hold a local inquiry in pursuance of any statutory provision;

(e) any other tribunal, board, committee or body constituted by or under, and exercising functions under, any statutory provision.

(1A) In the case of a local authority which are operating executive arrangements, a fair and accurate record of any decision made by any member of the executive where that record is required to be made and available for public inspection by virtue of section 22 of the Local Government Act 2000 or of any provision in regulations made under that section.

(2) In sub-paragraphs (1)(a), (1)(aa) and (1A)—

"local authority" means—

(a) in relation to England and Wales, a principal council within the meaning of the Local Government Act 1972, any body falling within any paragraph of section 100J(1) of that Act or an authority or body to which the Public Bodies (Admission to Meetings) Act 1960 applies,

(b) in relation to Scotland, a council constituted under section 2 of the Local Government etc. (Scotland) Act 1994 or an authority or body to which the Public Bodies (Admission to Meetings) Act 1960 applies,

(c) in relation to Northern Ireland, any authority or body to which sections 23 to 27 of the Local Government Act (Northern Ireland) 1972 apply; and

"local authority committee" means any committee of a local authority or of local authorities, and includes—

(a) any committee or sub-committee in relation to which sections 100A to 100D of the Local Government Act 1972 apply by virtue of section 100E of that Act (whether or not also by virtue of section 100J of that Act), and

(b) any committee or sub-committee in relation to which sections 50A to 50D of the Local Government (Scotland) Act 1973 apply by virtue of section 50E of that Act.

(2A) In sub-paragraphs (1) and (1A)—

"executive" and "executive arrangements" have the same meaning as in Part II of the Local Government Act 2000.

(3) A fair and accurate report of any corresponding proceedings in any of the Channel Islands or the Isle of Man or in another member State.

11. (Scotland and Wales)

(1) A fair and accurate report of proceedings at any public meeting or sitting in the United Kingdom of—

(a) a local authority, local authority committee or in the case of a local authority which are operating executive arrangements the executive of that authority or a committee of that executive;

(b) a justice or justices of the peace acting otherwise than as a court exercising judicial authority;

(c) a commission, tribunal, committee or person appointed for the purposes of any inquiry by any statutory provision, by Her Majesty or by a Minister of the Crown, a member of the Scottish Executive,] the Welsh Ministers or the Counsel General to the Welsh Assembly Government,or a Northern Ireland Department;

(d) a person appointed by a local authority to hold a local inquiry in pursuance of any statutory provision;

(e) any other tribunal, board, committee or body constituted by or under, and exercising functions under, any statutory provision.

(1A) In the case of a local authority which are operating executive arrangements, a fair and accurate record of any decision made by any member of the executive where that record is required to be made and available for public inspection by virtue of section 22 of the Local Government Act 2000 or of any provision in regulations made under that section.

(2) [In sub-paragraphs (1)(a) and (1A)] 1 —

"executive" and "executive arrangements" have the same meaning as in Part II of the Local Government Act 2000;

"local authority" means —
(a) in relation to England and Wales, a principal council within the meaning of the Local Government Act 1972, any body falling within any paragraph of section 100J(1) of that Act or an authority or body to which the Public Bodies (Admission to Meetings) Act 1960 applies,
(b) in relation to Scotland, a council constituted under section 2 of the Local Government etc. (Scotland) Act 1994 or an authority or body to which the Public Bodies (Admission to Meetings) Act 1960 applies,
(c) in relation to Northern Ireland, any authority or body to which sections 23 to 27 of the Local Government Act (Northern Ireland) 1972 apply; and

"local authority committee" means any committee of a local authority or of local authorities, and includes—
(a) any committee or sub-committee in relation to which sections 100A to 100D of the Local Government Act 1972 apply by virtue of section 100E of that Act (whether or not also by virtue of section 100J of that Act), and
(b) any committee or sub-committee in relation to which sections 50A to 50D of the Local Government (Scotland) Act 1973 apply by virtue of section 50E of that Act.

(3) A fair and accurate report of any corresponding proceedings in any of the Channel Islands or the Isle of Man or in another member State.

12.—(1) A fair and accurate report of proceedings at any public meeting held in a member State.

(2) In this paragraph a "public meeting" means a meeting bona fide and lawfully held for a lawful purpose and for the furtherance or discussion of a matter of public concern, whether admission to the meeting is general or restricted.

13.—(1) A fair and accurate report of proceedings at a general meeting of a UK public company.

(2) A fair and accurate copy of or extract from any document circulated to members of a UK public company—
(a) by or with the authority of the board of directors of the company,
(b) by the auditors of the company, or
(c) by any member of the company in pursuance of a right conferred by any statutory provision.

(3) A fair and accurate copy of or extract from any document circulated to members of a UK public company which relates to the appointment, resignation, retirement or dismissal of directors of the company.

(4) In this paragraph "UK public company" means—
   (a) a public company within the meaning of section 4(2) of the Companies Act 2006, or
   (b) a body corporate incorporated by or registered under any other statutory provision, or by Royal Charter, or formed in pursuance of letters patent.

(5) A fair and accurate report of proceedings at any corresponding meeting of, or copy of or extract from any corresponding document circulated to members of, a public company formed under the law of any of the Channel Islands or the Isle of Man or of another member State.

14.   A fair and accurate report of any finding or decision of any of the following descriptions of association, formed in the United Kingdom or another member State, or of any committee or governing body of such an association—
   (a) an association formed for the purpose of promoting or encouraging the exercise of or interest in any art, science, religion or learning, and empowered by its constitution to exercise control over or adjudicate on matters of interest or concern to the association, or the actions or conduct of any person subject to such control or adjudication;
   (b) an association formed for the purpose of promoting or safeguarding the interests of any trade, business, industry or profession, or of the persons carrying on or engaged in any trade, business, industry or profession, and empowered by its constitution to exercise control over or adjudicate upon matters connected with that trade, business, industry or profession, or the actions or conduct of those persons;
   (c) an association formed for the purpose of promoting or safeguarding the interests of a game, sport or pastime to the playing or exercise of which members of the public are invited or admitted, and empowered by its constitution to exercise control over or adjudicate upon persons connected with or taking part in the game, sport or pastime;
   (d) an association formed for the purpose of promoting charitable objects or other objects beneficial to the community and empowered by its constitution to exercise control over or to adjudicate on matters of interest or concern to the association, or the actions or conduct of any person subject to such control or adjudication.

15.—(1) A fair and accurate report of, or copy of or extract from, any adjudication, report, statement or notice issued by a body, officer or other person designated for the purposes of this paragraph—
   (a) for England and Wales by order of the Lord Chancellor, and
   (b) for Scotland, by order of the Secretary of State, and
   (c) for Northern Ireland, by order of the Department of Justice in Northern Ireland.

(2) An order under this paragraph shall be made by statutory instrument which shall be subject to annulment in pursuance of a resolution of either House of Parliament.

Part III SUPPLEMENTARY PROVISIONS
16.—(1) In this Schedule—

"court" includes any tribunal or body exercising the judicial power of the State;

"international conference" means a conference attended by representatives of two or more governments;

"international organisation" means an organisation of which two or more governments are members, and includes any committee or other subordinate body of such an organisation; and

"legislature" includes a local legislature.

(2) References in this Schedule to a member State include any European dependent territory of a member State.

(3) In paragraphs 2 and 6 "court" includes—
  (a) the European Court of Justice (or any court attached to that court) and the Court of Auditors of the European Communities,
  (b) the European Court of Human Rights,
  (c) any international criminal tribunal established by the Security Council of the United Nations or by an international agreement to which the United Kingdom is a party, and
  (d) the International Court of Justice and any other judicial or arbitral tribunal deciding matters in dispute between States.

(4) In paragraphs 1, 3 and 7 "legislature" includes the European Parliament.

17.—(1) Provision may be made by order identifying—
  (a) for the purposes of paragraph 11, the corresponding proceedings referred to in sub-paragraph (3);
  (b) for the purposes of paragraph 13, the corresponding meetings and documents referred to in sub-paragraph (5).

(2) An order under this paragraph may be made—
  (a) for England and Wales by the Lord Chancellor, and
  (b) for Scotland, by the Secretary of State, and
  (c) for Northern Ireland, by the Department of Justice in Northern Ireland.

(3) An order under this paragraph shall be made by statutory instrument which shall be subject to annulment in pursuance of a resolution of either House of Parliament.

DAMAGES ACT 1996
(c.48)

1 ASSUMED RATE OF RETURN ON INVESTMENT OF DAMAGES

(1) In determining the return to be expected from the investment of a sum awarded as damages for future pecuniary loss in an action for personal injury the court shall, subject to and in accordance with rules of court made for the purposes of this section, take into account such rate of return (if any) as may from time to time be prescribed by an order made by the Lord Chancellor.

(2) Subsection (1) above shall not however prevent the court taking a different rate of return into account if any party to the proceedings shows that it is more appropriate in the case in question.

(3) An order under subsection (1) above may prescribe different rates of return for different classes of case.

(4) Before making an order under subsection (1) above the Lord Chancellor shall consult the Government Actuary and the Treasury; and any order under that subsection shall be made by statutory instrument subject to annulment in pursuance of a resolution of either House of Parliament.

(5) In the application of this section to Scotland—
  (a) for the reference to the Lord Chancellor in subsections (1) and (4) there is substituted a reference to the Scottish Ministers; and

(b) in subsection (4)—
    (i) "and the Treasury" is omitted; and
    (ii) for "either House of Parliament" there is substituted "the Scottish Parliament".

2 PERIODICAL PAYMENTS (ENGLAND AND WALES)

(A1) In cases where Regulation (EC) No. 1371/2007 of the European Parliament and of the Council of 23rd October 2007 on rail passengers' rights and obligations applies, this section needs to be read in the light of Article 30 of the Uniform Rules concerning the contract for the international carriage of passengers and luggage by rail (damages to be awarded as annuity on request), as set out in Annex I to that Regulation.

(1) A court awarding damages for future pecuniary loss in respect of personal injury–
    (a) may order that the damages are wholly or partly to take the form of periodical payments, and
    (b) shall consider whether to make that order.

(2) A court awarding other damages in respect of personal injury may, if the parties consent, order that the damages are wholly or partly to take the form of periodical payments.

(3) A court may not make an order for periodical payments unless satisfied that the continuity of payment under the order is reasonably secure.

(4) For the purpose of subsection (3) the continuity of payment under an order is reasonably secure if–
    (a) it is protected by a guarantee given under section 6 of or the Schedule to this Act,
    (b) it is protected by a scheme under section 213 of the Financial Services and Markets Act 2000 (compensation) (whether or not as modified by section 4 of this Act), or
    (c) the source of payment is a government or health service body.

(5) An order for periodical payments may include provision–
    (a) requiring the party responsible for the payments to use a method (selected or to be selected by him) under which the continuity of payment is reasonably secure by virtue of subsection (4);
    (b) about how the payments are to be made, if not by a method under which the continuity of payment is reasonably secure by virtue of subsection (4);
    (c) requiring the party responsible for the payments to take specified action to secure continuity of payment, where continuity is not reasonably secure by virtue of subsection (4);
    (d) enabling a party to apply for a variation of provision included under paragraph (a), (b) or (c).

(6) Where a person has a right to receive payments under an order for periodical payments, or where an arrangement is entered into in satisfaction of an order which gives a person a right to receive periodical payments, that person's right under the order or arrangement may not be assigned or charged without the approval of the court which made the order; and–
    (a) a court shall not approve an assignment or charge unless satisfied that special circumstances make it necessary, and
    (b) a purported assignment or charge, or agreement to assign or charge, is void unless approved by the court.

(7) Where an order is made for periodical payments, an alteration of the method by which the payments are made shall be treated as a breach of the order (whether or not the method was specified under subsection (5)(b)) unless–

(a) the court which made the order declares its satisfaction that the continuity of payment under the new method is reasonably secure,

(b) the new method is protected by a guarantee given under section 6 of or the Schedule to this Act,

(c) the new method is protected by a scheme under section 213 of the Financial Services and Markets Act 2000 (compensation) (whether or not as modified by section 4 of this Act), or

(d) the source of payment under the new method is a government or health service body.

(8) An order for periodical payments shall be treated as providing for the amount of payments to vary by reference to the retail prices index (within the meaning of section 833(2) of the Income and Corporation Taxes Act 1988) at such times, and in such a manner, as may be determined by or in accordance with Civil Procedure Rules.

(9) But an order for periodical payments may include provision–
(a) disapplying subsection (8), or
(b) modifying the effect of subsection (8).

2 PEROIDCAL PAYMENTS (SCOTLAND)

(A1) In cases where Regulation (EC) No. 1371/2007 of the European Parliament and of the Council of 23rd October 2007 on rail passengers' rights and obligations applies, this section needs to be read in the light of Article 30 of the Uniform Rules concerning the contract for the international carriage of passengers and luggage by rail (damages to be awarded as annuity on request), as set out in Annex I to that Regulation.

(1) A court awarding damages in an action for personal injury may, with the consent of the parties, make an order under which the damages are wholly or partly to take the form of periodical payments.

(2) In this section "damages" includes an interim payment which the court, by virtue of rules of court in that behalf, orders the defendant to make to the plaintiff (or, in the application of this section to Scotland, the defender to make to the pursuer).

(3) This section is without prejudice to any powers exerciseable apart from this section.

2A PERIODICAL PAYMENTS: SUPPLEMENTARY

(1) Civil Procedure Rules may require a court to take specified matters into account in considering—
(a) whether to order periodical payments;
(b) the security of the continuity of payment;
(c) whether to approve an assignment or charge.

(2) For the purposes of section 2(4)(c) and (7)(d) "government or health service body" means a body designated as a government body or a health service body by order made by the Lord Chancellor.

(3) An order under subsection (2)—
(a) shall be made by statutory instrument, and
(b) shall be subject to annulment in pursuance of a resolution of either House of Parliament.

(4) Section 2(6) is without prejudice to a person's power to assign a right to the scheme manager established under section 212 of the Financial Services and Markets Act 2000.

(5)   In section 2 "damages" includes an interim payment which a court orders a defendant to make to a claimant.

(6)   In the application of this section to Northern Ireland—
    (a)   a reference to Civil Procedure Rules shall be taken as a reference to rules of court, and
    (b)   a reference to a claimant shall be taken as a reference to a plaintiff.

(7)   Section 2 is without prejudice to any power exercisable apart from that section.

2B   VARIATION OF ORDERS AND SETTLEMENTS

(1)   The Lord Chancellor may by order enable a court which has made an order for periodical payments to vary the order in specified circumstances (otherwise than in accordance with section 2(5)(d)).

(2)   The Lord Chancellor may by order enable a court in specified circumstances to vary the terms on which a claim or action for damages for personal injury is settled by agreement between the parties if the agreement—
    (a)   provides for periodical payments, and
    (b)   expressly permits a party to apply to a court for variation in those circumstances.

(3)   An order under this section may make provision—
    (a)   which operates wholly or partly by reference to a condition or other term of the court's order or of the agreement;
    (b)   about the nature of an order which may be made by a court on a variation;
    (c)   about the matters to be taken into account on considering variation;
    (d)   of a kind that could be made by Civil Procedure Rules or, in relation to Northern Ireland, rules of court (and which may be expressed to be with or without prejudice to the power to make those rules).

(4)   An order under this section may apply (with or without modification) or amend an enactment about provisional or further damages.

(5)   An order under this section shall be subject to any order under section 1 of the Courts and Legal Services Act 1990 (allocation between High Court and county courts).

(6)   An order under this section—
    (a)   shall be made by statutory instrument,
    (b)   may not be made unless the Lord Chancellor has consulted such persons as he thinks appropriate,
    (c)   may not be made unless a draft has been laid before and approved by resolution of each House of Parliament, and
    (d)   may include transitional, consequential or incidental provision.

(7)   In subsection (4)—

"provisional damages" means damages awarded by virtue of subsection (2)(a) of section 32A of the Senior Courts Act 1981 or section 51 of the County Courts Act 1984 (or, in relation to Northern Ireland, paragraph 10(2)(a) of Schedule 6 to the Administration of Justice Act 1982), and

"further damages" means damages awarded by virtue of subsection (2)(b) of either of those sections (or, in relation to Northern Ireland, paragraph 10(2)(b) of Schedule 6 to the Administration of Justice Act 1982).

3 PROVISIONAL DAMAGES AND FATAL ACCIDENT CLAIMS

(1)   This section applies where a person—
    (a)   is awarded provisional damages; and
    (b)   subsequently dies as a result of the act or omission which gave rise to the cause of action for which the damages were awarded.

(2)   The award of the provisional damages shall not operate as a bar to an action in respect of that person's death under the Fatal Accidents Act 1976.

(3)   Such part (if any) of—
    (a)   the provisional damages; and
    (b)   any further damages awarded to the person in question before his death,
    as was intended to compensate him for pecuniary loss in a period which in the event falls after his death shall be taken into account in assessing the amount of any loss of support suffered by the person or persons for whose benefit the action under the Fatal Accidents Act 1976 is brought.

(4)   No award of further damages made in respect of that person after his death shall include any amount for loss of income in respect of any period after his death.

(5)   In this section "provisional damages" means damages awarded by virtue of subsection (2) (a) of section 32A of the Senior Courts Act 1981 or section 51 of the County Courts Act 1984 and "further damages" means damages awarded by virtue of subsection (2)(b) of either of those sections.

(6)   Subsection (2) above applies whether the award of provisional damages was before or after the coming into force of that subsection; and subsections (3) and (4) apply to any award of damages under the 1976 Act or, as the case may be, further damages after the coming into force of those subsections.

(7)   In the application of this section to Northern Ireland—
    (a)   for references to the Fatal Accidents Act 1976 there shall be substituted references to the Fatal Accidents (Northern Ireland) Order 1977;
    (b)   for the reference to subsection (2)(a) and (b) of section 32A of the Senior Courts Act 1981 and section 51 of the County Courts Act 1984 there shall be substituted a reference to paragraph 10(2)(a) and (b) of Schedule 6 to the Administration of Justice Act 1982.

4 ENHANCED PROTECTION FOR PERIODICAL PAYMENTS

(1)   Subsection (2) applies where—
    (a)   a person has a right to receive periodical payments, and
    (b)   his right is protected by a scheme under section 213 of the Financial Services and Markets Act 2000 (compensation), but only as to part of the payments.

(2)   The protection provided by the scheme shall extend by virtue of this section to the whole of the payments.

(3)   Subsection (4) applies where—
    (a)   one person ("the claimant") has a right to receive periodical payments from another person ("the defendant"),
    (b)   a third person ("the insurer") is required by or in pursuance of an arrangement entered into with the defendant (whether or not together with other persons and whether before or after the creation of the claimant's right) to make payments in satisfaction of the claimant's right or for the purpose of enabling it to be satisfied, and

(c) the claimant's right to receive the payments would be wholly or partly protected by a scheme under section 213 of the Financial Services and Markets Act 2000 if it arose from an arrangement of the same kind as that mentioned in paragraph (b) but made between the claimant and the insurer.

(4) For the purposes of the scheme under section 213 of that Act—
(a) the claimant shall be treated as having a right to receive the payments from the insurer under an arrangement of the same kind as that mentioned in subsection (3)(b),
(b) the protection under the scheme in respect of those payments shall extend by virtue of this section to the whole of the payments, and
(c) no person other than the claimant shall be entitled to protection under the scheme in respect of the payments.

(5) In this section "periodical payments" means periodical payments made pursuant to—
(a) an order of a court in so far as it is made in reliance on section 2 above (including an order as varied), or
(b) an agreement in so far as it settles a claim or action for damages in respect of personal injury (including an agreement as varied).

(6) In subsection (5)(b) the reference to an agreement in so far as it settles a claim or action for damages in respect of personal injury includes a reference to an undertaking given by the Motor Insurers' Bureau (being the company of that name incorporated on 14th June 1946 under the Companies Act 1929), or an Article 75 insurer under the Bureau's Articles of Association, in relation to a claim or action in respect of personal injury.

6 GUARANTEES FOR PUBLIC SECTOR SETTLEMENTS

(1) This section applies where—
(a) a claim or action for damages for personal injury is settled on terms corresponding to those of a structured settlement as defined in section 5 above except that the person to whom the payments are to be made is not to receive them as mentioned in subsection (1)(b) of that section; or
(b) a court awarding damages for personal injury makes an order incorporating such terms.

(2) If it appears to a Minister of the Crown that the payments are to be made by a body in relation to which he has, by virtue of this section, power to do so, he may guarantee the payments to be made under the agreement or order.

(3) The bodies in relation to which a Minister may give such a guarantee shall, subject to subsection (4) below, be such bodies as are designated in relation to the relevant government department by guidelines agreed upon between that department and the Treasury.

(4) A guarantee purporting to be given by a Minister under this section shall not be invalidated by any failure on his part to act in accordance with such guidelines as are mentioned in subsection (3) above.

(5) A guarantee under this section shall be given on such terms as the Minister concerned may determine but those terms shall in every case require the body in question to reimburse the Minister, with interest, for any sums paid by him in fulfilment of the guarantee.

(6) Any sums required by a Minister for fulfilling a guarantee under this section shall be defrayed out of money provided by Parliament and any sums received by him by way of reimbursement or interest shall be paid into the Consolidated Fund.

(7)   A Minister who has given one or more guarantees under this section shall, as soon as possible after the end of each financial year, lay before each House of Parliament a statement showing what liabilities are outstanding in respect of the guarantees in that year, what sums have been paid in that year in fulfilment of the guarantees and what sums (including interest) have been recovered in that year in respect of the guarantees or are still owing.

(8)   In this section "government department" means any department of Her Majesty's government in the United Kingdom and for the purposes of this section a government department is a relevant department in relation to a Minister if he has responsibilities in respect of that department.

(8A)   In the application of subsection (3) above to Scotland, for the words from "guidelines" to the end there shall be substituted "the Minister".

(8B)   In the application of this section to Scotland, "relevant government department" shall be read as if it was a reference to any part of the Scottish Administration and subsection (8) shall cease to have effect.

(9)   The Schedule to this Act has effect for conferring corresponding powers on Northern Ireland departments.

7 INTERPRETATION

(1)   Subject to subsection (2) below, in this Act "personal injury" includes any disease and any impairment of a person's physical or mental condition and references to a claim or action for personal injury include references to such a claim or action brought by virtue of the Law Reform (Miscellaneous Provisions) Act 1934 and to a claim or action brought by virtue of the Fatal Accidents Act 1976.

(2)   In the application of this Act to Scotland "personal injury" has the same meaning as in the Damages (Scotland) Act 2011.

(3)   In the application of subsection (1) above to Northern Ireland for the references to the Law Reform (Miscellaneous Provisions) Act 1934 and to the Fatal Accidents Act 1976 there shall be substituted respectively references to the Law Reform (Miscellaneous Provisions) Act (Northern Ireland) 1937 and the Fatal Accidents (Northern Ireland) Order 1977.

8 SHORT TITLE, EXTENT AND COMMENCEMENT

(2)   Section 3 does not extend to Scotland but, subject to that, this Act extends to the whole of the United Kingdom.

EDUCATION ACT 1996
(c.56)

550ZA POWER OF MEMBERS OF STAFF TO SEARCH PUPILS FOR PROHIBITED ITEMS: ENGLAND

(1)   This section applies where a member of staff of a school in England—
    (a) has reasonable grounds for suspecting that a pupil at the school may have a prohibited item with him or her or in his or her possessions; and
    (b) falls within section 550ZB(1).

(2)   The member of staff may search the pupil ("P") or P's possessions for that item.

(3)   For the purposes of this section and section 550ZC each of the following is a "prohibited item"—
   (a)   an article to which section 139 of the Criminal Justice Act 1988 applies (knives and blades etc);
   (b)   an offensive weapon, within the meaning of the Prevention of Crime Act 1953;
   (c)   alcohol, within the meaning of section 191 of the Licensing Act 2003;
   (d)   a controlled drug, within the meaning of section 2 of the Misuse of Drugs Act 1971, which section 5(1) of that Act makes it unlawful for P to have in P's possession;
   (e)   a stolen article;
   (ea)   an article that the member of staff reasonably suspects has been, or is likely to be, used—
      (i)   to commit an offence, or
      (ii)   to cause personal injury to, or damage to the property of, any person (including P);
   (f)   an article of a kind specified in regulations.
   (g)   any other item which the school rules identify as an item for which a search may be made.

550ZB POWER OF SEARCH UNDER SECTION 550ZA: SUPPLEMENTARY

(1)   A person may carry out a search under section 550ZA only if that person—
   (a)   is the head teacher of the school; or
   (b)   has been authorised by the head teacher to carry out the search.

(2)   An authorisation for the purposes of subsection (1)(b) may be given in relation to—
   (a)   searches under section 550ZA generally;
   (b)   a particular search under that section;
   (c)   a particular description of searches under that section.

(3)   Nothing in any enactment, instrument or agreement shall be construed as authorising a head teacher of a school in England to require a person other than a member of the security staff of the school to carry out a search under section 550ZA.

(4)   A search under section 550ZA may be carried out only where—
   (a)   the member of staff and P are on the premises of the school; or
   (b)   they are elsewhere and the member of staff has lawful control or charge of P.

(5)   A person exercising the power in to search for an item within section 550ZA(3)(a) to (f) may use such force as is reasonable in the circumstances for exercising that power.

(6)   A person carrying out a search of P under section 550ZA—
   (a)   may not require P to remove any clothing other than outer clothing;
   (b)   must be of the same sex as P, unless the condition in subsection (6A) is satisfied;

550ZC POWER TO SEIZE ITEMS FOUND DURING SEARCH UNDER SECTION 550ZA

(1)   A person carrying out a search under section 550ZA may seize any of the following found in the course of the search—
   (a)   anything which that person has reasonable grounds for suspecting is a prohibited item;
   (b)   any other thing which that person has reasonable grounds for suspecting is evidence in relation to an offence.

(2)   A person exercising the power in subsection (1) to seize an item within section 550ZA(3) (a) to (f) or anything within subsection (1)(b)may use such force as is reasonable in the circumstances for exercising that power.

SOCIAL SECURITY (RECOVERY OF BENEFITS) ACT 1997
(c.27)

Introductory

1 CASES IN WHICH THIS ACT APPLIES

(1)   This Act applies in cases where—
   (a)   a person makes a payment (whether on his own behalf or not) to or in respect of any other person in consequence of any accident, injury or disease suffered by the other, and
   (b)   any listed benefits have been, or are likely to be, paid to or for the other during the relevant period in respect of the accident, injury or disease.

(2)   The reference above to a payment in consequence of any accident, injury or disease is to a payment made—
   (a)   by or on behalf of a person who is, or is alleged to be, liable to any extent in respect of the accident, injury or disease, or
   (b)   in pursuance of a compensation scheme for motor accidents;
but does not include a payment mentioned in Part I of Schedule 1.

(3)   Subsection (1)(a) applies to a payment made—
   (a)   voluntarily, or in pursuance of a court order or an agreement, or otherwise, and
   (b)   in the United Kingdom or elsewhere.

(4)   In a case where this Act applies—
   (a)   the "injured person" is the person who suffered the accident, injury or disease,
   (b)   the "compensation payment" is the payment within subsection (1)(a), and
   (c)   "recoverable benefit" is any listed benefit which has been or is likely to be paid as mentioned in subsection (1)(b).

1A LUMP SUM PAYMENTS: REGULATION-MAKING POWER

(1)   The Secretary of State may by regulations make provision about the recovery of the amount of a payment to which subsection (2) applies (a "lump sum payment") where—
   (a)   a compensation payment in consequence of a disease is made to or in respect of a person ("P") to whom, or in respect of whom, a lump sum payment has been, or is likely to be, made, and
   (b)   the compensation payment is made in consequence of the same disease as the lump sum payment.

(2)   This subsection applies to—
   (a)   a payment made in accordance with the Pneumoconiosis etc. (Workers' Compensation) Act 1979 ("the 1979 Act"),
   (b)   a payment made in accordance with Part 4 of the Child Maintenance and Other Payments Act 2008, and
   (c)   an extra-statutory payment (within the meaning given by subsection (5)(d) below).

(3)   Regulations under this section may, in particular—

    (a) make provision about the recovery of the amount of a lump sum payment made to or in respect of a dependant of P;

    (b) make provision enabling the recovery of the amount of a lump sum payment from a compensation payment (including provision enabling the recovery of an amount which reduces the compensation payment to nil);

    (c) enable the amount of a lump sum payment made before commencement to be recovered from a compensation payment made after commencement;

    (d) make provision about certificates in respect of lump sum payments;

    (e) apply any provision of this Act, with or without modifications.

(4)   References in subsection (1) to a payment made in consequence of a disease—

    (a) are references to a payment made by or on behalf of a person who is, or is alleged to be, liable to any extent in respect of the disease, but

    (b) do not include references to a payment mentioned in Part 1 of Schedule 1.

(5)   In this section—

    (a) "commencement" means the date on which this section comes into force,

    (b) "compensation payment" means a payment within section 1(1)(a) above,

    (c) "dependant" has the meaning given by section 3 of the 1979 Act, and

    (d) "extra-statutory payment" means a payment made by the Secretary of State to or in respect of a person following the rejection by the Secretary of State of a claim under the 1979 Act.

2 COMPENSATION PAYMENTS TO WHICH THIS ACT APPLIES

This Act applies in relation to compensation payments made on or after the day on which this section comes into force, unless they are made in pursuance of a court order or agreement made before that day.

3 "THE RELEVANT PERIOD"

(1)   In relation to a person ("the claimant") who has suffered any accident, injury or disease, "the relevant period" has the meaning given by the following subsections.

(2)   Subject to subsection (4), if it is a case of accident or injury, the relevant period is the period of five years immediately following the day on which the accident or injury in question occurred.

(3)   Subject to subsection (4), if it is a case of disease, the relevant period is the period of five years beginning with the date on which the claimant first claims a listed benefit in consequence of the disease.

(4)   If at any time before the end of the period referred to in subsection (2) or (3)—

    (a) a person makes a compensation payment in final discharge of any claim made by or in respect of the claimant and arising out of the accident, injury or disease, or

    (b) an agreement is made under which an earlier compensation payment is treated as having been made in final discharge of any such claim,

the relevant period ends at that time.

Certificates of recoverable benefits

4 APPLICATIONS FOR CERTIFICATES OF RECOVERABLE BENEFITS

(1)   Before a person ("the compensator") makes a compensation payment he must apply to the Secretary of State for a certificate of recoverable benefits.

5 INFORMATION CONTAINED IN CERTIFICATES

(1)   A certificate of recoverable benefits must specify, for each recoverable benefit—
    (a) the amount which has been or is likely to have been paid on or before a specified date, and
    (b) if the benefit is paid or likely to be paid after the specified date, the rate and period for which, and the intervals at which, it is or is likely to be so paid.

(2)   In a case where the relevant period has ended before the day on which the Secretary of State receives the application for the certificate, the date specified in the certificate for the purposes of subsection (1) must be the day on which the relevant period ended.

(3)   In any other case, the date specified for those purposes must not be earlier than the day on which the Secretary of State received the application.

(4)   The Secretary of State may estimate, in such manner as he thinks fit, any of the amounts, rates or periods specified in the certificate.

(5)   Where the Secretary of State issues a certificate of recoverable benefits, he must provide the information contained in the certificate to—
    (a) the person who appears to him to be the injured person, or
    (b) any person who he thinks will receive a compensation payment in respect of the injured person.

(6)   A person to whom a certificate of recoverable benefits is issued or who is provided with information under subsection (5) is entitled to particulars of the manner in which any amount, rate or period specified in the certificate has been determined, if he applies to the Secretary of State for those particulars.

Liability of person paying compensation

6 LIABILITY TO PAY SECRETARY OF STATE AMOUNT OF BENEFITS

(1)   A person who makes a compensation payment in any case is liable to pay to the Secretary of State an amount equal to the total amount of the recoverable benefits.

(2)   The liability referred to in subsection (1) arises immediately before the compensation payment or, if there is more than one, the first of them is made.

(3)   No amount becomes payable under this section before the end of the period of 14 days following the day on which the liability arises.

(4)   Subject to subsection (3), an amount becomes payable under this section at the end of the period of 14 days beginning with the day on which a certificate of recoverable benefits is first issued showing that the amount of recoverable benefit to which it relates has been or is likely to have been paid before a specified date.

7 RECOVERY OF PAYMENTS DUE UNDER SECTION 6

(1)   This section applies where a person has made a compensation payment but—
    (a) has not applied for a certificate of recoverable benefits, or
    (b) has not made a payment to the Secretary of State under section 6 before the end of the period allowed under that section.

(2)   The Secretary of State may—
    (a) issue the person who made the compensation payment with a certificate of recoverable benefits, if none has been issued, or

(b) issue him with a copy of the certificate of recoverable benefits or (if more than one has been issued) the most recent one,

and (in either case) issue him with a demand that payment of any amount due under section 6 be made immediately.

(3) The Secretary of State may, in accordance with subsections (4) and (5), recover the amount for which a demand for payment is made under subsection (2) from the person who made the compensation payment.

(4) If the person who made the compensation payment resides or carries on business in England and Wales and a county court so orders, any amount recoverable under subsection (3) is recoverable under section 85 of the County Courts Act 1984 or otherwise as if it were payable under an order of that court.

(5) If the person who made the payment resides or carries on business in Scotland, any amount recoverable under subsection (3) may be enforced in like manner as an extract registered decree arbitral bearing a warrant for execution issued by the sheriff court of any sheriffdom in Scotland.

(6) A document bearing a certificate which—
(a) is signed by a person authorised to do so by the Secretary of State, and
(b) states that the document, apart from the certificate, is a record of the amount recoverable under subsection (3),
is conclusive evidence that that amount is so recoverable.

(7) A certificate under subsection (6) purporting to be signed by a person authorised to do so by the Secretary of State is to be treated as so signed unless the contrary is proved.

Reduction of compensation payment

8 REDUCTION OF COMPENSATION PAYMENT

(1) This section applies in a case where, in relation to any head of compensation listed in column 1 of Schedule 2—
(a) any of the compensation payment is attributable to that head, and
(b) any recoverable benefit is shown against that head in column 2 of the Schedule.

(2) In such a case, any claim of a person to receive the compensation payment is to be treated for all purposes as discharged if—
(a) he is paid the amount (if any) of the compensation payment calculated in accordance with this section, and
(b) if the amount of the compensation payment so calculated is nil, he is given a statement saying so by the person who (apart from this section) would have paid the gross amount of the compensation payment.

(3) For each head of compensation listed in column 1 of the Schedule for which paragraphs (a) and (b) of subsection (1) are met, so much of the gross amount of the compensation payment as is attributable to that head is to be reduced (to nil, if necessary) by deducting the amount of the recoverable benefit or, as the case may be, the aggregate amount of the recoverable benefits shown against it.

(4) Subsection (3) is to have effect as if a requirement to reduce a payment by deducting an amount which exceeds that payment were a requirement to reduce that payment to nil.

(5) The amount of the compensation payment calculated in accordance with this section is—
(a) the gross amount of the compensation payment,
less

(b) the sum of the reductions made under subsection (3),
(and, accordingly, the amount may be nil).

9 SECTION 8: SUPPLEMENTARY

(1)   A person who makes a compensation payment calculated in accordance with section 8 must inform the person to whom the payment is made—
(a)   that the payment has been so calculated, and
(b)   of the date for payment by reference to which the calculation has been made.

(2)   If the amount of a compensation payment calculated in accordance with section 8 is nil, a person giving a statement saying so is to be treated for the purposes of this Act as making a payment within section 1(1)(a) on the day on which he gives the statement.

(3)   Where a person—
(a)   makes a compensation payment calculated in accordance with section 8, and
(b)   if the amount of the compensation payment so calculated is nil, gives a statement saying so,
he is to be treated, for the purpose of determining any rights and liabilities in respect of contribution or indemnity, as having paid the gross amount of the compensation payment.

(4)   For the purposes of this Act—
(a)   the gross amount of the compensation payment is the amount of the compensation payment apart from section 8, and
(b)   the amount of any recoverable benefit is the amount determined in accordance with the certificate of recoverable benefits.

Reviews and appeals

10 REVIEW OF CERTIFICATES OF RECOVERABLE BENEFITS

(1)   Any certificate of recoverable benefits may be reviewed by the Secretary of State—
(a)   either within the prescribed period or in prescribed cases or circumstances; and
(b)   either on an application made for the purpose or on his own initiative.

(2)   On a review under this section the Secretary of State may either—
(a)   confirm the certificate, or
(b)   (subject to subsection (3)) issue a fresh certificate containing such variations as he considers appropriate or
(c)   revoke the certificate.

(3)   The Secretary of State may not vary the certificate so as to increase the total amount of the recoverable benefits unless it appears to him that the variation is required as a result of the person who applied for the certificate supplying him with incorrect or insufficient information.

11 APPEALS AGAINST CERTIFICATES OF RECOVERABLE BENEFITS

(1)   An appeal against a certificate of recoverable benefits may be made on the ground—
(a)   that any amount, rate or period specified in the certificate is incorrect, or
(b)   that listed benefits which have been, or are likely to be, paid otherwise than in respect of the accident, injury or disease in question have been brought into account or.
(c)   that listed benefits which have not been, and are not likely to be, paid to the injured person during the relevant period have been brought into account, or

(d) that the payment on the basis of which the certificate was issued is not a payment within section 1(1)(a)

(2) An appeal under this section may be made by—
(a) the person who applied for the certificate of recoverable benefits, or
(aa) (in a case where that certificate was issued under section 7(2)(a)) the person to whom it was so issued, or
(b) (in a case where the amount of the compensation payment has been calculated under section 8) the injured person or other person to whom the payment is made.

(2A) Regulations may provide that, in such cases or circumstances as may be prescribed, an appeal may be made under this section only if the Secretary of State has reviewed the certificate under section 10.

(2B) The regulations may in particular provide that that condition is met only where—
(a) the review by the Secretary of State was on an application,
(b) the Secretary of State considered issues of a specified description, or
(c) the review by the Secretary of State satisfied any other condition specified in the regulations.

(3) No appeal may be made under this section until—
(a) the claim giving rise to the compensation payment has been finally disposed of, and
(b) the liability under section 6 has been discharged.

(4) For the purposes of subsection (3)(a), if an award of damages in respect of a claim has been made under or by virtue of—
(a) section 32A(2)(a) of the Senior Courts Act 1981,
(b) section 12(2)(a) of the Administration of Justice Act 1982, or
(c) section 51(2)(a) of the County Courts Act 1984,
(orders for provisional damages in personal injury cases), the claim is to be treated as having been finally disposed of.

(5) Regulations may make provision—
(a) as to the manner in which, and the time within which, appeals under this section may be made,
. . .
(c) for the purpose of enabling any such appeal or where in accordance with the regulations under subsection (2A) there is no right of appeal or purported appeal to be treated as an application for review under section 10.

12 REFERENCE OF QUESTIONS TO THE FIRST TIER TRIBUNAL

(1) The Secretary of State must refer an appeal under section 11 to the First Tier Tribunal.

(3) In determining any appeal under section 11, the First-tier Tribunal must take into account any decision of a court relating to the same, or any similar, issue arising in connection with the accident, injury or disease in question.

(4) On an appeal under sub-section 1 the First-tier Tribunal may either—
(a) confirm the amounts, rates and periods specified in the certificate of recoverable benefits,
(b) specify any variations which are to be made on the issue of a fresh certificate under subsection (5) or.
(c) declare that the certificate of recoverable benefits is to be revoked.

(5) When the Secretary of State has received the decision of the tribunal on the appeal under section 11, he must in accordance with that decision either—

(a) confirm the certificate against which the appeal was brought, or

(b) issue a fresh certificate or,

(c) revoke the certificate.

(7)   Regulations . . . may (among other things) provide for the non-disclosure of medical advice or medical evidence given or submitted following a reference under subsection (1).

13 APPEAL TO THE UPPER TRIBUNAL

(2)   An appeal to the Upper Tribunal under section 11 of the Tribunals, Courts and Enforcement Act 2007 which arises from any decision of the First-Tier Tribunal made under section 12 of this Act may be made by—

(a) the Secretary of State,

(b) the person who applied for the certificate of recoverable benefits,

(bb)(in a case where that certificate was issued under section 7(2)(a)) the person to whom it was so issued, or

(c) (in a case where the amount of the compensation payment has been calculated in accordance with section 8) the injured person or other person to whom the payment is made.

14 REVIEWS AND APPEALS: SUPPLEMENTARY

(1)   This section applies in cases where a fresh certificate of recoverable benefits is issued as a result of a review under section 10 or an appeal under section 11.

(2)   If—

(a) a person has made one or more payments to the Secretary of State under section 6, and

(b) in consequence of the review or appeal, it appears that the total amount paid is more than the amount that ought to have been paid,

regulations may provide for the Secretary of State to pay the difference to that person, or to the person to whom the compensation payment is made, or partly to one and partly to the other.

(3)   If—

(a) a person has made one or more payments to the Secretary of State under section 6, and

(b) in consequence of the review or appeal, it appears that the total amount paid is less than the amount that ought to have been paid,

regulations may provide for that person to pay the difference to the Secretary of State.

(4)   Regulations under this section may provide—

(a) for the re-calculation in accordance with section 8 of the amount of any compensation payment,

(b) for giving credit for amounts already paid, and

(c) for the payment by any person of any balance or the recovery from any person of any excess,

and may provide for any matter by modifying this Act.

Courts

15 COURT ORDERS

(1)   This section applies where a court makes an order for a compensation payment to be made in any case, unless the order is made with the consent of the injured person and the person by whom the payment is to be made.

(2)   The court must, in the case of each head of compensation listed in column 1 of Schedule 2 to which any of the compensation payment is attributable, specify in the order the amount of the compensation payment which is attributable to that head.

16 PAYMENTS INTO COURT

(1)   Regulations may make provision (including provision modifying this Act) for any case in which a payment into court is made.

(2)   The regulations may (among other things) provide—
   (a) for the making of a payment into court to be treated in prescribed circumstances as the making of a compensation payment,
   (b) for application for, and issue of, certificates of recoverable benefits, and
   (c) for the relevant period to be treated as ending on a date determined in accordance with the regulations.

(3)   Rules of court may make provision governing practice and procedure in such cases.

(4)   This section does not extend to Scotland.

17 BENEFITS IRRELEVANT TO ASSESSMENT OF DAMAGES

In assessing damages in respect of any accident, injury or disease, the amount of any listed benefits paid or likely to be paid is to be disregarded.

Reduction of compensation: complex cases

18 LUMP SUM AND PERIODICAL PAYMENTS

(1)   Regulations may make provision (including provision modifying this Act) for any case in which two or more compensation payments in the form of lump sums are made by the same person to or in respect of the injured person in consequence of the same accident, injury or disease.

(2)   The regulations may (among other things) provide—
   (a) for the re-calculation in accordance with section 8 of the amount of any compensation payment,
   (b) for giving credit for amounts already paid, and
   (c) for the payment by any person of any balance or the recovery from any person of any excess.

(3)   For the purposes of subsection (2), the regulations may provide for the gross amounts of the compensation payments to be aggregated and for—
   (a) the aggregate amount to be taken to be the gross amount of the compensation payment for the purposes of section 8,
   (b) so much of the aggregate amount as is attributable to a head of compensation listed in column 1 of Schedule 2 to be taken to be the part of the gross amount which is attributable to that head;
   and for the amount of any recoverable benefit shown against any head in column 2 of that Schedule to be taken to be the amount determined in accordance with the most recent certificate of recoverable benefits.

(4)   Regulations may make provision (including provision modifying this Act) for any case in which, in final settlement of the injured person's claim, an agreement is entered into for the making of—
   (a) periodical compensation payments (whether of an income or capital nature), or

(b) periodical compensation payments and lump sum compensation payments.

(5) Regulations made by virtue of subsection (4) may (among other things) provide—
(a) for the relevant period to be treated as ending at a prescribed time,
(b) for the person who is to make the payments under the agreement to be treated for the purposes of this Act as if he had made a single compensation payment on a prescribed date.

(6) A periodical payment may be a compensation payment for the purposes of this section even though it is a small payment (as defined in Part II of Schedule 1).

19 PAYMENTS BY MORE THAN ONE PERSON

(1) Regulations may make provision (including provision modifying this Act) for any case in which two or more persons ("the compensators") make compensation payments to or in respect of the same injured person in consequence of the same accident, injury or disease.

(2) In such a case, the sum of the liabilities of the compensators under section 6 is not to exceed the total amount of the recoverable benefits, and the regulations may provide for determining the respective liabilities under that section of each of the compensators.

(3) The regulations may (among other things) provide in the case of each compensator—
(a) for determining or re-determining the part of the recoverable benefits which may be taken into account in his case,
(b) for calculating or re-calculating in accordance with section 8 the amount of any compensation payment,
(c) for giving credit for amounts already paid, and
(d) for the payment by any person of any balance or the recovery from any person of any excess.

Miscellaneous

20 AMOUNTS OVERPAID UNDER SECTION 6

(1) Regulations may make provision (including provision modifying this Act) for cases where a person has paid to the Secretary of State under section 6 any amount ("the amount of the overpayment") which he was not liable to pay.

(2) The regulations may provide—
(a) for the Secretary of State to pay the amount of the overpayment to that person, or to the person to whom the compensation payment is made, or partly to one and partly to the other, or
(b) for the receipt by the Secretary of State of the amount of the overpayment to be treated as the recovery of that amount.

(3) Regulations made by virtue of subsection (2)(b) are to have effect in spite of anything in section 71 of the Social Security Administration Act 1992 (overpayments—general).

(4) The regulations may also (among other things) provide—
(a) for the re-calculation in accordance with section 8 of the amount of any compensation payment,
(b) for giving credit for amounts already paid, and
(c) for the payment by any person of any balance or the recovery from any person of any excess.

(5) This section does not apply in a case where section 14 applies.

21 COMPENSATION PAYMENTS TO BE DISREGARDED

(1) If, when a compensation payment is made, the first and second conditions are met, the payment is to be disregarded for the purposes of sections 6 and 8.

(2) The first condition is that the person making the payment—
(a) has made an application for a certificate of recoverable benefits which complies with subsection (3), and
(b) has in his possession a written acknowledgment of the receipt of his application.

(3) An application complies with this subsection if it—
(a) accurately states the prescribed particulars relating to the injured person and the accident, injury or disease in question, and
(b) specifies the name and address of the person to whom the certificate is to be sent.

(4) The second condition is that the Secretary of State has not sent the certificate to the person, at the address, specified in the application, before the end of the period allowed under section 4.

(5) In any case where—
(a) by virtue of subsection (1), a compensation payment is disregarded for the purposes of sections 6 and 8, but
(b) the person who made the compensation payment nevertheless makes a payment to the Secretary of State for which (but for subsection (1)) he would be liable under section 6,
subsection (1) is to cease to apply in relation to the compensation payment.

(6) If, in the opinion of the Secretary of State, circumstances have arisen which adversely affect normal methods of communication—
(a) he may by order provide that subsection (1) is not to apply during a specified period not exceeding three months, and
(b) he may continue any such order in force for further periods not exceeding three months at a time.

22 LIABILITY OF INSURERS

(1) If a compensation payment is made in a case where—
(a) a person is liable to any extent in respect of the accident, injury or disease, and
(b) the liability is covered to any extent by a policy of insurance,
the policy is also to be treated as covering any liability of that person under section 6.

(2) Liability imposed on the insurer by subsection (1) cannot be excluded or restricted.

(3) For that purpose excluding or restricting liability includes—
(a) making the liability or its enforcement subject to restrictive or onerous conditions,
(b) excluding or restricting any right or remedy in respect of the liability, or subjecting a person to any prejudice in consequence of his pursuing any such right or remedy, or
(c) excluding or restricting rules of evidence or procedure.

(4) Regulations may in prescribed cases limit the amount of the liability imposed on the insurer by subsection (1).

(5) This section applies to policies of insurance issued before (as well as those issued after) its coming into force.

(6) References in this section to policies of insurance and their issue include references to contracts of insurance and their making.

23 PROVISION OF INFORMATION

(1)   Where compensation is sought in respect of any accident, injury or disease suffered by any person ("the injured person"), the following persons must give the Secretary of State the prescribed information about the injured person—
(a) anyone who is, or is alleged to be, liable in respect of the accident, injury or disease, and
(b) anyone acting on behalf of such a person.

(2)   A person who receives or claims a listed benefit which is or is likely to be paid in respect of an accident, injury or disease suffered by him, must give the Secretary of State the prescribed information about the accident, injury or disease.

(3)   Where a person who has received a listed benefit dies, the duty in subsection (2) is imposed on his personal representative.

(4)   Any person who makes a payment (whether on his own behalf or not)—
(a) in consequence of, or
(b) which is referable to any costs (in Scotland, expenses) incurred by reason of,
any accident, injury or disease, or any damage to property, must, if the Secretary of State requests him in writing to do so, give the Secretary of State such particulars relating to the size and composition of the payment as are specified in the request.

(5)   The employer of a person who suffers or has suffered an accident, injury or disease, and anyone who has been the employer of such a person at any time during the relevant period, must give the Secretary of State the prescribed information about the payment of statutory sick pay in respect of that person.

(6)   In subsection (5) "employer" has the same meaning as it has in Part XI of the Social Security Contributions and Benefits Act 1992.

(7)   A person who is required to give information under this section must do so in the prescribed manner, at the prescribed place and within the prescribed time.

(8)   Section 1 does not apply in relation to this section.

28 THE CROWN

This Act applies to the Crown.

SCHEDULE 1

Section 1

COMPENSATION PAYMENTS

Part I EXEMPTED PAYMENTS
1.   Any small payment (defined in Part II of this Schedule).

2.   Any payment made to or for the injured person under section 130 of the Powers of Criminal Courts (Sentencing) Act 2000 or s 175 Armed Forces Act 2006 or section 249 of the Criminal Procedure (Scotland) Act 1995 (compensation orders against convicted persons).

3.   Any payment made in the exercise of a discretion out of property held subject to a trust in a case where no more than 50 per cent. by value of the capital contributed to

the trust was directly or indirectly provided by persons who are, or are alleged to be, liable in respect of—

(a) the accident, injury or disease suffered by the injured person, or

(b) the same or any connected accident, injury or disease suffered by another.

4.   Any payment made out of property held for the purposes of any prescribed trust (whether the payment also falls within paragraph 3 or not).

5.—(1) Any payment made to the injured person by an insurer under the terms of any contract of insurance entered into between the injured person and the insurer before—

(a) the date on which the injured person first claims a listed benefit in consequence of the disease in question, or

(b) the occurrence of the accident or injury in question.

(2) "Insurer" means—

(a) a person who has permission under Part 4 of the Financial Services and Markets Act 2000 to effect or carry out contracts of insurance; or

(b) an EEA firm of the kind mentioned in paragraph 5(d) of Schedule 3 to that Act which has permission under paragraph 15 of that Schedule (as a result of qualifying for authorisation under paragraph 12 of that Schedule) to effect or carry out contracts of insurance.

(3) Sub-paragraph (2) must be read with—

(a) section 22 of the Financial Services and Markets Act 2000;

(b) any relevant order under that section; and

(c) Schedule 2 to that Act.

6.   Any redundancy payment falling to be taken into account in the assessment of damages in respect of an accident, injury or disease.

7.   So much of any payment as is referable to costs.

8.   Any prescribed payment.

Part II POWER TO DISREGARD SMALL PAYMENTS

9.—(1) Regulations may make provision for compensation payments to be disregarded for the purposes of sections 6 and 8 in prescribed cases where the amount of the compensation payment, or the aggregate amount of two or more connected compensation payments, does not exceed the prescribed sum.

(2) A compensation payment disregarded by virtue of this paragraph is referred to in paragraph 1 as a "small payment".

(3) For the purposes of this paragraph—

(a) two or more compensation payments are "connected" if each is made to or in respect of the same injured person and in respect of the same accident, injury or disease, and

(b) any reference to a compensation payment is a reference to a payment which would be such a payment apart from paragraph 1.

SCHEDULE 2

Section 8. Calculation of compensation payment

Head of compensation	Benefit
1. Compensation for earnings lost during section 103 the relevant period	Disablement pension payable under of the 1992 Act
	Employment and support allowance Incapacity Benefit & Income Support Invalidity pension and allowance Jobseeker's allowance Reduced earnings allowance Severe disablement allowance Sickness benefit Statutory sick pay Unemployability supplement Unemployment benefit
2. Compensation for cost of care incurred during the relevant period	Attendance allowance Care component of disability living allowance Disablement pension increase payable under section 104 or 105 of the 1992 Act
3. Compensation for loss of mobility relevant period living allowance	Mobility allowance during the Mobility component of disability

NOTES

1.—(1) References to incapacity benefit, invalidity pension and allowance, severe disablement allowance, sickness benefit and unemployment benefit also include any income support paid with each of those benefits on the same instrument of payment or paid concurrently with each of those benefits by means of an instrument for benefit payment.

(2) For the purpose of this Note, income support includes personal expenses addition, special transitional additions and transitional addition as defined in the Income Support (Transitional) Regulations 1987.

2.   Any reference to statutory sick pay—
(a) includes only 80 per cent. of payments made between 6th April 1991 and 5th April 1994, and
(b) does not include payments made on or after 6th April 1994.

3.   In this Schedule "the 1992 Act" means the Social Security Contributions and Benefits Act 1992.

Editor's Note: s 11(2A) introduced by Welfare Reform Act 2012 sch. 11 para 10(2) and in force from a date to be appointed.

CONTRACT (SCOTLAND) ACT 1997
(c.34)

1 EXTRINSIC EVIDENCE OF ADDITIONAL CONTRACT TERM ETC.

(1)　Where a document appears (or two or more documents appear) to comprise all the express terms of a contract or unilateral voluntary obligation, it shall be presumed, unless the contrary is proved, that the document does (or the documents do) comprise all the express terms of the contract or unilateral voluntary obligation.

(2)　Extrinsic oral or documentary evidence shall be admissible to prove, for the purposes of subsection (1) above, that the contract or unilateral voluntary obligation includes additional express terms (whether or not written terms).

(3)　Notwithstanding the foregoing provisions of this section, where one of the terms in the document (or in the documents) is to the effect that the document does (or the documents do) comprise all the express terms of the contract or unilateral voluntary obligation, that term shall be conclusive in the matter.

(4)　This section is without prejudice to any enactment which makes provision as respects the constitution, or formalities of execution, of a contract or unilateral voluntary obligation.

2 SUPERSESSION

(1)　Where a deed is executed in implement, or purportedly in implement, of a contract, an unimplemented, or otherwise unfulfilled, term of the contract shall not be taken to be superseded by virtue only of that execution or of the delivery and acceptance of the deed.

(2)　Subsection (1) above is without prejudice to any agreement which the parties to a contract may reach (whether or not an agreement incorporated into the contract) as to supersession of the contract.

3 DAMAGES FOR BREACH OF CONTRACT OF SALE

Any rule of law which precludes the buyer in a contract of sale of property from obtaining damages for breach of that contract by the seller unless the buyer rejects the property and rescinds the contract shall cease to have effect.

4 SHORT TITLE, EXTENT ETC.

(1)　This Act may be cited as the Contract (Scotland) Act 1997.

(2)　This Act shall come into force at the end of that period of three months which begins with the day on which the Act is passed.

(3)　Section 1 of this Act applies only for the purposes of proceedings commenced on or after, and sections 2 and 3 only as respects contracts entered into on or after, the date on which this Act comes into force.

(4)　This Act extends to Scotland only.

PROTECTION FROM HARASSMENT ACT 1997
(c.40)

England and Wales

1 PROHIBITION OF HARASSMENT

(1) A person must not pursue a course of conduct—
   (a) which amounts to harassment of another, and
   (b) which he knows or ought to know amounts to harassment of the other.

(1A) A person must not pursue a course of conduct—
   (a) which involved the harassment of two persons, and
   (b) which he knows or ought to know involves harassment of those persons, and
   (c) which he intends to persuade any person (whether or not one of those mentioned above)—
      (i) not to something he is required to do, or
      (ii) to do something that he is not under any obligation to do.

(2) For the purposes of this section or s 2A(2)(c), the person whose course of conduct is in question ought to know that it amounts to or involves harassment of another if a reasonable person in possession of the same information would think the course of conduct amounted to or involved harassment of the other.

(3) Subsection (1) or (1A) does not apply to a course of conduct if the person who pursued it shows—
   (a) that it was pursued for the purpose of preventing or detecting crime,
   (b) that it was pursued under any enactment or rule of law or to comply with any condition or requirement imposed by any person under any enactment, or
   (c) that in the particular circumstances the pursuit of the course of conduct was reasonable.

2 OFFENCE OF HARASSMENT

(1) A person who pursues a course of conduct in breach of section 1(1) or (1A) is guilty of an offence.

(2) A person guilty of an offence under this section is liable on summary conviction to imprisonment for a term not exceeding six months, or a fine not exceeding level 5 on the standard scale, or both.

2A OFFENCE OF STALKING

(1) A person is guilty of an offence if—
   (a) the person pursues a course of conduct in breach of section 1(1), and
   (b) the course of conduct amounts to stalking.

(2) For the purposes of subsection (1)(b) (and section 4A(1)(a)) a person's course of conduct amounts to stalking of another person if—
   (a) it amounts to harassment of that person,
   (b) the acts or omissions involved are ones associated with stalking, and
   (c) the person whose course of conduct it is knows or ought to know that the course of conduct amounts to harassment of the other person.

(3)   The following are examples of acts or omissions which, in particular circumstances, are ones associated with stalking—

(a)   following a person,

(b)   contacting, or attempting to contact, a person by any means,

(c)   publishing any statement or other material—

(i)   relating or purporting to relate to a person, or

(ii)   purporting to originate from a person,

(d)   monitoring the use by a person of the internet, email or any other form of electronic communication,

(e)   loitering in any place (whether public or private),

(f)   interfering with any property in the possession of a person,

(g)   watching or spying on a person.

(4)   A person guilty of an offence under this section is liable on summary conviction to imprisonment for a term not exceeding 51 weeks, or a fine not exceeding level 5 on the standard scale, or both.

(5)   In relation to an offence committed before the commencement of section 281(5) of the Criminal Justice Act 2003, the reference in subsection (4) to 51 weeks is to be read as a reference to six months.

(6)   This section is without prejudice to the generality of section 2.

2B POWER OF ENTRY IN RELATION TO OFFENCE OF STALKING

(1)   A justice of the peace may, on an application by a constable, issue a warrant authorising a constable to enter and search premises if the justice of the peace is satisfied that there are reasonable grounds for believing that—

(a)   an offence under section 2A has been, or is being, committed,

(b)   there is material on the premises which is likely to be of substantial value (whether by itself or together with other material) to the investigation of the offence,

(c)   the material—

(i)   is likely to be admissible in evidence at a trial for the offence, and

(ii)   does not consist of, or include, items subject to legal privilege, excluded material or special procedure material (within the meanings given by sections 10, 11 and 14 of the Police and Criminal Evidence Act 1984), and

(d)   either—

(i)   entry to the premises will not be granted unless a warrant is produced, or

(ii)   the purpose of a search may be frustrated or seriously prejudiced unless a constable arriving at the premises can secure immediate entry to them.

(2)   A constable may seize and retain anything for which a search has been authorised under subsection (1).

(3)   A constable may use reasonable force, if necessary, in the exercise of any power conferred by virtue of this section.

(4)   In this section "premises" has the same meaning as in section 23 of the Police and Criminal Evidence Act 1984.

3 CIVIL REMEDY

(1)   An actual or apprehended breach of section 1(1) may be the subject of a claim in civil proceedings by the person who is or may be the victim of the course of conduct in question.

(2)   On such a claim, damages may be awarded for (among other things) any anxiety caused by the harassment and any financial loss resulting from the harassment.

(3)   Where—
　　(a)　in such proceedings the High Court or a county court grants an injunction for the purpose of restraining the defendant from pursuing any conduct which amounts to harassment, and
　　(b)　the plaintiff considers that the defendant has done anything which he is prohibited from doing by the injunction,
　　the plaintiff may apply for the issue of a warrant for the arrest of the defendant.

(4)   An application under subsection (3) may be made—
　　(a)　where the injunction was granted by the High Court, to a judge of that court, and
　　(b)　where the injunction was granted by a county court, to a judge or district judge of that or any other county court.

(5)   The judge or district judge to whom an application under subsection (3) is made may only issue a warrant if—
　　(a)　the application is substantiated on oath, and
　　(b)　the judge or district judge has reasonable grounds for believing that the defendant has done anything which he is prohibited from doing by the injunction.

(6)   Where—
　　(a)　the High Court or a county court grants an injunction for the purpose mentioned in subsection (3)(a), and
　　(b)　without reasonable excuse the defendant does anything which he is prohibited from doing by the injunction,
　　he is guilty of an offence.

(7)   Where a person is convicted of an offence under subsection (6) in respect of any conduct, that conduct is not punishable as a contempt of court.

(8)   A person cannot be convicted of an offence under subsection (6) in respect of any conduct which has been punished as a contempt of court.

(9)   A person guilty of an offence under subsection (6) is liable—
　　(a)　on conviction on indictment, to imprisonment for a term not exceeding five years, or a fine, or both, or
　　(b)　on summary conviction, to imprisonment for a term not exceeding six months, or a fine not exceeding the statutory maximum, or both.

3A INJUNCTIONS TO PROTECT PERSONS FROM HARASSMENT WITHIN SECTION 1(1A)

(1)   This section applies where there is an actual or apprehended breach of section 1(1A) by any person ("the relevant person").

(2)   In such a case—
　　(a)　any person who is or may be a victim of the course of conduct in question, or
　　(b)　any person who is or may be a person falling within section 1(1A)(c),
　　may apply to the High Court or a county court for an injunction restraining the relevant person from pursuing any conduct which amounts to harassment in relation to any person or persons mentioned or described in the injunction.

(3)   Section 3(3) to (9) apply in relation to an injunction granted under subsection (2) above as they apply in relation to an injunction granted as mentioned in section 3(3)(a).

4 PUTTING PEOPLE IN FEAR OF VIOLENCE

(1)   A person whose course of conduct causes another to fear, on at least two occasions, that violence will be used against him is guilty of an offence if he knows or ought to know that his course of conduct will cause the other so to fear on each of those occasions.

(2)   For the purposes of this section, the person whose course of conduct is in question ought to know that it will cause another to fear that violence will be used against him on any occasion if a reasonable person in possession of the same information would think the course of conduct would cause the other so to fear on that occasion.

(3)   It is a defence for a person charged with an offence under this section to show that
(a)   his course of conduct was pursued for the purpose of preventing or detecting crime,
(b)   his course of conduct was pursued under any enactment or rule of law or to comply with any condition or requirement imposed by any person under any enactment, or
(c)   the pursuit of his course of conduct was reasonable for the protection of himself or another or for the protection of his or another's property.

(4)   A person guilty of an offence under this section is liable—
(a)   on conviction on indictment, to imprisonment for a term not exceeding five years, or a fine, or both, or
(b)   on summary conviction, to imprisonment for a term not exceeding six months, or a fine not exceeding the statutory maximum, or both.

(5)   If on the trial on indictment of a person charged with an offence under this section the jury find him not guilty of the offence charged, they may find him guilty of an offence under section 2 or 2A.

(6)   The Crown Court has the same powers and duties in relation to a person who is by virtue of subsection (5) convicted before it of an offence under section 2 or s 2A as a magistrates' court would have on convicting him of the offence.

4A STALKING INVOLVING FEAR OF VIOLENCE OR SERIOUS ALARM OR DISTRESS

(1)   A person ("A") whose course of conduct—
(a)   amounts to stalking, and
(b)   either—
(i)   causes another ("B") to fear, on at least two occasions, that violence will be used against B, or
(ii)   causes B serious alarm or distress which has a substantial adverse effect on B's usual day-to-day activities,
is guilty of an offence if A knows or ought to know that A's course of conduct will cause B so to fear on each of those occasions or (as the case may be) will cause such alarm or distress.

(2)   For the purposes of this section A ought to know that A's course of conduct will cause B to fear that violence will be used against B on any occasion if a reasonable person in possession of the same information would think the course of conduct would cause B so to fear on that occasion.

(3)   For the purposes of this section A ought to know that A's course of conduct will cause B serious alarm or distress which has a substantial adverse effect on B's usual day-to-day activities if a reasonable person in possession of the same information would think the course of conduct would cause B such alarm or distress.

(4)   It is a defence for A to show that—

  (a)   A's course of conduct was pursued for the purpose of preventing or detecting crime,

  (b)   A's course of conduct was pursued under any enactment or rule of law or to comply with any condition or requirement imposed by any person under any enactment, or

  (c)   the pursuit of A's course of conduct was reasonable for the protection of A or another or for the protection of A's or another's property.

(5)   A person guilty of an offence under this section is liable—

  (a)   on conviction on indictment, to imprisonment for a term not exceeding five years, or a fine, or both, or

  (b)   on summary conviction, to imprisonment for a term not exceeding twelve months, or a fine not exceeding the statutory maximum, or both.

(6)   In relation to an offence committed before the commencement of section 154(1) of the Criminal Justice Act 2003, the reference in subsection (5)(b) to twelve months is to be read as a reference to six months.

(7)   If on the trial on indictment of a person charged with an offence under this section the jury find the person not guilty of the offence charged, they may find the person guilty of an offence under section 2 or 2A.

(8)   The Crown Court has the same powers and duties in relation to a person who is by virtue of subsection (7) convicted before it of an offence under section 2 or 2A as a magistrates' court would have on convicting the person of the offence.

(9)   This section is without prejudice to the generality of section 4.

5   RESTRAINING ORDERS ON CONVICTION

(1)   A court sentencing or otherwise dealing with a person ("the defendant") convicted of an offence may (as well as sentencing him or dealing with him in any other way) make an order under this section.

(2)   The order may, for the purpose of protecting the victim or victims of the offence, or any other person mentioned in the order, from conduct which—

  (a)   amounts to harassment, or

  (b)   will cause a fear of violence,

  prohibit the defendant from doing anything described in the order.

(3)   The order may have effect for a specified period or until further order.

(3A)   In proceedings under this section both the prosecution and the defence may lead, as further evidence, any evidence that would be admissible in proceedings for an injunction under section 3.

(4)   The prosecutor, the defendant or any other person mentioned in the order may apply to the court which made the order for it to be varied or discharged by a further order.

(4A)   Any person mentioned in the order is entitled to be heard on the hearing of an application under subsection (4).

(5)   If without reasonable excuse the defendant does anything which he is prohibited from doing by an order under this section, he is guilty of an offence.

(6)   A person guilty of an offence under this section is liable—

  (a)   on conviction on indictment, to imprisonment for a term not exceeding five years, or a fine, or both, or

(b) on summary conviction, to imprisonment for a term not exceeding six months, or a fine not exceeding the statutory maximum, or both.

(7)   A court dealing with a person for an offence under this section may vary or discharge the order in question by a further order.

5A RESTRAINING ORDERS ON ACQUITTAL

(1)   A court before which a person ("the defendant") is acquitted of an offence may, if it considers it necessary to do so to protect a person from harassment by the defendant, make an order prohibiting the defendant from doing anything described in the order.

(2)   Subsections (3) to (7) of section 5 apply to an order under this section as they apply to an order under that one.

(3)   Where the Court of Appeal allow an appeal against conviction they may remit the case to the Crown Court to consider whether to proceed under this section.

(4)   Where–
(a) the Crown Court allows an appeal against conviction, or
(b) a case is remitted to the Crown Court under subsection (3),
the reference in subsection (1) to a court before which a person is acquitted of an offence is to be read as referring to that court.

(5)   A person made subject to an order under this section has the same right of appeal against the order as if—
(a) he had been convicted of the offence in question before the court which made the order, and
(b) the order had been made under section 5.

7 INTERPRETATION OF THIS GROUP OF SECTIONS

(1)   This section applies for the interpretation of sections 1 to 5.

(2)   References to harassing a person include alarming the person or causing the person distress.

(3)   A "course of conduct" must involve—
(a) in the case of conduct in relation to a single person (see section 1(1)), conduct on at least two occasions in relation to that person, or
(b) in the case of conduct in relation to two or more persons (see section 1(1A)), conduct on at least one occasion in relation to each of those persons.

(3A) A person's conduct on any occasion shall be taken, if aided, abetted, counselled or procured by another
(a) to be conduct on that occasion of the other (as well as conduct of the person whose conduct it is); and
(b) to be conduct in relation to which the other's knowledge and purpose, and what he ought to have known, are the same as they were in relation to what was contemplated or reasonably foreseeable at the time of the aiding, abetting, counselling or procuring.

(4)   "Conduct" includes speech.

(5)   References to a person, in the context of the harassment of a person, are references to a person who is an individual.

Scotland

8 HARASSMENT

(1)   Every individual has a right to be free from harassment and, accordingly, a person must not pursue a course of conduct which amounts to harassment of another and—

(a)   is intended to amount to harassment of that person; or

(b)   occurs in circumstances where it would appear to a reasonable person that it would amount to harassment of that person.

(1A) Subsection (1) is subject to section 8A

(2)   An actual or apprehended breach of subsection (1) may be the subject of a claim in civil proceedings by the person who is or may be the victim of the course of conduct in question; and any such claim shall be known as an action of harassment.

(3)   For the purposes of this section—

"conduct" includes speech;

"harassment" of a person includes causing the person alarm or distress; and a course of conduct must involve conduct on at least two occasions.

(4)   It shall be a defence to any action of harassment to show that the course of conduct complained of—

(a)   was authorised by, under or by virtue of any enactment or rule of law;

(b)   was pursued for the purpose of preventing or detecting crime; or

(c)   was, in the particular circumstances, reasonable.

(5)   In an action of harassment the court may, without prejudice to any other remedies which it may grant—

(a)   award damages;

(b)   grant—

(i)   interdict or interim interdict;

(ii) if it is satisfied that it is appropriate for it to do so in order to protect the person from further harassment, an order, to be known as a "non-harassment order", requiring the defender to refrain from such conduct in relation to the pursuer as may be specified in the order for such period (which includes an indeterminate period) as may be so specified,

but a person may not be subjected to the same prohibitions in an interdict or interim interdict and a non-harassment order at the same time.

(6)   The damages which may be awarded in an action of harassment include damages for any anxiety caused by the harassment and any financial loss resulting from it.

(7)   Without prejudice to any right to seek review of any interlocutor, a person against whom a non-harassment order has been made, or the person for whose protection the order was made, may apply to the court by which the order was made for revocation of or a variation of the order and, on any such application, the court may revoke the order or vary it in such manner as it considers appropriate.

8A HARASSMENT AMOUNTING TO DOMESTIC ABUSE

(1)   Every individual has a right to be free from harassment and, accordingly, a person must not engage in conduct which amounts to harassment of another and—

(a)   is intended to amount to harassment of that person; or

(b)   occurs in circumstances where it would appear to a reasonable person that it would amount to harassment of that person.

(2)   Subsection (1) only applies where the conduct referred to amounts to domestic abuse.

(3)   Subsections (2) to (7) of section 8 apply in relation to subsection (1) as they apply in relation to subsection (1) of that section but with the following modifications—
    (a) in subsections (2) and (4), the words "course of" are omitted;
    (b) for subsection (3) there is substituted—

(3) For the purposes of this section—

- "conduct"—
    (a) may involve behaviour on one or more than one occasion; and
    (b) includes—
        (i)   speech; and
        (ii) presence in any place or area; and

- "harassment" of a person includes causing the person alarm or distress;

and

    (c) in subsection (4)(b), for "pursued" substitute "engaged in".

9 BREACH OF NON-HARASSMENT ORDER

(1)   Any person who is . . . in breach of a non-harassment order made under section 8 or section 8A is guilty of an offence and liable—
    (a) on conviction on indictment, to imprisonment for a term not exceeding five years or to a fine, or to both such imprisonment and such fine; and
    (b) on summary conviction, to imprisonment for a period not exceeding six months or to a fine not exceeding the statutory maximum, or to both such imprisonment and such fine.

(2)   A breach of a non-harassment order shall not be punishable other than in accordance with subsection (1).

11 NON-HARASSMENT ORDER FOLLOWING CRIMINAL OFFENCE

After section 234 of the Criminal Procedure (Scotland) Act 1995 there is inserted the following section—

Non-harassment orders

234A NON-HARASSMENT ORDERS

(1)   Where a person is convicted of an offence involving harassment of a person ("the victim"), the prosecutor may apply to the court to make a non-harassment order against the offender requiring him to refrain from such conduct in relation to the victim as may be specified in the order for such period (which includes an indeterminate period) as may be so specified, in addition to any other disposal which may be made in relation to the offence.

(2)   On an application under subsection (1) above the court may, if it is satisfied on a balance of probabilities that it is appropriate to do so in order to protect the victim from further harassment, make a non-harassment order.

(3)   A non-harassment order made by a criminal court shall be taken to be a sentence for the purposes of any appeal and, for the purposes of this subsection "order" includes any variation or revocation of such an order made under subsection (6) below.

(4)   Any person who is found to be in breach of a non-harassment order shall be guilty of an offence and liable—
    (a) on conviction on indictment, to imprisonment for a term not exceeding 5 years or to
    (b) on summary conviction, to imprisonment for a period not exceeding 6 months or to a fine not exceeding the statutory maximum, or to both such imprisonment and such fine.

(5)   The Lord Advocate, in solemn proceedings, and the prosecutor, in summary proceedings, may appeal to the High Court against any decision by a court to refuse an application under subsection (1) above; and on any such appeal the High Court may make such order as it considers appropriate.

(6)   The person against whom a non-harassment order is made, or the prosecutor at whose instance the order is made, may apply to the court which made the order for its revocation or variation and, in relation to any such application the court concerned may, if it is satisfied on a balance of probabilities that it is appropriate to do so, revoke the order or vary it in such manner as it thinks fit, but not so as to increase the period for which the order is to run.

(7)   For the purposes of this section "harassment" shall be construed in accordance with section 8 of the Protection from Harassment Act 1997.

General

12 NATIONAL SECURITY, ETC.

(1)   If the Secretary of State certifies that in his opinion anything done by a specified person on a specified occasion related to
    (a) national security,
    (b) the economic well-being of the United Kingdom, or
    (c) the prevention or detection of serious crime,
    and was done on behalf of the Crown, the certificate is conclusive evidence that this Act does not apply to any conduct of that person on that occasion.

(2)   In subsection (1), "specified" means specified in the certificate in question.

(3)   A document purporting to be a certificate under subsection (1) is to be received in evidence and, unless the contrary is proved, be treated as being such a certificate.

Editor's Note: Sections 2A, 2B and 4A inserted by ss 111–112 Protection of Freedoms Act 2012 to be brought into force on a date to be appointed.

DATA PROTECTION ACT 1998
(c.29)

10 RIGHT TO PREVENT PROCESSING LIKELY TO CAUSE DAMAGE OR DISTRESS

(1)   Subject to subsection (2), an individual is entitled at any time by notice in writing to a data controller to require the data controller at the end of such period as is reasonable in the circumstances to cease, or not to begin, processing, or processing for a specified purpose or in a specified manner, any personal data in respect of which he is the data subject, on the ground that, for specified reasons—

(a) the processing of those data or their processing for that purpose or in that manner is causing or is likely to cause substantial damage or substantial distress to him or to another, and

(b) that damage or distress is or would be unwarranted.

(2) Subsection (1) does not apply—
(a) in a case where any of the conditions in paragraphs 1 to 4 of Schedule 2 is met, or
(b) in such other cases as may be prescribed by the Secretary of State by order.

(3) The data controller must within twenty-one days of receiving a notice under subsection (1)("the data subject notice") give the individual who gave it a written notice—
(a) stating that he has complied or intends to comply with the data subject notice, or
(b) stating his reasons for regarding the data subject notice as to any extent unjustified and the extent (if any) to which he has complied or intends to comply with it.

(4) If a court is satisfied, on the application of any person who has given a notice under subsection (1) which appears to the court to be justified (or to be justified to any extent), that the data controller in question has failed to comply with the notice, the court may order him to take such steps for complying with the notice (or for complying with it to that extent) as the court thinks fit.

(5) The failure by a data subject to exercise the right conferred by subsection (1) or section 11(1) does not affect any other right conferred on him by this Part.

13 COMPENSATION FOR FAILURE TO COMPLY WITH CERTAIN REQUIREMENTS

(1) An individual who suffers damage by reason of any contravention by a data controller of any of the requirements of this Act is entitled to compensation from the data controller for that damage.

(2) An individual who suffers distress by reason of any contravention by a data controller of any of the requirements of this Act is entitled to compensation from the data controller for that distress if—
(a) the individual also suffers damage by reason of the contravention, or
(b) the contravention relates to the processing of personal data for the special purposes.

(3) In proceedings brought against a person by virtue of this section it is a defence to prove that he had taken such care as in all the circumstances was reasonably required to comply with the requirement concerned.

14 RECTIFICATION, BLOCKING, ERASURE AND DESTRUCTION

(1) If a court is satisfied on the application of a data subject that personal data of which the applicant is the subject are inaccurate, the court may order the data controller to rectify, block, erase or destroy those data and any other personal data in respect of which he is the data controller and which contain an expression of opinion which appears to the court to be based on the inaccurate data.

(2) Subsection (1) applies whether or not the data accurately record information received or obtained by the data controller from the data subject or a third party but where the data accurately record such information, then—
(a) if the requirements mentioned in paragraph 7 of Part II of Schedule 1 have been complied with, the court may, instead of making an order under subsection (1), make an order requiring the data to be supplemented by such statement of the true facts relating to the matters dealt with by the data as the court may approve, and

(b) if all or any of those requirements have not been complied with, the court may, instead of making an order under that subsection, make such order as it thinks fit for securing compliance with those requirements with or without a further order requiring the data to be supplemented by such a statement as is mentioned in paragraph (a).

(3) Where the court—
(a) makes an order under subsection (1), or
(b) is satisfied on the application of a data subject that personal data of which he was the data subject and which have been rectified, blocked, erased or destroyed were inaccurate, it may, where it considers it reasonably practicable, order the data controller to notify third parties to whom the data have been disclosed of the rectification, blocking, erasure or destruction.

(4) If a court is satisfied on the application of a data subject—
(a) that he has suffered damage by reason of any contravention by a data controller of any of the requirements of this Act in respect of any personal data, in circumstances entitling him to compensation under section 13, and
(b) that there is a substantial risk of further contravention in respect of those data in such circumstances,
the court may order the rectification, blocking, erasure or destruction of any of those data.

(5) Where the court makes an order under subsection (4) it may, where it considers it reasonably practicable, order the data controller to notify third parties to whom the data have been disclosed of the rectification, blocking, erasure or destruction.

(6) In determining whether it is reasonably practicable to require such notification as is mentioned in subsection (3) or (5) the court shall have regard, in particular, to the number of persons who would have to be notified.

HUMAN RIGHTS ACT 1998
(c.42)

12 FREEDOM OF EXPRESSION

(1) This section applies if a court is considering whether to grant any relief which, if granted, might affect the exercise of the Convention right to freedom of expression.

(2) If the person against whom the application for relief is made ("the respondent") is neither present nor represented, no such relief is to be granted unless the court is satisfied—
(a) that the applicant has taken all practicable steps to notify the respondent; or
(b) that there are compelling reasons why the respondent should not be notified.

(3) No such relief is to be granted so as to restrain publication before trial unless the court is satisfied that the applicant is likely to establish that publication should not be allowed.

(4) The court must have particular regard to the importance of the Convention right to freedom of expression and, where the proceedings relate to material which the respondent claims, or which appears to the court, to be journalistic, literary or artistic material (or to conduct connected with such material), to—
(a) the extent to which—
(i) the material has, or is about to, become available to the public; or
(ii) it is, or would be, in the public interest for the material to be published;
(b) any relevant privacy code.

(5)   In this section—

"court" includes a tribunal; and

"relief" includes any remedy or order (other than in criminal proceedings).

13 FREEDOM OF THOUGHT, CONSCIENCE AND RELIGION

(1)   If a court's determination of any question arising under this Act might affect the exercise by a religious organisation (itself or its members collectively) of the Convention right to freedom of thought, conscience and religion, it must have particular regard to the importance of that right.

(2)   In this section "court" includes a tribunal.

SCHEDULE 1

Section 1(3)

THE ARTICLES

Part I THE CONVENTION

RIGHTS AND FREEDOMS

Article 8 Right to respect for private and family life
1.   Everyone has the right to respect for his private and family life, his home and his correspondence.

2.   There shall be no interference by a public authority with the exercise of this right except such as is in accordance with the law and is necessary in a democratic society in the interests of national security, public safety or the economic well-being of the country, for the prevention of disorder or crime, for the protection of health or morals, or for the protection of the rights and freedoms of others.

Article 9 Freedom of thought, conscience and religion
1.   Everyone has the right to freedom of thought, conscience and religion; this right includes freedom to change his religion or belief and freedom, either alone or in community with others and in public or private, to manifest his religion or belief, in worship, teaching, practice and observance.

2.   Freedom to manifest one's religion or beliefs shall be subject only to such limitations as are prescribed by law and are necessary in a democratic society in the interests of public safety, for the protection of public order, health or morals, or for the protection of the rights and freedoms of others.

Article 10 Freedom of expression
1.   Everyone has the right to freedom of expression. This right shall include freedom to hold opinions and to receive and impart information and ideas without interference by public authority and regardless of frontiers. This Article shall not prevent States from requiring the licensing of broadcasting, television or cinema enterprises.

2.   The exercise of these freedoms, since it carries with it duties and responsibilities, may be subject to such formalities, conditions, restrictions or penalties as are prescribed by law and are necessary in a democratic society, in the interests of national security, territorial integrity or public safety, for the prevention of disorder or crime, for the protection of

health or morals, for the protection of the reputation or rights of others, for preventing the disclosure of information received in confidence, or for maintaining the authority and impartiality of the judiciary.

Article 14 Prohibition of discrimination
The enjoyment of the rights and freedoms set forth in this Convention shall be secured without discrimination on any ground such as sex, race, colour, language, religion, political or other opinion, national or social origin, association with a national minority, property, birth or other status.

Article 17 Prohibition of abuse of rights
Nothing in this Convention may be interpreted as implying for any State, group or person any right to engage in any activity or perform any act aimed at the destruction of any of the rights and freedoms set forth herein or at their limitation to a greater extent than is provided for in the Convention.

Part II THE FIRST PROTOCOL

Article 1 Protection of property
Every natural or legal person is entitled to the peaceful enjoyment of his possessions. No one shall be deprived of his possessions except in the public interest and subject to the conditions provided for by law and by the general principles of international law.

The preceding provisions shall not, however, in any way impair the right of a State to enforce such laws as it deems necessary to control the use of property in accordance with the general interest or to secure the payment of taxes or other contributions or penalties

WELFARE REFORM AND PENSIONS ACT 1999
(c.30)

68 CERTAIN OVERPAYMENTS OF BENEFIT NOT TO BE RECOVERABLE

(1)   An overpayment to which this section applies shall not be recoverable from the payee, whether by the Secretary of State or a local authority, under any provision made by or under Part III of the Administration Act (overpayments and adjustments of benefit).

(2)   This section applies to an overpayment if—
(a) it is in respect of a qualifying benefit;
(b) it is referable to a decision given on a review that there has been an alteration in the relevant person's condition, being a decision to which effect is required to be given as from a date earlier than that on which it was given;
(c) the decision was given before 1st June 1999; and
(d) the overpayment is not excluded by virtue of subsection (6).

(3)   In subsection (2)(b) the reference to a decision on a review that there has been an alteration in the relevant person's condition is a reference to a decision so given that that person's physical or mental condition either was at the time when the original decision was given, or has subsequently become, different from that on which that decision was based, with the result—
(a) that he did not at that time, or (as the case may be) has subsequently ceased to, meet any of the conditions contained in the following provisions of the Contributions and Benefits Act, namely—

   (i) section 64 (attendance allowance),

   (ii) section 72(1) or (2)(care component of disability living allowance), and

   (iii) section 73(1) or (2)(mobility component of that allowance); or

 (b) that he was at that time, or (as the case may be) has subsequently become, capable of work in accordance with regulations made under section 171C(2) of that Act (the all work test).

(4) For the purposes of this section "qualifying benefit" means—

 (a) attendance allowance;

 (b) disability living allowance;

 (c) any benefit awarded wholly or partly by reason of a person being (or being treated as being) in receipt of a component (at any rate) of disability living allowance or in receipt of attendance allowance;

 (d) incapacity benefit;

 (e) any benefit (other than incapacity benefit) awarded wholly or partly by reason of a person being (or being treated as being) incapable of work; or

 (f) any benefit awarded wholly or partly by reason of a person being (or being treated as being) in receipt of any benefit falling within paragraph (c), (d) or (e).

(5) For the purposes of this section—

 (a) "review" means a review taking place by virtue of section 25(1)(a) or (b), 30(2)(a) or (b) or 35(1)(a) or (b) of the Administration Act;

 (b) "the relevant person", in relation to a review, means the person to whose entitlement to a qualifying benefit or to whose incapacity for work the review related; and

 (c) "the original decision", in relation to a review, means the decision as to any such entitlement or incapacity to which the review related.

(6) An overpayment is excluded by virtue of this subsection if (before or after the passing of this Act)—

 (a) the payee has agreed to pay a penalty in respect of the overpayment under section 115A of the Administration Act,

 (b) the payee has been convicted of any offence (under section 111A or 112(1) or (1A) of that Act or otherwise) in connection with the overpayment, or

 (c) proceedings have been instituted against the payee for such an offence and the proceedings have not been determined or abandoned.

(7) Nothing in this section applies to an overpayment to the extent that it was recovered from the payee (by any means) before 26th February 1999.

(8) In this section—

"benefit" includes any amount included in—

 (a) the applicable amount in relation to an income-related benefit (as defined by section 135(1) of the Contributions and Benefits Act), or

 (b) the applicable amount in relation to a jobseeker's allowance (as defined by section 4(5) of the Jobseekers Act 1995);

"income-related benefit" has the meaning given by section 123(1) of the Contributions and Benefits Act;

"overpayment" means an amount of benefit paid in excess of entitlement;

"the payee", in relation to an overpayment, means the person to whom that amount was paid.

CONTRACTS (RIGHTS OF THIRD PARTIES) ACT 1999
(c.31)

1 RIGHT OF THIRD PARTY TO ENFORCE CONTRACTUAL TERM

(1)   Subject to the provisions of this Act, a person who is not a party to a contract (a "third party") may in his own right enforce a term of the contract if—
(a)   the contract expressly provides that he may, or
(b)   subject to subsection (2), the term purports to confer a benefit on him.

(2)   Subsection (1)(b) does not apply if on a proper construction of the contract it appears that the parties did not intend the term to be enforceable by the third party.

(3)   The third party must be expressly identified in the contract by name, as a member of a class or as answering a particular description but need not be in existence when the contract is entered into.

(4)   This section does not confer a right on a third party to enforce a term of a contract otherwise than subject to and in accordance with any other relevant terms of the contract.

(5)   For the purpose of exercising his right to enforce a term of the contract, there shall be available to the third party any remedy that would have been available to him in an action for breach of contract if he had been a party to the contract (and the rules relating to damages, injunctions, specific performance and other relief shall apply accordingly).

(6)   Where a term of a contract excludes or limits liability in relation to any matter references in this Act to the third party enforcing the term shall be construed as references to his availing himself of the exclusion or limitation.

(7)   In this Act, in relation to a term of a contract which is enforceable by a third party—

"the promisor" means the party to the contract against whom the term is enforceable by the third party, and

"the promisee" means the party to the contract by whom the term is enforceable against the promisor.

2 VARIATION AND RESCISSION OF CONTRACT

(1)   Subject to the provisions of this section, where a third party has a right under section 1 to enforce a term of the contract, the parties to the contract may not, by agreement, rescind the contract, or vary it in such a way as to extinguish or alter his entitlement under that right, without his consent if—
(a)   the third party has communicated his assent to the term to the promisor,
(b)   the promisor is aware that the third party has relied on the term, or
(c)   the promisor can reasonably be expected to have foreseen that the third party would rely on the term and the third party has in fact relied on it.

(2)   The assent referred to in subsection (1)(a)—
(a)   may be by words or conduct, and
(b)   if sent to the promisor by post or other means, shall not be regarded as communicated to the promisor until received by him.

(3)   Subsection (1) is subject to any express term of the contract under which—
(a)   the parties to the contract may by agreement rescind or vary the contract without the consent of the third party, or

(b) the consent of the third party is required in circumstances specified in the contract instead of those set out in subsection (1)(a) to (c).

(4) Where the consent of a third party is required under subsection (1) or (3), the court or arbitral tribunal may, on the application of the parties to the contract, dispense with his consent if satisfied—
(a) that his consent cannot be obtained because his whereabouts cannot reasonably be ascertained, or
(b) that he is mentally incapable of giving his consent.

(5) The court or arbitral tribunal may, on the application of the parties to a contract, dispense with any consent that may be required under subsection (1)(c) if satisfied that it cannot reasonably be ascertained whether or not the third party has in fact relied on the term.

(6) If the court or arbitral tribunal dispenses with a third party's consent, it may impose such conditions as it thinks fit, including a condition requiring the payment of compensation to the third party.

(7) The jurisdiction conferred on the court by subsections (4) to (6) is exercisable by both the High Court and a county court.

3 DEFENCES ETC. AVAILABLE TO PROMISOR

(1) Subsections (2) to (5) apply where, in reliance on section 1, proceedings for the enforcement of a term of a contract are brought by a third party.

(2) The promisor shall have available to him by way of defence or set-off any matter that—
(a) arises from or in connection with the contract and is relevant to the term, and
(b) would have been available to him by way of defence or set-off if the proceedings had been brought by the promisee.

(3) The promisor shall also have available to him by way of defence or set-off any matter if—
(a) an express term of the contract provides for it to be available to him in proceedings brought by the third party, and
(b) it would have been available to him by way of defence or set-off if the proceedings had been brought by the promisee.

(4) The promisor shall also have available to him—
(a) by way of defence or set-off any matter, and
(b) by way of counterclaim any matter not arising from the contract,
that would have been available to him by way of defence or set-off or, as the case may be, by way of counterclaim against the third party if the third party had been a party to the contract.

(5) Subsections (2) and (4) are subject to any express term of the contract as to the matters that are not to be available to the promisor by way of defence, set-off or counterclaim.

(6) Where in any proceedings brought against him a third party seeks in reliance on section 1 to enforce a term of a contract (including, in particular, a term purporting to exclude or limit liability), he may not do so if he could not have done so (whether by reason of any particular circumstances relating to him or otherwise) had he been a party to the contract.

4 ENFORCEMENT OF CONTRACT BY PROMISEE

Section 1 does not affect any right of the promisee to enforce any term of the contract.

5 PROTECTION OF PROMISOR FROM DOUBLE LIABILITY

Where under section 1 a term of a contract is enforceable by a third party, and the promisee has recovered from the promisor a sum in respect of—

(a)   the third party's loss in respect of the term, or

(b)   the expense to the promisee of making good to the third party the default of the promisor,

then, in any proceedings brought in reliance on that section by the third party, the court or arbitral tribunal shall reduce any award to the third party to such extent as it thinks appropriate to take account of the sum recovered by the promisee.

6 EXCEPTIONS

(1)   Section 1 confers no rights on a third party in the case of a contract on a bill of exchange, promissory note or other negotiable instrument.

(2)   Section 1 confers no rights on a third party in the case of any contract binding on a company and its members under section 33 of the Companies Act 2006 (effect of company's constitution).

(2A)   Section 1 confers no rights on a third party in the case of any incorporation document of a limited liability partnership or any agreement (express or implied) between the members of a limited liability partnership, or between a limited liability partnership and its members, that determines the mutual rights and duties of the members and their rights and duties in relation to the limited liability partnership.

(3)   Section 1 confers no right on a third party to enforce—
       (a) any term of a contract of employment against an employee,
       (b) any term of a worker's contract against a worker (including a home worker), or
       (c) any term of a relevant contract against an agency worker.

(4)   In subsection (3)—
       (a) "contract of employment", "employee", "worker's contract", and "worker" have the meaning given by section 54 of the National Minimum Wage Act 1998,
       (b) "home worker" has the meaning given by section 35(2) of that Act,
       (c) "agency worker" has the same meaning as in section 34(1) of that Act, and
       (d) "relevant contract" means a contract entered into, in a case where section 34 of that Act applies, by the agency worker as respects work falling within subsection (1)(a) of that section.

(5)   Section 1 confers no rights on a third party in the case of—
       (a) a contract for the carriage of goods by sea, or
       (b) a contract for the carriage of goods by rail or road, or for the carriage of cargo by air, which is subject to the rules of the appropriate international transport convention,
       except that a third party may in reliance on that section avail himself of an exclusion or limitation of liability in such a contract.

(6)   In subsection (5) "contract for the carriage of goods by sea" means a contract of carriage—
       (a) contained in or evidenced by a bill of lading, sea waybill or a corresponding electronic transaction, or
       (b) under or for the purposes of which there is given an undertaking which is contained in a ship's delivery order or a corresponding electronic transaction.

(7)   For the purposes of subsection (6)—
       (a) "bill of lading", "sea waybill" and "ship's delivery order" have the same meaning as in the Carriage of Goods by Sea Act 1992, and

(b) a corresponding electronic transaction is a transaction within section 1(5) of that Act which corresponds to the issue, indorsement, delivery or transfer of a bill of lading, sea waybill or ship's delivery order.

(8) In subsection (5) "the appropriate international transport convention" means—
    (a) in relation to a contract for the carriage of goods by rail, the Convention which has the force of law in the United Kingdom under regulation 3 of the Railways (Convention on International Carriage by Rail) Regulations 2005,
    (b) in relation to a contract for the carriage of goods by road, the Convention which has the force of law in the United Kingdom under section 1 of the Carriage of Goods by Road Act 1965, and
    (c) in relation to a contract for the carriage of cargo by air—
        (i) the Convention which has the force of law in the United Kingdom under section 1 of the Carriage by Air Act 1961, or
        (ii) the Convention which has the force of law under section 1 of the Carriage by Air (Supplementary Provisions) Act 1962, or

. . .

7 SUPPLEMENTARY PROVISIONS RELATING TO THIRD PARTY

(1) Section 1 does not affect any right or remedy of a third party that exists or is available apart from this Act.

(2) Section 2(2) of the Unfair Contract Terms Act 1977 (restriction on exclusion etc. of liability for negligence) shall not apply where the negligence consists of the breach of an obligation arising from a term of a contract and the person seeking to enforce it is a third party acting in reliance on section 1.

(3) In sections 5 and 8 of the Limitation Act 1980 the references to an action founded on a simple contract and an action upon a specialty shall respectively include references to an action brought in reliance on section 1 relating to a simple contract and an action brought in reliance on that section relating to a specialty.

(4) A third party shall not, by virtue of section 1(5) or 3(4) or (6), be treated as a party to the contract for the purposes of any other Act (or any instrument made under any other Act).

8 ARBITRATION PROVISIONS

(1) Where—
    (a) a right under section 1 to enforce a term ("the substantive term") is subject to a term providing for the submission of disputes to arbitration ("the arbitration agreement"), and
    (b) the arbitration agreement is an agreement in writing for the purposes of Part I of the Arbitration Act 1996,
the third party shall be treated for the purposes of that Act as a party to the arbitration agreement as regards disputes between himself and the promisor relating to the enforcement of the substantive term by the third party.

(2) Where—
    (a) a third party has a right under section 1 to enforce a term providing for one or more descriptions of dispute between the third party and the promisor to be submitted to arbitration ("the arbitration agreement"),
    (b) the arbitration agreement is an agreement in writing for the purposes of Part I of the Arbitration Act 1996, and

(c) the third party does not fall to be treated under subsection (1) as a party to the arbitration agreement,

the third party shall, if he exercises the right, be treated for the purposes of that Act as a party to the arbitration agreement in relation to the matter with respect to which the right is exercised, and be treated as having been so immediately before the exercise of the right.

. . .

10 SHORT TITLE, COMMENCEMENT AND EXTENT

(1) This Act may be cited as the Contracts (Rights of Third Parties) Act 1999.

(2) This Act comes into force on the day on which it is passed but, subject to subsection (3), does not apply in relation to a contract entered into before the end of the period of six months beginning with that day.

(3) The restriction in subsection (2) does not apply in relation to a contract which—
(a) is entered into on or after the day on which this Act is passed, and
(b) expressly provides for the application of this Act.

(4) This Act extends as follows—
(a) section 9 extends to Northern Ireland only;
(b) the remaining provisions extend to England and Wales. . .

As amended by Limited Liability Partnerships Regulations 2001, Sch. 5; Railways (Convention on International Carriage by Rail) Regulations 2005, Sch. 3; Companies Act 2006 (Consequential Amendments, Transitional Provisions and Savings) Order 2009, Sch. 1.

POSTAL SERVICES ACT 2000
(c.26)

89 SCHEMES AS TO TERMS AND CONDITIONS FOR PROVISION OF UNIVERSAL POSTAL SERVICE

. . .

90 EXCLUSION OF LIABILITY

(A1) This section applies in relation to—
(a) the provision by a universal service provider of a universal postal service, and
(b) the provision by a postal operator of a service in relation to which a scheme under section 89 (made by the operator) applies.

(A2) In this section—
(a) "the operator" means the universal service provider or the postal operator concerned, and
(b) "the service" means the service mentioned in subsection (A1)(a) or (b) (as the case may be).

(1) No proceedings in tort shall lie or, in Scotland, be competent against the operator provider in respect of loss or damage suffered by any person in connection with the provision of the service because of—

(a) anything done or omitted to be done in relation to any postal packet in the course of transmission by post, or

(b) any omission to carry out arrangements for the collection of anything to be conveyed by post.

(2) No officer, servant, employee, agent or sub-contractor of the operator shall be subject, except at the suit or instance of the operator, to any civil liability for—

(a) any loss or damage in the case of which liability of the operator is excluded by subsection (1), or

(b) any loss of, or damage to, a postal packet to which section 91 applies.

(3) No person engaged in or about the conveyance of postal packets and no officer, servant, employee, agent or sub-contractor of any such person shall be subject, except at the suit or instance of the operator concerned, to any civil liability for—

(a) any loss or damage in the case of which liability of the operator is excluded by subsection (1), or

(b) any loss of, or damage to, a postal packet to which section 91 applies.

(4) In the application of subsection (1) to Scotland, the reference to proceedings in tort shall be construed in the same way as in section 43(b) of the Crown Proceedings Act 1947.

(5) This section is subject to section 91.

91 LIMITED LIABILITY FOR REGISTERED INLAND PACKETS

(1) Proceedings shall lie or, in Scotland, be competent against a postal operator under this section, but not otherwise, in respect of relevant loss of, or relevant damage to, a postal packet in respect of which the the operator accepts liability under this section in pursuance of a scheme made under section 89.

(2) The references in subsection (1) to relevant loss or damage are to loss or damage so far as it is due to any wrongful act of, or any neglect or default by, an officer, servant, employee, agent or sub-contractor of the universal service provider while performing or purporting to perform in that capacity his functions in relation to the receipt, conveyance, delivery or other dealing with the packet.

(3) No proceedings shall lie or, in Scotland, be competent under this section in relation to a packet unless they are begun within the period of twelve months starting with the day on which the packet was posted.

(4) A universal service provider shall not be liable under this section in respect of a packet of any description unless such conditions (if any) as are required by a scheme under section 89 to be complied with in relation to packets of that description at the time when they are posted have been complied with in the case of the packet.

(5) For the purposes of this section and section 92 a scheme under section 89 may define a description of packet by reference to any circumstances whatever (including, in particular, the amount of any fee paid in respect of the packet in pursuance of the scheme).

(6) In this section "inland packet" means any postal packet which is posted in the United Kingdom for delivery at a place in the United Kingdom to the person to whom it is addressed.

HEALTH AND SOCIAL CARE (COMMUNITY HEALTH AND STANDARDS) ACT 2003
(c.43)

Part 3 RECOVERY OF NHS CHARGES

NHS charges

150 LIABILITY TO PAY NHS CHARGES

(1) This section applies if—
    (a) a person makes a compensation payment to or in respect of any other person (the "injured person") in consequence of any injury, whether physical or psychological, suffered by the injured person, and
    (b) the injured person has—
        (i) received NHS treatment at a health service hospital as a result of the injury,
        (ii) been provided with NHS ambulance services as a result of the injury for the purpose of taking him to a health service hospital for NHS treatment (unless he was dead on arrival at that hospital), or
        (iii) received treatment as mentioned in sub-paragraph (i) and been provided with ambulance services as mentioned in sub-paragraph (ii).

(2) The person making the compensation payment is liable to pay the relevant NHS charges—
    (a) in respect of—
        (i) the treatment, in so far as received at a hospital in England or Wales,
        (ii) the ambulance services, in so far as provided to take the injured person to such a hospital,
  to the Secretary of State,

    (b) in respect of—
        (i) the treatment, in so far as received at a hospital in Scotland,
        (ii) the ambulance services, in so far as provided to take the injured person to such a hospital,
    to the Scottish Ministers.

(3) "Compensation payment" means a payment, including a payment in money's worth, made—
    (a) by or on behalf of a person who is, or is alleged to be, liable to any extent in respect of the injury, or
    (b) in pursuance of a compensation scheme for motor accidents,

  but does not include a payment mentioned in Schedule 10.

(4) Subsection (1)(a) applies—
    (a) to a payment made—
        (i) voluntarily, or in pursuance of a court order or an agreement, or otherwise, and
        (ii) in the United Kingdom or elsewhere, and
    (b) if more than one payment is made, to each payment.

(5) "Injury" does not include any disease.

(6) Nothing in subsection (5) prevents this Part from applying to—
    (a) treatment received as a result of any disease suffered by the injured person, or
    (b) ambulance services provided as a result of any disease suffered by him,

if the disease in question is attributable to the injury suffered by the injured person (and accordingly that treatment is received or those services are provided as a result of the injury).

(7)   "NHS treatment" means any treatment (including any examination of the injured person) other than–

(a)   treatment provided by virtue of–

(i)   section 21(4) or 44(6) of the 2006 Act,

(ii)   paragraph 15 of Schedule 2 to, or paragraph 11 of Schedule 6 to, the 2006 Act,

(iii)   paragraph 15 of Schedule 2 to, or paragraph 11 of Schedule 5 to, the National Health Service (Wales) Act 2006, or

(iv)   section 57 of, or paragraph 14 of Schedule 7A to, the 1978 Act,

(accommodation and services for private patients),

(b)   other treatment provided by an NHS foundation trust in pursuance of an undertaking to pay in respect of the treatment given by or on behalf of the injured person,

(c)   treatment provided at a health service hospital by virtue of section 267 of the 2006 Act or section 198 of the National Health Service (Wales) Act 2006 or section 64 of the 1978 Act (permission for use of national health service accommodation or facilities in private practice), or

(d)   treatment provided by virtue of–

(i)   section 83, 84, 92, 99, 100 or 107 of the 2006 Act, or section 41, 42, 50, 56, 57 or 64 of the National Health Service (Wales) Act 2006 (primary medical and dental services), or

(ii)   section 2C, 17C, 17J or 25 of the 1978 Act (primary medical services or personal or general dental services). . . . .

(10)   "Relevant NHS charges" means the amount (or amounts) specified in a certificate of NHS charges—

(a)   issued under this Part, in respect of the injured person, to the person making the compensation payment, and

(b)   in force.

(11)   "Compensation scheme for motor accidents" means any scheme or arrangement under which funds are available for the payment of compensation in respect of motor accidents caused, or alleged to have been caused, by uninsured or unidentified persons.

(12)   Regulations may amend Schedule 10 by omitting or modifying any payment for the time being specified in that Schedule.

(13)   This section applies in relation to any injury which occurs after the date on which this section comes into force.

(14)   For the purposes of this Part, it is irrelevant whether a compensation payment is made with or without an admission of liability.

Certificates of NHS charges

151   APPLICATIONS FOR CERTIFICATES OF NHS CHARGES

(1)   Before a person makes a compensation payment in consequence of any injury suffered by an injured person, he may apply for a certificate to the Secretary of State, the Scottish Ministers or both, according to whether he believes the relevant NHS charges payable by him (if any) would be due to the Secretary of State, the Scottish Ministers or both.

(2)   If the Secretary of State receives or the Scottish Ministers receive an application under subsection (1), he or they must arrange for a certificate to be issued as soon as is reasonably practicable (subject to section 152).

(3)   A certificate may provide that it is to remain in force—
    (a)   until a specified date,
    (b)   until the occurrence of a specified event, or
    (c)   indefinitely.

153 INFORMATION CONTAINED IN CERTIFICATES

(1)   A certificate must specify the amount (or amounts) for which the person to whom it is issued is liable under section 150(2).

(2)   The amount (or amounts) to be specified is (or are) to be that (or those) set out in, or determined in accordance with, regulations, reduced if applicable in accordance with subsection (3) or regulations under subsection (10).

(3)   If a certificate relates to a claim made by or on behalf of an injured person—
    (a)   in respect of which a court in England and Wales or Scotland has ordered a reduction of damages in accordance with section 1 of the Law Reform (Contributory Negligence) Act 1945 (c. 28),
    (b)   in respect of which a court in Northern Ireland has ordered a reduction of damages in accordance with section 2 of the Law Reform (Miscellaneous Provisions) Act (Northern Ireland) 1948 (c. 23),
    (c)   in respect of which a court in a country other than England and Wales, Scotland or Northern Ireland has ordered a reduction of damages under any provision of the law of that country which appears to the Secretary of State or the Scottish Ministers (as the case may be) to correspond to section 1 of the Law Reform (Contributory Negligence) Act 1945,
    (d)   in respect of which an officer of a court in England and Wales or Northern Ireland has entered or sealed an agreed judgment or order which specifies—
        (i)   that the damages are to be reduced to reflect the injured person's share in the responsibility for the injury in question, and
        (ii)   the amount or proportion by which they are to be so reduced,
    (e)   in the case of which the parties to any resulting action before a court in Scotland have executed a joint minute which specifies—
        (i)   that the action has been settled extra-judicially, and
        (ii)   the matters mentioned in paragraph (d)(i) and (ii),
    (f)   in respect of which a document has been made under any provision of the law of a country other than England and Wales, Scotland or Northern Ireland—
        (i)   which appears to the Secretary of State to correspond to an agreed judgment or order entered or sealed by an officer of a court in England and Wales, and
        (ii)   which specifies the matters mentioned in paragraph (d)(i) and (ii), or
    (g)   in the case of which a document has been made under any provision of the law of a country other than England and Wales, Scotland or Northern Ireland—
        (i)   which appears to the Scottish Ministers to correspond to a joint minute executed by the parties to a resulting action before a court in Scotland specifying that the action has been settled extra-judicially, and
        (ii)   which specifies the matters mentioned in paragraph (d)(i) and (ii),
    the amount (or amounts) specified in the certificate is (or are) to be that (or those) which would be so specified apart from this subsection, reduced by the same proportion as the reduction of damages.

(4)   If a certificate relates to an injured person who has not received NHS treatment at a health service hospital or been provided with NHS ambulance services as a result of the injury, it must indicate that no amount is payable to the Secretary of State or the Scottish Ministers (as the case may be) by reference to that certificate.

Recovery of NHS charges

155 RECOVERY OF NHS CHARGES

(1) This section applies if a person has made a compensation payment and either—
   (a) subsection (7) of section 151 applies but he has not applied for a certificate as required by that subsection, or
   (b) he has not made payment, in full, of any amount due under section 150(2) by the end of the period allowed under section 154.

(2) The Secretary of State, the Scottish Ministers or both, according to the circumstances of the case, may—
   (a) in a case within subsection (1)(a), issue the person who made the compensation payment with a certificate, and
   (b) in a case within subsection (1)(b), issue him with a copy of the certificate or (if more than one has been issued) the most recent one,
   and, in either case, issue him with a demand that payment of any amount due under section 150(2) be made immediately.

(3) Subsections (5) and (6) of section 152 apply to certificates issued under subsection (2) above as they apply to certificates issued under section 151.

(4) A demand issued under subsection (2) may be issued jointly by the Secretary of State and the Scottish Ministers specifying—
   (a) an amount due under subsection (2) of section 150 to the Secretary of State, and
   (b) an amount due under that subsection to the Scottish Ministers,
   in respect of the same injured person in consequence of the same injury.

(5) In the case of a demand specifying amounts as mentioned in subsection (4)(a) and (b), references in the following provisions of this section to a demand are to be taken as being (as the case may require) to—
   (a) the demand in so far as it relates to any amount due to the Secretary of State, or
   (b) the demand in so far as it relates to any amount due to the Scottish Ministers,
   and related expressions are to be read accordingly.

(6) The Secretary of State or the Scottish Ministers may recover the amount for which a demand for payment is made under subsection (2) from the person who made the compensation payment.

(7) If the person who made the compensation payment resides or carries on business in England or Wales and a county court so orders, the amount demanded is recoverable under section 85 of the County Courts Act 1984 or otherwise as if it were payable under an order of that court.

(8) If the person who made the compensation payment resides or carries on business in Scotland, the demand may be enforced as if it were an extract registered decree arbitral bearing a warrant for execution issued by the sheriff court of any sheriffdom in Scotland.

(9) A document which states that it is a record of the amount recoverable under subsection (6) is conclusive evidence that the amount is so recoverable if it is signed by a person authorised to do so by the Secretary of State or the Scottish Ministers (as the case may be).

(10) For the purposes of subsection (9), a document purporting to be signed by a person authorised to do so by the Secretary of State or the Scottish Ministers (as the case may be) is to be treated as so signed unless the contrary is proved.

Payments to hospitals or ambulance trusts

162 PAYMENT OF NHS CHARGES TO HOSPITALS OR AMBULANCE TRUSTS

(1)   If the Secretary of State receives or the Scottish Ministers receive a payment of relevant NHS charges under section 150(2)—
(a)   if the payment relates only to NHS treatment received at a health service hospital, he or they must pay the amount received to the responsible body of the health service hospital,
(b)   if the payment relates only to the provision of NHS ambulance services, he or they must pay the amount received to the relevant ambulance trust,
(c)   if the payment relates to NHS treatment received at more than one health service hospital, he or they must divide the amount received among the responsible bodies of the hospitals concerned in such manner as he considers or they consider appropriate,
(d)   if the payment relates to NHS treatment received at one or more health service hospitals and the provision of NHS ambulance services, he or they must divide the amount received among the responsible body or bodies of the hospital or hospitals and any relevant ambulance trusts concerned in such manner as he considers or they consider appropriate.

(2)   Subsection (1) does not apply to any amount received by the Secretary of State or the Scottish Ministers under section 150(2) which he is or they are required to repay in accordance with regulations under section 153(2).

(3)   Regulations under this section may—
(a)   make provision for the manner in which and intervals at which any payments due under this section are to be made,
(b)   make provision for cases where the responsible body of the health service hospital or relevant ambulance trust concerned has ceased to exist (including provision modifying this Part).

(4)   Any amounts received under this section by the responsible bodies of the health service hospitals concerned must be used for the purposes of providing goods and services for the benefit of patients receiving NHS treatment at those hospitals.

(5)   Any amounts received under this section by the relevant ambulance trusts concerned must be used for the purposes of NHS ambulance services.

163 REGULATIONS GOVERNING LUMP SUMS, PERIODICAL PAYMENTS ETC.

(1)   Regulations may make provision (including provision modifying this Part)—
(a)   for cases to which section 150(2) applies in which two or more compensation payments in the form of lump sums are made by the same person in respect of the same injury,
(b)   for cases to which section 150(2) applies in which an agreement is entered into for the making of—
(i)   periodical compensation payments (whether of an income or capital nature), or
(ii)   periodical compensation payments and lump sum compensation payments,
(c)   for cases in which the compensation payment to which section 150(2) applies is an interim payment of damages which a court orders to be repaid.

(2)   Regulations made by virtue of subsection (1)(a) may (among other things) provide—
(a)   for giving credit for amounts already paid, and

(b) for the payment by any person of any balance or the recovery from any person of any excess.

(3) Regulations may make provision modifying the application of this Part in relation to cases in which a payment into court is made and, in particular, may provide—
    (a) for the making of a payment into court to be treated in prescribed circumstances as the making of a compensation payment,
    (b) for application for, and issue of, certificates.

164 LIABILITY OF INSURERS

(1) If a compensation payment is made in a case where—
    (a) a person is liable to any extent in respect of the injury, and
    (b) the liability is covered to any extent by a policy of insurance,
the policy is also to be treated as covering any liability of that person under section 150(2).

(2) Liability imposed on the insurer by subsection (1) cannot be excluded or restricted.

(3) For that purpose excluding or restricting liability includes—
    (a) making the liability or its enforcement subject to restrictive or onerous conditions,
    (b) excluding or restricting any right or remedy in respect of the liability, or subjecting a person to any prejudice in consequence of his pursuing any such right or remedy, or
    (c) excluding or restricting rules of evidence or procedure.

(4) Regulations may in prescribed cases limit the amount of the liability imposed on the insurer by subsection (1).

(5) This section applies in relation to policies of insurance issued before (as well as those issued after) the date on which it comes into force.

(6) References in this section to policies of insurance and their issue include references to contracts of insurance and their making.

166 THE CROWN

This Part binds the Crown.

CRIMINAL JUSTICE ACT 2003
(c.44)

329 CIVIL PROCEEDINGS FOR TRESPASS TO THE PERSON BROUGHT BY OFFENDER

(1) This section applies where—
    (a) a person ("the claimant") claims that another person ("the defendant") did an act amounting to trespass to the claimant's person, and
    (b) the claimant has been convicted in the United Kingdom of an imprisonable offence committed on the same occasion as that on which the act is alleged to have been done.

(2) Civil proceedings relating to the claim may be brought only with the permission of the court.

(3) The court may give permission for the proceedings to be brought only if there is evidence that either—
    (a) the condition in subsection (5) is not met, or

(b) in all the circumstances, the defendant's act was grossly disproportionate.

(4) If the court gives permission and the proceedings are brought, it is a defence for the defendant to prove both—
   (a) that the condition in subsection (5) is met, and
   (b) that, in all the circumstances, his act was not grossly disproportionate.

(5) The condition referred to in subsection (3)(a) and (4)(a) is that the defendant did the act only because—
   (a) he believed that the claimant—
      (i) was about to commit an offence,
      (ii) was in the course of committing an offence, or
      (iii) had committed an offence immediately beforehand; and
   (b) he believed that the act was necessary to—
      (i) defend himself or another person,
      (ii) protect or recover property,
      (iii) prevent the commission or continuation of an offence, or
      (iv) apprehend, or secure the conviction, of the claimant after he had committed an offence;
   or was necessary to assist in achieving any of those things.

(6) Subsection (4) is without prejudice to any other defence.

(7) Where—
   (a) a person is convicted of an offence under s 42 of the Armed Forces Act 2006 (criminal conduct),
   and

   (b) the corresponding civil offence (within the meaning of that Act) was an imprisonable offence,
   he is to be treated for the purposes of this section as having been convicted in the United Kingdom of the corresponding offence, and in paragraph (a) the reference to conviction includes anything that under section 376(1) and (2) of that Act is to be treated as a conviction.

(8) In this section—
   (a) the reference to trespass to the person is a reference to—
      (i) assault,
      (ii) battery, or
      (iii) false imprisonment;
   (b) references to a defendant's belief are to his honest belief, whether or not the belief was also reasonable;
   (c) "court" means the High Court or a county court; and
   (d) "imprisonable offence" means an offence which, in the case of a person aged 18 or over, is punishable by imprisonment.

FIRE AND RESCUE SERVICES ACT 2004
(c.21)

11 POWER TO RESPOND TO OTHER EVENTUALITIES

(1) A fire and rescue authority may take any action it considers appropriate—
   (a) in response to an event or situation of a kind mentioned in subsection (2);
   (b) for the purpose of enabling action to be taken in response to such an event or situation.

(2)   The event or situation is one that causes or is likely to cause—
    (a)   one or more individuals to die, be injured or become ill;
    (b)   harm to the environment (including the life and health of plants and animals).

(3)   The power conferred by subsection (1) includes power to secure the provision of equipment.

(4)   The power conferred by subsection (1) may be exercised by an authority outside as well as within the authority's area.

58 MEANING OF "EMERGENCY"

In this Act "emergency" means an event or situation that causes or is likely to cause—
(a)   one or more individuals to die, be seriously injured or become seriously ill, or

(b)   serious harm to the environment (including the life and health of plants and animals).

CIVIL PARTNERSHIP ACT 2004
(c.33)

Part 1 INTRODUCTION

1 CIVIL PARTNERSHIP

(1)   A civil partnership is a relationship between two people of the same sex ("civil partners")—
    (a)   which is formed when they register as civil partners of each other—
        (i)   in England or Wales (under Part 2),
        (ii)   in Scotland (under Part 3),
        (iii) in Northern Ireland (under Part 4), or
        (iv)   outside the United Kingdom under an Order in Council made under Chapter 1 of Part 5 (registration at British consulates etc. or by armed forces personnel), or
    (b)   which they are treated under Chapter 2 of Part 5 as having formed (at the time determined under that Chapter) by virtue of having registered an overseas relationship.

69 ACTIONS IN TORT BETWEEN CIVIL PARTNERS

(1)   This section applies if an action in tort is brought by one civil partner against the other during the subsistence of the civil partnership.

(2)   The court may stay the proceedings if it appears—
    (a)   that no substantial benefit would accrue to either civil partner from the continuation of the proceedings, or
    (b)   that the question or questions in issue could more conveniently be disposed of on an application under section 66.

(3)   Without prejudice to subsection (2)(b), the court may in such an action—
    (a)   exercise any power which could be exercised on an application under section 66, or
    (b)   give such directions as it thinks fit for the disposal under that section of any question arising in the proceedings.

73 CIVIL PARTNERSHIP AGREEMENTS UNENFORCEABLE

(1)   A civil partnership agreement does not under the law of England and Wales have effect as a contract giving rise to legal rights.

(2)   No action lies in England and Wales for breach of a civil partnership agreement, whatever the law applicable to the agreement.

(3)   In this section and section 74 "civil partnership agreement" means an agreement between two people—
   (a) to register as civil partners of each other—
       (i)   in England and Wales (under this Part),
       (ii) in Scotland (under Part 3),
       (iii) in Northern Ireland (under Part 4), or
       (iv) outside the United Kingdom under an Order in Council made under Chapter 1 of Part 5 (registration at British consulates etc. or by armed forces personnel), or
   (b) to enter into an overseas relationship.

(4)   This section applies in relation to civil partnership agreements whether entered into before or after this section comes into force, but does not affect any action commenced before it comes into force.

. . .

128 PROMISE OR AGREEMENT TO ENTER INTO CIVIL PARTNERSHIP

No promise or agreement to enter into civil partnership creates any rights or obligations under the law of Scotland; and no action for breach of such a promise or agreement may be brought in any court in Scotland, whatever the law applicable to the promise or agreement.

MENTAL CAPACITY ACT 2005
(c.9)

Preliminary

2 PEOPLE WHO LACK CAPACITY

(1)   For the purposes of this Act, a person lacks capacity in relation to a matter if at the material time he is unable to make a decision for himself in relation to the matter because of an impairment of, or a disturbance in the functioning of, the mind or brain.

(2)   It does not matter whether the impairment or disturbance is permanent or temporary.

(3)   A lack of capacity cannot be established merely by reference to—
   (a) a person's age or appearance, or
   (b) a condition of his, or an aspect of his behaviour, which might lead others to make unjustified assumptions about his capacity.

(4)   In proceedings under this Act or any other enactment, any question whether a person lacks capacity within the meaning of this Act must be decided on the balance of probabilities.

(5)   No power which a person ("D") may exercise under this Act—
   (a) in relation to a person who lacks capacity, or
   (b) where D reasonably thinks that a person lacks capacity,
   is exercisable in relation to a person under 16.

(6)   Subsection (5) is subject to section 18(3).

. . .

7 PAYMENT FOR NECESSARY GOODS AND SERVICES

(1)   If necessary goods or services are supplied to a person who lacks capacity to contract for the supply, he must pay a reasonable price for them.

(2)   "Necessary" means suitable to a person's condition in life and to his actual requirements at the time when the goods or services are supplied.

. . .

68 COMMENCEMENT AND EXTENT

. . .

(4)   Subject to subsections (5) and (6), this Act extends to England and Wales only.

(5)   The following provisions extend to the United Kingdom—
 (a)   paragraph 16(1) of Schedule 1 (evidence of instruments and of registration of lasting powers of attorney),
 (b)   paragraph 15(3) of Schedule 4 (evidence of instruments and of registration of enduring powers of attorney).

INQUIRIES ACT 2005
(c.12)

37 IMMUNITY FROM SUIT

(1)   No action lies against—
 (a)   a member of an inquiry panel,
 (b)   an assessor, counsel or solicitor to an inquiry, or
 (c)   a person engaged to provide assistance to an inquiry,
in respect of any act done or omission made in the execution of his duty as such, or any act done or omission made in good faith in the purported execution of his duty as such.

(2)   Subsection (1) applies only to acts done or omissions made during the course of the inquiry, otherwise than during any period of suspension (within the meaning of section 13).

(3)   For the purposes of the law of defamation, the same privilege attaches to—
 (a)   any statement made in or for the purposes of proceedings before an inquiry (including the report and any interim report of the inquiry), and
 (b)   reports of proceedings before an inquiry,
as would be the case if those proceedings were proceedings before a court in the relevant part of the United Kingdom.

COMPENSATION ACT 2006
(c.29)

Part 1 STANDARD OF CARE

1 DETERRENT EFFECT OF POTENTIAL LIABILITY

A court considering a claim in negligence or breach of statutory duty may, in determining whether the defendant should have taken particular steps to meet a standard of care (whether by taking precautions against a risk or otherwise), have regard to whether a requirement to take those steps might—

(a)   prevent a desirable activity from being undertaken at all, to a particular extent or in a particular way, or

(b)   discourage persons from undertaking functions in connection with a desirable activity.

2   APOLOGIES, OFFERS OF TREATMENT OR OTHER REDRESS

An apology, an offer of treatment or other redress, shall not of itself amount to an admission of negligence or breach of statutory duty.

3   MESOTHELIOMA: DAMAGES

(1)   This section applies where—
    (a)   a person ("**the responsible person**") has negligently or in breach of statutory duty caused or permitted another person ("**the victim**") to be exposed to asbestos,
    (b)   the victim has contracted mesothelioma as a result of exposure to asbestos,
    (c)   because of the nature of mesothelioma and the state of medical science, it is not possible to determine with certainty whether it was the exposure mentioned in paragraph (a) or another exposure which caused the victim to become ill, and
    (d)   the responsible person is liable in tort, by virtue of the exposure mentioned in paragraph (a), in connection with damage caused to the victim by the disease (whether by reason of having materially increased a risk or for any other reason).

(2)   The responsible person shall be liable—
    (a)   in respect of the whole of the damage caused to the victim by the disease (irrespective of whether the victim was also exposed to asbestos—
        (i)   other than by the responsible person, whether or not in circumstances in which another person has liability in tort, or
        (ii)   by the responsible person in circumstances in which he has no liability in tort), and
    (b)   jointly and severally with any other responsible person.

(3)   Subsection (2) does not prevent—
    (a)   one responsible person from claiming a contribution from another, or
    (b)   a finding of contributory negligence.

(4)   In determining the extent of contributions of different responsible persons in accordance with subsection (3)(a), a court shall have regard to the relative lengths of the periods of exposure for which each was responsible; but this subsection shall not apply—
    (a)   if or to the extent that responsible persons agree to apportion responsibility amongst themselves on some other basis, or
    (b)   if or to the extent that the court thinks that another basis for determining contributions is more appropriate in the circumstances of a particular case.

(5)   In subsection (1) the reference to causing or permitting a person to be exposed to asbestos includes a reference to failing to protect a person from exposure to asbestos.

(6)   In the application of this section to Scotland—
    (a)   a reference to tort shall be taken as a reference to delict, and
    (b)   a reference to a court shall be taken to include a reference to a jury.

(7)   The Treasury may make regulations about the provision of compensation to a responsible person where—

(a) he claims, or would claim, a contribution from another responsible person in accordance with subsection (3)(a), but

(b) he is unable or likely to be unable to obtain the contribution, because an insurer of the other responsible person is unable or likely to be unable to satisfy the claim for a contribution.

(8) The regulations may, in particular—

(a) replicate or apply (with or without modification) a provision of the Financial Services Compensation Scheme;

(b) replicate or apply (with or without modification) a transitional compensation provision;

(c) provide for a specified person to assess and pay compensation;

(d) provide for expenses incurred (including the payment of compensation) to be met out of levies collected in accordance with section 213(3)(b) of the Financial Services and Markets Act 2000 (c. 8)(the Financial Services Compensation Scheme);

(e) modify the effect of a transitional compensation provision;

(f) enable the Financial Services Authority to amend the Financial Services Compensation Scheme;

(g) modify the Financial Services and Markets Act 2000 in its application to an amendment pursuant to paragraph (f);

(h) make, or require the making of, provision for the making of a claim by a responsible person for compensation whether or not he has already satisfied claims in tort against him;

(i) make, or require the making of, provision which has effect in relation to claims for contributions made on or after the date on which this Act is passed.

(9) Provision made by virtue of subsection (8)(a) shall cease to have effect when the Financial Services Compensation Scheme is amended by the Financial Services Authority by virtue of subsection (8)(f).

(10) In subsections (7) and (8)—

(a) a reference to a responsible person includes a reference to an insurer of a responsible person, and

(b) "transitional compensation provision" means a provision of an enactment which is made under the Financial Services and Markets Act 2000 and—

(i) preserves the effect of the Policyholders Protection Act 1975 (c. 75), or

(ii) applies the Financial Services Compensation Scheme in relation to matters arising before its establishment.

(11) Regulations under subsection (7)—

(a) may include consequential or incidental provision,

(b) may make provision which has effect generally or only in relation to specified cases or circumstances,

(c) may make different provision for different cases or circumstances,

(d) shall be made by statutory instrument, and

(e) may not be made unless a draft has been laid before and approved by resolution of each House of Parliament.

Part 2 CLAIMS MANAGEMENT SERVICES

4 PROVISION OF REGULATED CLAIMS MANAGEMENT SERVICES

(1) A person may not provide regulated claims management services unless—

(a) he is an authorised person,

(b) he is an exempt person,

      (c) the requirement for authorisation has been waived in relation to him in accordance with regulations under section 9, or

      (d) he is an individual acting otherwise than in the course of a business.

(2)   In this Part—

      (a) "authorised person" means a person authorised by the Regulator under section 5(1)(a),

      (b) "claims management services" means advice or other services in relation to the making of a claim,

      (c) "claim" means a claim for compensation, restitution, repayment or any other remedy or relief in respect of loss or damage or in respect of an obligation, whether the claim is made or could be made—

          (i) by way of legal proceedings,

          (ii) in accordance with a scheme of regulation (whether voluntary or compulsory), or

          (iii) in pursuance of a voluntary undertaking,

      (d) "exempt person" has the meaning given by section 6(5), and

      (e) services are regulated if they are—

          (i) of a kind prescribed by order of the Secretary of State, or

          (ii) provided in cases or circumstances of a kind prescribed by order of the Secretary of State.

(2A) The Secretary of State may not make an order under subsection (2)(e) unless–

      (a) it is made in accordance with a recommendation made by the Legal Services Board, or

      (b) the Secretary of State has consulted the Legal Services Board about the making of an order.

(3)   For the purposes of this section—

      (a) a reference to the provision of services includes, in particular, a reference to—

          (i) the provision of financial services or assistance,

          (ii) the provision of services by way of or in relation to legal representation,

          (iii) referring or introducing one person to another, and

          (iv) making inquiries, and

      (b) a person does not provide claims management services by reason only of giving, or preparing to give, evidence (whether or not expert evidence).

(4)   For the purposes of subsection (1)(d) an individual acts in the course of a business if, in particular—

      (a) he acts in the course of an employment, or

      (b) he otherwise receives or hopes to receive money or money's worth as a result of his action.

(5)   The Secretary of State may by order provide that a claim for a specified benefit shall be treated as a claim for the purposes of this Part.

(6)   The Secretary of State may specify a benefit under subsection (5) only if it appears to him to be a United Kingdom social security benefit designed to provide compensation for industrial injury.

FRAUD ACT 2006
(c.35)

Fraud

1 FRAUD

(1)   A person is guilty of fraud if he is in breach of any of the sections listed in subsection (2) (which provide for different ways of committing the offence).

(2)   The sections are—
(a)   section 2 (fraud by false representation),
(b)   section 3 (fraud by failing to disclose information), and
(c)   section 4 (fraud by abuse of position).

(3)   A person who is guilty of fraud is liable—
(a)   on summary conviction, to imprisonment for a term not exceeding 12 months or to a fine not exceeding the statutory maximum (or to both);
(b)   on conviction on indictment, to imprisonment for a term not exceeding 10 years or to a fine (or to both).

(4)   Subsection (3)(a) applies in relation to Northern Ireland as if the reference to 12 months were a reference to 6 months.

2 FRAUD BY FALSE REPRESENTATION

(1)   A person is in breach of this section if he—
(a)   dishonestly makes a false representation, and
(b)   intends, by making the representation—
(i)   to make a gain for himself or another, or
(ii) to cause loss to another or to expose another to a risk of loss.

(2)   A representation is false if—
(a)   it is untrue or misleading, and
(b)   the person making it knows that it is, or might be, untrue or misleading.

(3)   "Representation" means any representation as to fact or law, including a representation as to the state of mind of—
(a)   the person making the representation, or
(b)   any other person.

(4)   A representation may be express or implied.

(5)   For the purposes of this section a representation may be regarded as made if it (or anything implying it) is submitted in any form to any system or device designed to receive, convey or respond to communications (with or without human intervention).

3 FRAUD BY FAILING TO DISCLOSE INFORMATION

A person is in breach of this section if he—
(a)   dishonestly fails to disclose to another person information which he is under a legal duty to disclose, and

(b)   intends, by failing to disclose the information—
(i)   to make a gain for himself or another, or
(ii) to cause loss to another or to expose another to a risk of loss.

4 FRAUD BY ABUSE OF POSITION

(1)   A person is in breach of this section if he—
    (a)   occupies a position in which he is expected to safeguard, or not to act against, the financial interests of another person,
    (b)   dishonestly abuses that position, and
    (c)   intends, by means of the abuse of that position—
        (i)   to make a gain for himself or another, or
        (ii)   to cause loss to another or to expose another to a risk of loss.

(2)   A person may be regarded as having abused his position even though his conduct consisted of an omission rather than an act.

5 "GAIN" AND "LOSS"

(1)   The references to gain and loss in sections 2 to 4 are to be read in accordance with this section.

(2)   "Gain" and "loss"—
    (a)   extend only to gain or loss in money or other property;
    (b)   include any such gain or loss whether temporary or permanent;
and "property" means any property whether real or personal (including things in action and other intangible property).

(3)   "Gain" includes a gain by keeping what one has, as well as a gain by getting what one does not have.

(4)   "Loss" includes a loss by not getting what one might get, as well as a loss by parting with what one has.

EDUCATION AND INSPECTIONS ACT 2006
(c.40)

93 POWER OF MEMBERS OF STAFF TO USE FORCE

(1)   A person to whom this section applies may use such force as is reasonable in the circumstances for the purpose of preventing a pupil from doing (or continuing to do) any of the following, namely—
    (a)   committing any offence,
    (b)   causing personal injury to, or damage to the property of, any person (including the pupil himself), or
    (c)   prejudicing the maintenance of good order and discipline at the school or among any pupils receiving education at the school, whether during a teaching session or otherwise.

(2)   This section applies to a person who is, in relation to a pupil, a member of the staff of any school at which education is provided for the pupil.

(3)   The power conferred by subsection (1) may be exercised only where—
    (a)   the member of the staff and the pupil are on the premises of the school in question, or
    (b)   they are elsewhere and the member of the staff has lawful control or charge of the pupil concerned.

(4)   Subsection (1) does not authorise anything to be done in relation to a pupil which constitutes the giving of corporal punishment within the meaning of section 548 of EA 1996.

(5)   The powers conferred by subsection (1) are in addition to any powers exercisable apart from this section and are not to be construed as restricting what may lawfully be done apart from this section.

(6)   In this section, "offence" includes anything that would be an offence but for the operation of any presumption that a person under a particular age is incapable of committing an offence.

93A RECORDING AND REPORTING THE USE OF FORCE BY MEMBERS OF STAFF: ENGLAND

(1)   The governing body of a school in England must ensure that a procedure is in place for—
   (a)   recording each significant incident in which a member of the staff uses force on a pupil for whom education is being provided at the school (a "use of force incident"); and
   (b)   reporting each use of force incident (except those where the pupil is aged 20 or over or provision made under subsection (5) applies) to each parent of the pupil as soon as practicable after the incident.

(2)   The governing body must take all reasonable steps to ensure that the procedure is complied with.

(3)   The procedure must require that a record of a use of force incident is made in writing as soon as practicable after the incident.

(4)   In discharging their duty under subsection (1), the governing body must have regard to any guidance issued by the Secretary of State for the purposes of that subsection.

(5)   A procedure under subsection (1) must include provision to the effect—
   (a)   that a person ("R") who would otherwise be required by the procedure to report an incident to a parent must not report it to that parent if it appears to R that doing so would be likely to result in significant harm to the pupil; and
   (b)   that if it appears to R that there is no parent of the pupil to whom R could report the incident without that being likely to result in significant harm to the pupil, R must report the incident to the local authority within whose area the pupil is ordinarily resident.

(6)   In deciding for the purposes of provision made under subsection (5) whether reporting an incident to a parent would be likely to result in significant harm to the pupil, R must have regard to any guidance issued by the Secretary of State about the meaning of "significant harm" for those purposes.

(7)   In this section—

"governing body", in relation to a school which is not a maintained school, means the proprietor of the school;

"maintained school" means—
   (a)   a community, foundation or voluntary school;
   (b)   a community or foundation special school;
   (c)   a maintained nursery school;

"parent", in relation to a pupil, has the meaning given by section 576 of EA 1996 in relation to a child or young person, but includes a local authority which provides accommodation for the pupil under section 20 of the Children Act 1989.

94 DEFENCE WHERE CONFISCATION LAWFUL

(1)   This section applies where, as a disciplinary penalty—
(a)   an item which a pupil has with him or in his possessions is seized, and
(b)   the item is retained for any period or is disposed of.

(2)   A person who seizes, retains or disposes of the item is not liable in any proceedings in respect of—
(a)   the seizure, retention or disposal (as the case may be), or
(b)   any damage or loss which arises in consequence of it,
if he proves that the seizure, retention or disposal (as the case may be) was lawful (whether or not by virtue of section 91).

(3)   Nothing in this section applies where an item is seized under section 550ZC or 550AA of EA 1996 (provision as to what is to be done with such an item being made by that section).

(4)   This section is not to be construed as preventing any person relying on any defence on which he is entitled to rely apart from this section.

Editor's Note: s 93A not yet in force.

NHS REDRESS ACT 2006
(c.44)

England

1 POWER TO ESTABLISH REDRESS SCHEME

(1)   The Secretary of State may by regulations establish a scheme for the purpose of enabling redress to be provided without recourse to civil proceedings in circumstances in which this section applies.

(2)   This section applies where under the law of England and Wales qualifying liability in tort on the part of a body or other person mentioned in subsection (3) arises in connection with the provision, as part of the health service in England, of qualifying services.

(3)   he bodies and other persons referred to are—
(a)   the Secretary of State,
(b)   a Primary Care Trust,
(c)   a designated Strategic Health Authority, and
(d)   a body or other person providing, or arranging for the provision of, services whose provision is the subject of arrangements with a body or other person mentioned in paragraph (a), (b) or (c).

(4)   The reference in subsection (2) to qualifying liability in tort is to liability in tort owed—
(a)   in respect of or consequent upon personal injury or loss arising out of or in connection with breach of a duty of care owed to any person in connection with the diagnosis of illness, or the care or treatment of any patient, and
(b)   in consequence of any act or omission by a health care professional.

(5)   For the purposes of subsection (2), services are qualifying services if—
(a)   they are provided in a hospital (in England or elsewhere), or
(b)   they are of such other description (including a description involving provision outside England) as the Secretary of State may specify by regulations.

(6) Regulations under subsection (5)(b) may not specify services of any of the following descriptions—
    (a) primary dental services,
    (b) primary medical services,
    (c) services provided under section 38 of the National Health Service Act 1977 (c. 49) (general ophthalmic services),
    (d) services provided under section 126 of the National Health Service Act 2006 (arrangements for pharmaceutical services) or by virtue of section 127 of that Act (arrangements for additional pharmaceutical services), and
    (e) services of a kind which may be provided under section 126 of that Act, or by virtue of section 127 of that Act, which are provided under Schedule 12 to that Act (local pharmaceutical services schemes) or under section 134 of that Act (local pharmaceutical services pilot schemes).

(7) The references in subsection (6) to primary dental services and primary medical services are to primary dental services and primary medical services under the National Health Services Act 2006, except that the Secretary of State may by regulations provide that services of a description specified in the regulations are not to be regarded as primary dental services or primary medical services for the purposes of that subsection.

(8) Regulations under subsection (5)(b) or (7) may, in particular, describe services by reference to the manner or circumstances in which they are provided.

(9) In subsection (3)(d), the reference to a person providing services does not include a person providing services under a contract of employment.

(10) In subsection (4), the reference to a health care professional is to a member of a profession (whether or not regulated by, or by virtue of, any enactment) which is concerned (wholly or partly) with the physical or mental health of individuals.

(11) In this section, "hospital" has the same meaning as in the National Health Service Act 2006.

2 APPLICATION OF SCHEME

(1) Subject to subsection (2), a scheme may make such provision defining its application as the Secretary of State thinks fit.

(2) A scheme must provide that it does not apply in relation to a liability that is or has been the subject of civil proceedings.

3 REDRESS UNDER SCHEME

(1) Subject to subsections (2) and (5), a scheme may make such provision as the Secretary of State thinks fit about redress under the scheme.

(2) A scheme must provide for redress ordinarily to comprise—
    (a) the making of an offer of compensation in satisfaction of any right to bring civil proceedings in respect of the liability concerned,
    (b) the giving of an explanation,
    (c) the giving of an apology, and
    (d) the giving of a report on the action which has been, or will be, taken to prevent similar cases arising,
but may specify circumstances in which one or more of those forms of redress is not required.

(3)   A scheme may, in particular—
    (a)   make provision for the compensation that may be offered to take the form of entry into a contract to provide care or treatment or of financial compensation, or both;
    (b)   make provision about the circumstances in which different forms of compensation may be offered.

(4)   A scheme that provides for financial compensation to be offered may, in particular—
    (a)   make provision about the matters in respect of which financial compensation may be offered;
    (b)   make provision with respect to the assessment of the amount of any financial compensation.

(5)   A scheme that provides for financial compensation to be offered—
    (a)   may specify an upper limit on the amount of financial compensation that may be included in an offer under the scheme;
    (b)   if it does not specify a limit under paragraph (a), must specify an upper limit on the amount of financial compensation that may be included in such an offer in respect of pain and suffering;
    (c)   may not specify any other limit on what may be included in such an offer by way of financial compensation.

4   COMMENCEMENT OF PROCEEDINGS UNDER SCHEME

(1)   A scheme may make such provision as the Secretary of State thinks fit about the commencement of proceedings under the scheme.

(2)   A scheme may, in particular, make provision—
    (a)   about who may commence proceedings under the scheme;
    (b)   about how proceedings under the scheme may be commenced;
    (c)   for time limits in relation to the commencement of proceedings under the scheme;
    (d)   about circumstances in which proceedings under the scheme may not be commenced;
    (e)   requiring proceedings under the scheme to be commenced in specified circumstances;
    (f)   for notification of the commencement of proceedings under the scheme in specified circumstances.

5   DUTY TO CONSIDER POTENTIAL APPLICATION OF SCHEME

(1)   The Secretary of State may by regulations make provision requiring any body or other person mentioned in subsection (2)—
    (a)   to consider, in such circumstances as the regulations may provide, whether a case that the body or other person is investigating or reviewing involves liability to which a scheme applies, and
    (b)   if it appears that it does, to take such steps as the regulations may provide.

(2)   The bodies and other persons referred to are—
    (a)   any body or other person to whose liability a scheme applies, and
    (b)   the Care Quality Commission.

6   PROCEEDINGS UNDER SCHEME

(1)   Subject to subsections (3) to (6), a scheme may make such provision as the Secretary of State thinks fit about proceedings under the scheme.

(2)   A scheme may, in particular, make provision—

(a) about the investigation of cases under the scheme (including provision for the overseeing of the investigation by an individual of a specified description);

(b) about the making of decisions about the application of the scheme;

(c) for time limits in relation to acceptance of an offer of compensation under the scheme;

(d) about the form and content of settlement agreements under the scheme;

(e) for settlement agreements under the scheme to be subject in cases of a specified description to approval by a court;

(f) about the termination of proceedings under the scheme.

(3) A scheme must—

(a) make provision for the findings of an investigation of a case under the scheme to be recorded in a report, and

(b) subject to subsection (4), make provision for a copy of the report to be provided on request to the individual seeking redress.

(4) A scheme may provide that no copy of an investigation report need be provided—

(a) before an offer is made under the scheme or proceedings under the scheme are terminated, or

(b) in such other circumstances as may be specified.

(5) A scheme must provide for a settlement agreement under the scheme to include a waiver of the right to bring civil proceedings in respect of the liability to which the settlement relates.

(6) A scheme must provide for the termination of proceedings under the scheme if the liability to which the proceedings relate becomes the subject of civil proceedings.

7 SUSPENSION OF LIMITATION PERIOD

(1) A scheme must make provision for the period during which a liability is the subject of proceedings under the scheme to be disregarded for the purposes of calculating whether any relevant limitation period has expired.

(2) In subsection (1), the reference to any relevant limitation period is to any period of time for the bringing of civil proceedings in respect of the liability which is prescribed by or under the Limitation Act 1980 (c. 58) or any other enactment.

(3) A scheme may define for the purposes of provision in pursuance of subsection (1) when liability is the subject of proceedings under the scheme.

8 LEGAL ADVICE ETC.

(1) Subject to subsections (2) and (4), a scheme may make such provision as the Secretary of State thinks fit—

(a) for the provision of legal advice without charge to individuals seeking redress under the scheme;

(b) for the provision in connection with proceedings under the scheme of other services, including the services of medical experts.

(2) A scheme must make such provision as the Secretary of State considers appropriate in order to secure that individuals to whom an offer under the scheme is made have access to legal advice without charge in relation to—

(a) the offer, and

(b) any settlement agreement.

(3)   Provision under subsection (1)(a) or (2) about who may provide the legal advice may operate by reference to whether a potential provider is included in a list prepared by a specified person.

(4)   A scheme that makes provision for the provision of the services of medical experts must provide for such experts to be instructed jointly by the scheme authority and the individual seeking redress under the scheme.

9 ASSISTANCE FOR INDIVIDUALS SEEKING REDRESS UNDER SCHEME

(1)   It is the duty of the Secretary of State to arrange, to such extent as he considers necessary to meet all reasonable requirements, for the provision of assistance (by way of representation or otherwise) to individuals seeking, or intending to seek, redress under a scheme.

(2)   The Secretary of State may make such other arrangements as he thinks fit for the provision of assistance to individuals in connection with cases which are the subject of proceedings under a scheme.

(3)   The Secretary of State may make payments to any person in pursuance of arrangements under this section.

(4)   In making arrangements under this section, the Secretary of State must have regard to the principle that the provision of services under the arrangements in connection with a particular case should, so far as practicable, be independent of any person to whose conduct the case relates or who is involved in dealing with the case.

10 SCHEME MEMBERS

(1)   Subject to subsection (3), a scheme may make such provision as the Secretary of State thinks fit—
   (a) about membership of the scheme on the part of any body or other person to whose liability the scheme applies, and
   (b) about the functions of members in connection with the scheme.

11 SCHEME AUTHORITY

(1)   A scheme must make provision for a specified Special Health Authority (in this Act referred to as "the scheme authority") to have such functions in connection with the scheme as the Secretary of State thinks fit.

12 GENERAL DUTY TO PROMOTE RESOLUTION UNDER SCHEME

A scheme must include provision requiring the scheme authority and the members of the scheme, in carrying out their functions under the scheme, to have regard in particular to the desirability of redress being provided without recourse to civil proceedings.

13 DUTIES OF CO-OPERATION

(1)   The scheme authority under a scheme and the Care Quality Commission must co-operate with each other where it appears to them that it is appropriate to do so for the efficient and effective discharge of their respective functions.

14 COMPLAINTS

(1) The Secretary of State may by regulations make provision about the handling and consideration of complaints made under the regulations about maladministration by any body or other person—

    (a) in the exercise of functions under a scheme,

    (b) in the exercise of other functions relating to proceedings under a scheme, or

    (c) in connection with a settlement agreement entered into under a scheme.

Editor's Note: This Act has yet to be brought into force.

COMPANIES ACT 2006
(c.46)

Part 3 A COMPANY'S CONSTITUTION

Chapter 1 INTRODUCTORY

17 A COMPANY'S CONSTITUTION

Unless the context otherwise requires, references in the Companies Acts to a company's constitution include—

(a) the company's articles, and

(b) any resolutions and agreements to which Chapter 3 applies . . .

. . .

Other provisions with respect to a company's constitution

. . .

33 EFFECT OF COMPANY'S CONSTITUTION

(1) The provisions of a company's constitution bind the company and its members to the same extent as if there were covenants on the part of the company and of each member to observe those provisions.

(2) Money payable by a member to the company under its constitution is a debt due from him to the company.

    In England and Wales . . . it is of the nature of an ordinary contract debt.

. . .

Part 4 A COMPANY'S CAPACITY AND RELATED MATTERS

Capacity of company and power of directors to bind it

39 A COMPANY'S CAPACITY

(1) The validity of an act done by a company shall not be called into question on the ground of lack of capacity by reason of anything in the company's constitution.

(2) This section has effect subject to section 42 (companies that are charities).

40 POWER OF DIRECTORS TO BIND THE COMPANY

(1)   In favour of a person dealing with a company in good faith, the power of the directors to bind the company, or authorise others to do so, is deemed to be free of any limitation under the company's constitution.

(2)   For this purpose—
      (a) a person "deals with" a company if he is a party to any transaction or other act to which the company is a party,
      (b) a person dealing with a company—
           (i)   is not bound to enquire as to any limitation on the powers of the directors to bind the company or authorise others to do so,
           (ii) is presumed to have acted in good faith unless the contrary is proved, and
           (iii) is not to be regarded as acting in bad faith by reason only of his knowing that an act is beyond the powers of the directors under the company's constitution.

(3)   The references above to limitations on the directors' powers under the company's constitution include limitations deriving—
      (a) from a resolution of the company or of any class of shareholders, or
      (b) from any agreement between the members of the company or of any class of shareholders.

(4)   This section does not affect any right of a member of the company to bring proceedings to restrain the doing of an action that is beyond the powers of the directors.

      But no such proceedings lie in respect of an act to be done in fulfilment of a legal obligation arising from a previous act of the company.

(5)   This section does not affect any liability incurred by the directors, or any other person, by reason of the directors' exceeding their powers.

(6)   This section has effect subject to—

      section 41 (transactions with directors or their associates), and
      section 42 (companies that are charities).

Formalities of doing business under the law of England and Wales . . .

43 COMPANY CONTRACTS

(1)   Under the law of England and Wales . . . a contract may be made—
      (a) by a company, by writing under its common seal, or
      (b) on behalf of a company, by a person acting under its authority, express or implied.

(2)   Any formalities required by law in the case of a contract made by an individual also apply, unless a contrary intention appears, to a contract made by or on behalf of a company.

. . .

Formalities of doing business under the law of Scotland

48 EXECUTION OF DOCUMENTS BY COMPANIES

(1)   The following provisions form part of the law of Scotland only.

(2)   Notwithstanding the provisions of any enactment, a company need not have a company seal.

(3)   For the purposes of any enactment—
    (a) providing for a document to be executed by a company by affixing its common seal, or
    (b) referring (in whatever terms) to a document so executed,
a document signed or subscribed by or on behalf of the company in accordance with the provisions of the Requirements of Writing (Scotland) Act 1995 (c. 7) has effect as if so executed.

Other matters

. . .

51   PRE-INCORPORATION CONTRACTS, DEEDS AND OBLIGATIONS

(1)   A contract that purports to be made by or on behalf of a company at a time when the company has not been formed has effect, subject to any agreement to the contrary, as one made with the person purporting to act for the company or as agent for it, and he is personally liable on the contract accordingly.

(2)   Subsection (1) applies—
    (a) to the making of a deed under the law of England and Wales . . . and
    (b) to the undertaking of an obligation under the law of Scotland,
as it applies to the making of a contract.

170   SCOPE AND NATURE OF GENERAL DUTIES

(1)   The general duties specified in sections 171 to 177 are owed by a director of a company to the company.

(2)   A person who ceases to be a director continues to be subject—
    (a) to the duty in section 175 (duty to avoid conflicts of interest) as regards the exploitation of any property, information or opportunity of which he became aware at a time when he was a director, and
    (b) to the duty in section 176 (duty not to accept benefits from third parties) as regards things done or omitted by him before he ceased to be a director.
To that extent those duties apply to a former director as to a director, subject to any necessary adaptations.

(3)   The general duties are based on certain common law rules and equitable principles as they apply in relation to directors and have effect in place of those rules and principles as regards the duties owed to a company by a director.

(4)   The general duties shall be interpreted and applied in the same way as common law rules or equitable principles, and regard shall be had to the corresponding common law rules and equitable principles in interpreting and applying the general duties.

(5)   The general duties apply to shadow directors where, and to the extent that, the corresponding common law rules or equitable principles so apply.

174   DUTY TO EXERCISE REASONABLE CARE, SKILL AND DILIGENCE

(1)   A director of a company must exercise reasonable care, skill and diligence.

(2)   This means the care, skill and diligence that would be exercised by a reasonably diligent person with—

(a)   the general knowledge, skill and experience that may reasonably be expected of a person carrying out the functions carried out by the director in relation to the company, and

(b)   the general knowledge, skill and experience that the director has.

175 DUTY TO AVOID CONFLICTS OF INTEREST

(1)   A director of a company must avoid a situation in which he has, or can have, a direct or indirect interest that conflicts, or possibly may conflict, with the interests of the company.

(2)   This applies in particular to the exploitation of any property, information or opportunity (and it is immaterial whether the company could take advantage of the property, information or opportunity).

(3)   This duty does not apply to a conflict of interest arising in relation to a transaction or arrangement with the company.

(4)   This duty is not infringed—
(a)   if the situation cannot reasonably be regarded as likely to give rise to a conflict of interest; or
(b)   if the matter has been authorised by the directors.

(5)   Authorisation may be given by the directors—
(a)   where the company is a private company and nothing in the company's constitution invalidates such authorisation, by the matter being proposed to and authorised by the directors; or
(b)   where the company is a public company and its constitution includes provision enabling the directors to authorise the matter, by the matter being proposed to and authorised by them in accordance with the constitution.

(6)   The authorisation is effective only if—
(a)   any requirement as to the quorum at the meeting at which the matter is considered is met without counting the director in question or any other interested director, and
(b)   the matter was agreed to without their voting or would have been agreed to if their votes had not been counted.

(7)   Any reference in this section to a conflict of interest includes a conflict of interest and duty and a conflict of duties.

178 CIVIL CONSEQUENCES OF BREACH OF GENERAL DUTIES

(1)   The consequences of breach (or threatened breach) of sections 171 to 177 are the same as would apply if the corresponding common law rule or equitable principle applied.

(2)   The duties in those sections (with the exception of section 174 (duty to exercise reasonable care, skill and diligence)) are, accordingly, enforceable in the same way as any other fiduciary duty owed to a company by its directors.

222 PAYMENTS MADE WITHOUT APPROVAL: CIVIL CONSEQUENCES

(1)   If a payment is made in contravention of section 217 (payment by company)—
(a)   it is held by the recipient on trust for the company making the payment, and
(b)   any director who authorised the payment is jointly and severally liable to indemnify the company that made the payment for any loss resulting from it.

(2) If a payment is made in contravention of section 218 (payment in connection with transfer of undertaking etc.), it is held by the recipient on trust for the company whose undertaking or property is or is proposed to be transferred.

(3) If a payment is made in contravention of section 219 (payment in connection with share transfer)—
   (a) it is held by the recipient on trust for persons who have sold their shares as a result of the offer made, and
   (b) the expenses incurred by the recipient in distributing that sum amongst those persons shall be borne by him and not retained out of that sum.

(4) If a payment is in contravention of section 217 and section 218, subsection (2) of this section applies rather than subsection (1).

(5) If a payment is in contravention of section 217 and section 219, subsection (3) of this section applies rather than subsection (1), unless the court directs otherwise.

232 PROVISIONS PROTECTING DIRECTORS FROM LIABILITY

(1) Any provision that purports to exempt a director of a company (to any extent) from any liability that would otherwise attach to him in connection with any negligence, default, breach of duty or breach of trust in relation to the company is void.

(2) Any provision by which a company directly or indirectly provides an indemnity (to any extent) for a director of the company, or of an associated company, against any liability attaching to him in connection with any negligence, default, breach of duty or breach of trust in relation to the company of which he is a director is void, except as permitted by—
   (a) section 233 (provision of insurance),
   (b) section 234 (qualifying third party indemnity provision), or
   (c) section 235 (qualifying pension scheme indemnity provision).

(3) This section applies to any provision, whether contained in a company's articles or in any contract with the company or otherwise.

(4) Nothing in this section prevents a company's articles from making such provision as has previously been lawful for dealing with conflicts of interest.

463 LIABILITY FOR FALSE OR MISLEADING STATEMENTS IN REPORTS

(1) The reports to which this section applies are—
   (a) the directors' report,
   (b) the directors' remuneration report, and
   (c) a summary financial statement so far as it is derived from either of those reports.

(2) A director of a company is liable to compensate the company for any loss suffered by it as a result of—
   (a) any untrue or misleading statement in a report to which this section applies, or
   (b) the omission from a report to which this section applies of anything required to be included in it.

(3) He is so liable only if—
   (a) he knew the statement to be untrue or misleading or was reckless as to whether it was untrue or misleading, or
   (b) he knew the omission to be dishonest concealment of a material fact.

(4)   No person shall be subject to any liability to a person other than the company resulting from reliance, by that person or another, on information in a report to which this section applies.

(5)   The reference in subsection (4) to a person being subject to a liability includes a reference to another person being entitled as against him to be granted any civil remedy or to rescind or repudiate an agreement.

(6)   This section does not affect—
       (a)   liability for a civil penalty, or
       (b)   liability for a criminal offence.

532 VOIDNESS OF PROVISIONS PROTECTING AUDITORS FROM LIABILITY

(1)   This section applies to any provision—
       (a)   for exempting an auditor of a company (to any extent) from any liability that would otherwise attach to him in connection with any negligence, default, breach of duty or breach of trust in relation to the company occurring in the course of the audit of accounts, or
       (b)   by which a company directly or indirectly provides an indemnity (to any extent) for an auditor of the company, or of an associated company, against any liability attaching to him in connection with any negligence, default, breach of duty or breach of trust in relation to the company of which he is auditor occurring in the course of the audit of accounts.

(2)   Any such provision is void, except as permitted by—
       (a)   section 533 (indemnity for costs of successfully defending proceedings), or
       (b)   sections 534 to 536 (liability limitation agreements).

(3)   This section applies to any provision, whether contained in a company's articles or in any contract with the company or otherwise.

(4)   For the purposes of this section companies are associated if one is a subsidiary of the other or both are subsidiaries of the same body corporate.

847 CONSEQUENCES OF UNLAWFUL DISTRIBUTION

(1)   This section applies where a distribution, or part of one, made by a company to one of its members is made in contravention of this Part.

(2)   If at the time of the distribution the member knows or has reasonable grounds for believing that it is so made, he is liable—
       (a)   to repay it (or that part of it, as the case may be) to the company, or
       (b)   in the case of a distribution made otherwise than in cash, to pay the company a sum equal to the value of the distribution (or part) at that time.

(3)   This is without prejudice to any obligation imposed apart from this section on a member of a company to repay a distribution unlawfully made to him.

(4)   This section does not apply in relation to—
       (a)   financial assistance given by a company in contravention of section 678 or 679, or
       (b)   any payment made by a company in respect of the redemption or purchase by the company of shares in itself.

956 NO ACTION FOR BREACH OF STATUTORY DUTY ETC.

(1)   Contravention of a rule-based requirement or a disclosure requirement does not give rise to any right of action for breach of statutory duty.

(2)   Contravention of a rule-based requirement does not make any transaction void or unenforceable or (subject to any provision made by rules) affect the validity of any other thing.

(3)   In this section—
       (a)   "contravention" includes failure to comply;
       (b)   "disclosure requirement" and "rule-based requirement" have the same meaning as in section 955.

1218 EXEMPTION FROM LIABILITY FOR DAMAGES

(1)   No person within subsection (2) is to be liable in damages for anything done or omitted in the discharge or purported discharge of functions to which this subsection applies.

(2)   The persons within this subsection are—
       (a)   any recognised supervisory body,
       (b)   any officer or employee of a recognised supervisory body, and
       (c)   any member of the governing body of a recognised supervisory body.

INCOME TAX ACT 2007
(c.3)

Transactions in Land

762 TRACING VALUE

(1)   This section applies if it is necessary to determine the extent to which the value of any property or right is derived from any other property or right for the purposes of this Chapter.

(2)   Value may be traced through any number of companies, partnerships and trusts.

(3)   The property held by a company, partnership or trust must be attributed to the shareholders, partners or beneficiaries at each stage in such manner as is appropriate in the circumstances.

Sales of Occupation Income

781 TRACING VALUE

(1)   This section applies if it is necessary to determine the extent to which the value of any property or right is derived from any other property or right for the purposes of this Chapter.

(2)   Value may be traced through any number of companies, partnerships and trusts.

(3)   The property held by a company, partnership or trust must be attributed to the shareholders, partners or beneficiaries at each stage in such manner as is appropriate in the circumstances.

FINANCE ACT 2007
(c.11)

107 LIMITATION PERIOD IN OLD ACTIONS FOR MISTAKE OF LAW RELATING TO DIRECT TAX

(1)   Section 32(1)(c) of the Limitation Act 1980 (c. 58) (extended period for bringing action in case of mistake) does not apply in relation to any action brought before 8th September 2003 for relief from the consequences of a mistake of law relating to a taxation matter under the care and management of the Commissioners of Inland Revenue.

(2)   Subsection (1) has effect regardless of how the grounds on which the action was brought were expressed and of whether it was also brought otherwise than for such relief.

(3)   But subsection (1) does not have effect in relation to an action, or so much of an action as relates to a cause of action, if—
(a) the action, or cause of action, has been the subject of a judgment of the House of Lords given before 6th December 2006 as to the application of section 32(1)(c) in relation to such relief, or
(b) the parties to the action are, in accordance with a group litigation order, bound in relation to the action, or cause of action, by a judgment of the House of Lords in another action given before that date as to the application of section 32(1)(c) in relation to such relief.

(4)   If the judgment of any court was given on or after 6th December 2006 but before the day on which this Act is passed, the judgment is to be taken to have been what it would have been had subsections (1) to (3) been in force at all times since the action was brought (and any defence of limitation which would have been available had been raised).

(5)   And any payment made to satisfy a liability under the judgment which (in consequence of subsection (4)) is to be taken not to have been imposed is repayable (with interest from the date of the payment).

(6)   In this section—

"group litigation order" means an order of a court providing for the case management of actions which give rise to common or related issues of fact or law, and

"judgment" includes order (and "given" includes made).

DORMANT BANK AND BUILDING SOCIETY ACCOUNTS ACT 2008
(c.31)

Part 1 TRANSFER OF BALANCES IN DORMANT ACCOUNTS

The general scheme

1 TRANSFER OF BALANCES TO RECLAIM FUND

(1)   This section applies where—
(a) a bank or building society transfers to an authorised reclaim fund the balance of a dormant account that a person ("the customer") holds with it, and

(b) the reclaim fund consents to the transfer.

(2) After the transfer—
    (a) the customer no longer has any right against the bank or building society to payment of the balance, but
    (b) the customer has against the reclaim fund whatever right to payment of the balance the customer would have against the bank or building society if the transfer had not happened.

(3) The reference in subsection (1) to an account that a person holds is to be read as including an account held by a deceased individual immediately before his or her death.

In such a case, a reference in subsection (2) to the customer is to be read as a reference to the person to whom the right to payment of the balance has passed.

Alternative scheme for smaller institutions

2 TRANSFER OF BALANCES TO CHARITIES, WITH PROPORTION TO RECLAIM FUND

(1) This section applies where—
    (a) a smaller bank or building society transfers to an authorised reclaim fund an agreed proportion of the balance of a dormant account that a person ("the customer") holds with it,
    (b) the bank or building society transfers the remainder of that balance to one or more charities,
    (c) the charity, or each of the charities, either—
        (i) is a charity that the bank or building society considers to have a special connection with it, or
        (ii) undertakes to apply the money in question for the benefit of members of communities that are local to the branches of the bank or building society,
    (d) the reclaim fund consents to the transfer to it, and
    (e) the charity, or each of the charities, consents to the transfer to it.

(2) After the transfers—
    (a) the customer no longer has any right against the bank or building society to payment of the balance, but
    (b) the customer has against the reclaim fund whatever right to payment of the balance the customer would have against the bank or building society if the transfers had not happened.

(3) The reference in subsection (1) to an account that a person holds is to be read as including an account held by a deceased individual immediately before his or her death.

In such a case, a reference in subsection (2) to the customer is to be read as a reference to the person to whom the right to payment of the balance has passed.

(4) In subsection (1) "agreed proportion" means a proportion agreed between the bank or building society and the reclaim fund.

In agreeing that proportion, the reclaim fund must take account of the need for the fund to have access at any given time to enough money to enable it to meet whatever repayment claims it is prudent to anticipate.

(5) For the purposes of this section—
    (a) "repayment claim" means a claim made by virtue of subsection (2)(b);

(b) a "smaller" bank or building society is one that meets the assets-limit condition (see section 3);

(c) a charity has a "special connection" with a bank if (and only if) the purpose, or any of the main purposes, of the charity is to benefit members of communities that are local to the branches of the bank;

(d) a charity has a "special connection" with a building society if (and only if) the purpose, or any of the main purposes, of the charity—

(i) is to benefit members of communities that are local to the branches of the building society, or

(ii) is especially consonant with any particular purposes that the building society has.

(6) The reference in subsection (5)(d)(ii) to particular purposes does not include the purpose mentioned in section 5(1)(a) of the Building Societies Act 1986 (c. 53) (making loans that are secured on residential property and substantially funded by members).

3 THE ASSETS-LIMIT CONDITION

(1) A bank or building society meets the assets-limit condition if the aggregate of the amounts shown in its balance sheet as assets on the last day of the latest financial year for which it has prepared accounts is less than £7,000 million.

(2) In relation to a bank or building society that was a member of a group on the day referred to in subsection (1), that subsection has effect as if the aggregate of the amounts shown in its balance sheet as assets on that day also included the aggregate of the amounts shown in each group member's balance sheet as assets—

(a) on that day, or

(b) (in the case of a group member whose financial year did not end on that day) on the last day of its latest financial year to end before that day.

Shareholding members of building societies

4 EFFECT OF BALANCE TRANSFER ON MEMBERSHIP RIGHTS

(1) This section applies where a person ("the member") holds a share in a building society represented by an account with the society, and either—

(a) a transfer is made to a reclaim fund with the result that section 1 applies in relation to the account, or

(b) transfers are made to a reclaim fund and one or more charities with the result that section 2 applies in relation to the account.

(2) After the transfer or transfers the member is to be treated as having whatever share in the building society the member would have if the transfer or transfers had not happened (and accordingly as having whatever rights, including distribution rights, a holder of that share would have as such).

(3) In subsection (2) "distribution rights" means rights to any distribution arising as mentioned in section 96 (amalgamation or transfer of engagements) or 100 (transfer of business) of the Building Societies Act 1986.

(4) Subsection (2) ceases to apply where the balance of the account is paid out following a claim made by virtue of section 1(2)(b) or 2(2)(b).

(5) But where the balance of the account is paid out following such a claim and, as soon as reasonably practical, the money is—

(a) paid back into the account, or

(b) paid into another share account with the building society in the member's name, subsection (2) continues to apply until the account is credited with the money.

(6)   Where, after the transfer or transfers referred to in subsection (1), the building society is succeeded by another building society as a result of an amalgamation or transfer of engagements, a reference in subsection (2) or (5) to the building society is to be read, in relation to any time after the amalgamation or transfer of engagements, as a reference to the successor building society (or to the successor building society of the successor, in relation to any time after a subsequent amalgamation or transfer; and so on).

Reclaim funds

5 FUNCTIONS ETC OF A RECLAIM FUND

(1)   A "reclaim fund" is a company the objects of which are restricted by its articles of association to the following—
(a) the meeting of repayment claims;
(b) the management of dormant account funds in such a way as to enable the company to meet whatever repayment claims it is prudent to anticipate;
(c) the transfer of money to the body or bodies for the time being specified in section 16(1), subject to the need for the company—
    (i) to have access at any given time to enough money to meet whatever repayment claims it is prudent to anticipate,
    (ii) to comply with any requirement with regard to its financial resources that is imposed on it by or under any enactment, and
    (iii) to defray its expenses;
(d) objects that are incidental or conducive to, or otherwise connected with, any of the above (including in particular the prudent investment of dormant account funds).

(2)   Schedule 1 makes further provision about provision that must be made in the articles of association of a reclaim fund.

8 "BALANCE"

(1)   The balance of a person's account at any particular time is the amount owing to the person in respect of the account at that time, after the appropriate adjustments have been made for such things as interest due and fees and charges payable.

(2)   In relation to a time after a transfer has been made as mentioned in section 1(1) or transfers have been made as mentioned in section 2(1), the adjustments referred to in subsection (1) above include those that would fall to be made but for the transfer or transfers.

9 "ACCOUNT"

(1)   "Account" means an account that has at all times consisted only of money.

(2)   A reference in this Part to an account held with a bank or building society is to an account provided by the bank or building society as part of its activity of accepting deposits.

(3)   In relation to a building society, "account" includes an account representing shares in the society, other than—
(a) preferential shares, or
(b) deferred shares within the meaning given in section 119(1) of the Building Societies Act 1986 (c. 53).

10 "DORMANT"

(1)   An account is "dormant" at a particular time if—
 (a) the account has been open throughout the period of 15 years ending at that time, but
 (b) during that period no transactions have been carried out in relation to the account by or on the instructions of the holder of the account.

(2)   But an account is to be treated as not dormant if at any time during that period—
 (a) the bank or building society in question was under instructions from the holder of the account not to communicate with that person about the account, or
 (b) under the terms of the account—
  (i) withdrawals were prevented, or
  (ii) there was a penalty or other disincentive for making withdrawals in all circumstances.

(3)   For the purposes of subsection (1) an account is to be treated as remaining open where it is closed otherwise than on the instructions of the holder of the account.

(4)   For the purposes of subsection (2)(b)(i) withdrawals are prevented if they are prevented except as permitted by provision made under subsection (4)(d) of section 3 of the Child Trust Funds Act 2004 (c. 6)(requirements to be satisfied by child trust funds).

12 DISCLOSURE OF INFORMATION

No obligation as to secrecy or other restriction on disclosure (however imposed) prevents a bank or building society from giving to an authorised reclaim fund information needed by the fund to enable it to deal with claims made by virtue of section 1(2)(b) or 2(2)(b).

16 DISTRIBUTION OF DORMANT ACCOUNT MONEY BY BIG LOTTERY FUND

(1)   Subject to the provisions of this Part, the Big Lottery Fund shall distribute dormant account money for meeting expenditure that has a social or environmental purpose.

(2)   In this Part "dormant account money" means money transferred to the Big Lottery Fund by a reclaim fund in pursuance of the object mentioned in section 5(1)(c), and also includes the proceeds of such money invested under—
 (a) paragraph 20(1) of Schedule 4A to the National Lottery etc. Act 1993 (c. 39), or
 (b) arrangements made under section 25(1).

(3)   The Fund may make grants or loans, or make or enter into other arrangements, for the purpose of complying with subsection (1).

(4)   A grant or loan may be subject to conditions (which may, in particular, include conditions as to repayment with interest).

(5)   For the purposes of this Part, distributing money for meeting expenditure of a particular description includes distributing money for the purpose of establishing, or contributing to, endowments (including permanent endowments) in connection with expenditure of that description.

(6)   Schedule 3 makes further provision about the functions of the Fund in relation to dormant account money.

NHS REDRESS (WALES) MEASURE 2008

1 POWER OF WELSH MINISTERS TO MAKE REGULATIONS IN RESPECT OF NHS REDRESS

(1)   The Welsh Ministers may make provision by regulations for the purpose of enabling redress to be provided without recourse to civil proceedings in circumstances in which this section applies.

(2)   This section applies where under the law of England and Wales qualifying liability in tort on the part of a body or person mentioned in subsection (3) arises in connection with the provision of qualifying services in Wales or elsewhere as part of the health service in Wales.

(3)   The bodies and persons referred to in subsection (2) are—
   (a)   an NHS Trust in Wales;
   (b)   a Local Health Board;
   (c)   a Special Health Authority;
   (d)   the Welsh Ministers;
   (e)   a body or person providing, or arranging for the provision of, services whose provision is the subject of arrangements with a body or person mentioned in paragraphs (a) to (d).

(4)   The reference in subsection (2) to qualifying liability in tort is to liability in tort owed in respect of, or consequent upon, personal injury or loss arising out of or in connection with breach of a duty of care owed to any person in connection with the diagnosis of illness, or in the care or treatment of any patient—
   (a)   in consequence of any act or omission by a health care professional, or
   (b)   in consequence of any act or omission by any other body or person as the Welsh Ministers may specify by the regulations.
(5)   For the purposes of subsection (2), services are qualifying services if they are of such description (including a description involving provision outside Wales) as the Welsh Ministers may specify by the regulations.

(6)   In subsection (3)(e), the reference to a person providing services does not include a person providing services under a contract of employment.

2 REDRESS UNDER THE REGULATIONS

(1)   Subject to subsections (2), (3) and (6), the regulations may make such provision as the Welsh Ministers think fit about redress.

(2)   The regulations must provide for redress ordinarily to comprise—
   (a)   the making of an offer of compensation in satisfaction of any right to bring civil proceedings in respect of the liability concerned;
   (b)   the giving of an explanation;
   (c)   the making of a written apology; and
   (d)   the giving of a report on the action which has been, or will be, taken to prevent similar cases arising;
   but the regulations may specify circumstances in which one or more of those forms of redress is not required.

(3)   The regulations must provide that redress does not apply in relation to a liability that is or has been the subject of civil proceedings.

(4)   The regulations may, in particular—
    (a)   make provision for the compensation that may be offered to take the form of entry into a contract to provide care or treatment or of financial compensation, or both;
    (b)   make provision about the circumstances in which different forms of compensation may be offered.

(5)   If the regulations provide for financial compensation to be offered, they may, in particular—
    (a)   make provision about the matters in respect of which financial compensation may be offered;
    (b)   make provision with respect to the assessment of the amount of any financial compensation.

(6)   The regulations which provide for financial compensation to be offered—
    (a)   may specify an upper limit on the amount of financial compensation that may be included in an offer of redress made in accordance with the regulations;
    (b)   must, if they do not specify a limit under paragraph (a), specify an upper limit on the amount of financial compensation that may be included in such an offer in respect of pain and suffering;
    (c)   may not specify any other limit on what may be included in such an offer by way of financial compensation.

3 ACCESSING REDRESS

(1)   The regulations may make such provision as the Welsh Ministers think fit about accessing redress.

(2)   The regulations may, in particular, make provision—
    (a)   about who may access redress;
    (b)   about how redress may be accessed;
    (c)   for time limits in relation to accessing redress;
    (d)   about circumstances in which redress may not be accessed.

4 DUTY TO CONSIDER THE POTENTIAL APPLICATION OF REDRESS ARRANGEMENTS

(1)   The regulations may make such provision as the Welsh Ministers think fit requiring any body or person mentioned in subsection (2)—
    (a)   to consider, in such circumstances as the regulations may provide, whether a case that the body or person is investigating or reviewing involves liability for which redress may be available, and
    (b)   if it appears that it does, to take such steps as the regulations may provide.

(2)   The bodies or persons referred to in subsection (1) are—
    (a)   any body or person to whose liability the regulations apply;
    (b)   any other body or person prescribed by the Welsh Ministers in the regulations.

5 METHOD OF DELIVERING REDRESS

(1)   Subject to subsections (3) to (6), the regulations may make such provision as the Welsh Ministers think fit regarding how redress is delivered.

(2)   The regulations may, in particular, make provision—
    (a)   regarding the investigation of applications for redress made under the regulations (including provision for the overseeing of the investigation by an individual of a specified description);

(b) regarding the form and content of settlement agreements under the regulations;

(c) for settlement agreements under the regulations to be subject in cases of a specified description to approval by a court;

(d) regarding the procedure to be followed when, and the circumstances in which, applications for redress under the regulations may no longer be pursued.

(3) The regulations must—

(a) make provision for time limits and any extensions of them in relation to—

(i)   the conduct and completion of an investigation;

(ii) the making of an offer of redress; and

(iii) the acceptance of such an offer,

under the regulations,

(b) make provision for the findings of an investigation of a case where an individual is seeking redress under the regulations to be recorded in a report, and

(c) subject to subsection (4), make provision for a copy of the report to be provided to the individual seeking redress.

(4) The regulations may provide that no copy of an investigation report need be provided—

(a) before an offer of redress under the regulations is made or proceedings are for any reason terminated;

(b) where the report contains information likely to cause the patient or other applicant significant harm or distress; or

(c) in such other circumstances as may be specified.

(5) The regulations must provide for a settlement agreement for redress entered into under the regulations to include a waiver of any right to bring civil proceedings in respect of the liability to which the settlement relates.

(6) The regulations must provide that redress may no longer be sought under the regulations if the liability in relation to which redress is being sought becomes the subject of civil proceedings.

6 SUSPENSION OF LIMITATION PERIOD

(1) The regulations must make provision for the period during which a liability is the subject of an application for redress under the regulations to be disregarded for the purposes of calculating whether any relevant limitation period has expired or not.

(2) The reference in subsection (1) to any relevant limitation period is to any period of time for the bringing of civil proceedings in respect of the liability which is prescribed by or under the Limitation Act 1980 (c. 58) or any other enactment.

(3) The regulations may define for the purposes of provision in accordance with subsection (1) when liability is the subject of an application for redress under the regulations.

7 LEGAL ADVICE, ETC.

(1) Subject to subsections (2) and (4), the regulations may make such provision as the Welsh Ministers think fit—

(a) for the provision of legal advice without charge to individuals seeking redress under the regulations;

(b) for the provision in connection with an application for redress under the regulations of other services, including the services of medical experts.

(2)   The regulations must make such provision as the Welsh Ministers consider appropriate in order to secure that individuals to whom an offer of redress under the regulations may be made have access to legal advice without charge in relation to—
(a)   any offer that is made,
(b)   any refusal to make such an offer; and
(c)   any settlement agreement.

(3)   Provision under subsection (1)(a) or (2) about who may provide the legal advice may operate by reference to whether a potential provider is included in a list prepared by a specified person or body.

(4)   If the regulations make provision for the services of medical experts, they must also provide for such experts to be instructed jointly by the body or person operating the redress arrangements under the regulations and the individual seeking redress.

8   ASSISTANCE FOR INDIVIDUALS SEEKING REDRESS

(1)   It is the duty of the Welsh Ministers to arrange, to such extent as they consider necessary to meet all reasonable requirements, for the provision of assistance (by way of representation or otherwise) to individuals seeking, or intending to seek, redress under the regulations.

(2)   The Welsh Ministers may make such other arrangements as they think fit for the provision of assistance (by way of representation or otherwise) to individuals in connection with cases which are the subject of an application for redress under the regulations.

(3)   The Welsh Ministers may make payments to any person or body in pursuance of arrangements under this section and section 7.

(4)   In making arrangements under this section, the Welsh Ministers must have regard to the principle that the provision of services under the arrangements in connection with a particular case should, as far as practicable, be independent of any person to whose conduct the case relates or who is involved in dealing with the application for redress.

9   FUNCTIONS WITH REGARD TO REDRESS ARRANGEMENTS

(1)   The regulations may make provision for any person or body within the health service in Wales to have such functions with regard to the operation of redress arrangements under this Measure as the Welsh Ministers think fit.

(2)   The regulations may, in particular, provide for such persons or bodies to have functions in relation to—
(a)   accessing redress;
(b)   payments under settlement agreements by way of redress;
(c)   the provision in connection with redress arrangements of advice or other guidance about specified matters;
(d)   the provision in connection with redress arrangements of legal advice without charge;
(e)   the monitoring of the carrying out by persons or bodies of their functions under the regulations;
(f)   the publication of annual data about the redress arrangements.

(3)   The regulations may require any body or person carrying out functions under the regulations to—
(a)   keep specified records in relation to carrying out such functions;
(b)   charge an individual of a specified description with responsibility for overseeing the carrying out of specified functions conferred on that body or person under the regulations;

(c) charge an individual of a specified description with responsibility for advising the body or person about lessons to be learnt from cases involving that body or person that are dealt with under the regulations.

(4) The regulations must require that such a body or person prepare and publish an annual report about cases involving that body or person that are dealt with under the regulations and the lessons to be learnt from them.

(5) The regulations may provide that any function exercisable by a body or person under the regulations may, by arrangement with that body or person and subject to such restrictions and conditions as that body or person may think fit, be exercised on behalf of that body or person by, or jointly with, another body or person.

(6) The regulations may require any body or person exercising functions under the regulations to have regard to any advice or guidance given from time to time by the Welsh Ministers.

(7) The provision that may be made under this section includes provision which has the effect that a body or person who has arranged for the provision of services shall have functions under the regulations which relate to someone else's liability in connection with the provision of those services.

10 COMPLAINTS

In section 113(2) of the Health and Social Care (Community Health and Standards) Act 2003 (c. 43), after paragraph (c) insert—

"(d) the provision of redress by or for a Welsh NHS body under the NHS Redress (Wales) Measure 2008."

11 ORDERS AND REGULATIONS

(1) Any power to make an order or regulations conferred by this Measure is exercisable by statutory instrument.

(2) Any power of the Welsh Ministers to make regulations under this Measure includes power—
   (a) to make provision conferring or imposing functions which involve the exercise of discretion;
   (b) to make provision generally or in relation to specific cases;
   (c) to make different provision for different cases; and
   (d) to make such incidental, supplementary, saving or transitional provision as the Welsh Ministers think fit.

(3) Any power of the Welsh Ministers to make regulations or orders under this Measure (as well as being exercisable in relation to all cases to which it extends) may be exercised in relation to all those cases subject to exceptions or in relation to any particular case or class of case.

(4) Any statutory instrument containing regulations made under this Measure is subject to annulment in pursuance of a resolution of the National Assembly for Wales.

(5) Subsection (4) does not apply to regulations to which subsection (6) applies.

(6) A statutory instrument which—
   (a) contains regulations made by the Welsh Ministers under section 12 which amend or repeal any part of the text of an Act of Parliament or an Assembly Measure, or

    (b) contains the first regulations under section 1(1), or

    (c) contains regulations making provision under section 1(4)(b), section 1(5), section 3 or section 5, or

    (d) contains the first regulations to make provision under sections 2, 4, 6, 7 or 9,

may not be made unless a draft of the instrument has been laid before, and approved by a resolution of, the National Assembly for Wales.

(7)   Nothing in this Measure is to be regarded as limiting the generality of sections 1(1) and 12(1).

12 POWER TO MAKE FURTHER SUPPLEMENTARY AND CONSEQUENTIAL PROVISION ETC.

(1)   The Welsh Ministers may at any time by regulations make—

    (a) such supplementary, incidental or consequential provision, or

    (b) such transitional or saving provision,

as they consider necessary or expedient for the purposes of, in consequence of, or for giving full effect to, any provision of this Measure.

(2)   Regulations under subsection (1) may, in particular, make provision—

    (a) amending or repealing any enactment passed before, or during the same Assembly year as, this Measure, and

    (b) amending or revoking any subordinate legislation (within the meaning of the Interpretation Act 1978 (c. 30)) made before the passing of this Measure.

13 INTERPRETATION

In this Measure—

- "a health care professional" ("*proffesiynolyn gofal iechyd*") means a member of a profession (whether or not regulated by, or by virtue of, any enactment) which is concerned (wholly or partly) with the physical or mental health of individuals;
- "the health service in Wales" ("*y gwasanaeth iechyd yng Nghymru*") means the health service continued under section 1(1) of the National Health Service (Wales) Act 2006 (c. 42);
- "illness" ("*salwch*") has the same meaning as in that Act;
- "patient" ("*claf*") has the same meaning as in that Act;
- "personal injury" ("*anaf personol*") includes any disease and any impairment of a person's physical or mental health.

14 SHORT TITLE AND COMMENCEMENT

(1)   This Measure may be cited as the NHS Redress (Wales) Measure 2008.

(2)   This section shall come into force on the day on which this Measure is approved by Her Majesty in Council.

(3)   The remaining provisions of this Measure shall come into force on such day as the Welsh Ministers may appoint by order.

DAMAGES (ASBESTOS-RELATED CONDITIONS) (SCOTLAND) ACT 2009
asp 4

1 PLEURAL PLAQUES

(1)   Asbestos-related pleural plaques are a personal injury which is not negligible.

(2)   Accordingly, they constitute actionable harm for the purposes of an action of damages for personal injuries.

(3)   Any rule of law the effect of which is that asbestos-related pleural plaques do not constitute actionable harm ceases to apply to the extent it has that effect.

(4)   But nothing in this section otherwise affects any enactment or rule of law which determines whether and in what circumstances a person may be liable in damages in respect of personal injuries.

2 PLEURAL THICKENING AND ASBESTOSIS

(1)   For the avoidance of doubt, a condition mentioned in subsection (2) which has not caused and is not causing impairment of a person's physical condition is a personal injury which is not negligible.

(2)   Those conditions are—
(a) asbestos-related pleural thickening; and
(b) asbestosis.

(3)   Accordingly, such a condition constitutes actionable harm for the purposes of an action of damages for personal injuries.

(4)   Any rule of law the effect of which is that such a condition does not constitute actionable harm ceases to apply to the extent it has that effect.

(5)   But nothing in this section otherwise affects any enactment or rule of law which determines whether and in what circumstances a person may be liable in damages in respect of personal injuries.

3 LIMITATION OF ACTIONS

(1)   This section applies to an action of damages for personal injuries—
(a) in which the damages claimed consist of or include damages in respect of—
(i)   asbestos-related pleural plaques; or
(ii) a condition to which section 2 applies; and
(b) which, in the case of an action commenced before the date this section comes into force, has not been determined by that date.

(2)   For the purposes of sections 17 and 18 of the Prescription and Limitation (Scotland) Act 1973 (c. 52) (limitation in respect of actions for personal injuries), the period beginning with 17 October 2007 and ending with the day on which this section comes into force is to be left out of account.

4 COMMENCEMENT AND RETROSPECTIVE EFFECT

(1)   This Act (other than this subsection and section 5) comes into force on such day as the Scottish Ministers may, by order made by statutory instrument, appoint.

(2)   Sections 1 and 2 are to be treated for all purposes as having always had effect.

(3)   But those sections have no effect in relation to—
       (a) a claim which is settled before the date on which subsection (2) comes into force (whether or not legal proceedings in relation to the claim have been commenced); or
       (b) legal proceedings which are determined before that date.

5 SHORT TITLE AND CROWN APPLICATION

(1)   This Act may be cited as the Damages (Asbestos-related Conditions) (Scotland) Act 2009.

(2)   This Act binds the Crown.

EQUALITY ACT 2010
(c.15)

Part 1 SOCIO-ECONOMIC INEQUALITIES

1 PUBLIC SECTOR DUTY REGARDING SOCIO-ECONOMIC INEQUALITIES

(1)   An authority to which this section applies must, when making decisions of a strategic nature about how to exercise its functions, have due regard to the desirability of exercising them in a way that is designed to reduce the inequalities of outcome which result from socio-economic disadvantage.

(2)   In deciding how to fulfil a duty to which it is subject under subsection (1), an authority must take into account any guidance issued by a Minister of the Crown.

(3)   The authorities to which this section applies are—
       (a) a Minister of the Crown;
       (b) a government department other than the Security Service, the Secret Intelligence Service or the Government Communications Headquarters;
       (c) a county council or district council in England;
       (d) the Greater London Authority;
       (e) a London borough council;

(f)   the Common Council of the City of London in its capacity as a local authority;

(g)   the Council of the Isles of Scilly;

(h)   a Strategic Health Authority established under section 13 of the National Health Service Act 2006, or continued in existence by virtue of that section;

(i)   a Primary Care Trust established under section 18 of that Act, or continued in existence by virtue of that section;

(j)   a regional development agency established by the Regional Development Agencies Act 1998;

(k)   a police authority established for an area in England.

(4)   This section also applies to an authority that—

(a)   is a partner authority in relation to a responsible local authority, and

(b)   does not fall within subsection (3),

but only in relation to its participation in the preparation or modification of a sustainable community strategy.

(5)   In subsection (4)—

"partner authority" has the meaning given by section 104 of the Local Government and Public Involvement in Health Act 2007;

"responsible local authority" has the meaning given by section 103 of that Act;

"sustainable community strategy" means a strategy prepared under section 4 of the Local Government Act 2000.

(6)   The reference to inequalities in subsection (1) does not include any inequalities experienced by a person as a result of being a person subject to immigration control within the meaning given by section 115(9) of the Immigration and Asylum Act 1999.

2 POWER TO AMEND SECTION 1

(1)   A Minister of the Crown may by regulations amend section 1 so as to—

(a)   add a public authority to the authorities that are subject to the duty under subsection (1) of that section;

(b)   remove an authority from those that are subject to the duty;

(c)   make the duty apply, in the case of a particular authority, only in relation to certain functions that it has;

(d)   in the case of an authority to which the application of the duty is already restricted to certain functions, remove or alter the restriction.

(2)   In subsection (1) "public authority" means an authority that has functions of a public nature.

(3)   Provision made under subsection (1) may not impose a duty on an authority in relation to any devolved Scottish functions or devolved Welsh functions.

(4)   The Scottish Ministers or the Welsh Ministers may by regulations amend section 1 so as to—

(a)   add a relevant authority to the authorities that are subject to the duty under subsection (1) of that section;

(b)   remove a relevant authority from those that are subject to the duty;

(c)   make the duty apply, in the case of a particular relevant authority, only in relation to certain functions that it has;

(d)   in the case of a relevant authority to which the application of the duty is already restricted to certain functions, remove or alter the restriction.

(5)   For the purposes of the power conferred by subsection (4) on the Scottish Ministers, "relevant authority" means an authority whose functions—

    (a)   are exercisable only in or as regards Scotland,

    (b)   are wholly or mainly devolved Scottish functions, and

    (c)   correspond or are similar to those of an authority for the time being specified in section 1(3).

(6)   For the purposes of the power conferred by subsection (4) on the Welsh Ministers, "relevant authority" means an authority whose functions—

    (a)   are exercisable only in or as regards Wales,

    (b)   are wholly or mainly devolved Welsh functions, and

    (c)   correspond or are similar to those of an authority for the time being specified in subsection (3) of section 1 or referred to in subsection (4) of that section.

(7)   Before making regulations under this section, the Scottish Ministers or the Welsh Ministers must consult a Minister of the Crown.

(8)   Regulations under this section may make any amendments of section 1 that appear to the Minister or Ministers to be necessary or expedient in consequence of provision made under subsection (1) or (as the case may be) subsection (4).

(9)   Provision made by the Scottish Ministers or the Welsh Ministers in reliance on subsection (8) may, in particular, amend section 1 so as to—

    (a)   confer on the Ministers a power to issue guidance;

    (b)   require a relevant authority to take into account any guidance issued under a power conferred by virtue of paragraph (a);

    (c)   disapply section 1(2) in consequence of the imposition of a requirement by virtue of paragraph (b).

(10)   Before issuing guidance under a power conferred by virtue of subsection (9)(a), the Ministers must—

    (a)   take into account any guidance issued by a Minister of the Crown under section 1;

    (b)   consult a Minister of the Crown.

(11)   For the purposes of this section—

    (a)   a function is a devolved Scottish function if it is exercisable in or as regards Scotland and it does not relate to reserved matters (within the meaning of the Scotland Act 1998);

    (b)   a function is a devolved Welsh function if it relates to a matter in respect of which functions are exercisable by the Welsh Ministers, the First Minister for Wales or the Counsel General to the Welsh Assembly Government, or to a matter within the legislative competence of the National Assembly for Wales.

3 ENFORCEMENT

A failure in respect of a performance of a duty under section 1 does not confer a cause of action at private law.

Part 2 EQUALITY: KEY CONCEPTS

Chapter 1 PROTECTED CHARACTERISTICS

4 THE PROTECTED CHARACTERISTICS

The following characteristics are protected characteristics—

    age;

    disability;

gender reassignment;
marriage and civil partnership;
pregnancy and maternity;
race;
religion or belief;
sex;
sexual orientation.

5 AGE

(1)   In relation to the protected characteristic of age—
   (a)   a reference to a person who has a particular protected characteristic is a reference to a person of a particular age group;
   (b)   a reference to persons who share a protected characteristic is a reference to persons of the same age group.

(2)   A reference to an age group is a reference to a group of persons defined by reference to age, whether by reference to a particular age or to a range of ages.

6 DISABILITY

(1)   A person (P) has a disability if—
   (a)   P has a physical or mental impairment, and
   (b)   the impairment has a substantial and long-term adverse effect on P's ability to carry out normal day-to-day activities.

(2)   A reference to a disabled person is a reference to a person who has a disability.

(3)   In relation to the protected characteristic of disability—
   (a)   a reference to a person who has a particular protected characteristic is a reference to a person who has a particular disability;
   (b)   a reference to persons who share a protected characteristic is a reference to persons who have the same disability.

(4)   This Act (except Part 12 and section 190) applies in relation to a person who has had a disability as it applies in relation to a person who has the disability; accordingly (except in that Part and that section)—
   (a)   a reference (however expressed) to a person who has a disability includes a reference to a person who has had the disability, and
   (b)   a reference (however expressed) to a person who does not have a disability includes a reference to a person who has not had the disability.

(5)   A Minister of the Crown may issue guidance about matters to be taken into account in deciding any question for the purposes of subsection (1).

(6)   Schedule 1 (disability: supplementary provision) has effect.

7 GENDER REASSIGNMENT

(1)   A person has the protected characteristic of gender reassignment if the person is proposing to undergo, is undergoing or has undergone a process (or part of a process) for the purpose of reassigning the person's sex by changing physiological or other attributes of sex.

(2)   A reference to a transsexual person is a reference to a person who has the protected characteristic of gender reassignment.

(3)   In relation to the protected characteristic of gender reassignment—
    (a)   a reference to a person who has a particular protected characteristic is a reference to a transsexual person;
    (b)   a reference to persons who share a protected characteristic is a reference to transsexual persons.

8 MARRIAGE AND CIVIL PARTNERSHIP

(1)   A person has the protected characteristic of marriage and civil partnership if the person is married or is a civil partner.

(2)   In relation to the protected characteristic of marriage and civil partnership—
    (a)   a reference to a person who has a particular protected characteristic is a reference to a person who is married or is a civil partner;
    (b)   a reference to persons who share a protected characteristic is a reference to persons who are married or are civil partners.

9 RACE

(1)   Race includes—
    (a)   colour;
    (b)   nationality;
    (c)   ethnic or national origins.

(2)   In relation to the protected characteristic of race—
    (a)   a reference to a person who has a particular protected characteristic is a reference to a person of a particular racial group;
    (b)   a reference to persons who share a protected characteristic is a reference to persons of the same racial group.

(3)   A racial group is a group of persons defined by reference to race; and a reference to a person's racial group is a reference to a racial group into which the person falls.

(4)   The fact that a racial group comprises two or more distinct racial groups does not prevent it from constituting a particular racial group.

(5)   A Minister of the Crown may by order—
    (a)   amend this section so as to provide for caste to be an aspect of race;
    (b)   amend this Act so as to provide for an exception to a provision of this Act to apply, or not to apply, to caste or to apply, or not to apply, to caste in specified circumstances.

(6)   The power under section 207(4)(b), in its application to subsection (5), includes power to amend this Act.

10 RELIGION OR BELIEF

(1)   Religion means any religion and a reference to religion includes a reference to a lack of religion.

(2)   Belief means any religious or philosophical belief and a reference to belief includes a reference to a lack of belief.

(3)   In relation to the protected characteristic of religion or belief—
    (a)   a reference to a person who has a particular protected characteristic is a reference to a person of a particular religion or belief;

(b)   a reference to persons who share a protected characteristic is a reference to persons who are of the same religion or belief.

11 SEX

In relation to the protected characteristic of sex—

(a)   a reference to a person who has a particular protected characteristic is a reference to a man or to a woman;

(b)   a reference to persons who share a protected characteristic is a reference to persons of the same sex.

12 SEXUAL ORIENTATION

(1)   Sexual orientation means a person's sexual orientation towards—
      (a) persons of the same sex,
      (b) persons of the opposite sex, or
      (c) persons of either sex.

(2)   In relation to the protected characteristic of sexual orientation—
      (a) a reference to a person who has a particular protected characteristic is a reference to a person who is of a particular sexual orientation;
      (b) a reference to persons who share a protected characteristic is a reference to persons who are of the same sexual orientation.

Chapter 2 PROHIBITED CONDUCT

Discrimination

13 DIRECT DISCRIMINATION

(1)   A person (A) discriminates against another (B) if, because of a protected characteristic, A treats B less favourably than A treats or would treat others.

(2)   If the protected characteristic is age, A does not discriminate against B if A can show A's treatment of B to be a proportionate means of achieving a legitimate aim.

(3)   If the protected characteristic is disability, and B is not a disabled person, A does not discriminate against B only because A treats or would treat disabled persons more favourably than A treats B.

(4)   If the protected characteristic is marriage and civil partnership, this section applies to a contravention of Part 5 (work) only if the treatment is because it is B who is married or a civil partner.

(5)   If the protected characteristic is race, less favourable treatment includes segregating B from others.

(6)   If the protected characteristic is sex—
      (a) less favourable treatment of a woman includes less favourable treatment of her because she is breast-feeding;
      (b) in a case where B is a man, no account is to be taken of special treatment afforded to a woman in connection with pregnancy or childbirth.

(7)   Subsection (6)(a) does not apply for the purposes of Part 5 (work).

(8)   This section is subject to sections 17(6) and 18(7).

14 COMBINED DISCRIMINATION: DUAL CHARACTERISTICS

(1)   A person (A) discriminates against another (B) if, because of a combination of two relevant protected characteristics, A treats B less favourably than A treats or would treat a person who does not share either of those characteristics.

(2)   The relevant protected characteristics are—
(a) age;
(b) disability;
(c) gender reassignment;
(d) race
(e) religion or belief;
(f)   sex;
(g) sexual orientation.

(3)   For the purposes of establishing a contravention of this Act by virtue of subsection (1), B need not show that A's treatment of B is direct discrimination because of each of the characteristics in the combination (taken separately).

(4)   But B cannot establish a contravention of this Act by virtue of subsection (1) if, in reliance on another provision of this Act or any other enactment, A shows that A's treatment of B is not direct discrimination because of either or both of the characteristics in the combination.

(5)   Subsection (1) does not apply to a combination of characteristics that includes disability in circumstances where, if a claim of direct discrimination because of disability were to be brought, it would come within section 116 (special educational needs).

(6)   A Minister of the Crown may by order amend this section so as to—
(a) make further provision about circumstances in which B can, or in which B cannot, establish a contravention of this Act by virtue of subsection (1);
(b) specify other circumstances in which subsection (1) does not apply.

(7)   The references to direct discrimination are to a contravention of this Act by virtue of section 13.

15 DISCRIMINATION ARISING FROM DISABILITY

(1)   A person (A) discriminates against a disabled person (B) if—
(a) A treats B unfavourably because of something arising in consequence of B's disability, and
(b) A cannot show that the treatment is a proportionate means of achieving a legitimate aim.

(2)   Subsection (1) does not apply if A shows that A did not know, and could not reasonably have been expected to know, that B had the disability.

16 GENDER REASSIGNMENT DISCRIMINATION: CASES OF ABSENCE FROM WORK

(1)   This section has effect for the purposes of the application of Part 5 (work) to the protected characteristic of gender reassignment.

(2)   A person (A) discriminates against a transsexual person (B) if, in relation to an absence of B's that is because of gender reassignment, A treats B less favourably than A would treat B if—
(a) B's absence was because of sickness or injury, or

(b) B's absence was for some other reason and it is not reasonable for B to be treated less favourably.

(3) A person's absence is because of gender reassignment if it is because the person is proposing to undergo, is undergoing or has undergone the process (or part of the process) mentioned in section 7(1).

17 PREGNANCY AND MATERNITY DISCRIMINATION: NON-WORK CASES

(1) This section has effect for the purposes of the application to the protected characteristic of pregnancy and maternity of—
(a) Part 3 (services and public functions);
(b) Part 4 (premises);
(c) Part 6 (education);
(d) Part 7 (associations).

(2) A person (A) discriminates against a woman if A treats her unfavourably because of a pregnancy of hers.

(3) A person (A) discriminates against a woman if, in the period of 26 weeks beginning with the day on which she gives birth, A treats her unfavourably because she has given birth.

(4) The reference in subsection (3) to treating a woman unfavourably because she has given birth includes, in particular, a reference to treating her unfavourably because she is breast-feeding.

(5) For the purposes of this section, the day on which a woman gives birth is the day on which—
(a) she gives birth to a living child, or
(b) she gives birth to a dead child (more than 24 weeks of the pregnancy having passed).

(6) Section 13, so far as relating to sex discrimination, does not apply to anything done in relation to a woman in so far as—
(a) it is for the reason mentioned in subsection (2), or
(b) it is in the period, and for the reason, mentioned in subsection (3).

18 PREGNANCY AND MATERNITY DISCRIMINATION: WORK CASES

(1) This section has effect for the purposes of the application of Part 5 (work) to the protected characteristic of pregnancy and maternity.

(2) A person (A) discriminates against a woman if, in the protected period in relation to a pregnancy of hers, A treats her unfavourably —
(a) because of the pregnancy, or
(b) because of illness suffered by her as a result of it.

(3) A person (A) discriminates against a woman if A treats her unfavourably because she is on compulsory maternity leave.

(4) A person (A) discriminates against a woman if A treats her unfavourably because she is exercising or seeking to exercise, or has exercised or sought to exercise, the right to ordinary or additional maternity leave.

(5) For the purposes of subsection (2), if the treatment of a woman is in implementation of a decision taken in the protected period, the treatment is to be regarded as occurring in that period (even if the implementation is not until after the end of that period).

(6)   The protected period, in relation to a woman's pregnancy, begins when the pregnancy begins, and ends—

   (a) if she has the right to ordinary and additional maternity leave, at the end of the additional maternity leave period or (if earlier) when she returns to work after the pregnancy;

   (b) if she does not have that right, at the end of the period of 2 weeks beginning with the end of the pregnancy.

(7)   Section 13, so far as relating to sex discrimination, does not apply to treatment of a woman in so far as—

   (a) it is in the protected period in relation to her and is for a reason mentioned in paragraph (a) or (b) of subsection (2), or

   (b) it is for a reason mentioned in subsection (3) or (4).

19 INDIRECT DISCRIMINATION

(1)   A person (A) discriminates against another (B) if A applies to B a provision, criterion or practice which is discriminatory in relation to a relevant protected characteristic of B's.

(2)   For the purposes of subsection (1), a provision, criterion or practice is discriminatory in relation to a relevant protected characteristic of B's if—

   (a) A applies, or would apply, it to persons with whom B does not share the characteristic,

   (b) it puts, or would put, persons with whom B shares the characteristic at a particular disadvantage when compared with persons with whom B does not share it,

   (c) it puts, or would put, B at that disadvantage, and

   (d) A cannot show it to be a proportionate means of achieving a legitimate aim.

(3)   The relevant protected characteristics are—

   age;
   disability;
   gender reassignment;
   marriage and civil partnership;
   race;
   religion or belief;
   sex;
   sexual orientation.

   . . .

Discrimination: supplementary

23 COMPARISON BY REFERENCE TO CIRCUMSTANCES

(1)   On a comparison of cases for the purposes of section 13, 14, or 19 there must be no material difference between the circumstances relating to each case.

(2)   The circumstances relating to a case include a person's abilities if—

   (a) on a comparison for the purposes of section 13, the protected characteristic is disability;

   (b) on a comparison for the purposes of section 14, one of the protected characteristics in the combination is disability.

(3)   If the protected characteristic is sexual orientation, the fact that one person (whether or not the person referred to as B) is a civil partner while another is married is not a material difference between the circumstances relating to each case.

24 IRRELEVANCE OF ALLEGED DISCRIMINATOR'S CHARACTERISTICS

(1)   For the purpose of establishing a contravention of this Act by virtue of section 13(1), it does not matter whether A has the protected characteristic.

(2)   For the purpose of establishing a contravention of this Act by virtue of section 14(1), it does not matter—
   (a)   whether A has one of the protected characteristics in the combination;
   (b)   whether A has both.

25 REFERENCES TO PARTICULAR STRANDS OF DISCRIMINATION

(1)   Age discrimination is—
   (a)   discrimination within section 13 because of age;
   (b)   discrimination within section 19 where the relevant protected characteristic is age.

(2)   Disability discrimination is—
   (a)   discrimination within section 13 because of disability;
   (b)   discrimination within section 15;
   (c)   discrimination within section 19 where the relevant protected characteristic is disability;
   (d)   discrimination within section 21.

(3)   Gender reassignment discrimination is—
   (a)   discrimination within section 13 because of gender reassignment;
   (b)   discrimination within section 16;
   (c)   discrimination within section 19 where the relevant protected characteristic is gender reassignment.

(4)   Marriage and civil partnership discrimination is—
   (a)   discrimination within section 13 because of marriage and civil partnership;
   (b)   discrimination within section 19 where the relevant protected characteristic is marriage and civil partnership.

(5)   Pregnancy and maternity discrimination is discrimination within section 17 or 18.

(6)   Race discrimination is—
   (a)   discrimination within section 13 because of race;
   (b)   discrimination within section 19 where the relevant protected characteristic is race.

(7)   Religious or belief-related discrimination is—
   (a)   discrimination within section 13 because of religion or belief;
   (b)   discrimination within section 19 where the relevant protected characteristic is religion or belief.

(8)   Sex discrimination is—
   (a)   discrimination within section 13 because of sex;
   (b)   discrimination within section 19 where the relevant protected characteristic is sex.

(9)   Sexual orientation discrimination is—
   (a)   discrimination within section 13 because of sexual orientation;
   (b)   discrimination within section 19 where the relevant protected characteristic is sexual orientation.

Other prohibited conduct

26 HARASSMENT

(1)   A person (A) harasses another (B) if—
    (a) A engages in unwanted conduct related to a relevant protected characteristic, and
    (b) the conduct has the purpose or effect of—
        (i)   violating B's dignity, or
        (ii) creating an intimidating, hostile, degrading, humiliating or offensive environment for B.

(2)   A also harasses B if—
    (a) A engages in unwanted conduct of a sexual nature, and
    (b) the conduct has the purpose or effect referred to in subsection (1)(b).

(3)   A also harasses B if—
    (a) A or another person engages in unwanted conduct of a sexual nature or that is related to gender reassignment or sex,
    (b) the conduct has the purpose or effect referred to in subsection (1)(b), and
    (c) because of B's rejection of or submission to the conduct, A treats B less favourably than A would treat B if B had not rejected or submitted to the conduct.

(4)   In deciding whether conduct has the effect referred to in subsection (1)(b), each of the following must be taken into account—
    (a) the perception of B;
    (b) the other circumstances of the case;
    (c) whether it is reasonable for the conduct to have that effect.

(5)   The relevant protected characteristics are—
age;
disability;
gender reassignment;
race;
religion or belief;
sex;
sexual orientation.

27 VICTIMISATION

(1)   A person (A) victimises another person (B) if A subjects B to a detriment because—
    (a) B does a protected act, or
    (b) A believes that B has done, or may do, a protected act.

(2)   Each of the following is a protected act—
    (a) bringing proceedings under this Act;
    (b) giving evidence or information in connection with proceedings under this Act;
    (c) doing any other thing for the purposes of or in connection with this Act;
    (d) making an allegation (whether or not express) that A or another person has contravened this Act.

(3)   Giving false evidence or information, or making a false allegation, is not a protected act if the evidence or information is given, or the allegation is made, in bad faith.

(4)   This section applies only where the person subjected to a detriment is an individual.

(5)   The reference to contravening this Act includes a reference to committing a breach of an equality clause or rule.

Part 3 SERVICES AND PUBLIC FUNCTIONS

Preliminary

28 APPLICATION OF THIS PART

(1)   This Part does not apply to the protected characteristic of—
    (a) age, so far as relating to persons who have not attained the age of 18;
    (b) marriage and civil partnership.

(2)   This Part does not apply to discrimination, harassment or victimisation—
    (a) that is prohibited by Part 4 (premises), 5 (work) or 6 (education), or
    (b) that would be so prohibited but for an express exception.

(3)   This Part does not apply to—
    (a) a breach of an equality clause or rule;
    (b) anything that would be a breach of an equality clause or rule but for section 69 or Part 2 of Schedule 7;
    (c) a breach of a non-discrimination rule.

Provision of services, etc.

29 PROVISION OF SERVICES, ETC.

(1)   A person (a "service-provider") concerned with the provision of a service to the public or a section of the public (for payment or not) must not discriminate against a person requiring the service by not providing the person with the service.

(2)   A service-provider (A) must not, in providing the service, discriminate against a person (B)—
    (a) as to the terms on which A provides the service to B;
    (b) by terminating the provision of the service to B;
    (c) by subjecting B to any other detriment.

(3)   A service-provider must not, in relation to the provision of the service, harass—
    (a) a person requiring the service, or
    (b) a person to whom the service-provider provides the service.

(4)   A service-provider must not victimise a person requiring the service by not providing the person with the service.

(5)   A service-provider (A) must not, in providing the service, victimise a person (B)—
    (a) as to the terms on which A provides the service to B;
    (b) by terminating the provision of the service to B;
    (c) by subjecting B to any other detriment.

(6)   A person must not, in the exercise of a public function that is not the provision of a service to the public or a section of the public, do anything that constitutes discrimination, harassment or victimisation.

(7)   A duty to make reasonable adjustments applies to—
    (a) a service-provider (and see also section 55(7));
    (b) a person who exercises a public function that is not the provision of a service to the public or a section of the public.

(8)   In the application of section 26 for the purposes of subsection (3), and subsection (6) as it relates to harassment, neither of the following is a relevant protected characteristic—

(a) religion or belief;

(b) sexual orientation.

(9) In the application of this section, so far as relating to race or religion or belief, to the granting of entry clearance (within the meaning of the Immigration Act 1971), it does not matter whether an act is done within or outside the United Kingdom.

(10) Subsection (9) does not affect the application of any other provision of this Act to conduct outside England and Wales or Scotland.

Supplementary

. . .

31 INTERPRETATION AND EXCEPTIONS

(1) This section applies for the purposes of this Part.

(2) A reference to the provision of a service includes a reference to the provision of goods or facilities.

(3) A reference to the provision of a service includes a reference to the provision of a service in the exercise of a public function.

(4) A public function is a function that is a function of a public nature for the purposes of the Human Rights Act 1998.

(5) Where an employer arranges for another person to provide a service only to the employer's employees—

(a) the employer is not to be regarded as the service-provider, but

(b) the employees are to be regarded as a section of the public.

(6) A reference to a person requiring a service includes a reference to a person who is seeking to obtain or use the service.

(7) A reference to a service-provider not providing a person with a service includes a reference to—

(a) the service-provider not providing the person with a service of the quality that the service-provider usually provides to the public (or the section of it which includes the person), or

(b) the service-provider not providing the person with the service in the manner in which, or on the terms on which, the service-provider usually provides the service to the public (or the section of it which includes the person).

(8) In relation to the provision of a service by either House of Parliament, the service-provider is the Corporate Officer of the House concerned; and if the service involves access to, or use of, a place in the Palace of Westminster which members of the public are allowed to enter, both Corporate Officers are jointly the service-provider.

(9) Schedule 2 (reasonable adjustments) has effect.

(10) Schedule 3 (exceptions) has effect.

Part 4 PREMISES

Preliminary

32 APPLICATION OF THIS PART

(1)   This Part does not apply to the following protected characteristics—
  (a)   age;
  (b)   marriage and civil partnership.

(2)   This Part does not apply to discrimination, harassment or victimisation—
  (a)   that is prohibited by Part 5 (work) or Part 6 (education), or
  (b)   that would be so prohibited but for an express exception.

(3)   This Part does not apply to the provision of accommodation if the provision—
  (a)   is generally for the purpose of short stays by individuals who live elsewhere, or
  (b)   is for the purpose only of exercising a public function or providing a service to the public or a section of the public.

(4)   The reference to the exercise of a public function, and the reference to the provision of a service, are to be construed in accordance with Part 3.

(5)   This Part does not apply to—
  (a)   a breach of an equality clause or rule;
  (b)   anything that would be a breach of an equality clause or rule but for section 69 or Part 2 of Schedule 7;
  (c)   a breach of a non-discrimination rule.

Disposal and management

33 DISPOSALS, ETC.

(1)   A person (A) who has the right to dispose of premises must not discriminate against another (B)—
  (a)   as to the terms on which A offers to dispose of the premises to B;
  (b)   by not disposing of the premises to B;
  (c)   in A's treatment of B with respect to things done in relation to persons seeking premises.

(2)   Where an interest in a commonhold unit cannot be disposed of unless a particular person is a party to the disposal, that person must not discriminate against a person by not being a party to the disposal.

(3)   A person who has the right to dispose of premises must not, in connection with anything done in relation to their occupation or disposal, harass—
  (a)   a person who occupies them;
  (b)   a person who applies for them.

(4)   A person (A) who has the right to dispose of premises must not victimise another (B)—
  (a)   as to the terms on which A offers to dispose of the premises to B;
  (b)   by not disposing of the premises to B;
  (c)   in A's treatment of B with respect to things done in relation to persons seeking premises.

(5)   Where an interest in a commonhold unit cannot be disposed of unless a particular person is a party to the disposal, that person must not victimise a person by not being a party to the disposal.

(6)   In the application of section 26 for the purposes of subsection (3), neither of the following is a relevant protected characteristic—
(a) religion or belief;
(b) sexual orientation.

34 PERMISSION FOR DISPOSAL

(1)   A person whose permission is required for the disposal of premises must not discriminate against another by not giving permission for the disposal of the premises to the other.

(2)   A person whose permission is required for the disposal of premises must not, in relation to an application for permission to dispose of the premises, harass a person—
(a) who applies for permission to dispose of the premises, or
(b) to whom the disposal would be made if permission were given.

(3)   A person whose permission is required for the disposal of premises must not victimise another by not giving permission for the disposal of the premises to the other.

(4)   In the application of section 26 for the purposes of subsection (2), neither of the following is a relevant protected characteristic—
(a) religion or belief;
(b) sexual orientation.

(5)   This section does not apply to anything done in the exercise of a judicial function.

35 MANAGEMENT

(1)   A person (A) who manages premises must not discriminate against a person (B) who occupies the premises—
(a) in the way in which A allows B, or by not allowing B, to make use of a benefit or facility;
(b) by evicting B (or taking steps for the purpose of securing B's eviction);
(c) by subjecting B to any other detriment.

(2)   A person who manages premises must not, in relation to their management, harass—
(a) a person who occupies them;
(b) a person who applies for them.

(3)   A person (A) who manages premises must not victimise a person (B) who occupies the premises—
(a) in the way in which A allows B, or by not allowing B, to make use of a benefit or facility;
(b) by evicting B (or taking steps for the purpose of securing B's eviction);
(c) by subjecting B to any other detriment.

(4)   In the application of section 26 for the purposes of subsection (2), neither of the following is a relevant protected characteristic—
(a) religion or belief;
(b) sexual orientation.
. . .

Supplementary

38 INTERPRETATION AND EXCEPTIONS

(1)   This section applies for the purposes of this Part.

(2)   A reference to premises is a reference to the whole or part of the premises.

(3)   A reference to disposing of premises includes, in the case of premises subject to a tenancy, a reference to—
      (a) assigning the premises,
      (b) sub-letting them, or
      (c) parting with possession of them.

(4)   A reference to disposing of premises also includes a reference to granting a right to occupy them.

(5)   A reference to disposing of an interest in a commonhold unit includes a reference to creating an interest in a commonhold unit.

(6)   A reference to a tenancy is to a tenancy created (whether before or after the passing of this Act)—
      (a) by a lease or sub-lease,
      (b) by an agreement for a lease or sub-lease,
      (c) by a tenancy agreement, or
      (d) in pursuance of an enactment,
      and a reference to a tenant is to be construed accordingly.

(7)   A reference to commonhold land, a commonhold association, a commonhold community statement, a commonhold unit or a unit-holder is to be construed in accordance with the Commonhold and Leasehold Reform Act 2002.

(8)   Schedule 4 (reasonable adjustments) has effect.

(9)   Schedule 5 (exceptions) has effect.

. . .

Part 5 WORK

. . .

Chapter 3 EQUALITY OF TERMS

Sex equality

64 RELEVANT TYPES OF WORK

(1)   Sections 66 to 70 apply where—
      (a) a person (A) is employed on work that is equal to the work that a comparator of the opposite sex (B) does;
      (b) a person (A) holding a personal or public office does work that is equal to the work that a comparator of the opposite sex (B) does.

(2)   The references in subsection (1) to the work that B does are not restricted to work done contemporaneously with the work done by A.

65 EQUAL WORK

(1)   For the purposes of this Chapter, A's work is equal to that of B if it is—
      (a) like B's work,
      (b) rated as equivalent to B's work, or
      (c) of equal value to B's work.

(2)   A's work is like B's work if—
    (a) A's work and B's work are the same or broadly similar, and
    (b) such differences as there are between their work are not of practical importance in relation to the terms of their work.

(3)   So on a comparison of one person's work with another's for the purposes of subsection (2), it is necessary to have regard to—
    (a) the frequency with which differences between their work occur in practice, and
    (b) the nature and extent of the differences.

(4)   A's work is rated as equivalent to B's work if a job evaluation study—
    (a) gives an equal value to A's job and B's job in terms of the demands made on a worker, or
    (b) would give an equal value to A's job and B's job in those terms were the evaluation not made on a sex-specific system.

(5)   A system is sex-specific if, for the purposes of one or more of the demands made on a worker, it sets values for men different from those it sets for women.

(6)   A's work is of equal value to B's work if it is—
    (a) neither like B's work nor rated as equivalent to B's work, but
    (b) nevertheless equal to B's work in terms of the demands made on A by reference to factors such as effort, skill and decision-making.

66 SEX EQUALITY CLAUSE

(1)   If the terms of A's work do not (by whatever means) include a sex equality clause, they are to be treated as including one.

(2)   A sex equality clause is a provision that has the following effect—
    (a) if a term of A's is less favourable to A than a corresponding term of B's is to B, A's term is modified so as not to be less favourable;
    (b) if A does not have a term which corresponds to a term of B's that benefits B, A's terms are modified so as to include such a term.

(3)   Subsection (2)(a) applies to a term of A's relating to membership of or rights under an occupational pension scheme only in so far as a sex equality rule would have effect in relation to the term.

(4)   In the case of work within section 65(1)(b), a reference in subsection (2) above to a term includes a reference to such terms (if any) as have not been determined by the rating of the work (as well as those that have).

67 SEX EQUALITY RULE

(1)   If an occupational pension scheme does not include a sex equality rule, it is to be treated as including one.

(2)   A sex equality rule is a provision that has the following effect—
    (a) if a relevant term is less favourable to A than it is to B, the term is modified so as not to be less favourable;
    (b) if a term confers a relevant discretion capable of being exercised in a way that would be less favourable to A than to B, the term is modified so as to prevent the exercise of the discretion in that way.

(3)   A term is relevant if it is—

(a) a term on which persons become members of the scheme, or

(b) a term on which members of the scheme are treated.

(4) A discretion is relevant if its exercise in relation to the scheme is capable of affecting—

(a) the way in which persons become members of the scheme, or

(b) the way in which members of the scheme are treated.

(5) The reference in subsection (3)(b) to a term on which members of a scheme are treated includes a reference to the term as it has effect for the benefit of dependants of members.

(6) The reference in subsection (4)(b) to the way in which members of a scheme are treated includes a reference to the way in which they are treated as the scheme has effect for the benefit of dependants of members.

(7) If the effect of a relevant matter on persons of the same sex differs according to their family, marital or civil partnership status, a comparison for the purposes of this section of the effect of that matter on persons of the opposite sex must be with persons who have the same status.

(8) A relevant matter is—

(a) a relevant term;

(b) a term conferring a relevant discretion;

(c) the exercise of a relevant discretion in relation to an occupational pension scheme.

(9) This section, so far as relating to the terms on which persons become members of an occupational pension scheme, does not have effect in relation to pensionable service before 8 April 1976.

(10) This section, so far as relating to the terms on which members of an occupational pension scheme are treated, does not have effect in relation to pensionable service before 17 May 1990.

68 SEX EQUALITY RULE: CONSEQUENTIAL ALTERATION OF SCHEMES

(1) This section applies if the trustees or managers of an occupational pension scheme do not have power to make sex equality alterations to the scheme.

(2) This section also applies if the trustees or managers of an occupational pension scheme have power to make sex equality alterations to the scheme but the procedure for doing so—

(a) is liable to be unduly complex or protracted, or

(b) involves obtaining consents which cannot be obtained or which can be obtained only with undue delay or difficulty.

(3) The trustees or managers may by resolution make sex equality alterations to the scheme.

(4) Sex equality alterations may have effect in relation to a period before the date on which they are made.

(5) Sex equality alterations to an occupational pension scheme are such alterations to the scheme as may be required to secure conformity with a sex equality rule.

69 DEFENCE OF MATERIAL FACTOR

(1) The sex equality clause in A's terms has no effect in relation to a difference between A's terms and B's terms if the responsible person shows that the difference is because of a material factor reliance on which—

      (a)   does not involve treating A less favourably because of A's sex than the responsible person treats B, and

      (b)   if the factor is within subsection (2), is a proportionate means of achieving a legitimate aim.

(2)   A factor is within this subsection if A shows that, as a result of the factor, A and persons of the same sex doing work equal to A's are put at a particular disadvantage when compared with persons of the opposite sex doing work equal to A's.

(3)   For the purposes of subsection (1), the long-term objective of reducing inequality between men's and women's terms of work is always to be regarded as a legitimate aim.

(4)   A sex equality rule has no effect in relation to a difference between A and B in the effect of a relevant matter if the trustees or managers of the scheme in question show that the difference is because of a material factor which is not the difference of sex.

(5)   "Relevant matter" has the meaning given in section 67.

(6)   For the purposes of this section, a factor is not material unless it is a material difference between A's case and B's.

70 EXCLUSION OF SEX DISCRIMINATION PROVISIONS

(1)   The relevant sex discrimination provision has no effect in relation to a term of A's that—

      (a)   is modified by, or included by virtue of, a sex equality clause or rule, or

      (b)   would be so modified or included but for section 69 or Part 2 of Schedule 7.

(2)   Neither of the following is sex discrimination for the purposes of the relevant sex discrimination provision—

      (a)   the inclusion in A's terms of a term that is less favourable as referred to in section 66(2)(a);

      (b)   the failure to include in A's terms a corresponding term as referred to in section 66(2)(b).

. . .

71 SEX DISCRIMINATION IN RELATION TO CONTRACTUAL PAY

(1)   This section applies in relation to a term of a person's work—

      (a)   that relates to pay, but

      (b)   in relation to which a sex equality clause or rule has no effect.

(2)   The relevant sex discrimination provision (as defined by section 70) has no effect in relation to the term except in so far as treatment of the person amounts to a contravention of the provision by virtue of section 13 or 14.

. . .

Part 8 PROHIBITED CONDUCT: ANCILLARY

108 RELATIONSHIPS THAT HAVE ENDED

(1)   A person (A) must not discriminate against another (B) if—

      (a)   the discrimination arises out of and is closely connected to a relationship which used to exist between them, and

      (b)   conduct of a description constituting the discrimination would, if it occurred during the relationship, contravene this Act.

(2) A person (A) must not harass another (B) if—
   (a) the harassment arises out of and is closely connected to a relationship which used to exist between them, and
   (b) conduct of a description constituting the harassment would, if it occurred during the relationship, contravene this Act.

(3) It does not matter whether the relationship ends before or after the commencement of this section.

(4) A duty to make reasonable adjustments applies to A if B is placed at a substantial disadvantage as mentioned in section 20.

(5) For the purposes of subsection (4), sections 20, 21 and 22 and the applicable Schedules are to be construed as if the relationship had not ended.

(6) For the purposes of Part 9 (enforcement), a contravention of this section relates to the Part of this Act that would have been contravened if the relationship had not ended.

(7) But conduct is not a contravention of this section in so far as it also amounts to victimisation of B by A.

109 LIABILITY OF EMPLOYERS AND PRINCIPALS

(1) Anything done by a person (A) in the course of A's employment must be treated as also done by the employer.

(2) Anything done by an agent for a principal, with the authority of the principal, must be treated as also done by the principal.

(3) It does not matter whether that thing is done with the employer's or principal's knowledge or approval.

(4) In proceedings against A's employer (B) in respect of anything alleged to have been done by A in the course of A's employment it is a defence for B to show that B took all reasonable steps to prevent A—
   (a) from doing that thing, or
   (b) from doing anything of that description.

(5) This section does not apply to offences under this Act (other than offences under Part 12 (disabled persons: transport)).

110 LIABILITY OF EMPLOYEES AND AGENTS

(1) A person (A) contravenes this section if—
   (a) A is an employee or agent,
   (b) A does something which, by virtue of section 109(1) or (2), is treated as having been done by A's employer or principal (as the case may be), and
   (c) the doing of that thing by A amounts to a contravention of this Act by the employer or principal (as the case may be).

(2) It does not matter whether, in any proceedings, the employer is found not to have contravened this Act by virtue of section 109(4).

(3) A does not contravene this section if—
   (a) A relies on a statement by the employer or principal that doing that thing is not a contravention of this Act, and
   (b) it is reasonable for A to do so.

(4)   A person (B) commits an offence if B knowingly or recklessly makes a statement mentioned in subsection (3)(a) which is false or misleading in a material respect.

(5)   A person guilty of an offence under subsection (4) is liable on summary conviction to a fine not exceeding level 5 on the standard scale.

(6)   Part 9 (enforcement) applies to a contravention of this section by A as if it were the contravention mentioned in subsection (1)(c).

(7)   The reference in subsection (1)(c) to a contravention of this Act does not include a reference to disability discrimination in contravention of Chapter 1 of Part 6 (schools).

111 INSTRUCTING, CAUSING OR INDUCING CONTRAVENTIONS

(1)   A person (A) must not instruct another (B) to do in relation to a third person (C) anything which contravenes Part 3, 4, 5, 6 or 7 or section 108(1) or (2) or 112(1) (a basic contravention).

(2)   A person (A) must not cause another (B) to do in relation to a third person (C) anything which is a basic contravention.

(3)   A person (A) must not induce another (B) to do in relation to a third person (C) anything which is a basic contravention.

(4)   For the purposes of subsection (3), inducement may be direct or indirect.

(5)   Proceedings for a contravention of this section may be brought—
(a) by B, if B is subjected to a detriment as a result of A's conduct;
(b) by C, if C is subjected to a detriment as a result of A's conduct;
(c) by the Commission.

(6)   For the purposes of subsection (5), it does not matter whether—
(a) the basic contravention occurs;
(b) any other proceedings are, or may be, brought in relation to A's conduct.

(7)   This section does not apply unless the relationship between A and B is such that A is in a position to commit a basic contravention in relation to B.

(8)   A reference in this section to causing or inducing a person to do something includes a reference to attempting to cause or induce the person to do it.

(9)   For the purposes of Part 9 (enforcement), a contravention of this section is to be treated as relating—
(a) in a case within subsection (5)(a), to the Part of this Act which, because of the relationship between A and B, A is in a position to contravene in relation to B;
(b) in a case within subsection (5)(b), to the Part of this Act which, because of the relationship between B and C, B is in a position to contravene in relation to C.

112 AIDING CONTRAVENTIONS

(1)   A person (A) must not knowingly help another (B) to do anything which contravenes Part 3, 4, 5, 6 or 7 or section 108(1) or (2) or 111 (a basic contravention).

(2)   It is not a contravention of subsection (1) if—
(a) A relies on a statement by B that the act for which the help is given does not contravene this Act, and
(b) it is reasonable for A to do so.

(3)   B commits an offence if B knowingly or recklessly makes a statement mentioned in subsection (2)(a) which is false or misleading in a material respect.

(4)   A person guilty of an offence under subsection (3) is liable on summary conviction to a fine not exceeding level 5 on the standard scale.

(5)   For the purposes of Part 9 (enforcement), a contravention of this section is to be treated as relating to the provision of this Act to which the basic contravention relates.

(6)   The reference in subsection (1) to a basic contravention does not include a reference to disability discrimination in contravention of Chapter 1 of Part 6 (schools).

Part 9 ENFORCEMENT

Chapter 1 INTRODUCTORY

113 PROCEEDINGS

(1)   Proceedings relating to a contravention of this Act must be brought in accordance with this Part.

(2)   Subsection (1) does not apply to proceedings under Part 1 of the Equality Act 2006.

(3)   Subsection (1) does not prevent—
(a)   a claim for judicial review;
(b)   proceedings under the Immigration Acts;
(c)   proceedings under the Special Immigration Appeals Commission Act 1997;
(d)   in Scotland, an application to the supervisory jurisdiction of the Court of Session.

(4)   This section is subject to any express provision of this Act conferring jurisdiction on a court or tribunal.

(5)   The reference to a contravention of this Act includes a reference to a breach of an equality clause or rule.

(6)   Chapters 2 and 3 do not apply to proceedings relating to an equality clause or rule except in so far as Chapter 4 provides for that.

(7)   This section does not apply to—
(a)   proceedings for an offence under this Act;
(b)   proceedings relating to a penalty under Part 12 (disabled persons: transport).

Chapter 2 CIVIL COURTS

114 JURISDICTION

(1)   A county court or, in Scotland, the sheriff has jurisdiction to determine a claim relating to—
(a)   a contravention of Part 3 (services and public functions);
(b)   a contravention of Part 4 (premises);
(c)   a contravention of Part 6 (education);
(d)   a contravention of Part 7 (associations);
(e)   a contravention of section 108, 111 or 112 that relates to Part 3, 4, 6 or 7.

(2)   Subsection (1)(a) does not apply to a claim within section 115.

(3)   Subsection (1)(c) does not apply to a claim within section 116.

(4)   Subsection (1)(d) does not apply to a contravention of section 106.

(5)   For the purposes of proceedings on a claim within subsection (1)(a)—
    (a)   a decision in proceedings on a claim mentioned in section 115(1) that an act is a contravention of Part 3 is binding;
    (b)   it does not matter whether the act occurs outside the United Kingdom.

(6)   The county court or sheriff—
    (a)   must not grant an interim injunction or interdict unless satisfied that no criminal matter would be prejudiced by doing so;
    (b)   must grant an application to stay or sist proceedings under subsection (1) on grounds of prejudice to a criminal matter unless satisfied the matter will not be prejudiced.

(7)   In proceedings in England and Wales on a claim within subsection (1), the power under section 63(1) of the County Courts Act 1984 (appointment of assessors) must be exercised unless the judge is satisfied that there are good reasons for not doing so.

(8)   In proceedings in Scotland on a claim within subsection (1), the power under rule 44.3 of Schedule 1 to the Sheriff Court (Scotland) Act 1907 (appointment of assessors) must be exercised unless the sheriff is satisfied that there are good reasons for not doing so.

(9)   The remuneration of an assessor appointed by virtue of subsection (8) is to be at a rate determined by the Lord President of the Court of Session.

. . .

119 REMEDIES

(1)   This section applies if a county court or the sheriff finds that there has been a contravention of a provision referred to in section 114(1).

(2)   The county court has power to grant any remedy which could be granted by the High Court—
    (a)   in proceedings in tort;
    (b)   on a claim for judicial review.

(3)   The sheriff has power to make any order which could be made by the Court of Session—
    (a)   in proceedings for reparation;
    (b)   on a petition for judicial review.

(4)   An award of damages may include compensation for injured feelings (whether or not it includes compensation on any other basis).

(5)   Subsection (6) applies if the county court or sheriff—
    (a)   finds that a contravention of a provision referred to in section 114(1) is established by virtue of section 19, but
    (b)   is satisfied that the provision, criterion or practice was not applied with the intention of discriminating against the claimant or pursuer.

(6)   The county court or sheriff must not make an award of damages unless it first considers whether to make any other disposal.

(7)   The county court or sheriff must not grant a remedy other than an award of damages or the making of a declaration unless satisfied that no criminal matter would be prejudiced by doing so.

. . .

Chapter 4 EQUALITY OF TERMS

127 JURISDICTION

(1) An employment tribunal has, subject to subsection (6), jurisdiction to determine a complaint relating to a breach of an equality clause or rule.

(2) The jurisdiction conferred by subsection (1) includes jurisdiction to determine a complaint arising out of a breach of an equality clause or rule; and a reference in this Chapter to a complaint relating to such a breach is to be read accordingly.

(3) An employment tribunal also has jurisdiction to determine an application by a responsible person for a declaration as to the rights of that person and a worker in relation to a dispute about the effect of an equality clause or rule.

(4) An employment tribunal also has jurisdiction to determine an application by the trustees or managers of an occupational pension scheme for a declaration as to their rights and those of a member in relation to a dispute about the effect of an equality rule.

(5) An employment tribunal also has jurisdiction to determine a question that—
(a) relates to an equality clause or rule, and
(b) is referred to the tribunal by virtue of section 128(2).

(6) This section does not apply to a complaint relating to an act done when the complainant was serving as a member of the armed forces unless—
(a) the complainant has made a service complaint about the matter, and
(b) the complaint has not been withdrawn.

(7) Subsections (2) to (5) of section 121 apply for the purposes of subsection (6) of this section as they apply for the purposes of subsection (1) of that section.

(8) In proceedings before an employment tribunal on a complaint relating to a breach of an equality rule, the employer—
(a) is to be treated as a party, and
(b) is accordingly entitled to appear and be heard.

(9) Nothing in this section affects such jurisdiction as the High Court, a county court, the Court of Session or the sheriff has in relation to an equality clause or rule.

128 REFERENCES BY COURT TO TRIBUNAL, ETC.

(1) If it appears to a court in which proceedings are pending that a claim or counter-claim relating to an equality clause or rule could more conveniently be determined by an employment tribunal, the court may strike out the claim or counter-claim.

(2) If in proceedings before a court a question arises about an equality clause or rule, the court may (whether or not on an application by a party to the proceedings)—
(a) refer the question, or direct that it be referred by a party to the proceedings, to an employment tribunal for determination, and
(b) stay or sist the proceedings in the meantime.

. . .

132 REMEDIES IN NON-PENSIONS CASES

(1) This section applies to proceedings before a court or employment tribunal on a complaint relating to a breach of an equality clause, other than a breach with respect to membership of or rights under an occupational pension scheme.

(2) If the court or tribunal finds that there has been a breach of the equality clause, it may—

    (a) make a declaration as to the rights of the parties in relation to the matters to which the proceedings relate;

    (b) order an award by way of arrears of pay or damages in relation to the complainant.

(3) The court or tribunal may not order a payment under subsection (2)(b) in respect of a time before the arrears day.

. . .

Chapter 5 MISCELLANEOUS

136 BURDEN OF PROOF

(1) This section applies to any proceedings relating to a contravention of this Act.

(2) If there are facts from which the court could decide, in the absence of any other explanation, that a person (A) contravened the provision concerned, the court must hold that the contravention occurred.

(3) But subsection (2) does not apply if A shows that A did not contravene the provision.

(4) The reference to a contravention of this Act includes a reference to a breach of an equality clause or rule.

(5) This section does not apply to proceedings for an offence under this Act.

(6) A reference to the court includes a reference to—

    (a) an employment tribunal;

    (b) the Asylum and Immigration Tribunal;

    (c) the Special Immigration Appeals Commission;

    (d) the First-tier Tribunal;

    (e) the Special Educational Needs Tribunal for Wales;

    (f) an Additional Support Needs Tribunal for Scotland.

. . .

Part 10 CONTRACTS, ETC.

Contracts and other agreements

142 UNENFORCEABLE TERMS

(1) A term of a contract is unenforceable against a person in so far as it constitutes, promotes or provides for treatment of that or another person that is of a description prohibited by this Act.

(2) A relevant non-contractual term is unenforceable against a person in so far as it constitutes, promotes or provides for treatment of that or another person that is of a description prohibited by this Act, in so far as this Act relates to disability.

(3) A relevant non-contractual term is a term which—

    (a) is a term of an agreement that is not a contract, and

    (b) relates to the provision of an employment service within section 56(2)(a) to (e) or to the provision under a group insurance arrangement of facilities by way of insurance.

(4) A reference in subsection (1) or (2) to treatment of a description prohibited by his Act does not include—

    (a) a reference to the inclusion of a term in a contract referred to in section 70(2)(a) or 76(2), or

    (b) a reference to the failure to include a term in a contract as referred to in section 70(2)(b).

(5) Subsection (4) does not affect the application of section 148(2) to this section.

143 REMOVAL OR MODIFICATION OF UNENFORCEABLE TERMS

(1) A county court or the sheriff may, on an application by a person who has an interest in a contract or other agreement which includes a term that is unenforceable as a result of section 142, make an order for the term to be removed or modified.

(2) An order under this section must not be made unless every person who would be affected by it—
    (a) has been given notice of the application (except where notice is dispensed with in accordance with rules of court), and
    (b) has been afforded an opportunity to make representations to the county court or sheriff.

(3) An order under this section may include provision in respect of a period before the making of the order.

144 CONTRACTING OUT

(1) A term of a contract is unenforceable by a person in whose favour it would operate in so far as it purports to exclude or limit a provision of or made under this Act.

(2) A relevant non-contractual term (as defined by section 142) is unenforceable by a person in whose favour it would operate in so far as it purports to exclude or limit a provision of or made under this Act, in so far as the provision relates to disability.

(3) This section does not apply to a contract which settles a claim within section 114.

(4) This section does not apply to a contract which settles a complaint within section 120 if the contract—
    (a) is made with the assistance of a conciliation officer, or
    (b) is a qualifying compromise contract.

(5) A contract within subsection (4) includes a contract which settles a complaint relating to a breach of an equality clause or rule or of a non-discrimination rule.

(6) A contract within subsection (4) includes an agreement by the parties to a dispute to submit the dispute to arbitration if—
    (a) the dispute is covered by a scheme having effect by virtue of an order under section 212A of the Trade Union and Labour Relations (Consolidation) Act 1992, and
    (b) the agreement is to submit the dispute to arbitration in accordance with the scheme.

Collective agreements and rules of undertakings

145 VOID AND UNENFORCEABLE TERMS

(1) A term of a collective agreement is void in so far as it constitutes, promotes or provides for treatment of a description prohibited by this Act.

(2)   A rule of an undertaking is unenforceable against a person in so far as it constitutes, promotes or provides for treatment of the person that is of a description prohibited by this Act.

146 DECLARATION IN RESPECT OF VOID TERM, ETC.

(1)   A qualifying person (P) may make a complaint to an employment tribunal that a term is void, or that a rule is unenforceable, as a result of section 145.

(2)   But subsection (1) applies only if—
(a)   the term or rule may in the future have effect in relation to P, and
(b)   where the complaint alleges that the term or rule provides for treatment of a description prohibited by this Act, P may in the future be subjected to treatment that would (if P were subjected to it in present circumstances) be of that description.

(3)   If the tribunal finds that the complaint is well-founded, it must make an order declaring that the term is void or the rule is unenforceable.

(4)   An order under this section may include provision in respect of a period before the making of the order.

(5)   In the case of a complaint about a term of a collective agreement, where the term is one made by or on behalf of a person of a description specified in the first column of the table, a qualifying person is a person of a description specified in the second column.

. . .

Part 15 FAMILY PROPERTY

198 ABOLITION OF HUSBAND'S DUTY TO MAINTAIN WIFE

The rule of common law that a husband must maintain his wife is abolished.

199 ABOLITION OF PRESUMPTION OF ADVANCEMENT

(1)   The presumption of advancement (by which, for example, a husband is presumed to be making a gift to his wife if he transfers property to her, or purchases property in her name) is abolished.

(2)   The abolition by subsection (1) of the presumption of advancement does not have effect in relation to—
(a)   anything done before the commencement of this section, or
(b)   anything done pursuant to any obligation incurred before the commencement of this section.

200 AMENDMENT OF MARRIED WOMEN'S PROPERTY ACT 1964

(1)   In section 1 of the Married Women's Property Act 1964 (money and property derived from housekeeping allowance made by husband to be treated as belonging to husband and wife in equal shares)—
(a)   for "the husband for" substitute "either of them for", and
(b)   for "the husband and the wife" substitute "them".

(2)   Accordingly, that Act may be cited as the Matrimonial Property Act 1964.

(3)   The amendments made by this section do not have effect in relation to any allowance made before the commencement of this section.

. . .

Part 16 GENERAL AND MISCELLANEOUS

. . .

216 COMMENCEMENT

(1)   The following provisions come into force on the day on which this Act is passed—
(a)   section 186(2) (rail vehicle accessibility: compliance);
(b)   this Part (except sections 202 (civil partnerships on religious premises), 206 (information society services) and 211 (amendments, etc).

(2)   Part 15 (family property) comes into force on such day as the Lord Chancellor may by order appoint.

(3)   The other provisions of this Act come into force on such day as a Minister of the Crown may by order appoint.

217 EXTENT

(1)   This Act forms part of the law of England and Wales.

(2)   This Act, apart from section 190 (improvements to let dwelling houses) and Part 15 (family property), forms part of the law of Scotland.

. . .

Please note that at the time of writing Equality Act 2010, ss. 1-3, 14, and 198-200 were not yet in force. Some of the other sections were only partially in force. Please also note that Equality Act 2010, s. 1 is prospectively amended by the Public Bodies Act 2011, Sch 6, by the Police Reform and Social Responsibility Act 2011, Sch 16 and by the Health and Social Care Act 2012, Sch 5.

THIRD PARTIES (RIGHTS AGAINST INSURERS) ACT 2010
(c.10)

Transfer of rights to third parties

1 RIGHTS AGAINST INSURER OF INSOLVENT PERSON ETC.

(1)   This section applies if—
(a)   a relevant person incurs a liability against which that person is insured under a contract of insurance, or
(b)   a person who is subject to such a liability becomes a relevant person.

(2)   The rights of the relevant person under the contract against the insurer in respect of the liability are transferred to and vest in the person to whom the liability is or was incurred (the "third party").

(3)   The third party may bring proceedings to enforce the rights against the insurer without having established the relevant person's liability; but the third party may not enforce those rights without having established that liability.

(4)   For the purposes of this Act, a liability is established only if its existence and amount are established; and, for that purpose, "establish" means establish—
    (a) by virtue of a declaration under section 2 or a declarator under section 3,
    (b) by a judgment or decree,
    (c) by an award in arbitral proceedings or by an arbitration, or
    (d) by an enforceable agreement.

(5)   In this Act—
    (a) references to an "insured" are to a person who incurs or who is subject to a liability to a third party against which that person is insured under a contract of insurance;
    (b) references to a "relevant person" are to a person within sections 4 to 7;
    (c) references to a "third party" are to be construed in accordance with subsection (2);
    (d) references to "transferred rights" are to rights under a contract of insurance which are transferred under this section.

2 ESTABLISHING LIABILITY IN ENGLAND AND WALES AND NORTHERN IRELAND—

(1)   This section applies where a person (P)—
    (a) claims to have rights under a contract of insurance by virtue of a transfer under section 1, but
    (b) has not yet established the insured's liability which is insured under that contract.

(2)   P may bring proceedings against the insurer for either or both of the following—
    (a) a declaration as to the insured's liability to P;
    (b) a declaration as to the insurer's potential liability to P.

(3)   In such proceedings P is entitled, subject to any defence on which the insurer may rely, to a declaration under subsection (2)(a) or (b) on proof of the insured's liability to P or (as the case may be) the insurer's potential liability to P.

(4)   Where proceedings are brought under subsection (2)(a) the insurer may rely on any defence on which the insured could rely if those proceedings were proceedings brought against the insured in respect of the insured's liability to P.

(5)   Subsection (4) is subject to section 12(1).

(6)   Where the court makes a declaration under this section, the effect of which is that the insurer is liable to P, the court may give the appropriate judgment against the insurer.

(7)   Where a person applying for a declaration under subsection (2)(b) is entitled or required, by virtue of the contract of insurance, to do so in arbitral proceedings, that person may also apply in the same proceedings for a declaration under subsection (2)(a).

(8)   In the application of this section to arbitral proceedings, subsection (6) is to be read as if "tribunal" were substituted for "court" and "make the appropriate award" for "give the appropriate judgment".

(9)   When bringing proceedings under subsection (2)(a), P may also make the insured a defendant to those proceedings.

(10) If (but only if) the insured is a defendant to proceedings under this section (whether by virtue of subsection (9) or otherwise), a declaration under subsection (2) binds the insured as well as the insurer.

(11) In this section, references to the insurer's potential liability to P are references to the insurer's liability in respect of the insured's liability to P, if established.

3 ESTABLISHING LIABILITY IN SCOTLAND

(1) This section applies where a person (P)—
   (a) claims to have rights under a contract of insurance by virtue of a transfer under section 1, but
   (b) has not yet established the insured's liability which is insured under that contract.

(2) P may bring proceedings against the insurer for either or both of the following—
   (a) a declarator as to the insured's liability to P;
   (b) a declarator as to the insurer's potential liability to P.

(3) Where proceedings are brought under subsection (2)(a) the insurer may rely on any defence on which the insured could rely if those proceedings were proceedings brought against the insured in respect of the insured's liability to P.

(4) Subsection (3) is subject to section 12(1).

(5) Where the court grants a declarator under this section, the effect of which is that the insurer is liable to P, the court may grant the appropriate decree against the insurer.

(6) Where a person applying for a declarator under subsection (2)(b) is entitled or required, by virtue of the contract of insurance, to do so in an arbitration, that person may also apply in the same arbitration for a declarator under subsection (2)(a).

(7) In the application of this section to an arbitration, subsection (5) is to be read as if "tribunal" were substituted for "court" and "make the appropriate award" for "grant the appropriate decree".

(8) When bringing proceedings under subsection (2)(a), P may also make the insured a defender to those proceedings.

(9) If (but only if) the insured is a defender to proceedings under this section (whether by virtue of subsection (8) or otherwise), a declarator under subsection (2) binds the insured as well as the insurer.

(10) In this section, the reference to the insurer's potential liability to P is a reference to the insurer's liability in respect of the insured's liability to P, if established.

Relevant persons

4 INDIVIDUALS

(1) An individual is a relevant person if any of the following is in force in respect of that individual in England and Wales—
   (a) a deed of arrangement registered in accordance with the Deeds of Arrangement Act 1914,
   (b) an administration order made under Part 6 of the County Courts Act 1984,
   (c) an enforcement restriction order made under Part 6A of that Act,
   (d) subject to subsection (4), a debt relief order made under Part 7A of the Insolvency Act 1986,

(e)   a voluntary arrangement approved in accordance with Part 8 of that Act, or

(f)   a bankruptcy order made under Part 9 of that Act.

(2)   An individual is a relevant person if any of the following is in force in respect of that individual (or, in the case of paragraph (a) or (b), that individual's estate) in Scotland—

(a)   an award of sequestration made under section 5 of the Bankruptcy (Scotland) Act 1985,

(b)   a protected trust deed within the meaning of that Act, or

(c)   a composition approved in accordance with Schedule 4 to that Act.

(3)   An individual is a relevant person if any of the following is in force in respect of that individual in Northern Ireland—

(a)   an administration order made under Part 6 of the Judgments Enforcement (Northern Ireland) Order 1981 (S.I. 1981/226 (N.I. 6)),

(b)   a deed of arrangement registered in accordance with Chapter 1 of Part 8 of the Insolvency (Northern Ireland) Order 1989 (S.I. 1989/2405 (N.I. 19)),

(c)   a voluntary arrangement approved under Chapter 2 of Part 8 of that Order, or

(d)   a bankruptcy order made under Part 9 of that Order.

(4)   If an individual is a relevant person by virtue of subsection (1)(d), that person is a relevant person for the purposes of section 1(1)(b) only.

(5)   Where an award of sequestration made under section 5 of the Bankruptcy (Scotland) Act 1985 is recalled or reduced, any rights which were transferred under section 1 as a result of that award are re-transferred to and vest in the person who became a relevant person as a result of the award.

(6)   Where an order discharging an individual from an award of sequestration made under section 5 of the Bankruptcy (Scotland) Act 1985 is recalled or reduced under paragraph 17 or 18 of Schedule 4 to that Act, the order is to be treated for the purposes of this section as never having been made.

5 INDIVIDUALS WHO DIE INSOLVENT

(1)   An individual who dies insolvent is a relevant person for the purposes of section 1(1)(b) only.

(2)   For the purposes of this section an individual (D) is to be regarded as having died insolvent if, following D's death—

(a)   D's estate falls to be administered in accordance with an order under section 421 of the Insolvency Act 1986 or Article 365 of the Insolvency (Northern Ireland) Order 1989 (S.I. 1989/2405 (N. I. 19)),

(b)   an award of sequestration is made under section 5 of the Bankruptcy (Scotland) Act 1985 in respect of D's estate and the award is not recalled or reduced, or

(c)   a judicial factor is appointed under section 11A of the Judicial Factors (Scotland) Act 1889 in respect of D's estate and the judicial factor certifies that the estate is absolutely insolvent within the meaning of the Bankruptcy (Scotland) Act 1985.

(3)   Where a transfer of rights under section 1 takes place as a result of an insured person being a relevant person by virtue of this section, references in this Act to an insured are, where the context so requires, to be read as references to the insured's estate.

6 CORPORATE BODIES ETC.

(1)   A body corporate or an unincorporated body is a relevant person if—

(a) a compromise or arrangement between the body and its creditors (or a class of them) is in force, having been sanctioned in accordance with section 899 of the Companies Act 2006, or

(b) the body has been dissolved under section 1000, 1001 or 1003 of that Act, and the body has not been—

    (i) restored to the register by virtue of section 1025 of that Act, or

    (ii) ordered to be restored to the register by virtue of section 1031 of that Act.

(2) A body corporate or an unincorporated body is a relevant person if, in England and Wales or Scotland—

(a) a voluntary arrangement approved in accordance with Part 1 of the Insolvency Act 1986 is in force in respect of it,

(b) an administration order made under Part 2 of that Act is in force in respect of it,

(c) there is a person appointed in accordance with Part 3 of that Act who is acting as receiver or manager of the body's property (or there would be such a person so acting but for a temporary vacancy),

(d) the body is, or is being, wound up voluntarily in accordance with Chapter 2 of Part 4 of that Act,

(e) there is a person appointed under section 135 of that Act who is acting as provisional liquidator in respect of the body (or there would be such a person so acting but for a temporary vacancy), or

(f) the body is, or is being, wound up by the court following the making of a winding-up order under Chapter 6 of Part 4 of that Act or Part 5 of that Act.

(3) A body corporate or an unincorporated body is a relevant person if, in Scotland—

(a) an award of sequestration has been made under section 6 of the Bankruptcy (Scotland) Act 1985 in respect of the body's estate, and the body has not been discharged under that Act,

(b) the body has been dissolved and an award of sequestration has been made under that section in respect of its estate,

(c) a protected trust deed within the meaning of the Bankruptcy (Scotland) Act 1985 is in force in respect of the body's estate, or

(d) a composition approved in accordance with Schedule 4 to that Act is in force in respect of the body.

(4) A body corporate or an unincorporated body is a relevant person if, in Northern Ireland—

(a) a voluntary arrangement approved in accordance with Part 2 of the Insolvency (Northern Ireland) Order 1989 (S.I. 1989/2405 (N. I. 19)) is in force in respect of the body,

(b) an administration order made under Part 3 of that Order is in force in respect of the body,

(c) there is a person appointed in accordance with Part 4 of that Order who is acting as receiver or manager of the body's property (or there would be such a person so acting but for a temporary vacancy),

(d) the body is, or is being, wound up voluntarily in accordance with Chapter 2 of Part 5 of that Order,

(e) there is a person appointed under Article 115 of that Order who is acting as provisional liquidator in respect of the body (or there would be such a person so acting but for a temporary vacancy), or

(f) the body is, or is being, wound up by the court following the making of a winding-up order under Chapter 6 of Part 5 of that Order or Part 6 of that Order.

(5) A body within subsection (1)(a) is not a relevant person in relation to a liability that is transferred to another body by the order sanctioning the compromise or arrangement.

(6)   Where a body is a relevant person by virtue of subsection (1)(a), section 1 has effect to transfer rights only to a person on whom the compromise or arrangement is binding.

(7)   Where an award of sequestration made under section 6 of the Bankruptcy (Scotland) Act 1985 is recalled or reduced, any rights which were transferred under section 1 as a result of that award are re-transferred to and vest in the person who became a relevant person as a result of the award.

(8)   Where an order discharging a body from an award of sequestration made under section 6 of the Bankruptcy (Scotland) Act 1985 is recalled or reduced under paragraph 17 or 18 of Schedule 4 to that Act, the order is to be treated for the purposes of this section as never having been made.

(9)   In this section—
    (a) a reference to a person appointed in accordance with Part 3 of the Insolvency Act 1986 includes a reference to a person appointed under section 101 of the Law of Property Act 1925;
    (b) a reference to a receiver or manager of a body's property includes a reference to a receiver or manager of part only of the property and to a receiver only of the income arising from the property or from part of it;
    (c) for the purposes of subsection (3) "body corporate or unincorporated body" includes any entity, other than a trust, the estate of which may be sequestrated under section 6 of the Bankruptcy (Scotland) Act 1985;
    (d) a reference to a person appointed in accordance with Part 4 of the Insolvency (Northern Ireland) Order 1989 (S.I. 1989/2405 (N. I. 19)) includes a reference to a person appointed under section 19 of the Conveyancing Act 1881.

7 SCOTTISH TRUSTS

(1)   A trustee of a Scottish trust is, in respect of a liability of that trustee that falls to be met out of the trust estate, a relevant person if—
    (a) an award of sequestration has been made under section 6 of the Bankruptcy (Scotland) Act 1985 in respect of the trust estate, and the trust has not been discharged under that Act,
    (b) a protected trust deed within the meaning of that Act is in force in respect of the trust estate, or
    (c) a composition approved in accordance with Schedule 4 to that Act is in force in respect of the trust estate.

(2)   Where an award of sequestration made under section 6 of the Bankruptcy (Scotland) Act 1985 is recalled or reduced any rights which were transferred under section 1 as a result of that award are re-transferred to and vest in the person who became a relevant person as a result of the award.

(3)   Where an order discharging an individual, body or trust from an award of sequestration made under section 6 of the Bankruptcy (Scotland) Act 1985 is recalled or reduced under paragraph 17 or 18 of Schedule 4 to that Act, the order is to be treated for the purposes of this section as never having been made.

(4)   In this section "Scottish trust" means a trust the estate of which may be sequestrated under section 6 of the Bankruptcy (Scotland) Act 1985.

Transferred rights: supplemental

8 LIMIT ON RIGHTS TRANSFERRED

Where the liability of an insured to a third party is less than the liability of the insurer to the insured (ignoring the effect of section 1), no rights are transferred under that section in respect of the difference.

9 CONDITIONS AFFECTING TRANSFERRED RIGHTS—

(1) This section applies where transferred rights are subject to a condition (whether under the contract of insurance from which the transferred rights are derived or otherwise) that the insured has to fulfil.

(2) Anything done by the third party which, if done by the insured, would have amounted to or contributed to fulfilment of the condition is to be treated as if done by the insured.

(3) The transferred rights are not subject to a condition requiring the insured to provide information or assistance to the insurer if that condition cannot be fulfilled because the insured is—
(a) an individual who has died, or
(b) a body corporate that has been dissolved.

(4) A condition requiring the insured to provide information or assistance to the insurer does not include a condition requiring the insured to notify the insurer of the existence of a claim under the contract of insurance.

(5) The transferred rights are not subject to a condition requiring the prior discharge by the insured of the insured's liability to the third party.

(6) In the case of a contract of marine insurance, subsection (5) applies only to the extent that the liability of the insured is a liability in respect of death or personal injury.

(7) In this section—

- "contract of marine insurance" has the meaning given by section 1 of the Marine Insurance Act 1906;
- "dissolved" means dissolved under—
  (a) Chapter 9 of Part 4 of the Insolvency Act 1986,
  (b) section 1000, 1001 or 1003 of the Companies Act 2006, or
  (c) Chapter 9 of Part 5 of the Insolvency (Northern Ireland) Order 1989 (S.I. 1989/2405 (N. I. 19));
- "personal injury" includes any disease and any impairment of a person's physical or mental condition.

10 INSURER'S RIGHT OF SET OFF—

(1) This section applies if—
(a) rights of an insured under a contract of insurance have been transferred to a third party under section 1,
(b) the insured is under a liability to the insurer under the contract ("the insured's liability"), and
(c) if there had been no transfer, the insurer would have been entitled to set off the amount of the insured's liability against the amount of the insurer's own liability to the insured.

(2)   The insurer is entitled to set off the amount of the insured's liability against the amount of the insurer's own liability to the third party in relation to the transferred rights.

Provision of information etc.

11 INFORMATION AND DISCLOSURE FOR THIRD PARTIES

Schedule 1 (information and disclosure for third parties) has effect.

Enforcement of transferred rights

12 LIMITATION AND PRESCRIPTION

(1)   Subsection (2) applies where a person brings proceedings for a declaration under section 2(2)(a), or for a declarator under section 3(2)(a), and the proceedings are started or, in Scotland, commenced—
   (a) after the expiry of a period of limitation applicable to an action against the insured to enforce the insured's liability, or of a period of prescription applicable to that liability, but
   (b) while such an action is in progress.

(2)   The insurer may not rely on the expiry of that period as a defence unless the insured is able to rely on it in the action against the insured.

(3)   For the purposes of subsection (1), an action is to be treated as no longer in progress if it has been concluded by a judgment or decree, or by an award, even if there is an appeal or a right of appeal.

(4)   Where a person who has already established an insured's liability to that person brings proceedings under this Act against the insurer, nothing in this Act is to be read as meaning—
   (a) that, for the purposes of the law of limitation in England and Wales, that person's cause of action against the insurer arose otherwise than at the time when that person established the liability of the insured,
   (b) that, for the purposes of the law of prescription in Scotland, the obligation in respect of which the proceedings are brought became enforceable against the insurer otherwise than at that time, or
   (c) that, for the purposes of the law of limitation in Northern Ireland, that person's cause of action against the insurer arose otherwise than at the time when that person established the liability of the insured.

13 JURISDICTION WITHIN THE UNITED KINGDOM—

(1)   Where a person (P) domiciled in a part of the United Kingdom is entitled to bring proceedings under this Act against an insurer domiciled in another part, P may do so in the part where P is domiciled or in the part where the insurer is domiciled (whatever the contract of insurance may stipulate as to where proceedings are to be brought).

(2)   The following provisions of the Civil Jurisdiction and Judgments Act 1982 (relating to determination of domicile) apply for the purposes of subsection (1)—
   (a) section 41(2), (3), (5) and (6) (individuals);
   (b) section 42(1), (3), (4) and (8) (corporations and associations);
   (c) section 45(2) and (3) (trusts);
   (d) section 46(1), (3) and (7) (the Crown).

(3)   In Schedule 5 to that Act (proceedings excluded from general provisions as to allocation of jurisdiction within the United Kingdom) at the end add—

"Proceedings by third parties against insurers

11 Proceedings under the Third Parties (Rights against Insurers) Act 2010."

Enforcement of insured's liability

14 EFFECT OF TRANSFER ON INSURED'S LIABILITY

(1)   Where rights in respect of an insured's liability to a third party are transferred under section 1, the third party may enforce that liability against the insured only to the extent (if any) that it exceeds the amount recoverable from the insurer by virtue of the transfer.

(2)   Subsection (3) applies if a transfer of rights under section 1 occurs because the insured person is a relevant person by virtue of—
(a)   section 4(1)(a) or (e), (2)(b) or (3)(b) or (c),
(b)   section 6(1)(a), (2)(a), (3)(c) or (4)(a), or
(c)   section 7(1)(b).

(3)   If the liability is subject to the arrangement, trust deed or compromise by virtue of which the insured is a relevant person, the liability is to be treated as subject to that arrangement, trust deed or compromise only to the extent that the liability exceeds the amount recoverable from the insurer by virtue of the transfer.

(4)   (4) Subsection (5) applies if a transfer of rights under section 1 occurs in respect of a liability which, after the transfer, becomes one that is subject to a composition approved in accordance with Schedule 4 to the Bankruptcy (Scotland) Act 1985.

(5)   The liability is to be treated as subject to the composition only to the extent that the liability exceeds the amount recoverable from the insurer by virtue of the transfer.

(6)   (For the purposes of this section the amount recoverable from the insurer does not include any amount that the third party is unable to recover as a result of—
(a)   a shortage of assets on the insurer's part, in a case where the insurer is a relevant person, or
(b)   a limit set by the contract of insurance on the fund available to meet claims in respect of a particular description of liability of the insured.

(7)   (Where a third party is eligible to make a claim in respect of the insurer's liability under or by virtue of rules made under Part 15 of the Financial Services and Markets Act 2000 (the Financial Services Compensation Scheme)—
(a)   subsection (6)(a) applies only if the third party has made such a claim, and
(b)   the third party is to be treated as being able to recover from the insurer any amount paid to, or due to, the third party as a result of the claim.

Application of Act

15 REINSURANCE

This Act does not apply to a case where the liability referred to in section 1(1) is itself a liability incurred by an insurer under a contract of insurance.

16 VOLUNTARILY-INCURRED LIABILITIES

It is irrelevant for the purposes of section 1 whether or not the liability of the insured is or was incurred voluntarily.

17 AVOIDANCE

(1)   A contract of insurance to which this section applies is of no effect in so far as it purports, whether directly or indirectly, to avoid or terminate the contract or alter the rights of the parties under it in the event of the insured—

    (a)   becoming a relevant person, or

    (b)   dying insolvent (within the meaning given by section 5(2)).

(2)   A contract of insurance is one to which this section applies if the insured's rights under it are capable of being transferred under section 1.

18 CASES WITH A FOREIGN ELEMENT

Except as expressly provided, the application of this Act does not depend on whether there is a connection with a part of the United Kingdom; and in particular it does not depend on—

(a)   whether or not the liability (or the alleged liability) of the insured to the third party was incurred in, or under the law of, England and Wales, Scotland or Northern Ireland;

(b)   the place of residence or domicile of any of the parties;

(c)   whether or not the contract of insurance (or a part of it) is governed by the law of England and Wales, Scotland or Northern Ireland;

(d)   the place where sums due under the contract of insurance are payable.

Supplemental

19 POWER TO AMEND ACT

(1)   The Secretary of State may by order made by statutory instrument amend section 4, 5 or 6 so as to—

    (a)   substitute a reference to a provision of Northern Ireland legislation with a reference to a different provision of Northern Ireland legislation, or

    (b)   add a reference to a provision of a description within subsection (2).

(2)   A provision is within this subsection if—

    (a)   it is made by or under Northern Ireland legislation, and

    (b)   in the opinion of the Secretary of State, it corresponds with a provision under the law of England and Wales or the law of Scotland that is referred to in the section being amended.

(3)   An order under this section may include consequential, incidental, supplementary, transitional, transitory or saving provision.

(4)   An order under this section may not be made unless a draft of the statutory instrument containing the order has been laid before, and approved by a resolution of, each House of Parliament.

21 SHORT TITLE, COMMENCEMENT AND EXTENT

(1)   This Act may be cited as the Third Parties (Rights against Insurers) Act 2010.

(2)   This Act comes into force on such day as the Secretary of State may by order made by statutory instrument appoint.

(3)   This Act extends to England and Wales, Scotland and Northern Ireland, subject as follows.

(4)   Section 2 and paragraphs 3 and 4 of Schedule 1 do not extend to Scotland.

(5)   Section 3 extends to Scotland only.

(6)   Any amendment, repeal or revocation made by this Act has the same extent as the provision to which it relates.

Editor's Note: This Act has yet to be brought into force.

BRIBERY ACT 2010
(c.23)

General bribery offences

1 OFFENCES OF BRIBING ANOTHER PERSON

(1)   A person ("P") is guilty of an offence if either of the following cases applies.

(2)   Case 1 is where—
       (a) P offers, promises or gives a financial or other advantage to another person, and
       (b) P intends the advantage—
            (i)   to induce a person to perform improperly a relevant function or activity, or
            (ii) to reward a person for the improper performance of such a function or activity.

(3)   Case 2 is where—
       (a) P offers, promises or gives a financial or other advantage to another person, and
       (b) P knows or believes that the acceptance of the advantage would itself constitute the improper performance of a relevant function or activity.

(4)   In case 1 it does not matter whether the person to whom the advantage is offered, promised or given is the same person as the person who is to perform, or has performed, the function or activity concerned.

(5)   In cases 1 and 2 it does not matter whether the advantage is offered, promised or given by P directly or through a third party.

2 OFFENCES RELATING TO BEING BRIBED

(1)   A person ("R") is guilty of an offence if any of the following cases applies.

(2)   Case 3 is where R requests, agrees to receive or accepts a financial or other advantage intending that, in consequence, a relevant function or activity should be performed improperly (whether by R or another person).

(3)   Case 4 is where—
       (a) R requests, agrees to receive or accepts a financial or other advantage, and
       (b) the request, agreement or acceptance itself constitutes the improper performance by R of a relevant function or activity.

(4)   Case 5 is where R requests, agrees to receive or accepts a financial or other advantage as a reward for the improper performance (whether by R or another person) of a relevant function or activity.

(5)   Case 6 is where, in anticipation of or in consequence of R requesting, agreeing to receive or accepting a financial or other advantage, a relevant function or activity is performed improperly—
(a) by R, or
(b) by another person at R's request or with R's assent or acquiescence.

(6)   In cases 3 to 6 it does not matter—
(a) whether R requests, agrees to receive or accepts (or is to request, agree to receive or accept) the advantage directly or through a third party,
(b) whether the advantage is (or is to be) for the benefit of R or another person.

(7)   In cases 4 to 6 it does not matter whether R knows or believes that the performance of the function or activity is improper.

(8)   In case 6, where a person other than R is performing the function or activity, it also does not matter whether that person knows or believes that the performance of the function or activity is improper.

3 FUNCTION OR ACTIVITY TO WHICH BRIBE RELATES

(1)   For the purposes of this Act a function or activity is a relevant function or activity if—
(a) it falls within subsection (2), and
(b) meets one or more of conditions A to C.

(2)   The following functions and activities fall within this subsection—
(a) any function of a public nature,
(b) any activity connected with a business,
(c) any activity performed in the course of a person's employment,
(d) any activity performed by or on behalf of a body of persons (whether corporate or unincorporate).

(3)   Condition A is that a person performing the function or activity is expected to perform it in good faith.

(4)   Condition B is that a person performing the function or activity is expected to perform it impartially.

(5)   Condition C is that a person performing the function or activity is in a position of trust by virtue of performing it.

(6)   A function or activity is a relevant function or activity even if it—
(a) has no connection with the United Kingdom, and
(b) is performed in a country or territory outside the United Kingdom.

(7)   In this section "business" includes trade or profession.

4 IMPROPER PERFORMANCE TO WHICH BRIBE RELATES

(1)   For the purposes of this Act a relevant function or activity—
(a) is performed improperly if it is performed in breach of a relevant expectation, and
(b) is to be treated as being performed improperly if there is a failure to perform the function or activity and that failure is itself a breach of a relevant expectation.

(2)   In subsection (1) "relevant expectation"—
(a) in relation to a function or activity which meets condition A or B, means the expectation mentioned in the condition concerned, and

(b) in relation to a function or activity which meets condition C, means any expectation as to the manner in which, or the reasons for which, the function or activity will be performed that arises from the position of trust mentioned in that condition.

(3) Anything that a person does (or omits to do) arising from or in connection with that person's past performance of a relevant function or activity is to be treated for the purposes of this Act as being done (or omitted) by that person in the performance of that function or activity.

5 EXPECTATION TEST

(1) For the purposes of sections 3 and 4, the test of what is expected is a test of what a reasonable person in the United Kingdom would expect in relation to the performance of the type of function or activity concerned.

(2) In deciding what such a person would expect in relation to the performance of a function or activity where the performance is not subject to the law of any part of the United Kingdom, any local custom or practice is to be disregarded unless it is permitted or required by the written law applicable to the country or territory concerned.

(3) In subsection (2) "written law" means law contained in—
(a) any written constitution, or provision made by or under legislation, applicable to the country or territory concerned, or
(b) any judicial decision which is so applicable and is evidenced in published written sources.

. . .

Failure of commercial organisations to prevent bribery

7 FAILURE OF COMMERCIAL ORGANISATIONS TO PREVENT BRIBERY

(1) A relevant commercial organisation ("C") is guilty of an offence under this section if a person ("A") associated with C bribes another person intending—
(a) to obtain or retain business for C, or
(b) to obtain or retain an advantage in the conduct of business for C.

(2) But it is a defence for C to prove that C had in place adequate procedures designed to prevent persons associated with C from undertaking such conduct.

(3) For the purposes of this section, A bribes another person if, and only if, A—
(a) is, or would be, guilty of an offence under section 1 or 6 (whether or not A has been prosecuted for such an offence), or
(b) would be guilty of such an offence if section 12(2)(c) and (4) were omitted.

(4) See section 8 for the meaning of a person associated with C and see section 9 for a duty on the Secretary of State to publish guidance.

(5) In this section—

"partnership" means—
(a) a partnership within the Partnership Act 1890, or
(b) a limited partnership registered under the Limited Partnerships Act 1907,
or a firm or entity of a similar character formed under the law of a country or territory outside the United Kingdom,

"relevant commercial organisation" means—

(a) a body which is incorporated under the law of any part of the United Kingdom and which carries on a business (whether there or elsewhere),

(b) any other body corporate (wherever incorporated) which carries on a business, or part of a business, in any part of the United Kingdom,

(c) a partnership which is formed under the law of any part of the United Kingdom and which carries on a business (whether there or elsewhere), or

(d) any other partnership (wherever formed) which carries on a business, or part of a business, in any part of the United Kingdom,

and, for the purposes of this section, a trade or profession is a business.

8 MEANING OF ASSOCIATED PERSON

(1) For the purposes of section 7, a person ("A") is associated with C if (disregarding any bribe under consideration) A is a person who performs services for or on behalf of C.

(2) The capacity in which A performs services for or on behalf of C does not matter.

(3) Accordingly A may (for example) be C's employee, agent or subsidiary.

(4) Whether or not A is a person who performs services for or on behalf of C is to be determined by reference to all the relevant circumstances and not merely by reference to the nature of the relationship between A and C.

(5) But if A is an employee of C, it is to be presumed unless the contrary is shown that A is a person who performs services for or on behalf of C.

. . .

11 PENALTIES

(1) An individual guilty of an offence under section 1, 2 or 6 is liable—
(a) on summary conviction, to imprisonment for a term not exceeding 12 months, or to a fine not exceeding the statutory maximum, or to both,
(b) on conviction on indictment, to imprisonment for a term not exceeding 10 years, or to a fine, or to both.

(2) Any other person guilty of an offence under section 1, 2 or 6 is liable—
(a) on summary conviction, to a fine not exceeding the statutory maximum,
(b) on conviction on indictment, to a fine.

(3) A person guilty of an offence under section 7 is liable on conviction on indictment to a fine.

(4) The reference in subsection (1)(a) to 12 months is to be read—
(a) in its application to England and Wales in relation to an offence committed before the commencement of section 154(1) of the Criminal Justice Act 2003, and
(b) in its application to Northern Ireland,
as a reference to 6 months.

. . .

13 DEFENCE FOR CERTAIN BRIBERY OFFENCES ETC.

(1) It is a defence for a person charged with a relevant bribery offence to prove that the person's conduct was necessary for—
(a) the proper exercise of any function of an intelligence service, or

(b) the proper exercise of any function of the armed forces when engaged on active service.

. . .

Supplementary and final provisions

. . .

18 EXTENT

(1) Subject as follows, this Act extends to England and Wales, Scotland and Northern Ireland.

. . .

19 COMMENCEMENT AND TRANSITIONAL PROVISION ETC.

(1) Subject to subsection (2), this Act comes into force on such day as the Secretary of State may by order made by statutory instrument appoint.

. . .

DAMAGES (SCOTLAND) ACT 2011
Asp 7

1 DAMAGES TO INJURED PERSON WHOSE EXPECTATION OF LIFE IS DIMINISHED

(1) This section applies to an action for damages in respect of personal injuries suffered by a pursuer whose date of death is expected to be earlier than had the injuries not been suffered.

(2) In assessing the amount of damages by way of solatium the court is, if the pursuer—
  (a) was at any time,
  (b) is, or
  (c) is likely to become,
  aware of the reduced expectation of life, to have regard to the extent to which the pursuer, in consequence of that awareness, has suffered or is likely to suffer.

(3) Subject to subsection (2), no damages by way of solatium are recoverable by the pursuer in respect of loss of expectation of life.

(4) In making an award of damages by way of solatium, the court is not required to ascribe specifically any part of the award to loss of expectation of life.

(5) In assessing the amount of any patrimonial loss in respect of the period after the date of decree the court is to assume that the pursuer will live until the date when death would have been expected had the injuries not been suffered (the "notional date of death").

(6) Such part of that amount as is attributable to the period between the expected date of death and the notional date of death (the "lost period") is to be assessed as follows—
  (a) the court is to estimate what (if anything) the pursuer would have earned during the lost period through the pursuer's own labour or own gainful activity had the injuries not been suffered,

(b) the court may, if it thinks fit, add to the amount so estimated (whether or not that amount is nil) an amount equivalent to all or part of what it estimates the pursuer would have received by way of relevant benefits during the lost period had the injuries not been suffered, and

(c) the court is then to deduct, from the total amount obtained by virtue of paragraphs (a) and (b), 25% of that amount (to represent what would have been the pursuer's living expenses during the lost period had the injuries not been suffered).

(7) But, if satisfied that it is necessary to do so for the purpose of avoiding a manifestly and materially unfair result, the court may apply a different percentage to that specified in subsection (6)(c).

(8) In paragraph (b) of subsection (6), "relevant benefits" means benefits in money or money's worth other than benefits—
   (a) derived from the pursuer's own estate, or
   (b) consisting of such earnings as are mentioned in paragraph (a) of that subsection.

2 TRANSMISSION OF DECEASED'S RIGHTS TO EXECUTOR

(1) There are transmissible to a deceased person's executor ("E") the like rights to damages, including a right to damages for non-patrimonial loss, in respect of injuries suffered by the deceased ("A") and vested in A immediately before A's death, being—
   (a) personal injuries, or
   (b) injuries which, though not personal injuries, are—
      (i) injuries to name or reputation, or
      (ii) injuries resulting from harassment actionable under section 8 or 8A of the Protection from Harassment Act 1997 (c.40).

(2) The "like rights" mentioned in subsection (1) do not include any right to damages by way of compensation for patrimonial loss attributable to any period after the date of death; and in determining the amount of damages for non-patrimonial loss payable to E by virtue of this section, the only period to which the court is to have regard is that ending immediately before A's death.

(3) In so far as a right to damages vested in A comprises a right to damages for non-patrimonial loss in respect of such injuries as are mentioned in sub-paragraph (i) of subsection (1)(b), that right is transmissible to E only if an action to enforce the right is brought by A and is not concluded before A's death.

(4) For the purposes of subsection (3) an action is not to be taken to be concluded—
   (a) while an appeal is competent, or
   (b) before any appeal taken is disposed of.

3 APPLICATION OF SECTIONS 4 TO 6

Sections 4 to 6 apply where a person ("A") dies in consequence of suffering personal injuries as the result of the act or omission of another person ("B") and the act or omission—

(a) gives rise to liability to pay damages to A (or to A's executor), or

(b) would have given rise to such liability but for A's death.

4 SUMS OF DAMAGES PAYABLE TO RELATIVES

(1) B is liable under this subsection to pay—
   (a) to any relative of A who is a member of A's immediate family, such sums of damages as are mentioned in paragraphs (a) and (b) of subsection (3),

(b) to any other relative of A, such sum of damages as is mentioned in paragraph (a) of that subsection.

(2) But, except as provided for in section 5, no such liability arises if the liability to pay damages to A (or to A's executor) in respect of the act or omission—
   (a) is excluded or discharged, whether by antecedent agreement or otherwise, by A before A's death, or
   (b) is excluded by virtue of an enactment.

(3) The sums of damages are—
   (a) such sum as will compensate for any loss of support which as a result of the act or omission is sustained, or is likely to be sustained, by the relative after the date of A's death together with any reasonable expenses incurred by the relative in connection with A's funeral, and
   (b) such sum, if any, as the court thinks just by way of compensation for all or any of the following—
      (i)   distress and anxiety endured by the relative in contemplation of the suffering of A before A's death,
      (ii) grief and sorrow of the relative caused by A's death,
      (iii) the loss of such non-patrimonial benefit as the relative might have been expected to derive from A's society and guidance if A had not died.

(4) The court, in making an award under paragraph (b) of subsection (3) is not required to ascribe any part of the award specifically to any of the sub-paragraphs of that paragraph.

(5) For the purpose of subsection (1)(a)—
   (a) a relative of A is a member of A's immediate family if the relative falls within any of paragraphs (a) to (d) of the definition of "relative" in section 14(1),
   (b) paragraphs (a)(i) and (b) of section 14(2) are to be disregarded.

5 DISCHARGE OF LIABILITY TO PAY DAMAGES: EXCEPTION FOR MESOTHELIOMA

(1) This section applies where—
   (a) the liability to pay damages to A (or to A's executor) is discharged, whether by antecedent agreement or otherwise, by A before A's death,
   (b) the personal injury in consequence of which A died is mesothelioma, and
   (c) the discharge and the death each occurred on or after 20th December 2006.

(2) Liability arises under section 4(1) but is limited to the payment of such sum of damages as is mentioned in paragraph (b) of section 4(3).

6 RELATIVE'S LOSS OF PERSONAL SERVICES

(1) A relative entitled to damages under paragraph (a) of section 4(3) is entitled to include, as a head of damages under that paragraph, a reasonable sum in respect of the loss to the relative of A's personal services as a result of the act or omission.

(2) In subsection (1), "personal services" has the same meaning as in section 9(1) of the Administration of Justice Act 1982 (c.53) (damages in respect of inability of injured person to render such services).

7 ASSESSMENT OF COMPENSATION FOR LOSS OF SUPPORT

(1)   Such part of an award under paragraph (a) of section 4(3) as consists of a sum in compensation for loss of support is to be assessed applying the following paragraphs—

(a) the total amount to be available to support A's relatives is an amount equivalent to 75% of A's net income,

(b) in the case of any other relative than—

(i) a person described in paragraph (a) of the definition of "relative" in section 14(1), or

(ii) a dependent child,

the relative is not to be awarded more in compensation for loss of support than the actual amount of that loss,

(c) if—

(i) no such other relative is awarded a sum in compensation for loss of support, the total amount mentioned in paragraph (a) is to be taken to be spent by A in supporting such of A's relatives as are mentioned in sub-paragraphs (i) and (ii) of paragraph (b),

(ii) any such other relative is awarded a sum in compensation for loss of support, the total amount mentioned in paragraph (a) is, after deduction of the amount of the sum so awarded, to be taken to be spent by A in supporting such of A's relatives as are mentioned in those subparagraphs, and

(d) any multiplier applied by the court—

(i) is to run from the date of the interlocutor awarding damages, and

(ii) is to apply only in respect of future loss of support.

(2)   But, if satisfied that it is necessary to do so for the purpose of avoiding a manifestly and materially unfair result, the court may apply a different percentage to that specified in subsection (1)(a).

(3)   In subsection (1)(b)(ii), "dependent child" means a child who as at the date of A's death—

(a) has not attained the age of 18 years, and

(b) is owed an obligation of aliment by A.

8 FURTHER PROVISION AS REGARDS RELATIVE'S ENTITLEMENT TO DAMAGES

(1)   Subject to subsection (3), in assessing for the purposes of section 4 or 6 the amount of any loss of support sustained by a relative of A no account is to be taken of—

(a) any patrimonial gain or advantage which has accrued or will or may accrue to the relative, by way of succession or settlement, from A or from any other person, or

(b) any insurance money, benefit, pension or gratuity which has been, or will or may be, paid as a result of A's death.

(2)   In subsection (1)—

"benefit" means benefit under the Social Security Contributions and Benefits Act 1992 (c.4) or the Social Security Contributions and Benefits (Northern Ireland) Act 1992 (c.7) and any payment by a friendly society or trade union for the relief or maintenance of a member's dependants,

"insurance money" includes a return of premiums, and

"pension" includes a return of contributions and any payment of a lump sum in respect of a person's employment.

(3)   Where A has been awarded a provisional award of damages under section 12(2) of the Administration of Justice Act 1982 (c.53), the making of that award does not prevent liability from arising under section 4(1); but in assessing for the purposes of section 4 or 6 the amount of any loss of support sustained by a relative the court is to take into account such part of the provisional award relating to future patrimonial loss as was intended to compensate A for a period beyond the date on which A died.

(4)   In order to establish loss of support for the purposes of section 4 or 6, it is not essential for a relative to show that A was, or might have become, subject to a duty in law to provide support for, or contribute to the support of, the relative; but if any such fact is established it may be taken into account in determining whether, and if so to what extent, A would (had A not died) have been likely to provide, or contribute to, such support.

(5)   Except as provided for in this Act or in any other enactment, no person is entitled by reason of relationship to damages in respect of the death of another person.

(6)   In subsection (5), "damages" includes damages by way of solatium.

9 TRANSMISSION OF RELATIVE'S RIGHTS TO EXECUTOR

(1)   This section applies where liability to pay damages to a relative ("R") has arisen under section 4 or 6 but R dies.

(2)   If the right to damages is vested in R immediately before R's death that right is transmissible to R's executor ("E"); but in determining the amount of damages payable to E by virtue of this section, the only period to which the court is to have regard is the period ending immediately before R's death.

(3)   In a case where—
   (a) section 5 applies, and
   (b) R died before 27th April 2007,
        any right of R to damages under that section is to be taken, for the purposes of subsection (2), to have vested in R on A's death.

10 ENFORCEMENT BY EXECUTOR OF RIGHTS TRANSMITTED UNDER SECTION 2 OR 9

(1)   Where a right is transmitted by virtue of section 2 or 9, the executor in question is entitled—
   (a) to bring an action to enforce it, or
   (b) if an action to enforce it was brought by the deceased but not concluded before the date of death, to be sisted as pursuer in that action.

(2)   For the purposes of subsection (1)(b) an action is not to be taken to be concluded—
   (a) while an appeal is competent, or
   (b) before any appeal taken is disposed of.

11 EXECUTOR'S CLAIM NOT EXCLUDED BY RELATIVE'S CLAIM ETC.

(1)   A claim made by virtue of this Act by a deceased's executor is not excluded by a claim so made by a relative of the deceased (or by such a relative's executor).

(2)   Nor is a claim so made by a such a relative (or by such a relative's executor) excluded by a claim so made by the deceased's executor.

12 LIMITATION OF TOTAL AMOUNT OF LIABILITY

(1)   This section applies to an action directed against a defender ("B") in which, following the death of a person ("A") from personal injuries, damages are claimed—
(a)   in respect of those injuries, by A's executor, or
(b)   in respect of A's death, by any relative of A or by the executor of any relative of A.

(2)   If it is shown that the liability arising in relation to B from the personal injuries in question—
(a)   had before A's death, by antecedent agreement or otherwise, been limited to damages of a specified or ascertainable amount, or
(b)   is so limited by virtue of an enactment,
nothing in this Act makes B liable to pay damages exceeding that amount.

(3)   Accordingly, where there are two or more pursuers, any damages to which they would (but for this section) respectively be entitled under this Act are, if necessary, to be reduced pro rata.

(4)   And where two or more actions are conjoined the conjoined actions are to be treated, for the purposes of this section, as if they were a single action.

13 AMENDMENT OF SECTION 9 OF ADMINISTRATION OF JUSTICE ACT 1982

In section 9 of the Administration of Justice Act 1982 (c.53) (services to injured person's relative)—
(a)   after subsection (1) there is inserted—

"(1A) In assessing the amount of damages payable by virtue of subsection (1) above to an injured person whose date of death is expected to be earlier than had the injuries not been sustained, the court is to assume that the person will live until the date when death would have been expected had the injuries not been sustained.",

(b)   subsection (2) is repealed,

(c)   in subsection (3), for the words "subsections (1) and (2)" there is substituted "subsection (1)", and

(d)   in subsection (4), for the words "subsection (2) above" there is substituted "section 6(1) of the Damages (Scotland) Act 2011 (asp 7) (relative's loss of personal services)".

14 INTERPRETATION

(1)   In this Act, unless the context otherwise requires—

"personal injuries" means—

(a)   any disease, and
(b)   any impairment of a person's physical or mental condition, and

"relative", in relation to a person who has died, means a person who—

(a)   immediately before the death is the deceased's spouse or civil partner or is living with the deceased as if married to, or in civil partnership with, the deceased,
(b)   is a parent or child of the deceased, accepted the deceased as a child of the person's family or was accepted by the deceased as a child of the deceased's family,
(c)   is the brother or sister of the deceased or was brought up in the same household as the deceased and accepted as a child of the family in which the deceased was a child,

(d) is a grandparent or grandchild of the deceased, accepted the deceased as a grandchild of the person or was accepted by the deceased as a grandchild of the deceased,

(e) is an ascendant or descendant of the deceased (other than a parent or grandparent or a child or grandchild of the deceased),

(f) is an uncle or aunt of the deceased,

(g) is a child or other issue of—
   (i) a brother or sister of the deceased, or
   (ii) an uncle or aunt of the deceased, or

(h) is a former spouse or civil partner of the deceased having become so by virtue of divorce or (as the case may be) dissolution of the partnership.

(2) In deducing a relationship for the purposes of the definition of "relative" in subsection (1)—
   (a) any relationship—
      (i) by affinity is to be treated as a relationship by consanguinity,
      (ii) of the half blood is to be treated as a relationship of the whole blood,
   (b) a stepchild of a person is to be treated as the person's child.

(3) In any enactment passed or made before this Act, unless the context otherwise requires, any reference to—
   (a) solatium in respect of the death of any person (however expressed), or
   (b) a loss of society award,
   is to be construed as a reference to an award under paragraph (b) of section 4(3)?. . .

17 SAVING

Nothing in this Act affects proceedings commenced before section 16 comes into force.
. . .

19 SHORT TITLE, CROWN APPLICATION AND COMMENCEMENT

(1) This Act may be cited as the Damages (Scotland) Act 2011.

(2) This Act binds the Crown.

(3) The provisions of this Act, except section 18 and this section, come into force on such day as the Scottish Ministers may by order made by statutory instrument appoint.

(4) An order under subsection (3) may include such transitional, transitory or saving provision as the Scottish Ministers consider necessary or expedient in connection with the commencement of this Act.

Statutory Instruments

PACKAGE TRAVEL, PACKAGE HOLIDAYS AND PACKAGE TOURS REGULATIONS 1992
(1992/3288)

Citation and commencement

1.　These Regulations may be cited as the Package Travel, Package Holidays and Package Tours Regulations 1992 and shall come into force on the day after the day on which they are made.

Interpretation

2.—(1)　In these Regulations—

"brochure" means any brochure in which packages are offered for sale;

"contract" means the agreement linking the consumer to the organiser or to the retailer, or to both, as the case may be;

"the Directive" means Council Directive 90/314/EEC on package travel, package holidays and package tours;

"member State" means a member State of the European Community or another State in the European Economic Area;

"offer" includes an invitation to treat whether by means of advertising or otherwise, and cognate expressions shall be construed accordingly;

"organiser" means the person who, otherwise than occasionally, organises packages and sells or offers them for sale, whether directly or through a retailer;

"the other party to the contract" means the party, other than the consumer, to the contract, that is, the organiser or the retailer, or both, as the case may be;

"package" means the pre-arranged combination of at least two of the following components when sold or offered for sale at an inclusive price and when the service covers a period of more than twenty-four hours or includes overnight accommodation—

(a)　transport;

(b)　accommodation;

(c)　other tourist services not ancillary to transport or accommodation and accounting for a significant proportion of the package, and

     (i)   the submission of separate accounts for different components shall not cause the arrangements to be other than a package;

    (ii)   the fact that a combination is arranged at the request of the consumer and in accordance with his specific instructions (whether modified or not) shall not of itself cause it to be treated as other than pre-arranged; and

"retailer" means the person who sells or offers for sale the package put together by the organiser.

(2) In the definition of "contract" in paragraph (1) above, "consumer" means the person who takes or agrees to take the package ("the principal contractor") and elsewhere in these Regulations "consumer" means, as the context requires, the principal contractor, any person on whose behalf the principal contractor agrees to purchase the package ("the other beneficiaries") or any person to whom the principal contractor or any of the other beneficiaries transfers the package ("the transferee").

Application of Regulations

3.—(1) These Regulations apply to packages sold or offered for sale in the territory of the United Kingdom.

(2) Regulations 4 to 15 apply to packages so sold or offered for sale on or after 31st December 1992.

(3) Regulations 16 to 22 apply to contracts which, in whole or part, remain to be performed on 31st December 1992.

Descriptive matter relating to packages must not be misleading

4.—(1) No organiser or retailer shall supply to a consumer any descriptive matter concerning a package, the price of a package or any other conditions applying to the contract which contains any misleading information.

(2) If an organiser or retailer is in breach of paragraph (1) he shall be liable to compensate the consumer for any loss which the consumer suffers in consequence.

Requirements as to brochures

5.—(1) Subject to paragraph (4) below, no organiser shall make available a brochure to a possible consumer unless it indicates in a legible, comprehensible and accurate manner the price and adequate information about the matters specified in Schedule 1 to these Regulations in respect of the packages offered for sale in the brochure to the extent that those matters are relevant to the packages so offered.

(2) Subject to paragraph (4) below, no retailer shall make available to a possible consumer a brochure which he knows or has reasonable cause to believe does not comply with the requirements of paragraph (1).

(3) An organiser who contravenes paragraph (1) of this regulation and a retailer who contravenes paragraph (2) thereof shall be guilty of an offence and liable—
(a) on summary conviction, to a fine not exceeding level 5 on the standard scale; and
(b) on conviction on indictment, to a fine.

(4) Where a brochure was first made available to consumers generally before 31st December 1992 no liability shall arise under this regulation in respect of an identical brochure being made available to a consumer at any time.

Circumstances in which particulars in brochure are to be binding

6.—(1) Subject to paragraphs (2) and (3) of this regulation, the particulars in the brochure (whether or not they are required by regulation 5(1) above to be included in the brochure) shall constitute implied warranties (or, as regards Scotland, implied terms) for the purposes of any contract to which the particulars relate.

(2) Paragraph (1) of this regulation does not apply—
   (a) in relation to information required to be included by virtue of paragraph 9 of Schedule 1 to these Regulations; or
   (b) where the brochure contains an express statement that changes may be made in the particulars contained in it before a contract is concluded and changes in the particulars so contained are clearly communicated to the consumer before a contract is concluded.

(3) Paragraph (1) of this regulation does not apply when the consumer and the other party to the contract agree after the contract has been made that the particulars in the brochure, or some of those particulars, should not form part of the contract.

Information to be provided before contract is concluded

7.—(1) Before a contract is concluded, the other party to the contract shall provide the intending consumer with the information specified in paragraph (2) below in writing or in some other appropriate form.

(2) The information referred to in paragraph (1) is—
   (a) general information about passport and visa requirements which apply to nationals of the member State or States concerned who purchase the package in question, including information about the length of time it is likely to take to obtain the appropriate passports and visas;
   (b) information about health formalities required for the journey and the stay; and
   (c) the arrangements for security for the money paid over and (where applicable) for the repatriation of the consumer in the event of insolvency.

(3) If the intending consumer is not provided with the information required by paragraph (1) in accordance with that paragraph the other party to the contract shall be guilty of an offence and liable—
   (a) on summary conviction, to a fine not exceeding level 5 on the standard scale; and
   (b) on conviction on indictment, to a fine.

Information to be provided in good time

8.—(1) The other party to the contract shall in good time before the start of the journey provide the consumer with the information specified in paragraph (2) below in writing or in some other appropriate form.

(2) The information referred to in paragraph (1) is the following—
   (a) the times and places of intermediate stops and transport connections and particulars of the place to be occupied by the traveller (for example, cabin or berth on ship, sleeper compartment on train);
   (b) the name, address and telephone number—
      (i) of the representative of the other party to the contract in the locality where the consumer is to stay,
      or, if there is no such representative,
      (ii) of an agency in that locality on whose assistance a consumer in difficulty would be able to call, or, if there is no such representative or agency, a telephone number or other information which will enable the consumer to contact the other party to the contract during the stay; and
   (c) in the case of a journey or stay abroad by a child under the age of 16 on the day when the journey or stay is due to start, information enabling direct contact to be made with the child or the person responsible at the place where he is to stay; and

(d) except where the consumer is required as a term of the contract to take out an insurance policy in order to cover the cost of cancellation by the consumer or the cost of assistance, including repatriation, in the event of accident or illness, information about an insurance policy which the consumer may, if he wishes, take out in respect of the risk of those costs being incurred.

(3) If the consumer is not provided with the information required by paragraph (1) in accordance with that paragraph the other party to the contract shall be guilty of an offence and liable—
(a) on summary conviction, to a fine not exceeding level 5 on the standard scale; and
(b) on conviction on indictment, to a fine.

Contents and form of contract

9.—(1) The other party to the contract shall ensure that—
(a) depending on the nature of the package being purchased, the contract contains at least the elements specified in Schedule 2 to these Regulations;
(b) subject to paragraph (2) below, all the terms of the contract are set out in writing or such other form as is comprehensible and accessible to the consumer and are communicated to the consumer before the contract is made; and
(c) a written copy of these terms is supplied to the consumer.

(2) Paragraph (1)(b) above does not apply when the interval between the time when the consumer approaches the other party to the contract with a view to entering into a contract and the time of departure under the proposed contract is so short that it is impracticable to comply with the sub-paragraph.

(3) It is an implied condition (or, as regards Scotland, an implied term) of the contract that the other party to the contract complies with the provisions of paragraph (1).

(4) In Scotland, any breach of the condition implied by paragraph (3) above shall be deemed to be a material breach justifying rescission of the contract.

Transfer of bookings

10.—(1) In every contract there is an implied term that where the consumer is prevented from proceeding with the package the consumer may transfer his booking to a person who satisfies all the conditions applicable to the package, provided that the consumer gives reasonable notice to the other party to the contract of his intention to transfer before the date when departure is due to take place.

(2) Where a transfer is made in accordance with the implied term set out in paragraph (1) above, the transferor and the transferee shall be jointly and severally liable to the other party to the contract for payment of the price of the package (or, if part of the price has been paid, for payment of the balance) and for any additional costs arising from such transfer.

Price revision

11.—(1) Any term in a contract to the effect that the prices laid down in the contract may be revised shall be void and of no effect unless the contract provides for the possibility of upward or downward revision and satisfies the conditions laid down in paragraph (2) below.

(2) The conditions mentioned in paragraph (1) are that—
(a) the contract states precisely how the revised price is to be calculated;
(b) the contract provides that price revisions are to be made solely to allow for variations in:—
(i) transportation costs, including the cost of fuel,

       (ii) dues, taxes or fees chargeable for services such as landing taxes or embarkation or disembarkation fees at ports and airports, or

      (iii) the exchange rates applied to the particular package; and

  (3) Notwithstanding any terms of a contract,

      (i) no price increase may be made in a specified period which may not be less than 30 days before the departure date stipulated; and

      (ii) as against an individual consumer liable under the contract, no price increase may be made in respect of variations which would produce an increase of less than 2%, or such greater percentage as the contract may specify, ("non-eligible variations") and that the non-eligible variations shall be left out of account in the calculation.

Significant alterations to essential terms

12.—In every contract there are implied terms to the effect that—

  (a) where the organiser is constrained before the departure to alter significantly an essential term of the contract, such as the price (so far as regulation 11 permits him to do so), he will notify the consumer as quickly as possible in order to enable him to take appropriate decisions and in particular to withdraw from the contract without penalty or to accept a rider to the contract specifying the alterations made and their impact on the price; and

  (b) the consumer will inform the organiser or the retailer of his decision as soon as possible.

Withdrawal by consumer pursuant to regulation 12 and cancellation by organiser

13.—(1) The terms set out in paragraphs (2) and (3) below are implied in every contract and apply where the consumer withdraws from the contract pursuant to the term in it implied by virtue of regulation 12(a), or where the organiser, for any reason other than the fault of the consumer, cancels the package before the agreed date of departure.

  (2) The consumer is entitled—

      (a) to take a substitute package of equivalent or superior quality if the other party to the contract is able to offer him such a substitute; or

      (b) to take a substitute package of lower quality if the other party to the contract is able to offer him one and to recover from the organiser the difference in price between the price of the package purchased and that of the substitute package; or

      (c) to have repaid to him as soon as possible all the monies paid by him under the contract.

  (3) The consumer is entitled, if appropriate, to be compensated by the organiser for non-performance of the contract except where—

      (a) the package is cancelled because the number of persons who agree to take it is less than the minimum number required and the consumer is informed of the cancellation, in writing, within the period indicated in the description of the package; or

      (b) the package is cancelled by reason of unusual and unforeseeable circumstances beyond the control of the party by whom this exception is pleaded, the consequences of which could not have been avoided even if all due care had been exercised.

  (4) Overbooking shall not be regarded as a circumstance falling within the provisions of sub-paragraph (b) of paragraph (3) above.

Significant proportion of services not provided

14.—(1) The terms set out in paragraphs (2) and (3) below are implied in every contract and apply where, after departure, a significant proportion of the services contracted for is not provided or the organiser becomes aware that he will be unable to procure a significant proportion of the services to be provided.

(2) The organiser will make suitable alternative arrangements, at no extra cost to the consumer, for the continuation of the package and will, where appropriate, compensate the consumer for the difference between the services to be supplied under the contract and those supplied.

(3) If it is impossible to make arrangements as described in paragraph (2), or these are not accepted by the consumer for good reasons, the organiser will, where appropriate, provide the consumer with equivalent transport back to the place of departure or to another place to which the consumer has agreed and will, where appropriate, compensate the consumer.

Liability of other party to the contract for proper performance of obligations under contract

15.—(1) The other party to the contract is liable to the consumer for the proper performance of the obligations under the contract, irrespective of whether such obligations are to be performed by that other party or by other suppliers of services but this shall not affect any remedy or right of action which that other party may have against those other suppliers of services.

(2) The other party to the contract is liable to the consumer for any damage caused to him by the failure to perform the contract or the improper performance of the contract unless the failure or the improper performance is due neither to any fault of that other party nor to that of another supplier of services, because—
   (a) the failures which occur in the performance of the contract are attributable to the consumer;
   (b) such failures are attributable to a third party unconnected with the provision of the services contracted for, and are unforeseeable or unavoidable; or
   (c) such failures are due to—
      (i) unusual and unforeseeable circumstances beyond the control of the party by whom this exception is pleaded, the consequences of which could not have been avoided even if all due care had been exercised; or
      (ii) an event which the other party to the contract or the supplier of services, even with all due care, could not foresee or forestall.

(3) In the case of damage arising from the non-performance or improper performance of the services involved in the package, the contract may provide for compensation to be limited in accordance with the international conventions which govern such services.

(4) In the case of damage other than personal injury resulting from the non-performance or improper performance of the services involved in the package, the contract may include a term limiting the amount of compensation which will be paid to the consumer, provided that the limitation is not unreasonable.

(5) Without prejudice to paragraph (3) and paragraph (4) above, liability under paragraphs (1) and (2) above cannot be excluded by any contractual term.

(6) The terms set out in paragraphs (7) and (8) below are implied in every contract.

(7) In the circumstances described in paragraph (2)(b) and (c) of this regulation, the other party to the contract will give prompt assistance to a consumer in difficulty.

(8) If the consumer complains about a defect in the performance of the contract, the other party to the contract, or his local representative, if there is one, will make prompt efforts to find appropriate solutions.

(9) The contract must clearly and explicitly oblige the consumer to communicate at the earliest opportunity, in writing or any other appropriate form, to the supplier of the services concerned and to the other party to the contract any failure which he perceives at the place where the services concerned are supplied.

. . .

Enforcement

23.　Schedule 3 to these Regulations (which makes provision about the enforcement of regulations 5, 7, 8, 16 and 22 of these Regulations) shall have effect.

Due diligence defence

24.—(1)　Subject to the following provisions of this regulation, in proceedings against any person for an offence under regulation 5, 7, 8, 16 or 22 of these Regulations, it shall be a defence for that person to show that he took all reasonable steps and exercised all due diligence to avoid committing the offence.

(2)　Where in any proceedings against any person for such an offence the defence provided by paragraph (1) above involves an allegation that the commission of the offence was due—
(a)　to the act or default of another; or
(b)　to reliance on information given by another,
that person shall not, without the leave of the court, be entitled to rely on the defence unless, not less than seven clear days before the hearing of the proceedings, or, in Scotland, the trial diet, he has served a notice under paragraph (3) below on the person bringing the proceedings.

(3)　A notice under this paragraph shall give such information identifying or assisting in the identification of the person who committed the act or default or gave the information as is in the possession of the person serving the notice at the time he serves it.

(4)　It is hereby declared that a person shall not be entitled to rely on the defence provided by paragraph (1) above by reason of his reliance on information supplied by another, unless he shows that it was reasonable in all the circumstances for him to have relied on the information, having regard in particular—
(a)　to the steps which he took, and those which might reasonably have been taken, for the purpose of verifying the information; and
(b)　to whether he had any reason to disbelieve the information.

. . .

Saving for civil consequences

27.　No contract shall be void or unenforceable, and no right of action in civil proceedings in respect of any loss shall arise, by reason only of the commission of an offence under regulations 5, 7, 8, 16 or 22 of these Regulations.

Terms implied in contract

28.　Where it is p-rovided in these Regulations that a term (whether so described or whether described as a condition or warranty) is implied in the contract it is so implied irrespective of the law which governs the contract.

SCHEDULE 1

Information to be included (in addition to the price) in brochures where relevant to packages offered

1. The destination and the means, characteristics and categories of transport used.

2. The type of accommodation, its location, category or degree of comfort and its main features and, where the accommodation is to be provided in a member State, its approval or tourist classification under the rules of that member State.

3. The meals which are included in the package.

4. The itinerary.

5. General information about passport and visa requirements which apply for nationals of the member State or States in which the brochure is made available and health formalities required for the journey and the stay.

6. Either the monetary amount or the percentage of the price which is to be paid on account and the timetable for payment of the balance.

7. Whether a minimum number of persons is required for the package to take place and, if so, the deadline for informing the consumer in the event of cancellation.

8. The arrangements (if any) which apply if consumers are delayed at the outward or homeward points of departure.

9. The arrangements for security for money paid over and for the repatriation of the consumer in the event of insolvency.

SCHEDULE 2

Elements to be included in the contract if relevant to the particular package

1. The travel destination(s) and, where periods of stay are involved, the relevant periods, with dates.

2. The means, characteristics and categories of transport to be used and the dates, times and points of departure and return.

3. Where the package includes accommodation, its location, its tourist category or degree of comfort, its main features and, where the accommodation is to be provided in a member State, its compliance with the rules of that member State.

4. The meals which are included in the package.

5. Whether a minimum number of persons is required for the package to take place and, if so, the deadline for informing the consumer in the event of cancellation.

6. The itinerary.

7. Visits, excursions or other services which are included in the total price agreed for the package.

8. The name and address of the organiser, the retailer and, where appropriate, the insurer.

9. The price of the package, if the price may be revised in accordance with the term which may be included in the contract under regulation 11, an indication of the possibility of such price revisions, and an indication of any dues, taxes or fees chargeable for certain services (landing, embarkation or disembarkation fees at ports and airports and tourist taxes) where such costs are not included in the package.

10.   The payment schedule and method of payment.

11.   Special requirements which the consumer has communicated to the organiser or retailer when making the booking and which both have accepted.

12.   The periods within which the consumer must make any complaint about the failure to perform or the inadequate performance of the contract.

As amended by Package Travel, Package Holidays and Package Tours Amendment Regulations 1995, regulation 2; Package Travel, Package Holidays and Package Tours Amendment Regulations 1998, regulations 4–5.

COMMERCIAL AGENTS (COUNCIL DIRECTIVE) REGULATIONS 1993
(1993/3053)

Part I GENERAL

Citation, commencement and applicable law

1.—(1)   These Regulations may be cited as the Commercial Agents (Council Directive) Regulations 1993 and shall come into force on 1st January 1994.

(2)   These Regulations govern the relations between commercial agents and their principals and, subject to paragraph (3), apply in relation to the activities of commercial agents in Great Britain.

(3)   A court or tribunal shall:
   (a)   apply the law of the other member State concerned in place of regulations 3 to 22 where the parties have agreed that the agency contract is to be governed by the law of that member State;
   (b)   (whether or not it would otherwise be required to do so) apply these regulations where the law of another member State corresponding to these regulations enables the parties to agree that the agency contract is to be governed by the law of a different member State and the parties have agreed that it is to be governed by the law of England and Wales or Scotland.

Interpretation, application and extent

2.—(1)   In these Regulations—
   "commercial agent" means a self-employed intermediary who has continuing authority to negotiate the sale or purchase of goods on behalf of another person (the "principal"), or to negotiate and conclude the sale or purchase of goods on behalf of and in the name of that principal; but shall be understood as not including in particular:
   (i)   a person who, in his capacity as an officer of a company or association, is empowered to enter into commitments binding on that company or association;
   (ii)   a partner who is lawfully authorised to enter into commitments binding on his partners;
   (iii)   a person who acts as an insolvency practitioner (as that expression is defined in section 388 of the Insolvency Act 1986) or the equivalent in any other jurisdiction;

"commission" means any part of the remuneration of a commercial agent which varies with the number or value of business transactions;

"EEA Agreement" means the Agreement on the European Economic Area signed at Oporto on 2nd May 1992 as adjusted by the Protocol signed at Brussels on 17th March 1993;

"member State" includes a State which is a contracting party to the EEA Agreement;

"restraint of trade clause" means an agreement restricting the business activities of a commercial agent following termination of the agency contract.

(2) These Regulations do not apply to—
    (a) commercial agents whose activities are unpaid;
    (b) commercial agents when they operate on commodity exchanges or in the commodity market;

. . .

(3) The provisions of the Schedule to these Regulations have effect for the purpose of determining the persons whose activities as commercial agents are to be considered secondary.

(4) These Regulations shall not apply to the persons referred to in paragraph (3) above.

. . .

Part II RIGHTS AND OBLIGATIONS

Duties of a commercial agent to his principal
3.—(1) In performing his activities a commercial agent must look after the interests of his principal and act dutifully and in good faith.

(2) In particular, a commercial agent must—
    (a) make proper efforts to negotiate and, where appropriate, conclude the transactions he is instructed to take care of;
    (b) communicate to his principal all the necessary information available to him;
    (c) comply with reasonable instructions given by his principal.

Duties of a principal to his commercial agent
4.—(1) In his relations with his commercial agent a principal must act dutifully and in good faith.

(2) In particular, a principal must—
    (a) provide his commercial agent with the necessary documentation relating to the goods concerned;
    (b) obtain for his commercial agent the information necessary for the performance of the agency contract, and in particular notify his commercial agent within a reasonable period once he anticipates that the volume of commercial transactions will be significantly lower than that which the commercial agent could normally have expected.

(3) A principal shall, in addition, inform his commercial agent within a reasonable period of his acceptance or refusal of, and of any non-execution by him of, a commercial transaction which the commercial agent has procured for him.

Prohibition on derogation from regulations 3 and 4 and consequence of breach
5.—(1) The parties may not derogate from regulations 3 and 4 above.

(2) The law applicable to the contract shall govern the consequence of breach of the rights and obligations under regulations 3 and 4 above.

Part III REMUNERATION

Form and amount of remuneration in absence of agreement

6.—(1)   In the absence of any agreement as to remuneration between the parties, a commercial agent shall be entitled to the remuneration that commercial agents appointed for the goods forming the subject of his agency contract are customarily allowed in the place where he carries on his activities and, if there is no such customary practice, a commercial agent shall be entitled to reasonable remuneration taking into account all the aspects of the transaction.

(2)   This regulation is without prejudice to the application of any enactment or rule of law concerning the level of remuneration.

(3)   Where a commercial agent is not remunerated (wholly or in part) by commission, regulations 7 to 12 below shall not apply.

Entitlement to commission on transactions concluded during agency contract

7.—(1)   A commercial agent shall be entitled to commission on commercial transactions concluded during the period covered by the agency contract—
   (a)   where the transaction has been concluded as a result of his action; or
   (b)   where the transaction is concluded with a third party whom he has previously acquired as a customer for transactions of the same kind.

(2)   A commercial agent shall also be entitled to commission on transactions concluded during the period covered by the agency contract where he has an exclusive right to a specific geographical area or to a specific group of customers and where the transaction has been entered into with a customer belonging to that area or group. Entitlement to commission on transactions concluded after agency contract has terminated.

8.   Subject to regulation 9 below, a commercial agent shall be entitled to commission on commercial transactions concluded after the agency contract has terminated if—

   (a)   the transaction is mainly attributable to his efforts during the period covered by the agency contract and if the transaction was entered into within a reasonable period after that contract terminated; or
   (b)   in accordance with the conditions mentioned in regulation 7 above, the order of the third party reached the principal or the commercial agent before the agency contract terminated.

Apportionment of commission between new and previous commercial agents

9.—(1)   A commercial agent shall not be entitled to the commission referred to in regulation 7 above if that commission is payable, by virtue of regulation 8 above, to the previous commercial agent, unless it is equitable because of the circumstances for the commission to be shared between the commercial agents.

(2)   The principal shall be liable for any sum due under paragraph (1) above to the person entitled to it in accordance with that paragraph, and any sum which the other commercial agent receives to which he is not entitled shall be refunded to the principal.

When commission due and date for payment

10.—(1)   Commission shall become due as soon as, and to the extent that, one of the following circumstances occurs:
   (a)   the principal has executed the transaction; or
   (b)   the principal should, according to his agreement with the third party, have executed the transaction; or
   (c)   the third party has executed the transaction.

(2) Commission shall become due at the latest when the third party has executed his part of the transaction or should have done so if the principal had executed his part of the transaction, as he should have.

(3) The commission shall be paid not later than on the last day of the month following the quarter in which it became due, and, for the purposes of these Regulations, unless otherwise agreed between the parties, the first quarter period shall run from the date the agency contract takes effect, and subsequent periods shall run from that date in the third month thereafter or the beginning of the fourth month, whichever is the sooner.

(4) Any agreement to derogate from paragraphs (2) and (3) above to the detriment of the commercial agent shall be void.

Extinction of right to commission
11.—(1) The right to commission can be extinguished only if and to the extent that—
(a) it is established that the contract between the third party and the principal will not be executed; and
(b) that fact is due to a reason for which the principal is not to blame.

(2) Any commission which the commercial agent has already received shall be refunded if the right to it is extinguished.

(3) Any agreement to derogate from paragraph (1) above to the detriment of the commercial agent shall be void. Periodic supply of information as to commission due and right of inspection of principal's books.

12.—(1) The principal shall supply his commercial agent with a statement of the commission due, not later than the last day of the month following the quarter in which the commission has become due, and such statement shall set out the main components used in calculating the amount of the commission.

(2) A commercial agent shall be entitled to demand that he be provided with all the information (and in particular an extract from the books) which is available to his principal and which he needs in order to check the amount of the commission due to him.

(3) Any agreement to derogate from paragraphs (1) and (2) above shall be void.

(4) Nothing in this regulation shall remove or restrict the effect of, or prevent reliance upon, any enactment or rule of law which recognises the right of an agent to inspect the books of a principal.

Part IV CONCLUSION AND TERMINATION OF THE AGENCY CONTRACT

Right to signed written statement of terms of agency contract
13.—(1) The commercial agent and principal shall each be entitled to receive from the other, on request, a signed written document setting out the terms of the agency contract including any terms subsequently agreed.

(2) Any purported waiver of the right referred to in paragraph (1) above shall be void.

Conversion of agency contract after expiry of fixed period
14.   An agency contract for a fixed period which continues to be performed by both parties after that period has expired shall be deemed to be converted into an agency contract for an indefinite period.

Minimum periods of notice for termination of agency contract
15.—(1)   Where an agency contract is concluded for an indefinite period either party may terminate it by notice.

(2)   The period of notice shall be—
(a)   1 month for the first year of the contract;
(b)   2 months for the second year commenced;
(c)   3 months for the third year commenced and for the subsequent years;
and the parties may not agree on any shorter periods of notice.

(3)   If the parties agree on longer periods than those laid down in paragraph (2) above, the period of notice to be observed by the principal must not be shorter than that to be observed by the commercial agent.

(4)   Unless otherwise agreed by the parties, the end of the period of notice must coincide with the end of a calendar month.

(5)   The provisions of this regulation shall also apply to an agency contract for a fixed period where it is converted under regulation 14 above into an agency contract for an indefinite period subject to the proviso that the earlier fixed period must be taken into account in the calculation of the period of notice.

Savings with regard to immediate termination
16.   These Regulations shall not affect the application of any enactment or rule of law which provides for the immediate termination of the agency contract—
(a)   because of the failure of one party to carry out all or part of his obligations under that contract; or
(b)   where exceptional circumstances arise.

Entitlement of commercial agent to indemnity or compensation on termination of agency contract
17.—(1)   This regulation has effect for the purpose of ensuring that the commercial agent is, after termination of the agency contract, indemnified in accordance with paragraphs (3) to (5) below or compensated for damage in accordance with paragraphs (6) and (7) below.

(2)   Except where the agency **contract** otherwise provides, the commercial agent shall be entitled to be compensated rather than indemnified.

(3)   Subject to paragraph (9) and to regulation 18 below, the commercial agent shall be entitled to an indemnity if and to the extent that—
(a)   he has brought the principal new customers or has significantly increased the volume of business with existing customers and the principal continues to derive substantial benefits from the business with such customers; and
(b)   the payment of this indemnity is equitable having regard to all the circumstances and, in particular, the commission lost by the commercial agent on the business transacted with such customers.

(4)   The amount of the indemnity shall not exceed a figure equivalent to an indemnity for one year calculated from the commercial agent's average annual remuneration over the preceding five years and if the contract goes back less than five years the indemnity shall be calculated on the average for the period in question.

(5)   The grant of an indemnity as mentioned above shall not prevent the commercial agent from seeking damages.

(6) Subject to paragraph (9) and to regulation 18 below, the commercial agent shall be entitled to compensation for the damage he suffers as a result of the termination of his relations with his principal.

(7) For the purpose of these Regulations such damage shall be deemed to occur particularly when the termination takes place in either or both of the following circumstances, namely circumstances which—

    (a) deprive the commercial agent of the commission which proper performance of the agency contract would have procured for him whilst providing his principal with substantial benefits linked to the activities of the commercial agent; or

    (b) have not enabled the commercial agent to amortize the costs and expenses that he had incurred in the performance of the agency contract on the advice of his principal.

(8) Entitlement to the indemnity or compensation for damage as provided for under paragraphs (2) to (7) above shall also arise where the agency contract is terminated as a result of the death of the commercial agent.

(9) The commercial agent shall lose his entitlement to the indemnity or compensation for damage in the instances provided for in paragraphs (2) to (8) above if within one year following termination of his agency contract he has not notified his principal that he intends pursuing his entitlement.

Grounds for excluding payment of indemnity or compensation under regulation 17

18.   The indemnity or compensation referred to in regulation 17 above shall not be payable to the commercial agent where—

    (a) the principal has terminated the agency contract because of default attributable to the commercial agent which would justify immediate termination of the agency contract pursuant to regulation 16 above; or

    (b) the commercial agent has himself terminated the agency contract, unless such termination is justified—

        (i) by circumstances attributable to the principal, or

        (ii) on grounds of the age, infirmity or illness of the commercial agent in consequence of which he cannot reasonably be required to continue his activities; or

    (c) the commercial agent, with the agreement of his principal, assigns his rights and duties under the agency contract to another person. Prohibition on derogation from regulations 17 and 18.

19.   The parties may not derogate from regulations 17 and 18 to the detriment of the commercial agent before the agency contract expires.

Restraint of trade clauses

20.—(1) A restraint of trade clause shall be valid only if and to the extent that—

    (a) it is concluded in writing; and

    (b) it relates to the geographical area or the group of customers and the geographical area entrusted to the commercial agent and to the kind of goods covered by his agency under the contract.

(2) A restraint of trade clause shall be valid for not more than two years after termination of the agency contract.

(3) Nothing in this regulation shall affect any enactment or rule of law which imposes other restrictions on the validity or enforceability of restraint of trade clauses or which enables a court to reduce the obligations on the parties resulting from such clauses.

Part V MISCELLANEOUS AND SUPPLEMENTAL

Disclosure of information

21. Nothing in these Regulations shall require information to be given where such disclosure would be contrary to public policy.

Service of notice etc

22.—(1) Any notice, statement or other document to be given or supplied to a commercial agent or to be given or supplied to the principal under these Regulations may be so given or supplied:

(a) by delivering it to him;

(b) by leaving it at his proper address addressed to him by name;

(c) by sending it by post to him addressed either to his registered address or to the address of his registered or principal office;

or by any other means provided for in the agency contract.

(2) Any such notice, statement or document may—

(a) in the case of a body corporate, be given or served on the secretary or clerk of that body;

(b) in the case of a partnership, be given to or served on any partner or on any person having the control or management of the partnership business.

. . .

THE SCHEDULE

1. The activities of a person as a commercial agent are to be considered secondary where it may reasonably be taken that the primary purpose of the arrangement with his principal is other than as set out in paragraph 2 below.

2. An arrangement falls within this paragraph if—

(a) the business of the principal is the sale, or as the case may be purchase, of goods of a particular kind; and

(b) the goods concerned are such that—

(i) transactions are normally individually negotiated and concluded on a commercial basis, and

(ii) procuring a transaction on one occasion is likely to lead to further transactions in those goods with that customer on future occasions, or to transactions in those goods with other customers in the same geographical area or among the same group of customers, and

that accordingly it is in the commercial interests of the principal in developing the market in those goods to appoint a representative to such customers with a view to the representative devoting effort, skill and expenditure from his own resources to that end.

3. The following are indications that an arrangement falls within paragraph 2 above, and the absence of any of them is an indication to the contrary—

(a) the principal is the manufacturer, importer or distributor of the goods;

(b) the goods are specifically identified with the principal in the market in question rather than, or to a greater extent than, with any other person;

(c) the agent devotes substantially the whole of his time to representative activities (whether for one principal or for a number of principals whose interests are not conflicting);

(d) the goods are not normally available in the market in question other than by means of the agent;

(e) the arrangement is described as one of commercial agency.

4. The following are indications that an arrangement does not fall within paragraph 2 above—
    (a) promotional material is supplied direct to potential customers;
    (b) persons are granted agencies without reference to existing agents in a particular area or in relation to a particular group;
    (c) customers normally select the goods for themselves and merely place their orders through the agent.

5. The activities of the following categories of persons are presumed, unless the contrary is established, not to fall within paragraph 2 above
    (a) Mail order catalogue agents for consumer goods.
    (b) Consumer credit agents.

As amended by Commercial Agents (Council Directive) (Amendment) Regulations 1993, regulation 2; Commercial Agents (Council Directive) (Amendment) Regulations 1998, regulation 2.

THE PROVISION AND USE OF WORK EQUIPMENT REGULATIONS 1998
(SI 2306)

Part I INTRODUCTION

Interpretation
2.—(1) In these Regulations, unless the context otherwise requires—

"the 1974 Act" means the Health and Safety at Work etc. Act 1974;

"employer" except in regulation 3(2) and (3) includes a person to whom the requirements imposed by these Regulations apply by virtue of regulation 3(3)(a) and (b);

"essential requirements" means requirements described in regulation 10(1);

"the Executive" means the Health and Safety Executive;

"inspection" in relation to an inspection under paragraph (1) or (2) of regulation 6—
(a) means such visual or more rigorous inspection by a competent person as is appropriate for the purpose described in the paragraph;
(b) where it is appropriate to carry out testing for the purpose, includes testing the nature and extent of which are appropriate for the purpose;

"power press" means a press or press brake for the working of metal by means of tools, or for die proving, which is power driven and which embodies a flywheel and clutch;

"thorough examination" in relation to a thorough examination under paragraph (1), (2), (3) or (4) of regulation 32—
(a) means a thorough examination by a competent person;
(b) includes testing the nature and extent of which are appropriate for the purpose described in the paragraph;

"use" in relation to work equipment means any activity involving work equipment and includes starting, stopping, programming, setting, transporting, repairing, modifying, maintaining, servicing and cleaning;

"work equipment" means any machinery, appliance, apparatus, tool or installation for use at work (whether exclusively or not);

and related expressions shall be construed accordingly.

Part II GENERAL

Suitability of work equipment

4.—(1) Every employer shall ensure that work equipment is so constructed or adapted as to be suitable for the purpose for which it is used or provided.

(2) In selecting work equipment, every employer shall have regard to the working conditions and to the risks to the health and safety of persons which exist in the premises or undertaking in which that work equipment is to be used and any additional risk posed by the use of that work equipment.

(3) Every employer shall ensure that work equipment is used only for operations for which, and under conditions for which, it is suitable.

(4) In this regulation "suitable"—
   (a) subject to sub-paragraph (b), means suitable in any respect which it is reasonably foreseeable will affect the health or safety of any person;
   (b) in relation to—
      (i) an offensive weapon within the meaning of section 1(4) of the Prevention of Crime Act 1953 provided for use as self-defence or as deterrent equipment; and
      (ii) work equipment provided for use for arrest or restraint,
   by a person who holds the office of constable or an appointment as police cadet, means suitable in any respect which it is reasonably foreseeable will affect the health or safety of such person.

Maintenance

5.—(1) Every employer shall ensure that work equipment is maintained in an efficient state, in efficient working order and in good repair.

(2) Every employer shall ensure that where any machinery has a maintenance log, the log is kept up to date.

Inspection

6.—(1) Every employer shall ensure that, where the safety of work equipment depends on the installation conditions, it is inspected—
   (a) after installation and before being put into service for the first time; or
   (b) after assembly at a new site or in a new location,
   to ensure that it has been installed correctly and is safe to operate.

(2) Every employer shall ensure that work equipment exposed to conditions causing deterioration which is liable to result in dangerous situations is inspected—
   (a) at suitable intervals; and
   (b) each time that exceptional circumstances which are liable to jeopardise the safety of the work equipment have occurred,
   to ensure that health and safety conditions are maintained and that any deterioration can be detected and remedied in good time.

(3) Every employer shall ensure that the result of an inspection made under this regulation is recorded and kept until the next inspection under this regulation is recorded.

(4) Every employer shall ensure that no work equipment—
(a) leaves his undertaking; or
(b) if obtained from the undertaking of another person, is used in his undertaking, unless it is accompanied by physical evidence that the last inspection required to be carried out under this regulation has been carried out.

Specific risks

7.—(1) Where the use of work equipment is likely to involve a specific risk to health or safety, every employer shall ensure that—
(a) the use of that work equipment is restricted to those persons given the task of using it; and
(b) repairs, modifications, maintenance or servicing of that work equipment is restricted to those persons who have been specifically designated to perform operations of that description (whether or not also authorised to perform other operations).

(2) The employer shall ensure that the persons designated for the purposes of sub-paragraph (b) of paragraph (1) have received adequate training related to any operations in respect of which they have been so designated.

Information and instructions

8.—(1) Every employer shall ensure that all persons who use work equipment have available to them adequate health and safety information and, where appropriate, written instructions pertaining to the use of the work equipment.

(2) Every employer shall ensure that any of his employees who supervises or manages the use of work equipment has available to him adequate health and safety information and, where appropriate, written instructions pertaining to the use of the work equipment.

(3) Without prejudice to the generality of paragraphs (1) or (2), the information and instructions required by either of those paragraphs shall include information and, where appropriate, written instructions on—
(a) the conditions in which and the methods by which the work equipment may be used;
(b) foreseeable abnormal situations and the action to be taken if such a situation were to occur; and
(c) any conclusions to be drawn from experience in using the work equipment.

(4) Information and instructions required by this regulation shall be readily comprehensible to those concerned.

Training

9.—(1) Every employer shall ensure that all persons who use work equipment have received adequate training for purposes of health and safety, including training in the methods which may be adopted when using the work equipment, any risks which such use may entail and precautions to be taken.

(2) Every employer shall ensure that any of his employees who supervises or manages the use of work equipment has received adequate training for purposes of health and safety, including training in the methods which may be adopted when using the work equipment, any risks which such use may entail and precautions to be taken.

Conformity with Community requirements

10.—(1) Every employer shall ensure that an item of work equipment conforms at all times with any essential requirements, other than requirements which, at the time of its being first supplied or put into service in any place in which these Regulations apply, did not apply to work equipment of its type.

(2) In this regulation "essential requirements", in relation to an item of work equipment, means requirements relating to the design and construction of work equipment of its type in any of the instruments listed in Schedule 1 (being instruments which give effect to Community directives concerning the safety of products);

(3) This regulation applies to items of work equipment provided for use in the premises or undertaking of the employer for the first time after 31st December 1992.

Dangerous parts of machinery

11.—(1) Every employer shall ensure that measures are taken in accordance with paragraph (2) which are effective—
    (a) to prevent access to any dangerous part of machinery or to any rotating stock-bar; or
    (b) to stop the movement of any dangerous part of machinery or rotating stock-bar before any part of a person enters a danger zone.

(2) The measures required by paragraph (1) shall consist of—
    (a) the provision of fixed guards enclosing every dangerous part or rotating stock-bar where and to the extent that it is practicable to do so, but where or to the extent that it is not, then
    (b) the provision of other guards or protection devices where and to the extent that it is practicable to do so, but where or to the extent that it is not, then
    (c) the provision of jigs, holders, push-sticks or similar protection appliances used in conjunction with the machinery where and to the extent that it is practicable to do so, but where or to the extent that it is not, then
and the provision of information, instruction, training and supervision as is necessary.

(3) All guards and protection devices provided under sub-paragraphs (a) or (b) of paragraph (2) shall—
    (a) be suitable for the purpose for which they are provided;
    (b) be of good construction, sound material and adequate strength;
    (c) be maintained in an efficient state, in efficient working order and in good repair;
    (d) not give rise to any increased risk to health or safety;
    (e) not be easily bypassed or disabled;
    (f) be situated at sufficient distance from the danger zone;
    (g) not unduly restrict the view of the operating cycle of the machinery, where such a view is necessary;
    (h) be so constructed or adapted that they allow operations necessary to fit or replace parts and for maintenance work, restricting access so that it is allowed only to the area where the work is to be carried out and, if possible, without having to dismantle the guard or protection device.

(4) All protection appliances provided under sub-paragraph (c) of paragraph (2) shall comply with sub-paragraphs (a) to (d) and (g) of paragraph (3).

(5) In this regulation—

"danger zone" means any zone in or around machinery in which a person is exposed to a risk to health or safety from contact with a dangerous part of machinery or a rotating stock-bar;

"stock-bar" means any part of a stock-bar which projects beyond the head-stock of a lathe.

Protection against specified hazards

12.—(1) Every employer shall take measures to ensure that the exposure of a person using work equipment to any risk to his health or safety from any hazard specified in paragraph (3) is either prevented, or, where that is not reasonably practicable, adequately controlled.

(2) The measures required by paragraph (1) shall—
  (a) be measures other than the provision of personal protective equipment or of information, instruction, training and supervision, so far as is reasonably practicable; and
  (b) include, where appropriate, measures to minimise the effects of the hazard as well as to reduce the likelihood of the hazard occurring.

(3) The hazards referred to in paragraph (1) are—
  (a) any article or substance falling or being ejected from work equipment;
  (b) rupture or disintegration of parts of work equipment;
  (c) work equipment catching fire or overheating;
  (d) the unintended or premature discharge of any article or of any gas, dust, liquid, vapour or other substance which, in each case, is produced, used or stored in the work equipment;
  (e) the unintended or premature explosion of the work equipment or any article or substance produced, used or stored in it.

(4) For the purposes of this regulation "adequately" means adequately having regard only to the nature of the hazard and the nature and degree of exposure to the risk.

High or very low temperature

13. Every employer shall ensure that work equipment, parts of work equipment and any article or substance produced, used or stored in work equipment which, in each case, is at a high or very low temperature shall have protection where appropriate so as to prevent injury to any person by burn, scald or sear.

Controls for starting or making a significant change in operating conditions

14.—(1) Every employer shall ensure that, where appropriate, work equipment is provided with one or more controls for the purposes of—
  (a) starting the work equipment (including re-starting after a stoppage for any reason); or
  (b) controlling any change in the speed, pressure or other operating conditions of the work equipment where such conditions after the change result in risk to health and safety which is greater than or of a different nature from such risks before the change.

(2) Subject to paragraph (3), every employer shall ensure that, where a control is required by paragraph (1), it shall not be possible to perform any operation mentioned in sub-paragraph (a) or (b) of that paragraph except by a deliberate action on such control.

(3) Paragraph (1) shall not apply to re-starting or changing operating conditions as a result of the normal operating cycle of an automatic device.

Stop controls

15.—(1) Every employer shall ensure that, where appropriate, work equipment is provided with one or more readily accessible controls the operation of which will bring the work equipment to a safe condition in a safe manner.

(2) Any control required by paragraph (1) shall bring the work equipment to a complete stop where necessary for reasons of health and safety.

(3) Any control required by paragraph (1) shall, if necessary for reasons of health and safety, switch off all sources of energy after stopping the functioning of the work equipment.

(4) Any control required by paragraph (1) shall operate in priority to any control which starts or changes the operating conditions of the work equipment.

Emergency stop controls

16.—(1) Every employer shall ensure that, where appropriate, work equipment is provided with one or more readily accessible emergency stop controls unless it is not necessary by reason of the nature of the hazards and the time taken for the work equipment to come to a complete stop as a result of the action of any control provided by virtue of regulation 15(1).

(2) Any control required by paragraph (1) shall operate in priority to any control required by regulation 15(1).

Controls

17.—(1) Every employer shall ensure that all controls for work equipment are clearly visible and identifiable, including by appropriate marking where necessary.

(2) Except where necessary, the employer shall ensure that no control for work equipment is in a position where any person operating the control is exposed to a risk to his health or safety.

(3) Every employer shall ensure where appropriate—
(a) that, so far as is reasonably practicable, the operator of any control is able to ensure from the position of that control that no person is in a place where he would be exposed to any risk to his health or safety as a result of the operation of that control, but where or to the extent that it is not reasonably practicable;
(b) that, so far as is reasonably practicable, systems of work are effective to ensure that, when work equipment is about to start, no person is in a place where he would be exposed to a risk to his health or safety as a result of the work equipment starting, but where neither of these is reasonably practicable;
(c) that an audible, visible or other suitable warning is given by virtue of regulation 24 whenever work equipment is about to start.

(4) Every employer shall take appropriate measures to ensure that any person who is in a place where he would be exposed to a risk to his health or safety as a result of the starting or stopping of work equipment has sufficient time and suitable means to avoid that risk.

Control systems

18.—(1) Every employer shall ensure, so far as is reasonably practicable, that all control systems of work equipment—

(a) are safe; and

(b) are chosen making due allowance for the failures, faults and constraints to be expected in the planned circumstances of use.

(2) Without prejudice to the generality of paragraph (1), a control system shall not be safe unless—

(a) its operation does not create any increased risk to health or safety;

(b) it ensures, so far as is reasonably practicable, that any fault in or damage to any part of the control system or the loss of supply of any source of energy used by the work equipment cannot result in additional or increased risk to health or safety;

(c) it does not impede the operation of any control required by regulation 15 or 16.

Isolation from sources of energy

19.—(1) Every employer shall ensure that where appropriate work equipment is provided with suitable means to isolate it from all its sources of energy.

(2) Without prejudice to the generality of paragraph (1), the means mentioned in that paragraph shall not be suitable unless they are clearly identifiable and readily accessible.

(3) Every employer shall take appropriate measures to ensure that re-connection of any energy source to work equipment does not expose any person using the work equipment to any risk to his health or safety.

Stability

20. Every employer shall ensure that work equipment or any part of work equipment is stabilised by clamping or otherwise where necessary for purposes of health or safety.

Lighting

21. Every employer shall ensure that suitable and sufficient lighting, which takes account of the operations to be carried out, is provided at any place where a person uses work equipment.

Maintenance operations

22. Every employer shall take appropriate measures to ensure that work equipment is so constructed or adapted that, so far as is reasonably practicable, maintenance operations which involve a risk to health or safety can be carried out while the work equipment is shut down, or in other cases—

(a) maintenance operations can be carried out without exposing the person carrying them out to a risk to his health or safety; or

(b) appropriate measures can be taken for the protection of any person carrying out maintenance operations which involve a risk to his health or safety.

Markings

23. Every employer shall ensure that work equipment is marked in a clearly visible manner with any marking appropriate for reasons of health and safety.

Warnings

24.—(1) Every employer shall ensure that work equipment incorporates any warnings or warning devices which are appropriate for reasons of health and safety.

(2) Without prejudice to the generality of paragraph (1), warnings given by warning devices on work equipment shall not be appropriate unless they are unambiguous, easily perceived and easily understood.

THE EMPLOYERS' LIABILITY (COMPULSORY INSURANCE) REGULATIONS 1998
(SI 2573)

Prohibition of certain conditions in policies of insurance

2.—(1) For the purposes of the 1969 Act, there is prohibited in any contract of insurance any condition which provides (in whatever terms) that no liability (either generally or in respect of a particular claim) shall arise under the policy, or that any such liability so arising shall cease, if—

(a) some specified thing is done or omitted to be done after the happening of the event giving rise to a claim under the policy;

(b) the policy holder does not take reasonable care to protect his employees against the risk of bodily injury or disease in the course of their employment;

(c) the policy holder fails to comply with the requirements of any enactment for the protection of employees against the risk of bodily injury or disease in the course of their employment; or

(d) the policy holder does not keep specified records or fails to provide the insurer with or make available to him information from such records.

(2) For the purposes of the 1969 Act there is also prohibited in a policy of insurance any condition which requires—

(a) a relevant employee to pay; or

(b) an insured employer to pay the relevant employee, the first amount of any claim or any aggregation of claims.

(3) Paragraphs (1) and (2) above do not prohibit for the purposes of the 1969 Act a condition in a policy of insurance which requires the employer to pay or contribute any sum to the insurer in respect of the satisfaction of any claim made under the contract of insurance by a relevant employee or any costs and expenses incurred in relation to any such claim.

Limit of amount of compulsory insurance

3.—(1) Subject to paragraph (2) below, the amount for which an employer is required by the 1969 Act to insure and maintain insurance in respect of relevant employees under one or more policies of insurance shall be, or shall in aggregate be not less than £5 million in respect of—

(a) a claim relating to any one or more of those employees arising out of any one occurrence; and

(b) any costs and expenses incurred in relation to any such claim.

UNFAIR TERMS IN CONSUMER CONTRACTS REGULATIONS 1999
(1999/2083)

Citation and commencement

1. These Regulations may be cited as the Unfair Terms in Consumer Contracts Regulations 1999 and shall come into force on 1st October 1999.

. . .

Interpretation

3.—(1)   In these Regulations—

"the Community" means the European Community;

"consumer" means any natural person who, in contracts covered by these Regulations, is acting for purposes which are outside his trade, business or profession;

"court" in relation to England and Wales . . . means a county court or the High Court, and in relation to Scotland, the Sheriff or the Court of Session;

"Director" means the Director General of Fair Trading;

"EEA Agreement" means the Agreement on the European Economic Area signed at Oporto on 2nd May 1992 as adjusted by the protocol signed at Brussels on 17th March 1993;

"Member State" means a State which is a contracting party to the EEA Agreement;

"notified" means notified in writing;

"qualifying body" means a person specified in Schedule 1;

"seller or supplier" means any natural or legal person who, in contracts covered by these Regulations, is acting for purposes relating to his trade, business or profession, whether publicly owned or privately owned;

"unfair terms" means the contractual terms referred to in regulation 5.

(1A)   The references—
(a)   in regulation 4(1) to a seller or a supplier, and
(b)   in regulation 8(1) to a seller or supplier,
include references to a distance supplier and to an intermediary.

(1B)   In paragraph (1A) and regulation 5(6)—
"distance supplier" means—
(a)   a supplier under a distance contract within the meaning of the Financial Services (Distance Marketing) Regulations 2004, or
(b)   a supplier of unsolicited financial services within regulation 15 of those Regulations; and
"intermediary" has the same meaning as in those Regulations.

(2)   In the application of these Regulations to Scotland for references to an "injunction" or an "interim injunction" there shall be substituted references to an "interdict" or "interim interdict" respectively.

Terms to which these Regulations apply

4.—(1)   These Regulations apply in relation to unfair terms in contracts concluded between a seller or a supplier and a consumer.

(2)   These Regulations do not apply to contractual terms which reflect—
(a)   mandatory statutory or regulatory provisions (including such provisions under the law of any Member State or in Community legislation having effect in the United Kingdom without further enactment);
(b)   the provisions or principles of international conventions to which the Member States or the Community are party.

Unfair terms

5.—(1)   A contractual term which has not been individually negotiated shall be regarded as unfair if, contrary to the requirement of good faith, it causes a significant imbalance in the parties' rights and obligations arising under the contract, to the detriment of the consumer.

(2)   A term shall always be regarded as not having been individually negotiated where it has been drafted in advance and the consumer has therefore not been able to influence the substance of the term.

(3)   Notwithstanding that a specific term or certain aspects of it in a contract has been individually negotiated, these Regulations shall apply to the rest of a contract if an overall assessment of it indicates that it is a pre-formulated standard contract.

(4)   It shall be for any seller or supplier who claims that a term was individually negotiated to show that it was.

(5)   Schedule 2 to these Regulations contains an indicative and non-exhaustive list of the terms which may be regarded as unfair.

(6)   Any contractual term providing that a consumer bears the burden of proof in respect of showing whether a distance supplier or an intermediary complied with any or all of the obligations placed upon him resulting from the Directive and any rule or enactment implementing it shall always be regarded as unfair.

(7)   In paragraph (6)—

"the Directive" means Directive 2002/65/EC of the European Parliament and of the Council of 23 September 2002 concerning the distance marketing of consumer financial services and amending Council Directive 90/619/EEC and Directives 97/7/EC and 98/27/EC; and

"rule" means a rule made by the Financial Services Authority under the Financial Services and Markets Act 2000 or by a designated professional body within the meaning of section 326(2) of that Act.

Assessment of unfair terms

6.—(1)   Without prejudice to regulation 12, the unfairness of a contractual term shall be assessed, taking into account the nature of the goods or services for which the contract was concluded and by referring, at the time of conclusion of the contract, to all the circumstances attending the conclusion of the contract and to all the other terms of the contract or of another contract on which it is dependent.

(2)   In so far as it is in plain intelligible language, the assessment of fairness of a term shall not relate—
(a)   to the definition of the main subject matter of the contract, or
(b)   to the adequacy of the price or remuneration, as against the goods or services supplied in exchange.

Written contracts

7.—(1)   A seller or supplier shall ensure that any written term of a contract is expressed in plain, intelligible language.

(2)   If there is doubt about the meaning of a written term, the interpretation which is most favourable to the consumer shall prevail but this rule shall not apply in proceedings brought under regulation 12.

Effect of unfair term

8.—(1)   An unfair term in a contract concluded with a consumer by a seller or supplier shall not be binding on the consumer.

(2)   The contract shall continue to bind the parties if it is capable of continuing in existence without the unfair term.

Choice of law clauses

9.   These Regulations shall apply notwithstanding any contract term which applies or purports to apply the law of a non-Member State, if the contract has a close connection with the territory of the Member States.

Complaints—consideration by Director

10.—(1)   It shall be the duty of the Director to consider any complaint made to him that any contract term drawn up for general use is unfair, unless—
   (a) the complaint appears to the Director to be frivolous or vexatious; or
   (b) a qualifying body has notified the Director that it agrees to consider the complaint.

(2)   The Director shall give reasons for his decision to apply or not to apply, as the case may be, for an injunction under regulation 12 in relation to any complaint which these Regulations require him to consider.

(3)   In deciding whether or not to apply for an injunction in respect of a term which the Director considers to be unfair, he may, if he considers it appropriate to do so, have regard to any undertakings given to him by or on behalf of any person as to the continued use of such a term in contracts concluded with consumers.

Complaints—consideration by qualifying bodies

11.—(1)   If a qualifying body specified in Part One of Schedule 1 notifies the Director that it agrees to consider a complaint that any contract term drawn up for general use is unfair, it shall be under a duty to consider that complaint.

(2)   Regulation 10(2) and (3) shall apply to a qualifying body which is under a duty to consider a complaint as they apply to the Director.

Injunctions to prevent continued use of unfair terms

12.—(1)   The Director or, subject to paragraph (2), any qualifying body may apply for an injunction (including an interim injunction) against any person appearing to the Director or that body to be using, or recommending use of, an unfair term drawn up for general use in contracts concluded with consumers.

(2)   A qualifying body may apply for an injunction only where—
   (a) it has notified the Director of its intention to apply at least fourteen days before the date on which the application is made, beginning with the date on which the notification was given; or
   (b) the Director consents to the application being made within a shorter period.

(3)   The court on an application under this regulation may grant an injunction on such terms as it thinks fit.

(4)   An injunction may relate not only to use of a particular contract term drawn up for general use but to any similar term, or a term having like effect, used or recommended for use by any person.

Powers of the Director and qualifying bodies to obtain documents and information

13.—(1) The Director may exercise the power conferred by this regulation for the
purpose of—

(a) facilitating his consideration of a complaint that a contract term drawn up for
general use is unfair; or

(b) ascertaining whether a person has complied with an undertaking or court order
as to the continued use, or recommendation for use, of a term in contracts
concluded with consumers.

(2) A qualifying body specified in Part One of Schedule 1 may exercise the power
conferred by this regulation for the purpose of—

(a) facilitating its consideration of a complaint that a contract term drawn up for
general use is unfair; or

(b) ascertaining whether a person has complied with—

(i) an undertaking given to it or to the court following an application by that
body, or

(ii) a court order made on an application by that body,

as to the continued use, or recommendation for use, of a term in contracts
concluded with consumers.

(3) The Director may require any person to supply to him, and a qualifying
body specified in Part One of Schedule 1 may require any person to supply
to it—

(a) a copy of any document which that person has used or recommended for use, at
the time the notice referred to in paragraph (4) below is given, as a pre-
formulated standard contract in dealings with consumers;

(b) information about the use, or recommendation for use, by that person of that
document or any other such document in dealings with consumers.

(4) The power conferred by this regulation is to be exercised by a notice in writing which
may—

(a) specify the way in which and the time within which it is to be complied with; and

(b) be varied or revoked by a subsequent notice.

(5) Nothing in this regulation compels a person to supply any document or information
which he would be entitled to refuse to produce or give in civil proceedings before the
court.

(6) If a person makes default in complying with a notice under this regulation, the court
may, on the application of the Director or of the qualifying body, make such order as
the court thinks fit for requiring the default to be made good, and any such order may
provide that all the costs or expenses of and incidental to the application shall be
borne by the person in default or by any officers of a company or other association
who are responsible for its default.

Notification of undertakings and orders to Director

14. A qualifying body shall notify the Director—

(a) of any undertaking given to it by or on behalf of any person as to the continued use
of a term which that body considers to be unfair in contracts concluded with
consumers;

(b) of the outcome of any application made by it under regulation 12, and of the terms of
any undertaking given to, or order made by, the court;

(c) of the outcome of any application made by it to enforce a previous order of the
court.

Publication, information and advice

15.—(1) The Director shall arrange for the publication in such form and manner as he considers appropriate, of—

(a) details of any undertaking or order notified to him under regulation 14;

(b) details of any undertaking given to him by or on behalf of any person as to the continued use of a term which the Director considers to be unfair in contracts concluded with consumers;

(c) details of any application made by him under regulation 12, and of the terms of any undertaking given to, or order made by, the court;

(d) details of any application made by the Director to enforce a previous order of the court.

(2) The Director shall inform any person on request whether a particular term to which these Regulations apply has been—

(a) the subject of an undertaking given to the Director or notified to him by a qualifying body; or

(b) the subject of an order of the court made upon application by him or notified to him by a qualifying body;

and shall give that person details of the undertaking or a copy of the order, as the case may be, together with a copy of any amendments which the person giving the undertaking has agreed to make to the term in question.

(3) The Director may arrange for the dissemination in such form and manner as he considers appropriate of such information and advice concerning the operation of these Regulations as may appear to him to be expedient to give to the public and to all persons likely to be affected by these Regulations.

The functions of the Financial Services Authority

16.   The functions of the Financial Services Authority under these Regulations shall be treated as functions of the Financial Services Authority under the Financial Services and Markets Act 2000.

SCHEDULE 1 QUALIFYING BODIES

PART ONE

1.   The Information Commissioner.

2.   The Gas and Electricity Markets Authority.

3.   The Director General of Electricity Supply for Northern Ireland.

4.   The Director General of Gas for Northern Ireland.

5.   The Office of Communications.

6.   The Water Services Regulation Authority.

7.   The Rail Regulator.

8.   Every weights and measures authority in Great Britain.

9.   The Department of Enterprise, Trade and Investment in Northern Ireland.

10.   The Financial Services Authority.

PART TWO

11.   Consumers' Association.

SCHEDULE 2 INDICATIVE AND NON-EXHAUSTIVE LIST OF TERMS WHICH MAY BE REGARDED AS UNFAIR

1.   Terms which have the object or effect of—

(a) excluding or limiting the legal liability of a seller or supplier in the event of the death of a consumer or personal injury to the latter resulting from an act or omission of that seller or supplier;

(b) inappropriately excluding or limiting the legal rights of the consumer vis-à-vis the seller or supplier or another party in the event of total or partial non-performance or inadequate performance by the seller or supplier of any of the contractual obligations, including the option of offsetting a debt owed to the seller or supplier against any claim which the consumer may have against him;

(c) making an agreement binding on the consumer whereas provision of services by the seller or supplier is subject to a condition whose realisation depends on his own will alone;

(d) permitting the seller or supplier to retain sums paid by the consumer where the latter decides not to conclude or perform the contract, without providing for the consumer to receive compensation of an equivalent amount from the seller or supplier where the latter is the party cancelling the contract;

(e) requiring any consumer who fails to fulfil his obligation to pay a disproportionately high sum in compensation;

(f) authorising the seller or supplier to dissolve the contract on a discretionary basis where the same facility is not granted to the consumer, or permitting the seller or supplier to retain the sums paid for services not yet supplied by him where it is the seller or supplier himself who dissolves the contract;

(g) enabling the seller or supplier to terminate a contract of indeterminate duration without reasonable notice except where there are serious grounds for doing so;

(h) automatically extending a contract of fixed duration where the consumer does not indicate otherwise, when the deadline fixed for the consumer to express his desire not to extend the contract is unreasonably early;

(i) irrevocably binding the consumer to terms with which he had no real opportunity of becoming acquainted before the conclusion of the contract;

(j) enabling the seller or supplier to alter the terms of the contract unilaterally without a valid reason which is specified in the contract;

(k) enabling the seller or supplier to alter unilaterally without a valid reason any characteristics of the product or service to be provided;

(l) providing for the price of goods to be determined at the time of delivery or allowing a seller of goods or supplier of services to increase their price without in both cases giving the consumer the corresponding right to cancel the contract if the final price is too high in relation to the price agreed when the contract was concluded;

(m) giving the seller or supplier the right to determine whether the goods or services supplied are in conformity with the contract, or giving him the exclusive right to interpret any term of the contract;

(n) limiting the seller's or supplier's obligation to respect commitments undertaken by his agents or making his commitments subject to compliance with a particular formality;

(o) obliging the consumer to fulfil all his obligations where the seller or supplier does not perform his;

(p) giving the seller or supplier the possibility of transferring his rights and obligations under the contract, where this may serve to reduce the guarantees for the consumer, without the latter's agreement;

(q) excluding or hindering the consumer's right to take legal action or exercise any other legal remedy, particularly by requiring the consumer to take disputes exclusively to arbitration not covered by legal provisions, unduly restricting the evidence available to him or imposing on him a burden of proof which, according to the applicable law, should lie with another party to the contract.

2.   Scope of paragraphs 1(g), (j) and (l)

(a)   Paragraph 1(g) is without hindrance to terms by which a supplier of financial services reserves the right to terminate unilaterally a contract of indeterminate duration without notice where there is a valid reason, provided that the supplier is required to inform the other contracting party or parties thereof immediately.

(b)   Paragraph 1(j) is without hindrance to terms under which a supplier of financial services reserves the right to alter the rate of interest payable by the consumer or due to the latter, or the amount of other charges for financial services without notice where there is a valid reason, provided that the supplier is required to inform the other contracting party or parties thereof at the earliest opportunity and that the latter are free to dissolve the contract immediately.

Paragraph 1(j) is also without hindrance to terms under which a seller or supplier reserves the right to alter unilaterally the conditions of a contract of indeterminate duration, provided that he is required to inform the consumer with reasonable notice and that the consumer is free to dissolve the contract.

(c)   Paragraphs 1(g), (j) and (l) do not apply to:
— transactions in transferable securities, financial instruments and other products or services where the price is linked to fluctuations in a stock exchange quotation or index or a financial market rate that the seller or supplier does not control;
— contracts for the purchase or sale of foreign currency, traveller's cheques or money orders denominated in foreign currency;

(d)   Paragraph 1(l) is without hindrance to price indexation clauses, where lawful, provided that the method by which prices vary is explicitly described.

As amended by Unfair Terms in Consumer Contracts (Amendment) Regulations 2001, regulation 2; Financial Services and Markets Act 2000 (Consequential Amendments and Repeals) Order 2001, Pt 9; Communications Act 2003 (Consequential Amendments No. 2) Order 2003, article 2; Financial Services (Distance Marketing) Regulations 2004, regulation 24; Unfair Terms in Consumer Contracts (Amendment) and Water Act 2003 (Transitional Provision) Regulations 2006, regulation 2.

CONSUMER PROTECTION (DISTANCE SELLING) REGULATIONS 2000

(2000/2334)

Title, commencement and extent

1.—(1)   These Regulations may be cited as the Consumer Protection (Distance Selling) Regulations 2000 and shall come into force on 31st October 2000.

. . .

Interpretation

3.—(1)   In these Regulations—

"the 2000 Act" means the Financial Services and Markets Act 2000;
"appointed representative" has the same meaning as in section 39(2) of the 2000 Act;

"authorised person" has the same meaning as in section 31(2) of the 2000 Act;

"breach" means contravention by a supplier of a prohibition in, or failure to comply with a requirement of, these Regulations;

"business" includes a trade or profession;

"consumer" means any natural person who, in contracts to which these Regulations apply, is acting for purposes which are outside his business;

"court" in relation to England and Wales . . . means a county court or the High Court, and in relation to Scotland means the Sheriff Court or the Court of Session;

"credit" includes a cash loan and any other form of financial accommodation, and for this purpose "cash" includes money in any form;

"Director" means the Director General of Fair Trading;

"distance contract" means any contract concerning goods or services concluded between a supplier and a consumer under an organised distance sales or service provision scheme run by the supplier who, for the purpose of the contract, makes exclusive use of one or more means of distance communication up to and including the moment at which the contract is concluded;

"EEA Agreement" means the Agreement on the European Economic Area signed at Oporto on 2 May 1992 as adjusted by the Protocol signed at Brussels on 17 March 1993;

"enactment" includes an enactment comprised in, or in an instrument made under, an Act of the Scottish Parliament;

"enforcement authority" means the Director, every weights and measures authority in Great Britain . . .;

"excepted contract" means a contract such as is mentioned in regulation 5(1);

"financial service" means any service of a banking, credit, insurance, personal pension, investment or payment nature;

"means of distance communication" means any means which, without the simultaneous physical presence of the supplier and the consumer, may be used for the conclusion of a contract between those parties; and an indicative list of such means is contained in Schedule 1;

"Member State" means a State which is a contracting party to the EEA Agreement;

"operator of a means of communication" means any public or private person whose business involves making one or more means of distance communication available to suppliers;

"period for performance" has the meaning given by regulation 19(2);

"personal credit agreement" has the meaning given by regulation 14(8);

"regulated activity" has the same meaning as in section 22 of the 2000 Act;

"related credit agreement" has the meaning given by regulation 15(5);

"supplier" means any person who, in contracts to which these Regulations apply, is acting in his commercial or professional capacity; and

"working days" means all days other than Saturdays, Sundays and public holidays.

(2) In the application of these Regulations to Scotland, for references to an "injunction" or an "interim injunction" there shall be substituted references to an "interdict" or an "interim interdict" respectively.

Contracts to which these Regulations apply

4.   These Regulations apply, subject to regulation 6, to distance contracts other than excepted contracts.

Excepted contracts

5.—(1) The following are excepted contracts, namely any contract—
   (a) for the sale or other disposition of an interest in land except for a rental agreement;
   (b) for the construction of a building where the contract also provides for a sale or other disposition of an interest in land on which the building is constructed, except for a rental agreement;
   (c) relating to financial services;
   (d) concluded by means of an automated vending machine or automated commercial premises;
   (e) concluded with a telecommunications operator through the use of a public pay-phone;
   (f) concluded at an auction.

(2) References in paragraph (1) to a rental agreement—
   (a) if the land is situated in England and Wales, are references to any agreement which does not have to be made in writing (whether or not in fact made in writing) because of section 2(5)(a) of the Law of Property (Miscellaneous Provisions) Act 1989;
   (b) if the land is situated in Scotland, are references to any agreement for the creation, transfer, variation or extinction of an interest in land, which does not have to be made in writing (whether or not in fact made in writing) as provided for in section 1(2) and (7) of the Requirements of Writing (Scotland) Act 1995; . . .

(3) Paragraph (2) shall not be taken to mean that a rental agreement in respect of land situated outside the United Kingdom is not capable of being a distance contract to which these Regulations apply.

Contracts to which only part of these Regulations apply

6.—(1) Regulations 7 to 20 shall not apply to a contract which is a regulated contract within the meaning of the Timeshare, Holiday Products, Resale and Exchange Contracts Regulations 2010.

(2) Regulations 7 to 19(1) shall not apply to—
   (a) contracts for the supply of food, beverages or other goods intended for everyday consumption supplied to the consumer's residence or to his workplace by regular roundsmen; or
   (b) contracts for the provision of accommodation, transport, catering or leisure services, where the supplier undertakes, when the contract is concluded, to provide these services on a specific date or within a specific period.

(3) Regulations 19(2) to (8) and 20 do not apply to a contract for a "package" within the meaning of the Package Travel, Package Holidays and Package Tours Regulations 1992 which is sold or offered for sale in the territory of the Member States.

(4) Regulations 7 to 14, 17 to 20 and 25 do not apply to any contract which is made, and regulation 24 does not apply to any unsolicited services which are supplied, by an authorised person where the making or performance of that contract or the supply of those services, as the case may be, constitutes or is part of a regulated activity carried on by him.

(5) Regulations 7 to 9, 17 to 20 and 25 do not apply to any contract which is made, and regulation 24 does not apply to any unsolicited services which are supplied, by an appointed representative where the making or performance of that contract or the supply of those services, as the case may be, constitutes or is part of a regulated activity carried on by him.

Information required prior to the conclusion of the contract
7.—(1) Subject to paragraph (4), in good time prior to the conclusion of the contract the supplier shall—
  (a) provide to the consumer the following information—
    (i) the identity of the supplier and, where the contract requires payment in advance, the supplier's address;
    (ii) a description of the main characteristics of the goods or services;
    (iii) the price of the goods or services including all taxes;
    (iv) delivery costs where appropriate;
    (v) the arrangements for payment, delivery or performance;
    (vi) the existence of a right of cancellation except in the cases referred to in regulation 13;
    (vii) the cost of using the means of distance communication where it is calculated other than at the basic rate;
    (viii) the period for which the offer or the price remains valid; and
    (ix) where appropriate, the minimum duration of the contract, in the case of contracts for the supply of goods or services to be performed permanently or recurrently;
  (b) inform the consumer if he proposes, in the event of the goods or services ordered by the consumer being unavailable, to provide substitute goods or services (as the case may be) of equivalent quality and price; and
  (c) inform the consumer that the cost of returning any such substitute goods to the supplier in the event of cancellation by the consumer would be met by the supplier.

(2) The supplier shall ensure that the information required by paragraph (1) is provided in a clear and comprehensible manner appropriate to the means of distance communication used, with due regard in particular to the principles of good faith in commercial transactions and the principles governing the protection of those who are unable to give their consent such as minors.

(3) Subject to paragraph (4), the supplier shall ensure that his commercial purpose is made clear when providing the information required by paragraph (1).

(4) In the case of a telephone communication, the identity of the supplier and the commercial purpose of the call shall be made clear at the beginning of the conversation with the consumer.

Written and additional information
8.—(1) Subject to regulation 9, the supplier shall provide to the consumer in writing, or in another durable medium which is available and accessible to the consumer, the information referred to in paragraph (2), either—

(a) prior to the conclusion of the contract, or

(b) thereafter, in good time and in any event—

    (i) during the performance of the contract, in the case of services; and

    (ii) at the latest at the time of delivery where goods not for delivery to third parties are concerned.

(2) The information required to be provided by paragraph (1) is—

    (a) the information set out in paragraphs (i) to (vi) of Regulation 7(1)(a);

    (b) information about the conditions and procedures for exercising the right to cancel under regulation 10, including—

        (i) where a term of the contract requires (or the supplier intends that it will require) that the consumer shall return the goods to the supplier in the event of cancellation, notification of that requirement;

        (ii) information as to whether the consumer or the supplier would be responsible under these Regulations for the cost of returning any goods to the supplier, or the cost of his recovering them, if the consumer cancels the contract under regulation 10;

        (iii) in the case of a contract for the supply of services, information as to how the right to cancel may be affected by the consumer agreeing to performance of the services beginning before the end of the seven working day period referred to in regulation 12;

    (c) the geographical address of the place of business of the supplier to which the consumer may address any complaints;

    (d) information about any after-sales services and guarantees; and

    (e) the conditions for exercising any contractual right to cancel the contract, where the contract is of an unspecified duration or a duration exceeding **one year**.

Services performed through the use of a means of distance communication

9.—(1) Regulation 8 shall not apply to a contract for the supply of services which are performed through the use of a means of distance communication, where those services are supplied on only one occasion and are invoiced by the operator of the means of distance communication.

(2) But the supplier shall take all necessary steps to ensure that a consumer who is a party to a contract to which paragraph (1) applies is able to obtain the supplier's geographical address and the place of business to which the consumer may address any complaints.

Right to cancel

10.—(1) Subject to regulation 13, if within the cancellation period set out in regulations 11 and 12, the consumer gives a notice of cancellation to the supplier, or any other person previously notified by the supplier to the consumer as a person to whom notice of cancellation may be given, the notice of cancellation shall operate to cancel the contract.

(2) Except as otherwise provided by these Regulations, the effect of a notice of cancellation is that the contract shall be treated as if it had not been made.

(3) For the purposes of these Regulations, a notice of cancellation is a notice in writing or in another durable medium available and accessible to the supplier (or to the other person to whom it is given) which, however expressed, indicates the intention of the consumer to cancel the contract.

(4) A notice of cancellation given under this regulation by a consumer to a supplier or other person is to be treated as having been properly given if the consumer—

(a) leaves it at the address last known to the consumer and addressed to the supplier or other person by name (in which case it is to be taken to have been given on the day on which it was left);

(b) sends it by post to the address last known to the consumer and addressed to the supplier or other person by name (in which case, it is to be taken to have been given on the day on which it was posted);

(c) sends it by facsimile to the business facsimile number last known to the consumer (in which case it is to be taken to have been given on the day on which it is sent); or

(d) sends it by electronic mail, to the business electronic mail address last known to the consumer (in which case it is to be taken to have been given on the day on which it is sent).

(5) Where a consumer gives a notice in accordance with paragraph (4)(a) or (b) to a supplier who is a body corporate or a partnership, the notice is to be treated as having been properly given if—

(a) in the case of a body corporate, it is left at the address of, or sent to, the secretary or clerk of that body; or

(b) in the case of a partnership, it is left with or sent to a partner or a person having control or management of the partnership business.

Cancellation period in the case of contracts for the supply of goods

11.—(1) For the purposes of regulation 10, the cancellation period in the case of contracts for the supply of goods begins with the day on which the contract is concluded and ends as provided in paragraphs (2) to (5).

(2) Where the supplier complies with regulation 8, the cancellation period ends on the expiry of the period of seven working days beginning with the day after the day on which the consumer receives the goods.

(3) Where a supplier who has not complied with regulation 8 provides to the consumer the information referred to in regulation 8(2), and does so in writing or in another durable medium available and accessible to the consumer, within the period of three months beginning with the day after the day on which the consumer receives the goods, the cancellation period ends on the expiry of the period of seven working days beginning with the day after the day on which the consumer receives the information.

(4) Where neither paragraph (2) nor (3) applies, the cancellation period ends on the expiry of the period of three months and seven working days beginning with the day after the day on which the consumer receives the goods.

(5) In the case of contracts for goods for delivery to third parties, paragraphs (2) to (4) shall apply as if the consumer had received the goods on the day on which they were received by the third party.

Cancellation period in the case of contracts for the supply of services

12.—(1) For the purposes of regulation 10, the cancellation period in the case of contracts for the supply of services begins with the day on which the contract is concluded and ends as provided in paragraphs (2) to (4).

(2) Where the supplier complies with regulation 8 on or before the day on which the contract is concluded, the cancellation period ends on the expiry of the period of seven working days beginning with the day after the day on which the contract is concluded.

(3) Subject to paragraph (3A) Where a supplier who has not complied with regulation 8 on or before the day on which the contract is concluded provides to the consumer the information referred to in regulation 8(2), and does so in writing or in another durable medium available and accessible to the consumer, within the period of three months beginning with the day after the day on which the contract is concluded, the cancellation period ends on the expiry of the period of seven working days beginning with the day after the day on which the consumer receives the information.

(3A) Where the performance of the contract has begun with the consumer's agreement before the expiry of the period of seven working days beginning with the day after the day on which the contract was concluded and the supplier has not complied with regulation 8 on or before the day on which performance began, but provides to the consumer the information referred to in regulation 8(2) in good time during the performance of the contract, the cancellation period ends—
   (a) on the expiry of the period of seven working days beginning with the day after the day on which the consumer receives the information; or
   (b) if the performance of the contract is completed before the expiry of the period referred to in sub-paragraph (a), on the day when the performance of the contract is completed.

(4) Where none of paragraphs (2) to (3A) applies, the cancellation period ends on the expiry of the period of three months and seven working days beginning with the day after the day on which the contract is concluded.

Exceptions to the right to cancel
13.—(1) Unless the parties have agreed otherwise, the consumer will not have the right to cancel the contract by giving notice of cancellation pursuant to regulation 10 in respect of contracts—
   (a) for the supply of services if the performance of the contract has begun with the consumer's agreement—
      (i) before the end of the cancellation period applicable under regulation 12(2); and
      (ii) after the supplier has provided the information referred to in regulation 8(2);
   (b) for the supply of goods or services the price of which is dependent on fluctuations in the financial market which cannot be controlled by the supplier;
   (c) for the supply of goods made to the consumer's specifications or clearly personalised or which by reason of their nature cannot be returned or are liable to deteriorate or expire rapidly;
   (d) for the supply of audio or video recordings or computer software if they are unsealed by the consumer;
   (e) for the supply of newspapers, periodicals or magazines; or
   (f) for gaming, betting or lottery services.

Recovery of sums paid by or on behalf of the consumer on cancellation, and return of security
14.—(1) On the cancellation of a contract under regulation 10, the supplier shall reimburse any sum paid by or on behalf of the consumer under or in relation to the contract to the person by whom it was made free of any charge, less any charge made in accordance with paragraph(5).

(2) The reference in paragraph (1) to any sum paid on behalf of the consumer includes any sum paid by a creditor who is not the same person as the supplier under a personal credit agreement with the consumer.

(3) The supplier shall make the reimbursement referred to in paragraph (1) as soon as possible and in any case within a period not exceeding 30 days beginning with the day on which the notice of cancellation was given.

(4) Where any security has been provided in relation to the contract, the security (so far as it is so provided) shall, on cancellation under regulation 10, be treated as never having had effect and any property lodged with the supplier solely for the purposes of the security as so provided shall be returned by him forthwith.

(5) Subject to paragraphs (6) and (7), the supplier may make a charge, not exceeding the direct costs of recovering any goods supplied under the contract, where a term of the contract provides that the consumer must return any goods supplied if he cancels the contract under regulation 10 but the consumer does not comply with this provision or returns the goods at the expense of the supplier.

(6) Paragraph (5) shall not apply where—
   (a) the consumer cancels in circumstances where he has the right to reject the goods under a term of the contract, including a term implied by virtue of any enactment, or
   (b) the term requiring the consumer to return any goods supplied if he cancels the contract is an "unfair term" within the meaning of the Unfair Terms in Consumer Contracts Regulations 1999.

(7) Paragraph (5) shall not apply to the cost of recovering any goods which were supplied as substitutes for the goods ordered by the consumer.

(8) For the purposes of these Regulations, a personal credit agreement is an agreement between the consumer and any other person ("the creditor") by which the creditor provides the consumer with credit of any amount.

Automatic cancellation of a related credit agreement

15.—(1) Where a notice of cancellation is given under regulation 10 which has the effect of cancelling the contract, the giving of the notice shall also have the effect of cancelling any related credit agreement.

(2) Where a related credit agreement is cancelled by virtue of paragraph (1), the supplier shall, if he is not the same person as the creditor under that agreement, forthwith on receipt of the notice of cancellation inform the creditor that the notice has been given.

(3) Where a related credit agreement is cancelled by virtue of paragraph (1)—
   (a) any sum paid by or on behalf of the consumer under, or in relation to, the credit agreement which the supplier is not obliged to reimburse under regulation 14(1) shall be reimbursed, except for any sum which, if it had not already been paid, would have to be paid under subparagraph (b);
   (b) the agreement shall continue in force so far as it relates to repayment of the credit and payment of interest, subject to regulation 16; and
   (c) subject to subparagraph (b), the agreement shall cease to be enforceable.

(4) Where any security has been provided under a related credit agreement, the security, so far as it is so provided, shall be treated as never having had effect and any property lodged with the creditor solely for the purposes of the security as so provided shall be returned by him forthwith.

(5) For the purposes of this regulation and regulation 16, a "related credit agreement" means an agreement under which fixed sum credit which fully or partly covers the price under a contract cancelled under regulation 10 is granted—

(a) by the supplier, or

(b) by another person, under an arrangement between that person and the supplier.

(6) For the purposes of this regulation and regulation 16—

(a) "creditor" is a person who grants credit under a related credit agreement;

(b) "fixed sum credit" has the same meaning as in section 10 of the Consumer Credit Act 1974;

(c) "repayment" in relation to credit means repayment of money received by the consumer, and cognate expressions shall be construed accordingly; and

(d) "interest" means interest on money so received.

Repayment of credit and interest after cancellation of a related credit agreement

16.—(1) This regulation applies following the cancellation of a related credit agreement by virtue of regulation 15(1).

(2) If the consumer repays the whole or a portion of the credit—

(a) before the expiry of one month following the cancellation of the credit agreement, or

(b) in the case of a credit repayable by instalments, before the date on which the first instalment is due,

no interest shall be payable on the amount repaid.

(3) If the whole of a credit repayable by instalments is not repaid on or before the date referred to in paragraph (2)(b), the consumer shall not be liable to repay any of the credit except on receipt of a request in writing, signed by the creditor, stating the amounts of the remaining instalments (recalculated by the creditor as nearly as may be in accordance with the agreement and without extending the repayment period), but excluding any sum other than principal and interest.

(4) Where any security has been provided under a related credit agreement the duty imposed on the consumer to repay credit and to pay interest shall not be enforceable before the creditor has discharged any duty imposed on him by regulation 15(4) to return any property lodged with him as security on cancellation.

Restoration of goods by consumer after cancellation

17.—(1) This regulation applies where a contract is cancelled under regulation 10 after the consumer has acquired possession of any goods under the contract other than any goods mentioned in regulation 13(1)(b) to (e).

(2) The consumer shall be treated as having been under a duty throughout the period prior to cancellation—

(a) to retain possession of the goods, and

(b) to take reasonable care of them.

(3) On cancellation, the consumer shall be under a duty to restore the goods to the supplier in accordance with this regulation, and in the meanwhile to retain possession of the goods and take reasonable care of them.

(4) The consumer shall not be under any duty to deliver the goods except at his own premises and in pursuance of a request in writing, or in another durable medium available and accessible to the consumer, from the supplier and given to the consumer either before, or at the time when, the goods are collected from those premises.

(5) If the consumer—

(a) delivers the goods (whether at his own premises or elsewhere) to any person to whom, under regulation 10(1), a notice of cancellation could have been given; or

(b) sends the goods at his own expense to such a person,
he shall be discharged from any duty to retain possession of the goods or restore them to the supplier.

(6) Where the consumer delivers the goods in accordance with paragraph (5)(a), his obligation to take care of the goods shall cease; and if he sends the goods in accordance with paragraph (5)(b), he shall be under a duty to take reasonable care to see that they are received by the supplier and not damaged in transit, but in other respects his duty to take care of the goods shall cease when he sends them.

(7) Where, at any time during the period of 21 days beginning with the day notice of cancellation was given, the consumer receives such a request as is mentioned in paragraph (4), and unreasonably refuses or unreasonably fails to comply with it, his duty to retain possession and take reasonable care of the goods shall continue until he delivers or sends the goods as mentioned in paragraph (5), but if within that period he does not receive such a request his duty to take reasonable care of the goods shall cease at the end of that period.

(8) Where—
(a) a term of the contract provides that if the consumer cancels the contract, he must return the goods to the supplier, and
(b) the consumer is not otherwise entitled to reject the goods under the terms of the contract or by virtue of any enactment,
paragraph (7) shall apply as if for the period of 21 days there were substituted the period of 6 months.

(9) Where any security has been provided in relation to the cancelled contract, the duty to restore goods imposed on the consumer by this regulation shall not be enforceable before the supplier has discharged any duty imposed on him by regulation 14(4) to return any property lodged with him as security on cancellation.

(10) Breach of a duty imposed by this regulation on a consumer is actionable as a breach of statutory duty.

Goods given in part-exchange

18.—(1) This regulation applies on the cancellation of a contract under regulation 10 where the supplier agreed to take goods in part-exchange (the "part-exchange goods") and those goods have been delivered to him.

(2) Unless, before the end of the period of 10 days beginning with the date of cancellation, the part-exchange goods are returned to the consumer in a condition substantially as good as when they were delivered to the supplier, the consumer shall be entitled to recover from the supplier a sum equal to the part-exchange allowance.

(3) In this regulation the part-exchange allowance means the sum agreed as such in the cancelled contract, or if no such sum was agreed, such sum as it would have been reasonable to allow in respect of the part-exchange goods if no notice of cancellation had been served.

(4) Where the consumer recovers from the supplier a sum equal to the part-exchange allowance, the title of the consumer to the part-exchange goods shall vest in the supplier (if it has not already done so) on recovery of that sum.

Performance

19.—(1) Unless the parties agree otherwise, the supplier shall perform the contract within a maximum of 30 days beginning with the day after the day the consumer sent his order to the supplier.

(2) Subject to paragraphs (7) and (8), where the supplier is unable to perform the contract because the goods or services ordered are not available, within the period for performance referred to in paragraph (1) or such other period as the parties agree ("the period for performance"), he shall—
(a) inform the consumer; and
(b) reimburse any sum paid by or on behalf of the consumer under or in relation to the contract to the person by whom it was made.

(3) The reference in paragraph (2)(b) to any sum paid on behalf of the consumer includes any sum paid by a creditor who is not the same person as the supplier under a personal credit agreement with the consumer.

(4) The supplier shall make the reimbursement referred to in paragraph (2)(b) as soon as possible and in any event within a period of 30 days beginning with the day after the day on which the period for performance expired.

(5) A contract which has not been performed within the period for performance shall be treated as if it had not been made, save for any rights or remedies which the consumer has under it as a result of the non-performance.

(6) Where any security has been provided in relation to the contract, the security (so far as it is so provided) shall, where the supplier is unable to perform the contract within the period for performance, be treated as never having had any effect and any property lodged with the supplier solely for the purposes of the security as so provided shall be returned by him forthwith.

(7) Where the supplier is unable to supply the goods or services ordered by the consumer, the supplier may perform the contract for the purposes of these Regulations by providing substitute goods or services (as the case may be) of equivalent quality and price provided that—
(a) this possibility was provided for in the contract;
(b) prior to the conclusion of the contract the supplier gave the consumer the information required by regulation 7(1)(b) and (c) in the manner required by regulation 7(2).

(8) In the case of outdoor leisure events which by their nature cannot be rescheduled, paragraph 2(b) shall not apply where the consumer and the supplier so agree.

Effect of non-performance on related credit agreement
23.   Where a supplier is unable to perform the contract within the period for performance—

(a) regulations 15 and 16 shall apply to any related credit agreement as if the consumer had given a valid notice of cancellation under regulation 10 on the expiry of the period for performance; and
(b) the reference in regulation 15(3)(a) to regulation 14(1) shall be read, for the purposes of this regulation, as a reference to regulation 19(2).

. . .

Inertia selling
24.—(1) Paragraphs (2) and (3) apply if—
(a) unsolicited goods are sent to a person ("the recipient") with a view to his acquiring them;
(b) the recipient has no reasonable cause to believe that they were sent with a view to their being acquired for the purposes of a business; and
(c) the recipient has neither agreed to acquire nor agreed to return them.

(2) The recipient may, as between himself and the sender, use, deal with or dispose of the goods as if they were an unconditional gift to him.

(3) The rights of the sender to the goods are extinguished.

(6) In this regulation—

"acquire" includes hire;

"send" includes deliver;

"sender", in relation to any goods, includes—
(a) any person on whose behalf or with whose consent the goods are sent;
(b) any other person claiming through or under the sender or any person mentioned in paragraph (a); and
(c) any person who delivers the goods; and
"unsolicited" means, in relation to goods sent or services supplied to any person, that they are sent or supplied without any prior request made by or on behalf of the recipient.

(10) This regulation applies only to goods sent and services supplied after the date on which it comes into force.

No contracting-out
25.—(1) A term contained in any contract to which these Regulations apply is void if, and to the extent that, it is inconsistent with a provision for the protection of the consumer contained in these Regulations.

(2) Where a provision of these Regulations specifies a duty or liability of the consumer in certain circumstances, a term contained in a contract to which these Regulations apply, other than a term to which paragraph (3) applies, is inconsistent with that provision if it purports to impose, directly or indirectly, an additional duty or liability on him in those circumstances.

(3) This paragraph applies to a term which requires the consumer to return any goods supplied to him under the contract if he cancels it under regulation 10.

(4) A term to which paragraph (3) applies shall, in the event of cancellation by the consumer under regulation 10, have effect only for the purposes of regulation 14(5) and 17(8).

(5) These Regulations shall apply notwithstanding any contract term which applies or purports to apply the law of a non-Member State if the contract has a close connection with the territory of a Member State.

Consideration of complaints
26.—(1) It shall be the duty of an enforcement authority to consider any complaint made to it about a breach unless—
(a) the complaint appears to the authority to be frivolous or vexatious; or
(b) another enforcement authority has notified the Director that it agrees to consider the complaint.

(2) If an enforcement authority notifies the Director that it agrees to consider a complaint made to another enforcement authority, the first mentioned authority shall be under a duty to consider the complaint.

(3) An enforcement authority which is under a duty to consider a complaint shall give reasons for its decision to apply or not to apply, as the case may be, for an injunction under regulation 27.

(4) In deciding whether or not to apply for an injunction in respect of a breach an enforcement authority may, if it considers it appropriate to do so, have regard to any undertaking given to it or another enforcement authority by or on behalf of any person as to compliance with these Regulations.

Injunctions to secure compliance with these Regulations

27.—(1) The Director or, subject to paragraph (2), any other enforcement authority may apply for an injunction (including an interim injunction) against any person who appears to the Director or that authority to be responsible for a breach.

(2) An enforcement authority other than the Director may apply for an injunction only where—
(a) it has notified the Director of its intention to apply at least fourteen days before the date on which the application is to be made, beginning with the date on which the notification was given; or
(b) the Director consents to the application being made within a shorter period.

(3) The court on an application under this regulation may grant an injunction on such terms as it thinks fit to secure compliance with these Regulations.

Notification of undertakings and orders to the Director

28. An enforcement authority other than the Director shall notify the Director—

(a) of any undertaking given to it by or on behalf of any person who appears to it to be responsible for a breach;
(b) of the outcome of any application made by it under regulation 27 and of the terms of any undertaking given to or order made by the court;
(c) of the outcome of any application made by it to enforce a previous order of the court.

Publication, information and advice

29.—(1) The Director shall arrange for the publication in such form and manner as he considers appropriate of—
(a) details of any undertaking or order notified to him under regulation 28;
(b) details of any undertaking given to him by or on behalf of any person as to compliance with these Regulations;
(c) details of any application made by him under regulation 27, and of the terms of any undertaking given to, or order made by, the court;
(d) details of any application made by the Director to enforce a previous order of the court.

(2) The Director may arrange for the dissemination in such form and manner as he considers appropriate of such information and advice concerning the operation of these Regulations as it may appear to him to be expedient to give to the public and to all persons likely to be affected by these Regulations.

SCHEDULE 1 INDICATIVE LIST OF MEANS OF DISTANCE COMMUNICATION

1. Unaddressed printed matter.

2. Addressed printed matter.

3. Letter.

4.   Press advertising with order form.

5.   Catalogue.

6.   Telephone with human intervention.

7.   Telephone without human intervention (automatic calling machine, audiotext).

8.   Radio.

9.   Videophone (telephone with screen).

10.   Videotext (microcomputer and television screen) with keyboard or touch screen.

11.   Electronic mail.

12.   Facsimile machine (fax).

13.   Television (teleshopping).

As amended by Financial Services (Distance Marketing) Regulations 2004, regulation 25; Consumer Protection (Distance Selling) (Amendment) Regulations 2005, sch. 1; Consumer Protection from Unfair Trading Regulations 2008, sch. 4; Timeshare, Holiday Products, Resale and Exchange Contracts Regulations 2010, sch. 6.

ELECTRONIC COMMERCE (EC DIRECTIVE) REGULATIONS 2002
(2002/2013)

Citation and commencement
1.—(1)   These Regulations may be cited as the Electronic Commerce (EC Directive) Regulations 2002 and except for regulation 16 shall come into force on 21st August 2002.

. . .

Interpretation
2.—(1)   In these Regulations and in the Schedule—

. . .

"consumer" means any natural person who is acting for purposes other than those of his trade, business or profession;

. . .

"the Directive" means Directive 2000/31/EC of the European Parliament and of the Council of 8 June 2000 on certain legal aspects of information society services, in particular electronic commerce, in the Internal Market (Directive on electronic commerce);

. . .

"information society services" (which is summarised in recital 17 of the Directive as covering "any service normally provided for remuneration, at a distance, by means of electronic equipment for the processing (including digital compression) and storage of data, and at the individual request of a recipient of a service") has the meaning set out in Article 2(a) of the Directive, (which refers to Article 1(2) of Directive 98/34/EC of the European Parliament and of the Council of 22 June 1998 laying down a procedure for the provision of information in the field of technical standards and regulations, as amended by Directive 98/48/EC of 20 July 1998);

. . .

"recipient of the service" means any person who, for professional ends or otherwise, uses an information society service, in particular for the purposes of seeking information or making it accessible;

. . .

"service provider" means any person providing an information society service;
"the Treaty" means the treaty establishing the European Community.

. . .

Exclusions

3.—(1) Nothing in these Regulations shall apply in respect of—
   (a) the field of taxation;
   (b) questions relating to information society services covered by the Data Protection Directive and the Telecommunications Data Protection Directive and Directive 2002/58/EC of the European Parliament and of the Council of 12th July 2002 concerning the processing of personal data and the protection of privacy in the electronic communications sector (Directive on privacy and electronic communications);
   (c) questions relating to agreements or practices governed by cartel law; and
   (d) the following activities of information society services—
       (i) the activities of a public notary or equivalent professions to the extent that they involve a direct and specific connection with the exercise of public authority,
       (ii) the representation of a client and defence of his interests before the courts, and
       (iii) betting, gaming or lotteries which involve wagering a stake with monetary value.

(2) These Regulations shall not apply in relation to any Act passed on or after the date these Regulations are made or in relation to the exercise of a power to legislate after that date.

(3) In this regulation—

"cartel law" means so much of the law relating to agreements between undertakings, decisions by associations of undertakings or concerted practices as relates to agreements to divide the market or fix prices;

"Data Protection Directive" means Directive 95/46/EC of the European Parliament and of the Council of 24 October 1995 on the protection of individuals with regard to the processing of personal data and on the free movement of such data; and

"Telecommunications Data Protection Directive" means Directive 97/66/EC of the European Parliament and of the Council of 15 December 1997 concerning the processing of personal data and the protection of privacy in the telecommunications sector.

. . .

Information to be provided where contracts are concluded by electronic means

9.—(1) Unless parties who are not consumers have agreed otherwise, where a contract is to be concluded by electronic means a service provider shall, prior to an order being placed by the recipient of a service, provide to that recipient in a clear, comprehensible and unambiguous manner the information set out in (a) to (d) below—

(a) the different technical steps to follow to conclude the contract;

(b) whether or not the concluded contract will be filed by the service provider and whether it will be accessible;

(c) the technical means for identifying and correcting input errors prior to the placing of the order; and

(d) the languages offered for the conclusion of the contract.

(2) Unless parties who are not consumers have agreed otherwise, a service provider shall indicate which relevant codes of conduct he subscribes to and give information on how those codes can be consulted electronically.

(3) Where the service provider provides terms and conditions applicable to the contract to the recipient, the service provider shall make them available to him in a way that allows him to store and reproduce them.

(4) The requirements of paragraphs (1) and (2) above shall not apply to contracts concluded exclusively by exchange of electronic mail or by equivalent individual communications.

Other information requirements

10. Regulations 6, 7, 8 and 9(1) have effect in addition to any other information requirements in legislation giving effect to EU law.

Placing of the order

11.—(1) Unless parties who are not consumers have agreed otherwise, where the recipient of the service places his order through technological means, a service provider shall—

(a) acknowledge receipt of the order to the recipient of the service without undue delay and by electronic means; and

(b) make available to the recipient of the service appropriate, effective and accessible technical means allowing him to identify and correct input errors prior to the placing of the order.

(2) For the purposes of paragraph (1)(a) above—

(a) the order and the acknowledgement of receipt will be deemed to be received when the parties to whom they are addressed are able to access them; and

(b) the acknowledgement of receipt may take the form of the provision of the service paid for where that service is an information society service.

(3) The requirements of paragraph (1) above shall not apply to contracts concluded exclusively by exchange of electronic mail or by equivalent individual communications.

Meaning of the term "order"

12. Except in relation to regulation 9(1)(c) and regulation 11(1)(b) where "order" shall be the contractual offer, "order" may be but need not be the contractual offer for the purposes of regulations 9 and 11.

Liability of the service provider

13. The duties imposed by regulations 6, 7, 8, 9(1) and 11(1)(a) shall be enforceable, at the suit of any recipient of a service, by an action against the service provider for damages for breach of statutory duty.

Compliance with regulation 9(3)

14.   Where on request a service provider has failed to comply with the requirement in regulation 9(3), the recipient may seek an order from any court having jurisdiction in relation to the contract requiring that service provider to comply with that requirement.

Right to rescind contract

15.   Where a person—
(a)   has entered into a contract to which these Regulations apply, and
(b)   the service provider has not made available means of allowing him to identify and correct input errors in compliance with regulation 11(1)(b),
he shall be entitled to rescind the contract unless any court having jurisdiction in relation to the contract in question orders otherwise on the application of the service provider.

As amended by Electronic Commerce (EC Directive) (Extension) Regulations 2004, reg 3 and Treaty of Lisbon (Changes in Terminology Order) 2011.

ELECTRONIC SIGNATURES REGULATIONS 2002
(2002/318)

Citation and commencement

1.   These Regulations may be cited as the Electronic Signatures Regulations 2002 and shall come into force on 8th March 2002.

Interpretation

2.   In these Regulations—

"advanced electronic signature" means an electronic signature—
(a)   which is uniquely linked to the signatory,
(b)   which is capable of identifying the signatory,
(c)   which is created using means that the signatory can maintain under his sole control, and
(d)   which is linked to the data to which it relates in such a manner that any subsequent change of the data is detectable;

"certificate" means an electronic attestation which links signature-verification data to a person and confirms the identity of that person;

"certification-service-provider" means a person who issues certificates or provides other services related to electronic signatures;

"Directive" means Directive 1999/93/EC of the European Parliament and of the Council on a Community framework for electronic signatures;

"electronic signature" means data in electronic form which are attached to or logically associated with other electronic data and which serve as a method of authentication;

"qualified certificate" means a certificate which meets the requirements in Schedule 1 and is provided by a certification-service-provider who fulfils the requirements in Schedule 2;

"signatory" means a person who holds a signature-creation device and acts either on his own behalf or on behalf of the person he represents;

"signature-creation data" means unique data (including, but not limited to, codes or private cryptographic keys) which are used by the signatory to create an electronic signature;

"signature-creation device" means configured software or hardware used to implement the signature-creation data;

. . .

"voluntary accreditation" means any permission, setting out rights and obligations specific to the provision of certification services, to be granted upon request by the certification-service-provider concerned by the person charged with the elaboration of, and supervision of compliance with, such rights and obligations, where the certification-service-provider is not entitled to exercise the rights stemming from the permission until he has received the decision of that person.

Supervision of certification-service-providers

3.—(1) It shall be the duty of the Secretary of State to keep under review the carrying on of activities of certification-service-providers who are established in the United Kingdom and who issue qualified certificates to the public and the persons by whom they are carried on with a view to her becoming aware of the identity of those persons and the circumstances relating to the carrying on of those activities.

(2) It shall also be the duty of the Secretary of State to establish and maintain a register of certification-service-providers who are established in the United Kingdom and who issue qualified certificates to the public.

(3) The Secretary of State shall record in the register the names and addresses of those certification-service-providers of whom she is aware who are established in the United Kingdom and who issue qualified certificates to the public.

(4) The Secretary of State shall publish the register in such manner as she considers appropriate.

(5) The Secretary of State shall have regard to evidence becoming available to her with respect to any course of conduct of a certification-service-provider who is established in the United Kingdom and who issues qualified certificates to the public and which appears to her to be conduct detrimental to the interests of those persons who use or rely on those certificates with a view to making any of this evidence as she considers expedient available to the public in such manner as she considers appropriate.

Liability of certification-service-providers

4.—(1) Where—

(a) a certification-service-provider either—
(i) issues a certificate as a qualified certificate to the public, or
(ii) guarantees a qualified certificate to the public,
(b) a person reasonably relies on that certificate for any of the following matters—
(i) the accuracy of any of the information contained in the qualified certificate at the time of issue,
(ii) the inclusion in the qualified certificate of all the details referred to in Schedule 1,
(iii) the holding by the signatory identified in the qualified certificate at the time of its issue of the signature-creation data corresponding to the signature-verification data given or identified in the certificate, or

      (iv) the ability of the signature-creation data and the signature-verification data to be used in a complementary manner in cases where the certification-service-provider generates them both,

    (c) that person suffers loss as a result of such reliance, and

    (d) the certification-service-provider would be liable in damages in respect of any extent of the loss—

      (i) had a duty of care existed between him and the person referred to in sub-paragraph (b) above, and

      (ii) had the certification-service-provider been negligent,

then that certification-service-provider shall be so liable to the same extent notwithstanding that there is no proof that the certification-service-provider was negligent unless the certification-service-provider proves that he was not negligent.

(2) For the purposes of the certification-service-provider's liability under paragraph (1) above there shall be a duty of care between that certification-service-provider and the person referred to in paragraph (1)(b) above.

(3) Where—

    (a) a certification-service-provider issues a certificate as a qualified certificate to the public,

    (b) a person reasonably relies on that certificate,

    (c) that person suffers loss as a result of any failure by the certification-service-provider to register revocation of the certificate, and

    (d) the certification-service-provider would be liable in damages in respect of any extent of the loss—

      (i) had a duty of care existed between him and the person referred to in sub-paragraph (b) above, and

      (ii) had the certification-service-provider been negligent,

then that certification-service-provider shall be so liable to the same extent notwithstanding that there is no proof that the certification-service-provider was negligent unless the certification-service-provider proves that he was not negligent.

(4) For the purposes of the certification-service-provider's liability under paragraph (3) above there shall be a duty of care between that certification-service-provider and the person referred to in paragraph (3)(b) above.

Data protection

5.—(1) A certification-service-provider who issues a certificate to the public and to whom this paragraph applies in accordance with paragraph (6) below—

    (a) shall not obtain personal data for the purpose of issuing or maintaining that certificate otherwise than directly from the data subject or after the explicit consent of the data subject, and

    (b) shall not process the personal data referred to in sub-paragraph (a) above—

      (i) to a greater extent than is necessary for the purpose of issuing or maintaining that certificate, or

      (ii) to a greater extent than is necessary for any other purpose to which the data subject has explicitly consented,

unless the processing is necessary for compliance with any legal obligation, to which the certification-service-provider is subject, other than an obligation imposed by contract.

(2) The obligation to comply with paragraph (1) above shall be a duty owed to any data subject who may be affected by a contravention of paragraph (1).

(3) Where a duty is owed by virtue of paragraph (2) above to any data subject, any breach of that duty which causes that data subject to sustain loss or damage shall be actionable by him.

(4) Compliance with paragraph (1) above shall also be enforceable by civil proceedings brought by the Crown for an injunction or for an interdict or for any other appropriate relief or remedy.

(5) Paragraph (4) above shall not prejudice any right that a data subject may have by virtue of paragraph (3) above to bring civil proceedings for the contravention or apprehended contravention of paragraph (1) above.

(6) Paragraph (1) above applies to a certification-service-provider in respect of personal data only if the certification-service-provider is established in the United Kingdom and the personal data are processed in the context of that establishment.

(7) For the purposes of paragraph (6) above, each of the following is to be treated as established in the United Kingdom—
   (a) an individual who is ordinarily resident in the United Kingdom,
   (b) a body incorporated under the law of, or in any part of, the United Kingdom,
   (c) a partnership or other unincorporated association formed under the law of any part of the United Kingdom, and
   (d) any person who does not fall within sub-paragraph (a), (b) or (c) above but maintains in the United Kingdom—
      (i) an office, branch or agency through which he carries on any activity, or
      (ii) a regular practice.

(8) In this regulation—

"data subject" and "personal data" and "processing" shall have the same meanings as in section 1(1) of the Data Protection Act 1998, and

"obtain" shall bear the same interpretation as "obtaining" in section 1(2) of the Data Protection Act 1998.

SCHEDULE 1 (ANNEX I TO THE DIRECTIVE)

REQUIREMENTS FOR QUALIFIED CERTIFICATES

Qualified certificates must contain—

(a) an indication that the certificate is issued as a qualified certificate;

(b) the identification of the certification-service-provider and the State in which it is established;

(c) the name of the signatory or a pseudonym, which shall be identified as such;

(d) provision for a specific attribute of the signatory to be included if relevant, depending on the purpose for which the certificate is intended;

(e) signature-verification data which correspond to signature-creation data under the control of the signatory;

(f) an indication of the beginning and end of the period of validity of the certificate;

(g) the identity code of the certificate;

(h)   the advanced electronic signature of the certification-service-provider issuing it;

(i)   limitations on the scope of use of the certificate, if applicable; and

(j)   limits on the value of transactions for which the certificate can be used, if applicable.

SCHEDULE 2 (ANNEX II TO THE DIRECTIVE)

REQUIREMENTS FOR CERTIFICATION-SERVICE-PROVIDERS ISSUING QUALIFIED CERTIFICATES

Certification-service-providers must—

(a)   demonstrate the reliability necessary for providing certification services;

(b)   ensure the operation of a prompt and secure directory and a secure and immediate revocation service;

(c)   ensure that the date and time when a certificate is issued or revoked can be determined precisely;

(d)   verify, by appropriate means in accordance with national law, the identity and, if applicable, any specific attributes of the person to which a qualified certificate is issued;

(e)   employ personnel who possess the expert knowledge, experience, and qualifications necessary for the services provided, in particular competence at managerial level, expertise in electronic signature technology and familiarity with proper security procedures; they must also apply administrative and management procedures which are adequate and correspond to recognised standards;

(f)   use trustworthy systems and products which are protected against modification and ensure the technical and cryptographic security of the process supported by them;

(g)   take measures against forgery of certificates, and, in cases where the certification-service-provider generates signature-creation data, guarantee confidentiality during the process of generating such data;

(h)   maintain sufficient financial resources to operate in conformity with the requirements laid down in the Directive, in particular to bear the risk of liability for damages, for example, by obtaining appropriate insurance;

(i)   record all relevant information concerning a qualified certificate for an appropriate period of time, in particular for the purpose of providing evidence of certification for the purposes of legal proceedings. Such recording may be done electronically;

(j)   not store or copy signature-creation data of the person to whom the certification-service-provider provided key management services;

(k)   before entering into a contractual relationship with a person seeking a certificate to support his electronic signature inform that person by a durable means of communication of the precise terms and conditions regarding the use of the certificate, including any limitations on its use, the existence of a voluntary accreditation scheme and procedures for complaints and dispute settlement. Such information, which may be transmitted electronically, must be in writing and in readily understandable language. Relevant parts of this information must also be made available on request to third parties relying on the certificate;

(l)   use trustworthy systems to store certificates in a verifiable form so that:
     —   only authorised persons can make entries and changes,

- information can be checked for authenticity,
- certificates are publicly available for retrieval in only those cases for which the certificate-holder's consent has been obtained, and
- any technical changes compromising these security requirements are apparent to the operator.

SALE AND SUPPLY OF GOODS TO CONSUMERS REGULATIONS 2002
(2002/3045)

Title, commencement and extent

1.—(1)   These Regulations may be cited as the Sale and Supply of Goods to Consumers Regulations 2002 and shall come into force on 31st March 2003.

. . .

Interpretation

2.   In these Regulations—

"consumer" means any natural person who, in the contracts covered by these Regulations, is acting for purposes which are outside his trade, business or profession;

"consumer guarantee" means any undertaking to a consumer by a person acting in the course of his business, given without extra charge, to reimburse the price paid or to replace, repair or handle consumer goods in any way if they do not meet the specifications set out in the guarantee statement or in the relevant advertising;

"court" in relation to England and Wales . . . means a county court or the High Court, and in relation to Scotland, the sheriff or the Court of Session;

"enforcement authority" means the Director General of Fair Trading, every local weights and measures authority in Great Britain . . .;

"goods" has the same meaning as in section 61 of the Sale of Goods Act 1979;

"guarantor" means a person who offers a consumer guarantee to a consumer; and

"supply" includes supply by way of sale, lease, hire or hire-purchase.

. . .

Consumer guarantees

15.—(1)   Where goods are sold or otherwise supplied to a consumer which are offered with a consumer guarantee, the consumer guarantee takes effect at the time the goods are delivered as a contractual obligation owed by the guarantor under the conditions set out in the guarantee statement and the associated advertising.

(2)   The guarantor shall ensure that the guarantee sets out in plain intelligible language the contents of the guarantee and the essential particulars necessary for making claims under the guarantee, notably the duration and territorial scope of the guarantee as well as the name and address of the guarantor.

(2A)   The guarantor shall also ensure that the guarantee contains a statement that the consumer has statutory rights in relation to the goods which are sold or supplied and that those rights are not affected by the guarantee.

(3) On request by the consumer to a person to whom paragraph (4) applies, the guarantee shall within a reasonable time be made available in writing or in another durable medium available and accessible to him.

(4) This paragraph applies to the guarantor and any other person who offers to consumers the goods which are the subject of the guarantee for sale or supply.

(5) Where consumer goods are offered with a consumer guarantee, and where those goods are offered within the territory of the United Kingdom, then the guarantor shall ensure that the consumer guarantee is written in English.

(6) If the guarantor fails to comply with the provisions of paragraphs (2) or (5) above, or a person to whom paragraph (4) applies fails to comply with paragraph (3) then the enforcement authority may apply for an injunction or (in Scotland) an order of specific implement against that person requiring him to comply.

(7) The court on application under this Regulation may grant an injunction or (in Scotland) an order of specific implement on such terms as it thinks fit.

As amended by Consumer Protection from Unfair Trading Regulations 2008, sch. 2.

THE DAMAGES (VARIATION OF PERIODICAL PAYMENTS) ORDER 2005
(SI 841)

Citation, commencement, interpretation and extent

1.—(2) In this Order—
    (a) "the Act" means the Damages Act 1996;
    (b) "agreement" means an agreement by parties to a claim or action for damages which settles the claim or action and which provides for periodical payments;
    (c) "damages" means damages for future pecuniary loss in respect of personal injury
    (d) "defence society" means the Medical Defence Union or the Medical Protection Society;
    (e) "variable agreement" means an agreement which contains a provision referred to in Article 9(1);
    (f) "variable order" means an order for periodical payments which contains a provision referred to in Article 2.

(3) In the application of this Order to Northern Ireland—
    (a) "claimant" means plaintiff;
    (b) "permission" means leave;
    (c) "statements of case" means, in the High Court, the writ and pleadings and, in the county court, the civil bill and any notice of intention to defend, defence, notice for particulars, replies and counterclaim.

(4) This Order extends to England and Wales and Northern Ireland.

(5) This Order applies to proceedings begun on or after the date on which it comes into force.

Power to make variable orders

2. If there is proved or admitted to be a chance that at some definite or indefinite time in the future the claimant will—

    (a) as a result of the act or omission which gave rise to the cause of action, develop some serious disease or suffer some serious deterioration, or

    (b) enjoy some significant improvement in his physical or mental condition, where that condition had been adversely affected as a result of that act or omission,

    (c) the court may, on the application of a party, with the agreement of all the parties, or of its own initiative, provide in an order for periodical payments that it may be varied.

Defendant's financial resources

3. Unless—

    (a) the defendant is insured in respect of the claim,

    (b) the source of payment under the order for periodical payments is a government or health service body within the meaning of section 2A(2) of the Act,

    (c) the payment is guaranteed under section 6 of or the Schedule to the Act, or

    (d) the order is made by consent and the claimant is neither a child, nr a person who lacks capacity within the meaning of the Mental Capacity Act 2005 to administer and manage his property and affairs nor a patient within the meaning of Part VII of the Mental Health (Northern Ireland) Order 1996,

    the court will take into account the defendant's likely future financial resources in considering whether to make a variable order.

Award of provisional damages

4. The court may make a variable order in addition to an order for an award of provisional damages made by virtue of section 32A of the Senior Courts Act 1981 or section 51 of the County Courts Act 1984 or, in relation to Northern Ireland, paragraph 10(2)(a) of Schedule 6 to the Administration of Justice Act 1982.

Contents of variable order

5. Where the court makes a variable order—

    (a) the damages must be assessed or agreed on the assumption that the disease, deterioration or improvement will not occur;

    (b) the order must specify the disease or type of deterioration or improvement;

    (c) the order may specify a period within which an application for it to be varied may be made;

    (d) the order may specify more than one disease or type of deterioration or improvement and may, in respect of each, specify a different period within which an application for it to be varied may be made;

    (e) the order must provide that a party must obtain the court's permission to apply for it to be varied, unless the court otherwise orders.

Applications to extend period for applying for permission to vary

6. Where a period is specified under Article 5(c) or (d)—

    (a) a party may make more than one application to extend the period, and such an application is not to be treated as an application to vary a variable order for the purposes of Article 7;

    (b) a party may not make an application for the variable order to be varied after the end of the period specified or such period as extended by the court.

Limit on number of applications to vary

7. A party may make only one application to vary a variable order in respect of each specified disease or type of deterioration or improvement.

Case file

8.—(1) Where the court makes a variable order, the case file documents must be preserved by the court until the end of the period or periods specified under Article 5(c) or (d) or of any extension of them or, if no such period was specified, until the death of the claimant.

(2) The case file documents are, unless the court otherwise orders—
  (a) the judgment as entered;
  (b) the statements of case;
  (c) the schedule of expenses and losses;
  (d) a transcript of the judge's oral judgment;
  (e) all medical reports relied on;
  (f) a transcript of any parts of the claimant's own evidence which the judge considers necessary;
  (g) any subsequent orders.

(3) A court officer must ensure that the case file documents are provided by the parties where necessary and filed on the court file.

(4) Where a variable order has been made, the legal representatives of the parties and, if the parties are insured, their insurers, must also preserve their own case file until the end of the period or periods specified under Article 5(c) or (d) or of any extension of them or, if no such period was specified, until the death of the claimant.

Variable agreements

9.—(1) If there is agreed to be a chance that at some definite or indefinite time in the future the claimant will—
  (a) as a result of the act or omission which gave rise to the cause of action, develop some serious disease or suffer some serious deterioration, or
  (b) enjoy some significant improvement in his physical or mental condition, where that condition had been adversely affected as a result of that act or omission, the parties to an agreement may agree that a party to it may apply to the court subsequently for its terms to be varied.

(2) Where the parties agree to permit an application to vary the terms of an agreement, the agreement—
  (a) must expressly state that a party to it may apply to the court for its terms to be varied;
  (b) must specify the disease or type of deterioration or improvement;
  (c) may specify a period within which an application for it to be varied may be made
  (d) may specify more than one disease or type of deterioration or improvement and may, in respect of each, specify a different period within which an application for it to be varied may be made.

(3) A party who is permitted by an agreement to apply for its terms to be varied must obtain the court's permission to apply for it to be varied.

Application for permission

10.—(1) An application for permission to apply for a variable order or a variable agreement to be varied must be accompanied by evidence—
  (a) that the disease, deterioration or improvement specified in the order or agreement has occurred, and
  (b) that it has caused or is likely to cause an increase or decrease in the pecuniary loss suffered by the claimant.

(2) Where the applicant is the claimant and he knows that the defendant is insured in respect of the claim and the identity of the defendant's insurers, he must serve the application notice on the insurers as well as on the defendant.

(3) Where the applicant is the claimant and he knows that the defendant is a member of a defence society and the identity of the defence society, he must serve the application notice on the defence society as well as on the defendant.

(4) The respondent to the application may, within 28 days after service of the application, serve written representations on the applicant and, if he does, must file them with the court.

(5) The court will deal with the application without a hearing.

Refusal of permission
11.—(1) Where permission is refused, the applicant may, within 14 days after service of the order, request the decision to be reconsidered at a hearing.

(2) No appeal lies from an order refusing permission after reconsideration.

Grant of permission
12.—(1) Where permission is granted, the court will also give directions as to the application for the variation of the variable order or the variable agreement.

(2) Directions must include directions as to—
(a) the date by which the application for variation must be served and filed;
(b) the service and filing of evidence.

(3) No appeal lies from an order granting permission.

Order for variation
13.—(1) On an application for the variation of a variable order or a variable agreement, if the court is satisfied—
(a) that the disease, deterioration or improvement specified in the order or agreement has occurred, and
(b) that it has caused or is likely to cause an increase or decrease in the pecuniary loss suffered by the claimant,
it may order—

(i) the amount of annual payments to be varied, either from the date of the application for permission or from the date of the application to vary if the order did not require the permission of the court for an application to vary, or from such later date as it may specify in the order;
(ii) how each payment is to be made during the year and at what intervals;
(iii) lump sum to be paid in addition to the existing periodical payments.

(2) Section 2(3) to (9) of the Act applies to orders under this Order as it applies to orders for periodical payments.

Application of rules of court
14.   In England and Wales, the Civil Procedure Rules 1998 and in Northern Ireland, rules of court apply to applications under this Order, except where this Order makes provision inconsistent with Civil Procedure Rules or rules of court.

THE GENERAL PRODUCT SAFETY REGULATIONS 2005
(SI NO 1803)

Part 1 GENERAL

Interpretation

2.   In these Regulations—

"the 1987 Act" means the Consumer Protection Act 1987;

"EU law" includes a law in any part of the United Kingdom which implements an EU obligation and does not include Regulation (EC) No 765/2008 of the European Parliament and the Council setting out the requirements for accreditation and market surveillance relating to the marketing of products and repealing Regulation (EEC) No 339/93;

"contravention" includes a failure to comply and cognate expressions shall be construed accordingly;

"dangerous product" means a product other than a safe product;

"distributor" means a professional in the supply chain whose activity does not affect the safety properties of a product;

"enforcement authority" means the Secretary of State, any other Minister of the Crown in charge of a government department, any such department and any authority or council mentioned in regulation 10;

"general safety requirement" means the requirement that only safe products should be placed on the market;

"the GPS Directive" means Directive 2001/95/EC of the European Parliament and of the Council of 3 December 2001 on general product safety;

"magistrates' court" in relation to Northern Ireland, means a court of summary jurisdiction;

"Member State" means a member State, Norway, Iceland or Liechtenstein;

"notice" means a notice in writing;

"officer", in relation to an enforcement authority, means a person authorised in writing to assist the authority in carrying out its functions under or for the purposes of the enforcement of these Regulations and safety notices, except in relation to an enforcement authority which is a government department where it means an officer of that department;

(a)   the manufacturer of a product, when he is established in a Member State and any other person presenting himself as the manufacturer by affixing to the product his name, trade mark or other distinctive mark, or the person who reconditions the product;

(b)   when the manufacturer is not established in a Member State—

(i)   if he has a representative established in a Member State, the representative,

(ii)   into a Member State;

(c)   other professionals in the supply chain, insofar as their activities may affect the safety properties of a product;

"product" means a product which is intended for consumers or likely, under reasonably foreseeable conditions, to be used by consumers even if not intended for them and which is supplied or made available, whether for consideration or not, in the course of a commercial activity and whether it is new, used or reconditioned and includes a product that is supplied or made available to consumers for their own use in the context of providing a service. "product" does not include equipment used by service providers themselves to supply a service to consumers, in particular equipment on which consumers ride or travel which is operated by a service provider;

"recall" means any measure aimed at achieving the return of a dangerous product that has already been supplied or made available to consumers;

"recall notice" means a notice under regulation 15;

"record" includes any book or document and any record in any form;

"requirement to mark" means a notice under regulation 12;

"requirement to warn" means a notice under regulation 13;

"safe product" means a product which, under normal or reasonably foreseeable conditions of use including duration and, where applicable, putting into service, installation and maintenance requirements, does not present any risk or only the minimum risks compatible with the product's use, considered to be acceptable and consistent with a high level of protection for the safety and health of persons. In determining the foregoing, the following shall be taken into account in particular—
(a) assembly and, where applicable, instructions for installation and maintenance,
(b) the effect of the product on other products, where it is reasonably foreseeable that it will be used with other products,
(c) the presentation of the product, the labelling, any warnings and instructions for its use and disposal and any other indication or information regarding the product, and
(d) the categories of consumers at risk when using the product, in particular children and the elderly.

The feasibility of obtaining higher levels of safety or the availability of other products presenting a lesser degree of risk shall not constitute grounds for considering a product to be a dangerous product;

"safety notice" means a suspension notice, a requirement to mark, a requirement to warn, a withdrawal notice or a recall notice;

"serious risk" means a serious risk, including one the effects of which are not immediate, requiring rapid intervention;

"supply" in relation to a product includes making it available, in the context of providing a service, for use by consumers;

"suspension notice" means a notice under regulation 11;

"withdrawal" means any measure aimed at preventing the distribution, display or offer of a dangerous product to a consumer;

"withdrawal notice" means a notice under regulation 14.

Application
3.—(1) Each provision of these Regulations applies to a product in so far as there are no specific provisions with the same objective in rules of EU law governing the safety of the product other than the GPS Directive.

(2) Where a product is subject to specific safety requirements imposed by rules of EU law other than the GPS Directive, these Regulations shall apply only to the aspects and risks or category of risks not covered by those requirements. This means that:

(a) the definition of "safe product" and "dangerous product" in regulation 2 and regulations 5 and 6 shall not apply to such a product in so far as concerns the risks or category of risks covered by the specific rules, and

(b) the remainder of these Regulations shall apply except where there are specific provisions governing the aspects covered by those regulations with the same objective.

4.   These Regulations do not apply to a second-hand product supplied as a product to be repaired or reconditioned prior to being used, provided the supplier clearly informs the person to whom he supplies the product to that effect.

Part 2 OBLIGATIONS OF PRODUCERS AND DISTRIBUTORS

General safety requirement
5.—(1) No producer shall place a product on the market unless the product is a safe product.

(2) No producer shall offer or agree to place a product on the market or expose or possess a product for placing on the market unless the product is a safe product.

(3) No producer shall offer or agree to supply a product or expose or possess a product for supply unless the product is a safe product.

(4) No producer shall supply a product unless the product is a safe product.

Presumption of conformity
6.—(1) Where, in the absence of specific provisions in rules of EU law governing the safety of a product, the product conforms to the specific rules of the law of part of the United Kingdom laying down the health and safety requirements which the product must satisfy in order to be marketed in the United Kingdom, the product shall be deemed safe so far as concerns the aspects covered by such rules.

(2) Where a product conforms to a voluntary national standard of the United Kingdom giving effect to a European standard the reference of which has been published in the Official Journal of the European Union in accordance with Article 4 of the GPS Directive, the product shall be presumed to be a safe product so far as concerns the risks and categories of risk covered by that national standard. The Secretary of State shall publish the reference number of such national standards in such manner as he considers appropriate.

(3) In circumstances other than those referred to in paragraphs (1) and (2), the conformity of a product to the general safety requirement shall be assessed taking into account—

(a) any voluntary national standard of the United Kingdom giving effect to a European standard, other than one referred to in paragraph (2),

(b) other national standards drawn up in the United Kingdom,

(c) recommendations of the European Commission setting guidelines on product safety assessment,

(d) product safety codes of good practice in the sector concerned,

(e) the state of the art and technology, and

(f) reasonable consumer expectations concerning safety.

(4) Conformity of a product with the criteria designed to ensure the general safety requirement is complied with, in particular the provisions mentioned in paragraphs (1) to (3), shall not bar an enforcement authority from exercising its powers under these Regulations in relation to that product where there is evidence that, despite such conformity, it is dangerous.

Other obligations of producers

7.—(1) Within the limits of his activities, a producer shall provide consumers with the relevant information to enable them—

  (a) to assess the risks inherent in a product throughout the normal or reasonably foreseeable period of its use, where such risks are not immediately obvious without adequate warnings, and

  (b) to take precautions against those risks.

(2) The presence of warnings does not exempt any person from compliance with the other requirements of these Regulations.

(3) Within the limits of his activities, a producer shall adopt measures commensurate with the characteristics of the products which he supplies to enable him to—

  (a) be informed of the risks which the products might pose, and

  (b) take appropriate action including, where necessary to avoid such risks, withdrawal, adequately and effectively warning consumers as to the risks or, as a last resort, recall.

(4) The measures referred to in paragraph (3) include—

  (a) except where it is not reasonable to do so, an indication by means of the product or its packaging of—

  (i) the name and address of the producer, and

  (ii) the product reference or where applicable the batch of products to which it belongs; and

  (b) where and to the extent that it is reasonable to do so—

  (i) sample testing of marketed products,

  (ii) investigating and if necessary keeping a register of complaints concerning the safety of the product, and

  (iii) keeping distributors informed of the results of such monitoring where a product presents a risk or may present a risk.

Obligations of distributors

8.—(1) A distributor shall act with due care in order to help ensure compliance with the applicable safety requirements and in particular he—

  (a) shall not expose or possess for supply or offer or agree to supply, or supply, a product to any person which he knows or should have presumed, on the basis of the information in his possession and as a professional, is a dangerous product; and

  shall, within the limits of his activities, participate in monitoring the safety of a product placed on the market, in particular by—

  (i) passing on information on the risks posed by the product,

  (ii) keeping the documentation necessary for tracing the origin of the product,

  (iii) producing the documentation necessary for tracing the origin of the product, and cooperating in action taken by a producer or an enforcement authority to avoid the risks.

(2) Within the limits of his activities, a distributor shall take measures enabling him to cooperate efficiently in the action referred to in paragraph (1)(b)(iii).

Obligations of producers and distributors

9.—(1) Subject to paragraph (2), where a producer or a distributor knows that a product he has placed on the market or supplied poses risks to the consumer that are incompatible with the general safety requirement, he shall forthwith notify an enforcement authority in writing of that information and—

(a) the action taken to prevent risk to the consumer; and

(b) where the product is being or has been marketed or otherwise supplied to consumers outside the United Kingdom, of the identity of each Member State in which, to the best of his knowledge, it is being or has been so marketed or supplied.

(2) Paragraph (1) shall not apply—

(a) in the case of a second-hand product supplied as an antique or as a product to be repaired or reconditioned prior to being used, provided the supplier clearly informed the person to whom he supplied the product to that effect,

(b) in conditions concerning isolated circumstances or products.

(3) In the event of a serious risk the notification under paragraph (1) shall include the following—

(a) information enabling a precise identification of the product or batch of products in question,

(b) a full description of the risks that the product presents,

(c) all available information relevant for tracing the product, and

(d) a description of the action undertaken to prevent risks to the consumer.

(4) Within the limits of his activities, a person who is a producer or a distributor shall co-operate with an enforcement authority (at the enforcement authority's request) in action taken to avoid the risks posed by a product which he supplies or has supplied. Every enforcement authority shall maintain procedures for such co-operation, including procedures for dialogue with the producers and distributors concerned on issues related to product safety.

Part 3 ENFORCEMENT

Enforcement

10.—(1) It shall be the duty of every authority to which paragraph (4) applies to enforce within its area these Regulations and safety notices.

(2) An authority in England or Wales to which paragraph (4) applies shall have the power to investigate and prosecute for an alleged contravention of any provision imposed by or under these Regulations which was committed outside its area in any part of England and Wales.

(3) A district council in Northern Ireland shall have the power to investigate and prosecute for an alleged contravention of any provision imposed by or under these Regulations which was committed outside its area in any part of Northern Ireland.

(4) The authorities to which this paragraph applies are—

(a) in England, a county council, district council, London Borough Council, the Common Council of the City of London in its capacity as a local authority and the Council of the Isles of Scilly,

(b) in Wales, a county council or a county borough council,

(c) in Scotland, a council constituted under section 2 of the Local Government etc. (Scotland) Act 1994,

(d) in Northern Ireland any district council.

(5) An enforcement authority shall in enforcing these Regulations act in a manner proportionate to the seriousness of the risk and shall take due account of the precautionary principle. In this context, it shall encourage and promote voluntary action by producers and distributors. Notwithstanding the foregoing, an enforcement

authority may take any action under these Regulations urgently and without first encouraging and promoting voluntary action if a product poses a serious risk.

Suspension notices

11.—(1) Where an enforcement authority has reasonable grounds for suspecting that a requirement of these Regulations has been contravened in relation to a product, the authority may, for the period needed to organise appropriate safety evaluations, checks and controls, serve a notice ("a suspension notice") prohibiting the person on whom it is served from doing any of the following things without the consent of the authority, that is to say—

    (a) placing the product on the market, offering to place it on the market, agreeing to place it on the market or exposing it for placing on the market, or

    (b) supplying the product, offering to supply it, agreeing to supply it or exposing it for supply.

    (2) A suspension notice served by an enforcement authority in relation to a product may require the person on whom it is served to keep the authority informed of the whereabouts of any such product in which he has an interest.

    (3) A consent given by the enforcement authority for the purposes of paragraph (1) may impose such conditions on the doing of anything for which the consent is required as the authority considers appropriate.

Requirements to mark

12.—(1) Where an enforcement authority has reasonable grounds for believing that a product is a dangerous product in that it could pose risks in certain conditions, the authority may serve a notice ("a requirement to mark") requiring the person on whom the notice is served at his own expense to undertake either or both of the following, as specified in the notice—

    (a) to ensure that the product is marked in accordance with requirements specified in the notice with warnings as to the risks it may present,

    (b) to make the marketing of the product subject to prior conditions as specified in the notice so as to ensure the product is a safe product.

    (2) The requirements referred to in paragraph (1)(a) shall be such as to ensure that the product is marked with a warning which is suitable, clearly worded and easily comprehensible.

Requirements to warn

13. Where an enforcement authority has reasonable grounds for believing that a product is a dangerous product in that it could pose risks for certain persons, the authority may serve a notice ("a requirement to warn") requiring the person on whom the notice is served at his own expense to undertake one or more of the following, as specified in the notice—

    (a) where and to the extent it is practicable to do so, to ensure that any person who could be subject to such risks and who has been supplied with the product be given warning of the risks in good time and in a form specified in the notice,

    (b) to publish a warning of the risks in such form and manner as is likely to bring those risks to the attention of any such person,

    (c) to ensure that the product carries a warning of the risks in a form specified in the notice.

Withdrawal notices

14.—(1) Where an enforcement authority has reasonable grounds for believing that a product is a dangerous product, the authority may serve a notice ("a withdrawal notice") prohibiting the person on whom it is served from doing any of the following things without the consent of the authority, that is to say—

(a) placing the product on the market, offering to place it on the market, agreeing to place it on the market or exposing it for placing on the market, or

(b) supplying the product, offering to supply it, agreeing to supply it or exposing it for supply.

(2) A withdrawal notice may require the person on whom it is served to take action to alert consumers to the risks that the product presents.

(3) In relation to a product that is already on the market, a withdrawal notice may only be served by an enforcement authority where the action being undertaken by the producer or the distributor concerned in fulfilment of his obligations under these Regulations is unsatisfactory or insufficient to prevent the risks concerned to the health and safety of persons.

(4) Paragraph (3) shall not apply in the case of a product posing a serious risk requiring, in the view of the enforcement authority, urgent action.

(5) A withdrawal notice served by an enforcement authority in relation to a product may require the person on whom it is served to keep the authority informed of the whereabouts of any such product in which he has an interest.

(6) A consent given by the enforcement authority for the purposes of paragraph (1) may impose such conditions on the doing of anything for which the consent is required as the authority considers appropriate.

Recall notices

15.—(1) Subject to paragraph (4), where an enforcement authority has reasonable grounds for believing that a product is a dangerous product and that it has already been supplied or made available to consumers, the authority may serve a notice ("a recall notice") requiring the person on whom it is served to use his reasonable endeavours to organise the return of the product from consumers to that person or to such other person as is specified in the notice.

(2) A recall notice may require—

(a) the recall to be effected in accordance with a code of practice applicable to the product concerned, or

(b) the recipient of the recall notice to—

   (i) contact consumers who have purchased the product in order to inform them of the recall, where and to the extent it is practicable to do so,

   (ii) publish a notice in such form and such manner as is likely to bring to the attention of purchasers of the product the risk the product poses and the fact of the recall, or

   (iii) make arrangements for the collection or return of the product from consumers who have purchased it or for its disposal,

   and may impose such additional requirements on the recipient of the notice as are reasonable and practicable with a view to achieving the return of the product from consumers to the person specified in the notice or its disposal.

(3) In determining what requirements to include in a recall notice, the enforcement authority shall take into consideration the need to encourage distributors, users and consumers to contribute to its implementation.

(4) A recall notice may only be issued by an enforcement authority where—

(a) other action which it may require under these Regulations would not suffice to prevent the risks concerned to the health and safety of persons,

(b) the action being undertaken by the producer or the distributor concerned in fulfilment of his obligations under these Regulations is unsatisfactory or insufficient to prevent the risks concerned to the health and safety of persons, and

(c) the authority has given not less than seven days notice to the person on whom the recall notice is to be served of its intention to serve such a notice and where that person has before the expiry of that period by notice required the authority to seek the advice of such person as the Institute determines on the questions of—

    (i) whether the product is a dangerous product,

    (ii) whether the issue of a recall notice is proportionate to the seriousness of the risk, and the authority has taken account of such advice.

(5) Paragraphs (4)(b) and (c) shall not apply in the case of a product posing a serious risk requiring, in the view of the enforcement authority, urgent action.

(6) Where a person requires an enforcement authority to seek advice as referred to in paragraph (4)(c), that person shall be responsible for the fees, costs and expenses of the Institute and of the person appointed by the Institute to advise the authority.

(7) In paragraphs 4(c) and (6) "the Institute" means the charitable organisation with registered number 803725 and known as the Chartered Institute of Arbitrators.

(8) A recall notice served by an enforcement authority in relation to a product may require the person on whom it is served to keep the authority informed of the whereabouts of any such product to which the recall notice relates, so far as he is able to do so.

(9) Where the conditions in paragraph (1) for serving a recall notice are satisfied and either the enforcement authority has been unable to identify any person on whom to serve a recall notice, or the person on whom such a notice has been served has failed to comply with it, then the authority may itself take such action as could have been required by a recall notice.

(10) Where—

(a) an authority has complied with the requirements of paragraph (4); and

(b) the authority has exercised its powers under paragraph (9) to take action following the failure of the person on whom the recall notice has been served to comply with that notice,

then the authority may recover from the person on whom the notice was served summarily as a civil debt, any costs or expenses reasonably incurred by it in undertaking the action referred to in sub-paragraph (b).

(11) A civil debt recoverable under the preceding paragraph may be recovered—

(a) in England and Wales by way of complaint (as mentioned in section 58 of the Magistrates' Courts Act 1980,

(b) in Northern Ireland in proceedings under Article 62 of the Magistrate's Court (Northern Ireland) Order 1981.

Supplementary provisions relating to safety notices

16.—(1) Whenever feasible, prior to serving a safety notice the authority shall give an opportunity to the person on whom the notice is to be served to submit his views to the authority. Where, due to the urgency of the situation, this is not feasible the person shall be given an opportunity to submit his views to the authority after service of the notice.

(2) A safety notice served by an enforcement authority in respect of a product shall—
    (a) describe the product in a manner sufficient to identify it;
    (b) state the reasons on which the notice is based;
    (c) indicate the rights available to the recipient of the notice under these Regulations and (where applicable) the time limits applying to their exercise; and
    (d) in the case of a suspension notice, state the period of time for which it applies.

(3) A safety notice shall have effect throughout the United Kingdom.

(4) Where an enforcement authority serves a suspension notice in respect of a product, the authority shall be liable to pay compensation to a person having an interest in the product in respect of any loss or damage suffered by reason of the notice if—
    (a) there has been no contravention of any requirement of these Regulations in relation to the product; and
    (b) the exercise by the authority of the power to serve the suspension notice was not attributable to any neglect or default by that person.

(5) Where an enforcement authority serves a withdrawal notice in respect of a product, the authority shall be liable to pay compensation to a person having an interest in the product in respect of any loss or damage suffered by reason of the notice if—
    (a) the product was not a dangerous product; and
    (b) the exercise by the authority of the power to serve the withdrawal notice was not attributable to any neglect or default by that person.

(6) Where an enforcement authority serves a recall notice in respect of a product, the authority shall be liable to pay compensation to the person on whom the notice was served in respect of any loss or damage suffered by reason of the notice if—
    (a) the product was not a dangerous product; and
    (b) the exercise by the authority of the power to serve the recall notice was not attributable to any neglect or default by that person.

(7) An enforcement authority may vary or revoke a safety notice which it has served provided that the notice is not made more restrictive for the person on whom it is served or more onerous for that person to comply with.

(8) Wherever feasible prior to varying a safety notice the authority shall give an opportunity to the person on whom the original notice was served to submit his views to the authority.

Appeals against safety notices

17.—(1) A person on whom a safety notice has been served and a person having an interest in a product in respect of which a safety notice (other than a recall notice) has been served may, before the end of the period of 21 days beginning with the day on which the notice was served, apply for an order to vary or set aside the terms of the notice.

(2) On an application under paragraph (1) the court or the sheriff, as the case may be, shall make an order setting aside the notice only if satisfied that—
    (a) in the case of a suspension notice, there has been no contravention in relation to the product of any requirement of these Regulations,
    (b) in the case of a requirement to mark or a requirement to warn, the product is not a dangerous product,
    (c) (i) the product is not a dangerous product, or
        (ii) where applicable, regulation 14(3) has not been complied with by the enforcement authority concerned,
    (d) in the case of a recall notice—
        (i) the product is not a dangerous product, or

(ii) regulation 15(4) has not been complied with,
(c) in any case, the serving of the safety notice concerned was not proportionate to the seriousness of the risk.

(3) On an application concerning the period of time specified in a suspension notice as the period for which it applies, the court or the sheriff, as the case may be, may reduce the period to such period as it considers sufficient for organising appropriate safety evaluations, checks and controls.

(4) On an application to vary the terms of a notice, the court or the sheriff, as the case may be, may vary the requirements specified in the notice as it considers appropriate.

(5) A person on whom a recall notice has been served and who proposes to make an application under paragraph (1) in relation to the notice may, before the end of the period of seven days beginning with the day on which the notice was served, apply to the court or the sheriff for an order suspending the effect of the notice and the court or the sheriff may, in any case where it considers it appropriate to do so, make an order suspending the effect of the notice.

(6) If the court or the sheriff makes an order suspending the effect of a recall notice under paragraph (5) in the absence of the enforcement authority, the enforcement authority may apply for the revocation of such order.

(7) An order under paragraph (5) shall take effect from the time it is made until—
(a) it is revoked under paragraph (6),
(b) where no application is made under paragraph (1) in respect of the recall notice within the time specified in that paragraph, the expiration of that time,
(c) where such an application is made but is withdrawn or dismissed for want of prosecution, the date of dismissal or withdrawal of the application, or
(d) where such an application is made and is not withdrawn or dismissed for want of prosecution, the determination of the application.

(8) Subject to paragraph (6), in Scotland the sheriff's decision under paragraph (5) shall be final.

(9) An application under this regulation may be made—
(a) by way of complaint to any magistrates' court in which proceedings have been brought in England and Wales or Northern Ireland—
(i) in respect of a contravention in relation to the product of a requirement imposed by or under these Regulations; or
(ii) for the forfeiture of the product under regulation 18;
(b) where no such proceedings have been brought, by way of complaint to any magistrates' court; or
(c) in Scotland, by summary application to the sheriff.

(10) A person aggrieved by an order made pursuant to an application under paragraph (1) by a magistrates' court in England, Wales or Northern Ireland, or by a decision of such a court not to make such an order, may appeal against that order or decision—
(a) in England and Wales, to the Crown Court;
(b) in Northern Ireland, to the county court.

Forfeiture: England and Wales and Northern Ireland
18.—(1) An enforcement authority in England and Wales or Northern Ireland may apply for an order for the forfeiture of a product on the grounds that the product is a dangerous product.

(2) An application under paragraph (1) may be made—

    (a) where proceedings have been brought in a magistrates' court for an offence in respect of a contravention in relation to the product of a requirement imposed by or under these Regulations, to that court,

    (b) where an application with respect to the product has been made to a magistrates' court under regulation 17 (appeals against safety notices) or 25 (appeals against detention of products and records) to that court, and

    (c) otherwise, by way of complaint to a magistrates' court.

(3) An enforcement authority making an application under paragraph (1) shall serve a copy of the application on any person appearing to it to be the owner of, or otherwise to have an interest in, the product to which the application relates, together with a notice giving him the opportunity to appear at the hearing of the application to show cause why the product should not be forfeited.

(4) A person on whom notice is served under paragraph (3) and any other person claiming to be the owner of, or otherwise to have an interest in, the product to which the application relates shall be entitled to appear at the hearing of the application and show cause why the product should not be forfeited.

(5) The court shall not make an order for the forfeiture of a product—

    (a) if any person on whom notice is served under paragraph (3) does not appear, unless service of the notice on that person is proved, or

    (b) if no notice under paragraph (3) has been served, unless the court is satisfied that in the circumstances it was reasonable not to serve notice on any person.

(6) The court may make an order for the forfeiture of a product only if it is satisfied that the product is a dangerous product.

(7) Any person aggrieved by an order made by a magistrates' court for the forfeiture of a product, or by a decision of such a court not to make such an order, may appeal against that order or decision—

    (a) in England and Wales, to the Crown Court;

    (b) in Northern Ireland, to the county court.

(8) An order for the forfeiture of a product shall not take effect until the later of—

    (i) the end of the period within which an appeal under paragraph (7) may be brought or within which an application under section 111 of the Magistrates' Courts Act 1980 or article 146 of the Magistrates' Courts (Northern Ireland) Order 1981 (statement of case) may be made, or

    (ii) if an appeal or an application is so made, when the appeal or application is determined or abandoned.

(9) Subject to the following paragraph, where a product is forfeited it shall be destroyed in accordance with such directions as the court may give.

(10) On making an order for forfeiture of a product a magistrates' court may, if it considers it appropriate to do so, direct that the product shall (instead of being destroyed) be delivered up to such person as the court may specify, on condition that the person—

    (a) does not supply the product to any person otherwise than as mentioned in paragraph (11), and

    (b) costs or expenses (including any order under regulation 28) which has been made against him in the proceedings for the order for forfeiture.

(11) The supplies which may be permitted under the preceding paragraph are—

(a) a supply to a person who carries on a business of buying products of the same description as the product concerned and repairing or reconditioning them,

(b) a supply to a person as scrap (that is to say, for the value of materials included in the product rather than for the value of the product itself),

(c) a supply to any person, provided that being so supplied the product is repaired by or on behalf of the person to whom the product was delivered up by direction of the court and that following such repair it is not a dangerous product.

Forfeiture: Scotland

19.—(1) In Scotland a sheriff may make an order for forfeiture of a product on the grounds that the product is a dangerous product—

(a) on an application by a procurator-fiscal made in the manner specified in section 134 of the Criminal Procedure (Scotland) Act 1995, or

(b) where a person is convicted of any offence in respect of a contravention in relation to the product of a requirement imposed by or under these Regulations, in addition to any other penalty which the sheriff may impose.

(2) The procurator-fiscal making an application under paragraph (1)(a) shall serve on any person appearing to him to be the owner of, or otherwise to have an interest in, the product to which the application relates a copy of the application, together with a notice giving him the opportunity to appear at the hearing of the application to show cause why the product should not be forfeited.

(3) Service under paragraph (2) shall be carried out, and such service may be proved, in the manner specified for citation of an accused in summary proceedings under the Criminal Procedure (Scotland) Act 1995.

(4) A person upon whom notice is served under paragraph (2) and any other person claiming to be the owner of, or otherwise to have an interest in, the product to which the application relates shall be entitled to appear at the hearing of the application to show cause why the product should not be forfeited.

(5) The sheriff shall not make an order following an application under paragraph (1) (a)—

(a) if any person on whom notice is served under paragraph (2) does not appear, unless service of the notice on that person is proved; or

(b) if no notice under paragraph (2) has been served, unless the sheriff is satisfied that in the circumstances it was reasonable not to serve notice on any person.

(6) The sheriff may make an order under this regulation only if he is satisfied that the product is a dangerous product.

(7) Where an order for the forfeiture of a product is made following an application by the procurator-fiscal under paragraph (1)(a), any person who appeared, or was entitled to appear to show cause why the product should not be forfeited may, within twenty-one days of the making of the order, appeal to the High Court by Bill of Suspension on the ground of an alleged miscarriage of justice; and section 182(5)(a) to (e) of the Criminal Procedure (Scotland) Act 1995 shall apply to an appeal under this paragraph as it applies to a stated case under Part X of that Act.

(8) An order following an application under paragraph (1)(a) shall not take effect—

(a) until the end of the period of twenty-one days beginning with the day after the day on which the order is made; or

(b) if an appeal is made under paragraph (7) within that period, until the appeal is determined or abandoned.

(9) An order under paragraph (1)(b) shall not take effect—
   (a) until the end of the period within which an appeal against the order could be brought under the Criminal Procedure (Scotland) Act 1995; or
   (b) if an appeal is made within that period, until the appeal is determined or abandoned.

(10) Subject to paragraph (11), a product forfeited under this regulation shall be destroyed in accordance with such directions as the sheriff may give.

(11) If he thinks fit, the sheriff may direct that the product be released to such person as he may specify, on condition that that person does not supply the product to any other person otherwise than as mentioned in paragraph (11) of regulation 18.

Offences

20.—(1) A person who contravenes regulations 5 or 8(1)(a) shall be guilty of an offence and liable on conviction on indictment to imprisonment for a term not exceeding 12 months or to a fine not exceeding £20,000 or to both, or on summary conviction to imprisonment for a term not exceeding three months or to a fine not exceeding the statutory maximum or to both.

(2) A person who contravenes regulation 7(1), 7(3)(by failing to take any of the measures specified in regulation 7(4)), 8(1)(b)(i), (ii) or (iii) or 9(1) shall be guilty of an offence and liable on summary conviction to imprisonment for a term not exceeding three months or to a fine not exceeding level 5 on the standard scale or to both.

(3) A producer or distributor who does not give notice to an enforcement authority under regulation 9(1) in respect of a product he has placed on the market or supplied commits an offence where it is proved that he ought to have known that the product poses risks to consumers that are incompatible with the general safety requirement and he shall be liable on summary conviction to imprisonment for a term not exceeding three months or to a fine not exceeding level 5 on the standard scale or to both.

(4) A person who contravenes a safety notice shall be guilty of an offence and liable on conviction on indictment to imprisonment for a term not exceeding 12 months or to a fine not exceeding £20,000 or to both, or on summary conviction to imprisonment for a term not exceeding three months or to a fine not exceeding the statutory maximum or to both.

Test purchases

21.—(1) An enforcement authority shall have power to organise appropriate checks on the safety properties of a product, on an adequate scale, up to the final stage of use or consumption and for that purpose may make a purchase of a product or authorise an officer of the authority to make a purchase of a product.

(2) Where a product purchased under paragraph (1) is submitted to a test and the test leads to—
   (a) the bringing of proceedings for an offence in respect of a contravention in relation to the product of any requirement imposed by or under these Regulations or for the forfeiture of the product under regulation 18 or 19, or
   (b) the serving of a safety notice in respect of the product, and
   (c) the authority is requested to do so and it is practicable for the authority to comply with the request,
   then the authority shall allow the person from whom the product was purchased, a person who is a party to the proceedings, on whom the notice was served or who has an interest in the product to which the notice relates, to have the product tested.

Powers of entry and search etc.

22.—(1) An officer of an enforcement authority may at any reasonable hour and on production, if required, of his credentials exercise any of the powers conferred by the following provisions of this regulation.

(2) The officer may, for the purposes of ascertaining whether there has been a contravention of a requirement imposed by or under these Regulations, enter any premises other than premises occupied only as a person's residence and inspect any record or product.

(3) The officer may, for the purpose of ascertaining whether there has been a contravention of a requirement imposed by or under these Regulations, examine any procedure (including any arrangements for carrying out a test) connected with the production of a product.

(4) If the officer has reasonable grounds for suspecting that the product has not been placed on the market or supplied in the United Kingdom since it was manufactured or imported he may for the purpose of ascertaining whether there has been a contravention in relation to the product of a requirement imposed by or under these Regulations—
  (a) require a person carrying on a commercial activity, or employed in connection with a commercial activity, to supply all necessary information relating to the activity, including by the production of records,
  (b) require any record which is stored in an electronic form and is accessible from the premises to be produced in a form—
    (i) in which it can be taken away, and
    (ii) in which it is visible and legible.
  (c) for the purpose of ascertaining (by testing or otherwise) whether there has been any such contravention, seize and detain samples of the product,
  (d) take copies of, or of an entry in, any records produced by virtue of sub-paragraph (a).

(5) If the officer has reasonable grounds for suspecting that there has been a contravention in relation to a product of a requirement imposed by or under these Regulations, he may—
  (a) for the purpose of ascertaining whether there has been any such contravention, require a person carrying on a commercial activity, or employed in connection with a commercial activity, to supply all necessary information relating to the activity, including by the production of records,
  (b) any record which is stored in an electronic form and is accessible from the premises to be produced in a form—
    (i) in which it can be taken away, and
    (ii) in which it is visible and legible,
  (c) for the purpose of ascertaining (by testing or otherwise) whether there has been any such contravention, seize and detain samples of the product,
  (d) take copies of, or of an entry in, any records produced by virtue of sub-paragraph (a).

(6) The officer may seize and detain any products or records which he has reasonable grounds for believing may be required as evidence in proceedings for an offence in respect of a contravention of any requirement imposed by or under these Regulations.

(7) If and to the extent that it is reasonably necessary to do so to prevent a contravention of any requirement imposed by or under these Regulations, the officer may, for the purpose of exercising his power under paragraphs (4) to (6) to seize products or records—

(a) require any person having authority to do so to open any container or to open any vending machine; and

(b) himself open or break open any such container or machine where a

(c) requirement made under sub-paragraph (a) in relation to the container or machine has not been complied with.

Provisions supplemental to regulation 22 and search warrants etc.

23.—(1) An officer seizing any products or records shall, before he leaves the premises, provide to the person from whom they were seized a written notice—

(a) specifying the products (including the quantity thereof) and records seized,

(b) stating the reasons for their seizure, and

(c) explaining the right of appeal under regulation 25.

(2) References in paragraph (1) and regulation 25 to the person from whom something has been seized, in relation to a case in which the power of seizure was exercisable by reason of the product having been found on any premises, are references to the occupier of the premises at the time of the seizure.

(3) If a justice of the peace—

(a) is satisfied by written information on oath that there are reasonable grounds for believing either—

(i) that any products or records which an officer has power to inspect under regulation 22 are on any premises and that their inspection is likely to disclose evidence that there has been a contravention of any requirement imposed by or under these Regulations, or

(ii) that such a contravention has taken place, is taking place or is about to take place on any premises, and

(b) is also satisfied by such information either—

(i) that admission to the premises has been or is likely to be refused and that notice of the intention to apply for a warrant under this paragraph has been given to the occupier, or

(ii) that an application for admission, or the giving of such a notice, would defeat the object of the entry or that the premises are unoccupied or that the occupier is temporarily absent and it might defeat the object of the entry to await his return.

the justice may by warrant under his hand, which shall continue in force for a period of one month, authorise any officer of an enforcement authority to enter the premises, if need be by force.

(4) An officer entering premises by virtue of regulation 22 or a warrant under paragraph (3) may take him such other persons and equipment as may appear to him necessary.

(5) On leaving any premises which a person is authorised to enter by a warrant under paragraph (3), that person shall, if the premises are unoccupied or the occupier is temporarily absent—

(a) leave the premises as effectively secured against trespassers as he found them,

(b) attach a notice such as is mentioned in paragraph (1) in a prominent place at the premises.

(6) Where a product seized by an officer of an enforcement authority under regulation 22 or 23 is submitted to a test, the authority shall inform the person mentioned in paragraph (1) of the result of the test and, if—

(a) proceedings are brought for an offence in respect of a contravention in relation to a product of any requirement imposed by or under these Regulations or for the forfeiture of the product under regulation 18 or 19; or

(b) a safety notice is served in respect of the product

(c) the authority is requested to do so and it is practicable for him to comply with the request,

then the authority shall allow a person who is a party to the proceedings or, on whom the notice was served or who has an interest in the product to which the notice relates to have the product tested.

(7) If a person who is not an officer of an enforcement authority purports to act as such under regulation 22 or under this regulation he shall be guilty of an offence and liable on summary conviction to a fine not exceeding level 5 on the standard scale.

(8) In the application of this section to Scotland, the reference in paragraph (3) to a justice of the peace shall include a reference to a sheriff and the reference to written information on oath shall be construed as a reference to evidence on oath.

(9) In the application of this section to Northern Ireland, the reference in paragraph (3) to a justice of the peace shall include a reference to a lay magistrate and the references to an information on oath shall be construed as a reference to a complaint on oath.

Obstruction of officers

24.—(1) A person who—

(a) intentionally obstructs an officer of an enforcement authority who is acting in pursuance of any provision of regulations 22 or 23; or

(b) intentionally fails to comply with a requirement made of him by an officer of an enforcement authority under any provision of those regulations; or

(c) acting any other assistance or information which the officer may reasonably require of him for the purposes of the exercise of the officer's functions under any provision of those regulations,

shall be guilty of an offence and liable on summary conviction to a fine not exceeding level 5 on the standard scale.

(2) A person shall be guilty of an offence if, in giving any information which is required by him by virtue of paragraph (1)(c)—

(a) he makes a statement which he knows is false in a material particular; or

(b) he recklessly makes a statement which is false in a material particular.

(3) A person guilty of an offence under paragraph (2) shall be liable—

(a) on conviction on indictment, to a fine;

(b) on summary conviction, to a fine not exceeding the statutory maximum.

Appeals against detention of products and records

25.—(1) A person referred to in regulation 23(1) may apply for an order requiring any product or record which is for the time being detained under regulation 22 or 23 by an enforcement authority or by an officer of such an authority to be released to him or to another person.

(2) An application under the preceding paragraph may be made—

(a) to any magistrates' court in which proceedings have been brought in England and Wales or Northern Ireland—

(i) for an offence in respect of a contravention in relation to the product of a requirement imposed by or under these Regulation, or

(ii) for the forfeiture of the product under regulation 18,

(b) where no such proceedings have been brought, by way of complaint to a magistrates' court;

(c) in Scotland, by summary application to the sheriff.

(3) On an application under paragraph (1) to a magistrates' court or to the sheriff, the court or the sheriff may make an order requiring a product or record to be released only if the court or sheriff is satisfied—

(a) that proceedings

    (i) for an offence in respect of any contravention in relation to the product or, in the case of a record, the product to which the record relates, of any requirement imposed by or under these Regulations; or

    (ii) for the forfeiture of the product or, in the case of a record, the product to which the record relate, under regulation 18 or 19,

have not been brought or, having been brought, have been concluded without the product being forfeited; and

(b) where no such proceedings have been brought, that more than six months have elapsed since the product or records was seized.

(4) In determining whether to make an order under this regulation requiring the release of a product or record the court or sheriff shall take all the circumstances into account including the results of any tests on the product which have been carried out by or on behalf of the enforcement authority and any statement made by the enforcement authority to the court or sheriff as to its intention to bring proceedings for an offence in respect of a contravention in relation to the product of any requirement imposed by or under these Regulations.

(5) Where—

(a) more than 12 months have elapsed since a product or records were seized and the enforcement authority has not commenced proceedings for an offence in respect of a contravention in relation to the product (or, in the case of records, the product to which the records relate) of any requirement imposed by or under these Regulations or for the forfeiture of the product under regulation 18 or 19, or

(b) an enforcement authority has brought proceedings for an offence as mentioned in subparagraph (a) and the proceedings were dismissed and all rights of appeal have been exercised or the time for appealing has expired,

the authority shall be under a duty to return the product or records detained under regulation 22 or 23 to the person from whom they were seized.

(6) Where the authority is satisfied that some other person has a better right to a product or record than the person from whom they were seized, the authority shall, instead of the duty in paragraph (5), be under a duty to return it to that other person or, as the case may be, to the person appearing to the authority to have the best right to the product or record in question.

(7) Where different persons claim to be entitled to the return of a product or record that is required to be returned under paragraph (5), then it may be retained for as long as it reasonably necessary for the determination in accordance with paragraph (6) of the person to whom it must be returned.

(8) A person aggrieved by an order made under this regulation by a magistrates' court in England and Wales or Northern Ireland, or by a decision of such a court not to make such an order, may appeal against that order or decision—

(a) in England and Wales, to the Crown Court;

(b) in Northern Ireland, to the county court;

and an order so made may contain such provision as appears to the court to be appropriate for delaying the coming into force of the order pending the making and determination of any appeal (including any application under section 111 of the

Magistrates' Courts Act 1980 or article 146 of the Magistrates' Courts (Northern Ireland) Order 1981 (statement of case)).

Compensation for seizure and detention

26. Where an officer of an enforcement authority exercises any power under regulation 22 or 23 to seize and detain a product, the enforcement authority shall be liable to pay compensation to any person having an interest in the product in respect of any loss or damage caused by reason of the exercise of the power if—
   (a) there has been no contravention in relation to the product of any requirement imposed by or under these Regulations, and
   (b) the exercise of the power is not attributable to any neglect or default by that person.

Recovery of expenses of enforcement

27.—(1) This regulation shall apply where a court—
   (a) convicts a person of an offence in respect of a contravention in relation to a product of any requirement imposed by or under these Regulations, or
   (b) makes an order under regulation 18 or 19 for the forfeiture of a product.

   (2) The court may (in addition to any other order it may make as to costs or expenses) order the person convicted or, as the case may be, any person having an interest in the product to reimburse an enforcement authority for any expenditure which has been or may be incurred by that authority—
   (a) in connection with any seizure or detention of the product by or on behalf of the authority, or
   (b) in connection with any compliance by the authority with directions given by the court for the purposes of any order for the forfeiture of the product.

Power of Secretary of State to obtain information

28.—(1) If the Secretary of State considers that, for the purposes of deciding whether to serve a safety notice, or to vary or revoke a safety notice which he has already served, he requires information or a sample of a product he may serve on a person a notice requiring him:
   (a) to furnish to the Secretary of State, within a period specified in the notice, such information as is specified;
   (b) to produce such records as are specified in the notice at a time and place so specified (and to produce any such records which are stored in any electronic form in a form in which they are visible and legible) and to permit a person appointed by the Secretary of State for that purpose to take copies of the records at that time and place;
   (c) to produce such samples of a product as are specified in the notice at a time and place so specified.

   (2) A person shall be guilty of an offence if he—
   (a) fails, without reasonable cause, to comply with a notice served on him under paragraph (1); or
   (b) in purporting to comply with a requirement which by virtue of paragraph (1)(a) or (b) is contained in such a notice—
      (i) furnishes information or records which he knows are false in a material particular, or
      (ii) recklessly furnishes information or records which are false in a material particular.
   (3) A person guilty of an offence under paragraph (2) shall—

(a) in the case of an offence under sub-paragraph (a) of that paragraph, be liable on summary conviction to a fine not exceeding level 5 on the standard scale; and

(b) in the case of an offence under sub-paragraph (b) of that paragraph, be liable—
   (i) on conviction on indictment, to a fine;
   (ii) on summary conviction, to a fine not exceeding the statutory maximum.

Defence of due diligence

29.—(1) Subject to the following provisions of this regulation, in proceedings against a person for an offence under these Regulations it shall be a defence for that person to show that he took all reasonable steps and exercised all due diligence to avoid committing the offence.

(2) Where in any proceedings against any person for such an offence the defence provided by paragraph (1) involves an allegation that the commission of the offence was due—
(a) to the act or default of another, or
(b) to reliance on information given by another,
that person shall not, without the leave of the court, be entitled to rely on the defence unless, not less than seven clear days before, in England, Wales and Northern Ireland, the hearing of the proceedings or, in Scotland, the trial diet, he has served a notice under paragraph (3) on the person bringing the proceedings.

(3) A notice under this paragraph shall give such information identifying or assisting in the identification of the person who—
(a) committed the act or default, or
(b) gave the information,
as is in the possession of the person serving the notice at the time he serves it.

(4) A person may not rely on the defence provided by paragraph (1) by reason of his reliance on information supplied by another, unless he shows that it was reasonable in all the circumstances to have relied on the information, having regard in particular—
(a) to the steps which he took, and those which might reasonably have been taken, for the purpose of verifying the information; and
(b) to whether he had any reason to disbelieve the information.

Liability of person other than principal offender

31.—(1) Where the commission by a person of an offence under these Regulations is due to an act or default committed by some other person in the course of a commercial activity of his, the other person shall be guilty of the offence and may be proceeded against and punished by virtue of this paragraph whether or not proceedings are taken against the first-mentioned person.

(2) Where a body corporate is guilty of an offence under these Regulations (including where it is so guilty by virtue of paragraph (1)) in respect of any act or default which is shown to have been committed with the consent or connivance of, or to be attributable to any neglect on the part of, any director, manager, secretary or other similar officer of the body corporate or any person who was purporting to act in any such capacity he, as well as the body corporate, shall be guilty of that offence and shall be liable to be proceeded against and punished accordingly.

(3) Where the affairs of a body corporate are managed by its members, paragraph (2) shall apply in relation to the acts and defaults of a member in connection with his functions of management as if he were a director of the body corporate.

(4) Where a Scottish partnership is guilty of an offence under these Regulations (including where it is so guilty by virtue of paragraph (1)) in respect of any act or default which is shown to have been committed with the consent or connivance of, or to be attributable to any neglect on the part of, a partner in the partnership, he, as well as the partnership, shall be guilty of that offence and shall be liable to be proceeded against and punished accordingly.

Part 4 MISCELLANEOUS

Duty to notify Secretary of State and Commission

33.—(1) An enforcement authority which has received a notification under regulation 9(1) shall immediately pass the same on to the Secretary of State, who shall immediately pass it on to the competent authorities appointed for the purpose in the Member States where the product in question is or has been marketed or otherwise supplied to consumers.

(2) Where an enforcement authority takes a measure which restricts the placing on the market of a product, or requires its withdrawal or recall, it shall immediately notify the Secretary of State, specifying its reasons for taking the action. It shall also immediately notify the Secretary of State of any modification or lifting of such a measure.

(3) On receiving a notification under paragraph (2), or if he takes a measure which restricts the placing on the market of a product, or requires its withdrawal or recall, the Secretary of State shall (to the extent that such notification is not required under article 12 of the GPS Directive or any other Community legislation) immediately notify the European Commission of the measure taken, specifying the reasons for taking it. The Secretary of State shall also immediately notify the European Commission of any modification or lifting of such a measure. If the Secretary of State considers that the effects of the risk do not or cannot go beyond the territory of the United Kingdom, he shall notify the European Commission of the measure concerned insofar as it involves information likely to be of interest to Member States from the product safety standpoint, and in particular if it is in response to a new risk which has not yet been reported in other notifications.

(4) Where an enforcement authority adopts or decides to adopt, recommend or agree with producers and distributors, whether on a compulsory or voluntary basis, a measure or action to prevent, restrict or impose specific conditions on the possible marketing or use of a product (other than a pharmaceutical product) by reason of a serious risk, it shall immediately notify the Secretary of State. It shall also immediately notify the Secretary of State of any modification or withdrawal of any such measure or action.

(5) On receiving a notification under paragraph (4), or if he adopts or decides to adopt, recommend or agree with producers and distributors, whether on a compulsory or voluntary basis, a measure or action to prevent, restrict or impose specific conditions on the possible marketing or use of a product (other than a pharmaceutical product) by reason of a serious risk, the Secretary of State shall immediately notify the European Commission of it through the Community Rapid Information System, known as RAPEX. The Secretary of State shall also inform the European Commission without delay of any modification or withdrawal of any such measure or action.

(6) If the Secretary of State considers that the effects of the risk do not or cannot go beyond the territory of the United Kingdom, he shall notify the European Commission of the measures or action concerned insofar as they involve information

likely to be of interest to Member States of the European Union from the product safety standpoint, and in particular if they are in response to a new risk which has not been reported in other notifications.

(7) Before deciding to adopt such a measure or take such an action as is referred to in paragraph (5), the Secretary of State may pass on to the European Commission any information in his possession regarding the existence of a serious risk. Where he does so, he must inform the European Commission, within 45 days of the day of passing the information to it, whether he confirms or modifies that information.

(8) Upon receipt of a notification from the European Commission under article 12(2) of the GPS Directive, the Secretary of State shall notify the Commission of the following—
    (a) whether the product the subject of the notification has been marketed in the United Kingdom;
    (b) what measure concerning the product the enforcement authorities in the United Kingdom may be adopting, stating the reasons, including any differing assessment of risk or any other special circumstance justifying the decision as to the measure, in particular lack of action or follow-up; and
    (c) any relevant supplementary information he has obtained on the risk involved, including the results of any test or analysis carried out.

(9) The Secretary of State shall notify the European Commission without delay of any modification or withdrawal of any measures notified to it under paragraph (8)(b).

Implementation of Commission decisions

35.—(1) This regulation applies where the Commission adopts a decision pursuant to article 13 of the GPS Directive.

(2) The Secretary of State shall—
    (a) take such action under these Regulations, or
    (b) direct another enforcement authority to take such action under these Regulations as is necessary to comply with the decision.

(3) Where an enforcement authority serves a safety notice pursuant to paragraph (2), the following provisions of these Regulations shall not apply in relation to that notice, namely regulations 14(3), 15(4) to (6) and 16(1), 16(2)(c) and (d), 16(5) to (7) and 17.

(4) Unless the Commission's decision provides otherwise, export from the Community of a dangerous product which is the subject of such a decision is prohibited with effect from the date the decision comes into force.

(5) The enforcement of the prohibition in paragraph (4) shall be treated as an assigned matter within the meaning of section 1(1) of the Customs and Excise Management Act 1979.

(6) The measures necessary to implement the decision shall be taken within 20 days, unless the decision specifies a different period.

(7) The Secretary of State or, where the Secretary of State has directed another enforcement authority to take action under paragraph (2)(b), that enforcement authority shall, within one month, give the parties concerned an opportunity to submit their views and shall inform the Commission accordingly.

Civil proceedings
42.   These Regulations shall not be construed as conferring any right of action in civil proceedings in respect of any loss or damage suffered in consequence of a contravention of these Regulations.

THE CONSUMER PROTECTION FROM UNFAIR TRADING REGULATIONS 2008
(2008/1277)

Part 1 GENERAL

Citation and commencement
1.   These Regulations may be cited as the Consumer Protection from Unfair Trading Regulations 2008 and shall come into force on 26th May 2008.

Interpretation
2.—(1) In these Regulations—

"average consumer" shall be construed in accordance with paragraphs (2) to (6);

"business" includes a trade, craft or profession;

"code of conduct" means an agreement or set of rules (which is not imposed by legal or administrative requirements), which defines the behaviour of traders who undertake to be bound by it in relation to one or more commercial practices or business sectors;

"code owner" means a trader or a body responsible for—
(a) the formulation and revision of a code of conduct; or
(b) monitoring compliance with the code by those who have undertaken to be bound by it;

"commercial practice" means any act, omission, course of conduct, representation or commercial communication (including advertising and marketing) by a trader, which is directly connected with the promotion, sale or supply of a product to or from consumers, whether occurring before, during or after a commercial transaction (if any) in relation to a product;

"consumer" means any individual who in relation to a commercial practice is acting for purposes which are outside his business;

"enforcement authority" means the OFT, every local weights and measures authority in Great Britain (within the meaning of section 69 of the Weights and Measures Act 1985) . . .;

"goods" includes ships, aircraft, animals, things attached to land and growing crops;

"invitation to purchase" means a commercial communication which indicates characteristics of the product and the price in a way appropriate to the means of that commercial communication and thereby enables the consumer to make a purchase;

"materially distort the economic behaviour" means in relation to an average consumer, appreciably to impair the average consumer's ability to make an informed decision thereby causing him to take a transactional decision that he would not have taken otherwise;

"OFT" means the Office of Fair Trading;

"premises" includes any place and any stall, vehicle, ship or aircraft;

"product" means any goods or service and includes immovable property, rights and obligations;

"professional diligence" means the standard of special skill and care which a trader may reasonably be expected to exercise towards consumers which is commensurate with either—
(a) honest market practice in the trader's field of activity, or
(b) the general principle of good faith in the trader's field of activity;

"ship" includes any boat and any other description of vessel used in navigation;

"trader" means any person who in relation to a commercial practice is acting for purposes relating to his business, and anyone acting in the name of or on behalf of a trader;

"transactional decision" means any decision taken by a consumer, whether it is to act or to refrain from acting, concerning—
(a) whether, how and on what terms to purchase, make payment in whole or in part for, retain or dispose of a product; or
(b) whether, how and on what terms to exercise a contractual right in relation to a product.

(2) In determining the effect of a commercial practice on the average consumer where the practice reaches or is addressed to a consumer or consumers account shall be taken of the material characteristics of such an average consumer including his being reasonably well informed, reasonably observant and circumspect.

(3) Paragraphs (4) and (5) set out the circumstances in which a reference to the average consumer shall be read as in addition referring to the average member of a particular group of consumers.

(4) In determining the effect of a commercial practice on the average consumer where the practice is directed to a particular group of consumers, a reference to the average consumer shall be read as referring to the average member of that group.

(5) In determining the effect of a commercial practice on the average consumer—
(a) where a clearly identifiable group of consumers is particularly vulnerable to the practice or the underlying product because of their mental or physical infirmity, age or credulity in a way which the trader could reasonably be expected to foresee, and
(b) where the practice is likely to materially distort the economic behaviour only of that group,
a reference to the average consumer shall be read as referring to the average member of that group.

(6) Paragraph (5) is without prejudice to the common and legitimate advertising practice of making exaggerated statements which are not meant to be taken literally.

Part 2 PROHIBITIONS

Prohibition of unfair commercial practices

3.—(1) Unfair commercial practices are prohibited.

(2) Paragraphs (3) and (4) set out the circumstances when a commercial practice is unfair.

(3) A commercial practice is unfair if—
   (a) it contravenes the requirements of professional diligence; and
   (b) it materially distorts or is likely to materially distort the economic behaviour of the average consumer with regard to the product.

(4) A commercial practice is unfair if—
   (a) it is a misleading action under the provisions of regulation 5;
   (b) it is a misleading omission under the provisions of regulation 6;
   (c) it is aggressive under the provisions of regulation 7; or
   (d) it is listed in Schedule 1.

Prohibition of the promotion of unfair commercial practices

4. The promotion of any unfair commercial practice by a code owner in a code of conduct is prohibited.

Misleading actions

5.—(1) A commercial practice is a misleading action if it satisfies the conditions in either paragraph (2) or paragraph (3).

(2) A commercial practice satisfies the conditions of this paragraph—
   (a) if it contains false information and is therefore untruthful in relation to any of the matters in paragraph (4) or if it or its overall presentation in any way deceives or is likely to deceive the average consumer in relation to any of the matters in that paragraph, even if the information is factually correct; and
   (b) it causes or is likely to cause the average consumer to take a transactional decision he would not have taken otherwise.

(3) A commercial practice satisfies the conditions of this paragraph if—
   (a) it concerns any marketing of a product (including comparative advertising) which creates confusion with any products, trade marks, trade names or other distinguishing marks of a competitor; or
   (b) it concerns any failure by a trader to comply with a commitment contained in a code of conduct which the trader has undertaken to comply with, if—
      (i) the trader indicates in a commercial practice that he is bound by that code of conduct, and
      (ii) the commitment is firm and capable of being verified and is not aspirational,
   and it causes or is likely to cause the average consumer to take a transactional decision he would not have taken otherwise, taking account of its factual context and of all its features and circumstances.

(4) The matters referred to in paragraph (2)(a) are—
   (a) the existence or nature of the product;
   (b) the main characteristics of the product (as defined in paragraph 5);
   (c) the extent of the trader's commitments;
   (d) the motives for the commercial practice;
   (e) the nature of the sales process;
   (f) any statement or symbol relating to direct or indirect sponsorship or approval of the trader or the product;

(g) the price or the manner in which the price is calculated;

(h) the existence of a specific price advantage;

(i) the need for a service, part, replacement or repair;

(j) the nature, attributes and rights of the trader (as defined in paragraph 6);

(k) the consumer's rights or the risks he may face.

(5) In paragraph (4)(b), the "main characteristics of the product" include—

(a) availability of the product;

(b) benefits of the product;

(c) risks of the product;

(d) execution of the product;

(e) composition of the product;

(f) accessories of the product;

(g) after-sale customer assistance concerning the product;

(h) the handling of complaints about the product;

(i) the method and date of manufacture of the product;

(j) the method and date of provision of the product;

(k) delivery of the product;

(l) fitness for purpose of the product;

(m) usage of the product;

(n) quantity of the product;

(o) specification of the product;

(p) geographical or commercial origin of the product;

(q) results to be expected from use of the product; and

(r) results and material features of tests or checks carried out on the product.

(6) In paragraph (4)(j), the "nature, attributes and rights" as far as concern the trader include the trader's—

(a) identity;

(b) assets;

(c) qualifications;

(d) status;

(e) approval;

(f) affiliations or connections;

(g) ownership of industrial, commercial or intellectual property rights; and

(h) awards and distinctions.

(7) In paragraph (4)(k) "consumer's rights" include rights the consumer may have under Part 5A of the Sale of Goods Act 1979 or Part 1B of the Supply of Goods and Services Act 1982.

Misleading omissions

6.—(1) A commercial practice is a misleading omission if, in its factual context, taking account of the matters in paragraph (2)—

(a) the commercial practice omits material information,

(b) the commercial practice hides material information,

(c) the commercial practice provides material information in a manner which is unclear, unintelligible, ambiguous or untimely, or

(d) the commercial practice fails to identify its commercial intent, unless this is already apparent from the context,

and as a result it causes or is likely to cause the average consumer to take a transactional decision he would not have taken otherwise.

(2) The matters referred to in paragraph (1) are—

(a) all the features and circumstances of the commercial practice;

(b) the limitations of the medium used to communicate the commercial practice (including limitations of space or time); and

(c) where the medium used to communicate the commercial practice imposes limitations of space or time, any measures taken by the trader to make the information available to consumers by other means.

(3) In paragraph (1) "material information" means—

(a) the information which the average consumer needs, according to the context, to take an informed transactional decision; and

(b) any information requirement which applies in relation to a commercial communication as a result of a Community obligation.

(4) Where a commercial practice is an invitation to purchase, the following information will be material if not already apparent from the context in addition to any other information which is material information under paragraph (3)—

(a) the main characteristics of the product, to the extent appropriate to the medium by which the invitation to purchase is communicated and the product;

(b) the identity of the trader, such as his trading name, and the identity of any other trader on whose behalf the trader is acting;

(c) the geographical address of the trader and the geographical address of any other trader on whose behalf the trader is acting;

(d) either—

(i) the price, including any taxes; or

(ii) where the nature of the product is such that the price cannot reasonably be calculated in advance, the manner in which the price is calculated;

(e) where appropriate, either—

(i) all additional freight, delivery or postal charges; or

(ii) where such charges cannot reasonably be calculated in advance, the fact that such charges may be payable;

(f) the following matters where they depart from the requirements of professional diligence—

(i) arrangements for payment,

(ii) arrangements for delivery,

(iii) arrangements for performance,

(iv) complaint handling policy;

(g) for products and transactions involving a right of withdrawal or cancellation, the existence of such a right.

Aggressive commercial practices

7.—(1) A commercial practice is aggressive if, in its factual context, taking account of all of its features and circumstances—

(a) it significantly impairs or is likely significantly to impair the average consumer's freedom of choice or conduct in relation to the product concerned through the use of harassment, coercion or undue influence; and

(b) it thereby causes or is likely to cause him to take a transactional decision he would not have taken otherwise.

(2) In determining whether a commercial practice uses harassment, coercion or undue influence account shall be taken of—

(a) its timing, location, nature or persistence;

(b) the use of threatening or abusive language or behaviour;

(c) the exploitation by the trader of any specific misfortune or circumstance of such gravity as to impair the consumer's judgment, of which the trader is aware, to influence the consumer's decision with regard to the product;

    (d) any onerous or disproportionate non-contractual barrier imposed by the trader where a consumer wishes to exercise rights under the contract, including rights to terminate a contract or to switch to another product or another trader; and

    (e) any threat to take any action which cannot legally be taken.

  (3) In this regulation—

    (a) "coercion" includes the use of physical force; and

    (b) "undue influence" means exploiting a position of power in relation to the consumer so as to apply pressure, even without using or threatening to use physical force, in a way which significantly limits the consumer's ability to make an informed decision.

Part 3 OFFENCES

Offences relating to unfair commercial practices

8.—(1) A trader is guilty of an offence if—

    (a) he knowingly or recklessly engages in a commercial practice which contravenes the requirements of professional diligence under regulation 3(3)(a); and

    (b) the practice materially distorts or is likely to materially distort the economic behaviour of the average consumer with regard to the product under regulation 3(3)(b).

  (2) For the purposes of paragraph (1)(a) a trader who engages in a commercial practice without regard to whether the practice contravenes the requirements of professional diligence shall be deemed recklessly to engage in the practice, whether or not the trader has reason for believing that the practice might contravene those requirements.

9. A trader is guilty of an offence if he engages in a commercial practice which is a misleading action under regulation 5 otherwise than by reason of the commercial practice satisfying the condition in regulation 5(3)(b).

10. A trader is guilty of an offence if he engages in a commercial practice which is a misleading omission under regulation 6.

11. A trader is guilty of an offence if he engages in a commercial practice which is aggressive under regulation 7.

12. A trader is guilty of an offence if he engages in a commercial practice set out in any of paragraphs 1 to 10, 12 to 27 and 29 to 31 of Schedule 1.

Penalty for offences

13. A person guilty of an offence under regulation 8, 9, 10, 11 or 12 shall be liable—

    (a) on summary conviction, to a fine not exceeding the statutory maximum; or

    (b) on conviction on indictment, to a fine or imprisonment for a term not exceeding two years or both.

Time limit for prosecution

14.—(1) No proceedings for an offence under these Regulations shall be commenced after—

    (a) the end of the period of three years beginning with the date of the commission of the offence, or

    (b) the end of the period of one year beginning with the date of discovery of the offence by the prosecutor,

whichever is earlier.

. . .

Offences committed by bodies of persons

15.—(1) Where an offence under these Regulations committed by a body corporate is proved—

    (a) to have been committed with the consent or connivance of an officer of the body, or

    (b) to be attributable to any neglect on his part,

the officer as well as the body corporate is guilty of the offence and liable to be proceeded against and punished accordingly.

    (2) In paragraph (1) a reference to an officer of a body corporate includes a reference to—

    (a) a director, manager, secretary or other similar officer; and

    (b) a person purporting to act as a director, manager, secretary or other similar officer.

    (3) Where an offence under these Regulations committed by a Scottish partnership is proved—

    (a) to have been committed with the consent or connivance of a partner, or

    (b) to be attributable to any neglect on his part,

the partner as well as the partnership is guilty of the offence and liable to be proceeded against and punished accordingly.

    (4) In paragraph (3) a reference to a partner includes a person purporting to act as a partner.

Offence due to the default of another person

16.—(1) This regulation applies where a person "X"—

    (a) commits an offence under regulation 9, 10, 11 or 12, or

    (b) would have committed an offence under those regulations but for a defence under regulation 17 or 18,

and the commission of the offence, or of what would have been an offence but for X being able to rely on a defence under regulation 17 or 18, is due to the act or default of some other person "Y".

    (2) Where this regulation applies Y is guilty of the offence, subject to regulations 17 and 18, whether or not Y is a trader and whether or not Y's act or default is a commercial practice.

    (3) Y may be charged with and convicted of the offence by virtue of paragraph (2) whether or not proceedings are taken against X.

Due diligence defence

17.—(1) In any proceedings against a person for an offence under regulation 9, 10, 11 or 12 it is a defence for that person to prove—

    (a) that the commission of the offence was due to—

        (i) a mistake;

        (ii) reliance on information supplied to him by another person;

        (iii) the act or default of another person;

        (iv) an accident; or

        (v) another cause beyond his control; and

    (b) that he took all reasonable precautions and exercised all due diligence to avoid the commission of such an offence by himself or any person under his control.

    (2) A person shall not be entitled to rely on the defence provided by paragraph (1) by reason of the matters referred to in paragraph (ii) or (iii) of paragraph (1)(a) without leave of the court unless—

(a) he has served on the prosecutor a notice in writing giving such information identifying or assisting in the identification of that other person as was in his possession; and

(b) the notice is served on the prosecutor at least seven clear days before the date of the hearing.

Innocent publication of advertisement defence

18.—(1) In any proceedings against a person for an offence under regulation 9, 10, 11 or 12 committed by the publication of an advertisement it shall be a defence for a person to prove that—

(a) he is a person whose business it is to publish or to arrange for the publication of advertisements;

(b) he received the advertisement for publication in the ordinary course of business; and

(c) he did not know and had no reason to suspect that its publication would amount to an offence under the regulation to which the proceedings relate.

(2) In paragraph (1) "advertisement" includes a catalogue, a circular and a price list.

Part 4 ENFORCEMENT

Duty to enforce

19.—(1) It shall be the duty of every enforcement authority to enforce these Regulations.

(2) Where the enforcement authority is a local weights and measures authority the duty referred to in paragraph (1) shall apply to the enforcement of these Regulations within the authority's area.

. . .

(4) In determining how to comply with its duty of enforcement every enforcement authority shall have regard to the desirability of encouraging control of unfair commercial practices by such established means as it considers appropriate having regard to all the circumstances of the particular case.

(5) Nothing in this regulation shall authorise any enforcement authority to bring proceedings in Scotland for an offence.

Power to make test purchases

20. An enforcement authority may or may authorise any of its officers on its behalf to—

(a) make a purchase of a product, or

(b) enter into an agreement to secure the provision of a product,

for the purposes of determining whether these Regulations are being complied with.

Power of entry and investigation, etc.

21.—(1) A duly authorised officer of an enforcement authority may at all reasonable hours exercise the following powers—

(a) he may, for the purposes of ascertaining whether a breach of these Regulations has been committed, inspect any goods and enter any premises other than premises used only as a dwelling;

(b) if he has reasonable cause to suspect that a breach of these Regulations has been committed, he may, for the purpose of ascertaining whether it has been committed, require any trader to produce any documents relating to his business and may take copies of, or of any entry in, any such document;

    (c)   if he has reasonable cause to believe that a breach of these Regulations has been committed, he may seize and detain any goods for the purpose of ascertaining, by testing or otherwise, whether the breach has been committed; and

    (d)   he may seize and detain goods or documents which he has reason to believe may be required as evidence in proceedings for a breach of these Regulations.

(2)   If and to the extent that it is reasonably necessary to secure that the provisions of these Regulations are observed, the officer may for the purpose of exercising his powers under paragraphs (1)(c) and (d) to seize goods or documents—

    (a)   require any person having authority to do so to break open any container or open any vending machine; and

    (b)   himself open or break open any such container or open any vending machine where a requirement made under sub-paragraph (a) in relation to the container or vending machine has not been complied with.

(3)   An officer seizing any goods or documents in exercise of his powers under this regulation shall—

    (a)   inform the person from whom they are seized, and,

    (b)   where goods are seized from a vending machine, inform—

        (i)   the person whose name and address are stated on the machine as being the proprietor's; or

        (ii) if there is no such name or address stated on the machine the occupier of the premises on which the machine stands or to which it is affixed,

    that the goods or documents have been so seized.

(4)   In this regulation "document" includes information recorded in any form.

(5)   The reference in paragraph (1)(b) to the production of documents is, in the case of a document which contains information recorded otherwise than in legible form, a reference to the production of a copy of the information in legible form.

(6)   An officer seeking to exercise a power under this regulation must produce evidence of his identity and authority to a person (if there is one) who appears to the officer to be the occupier of the premises.

(7)   Where an officer seizes goods or documents in exercise of a power under this regulation they may not be detained—

    (a)   for a period of more than 3 months; or

    (b)   where the goods or documents are reasonably required by the enforcement authority in connection with the enforcement of these Regulations, for longer than they are so required.

(8)   An officer entering any premises under this regulation may take with him such other persons and such equipment as may appear to him to be necessary.

(9)   Nothing in this regulation or in regulation 22 gives any power to an officer of an enforcement authority—

    (a)   to require any person to produce, or

    (b)   to seize from another person,

    any document which the other person would be entitled to refuse to produce in proceedings in the High Court on the grounds of legal professional privilege or (in Scotland) in proceedings in the Court of Session on the grounds of confidentiality of communications.

(10) In paragraph (9) "communications" means—

    (a)   communications between a professional legal adviser and his client; or

(b) communications made in connection with or in contemplation of legal proceedings and for the purposes of those proceedings.

(11) If any person who is not an officer of an enforcement authority purports to act as such under this regulation or under regulation 22 he shall be guilty of an offence and liable on summary conviction to a fine not exceeding level 5 on the standard scale.

Power to enter premises with a warrant

22.—(1) If a justice of the peace by any written information on oath is satisfied—
  (a) that there are reasonable grounds for believing that Condition A or B is met, and
  (b) that Condition C, D or E is met,
  the justice may by warrant under his hand authorise an officer of an enforcement authority to enter the premises at all reasonable times, if necessary by force.

(2) Condition A is that there are on any premises goods or documents which a duly authorised officer of the enforcement authority has power under regulation 21(1) to inspect and that their inspection is likely to disclose evidence of a breach of these Regulations.

(3) Condition B is that a breach of these Regulations has been, is being or is about to be committed on any premises.

(4) Condition C is that the admission to the premises has been or is likely to be refused and that notice of intention to apply for a warrant under this regulation has been given to the occupier.

(5) Condition D is that an application for admission, or the giving of a notice of intention to apply for a warrant, would defeat the object of the entry.

(6) Condition E is that the premises are unoccupied or that the occupier is absent and it might defeat the object of the entry to await his return.

(7) A warrant under paragraph (1)—
  (a) ceases to have effect at the end of the period of one month beginning with the day it is issued;
  (b) must be produced for inspection to the person (if there is one) who appears to the officer to be the occupier of the premises.

(8) An officer entering any premises under this regulation may take with him such other persons and such equipment as may appear to him to be necessary.

(9) On leaving any premises which an officer is authorised to enter by warrant under this regulation the officer shall, if the premises are unoccupied or the occupier is temporarily absent, leave the premises as effectively secured against trespassers as he found them.

(10) In its application to Scotland, this regulation has effect as if—
  (a) the references in paragraph (1) to a justice of the peace included references to a sheriff; and
  (b) the reference in paragraph (1) to information on oath were a reference to evidence on oath.
  . . .

Obstruction of authorised officers

23.—(1) Any person who—
  (a) intentionally obstructs an officer of an enforcement authority acting in pursuance of these Regulations,

(b) intentionally fails to comply with any requirement properly made of him by such an officer under regulation 21, or

(c) without reasonable cause fails to give such an officer any other assistance or information which he may reasonably require of him for the purpose of the performance of his functions under these Regulations,

is guilty of an offence and liable, on summary conviction, to a fine not exceeding level 5 on the standard scale.

(2) Any person who, in giving any information which is required of him under paragraph (1)(c), makes any statement which he knows to be false in a material particular is guilty of an offence and liable—

(a) on summary conviction, to a fine not exceeding the statutory maximum; or

(b) on conviction on indictment, to a fine or imprisonment for a term not exceeding two years or both.

(3) Nothing in this regulation shall be construed as requiring a person to answer any question or give any information if to do so might incriminate him.

Notice of test and intended proceedings

24.—(1) Where goods purchased by an officer pursuant to regulation 20 are submitted to a test and the test leads to the institution of any proceedings for a breach of these Regulations the officer shall inform—

(a) the person from whom the goods were purchased, or

(b) where the goods were sold through a vending machine, the person mentioned in regulation 21(3)(b),

of the result of the test.

(2) Where goods seized by an officer pursuant to regulation 21 are submitted to a test then the officer shall inform the person mentioned in regulation 21(3) of the result of the test.

(3) Where, as a result of the test, any proceedings in respect of a breach of these Regulations are taken against any person, the officer shall allow him to have the goods tested on his behalf if it is reasonably practicable to do so.

Compensation

25.—(1) Where an officer of an enforcement authority seizes and detains goods in exercise of the powers under regulation 21 the enforcement authority shall be liable to pay compensation to any person having an interest in the goods in respect of any loss or damage caused by reason of the exercise of the power if—

(a) there has been no breach of these Regulations in relation to the goods, and

(b) the exercise of that power is not attributable to any neglect or default by that person.

(2) Any disputed question as to the right to or the amount of any compensation payable under this provision shall be determined by arbitration or, in Scotland, by a single arbiter appointed, failing agreement between the parties, by the sheriff.

. . .

Part 5 SUPPLEMENTARY

Crown

28.—(1) The powers conferred by regulations 21 and 22 are not exercisable in relation to premises occupied by the Crown.

(2) The Crown is not criminally liable as a result of any provision of these Regulations.

(3) Paragraph (2) does not affect the application of any provision of these Regulations in relation to a person in the public service of the Crown.

Validity of agreements

29. An agreement shall not be void or unenforceable by reason only of a breach of these Regulations.

. . .

SCHEDULE 1 COMMERCIAL PRACTICES WHICH ARE IN ALL CIRCUMSTANCES CONSIDERED UNFAIR

1. Claiming to be a signatory to a code of conduct when the trader is not.

2. Displaying a trust mark, quality mark or equivalent without having obtained the necessary authorisation.

3. Claiming that a code of conduct has an endorsement from a public or other body which it does not have.

4. Claiming that a trader (including his commercial practices) or a product has been approved, endorsed or authorised by a public or private body when the trader, the commercial practices or the product have not or making such a claim without complying with the terms of the approval, endorsement or authorisation.

5. Making an invitation to purchase products at a specified price without disclosing the existence of any reasonable grounds the trader may have for believing that he will not be able to offer for supply, or to procure another trader to supply, those products or equivalent products at that price for a period that is, and in quantities that are, reasonable having regard to the product, the scale of advertising of the product and the price offered (bait advertising).

6. Making an invitation to purchase products at a specified price and then—
    (a) refusing to show the advertised item to consumers,
    (b) refusing to take orders for it or deliver it within a reasonable time, or
    (c) demonstrating a defective sample of it,
    with the intention of promoting a different product (bait and switch).

7. Falsely stating that a product will only be available for a very limited time, or that it will only be available on particular terms for a very limited time, in order to elicit an immediate decision and deprive consumers of sufficient opportunity or time to make an informed choice.

8. Undertaking to provide after-sales service to consumers with whom the trader has communicated prior to a transaction in a language which is not an official language of the EEA State where the trader is located and then making such service available only in another language without clearly disclosing this to the consumer before the consumer is committed to the transaction.

9. Stating or otherwise creating the impression that a product can legally be sold when it cannot.

10. Presenting rights given to consumers in law as a distinctive feature of the trader's offer.

11. Using editorial content in the media to promote a product where a trader has paid for the promotion without making that clear in the content or by images or sounds clearly identifiable by the consumer (advertorial).

12. Making a materially inaccurate claim concerning the nature and extent of the risk to the personal security of the consumer or his family if the consumer does not purchase the product.

13. Promoting a product similar to a product made by a particular manufacturer in such a manner as deliberately to mislead the consumer into believing that the product is made by that same manufacturer when it is not.

14. Establishing, operating or promoting a pyramid promotional scheme where a consumer gives consideration for the opportunity to receive compensation that is derived primarily from the introduction of other consumers into the scheme rather than from the sale or consumption of products.

15. Claiming that the trader is about to cease trading or move premises when he is not.

16. Claiming that products are able to facilitate winning in games of chance.

17. Falsely claiming that a product is able to cure illnesses, dysfunction or malformations.

18. Passing on materially inaccurate information on market conditions or on the possibility of finding the product with the intention of inducing the consumer to acquire the product at conditions less favourable than normal market conditions.

19. Claiming in a commercial practice to offer a competition or prize promotion without awarding the prizes described or a reasonable equivalent.

20. Describing a product as 'gratis', 'free', 'without charge' or similar if the consumer has to pay anything other than the unavoidable cost of responding to the commercial practice and collecting or paying for delivery of the item.

21. Including in marketing material an invoice or similar document seeking payment which gives the consumer the impression that he has already ordered the marketed product when he has not.

22. Falsely claiming or creating the impression that the trader is not acting for purposes relating to his trade, business, craft or profession, or falsely representing oneself as a consumer.

23. Creating the false impression that after-sales service in relation to a product is available in an EEA State other than the one in which the product is sold.

24. Creating the impression that the consumer cannot leave the premises until a contract is formed.

25. Conducting personal visits to the consumer's home ignoring the consumer's request to leave or not to return, except in circumstances and to the extent justified to enforce a contractual obligation.

26. Making persistent and unwanted solicitations by telephone, fax, e-mail or other remote media except in circumstances and to the extent justified to enforce a contractual obligation.

27. Requiring a consumer who wishes to claim on an insurance policy to produce documents which could not reasonably be considered relevant as to whether the claim was valid, or failing systematically to respond to pertinent correspondence, in order to dissuade a consumer from exercising his contractual rights.

28. Including in an advertisement a direct exhortation to children to buy advertised products or persuade their parents or other adults to buy advertised products for them.

29. Demanding immediate or deferred payment for or the return or safekeeping of products supplied by the trader, but not solicited by the consumer, except where the product is a substitute supplied in accordance with regulation 19(7) of the Consumer Protection (Distance Selling) Regulations 2000 (inertia selling).

30. Explicitly informing a consumer that if he does not buy the product or service, the trader's job or livelihood will be in jeopardy.

31. Creating the false impression that the consumer has already won, will win, or will on doing a particular act win, a prize or other equivalent benefit, when in fact either—
     (a) there is no prize or other equivalent benefit, or
     (b) taking any action in relation to claiming the prize or other equivalent benefit is subject to the consumer paying money or incurring a cost.

BUSINESS PROTECTION FROM MISLEADING MARKETING REGULATIONS 2008
(2008/1276)

Part 1 DEFINITIONS AND PROHIBITIONS

Citation and commencement
1. These Regulations may be cited as the Business Protection from Misleading Marketing Regulations 2008 and shall come into force on 26th May 2008.

Interpretation
2.—(1) In these Regulations—

    "advertising" means any form of representation which is made in connection with a trade, business, craft or profession in order to promote the supply or transfer of a product and "advertiser" shall be construed accordingly;

. . .

Prohibition of advertising which misleads traders
3.—(1) Advertising which is misleading is prohibited.

  (2) Advertising is misleading which—
    (a) in any way, including its presentation, deceives or is likely to deceive the traders to whom it is addressed or whom it reaches; and by reason of its deceptive nature, is likely to affect their economic behaviour; or
    (b) for those reasons, injures or is likely to injure a competitor.

  (3) In determining whether advertising is misleading, account shall be taken of all its features, and in particular of any information it contains concerning—
    (a) the characteristics of the product (as defined in paragraph (4));
    (b) the price or manner in which the price is calculated;
    (c) the conditions on which the product is supplied or provided; and
    (d) the nature, attributes and rights of the advertiser (as defined in paragraph (5)).

  (4) In paragraph (3)(a) the "characteristics of the product" include—
    (a) availability of the product;
    (b) nature of the product;
    (c) execution of the product;
    (d) composition of the product;

(e) method and date of manufacture of the product;

(f) method and date of provision of the product;

(g) fitness for purpose of the product;

(h) uses of the product;

(i) quantity of the product;

(j) specification of the product;

(k) geographical or commercial origin of the product;

(l) results to be expected from use of the product; or

(m) results and material features of tests or checks carried out on the product.

(5) In paragraph (3)(d) the "nature, attributes and rights" of the advertiser include the advertiser's—

(a) identity;

(b) assets;

(c) qualifications;

(d) ownership of industrial, commercial or intellectual property rights; or

(e) awards and distinctions.

. . .

Part 2 OFFENCES

Misleading advertising

6. A trader is guilty of an offence if he engages in advertising which is misleading under regulation 3.

. . .

Part 4 INVESTIGATION POWERS

. . .

Validity of agreements

29. An agreement shall not be void or unenforceable by reason only of a breach of these Regulation

---

CANCELLATION OF CONTRACTS MADE IN A CONSUMER'S HOME OR PLACE OF WORK ETC. REGULATIONS 2008
(2008/1816)

Citation and commencement

1. These Regulations may be cited as the Cancellation of Contracts made in a Consumer's Home or Place of Work etc. Regulations 2008 and shall come into force on 1st October 2008.

Interpretation

2.—(1) In these Regulations:

"the 1974 Act" means the Consumer Credit Act 1974;

"cancellable agreement" has the same meaning as in section 189(1) of the 1974 Act;

"cancellation notice" means a notice in writing given by the consumer which indicates that he wishes to cancel the contract;

"cancellation period" means the period of 7 days starting with the date of receipt by the consumer of a notice of the right to cancel;

"consumer" means a natural person who in making a contract to which these Regulations apply is acting for purposes which can be regarded as outside his trade or profession;

"consumer credit agreement" means an agreement between the consumer and any other person by which the other person provides the consumer with credit of any amount;

"credit" includes a cash loan and any other form of financial accommodation, and for this purpose "cash" includes money in any form;

"enforcement authority" means any person mentioned in regulation 21;

"fixed sum credit" has the same meaning as in section 10(1) of the 1974 Act;

"notice of the right to cancel" means a notice given in accordance with regulation 7;

"related credit agreement" means a consumer credit agreement under which fixed sum credit which fully or partly covers the price under a contract which may be cancelled under regulation 7 is granted—
(i)   by the trader; or
(ii) by another person, under an arrangement made between that person and the trader;

"solicited visit" has the meaning given in regulation 6(3);

"specified contract" has the meaning given in regulation 9; and

"trader" means a person who, in making a contract to which these Regulations apply, is acting in his commercial or professional capacity and anyone acting in the name or on behalf of a trader.

(2) Paragraph 8(2) of Schedule 3 has effect for the purposes of paragraphs 7 and 8(1).

Consequential amendments, revocations and saving

. . .

4.—(1) Schedule 2 (Revocations) shall have effect.

(2) The Consumer Protection (Cancellation of Contracts Concluded away from Business Premises) Regulations 1987 ("the 1987 Regulations") shall continue to have effect in relation to a contract to which they applied before their revocation by these Regulations.

(3) These Regulations shall not apply to a contract to which the 1987 Regulations applied before their revocation.

Scope of application
5.   These Regulations apply to a contract, including a consumer credit agreement, between a consumer and a trader which is for the supply of goods or services to the consumer by a trader and which is made—
(a) during a visit by the trader to the consumer's home or place of work, or to the home of another individual;
(b) during an excursion organised by the trader away from his business premises; or
(c) after an offer made by the consumer during such a visit or excursion.

6.—(1) These Regulations do not apply to—

(a) any contracts listed in Schedule 3 (Excepted Contracts);

(b) a cancellable agreement;

(c) a consumer credit agreement which may be cancelled by the consumer in accordance with the terms of the agreement conferring upon him similar rights as if the agreement were a cancellable agreement;

(ca) a consumer credit agreement regulated under the 1974 Act to which the right of withdrawal applies under section 66A of that Act; or

(d) a contract made during a solicited visit or a contract made after an offer made by a consumer during a solicited visit where the contract is—

    (i) a regulated mortgage, home purchase plan or home reversion plan if the making or performance of such a contract constitutes a regulated activity for the purposes of the Financial Services and Markets Act 2000;

    (ii) a consumer credit agreement secured on land which is—

(aa) regulated under the 1974 Act; or

(bb) to the extent that it is not regulated under the 1974 Act, exempt under that Act; or

    (iii) any other consumer credit agreement regulated under the 1974 Act.

(2) Where any agreement referred to in paragraph (1)(b), (c), (ca) or (d)(iii) is a related credit agreement the provisions of regulations 11 and 12 shall apply to the cancellation of that agreement.

(3) A solicited visit means a visit by a trader, whether or not he is the trader who supplies the goods or services, to a consumer's home or place of work or to the home of another individual, which is made at the express request of the consumer but does not include—

(a) a visit by a trader which is made after he, or a person acting in his name or on his behalf—

    (i) telephones the consumer (otherwise than at the consumer's express request) and indicates during the course of the telephone call (either expressly or by implication) that he, or the trader in whose name or on whose behalf he is acting, is willing to visit the consumer; or

    (ii) visits the consumer (otherwise than at the consumer's express request) and indicates during the course of that visit (either expressly or by implication) that he, or the trader in whose name or on whose behalf he is acting, is willing to make a subsequent visit to the consumer; or

(b) a visit during which the contract which is made relates to goods and services other than those concerning which the consumer requested the visit of the trader, provided that when the visit was requested the consumer did not know, or could not reasonably have known, that the supply of such goods or services formed part of the trader's commercial or professional activities.

Right to cancel a contract to which these Regulations apply

7.—(1) A consumer has the right to cancel a contract to which these Regulations apply within the cancellation period.

(2) The trader must give the consumer a written notice of his right to cancel the contract and such notice must be given at the time the contract is made except in the case of a contract to which regulation 5(c) applies in which case the notice must be given at the time the offer is made by the consumer.

(3) The notice must—

(a) be dated;

(b) indicate the right of the consumer to cancel the contract within the cancellation period;

(c) be easily legible;
(d) contain—
    (i)   the information set out in Part I of Schedule 4; and
    (ii) a cancellation form in the form set out in Part II of that Schedule provided as a detachable slip and completed by or on behalf of the trader in accordance with the notes; and
(e) indicate if applicable—
    (i)   that the consumer may be required to pay for the goods or services supplied if the performance of the contract has begun with his written agreement before the end of the cancellation period;
    (ii) that a related credit agreement will be automatically cancelled if the contract for goods or services is cancelled.

(4) Where the contract is wholly or partly in writing the notice must be incorporated in the same document.

(5) If incorporated in the contract or another document the notice of the right to cancel must—
(a) be set out in a separate box with the heading "Notice of the Right to Cancel"; and
(b) have as much prominence as any other information in the contract or document apart from the heading and the names of the parties to the contract and any information inserted in handwriting.

(6) A contract to which these Regulations apply shall not be enforceable against the consumer unless the trader has given the consumer a notice of the right to cancel and the information required in accordance with this regulation.

Exercise of the right to cancel a contract
8.—(1) If the consumer serves a cancellation notice within the cancellation period then the contract is cancelled.

(2) A contract which is cancelled shall be treated as if it had never been entered into by the consumer except where these Regulations provide otherwise.

(3) The cancellation notice must indicate the intention of the consumer to cancel the contract and does not need to follow the form of cancellation notice set out in Part II of Schedule 4.

(4) The cancellation notice must be served on the trader or another person specified in the notice of the right to cancel as a person to whom the cancellation notice may be given.

(5) A cancellation notice sent by post is taken to have been served at the time of posting, whether or not it is actually received.

(6) Where a cancellation notice is sent by electronic mail it is taken to have been served on the day on which it is sent.

Cancellation of specified contracts commenced before expiry of the right to cancel
9.—(1) Where the consumer enters into a specified contract and he wishes the performance of the contract to begin before the end of the cancellation period, he must request this in writing.

(2) Where the consumer cancels a specified contract in accordance with regulation 8 he shall be under a duty to pay in accordance with the reasonable requirements of the cancelled contract for goods or services that were supplied before the cancellation.

(3) If the consumer fails to provide the request in writing referred to in paragraph (1) then—

    (a) the trader is not obliged to begin performance of the specified contract before the end of the cancellation period; and

    (b) the consumer is not bound by the duty referred to in paragraph (2) if he cancels the contract in accordance with regulation 8.

(4) For the purposes of this regulation and regulation 13, a "specified contract" means a contract for any of the following—

    (a) the supply of newspapers, periodicals or magazines;

    (b) advertising in any medium;

    (c) the supply of goods the price of which is dependent on fluctuations in the financial markets which cannot be controlled by the trader;

    (d) the supply of goods to meet an emergency;

    (e) the supply of goods made to a customer's specifications or clearly personalised and any services in connection with the provision of such goods;

    (f) the supply of perishable goods;

    (g) the supply of goods which by their nature are consumed by use and which, before the cancellation, were so consumed;

    (h) the supply of goods which, before the cancellation, had become incorporated in any land or thing not comprised in the cancelled contract;

    (i) the supply of goods or services relating to a funeral; or

    (j) the supply of services of any other kind.

Recovery of money paid by consumer

10.—(1) On the cancellation of a contract under regulation 8 any sum paid by or on behalf of the consumer in respect of the contract shall become repayable except where these Regulations provide otherwise.

(2) If the consumer or any person on his behalf is in possession of any goods under the terms of the cancelled contract then he shall have a lien on them for any sum repayable to him under paragraph (1).

(3) Where any security has been provided in relation to the cancelled contract, the security shall be treated as never having had effect for that purpose and the trader must immediately return any property lodged with him solely as security for the purposes of the cancelled contract.

Automatic cancellation of related credit agreement

11.—(1) A cancellation notice which cancels a contract for goods or services shall have the effect of cancelling any related credit agreement.

(2) Subject to paragraphs (3) and (4), where a related credit agreement has been cancelled under paragraph (1)—

    (a) the trader must, if he is not the same person as the creditor under that agreement, immediately on receipt of the cancellation notice inform the creditor that the notice has been given;

    (b) any sum paid by or on behalf of the consumer in relation to the credit agreement must be reimbursed, except for any sum which would have to be paid under sub-paragraph (c);

    (c) the agreement shall continue in force so far as it relates to repayment of the credit and payment of interest in accordance with regulation 12, but shall otherwise cease to be enforceable; and

(d) any security provided under the related credit agreement shall be treated as never having had effect for that purpose and the creditor must immediately return any property lodged with him solely as security for the purposes of the related credit agreement.

(3) Where a related credit agreement is a cancellable agreement—
  (a) its cancellation under paragraph (1) shall take effect as if a notice of cancellation within the meaning of the 1974 Act had been served;
  (b) that Act shall apply in respect of the consequences of such cancellation;
  (c) paragraph (2)(b) to (d) and regulation 12 shall not apply in respect of its cancellation; and
  (d) regulations 13 and 14 shall not apply in respect of the cancellation of the related contract for goods or services.

(4) Where a related credit agreement of a kind referred to in regulation 6(1)(c) is cancelled under paragraph (1)—
  (a) paragraph (2)(b) to (d) and regulation 12 shall not apply in respect of its cancellation; and
  (b) regulations 13 and 14 shall not apply in respect of the cancellation of the related contract for goods or services.

(5) Where a related credit agreement of a kind referred to in regulation 6(1)(ca) or 6(1)(d)(iii) is cancelled under paragraph (1)—
  (a) the provisions of this regulation and regulation 12 shall apply in respect of its cancellation; and
  (b) the provisions of regulations 13 and 14 shall apply in respect of the cancellation of the related contract for goods or services.

(6) For the purposes of this regulation and regulation 12 "creditor" is the person who grants credit under a related credit agreement.

Repayment of credit and interest
12.—(1) Where—
  (a) a contract under which credit is provided to the consumer is cancelled under regulation 8; or
  (b) a related credit agreement (other than a cancellable agreement or an agreement of a kind referred to in regulation 6(1)(c)) is cancelled as a result of the cancellation of a contract for goods or services,
  the contract or agreement shall continue in force so far as it relates to repayment of the credit and payment of interest.

(2) If, following the cancellation of a contract or related credit agreement to which paragraph (1) applies, the consumer repays the whole or a portion of the credit—
  (a) before the expiry of one month following service of the cancellation notice; or
  (b) in the case of a credit repayable by instalments, before the date on which the first instalment is due,
  no interest shall be payable on the amount repaid.

(3) If the whole of a credit repayable by instalments is not repaid on or before the date specified in paragraph (2)(b), the consumer shall not be liable to repay any of the credit except on receipt of a request in writing signed by the trader stating the amounts of the remaining instalments (recalculated by the trader as nearly as may be in accordance with the contract and without extending the repayment period), but excluding any sum other than principal and interest.

(4) Repayment of a credit, or payment of interest, under a cancelled contract or related credit agreement shall be treated as duly made if it is made to any person on whom, under regulation 8(4), a cancellation notice could have been served.

(5) Where any security has been provided in relation to the contract or consumer credit agreement, the duty imposed on the consumer by this regulation shall not be enforceable before the trader or creditor has discharged any duty imposed on him by regulation 10(3) or 11(2)(d) respectively.

Return of goods by consumer after cancellation

13.—(1) A consumer who has acquired possession of any goods by virtue of the contract shall on the cancellation of that contract be under a duty, subject to any lien, to restore the goods to the trader and meanwhile to retain possession of the goods and take reasonable care of them.

(2) The consumer shall not be under a duty to restore goods supplied under a specified contract in circumstances where—
   (a) he is required to pay, in accordance with the reasonable requirements of the cancelled contract, for the supply of such goods before cancellation; or
   (b) the trader has begun performance of the contract before the end of the cancellation period without a prior request in writing by the consumer.

(3) The consumer shall not be under any duty to deliver the goods except at his own premises and following a request in writing signed by the trader and served on the consumer either before, or at the time when, the goods are collected from those premises.

(4) If the consumer—
   (a) delivers the goods (whether at his own premises or elsewhere) to any person on whom, under regulation 8(4), a cancellation notice could have been served; or
   (b) sends the goods at his own expense to such a person,
   he shall be discharged from any duty to retain possession of the goods or restore them to the trader.

(5) Where the consumer delivers the goods as mentioned in paragraph (4)(a), his obligation to take care of the goods shall cease; and if he send the goods as mentioned in paragraph (4)(b), he shall be under a duty to take reasonable care to see that they are received by the trader and not damaged in transit, but in other respects his duty to take care of the goods shall cease.

(6) Where, at any time during the period of 21 days following the cancellation, the consumer receives such a request as is mentioned in paragraph (3) and unreasonably refuses or unreasonably fails to comply with it, his duty to retain possession and take reasonable care of the goods shall continue until he delivers or sends the goods as mentioned in paragraph (4); but if within that period he does not receive such a request his duty to take reasonable care of the goods shall cease at the end of that period.

(7) Where any security has been provided in relation to the cancelled contract, the duty imposed on the consumer to restore goods shall not be enforceable before the trader has discharged any duty imposed on him by regulation 10(3).

(8) Breach of a duty imposed on a consumer by this regulation is actionable as a breach of statutory duty.

Goods given in part-exchange

14.—(1) This regulation applies on the cancellation of a contract where the trader agreed to take goods in part-exchange (the "part-exchange goods") and those goods have been delivered to him.

(2) Unless, before the end of the period of ten days beginning with the date of cancellation, the part-exchange goods are returned to the consumer in a condition substantially as good as when they were delivered to the trader, the consumer shall be entitled to recover from the trader a sum equal to the part-exchange allowance.

(3) During the period of ten days beginning with the date of cancellation, the consumer, if he is in possession of goods to which the cancelled contract relates, shall have a lien on them for—
(a) delivery of the part-exchange goods in a condition substantially as good as when they were delivered to the trader; or
(b) a sum equal to the part-exchange allowance,
and if the lien continues to the end of that period it shall thereafter subsist only as a lien for a sum equal to the part-exchange allowance.

(4) In this regulation the part-exchange allowance means the sum agreed as such in the cancelled contract, or if no such sum was agreed, such sum as it would have been reasonable to allow in respect of the part-exchange goods if no notice of cancellation had been served.

No contracting-out of contracts to which these Regulations apply

15.—(1) A term contained in a contract is void if, and to the extent that, it is inconsistent with a provision for the protection of the consumer contained in these Regulations.

(2) Where a provision of these Regulations specifies the duty or liability of the consumer in certain circumstances, a term contained in a contract is inconsistent with that provision if it purports to impose, directly or indirectly, an additional or different duty or liability on the consumer in those circumstances.

Service of documents

16.—(1) A document to be served under these Regulations on a person may be so served—
(a) by delivering it to him, or by leaving it at his proper address or by sending it to him at that address;
(b) if the person is a body corporate, by serving it in accordance with sub-paragraph (a) on the secretary or clerk of that body;
(c) if the person is a partnership, by serving it in accordance with sub-paragraph (a) on a partner or on a person having the control or management of the partnership business; and
(d) if the person is an unincorporated body, by serving it in accordance with sub-paragraph (a) on a person having control or management of that body.

(2) For the purposes of paragraph (1), the proper address of any person on whom a document is to be served under these Regulations is his last known address except that—
(a) in the case of service on a body corporate or its secretary or clerk, it is the address of the registered or principal office of the body corporate in the United Kingdom; and
(b) in the case of service on a partnership or partner or person having the control or management of a partnership business, it is the partnership's principal place of business in the United Kingdom.

(3) A person's electronic mail address may also be his proper address for the purposes of paragraph (1).

Enforcement

Offence relating to the failure to give notice of the right to cancel

17.—(1) A trader is guilty of an offence if he enters into a contract to which these Regulations apply but fails to give the consumer a notice of the right to cancel in accordance with regulation 7.

(2) A person who is guilty of an offence under paragraph (1) shall be liable on summary conviction to a fine not exceeding level 5 on the standard scale.

Defence of due diligence

18.—(1) In any proceedings against a person for an offence under regulation 17 it is a defence for that person to prove—
    (a) that the commission of the offence was due to—
        (i) the act or default of another, or
        (ii) reliance on information given by another, and
    (b) that he took all reasonable precautions and exercised all due diligence to avoid the commission of such an offence by himself or any person under his control.

(2) A person shall not be entitled to rely on the defence provided by paragraph (1) without leave of the court unless—
    (a) he has served on the prosecutor a notice in writing giving such information identifying or assisting in the identification of that other person as was in his possession; and
    (b) the notice is served on the prosecutor not less than seven clear days before the hearing of the proceedings or, in Scotland, the diet of trial.

Liability of persons other than the principal offender

19. Where the commission by a person of an offence under regulation 17 is due to the act or default of another person, that other person is guilty of the offence and may be proceeded against and punished whether or not proceedings are taken against the first person.

Offences committed by bodies of persons

20.—(1) Where an offence under regulation 17 committed by a body corporate is proved—
    (a) to have been committed with the consent or connivance of an officer of the body corporate or
    (b) to be attributable to any neglect on his part,
the officer, as well as the body corporate shall be guilty of the offence and liable to be proceeded against and punished accordingly.

(2) In paragraph (1) a reference to an officer of a body corporate includes a reference to—
    (a) a director, manager, secretary or other similar officer; and
    (b) a person purporting to act as a director, manager, secretary or other similar officer.

(3) Where an offence under regulation 17 committed in Scotland by a Scottish partnership is proved—
    (a) to have been committed with the consent or connivance of a partner; or
    (b) to be attributable to any neglect on his part,
that partner, as well as the partnership shall be guilty of the offence and liable to be proceeded against and punished accordingly.

(4) In paragraph (3) a reference to a partner includes a person purporting to act as a partner.

Duty to enforce

21.—(1) Subject to paragraphs (2) and (3)—

    (a) it shall be the duty of every weights and measures authority in Great Britain to enforce regulation 17 within its area; . . .

(2) No proceedings for an offence under these Regulations may be instituted in England and Wales except by or on behalf of an enforcement authority.

(3) Nothing in paragraph (1) shall authorise any weights and measures authority to bring proceedings in Scotland for an offence.

Powers of investigation

22.—(1) If a duly authorised officer of an enforcement authority has reasonable grounds for suspecting that an offence has been committed under regulation 17, he may require a person carrying on or employed in a business to produce any document relating to the business, and take copies of it or any entry in it for the purposes of ascertaining whether such an offence has been committed.

(2) If the officer has reasonable grounds for believing that any documents may be required as evidence in proceedings for such an offence, he may seize and detain them and shall, if he does so, inform the person from whom they are seized.

(3) In this regulation "document" includes information recorded in any form.

(4) The reference in paragraph (1) to production of documents is, in the case of a document which contains information recorded otherwise than in a legible form, a reference to the production of a copy of the information in a legible form.

(5) An officer seeking to exercise a power under this regulation must do so only at a reasonable hour and on production (if required) of his identification and authority.

(6) Nothing in this regulation requires a person to produce, or authorises the taking from a person of, a document which the other person would be entitled to refuse to produce in proceedings in the High Court on the grounds of legal professional privilege or (in Scotland) in the Court of Session on the grounds of confidentiality of communications.

(7) In paragraph (6) "communications" means—

    (a) communications between a professional legal adviser and his client; or

    (b) communications made in connection with, or in contemplation of legal proceedings and for the purpose of those proceedings.

Obstruction of authorised officers

23.—(1) A person is guilty of an offence if he—

    (a) intentionally obstructs an officer of an enforcement authority acting in pursuance of his functions under these Regulations;

    (b) without reasonable cause fails to comply with any requirement properly made of him by such an officer under regulation 22; or

    (c) without reasonable cause fails to give such an officer any other assistance or information which he may reasonably require of him for the purpose of the performance of his functions under these Regulations.

(2) A person is guilty of an offence if, in giving any information which is required of him under paragraph (1)(c), he makes any statement which he knows to be false in a material particular.

(3) A person guilty of an offence under paragraph (1) or (2) shall be liable on summary conviction to a fine not exceeding level 3 on the standard scale.

24. Nothing in regulation 22 or 23 shall be construed as requiring a person to answer any question or give any information if to do so might incriminate him.

. . .

SCHEDULE 3 EXCEPTED CONTRACTS

1. A contract for the construction, sale or rental of immovable property or a contract concerning other rights relating to immovable property other than—
(a) a contract for the construction of extensions, patios, conservatories or driveways;
(b) a contract for the supply of goods and their incorporation in immovable property; and
(c) a contract for the repair, refurbishment or improvement of immovable property.

2. A contract for the supply of foodstuffs or beverages or other goods intended for current consumption in the household and supplied by a regular roundsman.

3. A contract for the supply of goods or services provided that each of the following conditions is met:
(a) the contract is concluded on the basis of a trader's catalogue which the consumer has a proper opportunity of reading in the absence of the trader's representative;
(b) there is intended to be continuity of contact between the trader's representative and the consumer in relation to that or any subsequent transaction; and
(c) both the catalogue and the contract contain a prominent notice informing the consumer of his rights to return goods to the supplier within a period of not less than seven days of receipt or otherwise to cancel the contract within that period without obligation of any kind other than to take reasonable care of the goods.

4. A contract of insurance.

5. Any contract under which credit within the meaning of the 1974 Act is provided not exceeding £35 other than a hire purchase or conditional sale agreement.

6. Any contract not falling within paragraph 5 under which the total payments to be made by the consumer do not exceed £35.

7. Any agreement the making or performance of which by either party constitutes a relevant regulated activity.

8.—(1) For the purposes of paragraph 7—
(a) "a relevant regulated activity" means an activity of the following kind—
(i)   dealing in investments, as principal or as agent;
(ii)   arranging deals in investments;
(iii) operating a multilateral trading facility;
(iv)   managing investments;
(v)   safeguarding and administering investments;
(vi)   establishing, operating or winding up a collective investment scheme; and
(b) for these purposes "investment" means—
(i)   shares;
(ii)   instruments creating or acknowledging indebtedness;

        (iii) instruments giving entitlement to investments

        (iv) certificates representing securities;

        (v)   units in a collective investment scheme;

        (vi) options;

        (vii) futures;

        (viii) contracts for differences; and

        (ix) rights to or interests in investments.

(2)   Paragraph 7 and this paragraph must be read with—

      (a) section 22 of the Financial Services and Markets Act 2000;

      (b) any relevant order under that section; and

      (c) Schedule 2 to that Act,

but any restriction on or exclusion from the meaning of a regulated activity for the purposes of paragraph 7 which arises from the identity of the person carrying on such activity is to be disregarded.

SCHEDULE 4 NOTICE OF THE RIGHT TO CANCEL

Part I INFORMATION TO BE CONTAINED IN NOTICE OF THE RIGHT TO CANCEL

1.   The identity of the trader including trading name if any.

2.   The trader's reference number, code or other details to enable the contract or offer to be identified.

3.   A statement that the consumer has a right to cancel the contract if he wishes and that this right can be exercised by delivering, or sending (including by electronic mail) a cancellation notice to the person mentioned in the next paragraph at any time within the period of 7 days starting with the day of receipt of a notice in writing of the right to cancel the contract.

4.   The name and address, (including any electronic mail address as well as the postal address), of a person to whom a cancellation notice may be given.

5.   A statement that notice of cancellation is deemed to be served as soon as it is posted or sent to a trader or in the case of an electronic communication from the day it is sent to the trader.

6.   A statement that the consumer can use the cancellation form provided if he wishes.

As amended by the Consumer Credit (EU Directive) Regulations 2010.

Proposed Legislation

PROPOSED UNFAIR CONTRACT TERMS BILL
(Law Commission (No. 292) and Scottish Law Commission (No. 199))

Part 1 BUSINESS LIABILITY FOR NEGLIGENCE

1. BUSINESS LIABILITY FOR NEGLIGENCE

(1) Business liability for death or personal injury resulting from negligence cannot be excluded or restricted by a contract term or a notice.

(2) Business liability for other loss or damage resulting from negligence cannot be excluded or restricted by a contract term or a notice unless the term or notice is fair and reasonable.

(3) "Business liability" means liability arising from—
   (a) anything that was or should have been done for purposes related to a business, or
   (b) the occupation of premises used for purposes related to the occupier's business.

(4) The reference in subsection (3)(a) to anything done for purposes related to a business includes anything done by an employee of that business within the scope of his employment.

(5) "Negligence" means the breach of—
   (a) an obligation to take reasonable care or exercise reasonable skill in the performance of a contract where the obligation arises from an express or implied term of the contract,
   (b) a common law duty to take reasonable care or exercise reasonable skill,
   (c) the common duty of care imposed by the Occupiers' Liability Act 1957 (c. 31) or the Occupiers' Liability Act (Northern Ireland) 1957 (c. 25 NI), or
   (d) the duty of reasonable care imposed by section 2(1) of the Occupiers' Liability (Scotland) Act 1960 (c. 30).

(6) It does not matter—
   (a) whether a breach of obligation or duty was, or was not, inadvertent, or
   (b) whether liability for it arises directly or vicariously.

2. EXCEPTIONS TO SECTION 1

(1) Section 1 does not prevent an employee from excluding or restricting his liability for negligence to his employer.

(2) Section 1 does not apply to the business liability of an occupier of premises to a person who obtains access to the premises for recreational or educational purposes if—
   (a) that person suffers loss or damage because of the dangerous state of the premises, and

    (b) allowing that person access to those premises for those purposes is not within the purposes of the occupier's business.

(3)   Subsection (2) does not extend to Scotland.

3. VOLUNTARY ACCEPTANCE OF RISK

The defence that a person voluntarily accepted a risk cannot be used against him just because he agreed to or knew about a contract term, or a notice, appearing to exclude or restrict business liability for negligence in the case in question.

Part 2 CONSUMER CONTRACTS

Contracts in general

4. TERMS OF NO EFFECT UNLESS FAIR AND REASONABLE

(1)   If a term of a consumer contract is detrimental to the consumer, the business cannot rely on the term unless the term is fair and reasonable.

(2)   But subsection (1) does not apply to a term which defines the main subject-matter of a consumer contract, if the definition is—
(a) transparent, and
(b) substantially the same as the definition the consumer reasonably expected.

(3)   Nor does subsection (1) apply to a term in so far as it sets the price payable under a consumer contract, if the price is—
(a) transparent,
(b) payable in circumstances substantially the same as those the consumer reasonably expected, and
(c) calculated in a way substantially the same as the way the consumer reasonably expected.

(4)   Nor does subsection (1) apply to a term which—
(a) is transparent, and
(b) leads to substantially the same result as would be produced as a matter of law if the term were not included.

(5)   The reference to the price payable under a consumer contract does not include any amount, payment of which would be incidental or ancillary to the main purpose of the contract.

(6)   "Price" includes remuneration.

Sale or supply of goods

5. SALE OR SUPPLY TO CONSUMER

(1)   This section applies to a consumer contract for the sale or supply of goods to the consumer.

(2)   In the case of a contract for the sale of the goods, the business cannot rely on a term of the contract to exclude or restrict liability arising under any of the following sections of the 1979 Act—
(a) section 12 (implied term that seller entitled to sell),
(b) section 13 (implied term that goods match description),
(c) section 14 (implied term that goods satisfactory and fit for the purpose),
(d) section 15 (implied term that goods match sample).

(3)   In the case of a contract for the hire-purchase of the goods, the business cannot rely on a term of the contract to exclude or restrict liability arising under any of the following sections of the 1973 Act—
(a) section 8 (implied term that supplier entitled to supply),
(b) section 9 (implied term that goods match description),
(c) section 10 (implied term that goods satisfactory and fit for the purpose),
(d) section 11 (implied term that goods match sample).

(4)   In the case of any other contract for the transfer of property in the goods, the business cannot rely on a term of the contract to exclude or restrict liability arising under any of the following sections of the 1982 Act—
(a) section 2 or 11B (implied term that supplier entitled to supply),
(b) section 3 or 11C (implied term that goods match description),
(c) section 4 or 11D (implied term that goods satisfactory and fit for the purpose),
(d) section 5 or 11E (implied term that goods match sample).

(5)   In the case of a contract for the hire of the goods, the business cannot rely on a term of the contract to exclude or restrict liability arising under any of the following sections of the 1982 Act—
(a) section 8 or 11I (implied term that goods match description),
(b) section 9 or 11J (implied term that goods satisfactory and fit for the purpose),
(c) section 10 or 11K (implied term that goods match sample).

(6)   Subsection (2)(b) to (d) does not apply if the contract is—
(a) for the sale of second-hand goods, and
(b) made at a public auction which the consumer had the opportunity to attend in person.

6. SALE OR SUPPLY TO BUSINESS

(1)   This section applies to a consumer contract for the sale or supply of goods to the business.

(2)   In the case of a contract for the sale of the goods, the consumer cannot rely on a term of the contract to exclude or restrict liability—
(a) arising under section 12 of the 1979 Act (implied term that seller entitled to sell), or
(b) unless the term is fair and reasonable, arising under either of the following sections of that Act—
(i)   section 13 (implied term that goods match description),
(ii) section 15 (implied term that goods match sample).

(3)   In the case of a contract for the hire-purchase of the goods, the consumer cannot rely on a term of the contract to exclude or restrict liability—
(a) arising under section 8 of the 1973 Act (implied term that supplier entitled to supply), or
(b) unless the term is fair and reasonable, arising under either of the following sections of that Act—
(i)   section 9 (implied term that goods match description),
(ii) section 11 (implied term that goods match sample).

Supplemental

7. REGULATION AND ENFORCEMENT

Schedule 1 confers functions on the OFT and regulators in relation to—
(a) consumer contract terms,

(b) terms drawn up or proposed for use as consumer contract terms,

(c) terms which a trade association recommends for use as consumer contract terms, and

(d) notices relating to the rights conferred or duties imposed by consumer contracts.

8. AMBIGUITY

(1)   If it is reasonable to read a written term of a consumer contract in two (or more) ways, the term is to be read in whichever of those ways it is reasonable to think the more (or the most) favourable to the consumer.

(2)   This section does not apply in relation to proceedings under Schedule 1 (regulation and enforcement of consumer contract terms, etc.).

Part 3 NON-CONSUMER CONTRACTS

Business contracts

9. WRITTEN STANDARD TERMS

(1)   This section applies where one party to a business contract ("A") deals on the written standard terms of business of the other ("B").

(2)   Unless the term is fair and reasonable, B cannot rely on any of those terms to exclude or restrict its liability to A for breach of the contract.

(3)   Unless the term is fair and reasonable, B cannot rely on any of those terms to claim that it has the right—
(a) to carry out its obligations under the contract in a way substantially different from the way in which A reasonably expected them to be carried out, or
(b) not to carry out all or part of those obligations.

10. SALE OR SUPPLY OF GOODS

(1)   In the case of a business contract for the sale of goods, the seller cannot rely on a term of the contract to exclude or restrict liability arising under section 12 of the 1979 Act (implied term that seller entitled to sell).

(2)   In the case of a business contract for the hire-purchase of goods, the supplier cannot rely on a term of the contract to exclude or restrict liability arising under section 8 of the 1973 Act (implied term that supplier entitled to supply).

(3)   In the case of any other business contract for the transfer of property in goods, the supplier cannot rely on a term of the contract to exclude or restrict liability arising under section 2 or 11B of the 1982 Act (implied term that supplier entitled to supply).

Small business contracts

11. NON-NEGOTIATED TERMS

(1)   This section applies where there is a small business contract and—
(a) the terms on which one party ("A") deals include a term which the other party ("B") put forward during the negotiation of the contract as one of its written standard terms of business,
(b) the substance of the term was not, as a result of negotiation, changed in favour of A, and
(c) at the time the contract is made, A is a small business.

(2)   If that term is detrimental to A, B cannot rely on the term unless the term is fair and reasonable.

(3)   But subsection (2) does not apply to a term which defines the main subject-matter of a small business contract, if the definition is—
   (a) transparent, and
   (b) substantially the same as the definition A reasonably expected.

(4)   Nor does subsection (2) apply to a term in so far as it sets the price payable under a small business contract, if the price is—
   (a) transparent,
   (b) payable in circumstances substantially the same as those A reasonably expected, and
   (c) calculated in a way substantially the same as the way A reasonably expected.

(5)   Nor does subsection (2) apply to a term which—
   (a) is transparent, and
   (b) leads to substantially the same result as would be produced as a matter of law if the term were not included.

(6)   The reference to the price payable under a small business contract does not include any amount, payment of which would be incidental or ancillary to the main purpose of the contract.

(7)   "Price" includes remuneration.

Employment contracts

12. WRITTEN STANDARD TERMS

(1)   This section applies in relation to an employment contract under which an individual ("the employee") is employed by a business on its written standard terms of employment.

(2)   Unless the term is fair and reasonable, the business cannot rely on any of those terms to exclude or restrict its liability for breach of the contract.

(3)   Unless the term is fair and reasonable, the business cannot rely on any of those terms to claim it has the right—
   (a) to carry out its obligations under the contract in a way substantially different from the way in which the employee reasonably expected them to be carried out, or
   (b) not to carry out all or part of those obligations.

Private contracts

13. SALE OR SUPPLY OF GOODS

(1)   This section applies if neither party to a contract for the sale or supply of goods enters into it for purposes related to a business of his.

(2)   In the case of a contract for the sale of the goods, the seller cannot rely on a term of the contract to exclude or restrict liability—
   (a) arising under section 12 of the 1979 Act (implied term that seller entitled to sell), or
   (b) unless the term is fair and reasonable, arising under either of the following sections of that Act—
      (i)   section 13 (implied term that goods match description),
      (ii) section 15 (implied term that goods match sample).

(3)   In the case of a contract for the hire-purchase of the goods, the supplier cannot rely on a term of the contract to exclude or restrict liability—
   (a) arising under section 8 of the 1973 Act (implied term that supplier entitled to supply), or
   (b) unless the term is fair and reasonable, arising under either of the following sections of

that Act—
(i)   section 9 (implied term that goods match description),
(ii) section 11 (implied term that goods match sample).

Part 4 THE "FAIR AND REASONABLE" TEST

The test

14. THE TEST

(1)   Whether a contract term is fair and reasonable is to be determined by taking into account—
(a) the extent to which the term is transparent, and
(b) the substance and effect of the term, and all the circumstances existing at the time it was agreed.

(2)   Whether a notice is fair and reasonable is to be determined by taking into account—
(a) the extent to which the notice is transparent, and
(b) the substance and effect of the notice, and all the circumstances existing at the time when the liability arose (or, but for the notice, would have arisen).

(3)   "Transparent" means—
(a) expressed in reasonably plain language,
(b) legible,
(c) presented clearly, and
(d) readily available to any person likely to be affected by the contract term or notice in question.

(4)   Matters relating to the substance and effect of a contract term, and to all the circumstances existing at the time it was agreed, include the following—
(a) the other terms of the contract,
(b) the terms of any other contract on which the contract depends,
(c) the balance of the parties' interests,
(d) the risks to the party adversely affected by the term,
(e) the possibility and probability of insurance,
(f) other ways in which the interests of the party adversely affected by the term might have been protected,
(g) the extent to which the term (whether alone or with others) differs from what would have been the case in its absence,
(h) the knowledge and understanding of the party adversely affected by the term,
(i) the strength of the parties' bargaining positions,
(j) the nature of the goods or services to which the contract relates.

(5)   Subsection (4) applies, with any necessary modifications, in relation to a notice as it applies in relation to a contract term.

(6)   Schedule 2 contains an indicative and non-exhaustive list of consumer contract terms and small business contract terms which may be regarded as not being fair and reasonable.

(7)   The Secretary of State may by order amend Schedule 2 so as to add, modify or omit an entry.

Burden of proof

15. BUSINESS LIABILITY FOR NEGLIGENCE

It is for a person wishing to rely on a contract term or a notice which purports to exclude or restrict liability of the kind mentioned in section 1(2) (business liability for negligence other than in case of death or personal injury) to prove that the term or notice is fair and reasonable.

16. CONSUMER CONTRACTS

(1) If an issue is raised as to whether a term in a consumer contract is fair and reasonable, it is for the business to prove that it is.

(2) But in proceedings under Schedule 1 (regulation and enforcement of consumer contracts) it is for a person claiming that a term in a consumer contract, or a notice, is not fair and reasonable to prove that it is not.

(3) It is for a person wishing to rely on a contract not being a consumer contract to prove that it is not.

17. BUSINESS CONTRACTS

(1) It is for a person wishing to rely on a term of a business contract to prove that the term is fair and reasonable.

(2) But in relation to a term to which section 11(2) (non-negotiated terms in small business contracts) applies, it is for a person claiming that the term is not fair and reasonable to prove that it is not.

. . .

Part 6 MISCELLANEOUS AND SUPPLEMENTARY

Miscellaneous

21. UNFAIRNESS ISSUE RAISED BY COURT

A court may, in proceedings before it, raise an issue about whether a contract term or a notice is fair and reasonable even if none of the parties to the proceedings has raised the issue or indicated that it intends to raise it.

22. EXCEPTIONS

Schedule 3 sets out types of contract, and of contract term, to which this Act does not apply or to which specified provisions of this Act do not apply.

23. SECONDARY CONTRACTS

(1) A term of a contract ("the secondary contract") which reduces the rights or remedies, or increases the obligations, of a person under another contract ("the main contract") is subject to the provisions of this Act that would apply to the term if it were in the main contract.

(2) It does not matter for the purposes of this section whether the parties to the secondary contract are the same as the parties to the main contract.

(3) This section does not apply if the secondary contract is a settlement of a claim arising under the main contract.

24. EFFECT OF UNFAIR TERM ON CONTRACT

Where a contract term cannot be relied on by a person as a result of this Act, the contract continues, so far as practicable, to have effect in every other respect.

Interpretation, etc.

25. PRELIMINARY

Sections 26 to 32 define or otherwise explain expressions for the purposes of this Act.

26. "CONSUMER CONTRACT" AND "BUSINESS CONTRACT"

(1)   "Consumer contract" means a contract (other than one of employment) between—
   (a)   an individual ("the consumer") who enters into it wholly or mainly for purposes unrelated to a business of his, and
   (b)   a person ("the business") who enters into it wholly or mainly for purposes related to his business.

(2)   "Business contract" means a contract between two persons, each of whom enters into it wholly or mainly for purposes related to his business.

27. "SMALL BUSINESS"

(1)   "Small business" means a person in whose business the number of employees does not exceed—
   (a)   nine, or
   (b)   where the Secretary of State specifies by order another number for the purposes of this section, that number.

(2)   But a person is not a small business if adding the number of employees in his business to the number of employees in any other business of his, or in any business of an associated person, gives a total exceeding the number which for the time being applies for the purposes of subsection (1).

(3)   A reference to the number of employees in a business is to the number calculated according to Schedule 4.

28. "ASSOCIATED PERSON"

(1)   For the purposes of this Act, two persons are associated if—
   (a)   one controls the other, or
   (b)   both are controlled by the same person.

(2)   A person ("A") controls a body corporate ("B") if A can secure that B's affairs are conducted according to A's wishes, directions or instructions.

(3)   The reference in subsection (2) to wishes, directions or instructions does not include advice given in a professional capacity.

(4)   Subsection (2) applies, with any necessary modifications, in relation to an unincorporated association (other than a partnership) as it applies in relation to a body corporate.

(5)   A person controls a partnership if he has the right to a share of more than half the assets or income of the partnership.

(6)   For the purposes of this section, one person does not control another just because he grants that other person a right to supply goods or services.

29. "SMALL BUSINESS CONTRACT"

(1)   "Small business contract" means a business contract—
   (a)   to which at least one of the parties is, at the time the contract is made, a small business, and
   (b)   which does not come within any of four exceptions.

(2)   The first exception is that the price payable under the contract exceeds £500,000.

(3) The second is that—
   (a) the transaction provided for by the contract forms part of a larger transaction, or part of a scheme or arrangement, and
   (b) the total price payable in respect of the larger transaction, or the scheme or arrangement, exceeds £500,000.

(4) The third is that—
   (a) a person agrees to carry on a regulated activity under the contract, and
   (b) he is an authorised person or, in relation to that activity, an exempt person.

(5) The fourth is that the contract is a series contract.

(6) A contract is a series contract if—
   (a) the transaction provided for by the contract forms part of a series, and
   (b) during the period of two years ending with the date of the contract, the total price payable under contracts providing for transactions in the series exceeds £500,000.

(7) A contract is also a series contract if, at the time the contract was made, both parties intended that—
   (a) the transaction provided for by the contract would form part of a series, and
   (b) the total price payable under contracts providing for transactions in the series and made during any period of two years, would exceed £500,000.

(8) Where a contract is a series contract, every subsequent contract providing for a transaction in the series is a series contract.

(9) The Secretary of State may by order vary the amount specified in subsections (2), (3), (6) and (7).

(10) "Authorised person", "exempt person" and "regulated activity" have the same meaning as in the Financial Services and Markets Act 2000 (c. 8).

30. "EXCLUDING OR RESTRICTING LIABILITY"

(1) A reference to excluding or restricting a liability includes—
   (a) making a right or remedy in respect of the liability subject to a restrictive or onerous condition;
   (b) excluding or restricting a right or remedy in respect of the liability;
   (c) putting a person at a disadvantage if he pursues a right or remedy in respect of the liability;
   (d) excluding or restricting rules of evidence or procedure.

(2) A reference in Part 1 or section 5, 6, 10 or 13 to excluding or restricting a liability includes preventing an obligation or duty arising or limiting its extent.

(3) A written agreement to submit current or future differences to arbitration is not to be regarded as excluding or restricting the liability in question.

31. "HIRE-PURCHASE" AND "HIRE"

(1) A reference to a contract for the hire-purchase of goods is to a hire-purchase agreement within the meaning of the Consumer Credit Act 1974 (c. 39).

(2) A reference to a contract for the hire of goods is to be read with the 1982 Act.

32. GENERAL INTERPRETATION

(1)   In this Act—

"the 1973 Act" means the Supply of Goods (Implied Terms) Act 1973 (c. 13),

"the 1979 Act" means the Sale of Goods Act 1979 (c. 54),

"the 1982 Act" means the Supply of Goods and Services Act 1982 (c. 29),

"associated person" has the meaning given in section 28,

"business contract" has the meaning given in section 26(2),

"business liability" has the meaning given in section 1(3) and (4),

"consumer", in relation to a party to a consumer contract, has the meaning given by section 26(1)(a),

"consumer contract" has the meaning given in section 26(1),

"court" means—
(a) in England and Wales and Northern Ireland, the High Court or a county court, and
(b) in Scotland, the Court of Session or a sheriff,
        and, except in Schedule 1, includes a tribunal, arbitrator or arbiter,

"enactment" includes—
(a) a provision of, or of an instrument made under, an Act of the Scottish Parliament or Northern Ireland legislation, and
(b) a provision of subordinate legislation (within the meaning of the Interpretation Act 1978 (c. 30)),

"fair and reasonable", in relation to a contract term or a notice, has the meaning given in section 14,

"goods" has the same meaning as in the 1979 Act,

"injunction" includes interim injunction,

"interdict" includes interim interdict,

"negligence" has the meaning given in section 1(5),

"notice" includes an announcement, whether or not in writing, and any other communication,

"the OFT" means the Office of Fair Trading,

"personal injury" includes any disease and any impairment of physical or mental condition,

"public authority" has the same meaning as in section 6 of the Human Rights Act 1998 (c. 42),

"regulator" has the meaning given in paragraph 10 of Schedule 1,

"small business" has the meaning given in section 27,

"small business contract" has the meaning given in section 29,

"statutory" means conferred by an enactment,

"supplier", in relation to a contract for the hire-purchase of goods or a contract for the hire of goods, means the person by whom goods are bailed or (in Scotland) hired to another person under the contract, and

"transparent" has the meaning given in section 14(3).

(2)   A reference to a business includes a profession and the activities of a public authority.

(3)   A reference to excluding or restricting liability is to be read with section 30.

(4)   A reference to a contract for the hire-purchase or hire of goods is to be read with section 31.

Final provisions

. . .

34. CONSEQUENTIAL AMENDMENTS AND REPEALS, ETC.

(1)   Schedule 5 contains minor and consequential amendments.

(2)   Schedule 6 contains repeals and revocations.

. . .

SCHEDULES

SCHEDULE 1

Section 7

CONSUMER CONTRACT TERMS, ETC.: REGULATION AND ENFORCEMENT

Cases where this Schedule applies
1.   (1) This Schedule applies to a complaint about—
        (a) a consumer contract term,
        (b) a term drawn up or proposed for use as a consumer contract term, or
        (c) a term which a trade association recommends for use as a consumer contract term.

        (2) This Schedule also applies to a complaint about—
        (a) a notice relating to the rights conferred or duties imposed by a consumer contract on the parties, or
        (b) any other notice purporting to exclude or restrict liability for negligence.

Consideration of complaints
2.   (1) If the OFT receives a complaint to which this Schedule applies, it must consider the complaint unless—
        (a) it thinks that the complaint is frivolous or vexatious,
        (b) it is notified by a regulator that that regulator intends to consider the complaint, or
        (c) in the case of a complaint under paragraph 1(2)(b), it thinks that subparagraph (2) applies in relation to the notice.

        (2) This sub-paragraph applies in relation to a notice which—
        (a) does not exclude or restrict business liability for negligence, or
        (b) excludes or restricts such liability only in relation to a person who, at the time when the liability arises, is acting for purposes related to a business.

        (3) If the regulator intends to consider a complaint to which this Schedule applies, it must—
        (a) notify the OFT that it intends to consider the complaint, and
        (b) consider the complaint.

Application for injunction or interdict

3.   (1) The OFT (or a regulator) may apply for an injunction or interdict against such persons as it considers appropriate if it thinks that the term or notice to which the complaint relates comes within this paragraph.

(2) A term or notice comes within this paragraph if it purports to exclude or restrict liability of the kind mentioned in—
(a) section 1(1) (business liability for death or personal injury resulting from negligence), or
(b) section 5 (implied terms in supply of goods to consumer).

(3) A term or notice also comes within this paragraph if it—
(a) is drawn up for general use, and
(b) is not fair and reasonable.

(4) A term also comes within this paragraph if—
(a) however it is expressed, it is in its effect a term of a kind which the business usually seeks to include in the kind of consumer contract in question, and
(b) it is not fair and reasonable.

(5) A term which comes within paragraph 1(b) or (c) (but not within paragraph 1(a)) is to be treated for the purposes of section 14 (the "fair and reasonable" test) as if it were a contract term.

Notification of application

4.   (1) If a regulator intends to make an application under paragraph 3—
(a) it must notify the OFT of its intention, and
(b) it may make the application only if this paragraph applies.

(2) This paragraph applies if—
(a) the period of 14 days beginning with the date of the notification to the OFT has ended, or
(b) before the end of that period, the OFT allows the regulator to make the application.

(3) Where the OFT (or a regulator), having considered a complaint to which this Schedule applies, decides not to make an application under paragraph 3 in response to the complaint, it must give its reasons to the person who made the complaint.

Determination of application

5.   (1) On an application under paragraph 3, the court may grant an injunction or interdict on such conditions, and against such of the respondents, as it thinks appropriate.

(2) The injunction or interdict may include provision about—
(a) a term or notice to which the application relates;
(b) any consumer contract term, or any notice, of a similar kind or like effect.

(3) It is not a defence to show that, because of a rule of law, a term to which the application relates is not, or could not be, an enforceable contract term.

(4) If a regulator makes the application, it must notify the OFT of—
(a) the outcome of the application, and
(b) if an injunction or interdict is granted, the conditions on which, and the identity of any person against whom, it is granted.

Undertakings

6. (1) The OFT (or a regulator) may accept from a relevant person an undertaking that he will comply with such conditions about the use of specified terms or notices, or of terms or notices of a specified kind, as he and the OFT (or the regulator) may agree.

    (2) If a regulator accepts an undertaking under this paragraph, it must notify the OFT of—
    (a) the conditions on which the undertaking is accepted, and
    (b) the identity of the person who gave it.

    (3) "Relevant person", in relation to the OFT or a regulator, means a person against whom it has applied, or thinks it is entitled to apply, for an injunction or interdict under paragraph 3.

    (4) "Specified", in relation to an undertaking, means specified in the undertaking.

Power to obtain information

7. (1) The OFT (or a regulator which is a public authority) may, for a purpose mentioned in sub-paragraph (2)(a) or (b), give notice to a person requiring him to provide it with specified information.

    (2) The purposes are—
    (a) to facilitate the exercise of the OFT's (or the regulator's) functions for the purposes of this Schedule,
    (b) to find out whether a person has complied, or is complying, with—
        (i) an injunction or interdict granted under paragraph 5 on an application by the OFT (or the regulator), or
        (ii) an undertaking accepted by it under paragraph 6.

    (3) The notice must—
    (a) be in writing,
    (b) specify the purpose for which the information is required, and
    (c) specify how and when the notice is to be complied with.

    (4) The notice may require the production of specified documents or documents of a specified description.

    (5) The OFT (or the regulator) may take copies of any documents produced in compliance with the notice.

    (6) The notice may be varied or revoked by a subsequent notice under this paragraph.

    (7) The notice may not require a person to provide information or produce documents which he would be entitled to refuse to provide or produce—
    (a) in proceedings in the High Court, on the grounds of legal professional privilege;
    (b) in proceedings in the Court of Session, on the grounds of confidentiality of communication.

    (8) "Specified", in relation to a notice under this paragraph, means specified in the notice.

Notices under paragraph 7: enforcement

8. (1) If the OFT (or the regulator) thinks that a person (a "defaulter") has failed, or is failing, to comply with a notice given under paragraph 7, it may apply to the court for an order under this paragraph (a "compliance order").

    (2) If the court thinks that the defaulter has failed to comply with the notice, it may make a compliance order.

(3) A compliance order—
  (a) must specify such things as the court thinks it reasonable for the defaulter to do to ensure compliance with the notice;
  (b) must require the defaulter to do those things;
  (c) may require the defaulter to pay some or all of the costs or expenses of the application for the order ("the application costs").

(4) If the defaulter is a company or association, the court may, when acting under sub-paragraph (3)(c), require payment of some or all of the application costs by an officer of the company or association whom the court thinks responsible for the failure.

(5) If a regulator applies for a compliance order, it must notify the OFT of—
  (a) the outcome of the application, and
  (b) if the order is made, the conditions on which, and the identity of any person against whom, it is made.

(6) "Officer"—
  (a) in relation to a company, means a director, manager, secretary or other similar officer of the company,
  (b) in relation to a partnership, means a partner,
  (c) in relation to any other association, means an officer of the association or a member of its governing body.

Publication, information and advice

9.   (1) The OFT must arrange to publish details of any—
  (a) application it makes for an injunction or interdict under paragraph 3;
  (b) injunction or interdict granted on an application by it under paragraph 3;
  (c) injunction or interdict notified to it under paragraph 5(4)(b);
  (d) undertaking it accepts under paragraph 6(1);
  (e) undertaking notified to it under paragraph 6(2);
  (f) application it makes for a compliance order under paragraph 8(1);
  (g) compliance order made under paragraph 8(2);
  (h) compliance order notified to it under paragraph 8(5)(b).

(2) Sub-paragraph (3) applies where a person tells the OFT about a term or notice and asks the OFT whether that term or notice, or one of a similar kind or like effect, is or has been the subject of an injunction, interdict or undertaking under this Schedule.

(3) The OFT must reply; and if it replies that the term or notice, or one of a similar kind or like effect, is or has been the subject of an injunction, interdict or undertaking under this Schedule, the OFT must give the person—
  (a) a copy of the injunction or interdict or details of the undertaking, and
  (b) if the person giving the undertaking has agreed to amend the term or notice concerned, a copy of the amendments.

(4) The OFT may arrange to publish advice and information about the provisions of this Act.

(5) A reference to an injunction or interdict under this Schedule is to an injunction or interdict—
  (a) granted on an application by the OFT under paragraph 3, or
  (b) notified to it under paragraph 5(4)(b).

(6) A reference to an undertaking under this Schedule is to an undertaking—
  (a) accepted by the OFT under paragraph 6(1), or
  (b) notified to it under paragraph 6(2).

Meaning of "regulator"

10. (1) For the purposes of this Schedule, "regulator" means—
    (a) the Financial Services Authority,
    (b) the Office of Communications,
    (c) the Information Commissioner,
    (d) the Gas and Electricity Markets Authority,
    (e) the Water Services Regulation Authority,
    (f) the Office of Rail Regulation,
    (g) the Northern Ireland Authority for Energy Regulation,
    (h) the Department of Enterprise, Trade and Investment in Northern Ireland,
    (i) a local weights and measures authority in Great Britain, or
    (j) a body designated as a regulator under sub-paragraph (3).

    (2) The Secretary of State may by order amend sub-paragraph (1) so as to add, modify or omit an entry.

    (3) Where the Secretary of State thinks that a body which is not a public authority represents the interests of consumers (or consumers of a particular description), he may by order designate the body as a regulator.

    (4) The Secretary of State may cancel the designation if he thinks that the body has failed, or is likely to fail, to comply with a duty imposed on it under this Act.

    (5) The Secretary of State must publish (and may from time to time vary) other criteria to be applied by him in deciding whether to make or cancel a designation under this paragraph.

The Financial Services Authority

11. Any function that the Financial Services Authority has under this Act is to be regarded, for the purposes of the Financial Services and Markets Act 2000 (c. 8), as a function that it has under that Act.

SCHEDULE 2

Section 14(6)

CONTRACT TERMS WHICH MAY BE REGARDED AS NOT FAIR AND REASONABLE

Part 1 INTRODUCTION

1.—(1) A term of a consumer contract or small business contract may be regarded as not being fair and reasonable if it—
    (a) has the object or effect of a term listed in Part 2, and
    (b) does not come within an exception mentioned in Part 3.

    (2) In this Schedule—
    (a) in relation to a consumer contract, "A" means the consumer and "B" means the business, and
    (b) in relation to a small business contract, "A" and "B" mean, respectively, the persons referred to as A and B in section 11.

Part 2 LIST OF TERMS

2. A term excluding or restricting liability to A for breach of contract.

3. A term imposing obligations on A in circumstances where B's obligation to perform depends on the satisfaction of a condition wholly within B's control.

4.   A term entitling B, if A exercises a right to cancel the contract or if B terminates the contract as a result of A's breach, to keep sums that A has paid, the amount of which is unreasonable.

5.   A term requiring A, when in breach of contract, to pay B a sum significantly above the likely loss to B.

6.   A term entitling B to cancel the contract without incurring liability, unless there is also a term entitling A to cancel it without incurring liability.

7.   A term entitling B, if A exercises a right to cancel the contract, to keep sums A has paid in respect of services which B has yet to supply.

8.   A term in a fixed-term contract or a contract of indefinite duration entitling B to terminate the contract without giving A reasonable advance notice (except in an urgent case).

9.   A term—
     (a) providing for a contract of fixed duration to be renewed unless A indicates otherwise, and
     (b) requiring A to give that indication a disproportionately long time before the contract is due to expire.

10. A term binding A to terms with which A did not have an opportunity to become familiar before the contract was made.

11. A term entitling B, without a good reason which is specified in the contract, to vary the terms of the contract.

12. A term entitling B, without a good reason, to vary the characteristics of the goods or services concerned.

13. A term requiring A to pay whatever price is set for the goods at the time of delivery (including a case where the price is set by reference to a list price), unless there is also a term entitling A to cancel the contract if that price is higher than the price indicated to A when the contract was made.

14. A term entitling B to increase the price specified in the contract, unless there is also a term entitling A to cancel the contract if the business does increase the price.

15. A term giving B the exclusive right (and, accordingly, excluding any power of a court) to determine—
     (a) whether the goods or services supplied match the definition of them given in the contract, or
     (b) the meaning of any term in the contract.

16. A term excluding or restricting B's liability for statements or promises made by B's employees or agents, or making B's liability for statements or promises subject to formalities.

17. A term requiring A to carry out its obligations in full (in particular, to pay the whole of the price specified in the contract) in circumstances where B has failed to carry out its obligations in full.

18. A term entitling B to transfer its obligations without A's consent.

19. A term entitling B to transfer its rights in circumstances where A's position might be weakened as a result.

20. A term excluding or restricting A's right—
     (a) to bring or defend any action or other legal proceedings, or
     (b) to exercise other legal remedies.

21. A term restricting the evidence on which A may rely.

Part 3 EXCEPTIONS

Financial services contracts

22.—(1) Sub-paragraph (2) applies where a term in a financial services contract of indefinite duration provides that B may terminate the contract—

(a) by giving A relatively short advance notice, or

(b) if B has a good reason for terminating the contract, without giving A any advance notice.

(2) Paragraph 8 (termination without reasonable notice) does not apply to the term if the contract also provides that B must immediately inform A of the termination.

(3) Sub-paragraph (4) applies where a term in a financial services contract of indefinite duration provides that B may vary the interest rate or other charges payable under it—

(a) by giving A relatively short advance notice, or

(b) if B has a good reason for making the variation, without giving A any advance notice.

(4) Paragraph 11 (variation without good reason) does not apply to a term if the contract also provides that—

(a) B must as soon as practicable inform A of the variation, and

(b) A may then cancel the contract, without incurring liability.

(5) "Financial services contract" means a contract for the supply by B of financial services to A.

Contracts of indefinite duration

23.— Paragraph 11 (variation without good reason) does not apply to a term in a contract of indefinite duration if the contract also provides that—

(a) B must give reasonable notice of the variation, and

(b) A may then cancel the contract, without incurring liability.

Contracts for sale of securities, foreign currency, etc.

24.—(1) None of the following paragraphs applies to a contract term if subparagraph (2) or (3) applies—

(a) paragraph 8 (termination without reasonable notice),

(b) paragraph 11 (variation without good reason),

(c) paragraph 13 (determination of price at time of delivery),

(d) paragraph 14 (increase in price).

(2) This sub-paragraph applies if the contract is for the transfer of securities, financial instruments or anything else, the price of which is linked to—

(a) fluctuations in prices quoted on a stock exchange, or

(b) a financial index or market rate that B does not control.

(3) This sub-paragraph applies if the contract is for the sale of foreign currency (and, for this purpose, that includes foreign currency in the form of traveller's cheques or international money orders).

Price index clauses

25.— Neither paragraph 13 nor paragraph 14 (determination of price at time of delivery or increase in price) applies to a contract term if—

(a) the term provides for the price of the goods or services to be varied by reference to an index of prices, and

(b) the contract specifies how a change to the index is to affect the price.

SCHEDULE 3

Section 22

EXCEPTIONS

Legal requirements
1.—(1) This Act does not apply to a contract term—
  (a) required by an enactment or a rule of law,
  (b) required or authorised by a provision in an international convention to which the United Kingdom or the European Community is a party, or
  (c) required by, or incorporated as a result of a decision or ruling of, a competent authority acting in the exercise of its statutory jurisdiction or any of its functions.

  (2) Sub-paragraph 1(c) does not apply if the competent authority is itself a party to the contract.

  (3) "Competent authority" means a public authority other than a local authority.

Settlements of claims
2. (1) This Act does not apply to a contract term in so far as it is, or forms part of—
  (a) a settlement of a claim in tort;
  (b) a discharge or indemnity given by a person in consideration of the receipt by him of compensation in settlement of any claim which he has.

  (2) In sub-paragraph (1)—
  (a) paragraph (a) does not extend to Scotland, and
  (b) paragraph (b) extends only to Scotland.

Insurance
3. The following sections do not apply to an insurance contract (including a contract to pay an annuity on human life)—
  (a) section 1 (exclusion of business liability for negligence),
  (b) section 9 (exclusion of liability for breach of business contract where one party deals on written standard terms of the other),
  (c) section 11 (non-negotiated terms in small business contracts),
  (d) section 12 (exclusion of employer's liability under employment contract).

Land
4. The following sections do not apply to a contract term in so far as it relates to the creation, transfer, variation or termination of an interest or real right in land—
  (a) section 1 (exclusion of business liability for negligence),
  (b) section 9 (exclusion of liability for breach of business contract where one party deals on written standard terms of the other),
  (c) section 11 (non-negotiated terms in small business contracts).

Intellectual property
5. Nor do those sections apply to a contract term in so far as it relates to the creation, transfer, variation or termination of a right or interest in any patent, trade mark, copyright or design right, registered design, technical or commercial information or other intellectual property.

Company formation, etc.
6. Nor do those sections apply to a contract term in so far as it relates to—
  (a) the formation or dissolution of a body corporate or unincorporated association (including a partnership),

(b) its constitution, or

(c) the rights and obligations of its members.

Securities

7. Nor do those sections apply to a contract term in so far as it relates to the creation or transfer of securities or of a right or interest in securities.

International supply contracts

8. The following provisions do not apply to a business contract for the supply of goods where the supply is to be made to a place outside the United Kingdom—

   (a) section 1(2) (business liability for negligence other than in case of death or personal injury),

   (b) sections 9 to 11 (unfair terms in business contracts),

   (c) sections 19 and 20 (choice of law in business contracts).

Shipping

9. (1) Section 1(2) does not apply to a shipping contract unless it is also a consumer contract.

   (2) Sections 9 and 11 do not apply to a shipping contract.

   (3) "Shipping contract" means—

      (a) a contract of marine salvage or towage,

      (b) a charterparty of a ship or hovercraft, or

      (c) a contract for the carriage of goods by ship or hovercraft.

10. (1) This paragraph applies where goods are carried by ship or hovercraft under a contract which—

      (a) specifies that as the means of transport for part of the journey, or

      (b) does not specify a means of transport but does not exclude that one.

   (2) Section 1(2) does not apply to the contract, unless it is also a consumer contract, in so far as it relates to the carriage of the goods by that means of transport.

   (3) Sections 9 and 11 do not apply to the contract in so far as it relates to the carriage of the goods by that means of transport.

SCHEDULE 4

Section 27

CALCULATING THE NUMBER OF EMPLOYEES IN A BUSINESS

. . .

SCHEDULE 5

Section 34(1)

MINOR AND CONSEQUENTIAL AMENDMENTS

. . .

SCHEDULE 6

Section 34(2)

REPEALS AND REVOCATIONS

DRAFT PENALTY CLAUSES (SCOTLAND) BILL

[*A Consultation on a Penalty Clauses (Scotland) Bill, July 2010*]
An Act of the Scottish Parliament to make new provision as respects the enforceability of
penalty clauses in contracts and in unilateral voluntary obligations; and for connected purposes.

1 ENFORCEABILITY OF PENALTY CLAUSES

(1)   A penalty clause in a contract is unenforceable in a particular case if the penalty for which
the clause provides is manifestly excessive (whether or not having regard to any loss
suffered) in that case.

(2)   Any rule of law under which such a clause is unenforceable if it is not founded in a pre-
estimate of damages ceases to have effect.

(3)   In subsection (1)—

"penalty" means a penalty of any kind (including, in particular, a forfeiture or an
obligation to transfer); and

"penalty clause"—
(a)   does not include a clause of irritancy of a lease of land; but
(b)   means any other clause, in whatever form, the substance of which is that a penalty is
incurred in the event of—
(i)   breach of, or early termination of, the contract; or
(ii)   failure to do, or to do in a particular way, something provided for in the contract.

(4)   In determining, for the purposes of subsection (1), whether a penalty is manifestly
excessive all circumstances which appear relevant are to be taken into account; and such
circumstances may include circumstances arising after the contract is entered into.

2 ONUS OF PROOF

The onus of proving that a penalty is manifestly excessive lies on the party so contending.

3 PURPORTED EVASION

Where a term of a contract would (but for this section) have the effect of excluding or
restricting the application of a provision of this Act in respect of that or any other contract, the
term is void.

4 POWER TO MODIFY A PENALTY

(1)   Where a court determines that a penalty provided for in a contract is manifestly excessive
in a particular case then on application it may, if it thinks fit, modify the penalty in that
case so as to make the penalty clause enforceable in the case.

(2)   In subsection (1), modifying a penalty includes imposing a condition as respects the penalty.

(3)   Subsection (1) applies to a tribunal or arbiter as it applies to a court (provided that the
tribunal or arbiter has power to adjudicate on the enforceability of the penalty).

5 APPLICATION OF ACT TO UNILATERAL VOLUNTARY OBLIGATIONS

This Act applies to unilateral voluntary obligations as it applies to contracts.

6 SHORT TITLE, COMMENCEMENT AND APPLICATION

(1)   This Act may be cited as the Penalty Clauses (Scotland) Act 2010.

(2)   This Act comes into force at the end of the period of 3 months beginning with Royal Assent.

(3)   This Act applies only as respects a penalty clause agreed to on or after the date on which the Act comes into force.

DEFAMATION BILL 2011

1 RESPONSIBLE PUBLICATION ON MATTERS OF PUBLIC INTEREST

(1)   Any defendant in an action for defamation has a defence if the defendant shows that—
       (a) the words or matters complained of were published for the purposes of, or otherwise in connection with, the discussion of a matter of public interest; and
       (b) the defendant acted responsibly in making the publication.

(2)   Subsection (1) applies irrespective of whether the publication contains statements of fact or inferences or opinions.

(3)   The court when deciding for the purposes of subsection (1)(b) whether the defendant has acted responsibly must have regard to all the circumstances of the case.

(4)   Those circumstances may include (among other things)—
       (a) the nature of the publication and its context;
       (b) the nature and seriousness of anything alleged about the claimant;
       (c) what information the defendant had before publication;
       (d) what steps (if any) were taken by the defendant to verify what was published;
       (e) if appropriate, whether the defendant gave the claimant an opportunity to comment before publication;
       (f) whether there were factors supporting urgent publication;
       (g) the extent of the defendant's compliance with any relevant code of conduct or other relevant guidelines; or
       (h) whether subsection (5) applies.

(5)   Where a publication reports accurately and impartially on a pre-existing matter (for example, that there is a dispute between two parties), a defendant may be regarded as acting responsibly to the extent that the court is satisfied that it is in the public interest for the existence of that matter, and anything reported in connection with it, to be the subject of a report or series of reports.

(6)   In determining for the purposes of subsection (5) whether publication is in the public interest, the court may disregard any question as to the truth of anything reported in connection with a pre-existing matter.

2 HONEST OPINION

In an action for defamation, the defence known before the commencement of this section as the defence of fair comment is, after commencement, to be known as the defence of honest opinion.

3 ESTABLISHING A DEFENCE OF HONEST OPINION

(1)   A defendant has a defence of honest opinion in an action for defamation if the defendant shows that Conditions 1 to 4 are satisfied (subject to subsections (7) and (8)).

(2)   Condition 1 is that the words or matters complained of relate to a matter of public interest.

(3)   Condition 2 is that, in the circumstances in which the words or matters are published, an ordinary person would reasonably consider those words or matters to be an opinion.

(4)   Condition 3 is that, at the time of publication, there existed—
    (a)   one or more facts;
    (b)   any material that falls within section 1 (responsible publication on matters of public interest);
    (c)   any material that falls within section 6, 7 or 8 (statutory privilege); or
    (d)   any material that is otherwise protected by privilege.

(5)   Condition 4 is that an honest person could form the opinion on the basis of the facts or material shown by the defendant in satisfying Condition 3.

(6)   In relation to the facts or material relied on by the defendant as providing a basis for the opinion, no account is to be taken of—
    (a)   anything that the defendant does not show, provided that the defendant shows that Condition 4 is satisfied on the basis of what is shown;
    (b)   whether the defendant first learned of the facts or material before or after publication; or
    (c)   whether the facts or material were or were not included (by reference or otherwise) in the publication.

(7)   There is no defence of honest opinion if the claimant shows that the defendant did not in fact hold the opinion.

(8)   Where the defendant was not the author ("A") of the words or matters complained of, there is no defence of honest opinion if the claimant shows that-
    (a)   the defendant knew that A did not in fact hold the opinion; or
    (b)   the defendant had reason to believe that A did not in fact hold the opinion and published without determining whether or not A did hold it.

4 TRUTH

In an action for defamation, the defence known before the commencement of this section as the defence of justification is, after commencement, to be known as the defence of truth.

5 ESTABLISHING A DEFENCE OF TRUTH

(1)   A defendant has a defence of truth in an action for defamation if the words or matters complained of are substantially true.

(2)   For these purposes, the defendant may show either that—
    (a)   the meaning (or meanings) alleged by the claimant are substantially true; or
    (b)   the words or matters complained of have a less serious meaning (or meanings) and each such meaning is substantially true.

(3)   A defence of justification does not fail only because a particular meaning alleged by the claimant is not shown as being substantially true, if that meaning would not materially

injure the claimant's reputation having regard to the truth of what the defendant has shown to be substantially true.

(4) Where—
(a) the words or matters complained of make two or more distinct allegations; and
(b) the truth of every allegation is not shown;
a defence of justification does not fail only because of paragraph (b) if anything not shown to be true does not materially injure the claimant's reputation having regard to the truth of the remaining allegations.

6 REPORTS OF COURT PROCEEDINGS PROTECTED BY ABSOLUTE PRIVILEGE

(1) A fair and accurate report of proceedings in public before a court to which this section applies, if published contemporaneously with the proceedings, is absolutely privileged.

(2) A report of proceedings which by an order of the court, or as a consequence of any statutory provision, is required to be postponed is to be treated as published contemporaneously if it is published as soon as practicable after publication is permitted.

(3) This section applies to—
(a) any court in the United Kingdom;
(b) the European Court of Justice or any court attached to that court;
(c) the European Court of Human Rights;
(d) any international criminal tribunal established by the Security Council of the United Nations or by an international agreement to which the United Kingdom is a party;
(e) any court established under the law of a country or territory outside the United Kingdom;
(f) the Inter-American Court of Human Rights;
(g) the African Court of Human and People's Rights;
(h) the International Court of Justice; and
(i) any other judicial or arbitral tribunal deciding matters in dispute between States.
In paragraph (a) "court" includes any tribunal or body exercising the judicial power of the State.

7 REPORTS ETC OF CERTAIN PARLIAMENTARY MATTERS PROTECTED BY ABSOLUTE PRIVILEGE

(1) The following are absolutely privileged—
(a) a fair and accurate report of proceedings in Parliament;
(b) a fair and accurate report of anything published by or on the authority of Parliament; and
(c) a fair and accurate copy of, extract from or summary of anything published by or on the authority of Parliament.

(2) The court must stay any proceedings where the defendant shows that—
(a) the proceedings relate to the publication of anything that falls within paragraph (a), (b) or (c) of subsection (1); or
(b) the proceedings seek to prevent or postpone the making of any such publication.

(3) This section also has effect in relation to the Welsh Assembly and the Northern Ireland Assembly (and any reference to Parliament is to be read as a reference to the Assembly in question).

8 OTHER REPORTS ETC PROTECTED BY QUALIFIED PRIVILEGE

(1)   The publication of any report or other statement mentioned in Schedule 1 to this Act is privileged unless the publication is shown to be made with malice, subject as follows.

(2)   In an action for defamation in respect of the publication of a report or other statement mentioned in Part 2 of Schedule 1, there is no defence under this section if the claimant shows that the defendant—
    (a) was requested by the claimant to publish in a suitable manner a reasonable letter or statement by way of explanation or contradiction;
    and
    (b) refused or neglected to do so without sufficient cause.

(3)   For this purpose "in a suitable manner" means in the same manner as the publication complained of or in a manner that is adequate and reasonable in the circumstances.

(4)   This section does not apply to the publication to the public, or a section of the public, of matter which is not of public concern and the publication of which is not for the public benefit.

(5)   Nothing in this section is to be construed—
    (a) as protecting the publication of matter the publication of which is prohibited by law; or
    (b) as limiting or abridging any privilege subsisting apart from this section.

9 RESPONSIBILITY FOR PUBLICATION

(1)   Any defendant in an action for defamation has a defence if the defendant shows that the defendant's only involvement in the publication of the words or matters complained of—
    (a) is as a facilitator; or
    (b) is as a broadcaster of a live programme in circumstances in which it was not reasonably foreseeable that those words or matters would be published.

(2)   Any defendant in an action for defamation, apart from a primary publisher, has a defence unless the claimant shows that—
    (a) the notice requirements specified in subsection (3) have been complied with;
    (b) the notice period specified in subsection (4) has expired; and
    (c) the words or matters complained of have not been removed from the publication.

(3)   The notice requirements are that the substance of the claimant's complaint must be communicated in writing to the defendant, specifying—
    (a) the words or matters complained of and the person (or persons) to whom they relate;
    (b) the publication that contains those words or matters;
    (c) why the claimant considers the words or matters to be defamatory;
    (d) the details of any matters relied on in the publication which the claimant considers to be untrue; and
    (e) why the claimant considers the words or matters to be harmful in the circumstances in which they were published.

(4)   The notice period is—
    (a) the period of 14 days starting with the date of receipt by the defendant of all the information required by subsection (3); or
    (b) such other period as the court may specify (whether of its own motion or on an application by any party to the action).

(5) Employees or agents of a primary publisher, or other person who publishes the words or matters complained of, are in the same position as their principal to the extent that they are responsible for the content of what is published or the decision to publish it.

(6) In this section—

"facilitator" means a person who is concerned only with the transmission or storage of the content of the publication and has no other influence or control over it; and

"primary publisher" means an author, an editor or a person who exercises effective control of an author or editor.

(7) For the purposes of the definition of "primary publisher" in subsection (6)—

"author" means—

(a) a person who originates the words or matters complained of;
   but

(b) does not include a person who does not intend that they be published; and "editor", in relation to a publication, means –

(a) a person who originates the words or matters complained of;

   but

(b) does not include a person who does not intend that they be published; and

"editor", in relation to a publication, means a person with editorial or equivalent responsibility for the content of the publication or the decision to publish it.

(8) This section does not apply to any cause of action which arose before the section came into force.

10 MULTIPLE PUBLICATIONS

(1) In any case to which subsection (2) applies—
   (a) the first occasion on which the publication is made available to the public generally (or to any section of the public) is to be regarded for all purposes as the date of publication of each subsequent publication; and
   (b) in an action for defamation based on any publication to which this section applies, the cause of action is to be treated as having accrued on that date.

(2) This subsection applies to any publication (such as a book, newspaper, periodical or material in an archive) which—
   (a) is published by the same person on multiple occasions; and
   (b) on each occasion, has the same, or substantially the same, content.

(3) Subsection (2) does not apply where a subsequent publication is made in a materially different manner, but this is without prejudice to that publication itself constituting a first publication for the purposes of subsection (1).

11 ACTION FOR DEFAMATION BROUGHT BY BODY CORPORATE

A body corporate which seeks to pursue an action for defamation must show that the publication of the words or matters complained of has caused, or is likely to cause, substantial financial loss to the body corporate.

12 STRIKING OUT WHERE CLAIMANT SUFFERS NO SUBSTANTIAL HARM

(1)   The court must strike out an action for defamation unless the claimant shows that—

(a) the publication of the words or matters complained of has caused substantial harm to the claimant's reputation; or

(b) it is likely that such harm will be caused to the claimant's reputation by the publication.

(2)   Subsection (1) does not apply if, in exceptional circumstances, the court is satisfied that it would be in the interests of justice not to strike out the action.

(3)   In determining whether a claimant's reputation is or may be substantially harmed, the court must have regard to all the circumstances of the case.

(4)   An order under subsection (1) may be made by the court of its own motion or on an application by any party to the action.

(5)   Subsection (1) does not limit any power to strike out proceedings which is exercisable apart from this section.

13 HARMFUL EVENT IN CASES OF PUBLICATION OUTSIDE THE JURISDICTION

(1)   This section applies in an action for defamation where the court is satisfied that the words or matters complained of have also been published outside the jurisdiction (including publication outside the jurisdiction of any words or matters that differ only in ways not affecting their substance).

(2)   No harmful event is to be regarded as having occurred in relation to the claimant unless the publication in the jurisdiction can reasonably be regarded as having caused substantial harm to the claimant's reputation having regard to the extent of publication elsewhere.

14 REVERSAL OF PRESUMPTION OF TRIAL BY A JURY IN DEFAMATION PROCEEDINGS

In section 69(1)(b) of the Senior Courts Act 1981 (trial by jury) omit the words "libel, slander".

15 DETERMINING AN APPLICATION FOR TRIAL BY A JURY

(1)   If the court is satisfied that it is in the interests of justice to do so, it may order trial by jury of such matter or matters arising in an action for defamation as are specified in the order.

(2)   An order under subsection (1) may be made on an application by any party to the action and the court determining the application must have regard to all the circumstances of the case.

(3)   Those circumstances may include (among other things)—

(a) whether there is a public interest in the subject matter of the action or anything arising in connection with it;

(b) the identity of any of the parties to the action;

(c) any office or other position held by any party to the action;

(d) whether it is in the interests of justice that the verdict of a jury or a reasoned judgment be obtained on any matter arising in the action;

(e) the extent to which early resolution of any matter (for example, as to the meaning of the words complained of) is likely to facilitate settlement of the action, improve active case management or assist in achieving a just and equitable outcome; and

(f)   whether the trial is likely to require the prolonged examination of documents or accounts or any scientific or local investigation which cannot conveniently be made with a jury.

(4)   An application must be made in accordance with such procedure as may be prescribed by rules of court.

16 EVIDENCE CONCERNING PROCEEDINGS IN PARLIAMENT

(1)   In this section "the relevant protection", in relation to the proceedings of either House of Parliament, means the protection of any enactment or rule of law which prevents proceedings in Parliament being impeached or questioned in any court or place out of Parliament.

(2)   The Speaker of either House of Parliament may, in accordance with Standing Orders of that House, by notice in writing waive the application of the relevant protection to such proceedings in an action for defamation as are specified in that notice.

(3)   Where the relevant protection is waived in relation to any proceedings in an action for defamation—
(a)   that protection is not to apply to prevent evidence being given, questions being asked or statements, submissions, comments or findings being made in those proceedings; and
(b)   none of those things is to be regarded as infringing the privilege of either House of Parliament.

(4)   Nothing in this section affects any enactment or rule of law so far as it protects a person from legal liability for words spoken or things done in the course of, or for the purposes of or incidental to, any proceedings in Parliament.

(5)   Without prejudice to the generality of subsection (4), that subsection applies to—
(a)   the giving of evidence before either House or a committee;
(b)   the presentation or submission of a document to either House or a committee;
(c)   the preparation of a document for the purposes of or incidental to the transacting of any such business;
(d)   the formulation, making or publication of a document, including a report, by or pursuant to an order of either House or a committee; and
(e)   any communication with the Parliamentary Commissioner for Standards or any person having functions in connection with the registration of members' interests.

In this subsection "a committee" means a committee of either House or a joint committee of both Houses of Parliament.

17 INTERPRETATION

(1)   In this Act—

"the 1996 Act" means the Defamation Act 1996;

"archive" includes any collection of sound recordings, images or other information however stored (including by electronic means);

"author" has the meaning given in section 9;

"publication" and "publish", in relation to a statement, have the meaning they have for the purposes of the law of defamation generally but "primary publisher" is specially defined for the purposes of section 9;

"statement" means words, pictures, visual images, gestures or any other method of signifying meaning;

"statutory provision" means—

(a) a provision contained in an Act or in subordinate legislation within the meaning of the Interpretation Act 1978;

(b) a provision contained in an Act of the Scottish Parliament or in an instrument made under such an Act; or

(c) a statutory provision within the meaning of the Interpretation Act (Northern Ireland) 1954.

(2) In this Act any reference to—

(a) a defendant in an action for defamation includes any person against whom a counterclaim for defamation is brought; and

(b) an action for defamation is to be construed accordingly.

. . .

20 EXTENT

(1) This Act extends to England, Wales and Northern Ireland.

(2) An amendment or repeal contained in this Act has the same extent as the enactment to which it relates.

(3) Subsection (2) does not apply to any amendment or repeal of an enactment which extends to Scotland.

21 COMMENCEMENT

(1) The following provisions of this Act come into force on the day this Act is passed—

(a) section 20;

(b) this section; and

(c) section 22.

(2) The other provisions of this Act come into force on such day as may be appointed by order of the Secretary of State; and different days may be appointed for different purposes.

(3) Any such order is to be made by statutory instrument.

EU Materials

DIRECTIVE 2011/83/EU OF THE EUROPEAN PARLIAMENT AND OF THE COUNCIL
of 25 October 2011

on consumer rights, amending Council Directive 93/13/EEC and Directive 1999/44/EC of the European Parliament and of the Council and repealing Council Directive 85/577/EEC and Directive 97/7/EC of the European Parliament and of the Council

. . .

HAVE ADOPTED THIS DIRECTIVE:

CHAPTER I

SUBJECT MATTER, DEFINITIONS AND SCOPE

Article 1

Subject matter
The purpose of this Directive is, through the achievement of a high level of consumer protection, to contribute to the proper functioning of the internal market by approximating certain aspects of the laws, regulations and administrative provisions of the Member States concerning contracts concluded between consumers and traders.

Article 2

Definitions
For the purpose of this Directive, the following definitions shall apply:

(1) 'consumer' means any natural person who, in contracts covered by this Directive, is acting for purposes which are outside his trade, business, craft or profession;

(2) 'trader' means any natural person or any legal person, irrespective of whether privately or publicly owned, who is acting, including through any other person acting in his name or on his behalf, for purposes relating to his trade, business, craft or profession in relation to contracts covered by this Directive;

(3) 'goods' means any tangible movable items, with the exception of items sold by way of execution or otherwise by authority of law; water, gas and electricity shall be considered as goods within the meaning of this Directive where they are put up for sale in a limited volume or a set quantity;

(4)   'goods made to the consumer's specifications' means non- prefabricated goods made on the basis of an individual choice of or decision by the consumer;

(5)   'sales contract' means any contract under which the trader transfers or undertakes to transfer the ownership of goods to the consumer and the consumer pays or undertakes to pay the price thereof, including any contract having as its object both goods and services;

(6)   'service contract' means any contract other than a sales contract under which the trader supplies or undertakes to supply a service to the consumer and the consumer pays or undertakes to pay the price thereof;

(7)   'distance contract' means any contract concluded between the trader and the consumer under an organised distance sales or service-provision scheme without the simultaneous physical presence of the trader and the consumer, with the exclusive use of one or more means of distance communication up to and including the time at which the contract is concluded;

(8)   'off-premises contract' means any contract between the trader and the consumer:
   (a)   concluded in the simultaneous physical presence of the trader and the consumer, in a place which is not the business premises of the trader;
   (b)   for which an offer was made by the consumer in the same circumstances as referred to in point (a);
   (c)   concluded on the business premises of the trader or through any means of distance communication immediately after the consumer was personally and individually addressed in a place which is not the business premises of the trader in the simultaneous physical presence of the trader and the consumer; or
   (d)   concluded during an excursion organised by the trader with the aim or effect of promoting and selling goods or services to the consumer;

(9)   'business premises' means:
   (a)   any immovable retail premises where the trader carries out his activity on a permanent basis; or
   (b)   any movable retail premises where the trader carries out his activity on a usual basis;

(10)   'durable medium' means any instrument which enables the consumer or the trader to store information addressed personally to him in a way accessible for future reference for a period of time adequate for the purposes of the information and which allows the unchanged reproduction of the information stored;

(11)   'digital content' means data which are produced and supplied in digital form;

(12)   'financial service' means any service of a banking, credit, insurance, personal pension, investment or payment

(13)   'public auction' means a method of sale where goods or services are offered by the trader to consumers, who attend or are given the possibility to attend the auction in person, through a transparent, competitive bidding procedure run by an auctioneer and where the successful bidder is bound to purchase the goods or services;

(14)   'commercial guarantee' means any undertaking by the trader or a producer (the guarantor) to the consumer, in addition to his legal obligation relating to the guarantee of conformity, to reimburse the price paid or to replace, repair or service goods in any way if they do not meet the specifications or any other requirements not related to conformity set out in the guarantee statement or in the relevant advertising available at the time of, or before the conclusion of the contract;

(15)   'ancillary contract' means a contract by which the consumer acquires goods or services related to a distance contract or an off-premises contract and where those goods are

supplied or those services are provided by the trader or by a third party on the basis of an arrangement between that third party and the trader.

Article 3

Scope
1. This Directive shall apply, under the conditions and to the extent set out in its provisions, to any contract concluded between a trader and a consumer. It shall also apply to contracts for the supply of water, gas, electricity or district heating, including by public providers, to the extent that these commodities are provided on a contractual basis.

2. If any provision of this Directive conflicts with a provision of another Union act governing specific sectors, the provision of that other Union act shall prevail and shall apply to those specific sectors.

3. This Directive shall not apply to contracts:
   (a) for social services, including social housing, childcare and support of families and persons permanently or temporarily in need, including long-term care;
   (b) for healthcare as defined in point (a) of Article 3 of Directive 2011/24/EU, whether or not they are provided via healthcare facilities;
   (c) for gambling, which involves wagering a stake with pecuniary value in games of chance, including lotteries, casino games and betting transactions;
   (d) for financial services;
   (e) for the creation, acquisition or transfer of immovable property or of rights in immovable property;
   (f) for the construction of new buildings, the substantial conversion of existing buildings and for rental of accommodation for residential purposes;
   (g) which fall within the scope of Council Directive 90/314/EEC of 13 June 1990 on package travel, package holidays and package tours. . .;
   (h) which fall within the scope of Directive 2008/122/EC of the European Parliament and of the Council of 14 January 2009 on the protection of consumers in respect of certain aspects of timeshare, long-term holiday product, resale and exchange contracts. . .;
   (i) which, in accordance with the laws of Member States, are established by a public office-holder who has a statutory obligation to be independent and impartial and who must ensure, by providing comprehensive legal information, that the consumer only concludes the contract on the basis of careful legal consideration and with knowledge of its legal scope;
   (j) for the supply of foodstuffs, beverages or other goods intended for current consumption in the household, and which are physically supplied by a trader on frequent and regular rounds to the consumer's home, residence or workplace;
   (k) for passenger transport services, with the exception of Article 8(2) and Articles 19 and 22;
   (l) concluded by means of automatic vending machines or automated commercial premises;
   (m) concluded with telecommunications operators through public payphones for their use or concluded for the use of one single connection by telephone, Internet or fax established by a consumer.

4. Member States may decide not to apply this Directive or not to maintain or introduce corresponding national provisions to off-premises contracts for which the payment to be made by the consumer does not exceed EUR 50. Member States may define a lower value in their national legislation.

5. This Directive shall not affect national general contract law such as the rules on the validity, formation or effect of a contract, in so far as general contract law aspects are not regulated in this Directive.

6. This Directive shall not prevent traders from offering consumers contractual arrangements which go beyond the protection provided for in this Directive.

Article 4

Level of harmonisation

Member States shall not maintain or introduce, in their national law, provisions diverging from those laid down in this Directive, including more or less stringent provisions to ensure a different level of consumer protection, unless otherwise provided for in this Directive.

CHAPTER II

CONSUMER INFORMATION FOR CONTRACTS OTHER THAN DISTANCE OR OFF-PREMISES CONTRACTS

Article 5

Information requirements for contracts other than distance or off-premises contracts

1. Before the consumer is bound by a contract other than a distance or an off-premises contract, or any corresponding offer, the trader shall provide the consumer with the following information in a clear and comprehensible manner, if that information is not already apparent from the context:
   (a) the main characteristics of the goods or services, to the extent appropriate to the medium and to the goods or services;
   (b) the identity of the trader, such as his trading name, the geographical address at which he is established and his telephone number;
   (c) the total price of the goods or services inclusive of taxes, or where the nature of the goods or services is such that the price cannot reasonably be calculated in advance, the manner in which the price is to be calculated, as well as, where applicable, all additional freight, delivery or postal charges or, where those charges cannot reasonably be calculated in advance, the fact that such additional charges may be payable;
   (d) where applicable, the arrangements for payment, delivery, performance, the time by which the trader undertakes to deliver the goods or to perform the service, and the trader's complaint handling policy;
   (e) in addition to a reminder of the existence of a legal guarantee of conformity for goods, the existence and the conditions of after-sales services and commercial guarantees, where applicable;
   (f) the duration of the contract, where applicable, or, if the contract is of indeterminate duration or is to be extended automatically, the conditions for terminating the contract;
   (g) where applicable, the functionality, including applicable technical protection measures, of digital content;
   (h) where applicable, any relevant interoperability of digital content with hardware and software that the trader is aware of or can reasonably be expected to have been aware of.

2. Paragraph 1 shall also apply to contracts for the supply of water, gas or electricity, where they are not put up for sale in a limited volume or set quantity, of district heating or of digital content which is not supplied on a tangible medium.

3.   Member States shall not be required to apply paragraph 1 to contracts which involve day-to-day transactions and which are performed immediately at the time of their conclusion.

4.   Member States may adopt or maintain additional pre- contractual information requirements for contracts to which this Article applies.

CHAPTER III

CONSUMER INFORMATION AND RIGHT OF WITHDRAWAL FOR DISTANCE AND OFF-PREMISES CONTRACTS

Article 6

Information requirements for distance and off-premises contracts
1.   Before the consumer is bound by a distance or off- premises contract, or any corresponding offer, the trader shall provide the consumer with the following information in a clear and comprehensible manner:
(a)   the main characteristics of the goods or services, to the extent appropriate to the medium and to the goods or services;
(b)   the identity of the trader, such as his trading name;
(c)   the geographical address at which the trader is established and the trader's telephone number, fax number and e-mail address, where available, to enable the consumer to contact the trader quickly and communicate with him efficiently and, where applicable, the geographical address and identity of the trader on whose behalf he is acting;
(d)   if different from the address provided in accordance with point (c), the geographical address of the place of business of the trader, and, where applicable, that of the trader on whose behalf he is acting, where the consumer can address any complaints;
(e)   the total price of the goods or services inclusive of taxes, or where the nature of the goods or services is such that the price cannot reasonably be calculated in advance, the manner in which the price is to be calculated, as well as, where applicable, all additional freight, delivery or postal charges and any other costs or, where those charges cannot reasonably be calculated in advance, the fact that such additional charges may be payable. In the case of a contract of indeterminate duration or a contract containing a subscription, the total price shall include the total costs per billing period. Where such contracts are charged at a fixed rate, the total price shall also mean the total monthly costs. Where the total costs cannot be reasonably calculated in advance, the manner in which the price is to be calculated shall be provided;
(f)   the cost of using the means of distance communication for the conclusion of the contract where that cost is calculated other than at the basic rate;
(g)   the arrangements for payment, delivery, performance, the time by which the trader undertakes to deliver the goods or to perform the services and, where applicable, the trader's complaint handling policy;
(h)   where a right of withdrawal exists, the conditions, time limit and procedures for exercising that right in accordance with Article 11(1), as well as the model withdrawal form set out in Annex I(B);
(i)   where applicable, that the consumer will have to bear the cost of returning the goods in case of withdrawal and, for distance contracts, if the goods, by their nature, cannot normally be returned by post, the cost of returning the goods;
(j)   that, if the consumer exercises the right of withdrawal after having made a request in accordance with Article 7(3) or Article 8(8), the consumer shall be liable to pay the trader reasonable costs in accordance with Article 14(3);

(k) where a right of withdrawal is not provided for in accordance with Article 16, the information that the consumer will not benefit from a right of withdrawal or, where applicable, the circumstances under which the consumer loses his right of withdrawal;

(l) a reminder of the existence of a legal guarantee of conformity for goods;

(m) where applicable, the existence and the conditions of after sale customer assistance, after-sales services and commercial guarantees;

(n) the existence of relevant codes of conduct, as defined in point (f) of Article 2 of Directive 2005/29/EC, and how copies of them can be obtained, where applicable;

(o) the duration of the contract, where applicable, or, if the contract is of indeterminate duration or is to be extended automatically, the conditions for terminating the contract;

(p) where applicable, the minimum duration of the consumer's obligations under the contract;

(q) where applicable, the existence and the conditions of deposits or other financial guarantees to be paid or provided by the consumer at the request of the trader;

(r) where applicable, the functionality, including applicable technical protection measures, of digital content;

(s) where applicable, any relevant interoperability of digital content with hardware and software that the trader is aware of or can reasonably be expected to have been aware of;

(t) where applicable, the possibility of having recourse to an out-of-court complaint and redress mechanism, to which the trader is subject, and the methods for having access to it.

2. Paragraph 1 shall also apply to contracts for the supply of water, gas or electricity, where they are not put up for sale in a limited volume or set quantity, of district heating or of digital content which is not supplied on a tangible medium.

3. In the case of a public auction, the information referred to in points (b), (c) and (d) of paragraph 1 may be replaced by the equivalent details for the auctioneer.

4. The information referred to in points (h), (i) and (j) of paragraph 1 may be provided by means of the model instructions on withdrawal set out in Annex I(A). The trader shall have fulfilled the information requirements laid down in points (h), (i) and (j) of paragraph 1 if he has supplied these instructions to the consumer, correctly filled in.

5. The information referred to in paragraph 1 shall form an integral part of the distance or off-premises contract and shall not be altered unless the contracting parties expressly agree otherwise.

6. If the trader has not complied with the information requirements on additional charges or other costs as referred to in point (e) of paragraph 1, or on the costs of returning the goods as referred to in point (i) of paragraph 1, the consumer shall not bear those charges or costs.

7. Member States may maintain or introduce in their national law language requirements regarding the contractual information, so as to ensure that such information is easily understood by the consumer.

8. The information requirements laid down in this Directive are in addition to information requirements contained in Directive 2006/123/EC and Directive 2000/31/EC and do not prevent Member States from imposing additional information requirements in accordance with those Directives.

Without prejudice to the first subparagraph, if a provision of Directive 2006/123/EC or Directive 2000/31/EC on the content and the manner in which the information is to be provided conflicts with a provision of this Directive, the provision of this Directive shall prevail.

9. As regards compliance with the information requirements laid down in this Chapter, the burden of proof shall be on the trader.

Article 7

Formal requirements for off-premises contracts

1. With respect to off-premises contracts, the trader shall give the information provided for in Article 6(1) to the consumer on paper or, if the consumer agrees, on another durable medium. That information shall be legible and in plain, intelligible language.

2. The trader shall provide the consumer with a copy of the signed contract or the confirmation of the contract on paper or, if the consumer agrees, on another durable medium, including, where applicable, the confirmation of the consumer's prior express consent and acknowledgement in accordance with point (m) of Article 16.

3. Where a consumer wants the performance of services or the supply of water, gas or electricity, where they are not put up for sale in a limited volume or set quantity, or of district heating to begin during the withdrawal period provided for in Article 9(2), the trader shall require that the consumer makes such an express request on a durable medium.

4. With respect to off-premises contracts where the consumer has explicitly requested the services of the trader for the purpose of carrying out repairs or maintenance for which the trader and the consumer immediately perform their contractual obligations and where the payment to be made by the consumer does not exceed EUR 200:
    (a) the trader shall provide the consumer with the information referred to in points (b) and (c) of Article 6(1) and information about the price or the manner in which the price is to be calculated together with an estimate of the total price, on paper or, if the consumer agrees, on another durable medium. The trader shall provide the information referred to in points (a), (h) and (k) of Article 6(1), but may choose not to provide it on paper or another durable medium if the consumer expressly agrees;
    (b) the confirmation of the contract provided in accordance with paragraph 2 of this Article shall contain the information provided for in Article 6(1).
    Member States may decide not to apply this paragraph.

5. Member States shall not impose any further formal pre- contractual information requirements for the fulfilment of the information obligations laid down in this Directive.

Article 8

Formal requirements for distance contracts

1. With respect to distance contracts, the trader shall give the information provided for in Article 6(1) or make that information available to the consumer in a way appropriate to the means of distance communication used in plain and intelligible language. In so far as that information is provided on a durable medium, it shall be legible.

2. If a distance contract to be concluded by electronic means places the consumer under an obligation to pay, the trader shall make the consumer aware in a clear and prominent manner, and directly before the consumer places his order, of the information provided for in points (a), (e), (o) and (p) of Article 6(1).

    The trader shall ensure that the consumer, when placing his order, explicitly acknowledges that the order implies an obligation to pay. If placing an order entails activating a button or a similar function, the button or similar function shall be labelled in an easily legible manner only with the words 'order with obligation to pay' or a corresponding unambiguous formulation indicating that placing the order entails an obligation to pay the trader. If the trader has not complied with this subparagraph, the consumer shall not be bound by the contract or order.

3.   Trading websites shall indicate clearly and legibly at the latest at the beginning of the ordering process whether any delivery restrictions apply and which means of payment are accepted.

4.   If the contract is concluded through a means of distance communication which allows limited space or time to display the information, the trader shall provide, on that particular means prior to the conclusion of such a contract, at least the pre-contractual information regarding the main characteristics of the goods or services, the identity of the trader, the total price, the right of withdrawal, the duration of the contract and, if the contract is of indeterminate duration, the conditions for terminating the contract, as referred to in points (a), (b), (e), (h) and (o) of Article 6(1). The other information referred to in Article 6(1) shall be provided by the trader to the consumer in an appropriate way in accordance with paragraph 1 of this Article.

5.   Without prejudice to paragraph 4, if the trader makes a telephone call to the consumer with a view to concluding a distance contract, he shall, at the beginning of the conversation with the consumer, disclose his identity and, where applicable, the identity of the person on whose behalf he makes that call, and the commercial purpose of the call.

6.   Where a distance contract is to be concluded by telephone, Member States may provide that the trader has to confirm the offer to the consumer who is bound only once he has signed the offer or has sent his written consent. Member States may also provide that such confirmations have to be made on a durable medium.

7.   The trader shall provide the consumer with the confirmation of the contract concluded, on a durable medium within a reasonable time after the conclusion of the distance contract, and at the latest at the time of the delivery of the goods or before the performance of the service begins. That confirmation shall include:
(a)   all the information referred to in Article 6(1) unless the trader has already provided that information to the consumer on a durable medium prior to the conclusion of the distance contract; and
(b)   where applicable, the confirmation of the consumer's prior express consent and acknowledgment in accordance with point (m) of Article 16.

8.   Where a consumer wants the performance of services, or the supply of water, gas or electricity, where they are not put up for sale in a limited volume or set quantity, or of district heating, to begin during the withdrawal period provided for in Article 9(2), the trader shall require that the consumer make an express request.

9.   This Article shall be without prejudice to the provisions on the conclusion of e-contracts and the placing of e-orders set out in Articles 9 and 11 of Directive 2000/31/EC.

10.   Member States shall not impose any further formal pre- contractual information requirements for the fulfilment of the information obligations laid down in this Directive.

Article 9

Right of withdrawal
1.   Save where the exceptions provided for in Article 16 apply, the consumer shall have a period of 14 days to withdraw from a distance or off-premises contract, without giving

any reason, and without incurring any costs other than those provided for in Article 13(2) and Article 14.

2.   Without prejudice to Article 10, the withdrawal period referred to in paragraph 1 of this Article shall expire after 14 days from:
(a) in the case of service contracts, the day of the conclusion of the contract;
(b) in the case of sales contracts, the day on which the consumer or a third party other than the carrier and indicated by the consumer acquires physical possession of the goods or:
    (i)   in the case of multiple goods ordered by the consumer in one order and delivered separately, the day on which the consumer or a third party other than the carrier and indicated by the consumer acquires physical possession of the last good;
    (ii) in the case of delivery of a good consisting of multiple lots or pieces, the day on which the consumer or a third party other than the carrier and indicated by the consumer acquires physical possession of the last lot or piece;
    (iii) in the case of contracts for regular delivery of goods during defined period of time, the day on which the consumer or a third party other than the carrier and indicated by the consumer acquires physical possession of the first good;
(c) in the case of contracts for the supply of water, gas or electricity, where they are not put up for sale in a limited volume or set quantity, of district heating or of digital content which is not supplied on a tangible medium, the day of the conclusion of the contract.

3.   The Member States shall not prohibit the contracting parties from performing their contractual obligations during the withdrawal period. Nevertheless, in the case of off-premises contracts, Member States may maintain existing national legislation prohibiting the trader from collecting the payment from the consumer during the given period after the conclusion of the contract.

Article 10

Omission of information on the right of withdrawal
1.   If the trader has not provided the consumer with the information on the right of withdrawal as required by point (h) of Article 6(1), the withdrawal period shall expire 12 months from the end of the initial withdrawal period, as determined in accordance with Article 9(2).

2.   If the trader has provided the consumer with the information provided for in paragraph 1 of this Article within 12 months from the day referred to in Article 9(2), the withdrawal period shall expire 14 days after the day upon which the consumer receives that information.

Article 11

Exercise of the right of withdrawal
1.   Before the expiry of the withdrawal period, the consumer shall inform the trader of his decision to withdraw from the contract. For this purpose, the consumer may either:
(a) use the model withdrawal form as set out in Annex I(B); or
(b) make any other unequivocal statement setting out his decision to withdraw from the contract.
Member States shall not provide for any formal requirements applicable to the model withdrawal form other than those set out in Annex I(B).

2.   The consumer shall have exercised his right of withdrawal within the withdrawal period referred to in Article 9(2) and Article 10 if the communication concerning the exercise of the right of withdrawal is sent by the consumer before that period has expired.

3.   The trader may, in addition to the possibilities referred to in paragraph 1, give the option to the consumer to electronically fill in and submit either the model withdrawal form set out in Annex I(B) or any other unequivocal statement on the trader's website. In those cases the trader shall communicate to the consumer an acknowledgement of receipt of such a withdrawal on a durable medium without delay.

4.   The burden of proof of exercising the right of withdrawal in accordance with this Article shall be on the consumer.

Article 12

Effects of withdrawal
The exercise of the right of withdrawal shall terminate the obligations of the parties:

(a)   to perform the distance or off-premises contract; or

(b)   to conclude the distance or off-premises contract, in cases where an offer was made by the consumer.

Article 13

Obligations of the trader in the event of withdrawal
1.   The trader shall reimburse all payments received from the consumer, including, if applicable, the costs of delivery without undue delay and in any event not later than 14 days from the day on which he is informed of the consumer's decision to withdraw from the contract in accordance with Article 11.

The trader shall carry out the reimbursement referred to in the first subparagraph using the same means of payment as the consumer used for the initial transaction, unless the consumer has expressly agreed otherwise and provided that the consumer does not incur any fees as a result of such reimbursement.

2.   Notwithstanding paragraph 1, the trader shall not be required to reimburse the supplementary costs, if the consumer has expressly opted for a type of delivery other than the least expensive type of standard delivery offered by the trader.

3.   Unless the trader has offered to collect the goods himself, with regard to sales contracts, the trader may withhold the reimbursement until he has received the goods back, or until the consumer has supplied evidence of having sent back the goods, whichever is the earliest.

Article 14

Obligations of the consumer in the event of withdrawal
1.   Unless the trader has offered to collect the goods himself, the consumer shall send back the goods or hand them over to the trader or to a person authorised by the trader to receive the goods, without undue delay and in any event not later than 14 days from the day on which he has communicated his decision to withdraw from the contract to the trader in accordance with Article 11. The deadline shall be met if the consumer sends back the goods before the period of 14 days has expired.

The consumer shall only bear the direct cost of returning the goods unless the trader has agreed to bear them or the trader failed to inform the consumer that the consumer has to bear them.

In the case of off-premises contracts where the goods have been delivered to the consumer's home at the time of the conclusion of the contract, the trader shall at his own expense collect the goods if, by their nature, those goods cannot normally be returned by post.

2.   The consumer shall only be liable for any diminished value of the goods resulting from the handling of the goods other than what is necessary to establish the nature, characteristics and functioning of the goods. The consumer shall in any event not be liable for diminished value of the goods where the trader has failed to provide notice of the right of withdrawal in accordance with point (h) of Article 6(1).

3.   Where a consumer exercises the right of withdrawal after having made a request in accordance with Article 7(3) or Article 8(8), the consumer shall pay to the trader an amount which is in proportion to what has been provided until the time the consumer has informed the trader of the exercise of the right of withdrawal, in comparison with the full coverage of the contract. The proportionate amount to be paid by the consumer to the trader shall be calculated on the basis of the total price agreed in the contract. If the total price is excessive, the proportionate amount shall be calculated on the basis of the market value of what has been provided.

4.   The consumer shall bear no cost for:
(a)   the performance of services or the supply of water, gas or electricity, where they are not put up for sale in a limited volume or set quantity, or of district heating, in full or in part, during the withdrawal period, where:
(i)   the trader has failed to provide information in accordance with points (h) or (j) of Article 6(1); or
(ii)   the consumer has not expressly requested performance to begin during the withdrawal period in accordance with Article 7(3) and Article 8(8); or
(b)   the supply, in full or in part, of digital content which is not supplied on a tangible medium where:
(i)   the consumer has not given his prior express consent to the beginning of the performance before the end of the 14-day period referred to in Article 9;
(ii)   the consumer has not acknowledged that he loses his right of withdrawal when giving his consent; or
(iii)   the trader has failed to provide confirmation in accordance with Article 7(2) or Article 8(7).

5.   Except as provided for in Article 13(2) and in this Article, the consumer shall not incur any liability as a consequence of the exercise of the right of withdrawal.

Article 15

Effects of the exercise of the right of withdrawal on ancillary contracts

1.   Without prejudice to Article 15 of Directive 2008/48/EC of the European Parliament and of the Council of 23 April 2008 on credit agreements for consumers . . ., if the consumer exercises his right of withdrawal from a distance or an off- premises contract in accordance with Articles 9 to 14 of this Directive, any ancillary contracts shall be automatically terminated, without any costs for the consumer, except as provided for in Article 13(2) and in Article 14 of this Directive.

2.   ʹThe Member States shall lay down detailed rules on the termination of such contracts.

Article 16

Exceptions from the right of withdrawal

Member States shall not provide for the right of withdrawal set out in Articles 9 to 15 in respect of distance and off-premises contracts as regards the following:
(a)   service contracts after the service has been fully performed if the performance has begun with the consumer's prior express consent, and with the acknowledgement that he will lose his right of withdrawal once the contract has been fully performed by the trader;

(b)   the supply of goods or services for which the price is dependent on fluctuations in the financial market which cannot be controlled by the trader and which may occur within the withdrawal period;

(c)   the supply of goods made to the consumer's specifications or clearly personalised;

(d)   the supply of goods which are liable to deteriorate or expire rapidly;

(e)   the supply of sealed goods which are not suitable for return due to health protection or hygiene reasons and were unsealed after delivery;

(f)   the supply of goods which are, after delivery, according to their nature, inseparably mixed with other items;

(g)   the supply of alcoholic beverages, the price of which has been agreed upon at the time of the conclusion of the sales contract, the delivery of which can only take place after 30 days and the actual value of which is dependent on fluctuations in the market which cannot be controlled by the trader;

(h)   contracts where the consumer has specifically requested a visit from the trader for the purpose of carrying out urgent repairs or maintenance. If, on the occasion of such visit, the trader provides services in addition to those specifically requested by the consumer or goods other than replacement parts necessarily used in carrying out the maintenance or in making the repairs, the right of withdrawal shall apply to those additional services or goods;

(i)   the supply of sealed audio or sealed video recordings or sealed computer software which were unsealed after delivery;

(j)   the supply of a newspaper, periodical or magazine with the exception of subscription contracts for the supply of such publications;

(k)   contracts concluded at a public auction;

(l)   the provision of accommodation other than for residential purpose, transport of goods, car rental services, catering or services related to leisure activities if the contract provides for a specific date or period of performance;

(m)   the supply of digital content which is not supplied on a tangible medium if the performance has begun with the consumer's prior express consent and his acknowledgment that he thereby loses his right of withdrawal.

CHAPTER IV

OTHER CONSUMER RIGHTS

Article 17

Scope

1.   Articles 18 and 20 shall apply to sales contracts. Those Articles shall not apply to contracts for the supply of water, gas or electricity, where they are not put up for sale in a limited volume or set quantity, of district heating or the supply of digital content which is not supplied on a tangible medium.

2.   Articles 19, 21 and 22 shall apply to sales and service contracts and to contracts for the supply of water, gas, electricity, district heating or digital content.

Article 18

Delivery

1. Unless the parties have agreed otherwise on the time of delivery, the trader shall deliver the goods by transferring the physical possession or control of the goods to the consumer without undue delay, but not later than 30 days from the conclusion of the contract.

2. Where the trader has failed to fulfil his obligation to deliver the goods at the time agreed upon with the consumer or within the time limit set out in paragraph 1, the consumer shall call upon him to make the delivery within an additional period of time appropriate to the circumstances. If the trader fails to deliver the goods within that additional period of time, the consumer shall be entitled to terminate the contract.

   The first subparagraph shall not be applicable to sales contracts where the trader has refused to deliver the goods or where delivery within the agreed delivery period is essential taking into account all the circumstances attending the conclusion of the contract or where the consumer informs the trader, prior to the conclusion of the contract, that delivery by or on a specified date is essential. In those cases, if the trader fails to deliver the goods at the time agreed upon with the consumer or within the time limit set out in paragraph 1, the consumer shall be entitled to terminate the contract immediately.

3. Upon termination of the contract, the trader shall, without undue delay, reimburse all sums paid under the contract.

4. In addition to the termination of the contract in accordance with paragraph 2, the consumer may have recourse to other remedies provided for by national law.

Article 19

Fees for the use of means of payment

Member States shall prohibit traders from charging consumers, in respect of the use of a given means of payment, fees that exceed the cost borne by the trader for the use of such means.

Article 20

Passing of risk

In contracts where the trader dispatches the goods to the consumer, the risk of loss of or damage to the goods shall pass to the consumer when he or a third party indicated by the consumer and other than the carrier has acquired the physical possession of the goods. However, the risk shall pass to the consumer upon delivery to the carrier if the carrier was commissioned by the consumer to carry the goods and that choice was not offered by the trader, without prejudice to the rights of the consumer against the carrier.

Article 21

Communication by telephone

Member States shall ensure that where the trader operates a telephone line for the purpose of contacting him by telephone in relation to the contract concluded, the consumer, when contacting the trader is not bound to pay more than the basic rate. The first subparagraph shall be without prejudice to the right of telecommunication services providers to charge for such calls.

Article 22

Additional payments

Before the consumer is bound by the contract or offer, the trader shall seek the express consent of the consumer to any extra payment in addition to the remuneration agreed upon for the trader's main contractual obligation. If the trader has not obtained the consumer's express consent but has inferred it by using default options which the consumer is required to reject in order to avoid the additional payment, the consumer shall be entitled to reimbursement of this payment.

CHAPTER V

GENERAL PROVISIONS

Article 23

Enforcement

1. Member States shall ensure that adequate and effective means exist to ensure compliance with this Directive.

2. The means referred to in paragraph 1 shall include provisions whereby one or more of the following bodies, as determined by national law, may take action under national law before the courts or before the competent administrative bodies to ensure that the national provisions transposing this Directive are applied:
   (a) public bodies or their representatives;
   (b) consumer organisations having a legitimate interest in protecting consumers;
   (c) professional organisations having a legitimate interest in acting.

Article 24

Penalties

1. Member States shall lay down the rules on penalties applicable to infringements of the national provisions adopted pursuant to this Directive and shall take all measures necessary to ensure that they are implemented. The penalties provided for must be effective, proportionate and dissuasive.

2. Member States shall notify those provisions to the Commission by 13 December 2013 and shall notify it without delay of any subsequent amendment affecting them.

Article 25

Imperative nature of the Directive

If the law applicable to the contract is the law of a Member State, consumers may not waive the rights conferred on them by the national measures transposing this Directive.

Any contractual terms which directly or indirectly waive or restrict the rights resulting from this Directive shall not be binding on the consumer.

Article 26

Information

Member States shall take appropriate measures to inform consumers and traders of the national provisions transposing this Directive and shall, where appropriate, encourage traders and code owners as defined in point (g) of Article 2 of Directive 2005/29/EC, to inform consumers of their codes of conduct.

Article 27

Inertia selling

The consumer shall be exempted from the obligation to provide any consideration in cases of unsolicited supply of goods, water, gas, electricity, district heating or digital content or unsolicited provision of services, prohibited by Article 5(5) and point 29 of Annex I to Directive 2005/29/EC. In such cases, the absence of a response from the consumer following such an unsolicited supply or provision shall not constitute consent.

Article 28

Transposition

1.   Member States shall adopt and publish, by 13 December 2013, the laws, regulations and administrative provisions necessary to comply with this Directive. They shall forthwith communicate to the Commission the text of these measures in the form of documents. The Commission shall make use of these documents for the purposes of the report referred to in Article 30.

They shall apply those measures from 13 June 2014.

When Member States adopt those measures, they shall contain a reference to this Directive or be accompanied by such a reference on the occasion of their official publication. Member States shall determine how such reference is to be made.

2.   The provisions of this Directive shall apply to contracts concluded after 13 June 2014.

. . .

CHAPTER VI

FINAL PROVISIONS

Article 31

Repeals

Directive 85/577/EEC and Directive 97/7/EC, as amended by Directive 2002/65/EC of the European Parliament and of the Council of 23 September 2002 concerning the distance marketing of consumer financial services. . .and by Directives 2005/29/EC and 2007/64/EC, are repealed as of 13 June 2014.

. . .

Appendix

CONSUMER INSURANCE (DISCLOSURE AND REPRESENTATIONS) ACT 2012
(c.6)

Main definitions

1 MAIN DEFINITIONS

In this Act—

"consumer insurance contract" means a contract of insurance between—

(a) an individual who enters into the contract wholly or mainly for purposes unrelated to the individual's trade, business or profession, and

(b) a person who carries on the business of insurance and who becomes a party to the contract by way of that business (whether or not in accordance with permission for the purposes of the Financial Services and Markets Act 2000);

"consumer" means the individual who enters into a consumer insurance contract, or proposes to do so;

"insurer" means the person who is, or would become, the other party to a consumer insurance contract.

Pre-contract and pre-variation information

2 DISCLOSURE AND REPRESENTATIONS BEFORE CONTRACT OR VARIATION

(1) This section makes provision about disclosure and representations by a consumer to an insurer before a consumer insurance contract is entered into or varied.

(2) It is the duty of the consumer to take reasonable care not to make a misrepresentation to the insurer.

(3) A failure by the consumer to comply with the insurer's request to confirm or amend particulars previously given is capable of being a misrepresentation for the purposes of this Act (whether or not it could be apart from this subsection).

(4) The duty set out in subsection (2) replaces any duty relating to disclosure or representations by a consumer to an insurer which existed in the same circumstances before this Act applied.

(5) Accordingly—
   (a) any rule of law to the effect that a consumer insurance contract is one of the utmost good faith is modified to the extent required by the provisions of this Act, and
   (b) the application of section 17 of the Marine Insurance Act 1906 (contracts of marine insurance are of utmost good faith), in relation to a contract of marine insurance which is a consumer insurance contract, is subject to the provisions of this Act.

3 REASONABLE CARE

(1) Whether or not a consumer has taken reasonable care not to make a misrepresentation is to be determined in the light of all the relevant circumstances.

(2) The following are examples of things which may need to be taken into account in making a determination under subsection (1)—
   (a) the type of consumer insurance contract in question, and its target market,
   (b) any relevant explanatory material or publicity produced or authorised by the insurer,
   (c) how clear, and how specific, the insurer's questions were,
   (d) in the case of a failure to respond to the insurer's questions in connection with the renewal or variation of a consumer insurance contract, how clearly the insurer communicated the importance of answering those questions (or the possible consequences of failing to do so),
   (e) whether or not an agent was acting for the consumer.

(3) The standard of care required is that of a reasonable consumer: but this is subject to subsections (4) and (5).

(4) If the insurer was, or ought to have been, aware of any particular characteristics or circumstances of the actual consumer, those are to be taken into account.

(5) A misrepresentation made dishonestly is always to be taken as showing lack of reasonable care.

Qualifying misrepresentations

4 QUALIFYING MISREPRESENTATIONS: DEFINITION AND REMEDIES

(1) An insurer has a remedy against a consumer for a misrepresentation made by the consumer before a consumer insurance contract was entered into or varied only if—
   (a) the consumer made the misrepresentation in breach of the duty set out in section 2(2), and
   (b) the insurer shows that without the misrepresentation, that insurer would not have entered into the contract (or agreed to the variation) at all, or would have done so only on different terms.

(2) A misrepresentation for which the insurer has a remedy against the consumer is referred to in this Act as a "qualifying misrepresentation".

(3) The only such remedies available are set out in Schedule 1.

5 QUALIFYING MISREPRESENTATIONS: CLASSIFICATION AND PRESUMPTIONS

(1) For the purposes of this Act, a qualifying misrepresentation (see section 4(2)) is either—
   (a) deliberate or reckless, or
   (b) careless.

(2)   A qualifying misrepresentation is deliberate or reckless if the consumer—
    (a)   knew that it was untrue or misleading, or did not care whether or not it was untrue or misleading, and
    (b)   knew that the matter to which the misrepresentation related was relevant to the insurer, or did not care whether or not it was relevant to the insurer.

(3)   A qualifying misrepresentation is careless if it is not deliberate or reckless.

(4)   It is for the insurer to show that a qualifying misrepresentation was deliberate or reckless.

(5)   But it is to be presumed, unless the contrary is shown—
    (a)   that the consumer had the knowledge of a reasonable consumer, and
    (b)   that the consumer knew that a matter about which the insurer asked a clear and specific question was relevant to the insurer.

Specific issues

6 WARRANTIES AND REPRESENTATIONS

(1)   This section applies to representations made by a consumer—
    (a)   in connection with a proposed consumer insurance contract, or
    (b)   in connection with a proposed variation to a consumer insurance contract.

(2)   Such a representation is not capable of being converted into a warranty by means of any provision of the consumer insurance contract (or of the terms of the variation), or of any other contract (and whether by declaring the representation to form the basis of the contract or otherwise).

7 GROUP INSURANCE

(1)   This section applies where—
    (a)   a contract of insurance is entered into by a person ("A") in order to provide cover for another person ("C"), or is varied or extended so as to do so,
    (b)   C is not a party to the contract,
    (c)   so far as the cover for C is concerned, the contract would have been a consumer insurance contract if entered into by C rather than by A, and
    (d)   C provided information directly or indirectly to the insurer before the contract was entered into, or before it was varied or extended to provide cover for C.

(2)   So far as the cover for C is concerned—
    (a)   sections 2 and 3 apply in relation to disclosure and representations by C to the insurer as if C were proposing to enter into a consumer insurance contract for the relevant cover with the insurer, and
    (b)   subject to subsections (3) to (5) and the modifications in relation to the insurer's remedies set out in Part 3 of Schedule 1, the remainder of this Act applies in relation to the cover for C as if C had entered into a consumer insurance contract for that cover with the insurer.

(3)   Section 4(1)(b) applies as if it read as follows—

"(b) the insurer shows that without the misrepresentation, that insurer would not have agreed to provide cover for C at all, or would have done so only on different terms."

(4)   If there is more than one C, a breach on the part of one of them of the duty imposed (by virtue of subsection (2)(a)) by section 2(2) does not affect the contract so far as it relates to the others.

(5)   Nothing in this section affects any duty owed by A to the insurer, or any remedy which the insurer may have against A for breach of such a duty.

8 INSURANCE ON LIFE OF ANOTHER

(1)   This section applies in relation to a consumer insurance contract for life insurance on the life of an individual ("L") who is not a party to the contract.

(2)   If this section applies—
    (a)   information provided to the insurer by L is to be treated for the purposes of this Act as if it were provided by the person who is the party to the contract, but
    (b)   in relation to such information, if anything turns on the state of mind, knowledge, circumstances or characteristics of the individual providing the information, it is to be determined by reference to L and not the party to the contract.

9 AGENTS

Schedule 2 applies for determining, for the purposes of this Act only, whether an agent through whom a consumer insurance contract is effected is the agent of the consumer or of the insurer.

10 CONTRACTING OUT

(1)   A term of a consumer insurance contract, or of any other contract, which would put the consumer in a worse position as respects the matters mentioned in subsection (2) than the consumer would be in by virtue of the provisions of this Act is to that extent of no effect.

(2)   The matters are—
    (a)   disclosure and representations by the consumer to the insurer before the contract is entered into or varied, and
    (b)   any remedies for qualifying misrepresentations (see section 4(2)).

(3)   This section does not apply in relation to a contract for the settlement of a claim arising under a consumer insurance contract.

    . . .

12 SHORT TITLE, COMMENCEMENT, APPLICATION AND EXTENT

(1)   This Act may be cited as the Consumer Insurance (Disclosure and Representations) Act 2012.

(2)   Section 1 and this section come into force on the day on which this Act is passed, but otherwise this Act comes into force on such day as the Treasury may by order made by statutory instrument appoint.

(3)   An order under subsection (2) may not appoint a day sooner than the end of the period of 1 year beginning with the day on which this Act is passed.

(4)   This Act applies only in relation to consumer insurance contracts entered into, and variations to consumer insurance contracts agreed, after the Act comes into force.

    In the case of group insurance (see section 7), that includes the provision of cover for C by means of an insurance contract entered into by A after the Act comes into force, or varied or extended so as to do so after the Act comes into force.

(5)   Nothing in this Act affects the circumstances in which a person is bound by the acts or omissions of that person's agent.

(6) Apart from the provisions listed in subsection (7), this Act extends to England and Wales, Scotland and Northern Ireland.

(7) In section 11—
   (a) subsection (3) extends to England and Wales and Scotland only;
   (b) subsection (4) extends to Northern Ireland only.

SCHEDULES

SCHEDULE 1

Section 4(3).

INSURERS' REMEDIES FOR QUALIFYING MISREPRESENTATIONS

PART 1

CONTRACTS

General
1   This Part of this Schedule applies in relation to qualifying misrepresentations made in connection with consumer insurance contracts (for variations to them, see Part 2).

Deliberate or reckless misrepresentations
2   If a qualifying misrepresentation was deliberate or reckless, the insurer—
   (a) may avoid the contract and refuse all claims, and
   (b) need not return any of the premiums paid, except to the extent (if any) that it would be unfair to the consumer to retain them.

Careless misrepresentations—claims
3   If the qualifying misrepresentation was careless, paragraphs 4 to 8 apply in relation to any claim.

4   The insurer's remedies are based on what it would have done if the consumer had complied with the duty set out in section 2(2), and paragraphs 5 to 8 are to be read accordingly.

5   If the insurer would not have entered into the consumer insurance contract on any terms, the insurer may avoid the contract and refuse all claims, but must return the premiums paid.

6   If the insurer would have entered into the consumer insurance contract, but on different terms (excluding terms relating to the premium), the contract is to be treated as if it had been entered into on those different terms if the insurer so requires.

7   In addition, if the insurer would have entered into the consumer insurance contract (whether the terms relating to matters other than the premium would have been the same or different), but would have charged a higher premium, the insurer may reduce proportionately the amount to be paid on a claim.

. . .

Careless misrepresentations—treatment of contract for the future
9   (1) This paragraph—

   (a) applies if the qualifying misrepresentation was careless, but
   (b) does not relate to any outstanding claim.

(2) Paragraphs 5 and 6 (as read with paragraph 4) apply as they apply where a claim has been made.

(3) Paragraph 7 (as read with paragraph 4) applies in relation to a claim yet to be made as it applies in relation to a claim which has been made.

(4) If by virtue of sub-paragraph (2) or (3), the insurer would have either (or both) of the rights conferred by paragraph 6 or 7, the insurer may—

    (a) give notice to that effect to the consumer, or

    (b) terminate the contract by giving reasonable notice to the consumer.

(5) But the insurer may not terminate a contract under sub-paragraph (4)(b) if it is wholly or mainly one of life insurance.

(6) If the insurer gives notice to the consumer under sub-paragraph (4)(a), the consumer may terminate the contract by giving reasonable notice to the insurer.

(7) If either party terminates the contract under this paragraph, the insurer must refund any premiums paid for the terminated cover in respect of the balance of the contract term.

(8) Termination of the contract under this paragraph does not affect the treatment of any claim arising under the contract in the period before termination.

(9) Nothing in this paragraph affects any contractual right to terminate the contract.

PART 2

VARIATIONS

10   This Part of this Schedule applies in relation to qualifying misrepresentations made in connection with variations to consumer insurance contracts.

11   If the subject-matter of a variation can reasonably be treated separately from the subject-matter of the rest of the contract, Part 1 of this Schedule applies (with any necessary modifications) in relation to the variation as it applies in relation to a contract.

12   Otherwise, Part 1 applies (with any necessary modifications) as if the qualifying misrepresentation had been made in relation to the whole contract (for this purpose treated as including the variation) rather than merely in relation to the variation.

PART 3

MODIFICATIONS FOR GROUP INSURANCE

13   Part 1 is to be read subject to the following modifications in relation to cover provided for C under a group insurance contract as mentioned in section 7 (and in this Part "A" and "C" mean the same as in that section).

14   References to the consumer insurance contract (however described) are to that part of the contract which provides for cover for C.

15   References to claims and premiums are to claims and premiums in relation to that cover.

16   The reference to the consumer is to be read—

    (a) in paragraph 2(b), as a reference to whoever paid the premiums, or the part of them that related to the cover for C,

    (b) in paragraph 9(4) and (6), as a reference to A.

PART 4

SUPPLEMENTARY

17   Section 84 of the Marine Insurance Act 1906 (return of premium for failure of consideration) is to be read subject to the provisions of this Schedule in relation to contracts of marine insurance which are consumer insurance contracts.

SCHEDULE 2

Section 9.

RULES FOR DETERMINING STATUS OF AGENTS

1   This Schedule sets out rules for determining, for the purposes of this Act only, whether an agent through whom a consumer insurance contract is effected is acting as the agent of the consumer or of the insurer.

2   The agent is to be taken as the insurer's agent in each of the following cases—

    (a)   when the agent does something in the agent's capacity as the appointed representative of the insurer for the purposes of the Financial Services and Markets Act 2000 (see section 39 of that Act),

    (b)   when the agent collects information from the consumer, if the insurer had given the agent express authority to do so as the insurer's agent,

    (c)   when the agent enters into the contract as the insurer's agent, if the insurer had given the agent express authority to do so.

3   (1)   In any other case, it is to be presumed that the agent is acting as the consumer's agent unless, in the light of all the relevant circumstances, it appears that the agent is acting as the insurer's agent.

    (2)   Some factors which may be relevant are set out below.

    (3)   Examples of factors which may tend to confirm that the agent is acting for the consumer are—

       (a)   the agent undertakes to give impartial advice to the consumer,

       (b)   the agent undertakes to conduct a fair analysis of the market,

       (c)   the consumer pays the agent a fee.

    (4)   Examples of factors which may tend to show that the agent is acting for the insurer are—

       (a)   the agent places insurance of the type in question with only one of the insurers who provide insurance of that type,

       (b)   the agent is under a contractual obligation which has the effect of restricting the number of insurers with whom the agent places insurance of the type in question,

       (c)   the insurer provides insurance of the type in question through only a small proportion of the agents who deal in that type of insurance,

       (d)   the insurer permits the agent to use the insurer's name in providing the agent's services,

       (e)   the insurance in question is marketed under the name of the agent,

       (f)   the insurer asks the agent to solicit the consumer's custom.

4   (1)   If it appears to the Treasury that the list of factors in sub-paragraph (3) or (4) of paragraph 3 has become outdated, the Treasury may by order made by statutory instrument bring the list up to date by amending the subparagraph so as to add, omit or alter any factor.

    (2)   A statutory instrument containing an order under sub-paragraph (1) may not be made unless a draft of the instrument has been laid before and approved by a resolution of each House of Parliament.

Thematic Index